Early Korea-Japan Interactions

Early Korea Project Occasional Series

Mark E. Byington, Series Editor

Early Korea-Japan Interactions

Edited by Mark E. Byington,
Ken'ichi Sasaki, and Martin T. Bale

Early Korea Project
Korea Institute
Harvard University
2018

Early Korea-Japan Interactions

Mark E. Byington, Ken'ichi Sasaki, and Martin T. Bale, Editors

Early Korea Project Occasional Series

Mark E. Byington, Series Editor

2018

Publisher: Korea Institute, Harvard University

The Early Korea Project Occasional Series is a peer-reviewed edited serial published by the Early Korea Project at the Korea Institute, Harvard University.
Operational funding for the Early Korea Project is provided by the Korea Foundation in Seoul, Korea.

ISSN 2159-0540
ISBN 978-0-9886928-7-9

Inquiries to: Early Korea, Korea Institute, Harvard University, Center for Government and International Studies, South Building, Room S228, 1730 Cambridge Street, Cambridge, MA 02138.

Phone: (617) 496-3403. Fax: (617) 495-9976.
Website: http://www.fas.harvard.edu/~ekp/
Email: ekp@fas.harvard.edu.

Printed in Seoul, Korea, by Haingraph Co., Ltd.
Distributed by the University of Hawai'i Press.
♾ Printed on acid-free paper

Contents

Preface

This volume is the result of a workshop held in May 2010 at Harvard University and organized by the editors as part of the workshop program of the Early Korea Project at Harvard. The workshop was intended to produce a survey in English that is representative of the current state of research in East Asia on early exchanges between the Korean peninsula and the Japanese archipelago from a primarily archaeological perspective. The participants of this workshop are all leading specialists in their fields in Japan and Korea, and all have conducted extensive research into interchange between these two regions during periods ranging from the early first millennium B.C. to the time of flourish of the first states in the seventh century A.D. The topic of the workshop was selected based on the editors' judgment that it represents a subject of significant interest among specialists of East Asian history that is greatly in need of an update in the English language, particularly in view of the great strides that have been made in recent decades in the field of archaeology.

The chapters that follow therefore represent the views of scholars who are currently leading the research on the target topic in Korea and Japan. The reader should expect to find that these views do not necessarily cohere, as the authors often differ in their interpretations of archaeological evidence, which is to be expected in an active field of scholarly inquiry. There are also some differences among the chapters in terms of chronology, periodization, and certain naming conventions. The editors have made no effort to impose a sense of interpretive unity among the chapters, as this would risk misleading the reader into the erroneous assumption that the major issues discussed in these pages are settled and beyond debate. The field represented here is a very active one, characterized by vigorous debate within academia and, we must acknowledge, subject to nationalistic distortion in the popular realm. The reader will also find a considerable degree of consistency among these chapters with regard to many of the major issues, which perhaps best reflects the remarkable advances in scholarship on this topic gained in recent decades.

The subject of this volume unavoidably touches upon certain issues that became greatly politicized over the course of the twentieth century and that are viewed as intimately associated with the contentious relationship between modern Koreans and Japanese during that time. This situation warrants a brief editorial account of certain naming conventions employed herein. Perhaps the most politically contentious matter dealt with here concerns the place or polity located in the southernmost part of the Korean peninsula and known in modern Korean as Imna 任那 or in modern Japanese pronunciation as Mimana. The choice of Japanese or Korean romanization might lead a reader to suppose a particular political view on the part of the editors with regard to the nature of that place or polity. To avoid creating such an impression, the convention adopted here is to use the Korean "Imna" when referring to the place or polity located on the peninsula and the Japanese "Mimana" when referring to the modern invocation of the term in Japanese context. Similarly, the name of the body of water separating Korea and Japan (referred to as the "East Sea" in Korea and as the "Sea of Japan" in Japan) is rendered herein with the term preferred by the individual authors, with the alternate name provided in parentheses. No particular political biases on the part of the editors should be assumed in either context.

We must also mention that in discussing the ancient societies and polities of the peninsula and archipelago it is often tempting to fall back on referring to these regions by their modern political names "Korea" and "Japan." Indeed, in many of the chapters here translated into English such modern terms have been used as shorthand for the geographical equivalents in antiquity. The authors and the editors are aware of the problematic nature of such a usage and the associated risks of conflating ancient societies with modern nations; however, because repetition of the terms "Korean peninsula" and "Japanese archipelago" sometimes makes for tedious reading, the editors have also adopted the occasional use of the shorthand terminology for stylistic reasons. Phrases such as "immigrants from Korea," for example, should therefore be understood to mean people coming from what is today referred to as the Korean peninsula.

Preface

This volume has been many years in the making, and the editors would like to acknowledge the many individuals and organizations that have contributed to both the workshop and this publication. We thank the staff and Executive Committee of the Korea Institute, Harvard University, for their support of the workshop. Susan Laurence and Myong-suk Chandra in particular provided administrative support for the event. Harvard graduate students Kyong-mi Kwon and Jae-ho Shin also worked tirelessly to make the workshop a success. In addition to the presenters whose work appears in this volume, we would like to thank the invaluable contributions made by those who served as discussants for the presentation, including Gina Barnes, Jonathan Best, Walter Edwards, William Wayne Ferris, Rowan Flad, and C. C. Lamberg-Karlovsky. Other scholars who participated actively in the discussions included Money Hickman, Junghee Lee, and Sunmi Park. We also thank the many attendees of the workshop for contributing to its success. Those who contributed their expertise toward the production of this volume include Jack Davey, Dennis Lee, Kelly Maccioli, and Nita Sembrowich.

The workshop enjoyed generous support from the Northeast Asian History Foundation and the Reishchauer Institute of Japanese Studies, while operational support for the Early Korea Project was provided by the Korea Foundation.

This publication was made possible by a generous publication subvention grant from the James Joo-Jin Kim Program in Korean Studies at the University of Pennsylvania and by funds provided by the Korea Institute, Harvard University.

Conventions for Classical Citations

In this volume, in-text references to classical sources are provided in an abbreviated form. Citations include the name of the classical source, followed in parentheses by volume, chapter, or section and page range or number if applicable. Although page numbers are specific to editions used in this volume, the other information provided is intended to direct the reader to a specific section of the source without reference to the pagination of particular editions.

Bitchū no kuni:

Bitchū no kuni taizei fu shibō nin chō 備中国大税負死亡人帳 [Notes on deceased taxpayers in the province of Bitchū]. In Nara ibun 寧樂遺文 [Writings of the Nara period], edited by Takeuchi Rizō 竹内理三, pp. 316–319. Tokyo: Yagi Shoten 八木書店 [1943-1944].

Hizen no kuni fudoki:

Hizen no kuni fudoki 肥前国風土記 [History of Hizen Province]. In *Bungo no kuni fudoki, Hizen no kuni fudoki* 豊後国風土記·肥前国風土記 [History of Bungo and history of Hizen], edited by Okimori Takuya 沖森卓也, Satō Makoto 佐藤信, and Yajima Izumi 矢嶋泉, pp. 39–64. Tokyo: Yamakawa Shuppansha 山川出版社, 2008.

Nihon ryōiki:

Keikai 景戒, *Nihon ryōiki* 日本霊異記 [Miraculous stories from Japan]. Edited and annotated by Endō Yoshimoto 遠藤嘉基 and Kasuga Kazuo 春日和男. Tokyo: Iwanami Shoten 岩波書店, 1967.

Nihon shoki:

Toneri Shinnō 舎人親王, et al., *Nihon shoki* 日本書紀 [Chronicles of Japan]. 2 vols. Tokyo: Iwanami Shoten 岩波書店, 1967.

Samguk sagi:

Kim Pu-sik 金富軾, *Samguk sagi* 三國史記 [History of the Three Kingdoms]. Edited by Yi Pyŏng-do 李丙燾. 2 vols. Seoul: Ŭryu Munhwasa 乙酉文化史, 1977.

Sanguozhi:

Chen Shou 陳壽, *Sanguozhi* 三國志 [Chronicles of the Three Kingdoms]. 5 vols. Beijing: Zhonghua Shuju 中华书局, 1992.

Shiji:

Sima Qian 司馬遷, *Shiji* 史記 [Records of the Grand Historian]. 10 vols. Beijing: Zhonghua Shuju 中华书局, 1982.

Songshu:

Shen Yue 沈約, *Songshu* 宋書 [History of the Liu Song dynasty]. 40 vols. Beijing: Zhonghua Shuju 中华书局, 1985.

Maps, Figures, and Tables

Maps, Figures, and Tables

Early Korea-Japan Interactions

Editors' Introduction

This volume in the Early Korea Project Occasional Series addresses a matter that has long drawn the interest of numerous scholars working in the English language but which nevertheless has not previously been addressed in the manner presented here. The subject is the nature of various interchanges that were conducted continuously between populations occupying the Korean peninsula and those of the Japanese archipelago. Of course, these people were not "Japanese" or "Korean" in the sense that we would understand the terms today, as political and ethnic boundaries in early times were softer and more porous than in the modern age, and their configurations underwent great change over time. Nevertheless, we should be aware that very modern sensibilities regarding national distinctions have tended to guide scholarship on this subject for well over a century, and it is often necessary to remind ourselves of the social and political context of the times in which these societies were transitioning into state-level polities.

The origins of this volume lie in a workshop held at Harvard University on May 3–4, 2010, titled "Early Korea-Japan Interactions: New Perspectives on Old Issues." The sometimes contentious issue of early relations between the polities and peoples of the peninsula and the archipelago was identified as a subject to be explored as a program of the Early Korea Project at Harvard. The idea for a workshop was fleshed out during informal meetings among the editors in the latter half of 2009, the impetus being the fortunate fact that Sasaki was then spending a year at Harvard and was available to work with Bale and Byington (then at the Early Korea Project) to organize the event and manage the participation of Japanese archaeologists specializing in the target subject. We decided to invite three archaeologists from Korea and three from Japan to discuss research in Korea-Japan interactions during the periods associated with the Bronze Age in Korea and the Yayoi period in Japan to the beginning of the seventh century. We also decided to invite as discussants a number of western scholars who had previously written on this topic in English in an effort to facilitate the transition of Japanese and Korean scholarship and its context into an accessible form in English.

The reasons for organizing such a conference and the resulting publication are simple. As is well known, the matter of early relations between "Korea" and "Japan" has tended to be tightly bound with political design (aggressive at times) and with nationalist sentiment, and much of the resulting scholarship on the topic has reflected those associations. This has not prevented the occasional publication of good scholarship in English capable of cutting through the haze, nor has it hindered a healthy and cooperative scholarly community in Korea and Japan from making remarkable progress in the past two or three decades, as will be shown below.

Nevertheless, the advances made in recent years have not come primarily from reinterpretation of historical texts (though progress has been made in this area as well), but rather from the successes of archaeology. And as the chapters of this volume will show, archaeology sometimes tells a story quite different from that related in historical records. To date there has yet to appear a volume in English that addresses these new understandings, and the motivation for the workshop and this publication was the desire to provide a volume featuring scholarship representative of this new phase of cooperative research in Japan and Korea.

For many decades scholarly and popular writings in English on early relations between the peninsula and archipelago tended to be dominated by interpretations centered on the nature of the entity referred to in certain sources as "Mimana" (Imna in Korean) said to have been an area of the southern peninsula governed by the Yamato state. Although this idea has been thoroughly debunked in scholarly circles, the name "Mimana" continues to appear, mostly outside of academia, often in politically charged rhetoric. A similar case is the hypothesis first offered by Egami Namio 江上波夫 suggesting that horse-riding warriors from the peninsula or Manchuria (he was not specific) were responsible for prompting early state formation in Japan (Egami 1964). This too was eventually disproved by archaeological analysis, yet the idea has had remarkable resilience, and variations on the horse-rider theme continue to appear in both scholarly and popular works.

For all their power as persistent themes, talk of Mimana and horse-riders has distracted many western readers from the real advances made possible by patient archaeological analysis over years and decades. Some of the results of those advances appear in the pages of this volume. In the remainder of this introduction, we will provide a brief background on the state of the fields of archaeology and early history in Korea and Japan as they pertain to the chapters of this volume.

As noted above, this volume marks a watershed in the study of the archaeology and early history of Korea and Japan. As with many of the titles of the Early Korea Project Occasional Series, never before has such a volume been published in English. This volume focuses on the ancient period from the first millennium B.C. to the mid-first millennium A.D. Yet, the ultimate antiquity and origin of interchange between the Korean peninsula and Japanese archipelago are even more ancient. For example, archaeologists have long hypothesized that some of the obsidian from Paleolithic archaeological sites in southeastern coastal Korea was obtained from the Japanese archipelago (Chang et al. 2007; Yi and Chwa 2015). Recently, in an effort led by the research of Chang Yong-jun of the Taegu National Museum, the source of some obsidian from the Wŏlsŏng-dong 月城洞 Paleolithic site in the Kŭmho 琴湖 River basin (Taegu) was traced to the Paektu Mountain 白頭山 area that straddles the border between North Korea and China (Chang 2017). Yet the picture for the relations between the Korean peninsula and the Japanese archipelago in the Paleolithic is likely a complex situation, and some of the Korean obsidian seems to be from a source in Kyushu (Chang et al. 2007).

Ilona Bausch proposes the "Korea Strait fishermen interaction sphere" to frame the long-term waxing and waning of cultural and technical changes in goods, ideas, people, and practices of the Korean Chŭlmun 櫛紋 period (the Korean Neolithic, ca. 8000–1500 B.C.) in the southeastern peninsula and Japanese Jōmon 縄文 period (ca. 14,500–1,000 or 800/700/600 B.C.) of northwestern Kyushu (Bausch 2017:432). In particular, Bausch describes fish hooks and other fishing tools, obsidian, and shell objects as the material culture that passed between the two regions. She posits that ideas were also exchanged between the two regions, namely knowledge about deep-sea fishing, ritual ideas, practices such as the exchange of goods, and the mobility and intermarriage of people (Bausch 2017:431). Dugout wooden canoes dating to the Chŭlmun and Jōmon found in both regions would have been sufficient means of transportation to carry out such prehistoric interactions.

Archaeologists recognize that obsidian in some Chŭlmun sites in Korea was obtained from the Japanese archipelago (Kuzmin 2012; Shimazu 1992). Among the well-known Korean sites with obsidian thought to have a source in the archipelago is the Tongsam-dong 東三洞 shell midden in Pusan. Shells of tropical shellfish that were fashioned into bracelets were also brought into the Korean peninsula to sites such as Changhang 獐項 in Kadŏk Island 加德島 and Yamaga 山鹿 in Fukuoka through exchange from as far away as the Ryukyu archipelago (Bausch 2017:416–421; Kungnip Cheju Pangmulgwan 2005:144–154). Many of these shell bracelets at Tongsam-dong are representative of contacts and exchanges that span the entire length of the multiple occupations there and at other sites over the *longue durée*. Anthropomorphic faces carved into shells from the Kurobashi 黒橋 and Adaka 阿高 shell midden sites in Kyushu and the Tongsam-dong site in Korea are an example of symbolic and ritualistic artifacts that to some degree demonstrate elements of a common prehistoric culture between the two regions (Bausch 2017:416–421).

Another issue in the archaeology of Korea-Japan interactions concerns the relationship between the two regions during the Korean Mumun 無文 period (the Korean Bronze Age, 1500–300 B.C.) and the corresponding Japanese Yayoi 弥生 period (c. 800/700/600 B.C.–A.D. 250). In his chapter, Lee Chungkyu addresses the changing nature of the interactions related to the production, classification, and distribution of metal objects in the first millennium B.C., but the vast breadth of the evidence for interactions cannot be discussed adequately in a single paper. In summary, an intensive series of complex ongoing interactions in the material culture of the southern Korean peninsula occurred from the Middle Mumun (c. 850–550 B.C.) and beyond with northern Kyushu that have a bearing on the onset of intensive agriculture, metallurgy, and incipient complex society in western Japan (see Iwanaga chapter, this volume). Among other kinds of material discussed in this volume, architectural technology and style for dwellings and mortuary features, in addition to a host of pottery and stone tool types, called *Songgung-ni* 松菊里 culture in Korea, are found in common in the southern peninsula and northern Kyushu. Archaeologists in both countries are divided about the meaning of and processes involved in such similarities. For instance, Japanese archaeologists have drawn up a number of detailed models proposing different scenarios of migration and internal development to account for the changes in northern Kyushu (Imamura Keiji 1996:127–146).

The basic theoretical orientation of the chapters in this volume, with the exception of the chapter by Sasaki, is the culture-historical or so-called "traditional" perspective that emphasizes artifact-centered description and the creation of seriations and types in order to explain material cultural change through time. As Habuta Yoshiyuki explains (this volume), Hamada Kōsaku 濱田耕作 (1881–1938) was the student of Sir W.M. Flinders Petrie (1853–1942), a pioneer of the culture-historical approach (Trigger 2006:221–222). Hamada was the first archaeologist at Kyoto University and went on to influence archaeologists in Japan and Korea with his excavations in both countries. Yet, as readers will see, all of the authors have explored their datasets far beyond the confines of traditional archaeology in order to create sophisticated models of culture change that will be useful for archaeologists working in North America and Europe, especially in the comparative context of archaeology of metallurgy, formation of complex societies, and early state-level societies. While the chapters in this book are relevant to broader theoretical issues, chapters on the Kofun period by Habuta, Kameda, and Sasaki primarily deal with material culture of the archipelago influenced by that of the peninsula. Typical or uniquely Japanese aspects of Kofun Period material culture, such as keyhole-shaped tumuli or mounded tombs, are not discussed in depth here.

The publication of this book would not have been possible if not for the current active and productive relationships between archaeologists and institutes in Korea and Japan. Yet, the enmity between the modern nation states of Japan, the Republic of Korea, and the Democratic People's Republic of Korea, exclusive of archaeology, can be traced back at least as early as the violent and turbulent episodes of history during the Japanese invasions of Korea (*Imjin Waeran* 壬辰倭亂) beginning in 1592. Such animosity still persists in contemporary Korean and Japanese societies from multiple perspectives; for example, in Korea a part of the historic anti-Japanese sentiment has merged with and transformed into fear of the radioactivity emanating from eastern Japan caused by the 2010 earthquake, tsunami, and nuclear meltdown in Fukushima. Further, friction has continued in both countries as a result of the failed agreement to resolve the so-called "comfort women" issue in 2015. These are but a few of the major irritants that characterize modern Korea-Japan relations.

Nevertheless, this book is one of the many testaments to the fact that in the archaeologies of Korea and Japan enmity has *not*, for the most part, characterized topics related to regional interchange between the peninsula and archipelago. The Yŏngnam-Kyushu Joint Archaeological Meetings 嶺南-九州合同考古學大會 are a good example of the positive ongoing cooperation between archaeologists of Korea and Japan since the early 1990s.

These meetings have taken place mostly biennially since that time, and the location for the conferences alternates between Korea and Japan. Conferences are organized though planning committees formed by the Yŏngnam Archaeological Society 嶺南考古學會 in Korea and the Kyushu Archaeological Society 九州考古学会 in Japan.

The Yŏngnam-Kyushu Joint Archaeological Meetings would not be possible without strong cooperative networks that have developed since the early 1980s between numerous universities and research institutes in Korea and Japan. Two of the Korean authors featured in this volume, Park Cheun Soo and Woo Jae-Pyoung, received their doctoral degrees from Osaka University 大阪大学 in the 1990s. Like Park and Woo, many other Korean archaeologists have received their graduate degrees in Japan and vice versa, and many others regularly conduct research in the other country as post-doctoral fellows and visiting scholars.

In Korea, interest in Korea-Japan interactions is strong among archaeologists across the country, but this is especially so in the southeast, particularly among the faculty, students, and former students of Kyungpook and Pusan National Universities and Dong-a and Dongguk Universities, as well as other universities, museums, and buried cultural heritage research institutes across Korea. The Japanese interest in the topic centers generally but not exclusively on western Japan and is especially strong at Osaka University and others in the Kansai region, in addition to Kyushu and Fukuoka Universities in the Fukuoka region. Research on aspects of prehistoric and ancient Korea-Japan interactions is active, as is evidenced by articles that regularly appear in the academic journals in both countries. It is because of these ever-intensifying interrelationships and interchanges that the level of research on Korea-Japan interaction has become highly sophisticated, advanced, and wide-ranging. This is partly reflected in this volume of the Early Korea Project Occasional Series.

Seven chapters constitute the present volume. The articles approach the subject mainly from an archaeological perspective, but in Korea and Japan archaeologists who do research that deals with metallurgy, the protohistoric in Korea and Japan (c. 300 B.C.–300 A.D.), and early historic periods are trained in early history out of necessity. Some of these topics have been covered in English from the exclusive perspective of Korea or Japan, but this volume takes an explicitly comparative approach that has not been seen in English until now. The chapters in this volume are meant to introduce new data and perspectives in English, to complement material presented in other publications, including the Early Korea Project *Early Korea* series as well as its Occasional Series, and to stimulate new interest in the study of early Korea and Japan.

The chapter by Lee Chungkyu is a detailed study from a Korean peninsular and Japanese archipelagic perspective of bronze and iron objects that were distributed mostly in mortuary contexts in northeastern Asia from the beginning of the first millennium B.C. to the first few centuries of the first millennium A.D. The author examines bronze mirrors in detail, partly because of their relative ubiquity and presence across northeastern China, the Korean peninsula, and the Japanese archipelago, and also because of the technological and social changes that took place in these regions of northeastern Asia. In particular we learn about the changes in social scale and metallurgical technology of polities in the Korean peninsula, leading up to and following the establishment of Han Chinese commanderies in the northern part of the peninsula in 108 B.C. From approximately this time more fine-grained differences can be discerned regarding how polities of the southern peninsula and the western archipelago dealt with Western and Eastern Han. These changes help us to understand the relative scalar trajectories in the development of complex societies in Korea and Japan.

The chapters by Park Cheun Soo and Woo Jae-Pyoung represent reexaminations of the relationships between a number of polities in the Korean peninsula and the Japanese archipelago, and both chapters are nothing short of revolutionary in their implications. This is because Park and Woo employ fundamental material cultural evidence to overturn the common perception that Paekche served as the nexus of peninsular relations with Wa between ca. 300–600 A.D. The chapter by Woo treats early historic interactions between Paekche and Wa. In the wake of the recent advances in the number and quality of archaeological excavations in the Paekche cultural area, in addition to the inscription of the Paekche Historic Areas of the Ungjin 熊津 and Sabi 泗沘 periods on the UNESCO World Heritage List in early 2016, scholars in Korea have emphasized that Paekche received culture and technologies from continental "Chinese" state-level societies, incorporated them to create their own unique culture, and spread that culture to Silla and Wa through various interactions (Republic of Korea 2015:12–13). In contrast, Woo tracks and characterizes the relations between Paekche and Wa technology, mortuary architecture, and political strategies.

The procurement of iron was a preoccupation of the Wa elites. In relation to that, both Park and Woo agree that Kaya was originally the focus of peninsular interactions with Wa in the third and fourth centuries. Yet, using archaeological evidence, Park shows clearly how peninsular political relations with Wa changed over time, from Kaya to Paekche and finally to Silla. Conventional wisdom gleaned from textual sources led us to believe that Wa and Silla had a relationship characterized by continuous animosity, but Park's relatively fine-grained examination of the material culture associated with the two polities reveals periods in which they were more closely aligned through trade. Both Park and Woo demonstrate that the relations between the peninsula and archipelago were intensely competitive, dynamic, and constantly in a state of change.

The publication of this volume is also timely in the context of Japanese archaeology. The chapters in this volume cover the Yayoi period (the chapter by Iwanaga) and the Kofun period (those by Habuta, Kameda, and Sasaki) in Japan. It is well known that methods of wet rice cultivation as well as bronze and iron objects were all introduced to Japan from the southern Korean peninsula and that this introduction marked the beginning of the Yayoi period. In addition, it has become evident from the perspective of biological anthropology that people from the Korean peninsula indeed immigrated to the Japanese islands, though Japanese archaeologists have been debating the scale of such migration. Nevertheless, the general flow of information, objects, and people was from the Korean peninsula to the Japanese islands.

At the same time, Japanese archaeologists began to notice that some Yayoi pottery and bronze objects that had been undoubtedly produced in Japan have been discovered in the Korean peninsula (Oda 1980; Oda and Han 1991). Therefore, some objects, information, and perhaps people did move from the Japanese islands to the Korean peninsula. The Chinese standard history *Sanguozhi* 三國志 (Chronicles of the Three Kingdoms) mentions that people of the Japanese archipelago came to the Korean peninsula to obtain iron. The discovery of a considerable quantity of Yayoi pottery in association with Korean attached-rim pottery at the Nŭk-to 勒島 site in Sach'ŏn 泗川 in 1985–6 stimulated discussion on the "interaction" between the Korean peninsula and Kyushu. In 1989, archaeological excavations at the Naesŏng 萊城 site in Pusan resulted in the discovery of a pottery assemblage, 90 percent of which was Yayoi pottery. These might be considered as evidence for people of the archipelago who came to acquire iron. In 1991, Oda Fujio and Han Pyŏng-sam published the definitive work on this subject: *Nikkan kōshō no kōkogaku: Yayoi jidai hen* [Archaeology of Korea-Japan interactions: Yayoi period] 日韓交渉の考古学: 弥生時代篇. They produced a compendium of almost all artifacts of Korean origin discovered at Yayoi-period sites in Japan and some artifacts of Yayoi cultural origins discovered in Korea.

Editors' Introduction

In the twenty-first century, the results of AMS (accelerator mass spectrometry) radiocarbon dating of the beginning of the Yayoi period, publicized by the National Museum of Japanese History (Imamura Mineo and Fujio 2003), have fueled Japanese archaeological discussion of Korea-Japan interaction. Members of the museum staff claim that the Yayoi period began in the ninth or perhaps the tenth century B.C. Prior to this publication, Japanese archaeologists believed that the methods of rice cultivation, iron tools, and bronze objects were introduced to Japan all at once around 400 B.C. If the AMS results produced by the National Museum of Japanese History were correct, it would mean that iron tools appeared in Japan earlier than in China and the Korean peninsula. This interpretation is, however, apparently at odds with recent findings in Korea that place the beginning of the Early Iron Age there as early as 550 cal. B.C. based on advances in AMS radiocarbon dating (Yi Ch'ang-hŭi 2010:89, 91).

In order to resolve this issue, Japanese archaeologists began to re-examine the archaeological contexts of iron tools at very early Yayoi sites in Japan, as well as chronologies of bronze objects discovered in the Korean peninsula (e.g. Imamura Mineo and Harunari 2004; Takakura and Tanaka 2011).[1] Chronologies of bronze objects, such as the Liaoning-style bronze dagger and Korean slender-type bronze dagger, are essential for cross-dating between the Korean Bronze Age and the Japanese Yayoi period. Iwanaga presents some aspects of this debate over the calendrical dates of the Yayoi period in this volume.

In recent years, Japanese research on Korea-Japan interactions during the Kofun period have gone through considerable changes in the fields of history and archaeology (e.g. Inoue 2014; Takada 2014). The hypothesis concerning the so-called Mimana Nihonfu 任那日本府 [Japanese Colony at Mimana (K. Imna)], formulated by Suematsu Yasukazu 末松保和 (1949), used to dominate the field of ancient Japanese history (see Moon 2012). Japanese historians (e.g. Ishimoda 1962) and archaeologists (e.g. Kobayashi 1962) believed that the central polity of fourth-century Japan dispatched military troops to the southern part of the Korean peninsula and established control over Kaya and its surrounding polities.

[1] Both Imamura and Harunari (2004) are professors at the National Museum of Japanese History, and their book collects papers mainly in support of the views of the National Museum of Japanese History. By contrast, Takakura and Tanaka (2011) collect papers critical of the views of the National Museum of Japanese History.

Although Japanese archaeologists are all aware that technological innovations of several kinds, such as firing stoneware in kilns, the practice of horse riding, the use of horse trappings, and new iron agricultural tools, were all introduced from the Korean peninsula, they tended to believe that these technological innovations were made possible by Japanese troops who brought back to Japan Korean specialists skilled in these technologies. Based on this "premise," an introduction to Kofun-period archaeology written by Onoyama Setsu (1975) presents the view that the central polity during the Kofun period had the power to occupy the southern part of the Korean peninsula and to exert control over all of the local polities in Japan.

Suematsu's Mimana hypothesis has been convincingly refuted by historians Yamao Yukihisa (e.g. 1989) and Tanaka Toshiaki (1992). Owing to their thorough critical analyses, it has become clear that events recorded in the *Nihon shoki* 日本書紀 (Chronicles of Japan) stated to have taken place in 369, including a dispatch of troops and the assertion of control over Mimana, would, if true, have taken place instead in 429 and thereafter. Certain records included in the *Paekche ki* 百済記 (Records of Paekche), one of the sources used in the *Nihon shoki*, have been shown to be fabrications, and the sections of the *Nihon shoki* written on the basis of the *Paekche ki* were themselves further distorted.

In the 1980s, when Japanese historians were re-examining and re-considering the Mimana hypothesis, new archaeological discoveries relevant to issues of Korea-Japan interactions were made in the southern Korean peninsula. For example, iron helmets and cuirasses undoubtedly made in Kofun-period Japan were excavated from Tomb 32 at Chisan-dong 池山洞 in Koryŏng 高靈 and Tomb 28 at Okchŏn 玉田 in Hapch'ŏn 陜川 in the late 1980s. The discoveries at Okchŏn, situated in the Tae Kaya 大加耶 region, also indicated that numerous gilt-bronze accessories and horse trappings discovered in Japan were in fact made in the Tae Kaya region. In the early 1990s, excavations at the Taesŏng-dong 大成洞 and Yangdong-ni 良洞里 cemeteries in Kimhae 金海 resulted in the discoveries of bronze and jade objects that used to be considered unique to the Kofun-period culture in Japan.

Investigations into "keyhole-shaped" mounded tombs in Korea also progressed considerably in the late 1980s and 1990s. These tombs are distributed only in the Yŏngsan River 榮山江 basin in the southwestern part of the Korean peninsula. So far, thirteen such tombs are known. In the late 1980s, in an attempt to prove that these tombs were indeed keyhole-shaped, Kang In-gu 姜仁求 (1987, 1992) surveyed and mapped three keyhole-shaped mounded tombs in southwestern Korea.

In June 1991, Tomb 1 at Sindŏk 新德 in Hamp'yŏng 咸平 was the first among the thirteen keyhole-shaped tombs to be excavated. (Sŏng 1992). Three keyhole-shaped tombs were excavated in 1993 and 1994 in the present city of Kwangju 光州. At Tomb 1 at Wŏlgye-dong 月桂洞, wooden objects in the form of the Iwami 石見 type shield-shaped *haniwa* 埴輪 ceramic object and parasol-shaped wooden objects were discovered in the moat enclosing the tomb, in association with *haniwa* ceramic cylinders (Im 1994). At the tomb at Myŏnghwa-dong 明花洞, *haniwa* ceramic cylinders were discovered, forming a line *in situ* (Kungnip Kwangju Pangmulgwan 1996). These results confirmed that these tombs were indeed keyhole-shaped and retained some features that were previously believed to be unique to keyhole-shaped mounded tombs of Kofun-period Japan. (For a comprehensive Japanese source, see Chōsen Gakkai 2002.)

In the early 1990s, as new data accumulated in the southern Korean peninsula, the Mimana hypothesis was no longer considered valid. Accordingly, a new conceptual framework became necessary to account for the new discoveries. It was Park Cheun Soo (1995) who responded to this need by presenting his "mutual interaction model."

In 1998, Park (1998) published another influential paper, in which he analyzes Kofun-period artifacts, previously identified only generally as coming from the Korean peninsula, and identifies them as more specifically artifacts of Kŭmgwan Kaya 金官加耶, Tae Kaya, and Paekche. He further finds that those artifacts of Korean origin dated to the fourth and early fifth centuries in Japan originated in Kŭmgwan Kaya, those of the late fifth century in Tae Kaya, and those of early sixth century and after in Paekche. Such regional shifts through time are clearly reflected also in artifacts of Japanese origin found in southern Korea. Kofun-period artifacts dated to the fourth and early fifth centuries are mainly discovered in the Kŭmgwan Kaya region, those of the late fifth century in the Tae Kaya region, and those of the early sixth century in the Paekche region. Park concludes that these phenomena were the results of the political situations in which Wa, Kaya, and Paekche were involved.

Along with Park, Azuma (1999) thoroughly analyzed iron ingots discovered both in the Japanese islands and the southern part of the Korean peninsula, taking into consideration the morphologies and their temporal change, the archaeological contexts of their discoveries, and their spatial distributions. Azuma finds that for one hundred years beginning from the end of the fourth century iron ingots were transported from southern Korea to the western Japanese islands. Until the mid-fifth century, the iron ingots originated from the lower tributary areas of the Naktong River 洛東江, in locations associated with Kŭmgwan Kaya, Ara Kaya 阿羅加耶, and So Kaya 小加耶. From the mid-fifth century iron ingots were also transported to Japan in the context of interaction with the Yŏngsan River region. Taking into consideration other material evidence, such as pottery and ritual bronze artifacts, Park concludes that the transportation of iron ingots to Japan was not a result of Japanese military invasions in the southern Korean peninsula, but rather a part of daily interaction between the Korean peninsula and Japanese islands.

Park spent the academic year of 2003–4 on sabbatical in Japan and examined Kofun-period artifacts of Korean origin discovered at numerous sites throughout Japan, identifying the polity in southern Korea from which each object originated. The results of his thorough and comprehensive examinations were published in 2007 as *Kaya to Wa: Han hantō to Nihon rettō no kōkogaku* 加耶と倭: 韓半島と日本列島の考古学 [Kaya and Wa: The archaeology of the Korean peninsula and the Japanese archipelago]. Park has made it clear that Kofun-period Japan closely interacted with Silla, although Japanese historical sources repeatedly state that Paekche was the official diplomatic partner. Park also hints that local polities in Japan interacted with local polities in southern Korea independently from the central polity of Kofun-period Japan.

Although some Japanese archaeologists, such as Tsude (1995), still contend that the central polity was so powerful that it monopolized all diplomatic rights, Takada (2014) and Sasaki (this volume) entirely agree with Park. In this sense, it is highly noteworthy that Kameda (1993), in a theoretical paper presenting models of various cases of immigration, has mentioned the possibility that immigrants traveled from the Korean peninsula to Japan without passing through the zone of authority controlled by the central polity.

Another important shift in the conceptual framework is the expansion of the geographical scope of Silla. In the 1980s, when Azuma and Tanaka (1983, 1989) wrote an introduction to archaeological sites in Korea, they and other Japanese scholars at that time were operating within the premise that Silla's territory was limited to the Kyŏngju area, that the surrounding regions were part of Kaya until the fifth century, and that Silla gradually conquered these surrounding regions. By contrast, Yi Hŭi-jun (2007) and other scholars at Kyungpook National University have suggested that the regions east of the Naktong River were already under Silla control. If this is indeed the case, the Pokch'ŏn-dong 福泉洞 cemetery in Pusan, usually considered as a part of Kaya culture, was included in Silla territory from the early stage of the development of the cemetery, and the artifacts discovered there would all have been produced by Silla. Park (2007) takes this framework for granted. At present, many Japanese archaeologists specializing in Korean archaeology such as Takada (2014) and Isahaya (2012), who consider issues focused on horse trappings, agree with this new framework.

As more data accumulate in southern Korea, and more thorough analyses of artifacts in Japan are conducted, the Japanese framework of the archaeology of Korea-Japan interactions is evolving considerably. The publication of this volume is indeed very timely.

As noted above, this volume consists of six chapters representing the research of the six scholars invited to the Early Korea Project workshop in 2010, with an additional chapter by Sasaki providing a case study that further illustrates the arguments presented in this volume. To accommodate the archaeological emphasis of these chapters, this volume of the Early Korea Project Occasional Series has departed somewhat from the style of earlier volumes in terms of both citation style and textual arrangement. The editors hope that this will make the content more accessible to western specialists as well as general readers.

Acknowledgement

The editors gratefully acknowledge the kind assistance provided by Drs. Isahaya Naoto and Takada Kanta in the preparation of this introduction.

References

Azuma Ushio 東潮
1999 *Kodai Higashi Asia no tetsu to Wa* 古代東アジアの鉄と倭 [Iron and Japan in ancient East Asian context]. Keisuisha 渓水社, Hiroshima.
Azuma Ushio 東潮, and Tanaka Toshiaki 田中俊明
1983 *Kankoku no kodai iseki 1: Shiragi hen (Keishū)* 韓国の古代遺跡 1: 新羅編 (慶州) [Ancient sites in Korea, volume 1: Silla (Kyŏngju)]. Chūō Kōronsha 中央公論社, Tokyo.
———
1989 *Kankoku no kodai iseki 2: (Kudara, Kaya hen)* 韓国の古代遺跡 2: 百済・加耶編 [Ancient sites in Korea, volume 2: Paekche and Kaya]. Chūō Kōronsha 中央公論社, Tokyo.
Bausch, Ilona R.
2017 Prehistoric Networks across the Korea Strait (5000–1000 BCE): 'Early Globalization' during the Jomon Period in North-West Kyushu? In *The Routledge Handbook of Archaeology and Globalization*, edited by Tamar Hodos, pp. 413–437. Routledge, Abingdon, Oxon.
Chang Yong-jun 장용준
2017 18,000 nyŏnjŏn Paektu-san hŭgyosŏk, Taegu esŏ hwagin: Taegu Wŏlsŏng-dong kusŏkki yujŏk ŭi hŭgyosŏk wŏnsanji punsŏk kyŏlkwa 18,000년전 백두산 흑요석, 대구에서 확인: 대구 월성동 구석기유적의 흑요석 원산지 분석결과 [Obsidian from Paektu mountain dated to 18,000 years ago confirmed in Taegu: The results of sourcing analysis of the obsidian from the Wŏlsŏng-dong Paleolithic site, Taegu]. *Munhwa ch'eyuk kwan'gwangbu podo charyo* 문화체육관광부 보도자료 [Press release from the Ministry of Culture, Sports, and Tourism] 5 January. Seoul.
Chang Yun-dŭk 장윤득, Pak T'ae-yun 박태윤, Yi Sang-mok 이상목, and Kim Chŏng-jin 김정진
2007 Wŏlsŏng-dong kusŏkgi yujŏk ch'ult'o hŭgyosŏkche sŏkki ŭi amsŏk mit kwangmulhakchŏk yŏn'gu rŭl t'onghan wŏnsanji ch'ujŏng 월성동 구석기 유적 출토 흑요석제 석기의 암석 및 광물학적 연구를 통한 원산지 추정 [Petrologic and mineralogic studies on the origin of Paleolithic obsidian implements from Wŏlsŏng-dong, Korea]. *Han'guk Chigu Kwahakhoe Chi* 韓國地球科學會誌 28(6): 733–742.
Chōsen Gakkai 朝鮮学会 [Society for Korean Studies] (editor)
2002 *Zempō-kōen-fun to kodai Nikkan kankei* 前方後円墳と古代日韓関係 [Keyhole-shaped mounded tombs and Korea-Japan relationship in ancient times]. Dōseisha 同成社, Tokyo.

Egami Namio.
1964. The Formation of the People and Origin of the State in Japan. *Memoirs of the Research Department of the Toyo Bunko* 23, pp. 35–70.
Im Yong-jin 林永珍
1994 Kwangju Wŏlgye-dong ŭi Changgo pun 2 ki 光州月桂洞의 長鼓墳2基 [Two tombs at Changgo in Wŏlgye-dong, Kwangju]. *Han'guk Kogo Hakpo* 韓國考古學報 31, pp. 237–264.
Imamura, Keiji
1996 *Prehistoric Japan: New Perspectives on Insular East Asia*. Hawai'i Press, Honolulu.
Imamura Mineo 今村峯雄, and Fujio Shin'ichirō 藤尾慎一郎
2003 *Tanso-14 nendai sokutei to kōkogaku* 炭素14年代測定と考古学 [Radiocarbon dating and archaeology]. Kokuritsu Rekishi Minzoku Hakubutsukan 国立歴史民俗博物館 [National Museum of Japanese History], Sakura.
Imamura Mineo 今村峯雄, and Harunari Hideji 春成秀爾 (editors)
2004 *Yayoi jidai no jitsu nendai* 弥生時代の実年代 [Calendrical dates of the Yayoi period]. Gakuseisha 学生社, Tokyo.
Inoue Chikara 井上主税
2014 *Chōsen hantō no Wa-kei ibutsu kara mita Nitchō kankei* 朝鮮半島の倭系遺物からみた日朝関係 [Korea-Japan relationship as seen from artifacts of Japanese origins discovered in the Korean peninsula]. Gakuseisha 学生社, Tokyo.
Isahaya Naoto 諫早直人
2012 *Tōhoku Asia ni okeru kiba bunka no kōkogaku-teki kenkyū* 東北アジアにおける騎馬文化の考古学的研究 [Archaeological study on cultures of horse riding in northeast Asia]. Yūzankaku 雄山閣, Tokyo.
Ishimoda Tadashi 石母田正
1962 Kodai-shi gaisetsu 古代史概説 [Ancient history: An overview]. *In Iwanami koza Nihon rekishi 1: Genshi, kodai* 岩波講座日本歴史 1: 原始・古代 [Iwanami introduction to Japanese history, volume 1: Proto-history and ancient history], edited by Ishimoda Tadashi, pp. 1–75. Iwanami Shoten 岩波書店, Tokyo.
Kameda Shūichi 亀田修一
1993 Kōkogaku kara mita toraijin 考古学から見た渡来人 [Immigrants from an archaeological perspective]. *Kobunka Dansō* 古文化談叢 30, pp. 747–778.
Kang In-gu 姜仁求
1987 *Han'guk ŭi chŏnbang huwŏnbun Mugi-san kwa Changgo-san ch'ŭngnyang chosa pogosŏ* 韓國의 前方後圓墳 舞妓山과 長鼓山 測量調査報告書 [Korea's keyhole-shaped tombs and report on surveys at Mugi-san and Changgo-san], Chosa Yŏn'gu Pogosŏ 調査研究報告書 [Survey Investigation Reports] 87-1. Han'guk Chŏngsin Munhwa Yŏn'guwŏn 韓國精神文化研究院, Sŏngnam.

———

1992 *Samguk sidae yujŏk ŭi chosa yŏn'gu 1: Chara-bong kobun* 三國時代遺蹟의調査研究 1: 자라봉古墳 [Studies of surveys of sites of the Three Kingdoms period 1: The Chara-bong tomb], Chosa Yŏn'gu Pogosŏ 調査研究報告書 [Survey Investigation Reports] 92-3. Han'guk Chŏngsin Munhwa Yŏn'guwŏn 韓國精神文化研究院, Sŏngnam.

Kobayashi Yukio 小林行雄

1962 Kofun bunka no keisei 古墳文化の形成 [Formation of Kofun culture]. In *Iwanami koza Nihon rekishi 1: Genshi, kodai* 岩波講座日本歴史 1: 原始・古代 [Iwanami introduction to Japanese history, volume 1: Proto-history and ancient history], edited by Ishimoda Tadashi 石母田正, pp. 237–272. Iwanami Shoten 岩波書店, Tokyo.

Kungnip Cheju Pangmulgwan 국립제주박물관 [National Cheju Museum]

2005 *Han'guk-Ilbon Ok'inawa ŭi chogae chep'um ŭl t'onghan sŏnsa sidae munhwa ŭi chaebalgyŏn* 한국-일본 오키나와의 조개제품을 통한 선사시대문화의 재발견 [The rediscovery of prehistorical culture from Korea-Japan shell products]. Kungnip Cheju Pangmulgwan, Cheju City.

Kungnip Kwangju Pangmulgwan 國立光州博物館 [Kwangju National Museum]

1996 *Kwangju Myŏnghwa-dong kobun* 光州明花洞古墳 [The Myŏnghwa-dong tomb in Kwangju]. Kungnip Kwangju Pangmulgwan Haksul Ch'ongsŏ 國立光州博物館學術叢書 [Academic Collection of the Kwangju National Museum] No. 29. Kungnip Kwangju Pangmulgwan, Kwangju.

Kuzmin, Yaroslav V.

2012 Long-Distance Obsidian Transport in Prehistoric Northeast Asia. *Bulletin of the Indo-Pacific Prehistory Association* 32: 1–5.

Moon Chang Rho

2012 Research on Kaya History and Issues of Academic Debate. In *Early Korea 3: The Rediscovery of Kaya in History and Archaeology*, edited by Mark E. Byington, pp. 49–104. Mark E. Byington, general editor, Korea Institute, Harvard University, Cambridge, MA.

Oda Fujio 小田富士雄

1980 Kyūshū-kei Yayoi bunbutsu no taigai dempa oboegaki 九州系弥生文物の対外伝播覚書 [Note on external diffusion of Yayoi artifacts of the Kyushu origins]. In *Nihon minzoku bunka to sono shūhen : Kōko hen* 日本民族文化とその周辺: 考古篇 [The culture of the Japanese people and their surrounding environment: Archaeology], edited by Kokubu Naoichi 国分直一, pp. 209–244. Shin Nihon Kyōiku Tosho 新日本教育図書, Shimonoseki.

Oda Fujio 小田富士雄, and Han Pyŏng-sam 韓炳三
1991 *Nikkan kōshō no kōkogaku: Yayoi jidai hen* 日韓交渉の考古学: 弥生時代編 [Archaeology of Korea-Japan interactions: Yayoi period]. Rokkō Shuppansha 六興出版, Tokyo.
Onoyama Setsu 小野山節
1975 *Kodai shi hakkutsu 6: Kofun to kokka no naritachi* 古代史発掘 6: 古墳と国家の成立ち [Excavations of ancient history, volume 6: State formation and mounded tombs]. Kōdansha 講談社, Tokyo.
Pak Ch'ŏn-su (Pak Cheun Soo) 朴天秀
1995 Torai-kei bumbutsu kara mita Kaya to Wa ni okeru seijiteki hendō 渡来系文物からみた伽耶と倭における政治的変動 [Political change in Kaya and Wa seen through imported goods]. In *Machikaneyama ronsō Shigaku hen* 待兼山論叢 史学篇 [Memoirs of the faculty of arts at Osaka University history section] 29, pp. 53–84. Ōsaka Daigaku Bungakubu 大阪大学文学部, Osaka.
———
1998 Kōkogaku kara mita kodai no Kan-Nichi kōshō 考古学から見た古代の韓・日交渉 [Ancient Korea-Japan exchanges seen through archaeology]. *Seikyū Gakujutsu Ronshū* 青丘学術論集 12: 77–122.
———
2007 *Kaya to Wa: Han hantō to Nihon rettō no kōkogaku* 加耶と倭: 韓半島と日本列島の考古学 [Kaya and Wa: The archaeology of the Korean peninsula and the Japanese archipelago]. Kōdansha 講談社, Tokyo.
Republic of Korea
2015 Nomination of the Baekje Historic Areas for inscription on the World Heritage List. Submitted to International Committee on Monuments and Sites (ICOMOS). Copies available from the World Heritage Centre website http://whc.unesco.org/uploads/nominations/1477.pdf. Republic of Korea, Seoul, accessed July 11, 2017.
Shimazu Yoshiaki 島津義昭
1992 Nikkan no bunbutsu kōryū 日韓の文物交流 [Exchange of Cultural Objects between Japan and Korea]. *Kikan Kōkogaku* 季刊考古学 38: 54–58.
Sŏng Nak-chun 成洛俊
1992 Hamp'yŏng Yedŏng-ni Sindŏk kobun kin'gŭp susŭp chosa yakpo 咸平禮德里 新德古墳 緊急收拾調査 略報 [Summary report of the emergency collection and survey of the Sindŏk tomb at Yedŏng-ni in Hamp'yŏng]. Che-35 hoe Chŏn'guk Yŏksahak Taehoe nonmun mit palp'yo yoji 제35회 전국역사학대회 논문및 발표요지 [Proceedings and abstracts of the thirty-fifth conference of the Korean Historical Society]. Location unknown.

Suematsu Yasukazu 末松保和
1949 *Mimana kōbō shi* 任那興亡史 [Rise and fall of Mimana]. Ōyashima Shuppan 大八州出版, Tokyo.
Takada Kanta 高田貫太
2014 *Kofun jidai no Nitchō kankei* 古墳時代の日朝関係 [Korea-Japan relationship during the Kofun period]. Yoshikawa Kōbunkan 吉川弘文館, Tokyo.
Takakura Hiroaki 高倉洋彰, and Tanaka Yoshiyuki 田中良之 (editors)
2011 *AMS nendai to kōkogaku* AMS 年代と考古学 [AMS dates and archaeology]. Gakuseisha 学生社, Tokyo.
Tanaka Toshiaki 田中俊明
1992 *Dai-Kaya renmei no kōbō to "Mimana"* 大伽耶連盟の興亡と「任那」 ["Mimana" and the rise and fall of the Tae Kaya confederacy]. Yoshikawa Kōbunkan 吉川弘文館, Tokyo.
Trigger, Bruce G.
2006 *A History of Archaeological Thought*. Cambridge University Press, Cambridge, UK.
Tsude Hiroshi 都出比呂志
1995 Zempō-kōen-fun taisei to chiiki kenryoku 前方後円墳体制と地域権力 [Regional authority and social system symbolized by keyhole-shaped mounded tombs]. In *Nihon kodai kokka no tenkai* 日本古代国家の展開 [Growth of ancient state in Japan], edited by Kadowaki Teiji 門脇禎二, pp. 49–72. Shibunkaku Shuppan 思文閣出版, Kyoto.
Yamao Yukihisa 山尾幸久
1989 *Kodai no Nitchō kankei* 古代の日朝関係 [Ancient Japan-Korea relationship]. Hanawa Shobō 塙書房, Tokyo.
Yi Ch'ang-hŭi 이창희
2010 Chŏmt'odae t'ogi ŭi siryŏndae: sehyŏng tonggŏm munhwa ŭi sŏngnip kwa ch'ŏlgi ŭi ch'urhyŏn yŏndae 점토대토기의 실연대: 세형동검문화의 성립과 철기의 출현연대 [The absolute dates of attached-rim pottery: The formation of slender bronze dagger culture and dates of the emergence of iron]. *Munhwajae* 문화재 43(3): 48-101.
Yi Hui-jun 李熙濬
2007 Silla kogohak yŏn'gu 新羅考古學研究 [Archaeological studies on Silla]. Sahoe P'yŏngnon 社會評論, Seoul.
Yi Sŏn-bok 이선복, and Chwa Yong-ju 좌용주
2015 Hŭgyosŏk sanji ch'ujŏng yŏn'gu ŭi chaegŏmt'o 흑요석 산지 추정 연구의 재검토 [On the provenance of prehistoric obsidian artifacts in Korea]. *Han'guk Kusŏkki Hakpo* 한국구석기학보 31: 156–180.

1 Bronze Mirrors and Exchange Between Southern Korea and Kyushu

Lee Chungkyu

Abstract

In this paper I consider metal artifacts from mortuary contexts in order to analyze diachronic exchange relations between the Korean peninsula and the Japanese archipelago from the first millennium B.C. to the earliest two centuries of the first millennium A.D. I explore the morphological chronological classification of bronze mirrors in connection with associated artifacts and molds. Mirrors were widely distributed in the peninsula and archipelago in a time-transgressive manner, and the center of production gradually moved eastward from western Liaoning into the northwestern part of the Korean peninsula in the fourth century B.C. As the polities of northwestern Korea became more complex, a bronze production complex developed in southwestern Korea in the second century B.C. The mortuary practices of southwestern Korea influenced those of polities in Kyushu, Japan, at approximately the same time when exchange also intensified between the two regions. Circumstances changed with the establishment of the Han commanderies in addition to the appearance of Han mirrors in Korea during the first century B.C. Mirrors were distributed widely at this time in southeastern Korea and Kyushu. Imitation mirrors are found in Japan from this time in connection with an intensification of exchange with southeastern Korea.

Introduction

The overall aim of this chapter is to analyze bronze mirrors and other bronze and iron objects found in mortuary context and to use them to explain the developmental transformations of exchange between the Korean peninsula and Japanese archipelago. This chapter first introduces the geographical distribution of mirrors in tombs, the bronze and iron objects that accompany them, and the differences in mirror morphology as well as the relative quantities in which they are found over time. We will then examine the internal circumstances of the production of bronze and iron objects and external exchange indirectly, through an examination of grave goods.

The 210-km-wide strait between the Korean peninsula and the Japanese archipelago formed as a result of a rise in sea level beginning at the end of the last glacial period approximately ten thousand years ago. From prehistoric times until today, the southern coast of the Korean peninsula and the northern coast of Kyushu, with the island of Tsushima as a midway point, have been footholds for the continuous movement of people and exchange between human groups. From the first half of the first millennium B.C., however, the method of this exchange changed. With the development of agriculture and other food production technologies came a dramatic rise in population, and the number of regional groups likewise increased. This prompted large-scale movements of populations and the spread of production techniques from the Korean peninsula to the Japanese archipelago.

In the second half of the first millennium B.C., exchange between Korea and Japan entered a new phase as bronze goods produced through advanced technologies began to appear in the Korean peninsula. Unlike the previous period, the principal exchange between the two regions was consistently conducted by certain levels of society in particular regional groups, and this exchange was centered on fixed bases of operation. In addition, the goods or skills that were the focus of trade were also restricted to an elite segment of the population.

Bronze goods require a consistent production process and a highly specialized skill-set at every stage of production—from the supply of raw materials to the creation of finished goods. Considering that bronze objects could be both weaponry to secure the safety of regional groups as well as ritual objects with ideological significance, they would have been strategic tools important in political, economic, and religious contexts beyond the simple production and exchange perspective. Though the proposition that bronze metallurgy was an important factor in state formation cannot be accepted uncritically, bronze ritual goods that required the highest level of skill in their production speak to the existence of hierarchical authority and regional polities.

This is reflected in the funerary ceremonies of individuals who owned the objects, as bronze goods came to be deposited as prestige items in high-status tombs in various regions of Korea and Japan. Among these bronze objects, mirrors (excluding a small number of crudely produced imitation mirrors) in particular exhibit a superlative level of specialized craftsmanship and production, and they must have been prestige goods of high-ranking individuals.

Written records indicate that the period during which mirrors with multiple knobs were produced and disseminated corresponds to the time when the polities of Old Chosŏn 古朝鮮, Puyŏ 夫餘, and the minor polities of the Samhan 三韓 were forming in northeastern China and the Korean peninsula. The minor polities, complex societies equivalent to the developmental level of chiefdoms as seen by the presence of leaders with such titles as *kunjang* 君長 or *sinji* 臣智, are to be distinguished from the subsequent developmental stage of the state-level (or *kuk* 國) society.[1] Tombs containing large quantities of burial goods, including multi-knobbed mirrors and various other types of bronze objects, are understood to be those of such leaders, and the regional groups with which these tombs are associated are thought to represent the minor polities (Yi Ch'ŏng-gyu 2000).

Mirrors with multiple knobs were no longer produced in the Korean peninsula after the destruction of Old Chosŏn by the Han empire in 108 B.C. Instead, Han-style mirrors of the Central Plains spread widely in regions of Korea and Japan and came to be recognized as high-status prestige goods.

Morphological Classification of Bronze Mirrors and Chronological Periodization

In order to explain in a systematic way the cultural changes involved in exchange related to mirrors between the Korean peninsula and the Japanese archipelago, it is necessary first to provide a brief outline of the distribution of mirrors over the entirety of Northeast Asia. In addition, other artifact assemblages such as iron and ceramic objects in the same contexts must be considered when organizing the chronology of mirrors and other bronze goods in Korea and Japan. For the morphological classification of bronze mirrors, the author uses his own system of classification as a basis for mirrors with multiple knobs (Yi Ch'ŏng-gyu 2010:45–89), and he relies on the systems devised by Chinese and Japanese archaeologists for Central Plains

[1] Editor's Note: These terms are derived from the descriptions of the Han polities included in the *Sanguozhi* 三國志 (Chronicles of the Three Kingdoms) compiled in the late third century on the basis of direct contact between these polities and the Wei empire of China.

mirrors with a single knob, referring also to the views of Korean scholars (Takakura 1972; Yi Yang-su 2006). For the chronological periodization of objects, the geographical scope will be limited to the Korean peninsula and follows the author's previous work (Yi Ch'ŏng-gyu 1997) as well as the opinions of Japanese and Chinese scholars.

Morphological Classification of Bronze Mirrors

The bronze mirrors that were distributed throughout the peninsula and the archipelago primarily include multi-knobbed mirrors produced in present-day northeastern China and in the Korean peninsula itself; mirrors with a single knob manufactured in the Central Plains that were imported into the region; and imitative mirrors produced in Korea and Japan based on the forms of those from the Central Plains. Whereas the multi-knobbed mirrors were extensively circulated prior to the fall of Wiman Chosŏn 衛滿朝鮮 in the second century B.C., the single-knobbed and imitative mirrors were distributed afterward.[2]

Classification of mirrors with multiple knobs can be made on the basis of the pattern of decorations on the back surface as well as from other attributes, including the outer rim and the shape of the knob (Miyazato 2008:1–32). Individual patterns are used first to classify multi-knobbed mirrors into three types: A, B, and C. Type A mirrors feature coarse-lined patterns with a zig-zag motif; Type B mirrors are also coarse-lined, but the lines are arranged in triangular patterns; and Type C mirrors display repeated triangle and square patterns of finely inscribed lines (Figures 1.1 and 1.2).

These three types of multi-knobbed mirror can be further subdivided. First, two variations of Type A mirrors can be distinguished (A1 and A2). The back faces of A1 mirrors maintain some form of the zig-zag pattern model, whereas A2 mirrors have a narrow outer band that follows the rim, and the pattern appears to be a precursor to the lined triangles common to Type B mirrors. If one looks at the shape of the rim, those of the A1 mirrors are flush with the plane of the inner portion of the mirror, while the outer edge of A2 mirrors appears triangular or trapezoidal in cross-section, and the inner section of the surface has a double protrusion.

[2] Editor's Note: Wiman Chosŏn refers to the early polity of Chosŏn based at present-day Pyongyang, control of which had been usurped in the early second century B.C. by a man of the Yan polity named Wei Man 衛滿, called Wi Man or Wiman in modern Korean. This polity was destroyed by the Han emperor Wu in 108 B.C.

Figure 1.1 Varieties of Type A and B Multi-knobbed Mirrors. From Yi Ch'ŏng-gyu 2010.

Type B mirrors are usually subdivided by the composition of their decorative patterns and shapes. B1 mirrors are completely unadorned. The main decorations of B2 mirrors are usually radial lines resembling leaf veins, lattices, or animal patterning. The surfaces of B3 mirrors are divided by several parallel lines and filled in with triangular line patterns. On B4 mirrors the surface is divided into outer and inner sections, with the inner portion

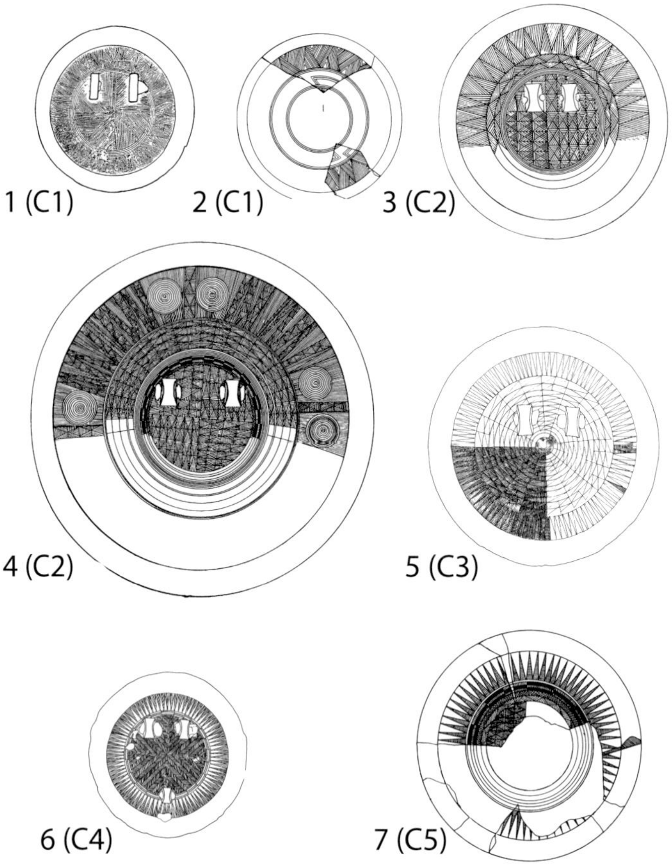

Figure 1.2 Varieties of Type C Multi-knobbed Mirrors.
From Yi Chŏng-gyu 2010.

arranged as triangular line patterns. B5 mirror surfaces have a single continuous pattern of triangular lines arranged around the center, and undecorated space or rectangular line patterns fill the center. Lastly, B6 mirrors are divided into two circular bands of triangular lined patterns that are filled with fine lines arranged in alternating directions.

In the case of Type C multi-knobbed mirrors, the patterned band of the outer section tends to correspond to those of the inner or central portions, so it is used as the basis of classification. C1 mirrors have no fixed patterning. C2 mirrors have a continuous outer band of triangular patterns, but the outward-pointing triangles have a different banded pattern from the inner-pointing ones. C3 mirrors feature a continuous banded triangular pattern, but the triangles that point toward the rim are filled in with lines parallel to the base of the triangle. C4 mirrors are inscribed with the same continuous triangular pattern as C3 mirrors, but the interior of the triangles that point toward the rim are blank. C5 mirrors also have the same continuous triangular pattern as C3 mirrors, but the interior of the triangles that point toward the center are blank (Yi Chŏng-gyu 2010:59–65).

The production techniques used for each of the three types of bronze mirrors with multiple knobs varied according to their molds. For Types A and B, the shape and pattern of the mirror were carved into a stone surface of talc or similar material, but in the case of Type C mirrors, a model of the overall shape of the mirror was sculpted in wax and the pattern detail was carved onto its surface. The model was then covered with a mixture of clay and fine sand to create the mirror mold. The earthen mold allowed patterns of minute lines to be created more easily, but required a much higher degree of craft specialization. The casting process would also destroy the earthen molds, making them different from the stone molds that could be used to cast multiple objects.

Unlike the simple geometric patterns of the previously discussed multi-knobbed mirrors, the decorative patterns on the back surfaces of Central Plains lineage mirrors with single knobs unearthed in Japan and Korea include a diverse range of animal and human motifs as well as Chinese character inscriptions. Using individual patterns and inscriptions as a reference for classifying these objects, mirrors with single knobs are generally designated as shown in Table 1.1.

Mirrors with coiled-dragon motifs are distinguished by their compound vine-like or similar pattern of a coiled dragon or snake on the primary band and a raised outer rim. Mirrors with grass leaves normally feature flower petals or other floral patterns, an interior rim decorated with patterns of linked arcs, and a checkerboard or circular arrangements of shapes or characters around the central knob. Mirrors with star-clouds feature sets of three to ten interconnected star-like small bumps or constellations, a rim decorated with inward facing linked arcs, and small bosses surrounding the central handle in a circular or floral style. The primary decoration on inscribed mirrors is an inscription of poetry, words of good fortune, or details relating to the origin of the mirror, and a flat band around

Table 1.1
Types of Single-knobbed Mirror

Mirror Type		Alternate Name	
Coiled-dragon mirrors	*pallimun kyŏng* 蟠螭文鏡		
Grass-leaf mirrors	*ch'oyŏpmun kyŏng* 草葉文鏡		
Star-cloud mirrors	*sŏngunmun kyŏng* 星雲文鏡		
Inscribed mirrors	*myŏngmun kyŏng* 銘文鏡		
Four-animal mirrors	*sayu kŭmsumun kyŏng* 四乳禽獸文鏡	Serpentine dragon mirrors	*hweyongmun kyŏng* 虺龍文鏡
TLV mirrors	*pakkuk kyŏng* 博局鏡	Checkerboard mirrors	*panggyŏk kyugu kyŏng* 方格規矩鏡
Floral-pattern mirrors	*naehaeng hwamun kyŏng* 內行花文鏡	Linked-arc mirrors	*yŏnhomun kyŏng* 連弧文鏡

the edge. In the central section of the mirror there are many examples composed of floral decoration or circular bands. Mirrors with four animals are distinguished by one of four faunal motifs: serpentine dragons, dragons and tigers, the four guardian animals, or birds. They also have a broad flat band around the edge. The inner section of so-called TLV mirrors features decorations such as the four guardian animals, other faunal motifs, or immortals that are divided by T-, L-, and V-shaped borders in a square or checkerboard arrangement surrounding the central knob. The distinguishing characteristics of floral-pattern mirrors are the primary decorative elements of quatrefoil or crescents and a plain outer rim (Figure 1.3).

It is thought that imitation mirrors based on these Han Chinese types were produced in the Korean peninsula and Japanese archipelago. They are classified by relative circumference size: small (under 10 cm), medium (approximately 15 cm), and large (over 20 cm). Small imitation mirrors are further subdivided into Types I, II, and III. Type I mirrors have a narrow edge that appears triangular or semicircular in cross-section and faithfully

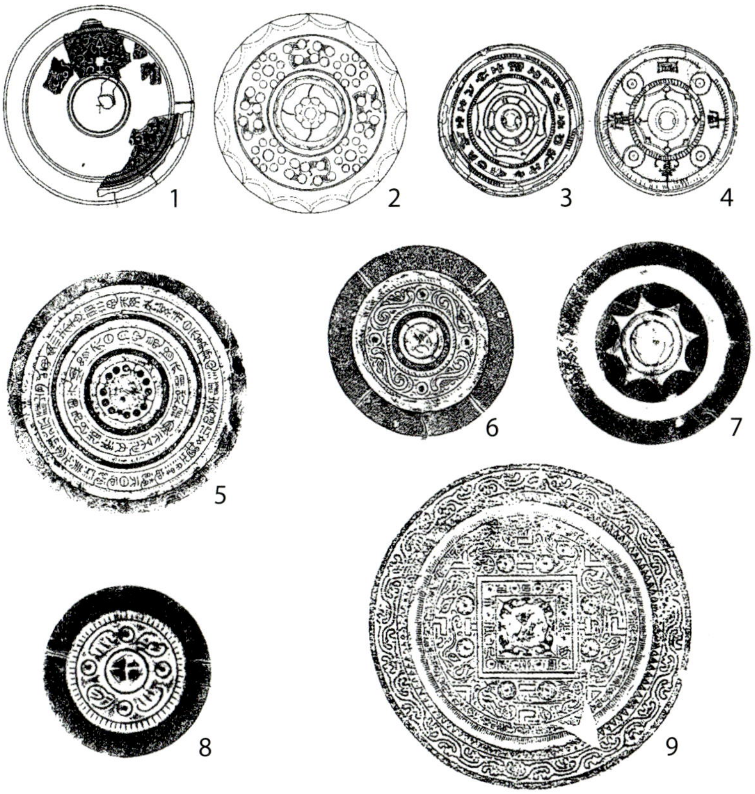

Figure 1.3 Varieties of Mirrors from the Central Plains of China. From Yi Chŏng-gyu 2010. 1. Coiled-dragon mirror; 2. Star-cloud mirror; 3–5. Inscribed mirrors; 6. Serpentine dragon mirror; 7. Floral-pattern mirror; 8. Water-animal mirror; 9. TLV mirror.

imitates Chinese floral and sunbeam mirror motifs. Type II small mirrors have a wide and flat edge and are more simplified. In Type III mirrors, which are mainly found in areas outside of Kyushu, the width of the flat edge is simplified rather than expanding. Among small imitation mirrors there are also a few examples with no decoration on the back surface at all. Other than their circumference, the distinguishing characteristic of medium-sized imitation mirrors is patterned bands divided into three concentric zones, these radial zones containing several sets of three to four parallel vertical lines arranged radially. As for large mirrors, the center or inner

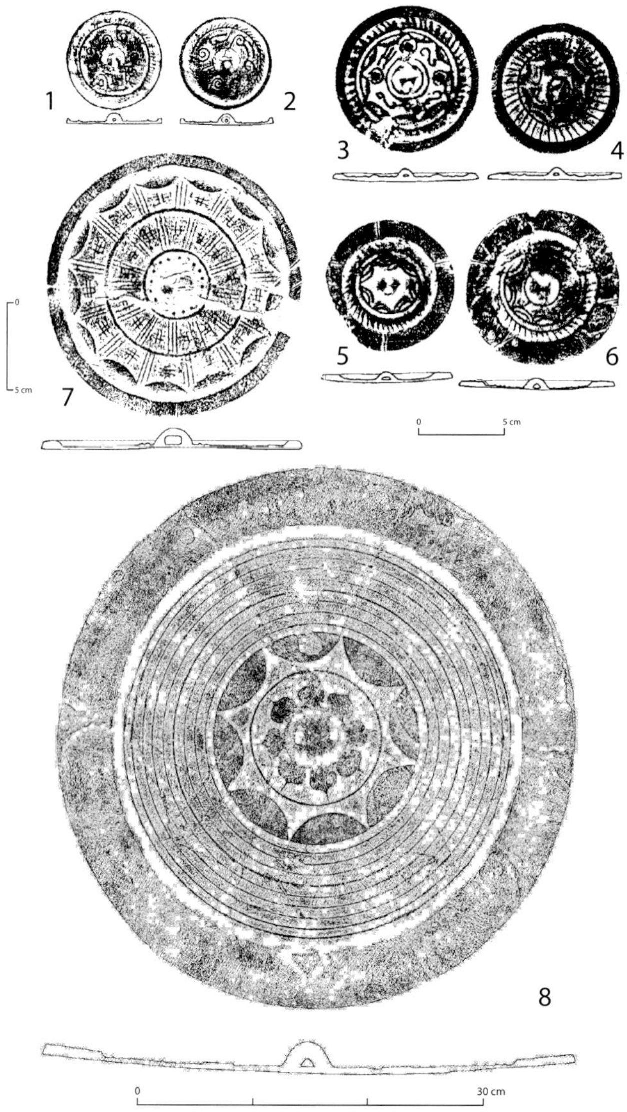

Figure 1.4 Varieties of Imitative Mirrors. From Takakura 1972.
1–4. Type I imitative mirror; 5. Type II imitative mirror; 6. Type III imitative mirror; 7. Medium imitative mirror; 8. Large imitative mirror.

portion of the object has an essentially floral decoration, and the outer portion is decorated with concentric circles (Takakura 1972:1–30; Morioka 1989) (Figure 1.4).

As is seen in the exquisitely expressed decoration of the Han mirrors of the Central Plains, the surface was created from an earthen mold made from a cut model of easy-to-carve wax or other material. Among Japanese imitation mirrors, there are some examples of large mirrors that suggest the possibility that earthen molds were used in their production, but it is widely assumed that the coarse patterns of small mirrors were produced with stone molds.

Periodization

The transition from mirrors with multiple knobs to Han mirrors with single knobs forms the basis for the periodization of bronze mirrors. Within this general two-stage sequence, multi-knobbed mirrors can be further divided into three stages (Types A, B, and C), while single-knobbed mirrors can be distinguished between those of the Western Han and those of the Eastern Han periods. This makes for a total of five morphological stages spread over two periods.

Stage I is marked by Type A mirrors with multiple knobs, and the earliest example (Type A1) comes from the Daling River 大凌河 basin in the Liaoxi region of western Liaoning. It intersects chronologically with Central Plains–lineage artifacts and thus provides a *terminus ante quem* at the end of the Western Zhou and the beginning of the Spring and Autumn period of the Eastern Zhou (approximately the ninth to eighth centuries B.C.). Type A bronze mirrors are concentrated in Liaoning as well as the northwestern portion of the Korean peninsula and are accompanied by lute-shaped bronze daggers. Bronze objects were not distributed in the Japanese archipelago during this period.

Stage II is characterized by the presence of Type B mirrors with multiple knobs that are distributed in the Liaodong region, Jilin Province, the Russian maritime region, and the western part of the Korean peninsula, but not in the Liaoxi region. At that time mirrors were not distributed in eastern Korea or Japan. B1 and B2 mirrors appeared in Liaodong and the Korean peninsula at almost the same time as slim bronze daggers. The latter subtypes of this stage, B5 and B6, were distributed with variform bronze objects in southwestern Korea. The Warring States polity of Yan 燕 spread Central Plains culture to Liaoxi generally around the first half of the fourth century B.C. and arrived in the Liaodong region in

Table 1.2
Stages of Mirror Types and Their Associated Artifacts

Stage	Chronology	Mirror Type	Associated Artifacts
I	Ninth to fifth centuries B.C.	Type A multi-knob mirrors	Lute-shaped bronze daggers 琵琶形銅劍
II	Fourth to third centuries B.C.	Type B multi-knob mirrors	Slim bronze daggers 細形銅劍 / variform bronze objects 異形銅器
III	Third to second centuries B.C.	Type C multi-knob mirrors	Slim bronze daggers 細形銅劍 / slim bronze dagger-axes 細形銅戈 / bronze bells 銅鈴具 / cast iron tools
IV	Second to first centuries B.C.	Western Han mirrors	Medium-thin bronze spears 中細形銅鉾 / iron swords 鍛造 鐵製短劍 / flat iron axes 板狀鐵斧
V	First to second centuries A.D.	Eastern Han mirrors / imitation mirrors	Medium-wide and wide bronze spears 中廣形 廣形銅鉾 / iron swords 鐵製長劍

the first half of the third century B.C., which defines an upper and lower limit for this stage.

Type C multi-knobbed mirrors appear in Stage III, and though this morphology has not yet been confirmed in the Liaodong or Jilin regions, they were distributed in western and eastern Korea as well as the Kyushu and Kinki regions of Japan. The C1 subtype is distributed in southwestern Korea, and later subtypes C2, C3, C4, and C5 spread to southeastern Korea and the Japanese archipelago. These mirrors are found concentrated in southwestern Korea in the same archaeological contexts as slim bronze dagger-axes, various bronze rattles, and cast iron tools. The upper limit of the stage is thought to be just after the Yan advance into Liaodong in the middle of the third century B.C., and the lower limit is the collapse of Wiman Chosŏn and the establishment of the Han commanderies at the beginning of the first century B.C.

The appearance of mirrors of the Western Han period (206 B.C.–9 A.D.) marks Stage IV, and they are concentrated in southeastern Korea and northern Kyushu. The mirrors with star-cloud motifs and those with variform characters are primarily distributed in the southeastern portion of Korea along with bronze weaponry, iron daggers, and flat iron axes. In northern Kyushu they are accompanied by medium-thin bronze weaponry. They date from the beginning of the first century B.C. to the end of the first century B.C. before the Wang Mang interregnum (9 A.D.–23 A.D.).

Eastern Han (23 A.D.–220 A.D.) mirrors appeared in Stage V, and those of this category are distributed in a concentrated pattern in southeastern Korea and northern Kyushu and are found as far as the Kinki region. Among other motifs, serpentine dragon and TLV mirrors as well as a diversity of imitation mirrors are distributed in southeastern Korea and are accompanied by long iron swords and various iron objects. Additionally, they are found in northern Kyushu with medium-wide and wide bronze spear heads. This stage dates from the first century A.D. to the middle of the second century. All stages are summarized in Table 1.2.

Stage I—Type A Mirrors (Ninth to Fifth Centuries B.C.)

The first half of this period (around the ninth to seventh centuries B.C.) marks the beginning of the large-scale inclusion of bronze objects in tombs. The largest concentration of such burials centers on the Liaoxi region, but they are not found in Liaodong or the Korean peninsula. The representative examples of these tombs can be found in the upper Liao River basin in the tombs at Xiaoheishigou 小黑石沟 (Neimenggu Zizhiqu Wenwu Kaogu Yanjiusuo and Ningchengxian Liao Zhongjing Bowuguan 2008), and in those at Nanshangen 南山根 (Zhongguo Shehui Kexueyuan Kaogu Yanjiusuo and Neimenggu Gongzuodui 1975:117–140), both in the Ningcheng 宁城 region of Inner Mongolia, as well as at Shiertaiyingzi 十二台营子 in Chaoyang, Liaoning Province, in the Daling River basin (Zhu Gui 朱贵 1960:63–72). The tombs in both sites in Ningcheng contain a number of different types of bronze objects, including weaponry, tools, personal adornments, horse-riding equipment, and containers. Yet the majority of these are morphologically distinct with no common precursors. Some scholars are of the opinion that the Ningcheng and Chaoyang tombs both fall within the Upper Xiajiadian 夏家店上层 culture, while others see the Chaoyang tomb as belonging to a separate Shiertaiyingzi or Linghe 凌河 culture. The connections between them based on ceramics and other artifact types are not clear, however, and no definite conclusions can be drawn (Wuenyuesitu 2007:224–251; Yi Ch'ŏng-gyu 2008:223–232) (Figures 1.5 and 1.6).

Nevertheless, the Ningcheng tombs contain weaponry and ornaments of the so-called Northern Zone cultural traditions, and they are accompanied by vessels either imported from the Central Plains or produced locally. In contrast, the characteristic multi-knobbed mirrors and lute-shaped

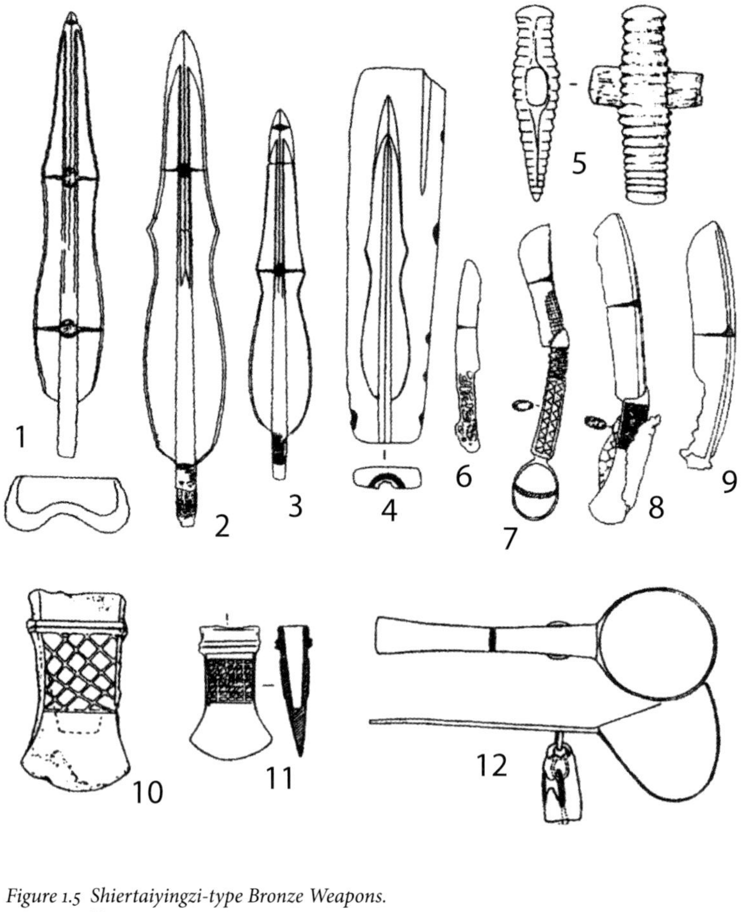

Figure 1.5 Shiertaiyingzi-type Bronze Weapons.
From Yi Chŏng-gyu 2008.

bronze daggers in the Shiertaiyingzi tomb are associated with bronze objects from the region to the east of the Liao River and the Korean peninsula. In other words, the bronze artifacts of the Ningcheng tombs tend to be related to the Central Plains or Northern Zone cultures, while those from the Shiertaiyingzi tomb are associated with the region to the east of the Liao River and the Korean peninsula.

Many scholars have pointed out that the Old Chosŏn polity, which clearly existed from the first half of the first millennium B.C., was

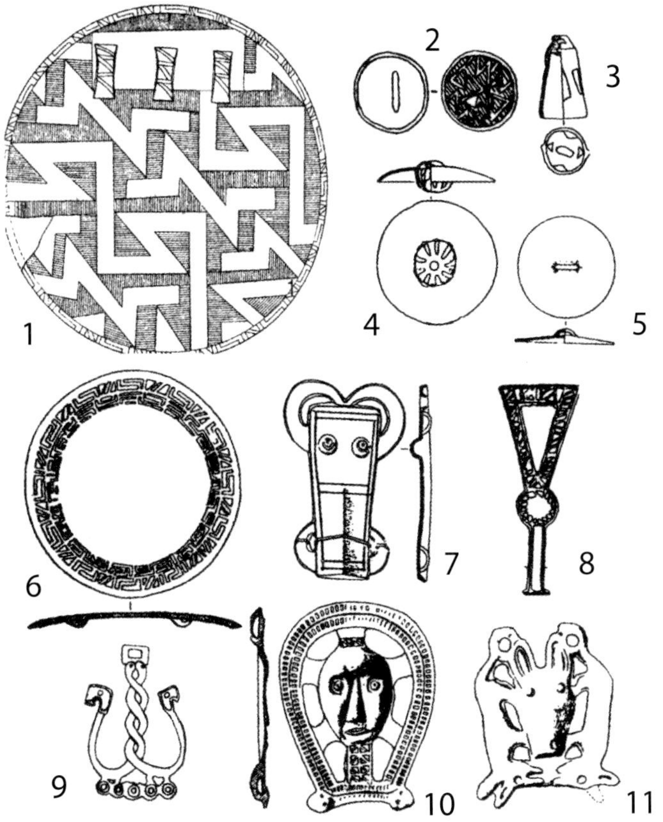

Figure 1.6 Shiertaiyingzi-type Bronze Mirrors and Ornaments. From Yi Chŏng-gyu 2008.

geographically associated with the Korean peninsula. If one considers this along with the fact that the tombs of the Shiertaiyingzi culture are characterized by multi-knobbed mirrors and lute-shaped bronze daggers as burial goods, we must conclude that such tombs could be associated also with Old Chosŏn. There are examples of Type A1 mirrors with multiple knobs, lute-shaped bronze daggers, and other bronze objects that are buried in tombs at almost the same time. Examples include the Dalahangou 大拉罕沟 and Paoshouyingzi 炮手营子 tombs in Jianping 建平 County in the Daling River

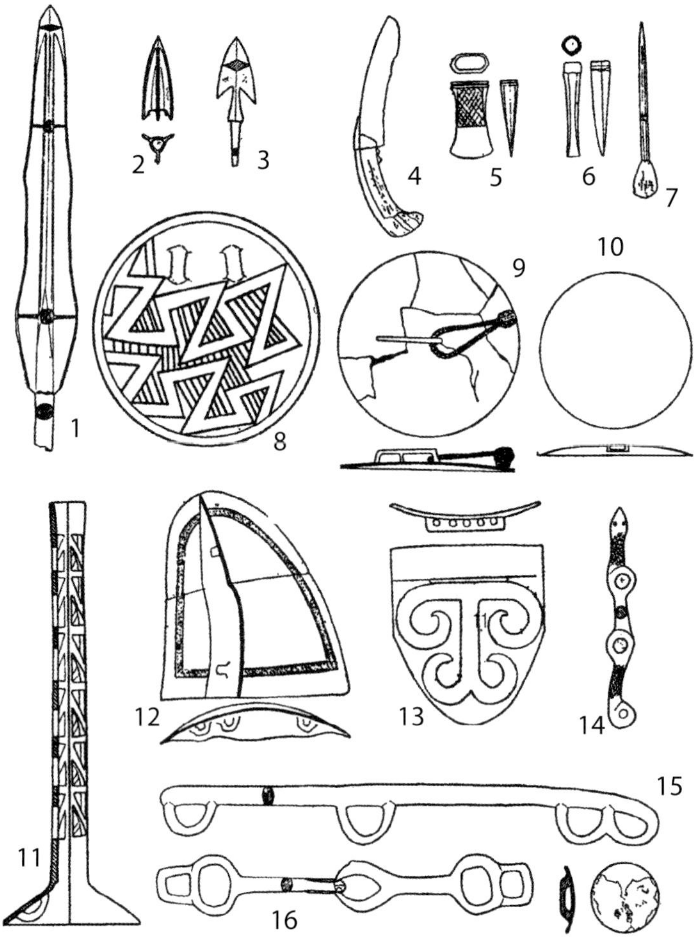

Figure 1.7 Bronzes from Tomb 6512 at Zhengjiawazi in Shenyang. From Shenyang Gugong Bowuguan et al. 1975.

region (Li Dianfu 1991:1–6), as well as the tomb at Liangjia Village 梁家村 in Benxi in the Liaodong region (Wei Haibo 1987). None have been discovered in the Korean peninsula. Among those that have been found, the Shiertaiyingzi tomb is most elaborate. Of the various polities that made up Old Chosŏn, the Shiertaiyingzi tomb would have been that of the leader of the most influential minor polity that linked the others together (Yi Ch'ŏng-gyu 2005:35–38).

The latter half of this stage, lasting from approximately the sixth to the fifth century B.C., seems to have seen a shift of the center of Old Chosŏn. In the Daling River basin of the Liaoxi region the Sanguandianzi 三官甸子 tomb at Lingyuan 凌源, dating from this time, contained a large quantity of bronze objects, including lute-shaped bronze daggers, but it did not include multi-knobbed mirrors, and its bronzes are mostly associated with those of the Central Plains. Like the Shiertaiyingzi burial, Tomb 6512 at Zhengjiawazi 郑家洼子 in Shenyang yielded large numbers of bronze objects, including multi-knobbed mirrors and lute-shaped daggers, and is likely the tomb of a high-level leader, but it is located on the middle reaches of the Liao River basin in the Liaodong region (Shenyang Gugong Bowuguan et al. 1975) (Figure 1.7). Various weapons, tools, horse-riding equipment, and variform bronze objects make up the bulk of the grave goods, and the tomb as a whole is understood to belong to the paramount leader of the various minor polities of Old Chosŏn that moved from the Liaoxi region to Liaodong.

Based on the examples found at Sinsŏng-dong 新成洞 in Pyongyang in northwestern Korea, it is presumed that the types of tombs that contain lute-shaped bronze daggers or multi-knobbed mirrors were constructed in the northwestern part of the Korean peninsula for the first time in the same period as the Zhengjiawazi tomb (Kungnip Chungang Pangmulgwan 2006:49–55). The bronze objects and the black long-necked jars found together with them are similar in form to those found in the Zhengjiawazi tomb (Map 1.1).

But unlike Zhengjiawazi, tombs in southern Korea do not contain bronze mirrors with diverse, multi-lined decoration. A Type A2 mirror was said to have been found in Taejŏn, but no tombs with bronze mirrors as burial goods have been confirmed. In this stage, the only similar examples in this region are burials such as that at Mundang-dong 文唐洞 in Kimch'ŏn, which was a wood-coffin tomb 木棺墓 that contained a bronze dagger and a black burnished long-necked pottery vessel (Kyŏngsang-pukto Munhwajae Yŏn'guwŏn 2008).

Dolmen tombs were constructed widely on the Korean peninsula during the first half of Stage I (Yi Yŏng-mun 2002). A minority of these contained polished groundstone daggers and arrowheads, and an even smaller number contained lute-shaped bronze daggers. Judging by these grave goods, it appears that the concept of prestige associated with the tombs of

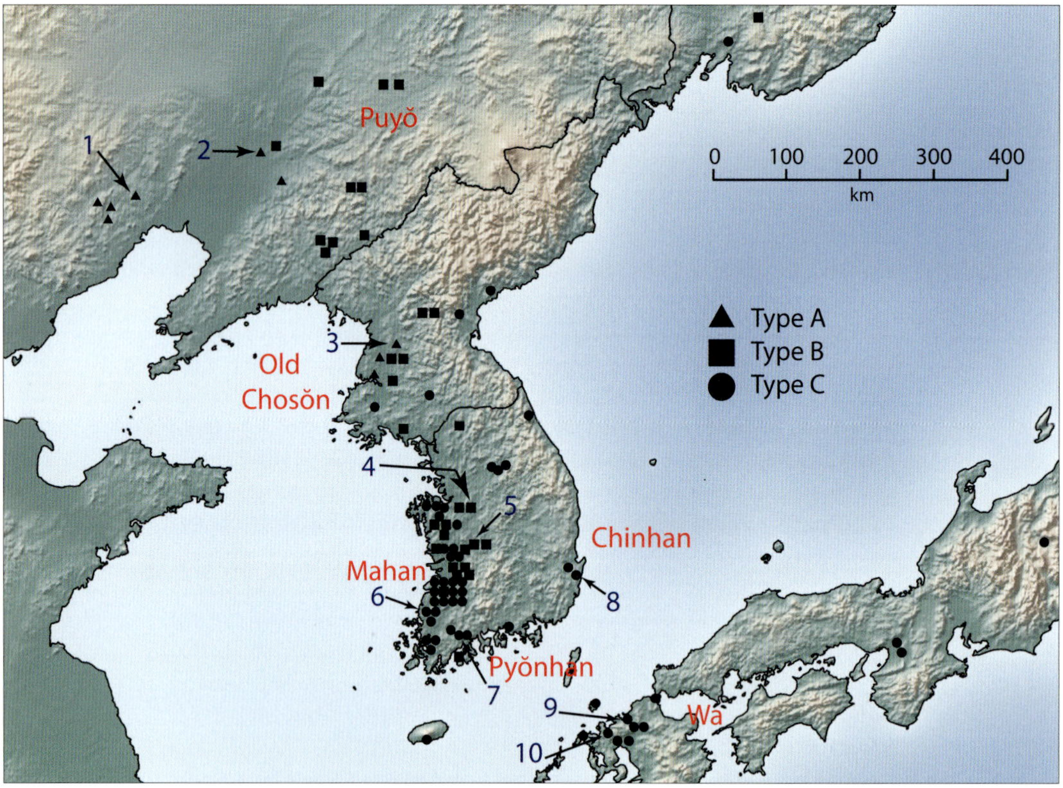

Map 1.1 Distribution of Multi-knobbed Mirrors.
1. Shiertaiyingzi in Chaoyang; 2. Zhengjiawazi in Shenyang; 3. Sinsŏng-dong in Pyongyang; 4. Namsŏng-ni in Asan; 5. Koejŏng-dong in Taejŏn; 6. Ch'op'o-ri in Hamp'yŏng; 7. Taegong-ni in Hwasun; 8. Ipsil-li in Kyŏngju; 9. Yoshitake-Takagi in Fukuoka; 10. Uki-Kunden in Karatsu.

prominent individuals had not yet appeared (Kim Sŭng-ok 2007:94–99). At the Chŏgyang-dong 積良洞 site in Yŏch'on 麗川, a large number of dolmen burials contained a single lute-shaped bronze dagger, which makes it difficult to accept the opinion that this represents the central group of a minor polity (Takesue 2002). The burial goods in dolmen tombs suggest that the social level of prestige goods associated with strong leaders of state-level societies had not yet developed. Further, it is likely that the mobilization of the considerable level of human labor necessary to build dolmen tombs was the result of a voluntary system of cooperation among members of a community; it is unlikely that it was due to the strong authority of a leader.

Nevertheless, the discovery of stone molds directly confirms that there was production of small-scale bronze tools in every region of southern Korea. More than twenty bronze daggers have also been discovered with a unique tang groove, suggesting that they were locally produced rather than imported during this stage. However, there was no demand or production system for objects requiring the use of high-level skill, such as horse harnesses, ritual equipment, or ornamentation. Considering this, it is unlikely that the social and economic conditions necessary for external exchange with the Japanese archipelago had arisen in this period.

It is also possible that construction of dolmen tombs centered on the Kyushu region began in the latter half of Stage I, though it is thought that this was not a wide-scale phenomenon until the following period. Polished groundstone daggers and arrowheads are the only artifacts to have been unearthed from these tombs in Kyushu, and bronze objects are completely nonexistent. Polished groundstone daggers may suggest military prestige, but these were much less potent symbols than bronze daggers (Chang and Hiragōri 2009:63–64). Even those tombs containing only polished groundstone daggers are rare, reflecting the fact that leaders with recognized prestige or socially stratified polities had not yet appeared in Japan at this stage.

Stage II—Type B Mirrors (Fourth to Third Centuries B.C.)

According to historical records, in approximately 300 B.C. the Yan general Qin Kai 秦開 led a military force eastward into Liaodong, and it is thought that this action forced Old Chosŏn to move its center from the Liaodong region to the northwestern part of the Korean peninsula.[3] Type B mirrors and other bronze objects such as weaponry and tools have been confirmed in many tombs dating to this period in both Liaodong and northwestern Korea. Therefore, it is possible that tombs with these mirrors reflect the two locations of the center of the Old Chosŏn polity before and after the Yan eastward campaigns. However, tombs with bronze goods in

[3] Editor's Note: The principal source for this information is found in the account of the Xiongnu in the *Shiji* 史記 (Records of the Grand Historian). See *Shiji* 110:2885.

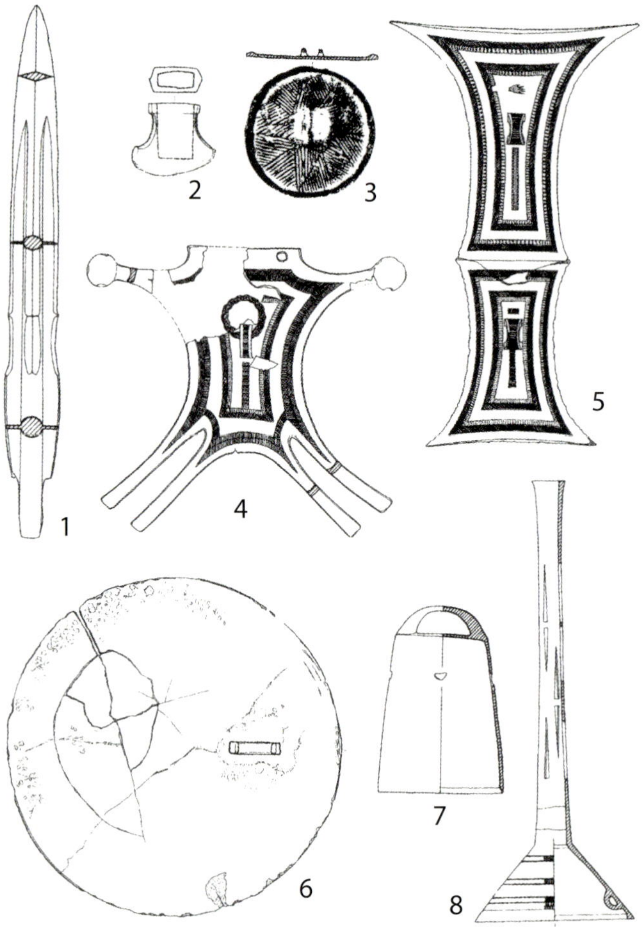

Figure 1.8 Namsŏng-ni–type Bronzes.
From Kungnip Chungang Pangmulgwan 1992.

numbers sufficient to correspond to the social status of a paramount leader of Old Chosŏn have not yet come to light.

In Stage II, bronze mirror tombs appeared in the southern part of the Korean peninsula. While there is an early example said to have come from present-day North Chŏlla Province, in which a Type B mirror was found together with an early slim bronze dagger (Chŏn 1977), formal excavations have yielded tombs with mirrors only from the latter half of Stage II. In addition to this, among these confirmed examples, tombs that yielded a number of grave goods sufficient to signify the highest leadership levels are concentrated not in northeastern China or in northwestern Korea as in the earlier stage—instead they are found in the southwestern part of the peninsula. Examples of these tombs include those at Namsŏng-ni 南城里 in Asan 牙山 (Han and Yi Kŏn-mu 1977), Koejŏng-dong 槐亭洞 in Taejŏn 大田 (Kungnip Pangmulgwan 1968), and Tongsŏ-ri 東西里 in Yesan 禮山 (Kang 1978:151–181), all in South Ch'ungch'ŏng Province (Figure 1.8). In addition to a range of two to five bronze mirrors, these tombs contain eight or nine bronze daggers, variform bronze objects in the shape of slender dagger handles, shields, and horns, as well as vessels with round lids, bells, and other artifacts. Not only are these the earliest examples of bronze-rich burials on the Korean peninsula, but they are comparable in wealth to that of the Zhengjiawazi tomb at Shenyang in the Liaoning region from Stage I.

It is thought that the variform bronze items unearthed from these tombs were mostly objects worn by the deceased or objects that were affixed to horses to enhance the prestige of the rider. When we compare this bronze assemblage with that found in the Stage III tombs (third to second centuries B.C.), which included Type C mirrors and various ceremonial rattles, it suggests that there were certain differences in the natures of the leaders who utilized these bronzes.

The slender rope-shaped loops and hollow bells attached to variform bronzes reveal that the objects were produced with the advanced casting technologies of wax models and earthen molds (Mifune 2007:25–58). Judging by the objects in the Stage I tombs at Xiaoheishigou and Shiertaiyingzi in Ningcheng, these techniques were already widely used in the Liaoxi region by 1000 B.C. It is likely that the leadership elites of the region that corresponds to South Ch'ungch'ŏng Province who possessed these variform bronzes also controlled the most highly skilled craft workshops and distribution supply.

The occupants of these tombs were likely the group that controlled the South Ch'ungch'ŏng area of southwestern Korea. According to historical records, when King Chun 準王 of Old Chosŏn was forced south by Wiman he encountered local groups known as the Han 韓. Although it is difficult to know if these Han groups were directly linked to the Mahan 馬韓 culture that was later recorded as existing in the first century

A.D., in terms of material culture they were clearly distinct from the Chinhan 辰韓 and Pyŏnhan 弁韓 groups of southeastern Korea, and for the sake of convenience I will use that name in the discussion below. (Yi Hyŏn-hye 1984:37–45).

In tandem with the appearance of Zhengjiawazi-style bronze objects is the large-scale adoption in the western coastal region of southern Korea of a new type of pottery with clay banding around the lip that is round in cross-section (*chŏmt'odae t'ogi* 粘土帶土器) (Pak Sun-bal 2004; Yi Sŏng-jae 2007). Examples of the style can be seen in ceramics from the settlement sites of Panje-ri 盤諸里 in Ansŏng 安城, Kyŏnggi Province, and of Kyosŏng-ni 校城里 in Poryŏng 保寧, South Ch'ungch'ŏng Province. As with mirrors, clay-banded pottery also first appeared in the Liao River region and is found together with bronzes in the Zhengjiawazi tomb. The adoption of sophisticated production techniques in southwestern Korea, seen from the inflow of the attached-band pottery of Liaodong, strongly suggests that the objects were connected with a population movement from Liaodong that also included craftspeople. Judging from the spread of attached-band pottery into southern Korea in the following stage, we may surmise that a group of people, including craftspeople, may have migrated to the Kyushu region of Japan (Kataoka 1999:176–201).

In the Japanese archipelago in Stage II there are stone-cist and wood-coffin tombs containing polished groundstone daggers and arrowheads, but there are few if any elite tombs that yield bronze objects. As discussed previously, there is an abundance of polished groundstone daggers and arrowheads from tombs in the southern portion of the Korean peninsula in Stage I, and it is generally understood that this cultural practice subsequently flowed into Kyushu. However, peninsular-style bronze objects had not yet found a place in the funeral rituals of this region.

There are two possible causes for these phenomena. The first possibility is that although elites had emerged in northern Kyushu, in this stage they had not yet established a tradition of funerary ceremonies that incorporated the burial of prestige goods in tombs. Another possibility is that rather than a hierarchical authority like the dolmen tomb societies of the Korean peninsula, society in Kyushu was still at the pre-state egalitarian level and had no role for prominent, individual leaders.

As examined in Stage I, peninsular dolmen tombs contained at most one lute-shaped dagger, and this lack of demand for bronze contrasts with the various bronze tools, weapons, and ritual objects buried in large quantities in tombs of the Liao River region. Similarities with the Korean peninsula in Stage I can be seen in the lack of bronze objects in Japan in this stage. As a result, as with the previous stage, we can see that there was very little exchange of bronze goods between Korea and Japan.

However, the appearance of Songgungni-style dwellings and pottery in Kyushu at this time suggests a significant population movement from the southern portion of Korea to the Kyushu region of Japan (Kataoka 1999:64–81). While peninsular bronze culture did not take root, the groups that removed to the Japanese archipelago appear to have spread the techniques of rice agriculture with relative ease, as suggested by finds of carbonized grains with stone tools related to agricultural production. This was likely a result of the fact that, unlike bronze production, rice agriculture does not require a steady supply of raw materials that are difficult to procure or a complex production process.

In contrast, evidence of population movement from Japan to the peninsula in the same period is extremely scarce (Takesue 2009:287–291). It is thought that an increase in the population on the southern coast of the peninsula at this time created an insufficiency of geographical space necessary for food procurement as well as overcrowded living spaces. Difficulties arising from increasing conflict for these resources between regional groups resulted in considerable population migration to the Japanese archipelago. Compared to the peninsula, there were abundant resources and ample living space in northern Kyushu. It may also be that while there were similar problems of overcrowding in northern Kyushu, it was easier for groups in this region to move to southern Kyushu or Honshu rather than advancing across the sea into the Korean peninsula. This is different from the circumstances in the previous Jōmon period, where forays into the ocean and occasional contact with the southern coast of the peninsula were inevitable because of the dependence of Jōmon groups on marine resources.

Stage III—Type C Mirrors (Third to Second Centuries B.C.)

Tombs with Type C mirrors have not been found in northeastern China. Instead they are concentrated in northwestern and southwestern Korea, and are distributed as well in southeastern Korea and northern Kyushu. A chronological scheme for the start of production of the fine-lined mirrors is based on an example that was excavated with a slender bronze dagger-axe found in Tomb 30 at Xinzhuangtou 辛庄头 at the site of Yan's Lower Capital (Xiadu 下都) in Beijing (Qiao Liang 2004:58–67; Kobayashi 2008a:24–38). This chronologically places the object before the third century B.C., which, according to historical records, was before the southward migration of King Chun of Old Chosŏn into the Mahan region of southwestern Korea. This type of dagger-axe developed from bronze dagger-axes produced during the Warring States period in the Liaoxi region and has also been found at several sites in northwestern Korea along with Type C mirrors. From this, we can surmise that Type C fine-line mirrors were produced in the workshops of highly skilled craftspeople with the support of Old Chosŏn elites before the time of King Chun in the third century B.C. and were buried in tombs of high-ranking elites.

Wiman Chosŏn, which was established in the early second century B.C. after King Chun was driven out by the Yan refugee Wiman 衛滿 and his followers, introduced various cultural changes. The Central Plains–style iron culture and ideology that members of the Wiman Chosŏn ruling class used while still in Yan territory replaced the earlier bronze culture and ritual ideology of Old Chosŏn as the basis of the highest authority. Thus, in the Wiman Chosŏn period, those who had adopted Type C mirrors as the highest prestige item were no longer the top-level leaders, but were rather members of the second-tier elite and lower.

In the Mahan region of southwestern Korea as well, there have been excavations of concentrations of early Type C mirrors in the process of transition from the Type B forms (Yi Kang-sŭng 1987) and of more developed Type C mirrors featuring a variety of decorative patterns. This suggests that bronze production workshops on a level equal to those of Old Chosŏn had been established in this region even before the southward migration of King Chun and his followers. Thus, the production of Type C mirrors seems to have resulted from developments upon an existing basis of bronze production techniques within a context of mutual exchange of new technological information from the northwestern region of Korea.

In sum, after the southward migration of King Chun, a fixed prestige network was created in which mirrors with multiple knobs symbolized the highest elites in Mahan territories, but in Wiman Chosŏn these multiple-knob mirrors were relegated to the secondary tier of elites. This is confirmed by the elite tombs of the Mahan region that contain Type C multi-knobbed mirrors as well as other types of bronze objects, such as weaponry, tools, and rattles seen at the sites of Ch'op'o-ri 草浦里 in Hamp'yŏng 咸平 (Yi Kŏn-mu and Sŏ Sŏng-hun 1988), and Taegong-ni 大谷里 in Hwasun 和順 (Cho 1984), both in South Chŏlla Province, and by artifacts said to have come from Nonsan 論山 in South Ch'ungch'ŏng Province (Figure 1.9). While there are examples of sets of rattles, but no weapons or tools, said to have been found in sites such as Tŏksan 德山 in

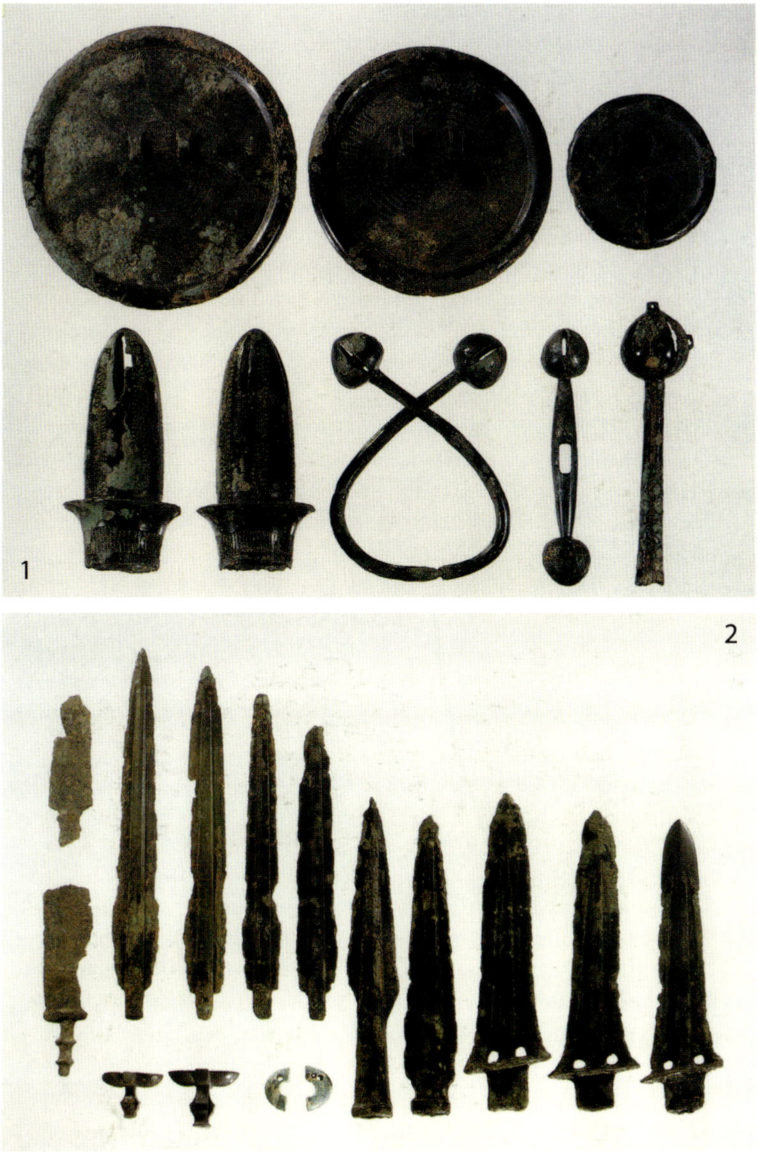

Figure 1.9 Bronzes from the Ch'op'o-ri Tomb in Hamp'yŏng. From Kungnip Chungang Pangmulgwan 1992.

South Ch'ungch'ŏng and Sangju 尙州 in North Kyŏngsang, these were all chance discoveries rather than systematically excavated artifacts (Kungnip Chungang Pangmulgwan 1992:102–107). Other examples from formal surveys suggest the likelihood that these bronzes were originally accompanied by mirrors and other bronze objects.

A new category of bronze rattle appeared in place of the variform bronzes of Stage II that took the shape of shields or sheaths. There were four types of rattles: twin-headed rattles 雙頭鈴, pole-cap rattles 竿頭鈴, two-headed rattles 二頭鈴, and eight-headed rattles 八珠鈴, with each type being composed of a pair. All are thought to have been used by shaking the hand rhythmically during ceremonies that were intended to invoke a deity and were buried in the tombs of religious leaders who presided over ancestral rites (Yi Hyŏn-hye 2003:1–34).

Mirrors show a regional distribution similar to the previous Stage II. Tombs containing these objects are concentrated in the western coastal region of South Ch'ungch'ŏng and show a tendency to spread to the western coastal region of South Chŏlla and the northern part of North Kyŏngsang. Political leaders of minor polities appeared in South Ch'ungch'ŏng and South Chŏlla. There is no way of knowing if both of these regions shared a sense of group identity, but they exhibit clear similarities in terms of material culture (bronze goods, pottery, tomb styles, and other artifact assemblages), and South Chŏlla can be seen as Mahan territory. The bronze rattle artifact assemblages said to have been found along the upper Naktong River 洛東江 in Sangju are identical to those in the North Kyŏngsang region, but they have not been confirmed in the middle and lower Naktong River, regions that are recognized as the central areas of Chinhan and Pyŏnhan. Considering this, there is a high likelihood that the political leaders in Sangju were connected with South Ch'ungch'ŏng via the upper Kŭm River and considered themselves to belong to the same polity.

The wax models, earthen molds, and complex patterns necessary to produce the minutely detailed fine-line sections of Type C mirrors and eight-headed bronze rattles could not have been possible without the presence of a much more highly developed technology than was present in Stage II. Evidence from several archaeological contexts suggests that, unlike that in Stage II, the development of this technology was gradual and occurred in southwestern Korea. The B6 mirror discovered at Namsŏng-ni 南城里 in Asan 牙山 and the C1 mirrors from Tongsŏ-ri 東西里 in Yesan 禮山 and Kubong-ni 九鳳里 in Puyŏ 扶餘 are thought to be the precursors of Types C2, C3, C4, and C5 mirrors found in the southeastern part of the

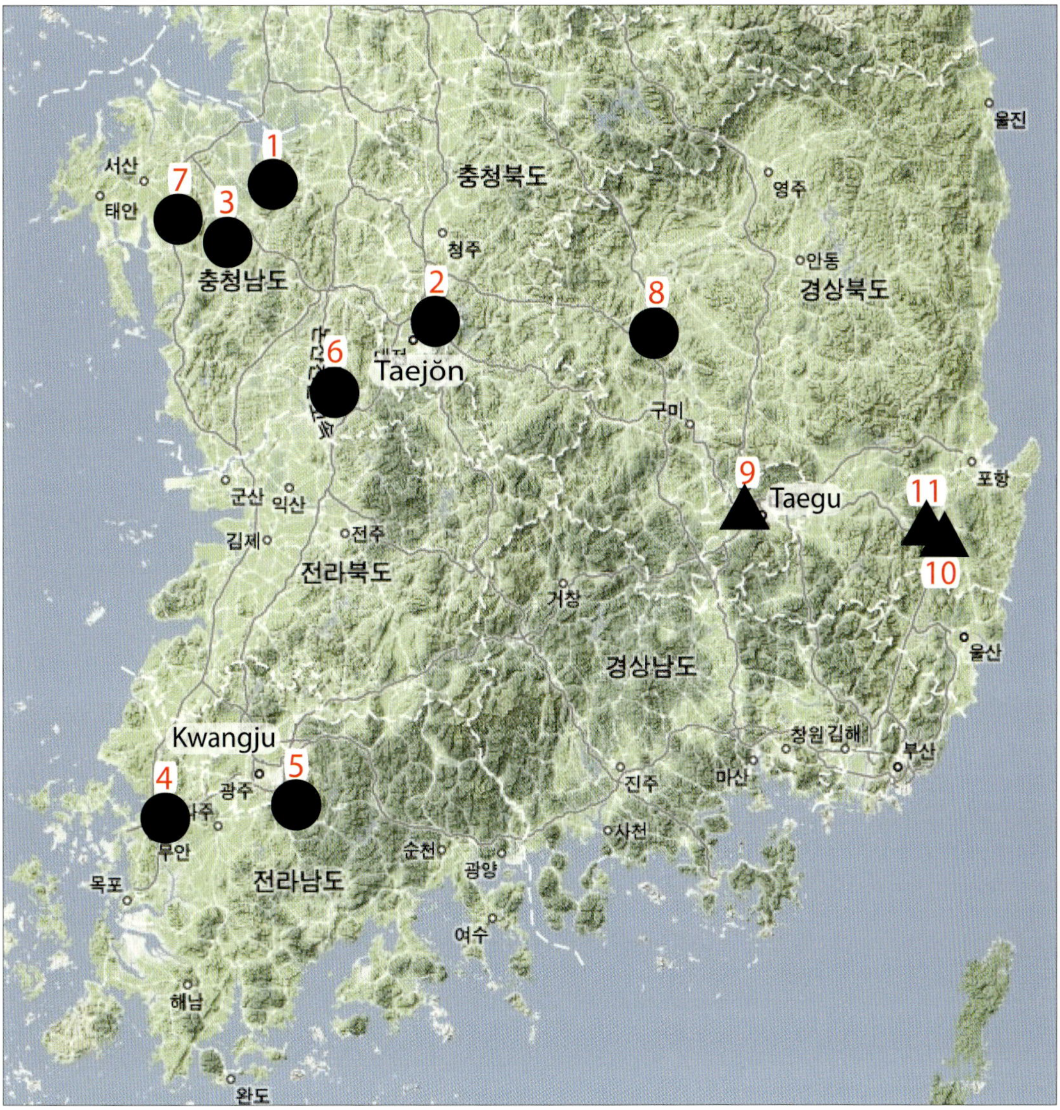

Map 1.2 Major Sites in Southern Korea Showing Stages of Multi-knobbed Mirrors.
Circles: Fourth to second centuries B.C.; Triangles: First century B.C. 1. Namsŏng-ni in Asan; 2. Koejŏng-dong in Taejŏn; 3. Tongsŏ-ri in Yesan; 4. Ch'op'o-ri in Hamp'yŏng; 5. Taegong-ni in Hwasun; 6. Nonsan; 7. Tŏksan; 8. Sangju; 9. Sinch'ŏn-dong in Taegu; 10. Ipsil-li in Kyŏngju; 11. Chuktong-ni in Kyŏngju.

peninsula. Bronze rattles also developed from the earlier shield-shaped bronze objects, such as those from Namsŏng-ni in Asan and other sites, into more diverse shapes and types.

The production of bronze rattles and Type C mirrors and the acquisition of highly skilled full-time craftspeople could not have occurred without the presence of elites who were capable of securing raw materials, facilities, and other commodities. These skilled production groups and elites who directed centers of bronze production are thought to have resided in those regions of the western portion of southern Korea where those same bronze goods are concentrated, a region that connects Tŏksan and Nonsan in South Ch'ungch'ŏng, Yŏngam 靈巖, Hamp'yŏng, and Hwasun in South Chŏlla, and Sangju in North Kyŏngsang (Map 1.2) (Sugiyama, Muramatsi, et al. 2005:339–381; Miyazato 2009:18–20).

In particular, it has been indirectly confirmed through finds of molds that various bronze objects were mass-produced by a group of skilled craftsmen in Yŏngam in South Chŏlla Province (Im 1987; Gotō 1996). However, despite the scale of production, no molds for bronze mirrors with thin-lined geometric patterns or bronze rattles—which would have required considerably more complex production processes and technologies—have been recovered. Mirrors with fine-lined geometric patterns and bronze rattles are thought to have been produced using earthen molds, and because they were probably destroyed after a single use, it is unlikely that they would have been curated or passed down like stone molds. Thus, although they have not survived in the archaeological record, it is possible that elaborate bronze items like Type C mirrors and rattles were produced in centers of bronze production like Yŏngam in South Chŏlla.

Very few multi-knobbed mirrors with extremely detailed fine-line patterns have been found in southeastern Korea or Kyushu, and it is unlikely that such sophisticated bronze objects were produced in these two regions. It is more likely that a large number of the Type C mirrors unearthed in southeastern Korea and Japan were produced in southwestern Korea and then distributed to other regions.

Bronze rattles dating to this period have not been found, but tombs containing Type C mirrors and large quantities of bronze weapons have been confirmed in over thirty sites on the Korean peninsula. Sites with these tombs are distributed along the eastern and southern coasts of the peninsula, the Han and Kŭm River regions, and the distribution area expands farther into the southern Korean peninsula as a whole. Single mirrors have also been found in wooden-chamber tombs at sites such as Kal-tong 葛洞 (Honam Munhwajae Yŏn'guwŏn 2005) and Tŏk-tong 悳洞 in Wanju 完州, North Chŏlla Province. Examples of sites with mirror fragments such as Sinp'ung-ni 新豊里 in Wanju, and Wŏlsŏng-ni 月城里 in Sach'ŏn 泗川, South Kyŏngsang, suggest that the distribution area of Type C mirrors increased and that they were possibly circulated among leaders in more peripheral areas.

In Japan, mirrors with multiple knobs were buried along with peninsular bronze weaponry and tools in tombs over a wide area. There are several examples of sites with mirror burials: a stone-cist tomb in Kajikurihama 梶栗浜 in Yamaguchi 山口 Prefecture; a wood-coffin tomb in Yoshitake-Takagi 吉武高木 in Fukuoka City; Tomb 12 at Uki-Kunden 宇木汲田 in Karatsu 唐津 City, Saga 佐賀 Prefecture; and four jar coffins at Honson-gomori 本村籠 in Saga 佐賀 City; and at Satotabaru 里田原 in Hirado 平戸 City, Nagasaki 長崎 Prefecture. The largest Japanese tomb with bronze objects that corresponds to this stage is Tomb 3 at Yoshitake-Takagi. It yielded a bronze mirror, dagger, spear, and dagger-axe (Fukuoka-shi Kyōiku Iinkai 1986) (Figure 1.10). While these tombs did not have the prestige artifacts of those of the highest elites in the Korean peninsula, the tombs of individual chiefs had multi-knobbed mirrors. Regarding Tomb 3 at Yoshitake-Takagi, Japanese researchers are united in the opinion that it was either the tomb of the leader of the most powerful polity of Wa or the tomb of a king (Takakura 1995; Terasawa 2000, 145–154; Tsunematsu 2006). This means that a polity had appeared in Kyushu and had expropriated Mahan region mirrors as the highest prestige good of a leader. These mirrors would have been considered as a rare, exotic product manufactured with sophisticated technology, and they would have had value as a ritual item that came down from Old Chosŏn. In other words, the Type C mirrors buried in the tombs of polity leaders of Wa in Kyushu can be explained as symbols of a ritual partnership linking them with pre-Wiman Old Chosŏn and Mahan (Suzuki 2005:31–34).

If one looks at the absence of tombs with bronze rattles, however, it seems that not all aspects of the peninsular ritual system were exported to Japan. In fact, there are depictions of rituals using only bronze dagger-axes and bells on painted pottery in Japan dating only from around the turn of the first century A.D. (Kobayashi 2008b). Taking this into account, it can be said that the same bronze cultural horizon existed in Japan and Korea, but that there were differences in the ritual activities of chief priests.

All six of the Type C mirrors found in Japanese tombs are small mirrors of 9 to 11 cm in diameter, and most of them are of the three-knobbed

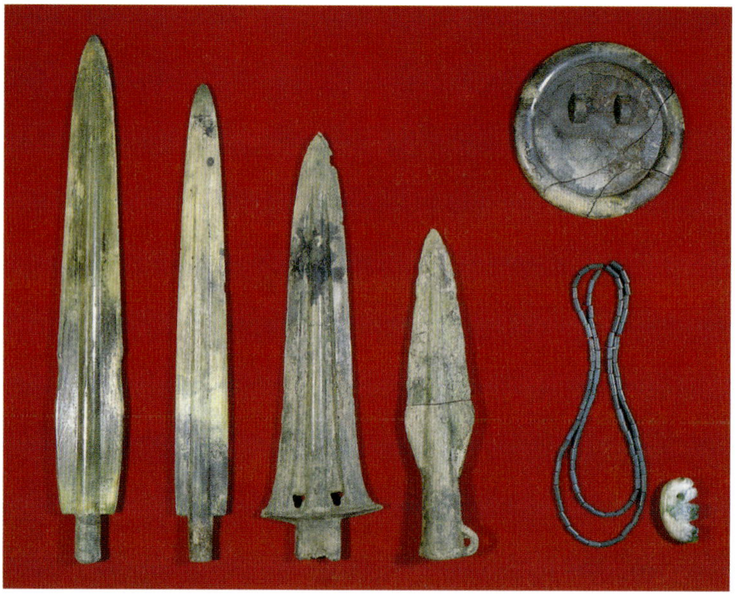

Figure 1.10 Bronzes from Yoshitake-Takagi Tomb 1 in Fukuoka. From Fukuoka-shi Kyōiku Iinkai 1986.

type. Those found in non-mortuary contexts at the sites of Wakayama 若山 in Ogōri 小郡 City, Fukuoka Prefecture, Ōgata 大県 in Kashiwara 柏原 City, Osaka Prefecture, and Nagara 名柄 in Gose 御所 City, Nara Prefecture, are medium-sized mirrors (15–22 cm) of the double-knobbed type. It seems that in Japan small mirrors were buried in tombs while medium ones were stored in ritual facilities, the difference in size suggesting a certain distinction in their symbolic significance. Such a difference in function between the small three-knobbed mirrors and the medium two-knobbed mirrors seems to have already existed in the Korean peninsula (Yi Yang-su 2004).

As in the Korean peninsula, tombs in the archipelago with bronze weaponry and an absence of mirrors are the majority. A representative example is the Taguma-Ishihatake site 田熊石畑 in Fukuoka. Tomb 1 at this site contained four daggers and a dagger-axe; Tomb 2 contained a dagger, a dagger-axe, and two spears; and Tomb 4 contained a dagger, a spear, and a dagger-axe. It is noteworthy that these are all wooden-coffin tombs rather than Japanese-style jar-coffin tombs (Munakata-shi Kyōiku Iinkai 2009).

Among tombs containing one of several varieties of weaponry, the majority of those including bronzes from the Korean peninsula are distributed in the Kyushu region of Japan, suggesting that funeral rituals in which bronze weapons were offered as grave goods in tombs spread widely in Japan in or around the second century B.C. The tombs of Yoshitake-Takagi and Taguma-Ishihatake are Korean-type wooden-coffin tombs with a stone mound rather than Japanese-type jar-coffin tombs. Local variation is mostly absent. It is difficult to say whether the individual interred in the tomb was a local elite who adopted Korean peninsula-type tomb architecture or if the individual was an immigrant from the Korean peninsula, but it is clear that peninsular mortuary styles and customs were practiced in Japan. It is possible that inhabitants of Kyushu were influenced by Korean bronzes and adopted the funeral custom of offering them as grave goods via various channels and processes.

Unlike Type C mirrors, finds of stone molds in Kyushu indicate the likelihood that bronze weaponry was produced in that region during the Middle Yayoi period (Yoshida 2008). Discoveries of peninsular-style clay-banded pottery with molds for bronzes strongly suggest that migrants from the Korean peninsula took the lead in bronze production. Although migrant craft specialists may have begun this practice, the locals would have learned the skills within a relatively short period and started producing them for themselves. Whereas weapons such as daggers, spears, and dagger-axes dating to this stage nearly all faithfully adhered to the Korean-type slender forms, in the following stage the Japanese-type medium-slender forms 中細形 were widely produced.

In conclusion, it can be said that an elite class based on the same concepts of prestige appeared among both the Samhan and Wa during this stage, given that the funeral ritual of placing bronze items (chiefly daggers, spears, and dagger-axes) in tombs along with Type C mirrors spread widely in Kyushu and perhaps Kinki, as it had in the Korean peninsula. It is also noteworthy that artifacts symbolizing the status of the highest authority or sophisticated goods like Type C mirrors were distributed far from their points of origin. Mirrors were produced in northwestern (late Old Chosŏn and Wiman Chosŏn) and southwestern Korea (Mahan) and were then distributed in Japan from the latter location. Even if the production technology was not transferred, the existence of a supply and demand for the objects indicates that a close network was maintained between Mahan and Wa.

Stage IV—Western Han Mirrors (Second to First Centuries B.C.)

As of today, no elite tombs with bronze mirrors dating from the first century B.C. have been systematically excavated. Only one relevant example of a Han-style coiled-dragon design mirror has been found in southwestern Korea (the territory of the Mahan polity that developed in Stage III) at the P'yŏngjang-ni 平障里 site in Iksan 益山, and it dates to approximately the second half of the second century B.C. It was discovered alongside a bronze spear and sword (Yi Kang-sŭng 1984). This contrasts with the previous period, in which large quantities of bronze objects, including Type C mirrors, were placed in elite tombs in the same region. In other words, at the end of the second century B.C. just after the collapse of Old Chosŏn and the establishment of the Han commanderies, the production and dissemination of multi-knobbed mirrors abruptly stopped, and they were no longer offered as grave goods in tombs in northwestern Korea or in the Mahan southwest.

There were apparently members of the leadership class in Wiman Chosŏn and Mahan who used Type C mirrors to display their status prior to the second century B.C., although there may have been differences in social positions between the two regions. Then, because the Type C mirrors lost their prestige following the collapse of Wiman Chosŏn, there was no longer a demand for the objects, and their production stopped. In other words, although there were still specialist craftspeople who could produce mirrors, without material support from elite patrons, their continued production had become untenable.

The ceasing of production in the Mahan region of southwestern Korea also brought about the almost simultaneous stoppage of the distribution and deposition of Type C mirrors in tombs in southeastern Korea (Chinhan region) and Kyushu (Wa polity), neither of which had a production center of its own. It is possible that the collapse of Wiman Chosŏn and the difficulty of exchange between the Han empire and the Samhan created problems in the supply of copper, tin, and other raw materials necessary for mirror production. However, the fact that at the same time in southeastern Korea there was production and dissemination of large-sized bronze weaponry makes this possibility unlikely.

In contrast to southwestern Korea, in the southeast, at the site of Ipsil-li 入室里 in Kyŏngju, Type C mirrors were unearthed alongside large amounts of bronze weaponry (Umehara and Fujita 1925:30–37). A lack of proper excavation reports for the site makes interpretations difficult, but if the finds are accepted, they indicate that Type C mirrors were replaced by

Figure 1.11 Bronzes from Sinch'ŏn-dong in Taegu.
From Kungnip Chungang Pangmulgwan 1992.

Han Chinese mirrors prior to the first century B.C. in southwestern Korea. However, this seems not to have been the case in the southeastern region.

In addition, at least some of the implements used for funeral ceremonies in the southwest during the previous period, such as bronze rattles, continue to be found in burials in southeastern Korea. Pole-cap rattles (a rattle fixed at

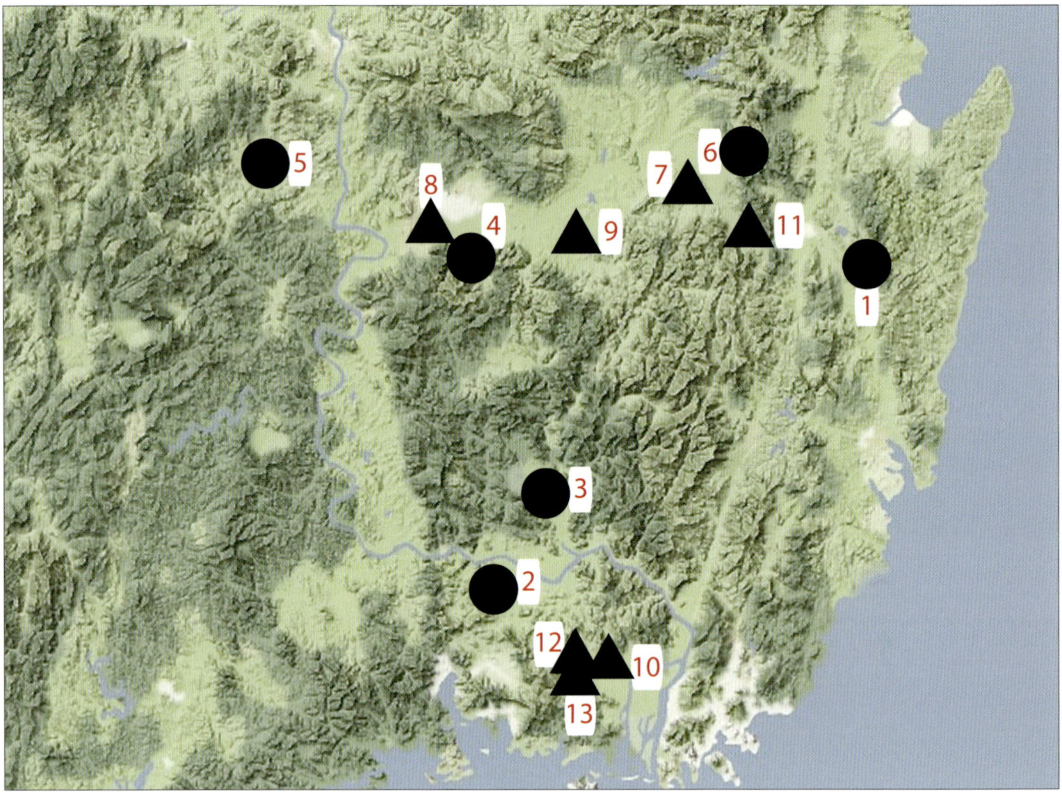

Map 1.3 Major Sites in Southwestern Korea Showing Stages of Han Mirrors.
Circles: first century B.C.; Triangles: First to second centuries A.D. 1. Choyang-dong in Kyŏngju; 2. Taho-ri in Ch'angwŏn; 3. Kyo-dong in Miryang; 4. Chisan-dong in Taegu; 5. Yesan-dong in Kyŏngju; 6. Yongjŏn-dong in Yŏngch'ŏn; 7. Ŏŭn-dong in Yŏng-ch'ŏn; 8. P'yŏngni-dong in Taegu; 9. Sindae-ri in Kyŏngsan; 10. Ponghwang-dong in Kimhae; 11. Sara-ri in Kyŏngju; 12. Yangdong-ni in Kimhae; 13. Naedŏng-ni in Kimhae.

the end of a wooden pole) are said to have been unearthed along with various bronze weapons in tombs at Ipsil-li and Chuktong-ni 竹東里 in Kyŏngju (Han 1987) as well as at Sinch'ŏn-dong 新川洞 in Taegu (Yun 1980) (Figure 1.11). Although these were not the complete bronze rattle sets comprising four pairs found in the previous stage, they suggest that the occupants of these tombs still maintained some form of the traditional position of a chief priest presiding over the same rituals as in the earlier period.

The development of the Chinhan polity, which appeared later than Mahan, is also seen indirectly at sites with tombs containing a large amount of bronze objects along the middle reaches of the Naktong River and in the Kŭmho 琴湖江 and Hyŏngsan 兄山江 River basins. In the latter half of this stage, sites on the middle Naktong containing Western Han mirrors, with such motifs as star-clouds and banded registers with inscribed characters, were excavated from graves, including Tomb 38 at Choyang-dong 朝陽洞 in Kyŏngju (Kungnip Kyŏngju Pangmulgwan 2003); Tomb 1 at Taho-ri 茶户里 in Ch'angwŏn 昌原 (Yi Kŏn-mu et al. 1989:14–26); and Tombs 3 and 7 at Kyo-dong 校洞 in Miryang 密陽 (Miryang Taehakkyo Pangmulgwan 2004); as well as one example recovered from a survey project at Chisan-dong 池山洞 in Taegu (Figures 1.12 and 1.13). In the cases of the tomb at Yongjŏn-ni 龍田里 in Yŏngch'ŏn 永川 (Kungnip Kyŏngju Pangmulgwan 2007) and Tomb 1 at Taho-ri, the large number of burial goods clearly suggests that each was the burial of a polity chief of its respective region, and their dates correspond with the emergence of Chinhan described in later historical records. Given its close proximity to Kimhae 金海 in the lower Naktong basin and the coastal area of South Kyŏngsang Province, which is associated with the territory of Pyŏnhan, it is thus possible to designate Taho-ri as a Pyŏnhan site. However, the Western Han mirrors and bronze weaponry at the site suggest that it is culturally closer to Chinhan in the middle Naktong basin (Map 1.3).

After a certain period of time following the collapse of Wiman Chosŏn and the establishment of the Han commanderies in its place, Han Chinese single-knobbed mirrors filtered into several regions of Chinhan from the commanderies and were offered as prestige goods in elite tombs. This development demonstrates that for the elites of southern Korea, the basis of external prestige had shifted from Wiman Chosŏn to the Han commanderies. In addition, in contrast with the previous stage, the vast majority of bronze mirrors have been recovered from the Chinhan region rather than the Mahan region. This change reflects the fact that as the political authority of northwestern Korea shifted from Wiman Chosŏn to the Han commanderies, Chinhan replaced Mahan as the peninsular polity with which the Han empire conducted primary relations. In the Mahan region, in this period as well as the next, there are no examples of Han mirrors as grave goods, and for a considerable period there appears to have been an absence of exchange of Han mirrors between Mahan and the commanderies. However, it is difficult to argue for an absence of the influence of a polity in the Mahan region based on this evidence alone.

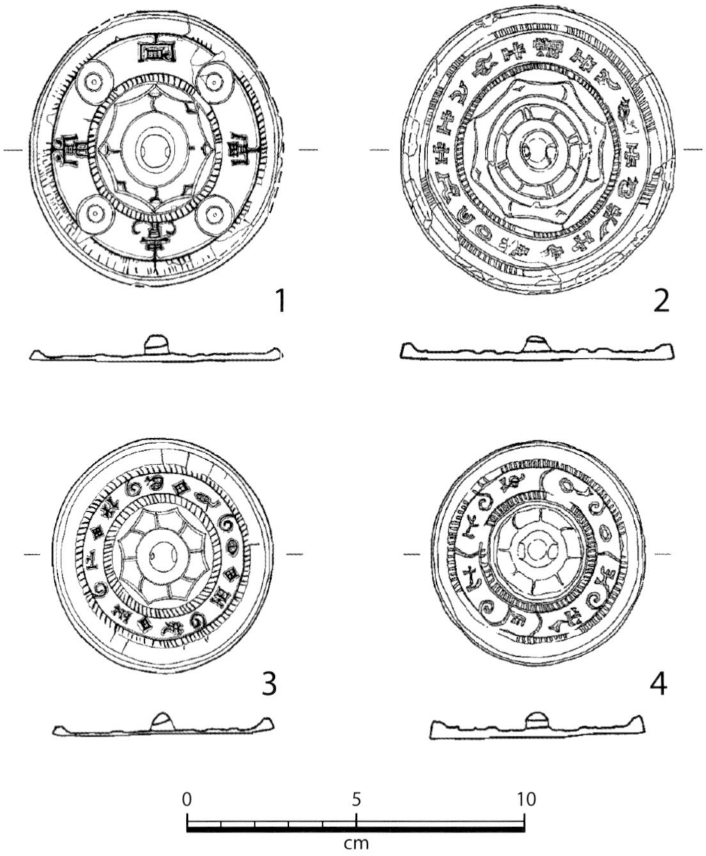

Figure 1.12 Bronzes from Tomb 38 at Choyang-dong in Kyŏngju. From Kungnip Kyŏngju Pangmulgwan 2003.

Burials containing bronze rattles are completely absent in Chinhan during the same period in which Han mirrors are found (the second half of the first century B.C.). This suggests that the importance of traditional ritual activities using rattles and the authority granted to priests officiating over these rituals had weakened. Instead, as shown at various sites such as Yesandong 禮山洞 in Sŏngju 星州 in North Kyŏngsang (Kyŏngsang-pukto Munhwajae Yŏn'guwŏn 2005) and Taho-ri in Ch'angwŏn in South Kyŏngsang,

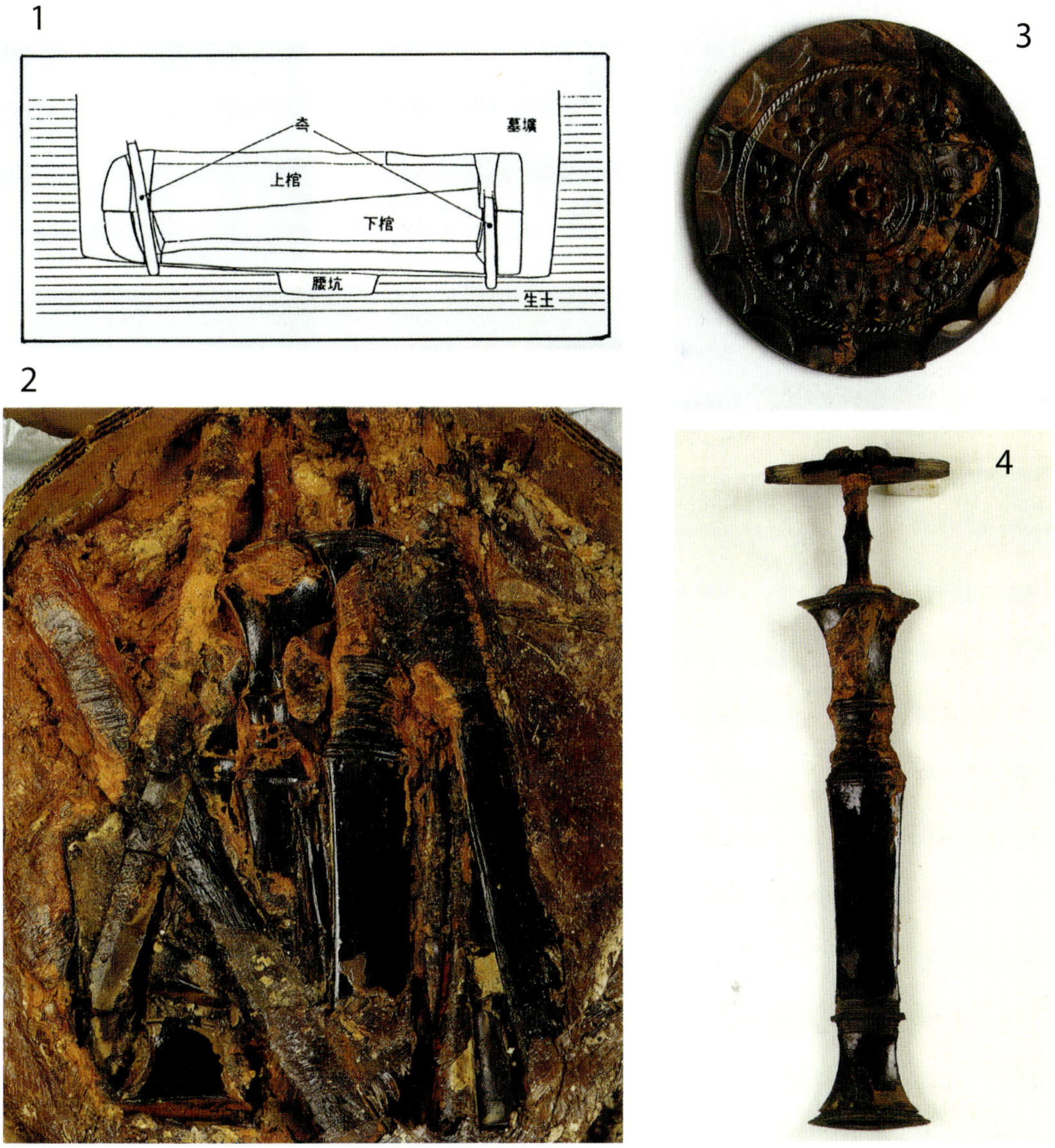

*Figure 1.13 Bronzes from Tomb 1 at Taho-ri in Ch'angwŏn.
From Kungnip Chungang Pangmulgwan 1992.*

Figure 1.14 Mikumo-Minami-shōji Tomb 1 with Bronze Mirror. From Kasuga-shi Nakoku no Oka Rekishi Shiryōkan 2000.

Figure 1.15 Suku-Okamoto Tomb D in Kasuga with Burial Goods. From Kasuga-shi Na-koku no Oka Rekishi Shiryōkan 2000.

horse-riding equipment—an object symbolic of power in the Central Plains that was absent in the previous stage—was offered as grave goods. Such artifacts are more suggestive of power derived from objects of secular utility rather than symbolic of religious ritual.

Burials from the same stage containing a large number of Han mirrors are also found in Fukuoka Prefecture, Kyushu, Japan, in burials such as Tombs 1 and 2 in Mikumo-Minami-shōji 三雲南小路, Maebaru 前原 City (Fukuoka-ken Kyōiku Iinkai 1985), and Area D at Suku-Okamoto 須玖

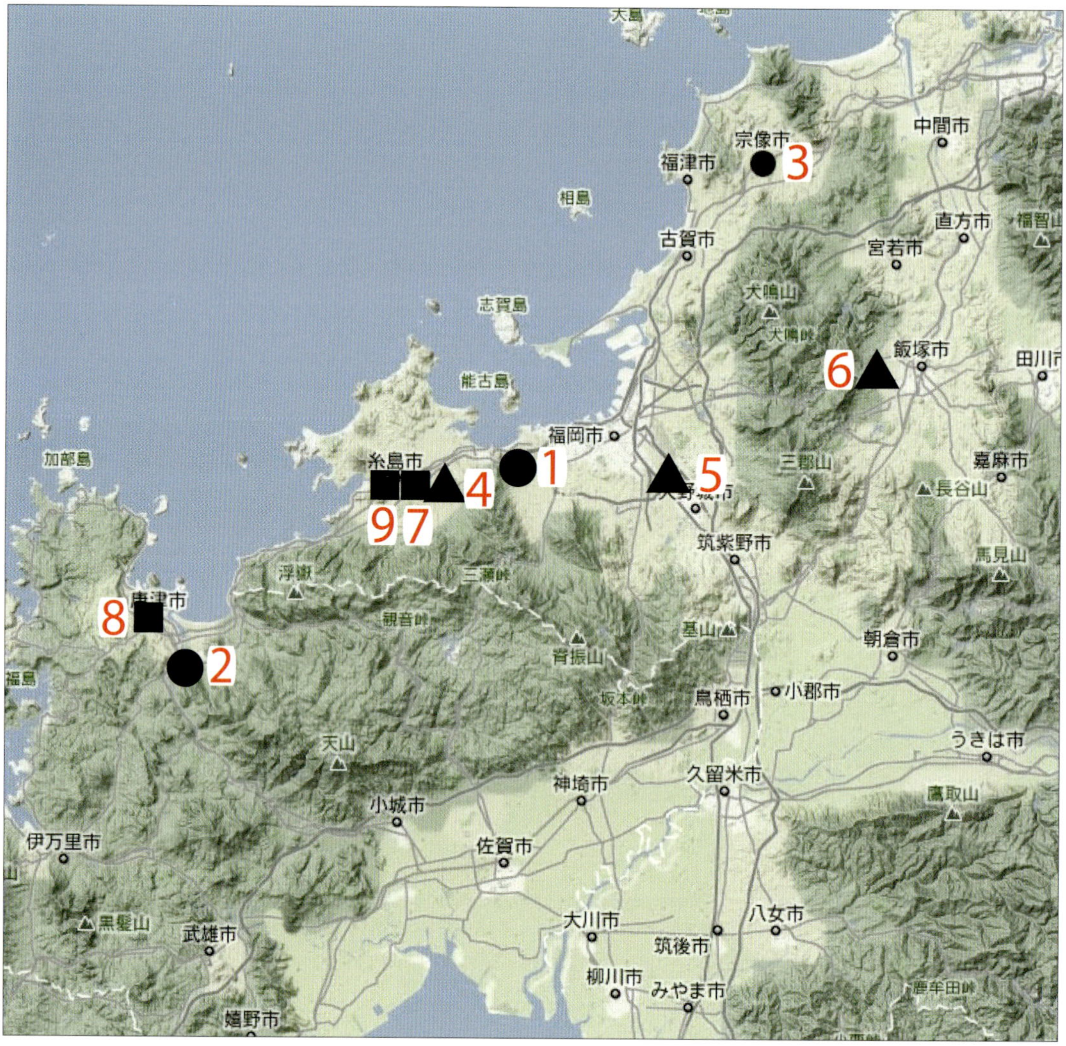

Map 1.4 Major Sites in Northern Kyushu Showing Stages of Multi-knobbed and Han Mirrors.
Circles: Multi-knobbed mirror stage; Triangles: Western Han mirror stage; Squares: Eastern Han mirror stage.
1. Yoshitake-Takagi in Fukuoka; 2. Uki-Kunden in Karatsu; 3. Takuma-Ishida in Munakata;
4. Mikumo-Minami-shōji in Fukuoka; 5. Suku-Okamoto in Kasuga; 6. Tateiwa in Iizuka;
7. Ihara-Yarimizo in Maebaru; 8. Sakuranobaba in Karatsu; 9. Hirabaru in Maebaru.

岡本, Kasuga 春日 City (Kyōto Teikoku Daigaku Bungakubu Kōkogaku Kyōshitsu 1930) (Figures 1.14 and 1.15). The quantity of Han mirrors unearthed from these tombs greatly outnumbers those found in Korea. The severely damaged tombs at Mikumo-Minami-shōji yielded more than twenty mirrors, while jar-coffin Tomb 10 at the grave-goods-rich site of Tateiwa Hotta 立岩堀田 in Iizuka 飯塚 City also contained six Han mirrors (Fukuoka-ken Iizuka-shi Tateiwa Iseki Chōsa Iinkai 1977) (Figure 1.16). In contrast, the Han mirrors found in tombs in the Chinhan region are much fewer in number and smaller in size than those found in Japan. Even those found within the territories of the Han commanderies have not produced a quantity of Han mirrors comparable to those in Japan (Takakura 1993). In any case, it may be that these examples are the tombs of the leaders of various minor polities that appeared in Kyushu following the Yoshitake-Takaki Tomb 3 of the previous stage. Japanese researchers suggest that the Mikumo-Minami-shōji site corresponds to the country of Ito 伊都國 mentioned in the *Sanguozhi* 三國志 (Oda Fujio 2000:4–9; Yanagida 2000) (Map 1.4).

The regional differences in the number of excavated Han mirrors are thought to reflect the policies of exchange that the Han commanderies maintained with the Samhan and Wa polities. The ideological context must also be considered. On the one hand, with the identification of priestly leadership with multi-knobbed mirrors and the enduring tradition of Type C mirrors within its ritual system, the Chinhan and Pyŏnhan regions could not readily accept Han mirrors as a replacement. However, in Japan the custom of Type C mirrors as grave goods was practiced only for a short period in the second century B.C., and so Han mirrors were more easily absorbed.

In Japan, Western Han mirrors are usually accompanied by other bronze objects. Jar-coffin Tomb 1 at Mikumo-Minami-shōji contained one medium-thin dagger-axe, one slender dagger, and two medium-thin spears. At Area D at Suku-Okamoto five spears, one dagger-axe, and one dagger were found in a jar burial. Jar-coffin Tomb 10 at Tateiwa contained one medium-thin bronze dagger-axe in addition to Han mirrors.

The burial in graves of Korean-style weaponry such as bronze daggers, dagger-axes, and pikes 銅矛 continued in southeastern Korea and the Kyushu region for more than half a century after the establishment of the Han commanderies. As these objects were produced in elongated sizes they became increasingly more symbolic rather than practical, but they did not deviate from the fundamental shape of peninsular weaponry (Iwanaga 2000:109–127). In Japan, prevalent thin bronze spears developed into the 40-cm-long

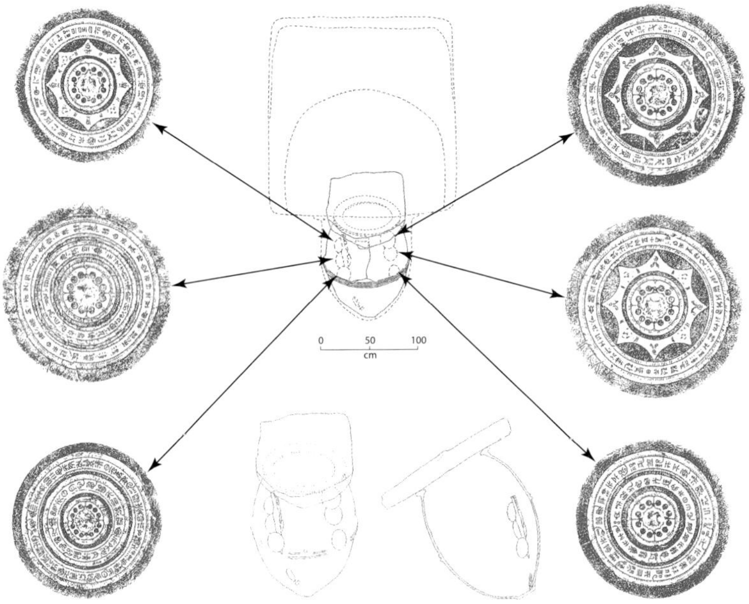

Figure 1.16 Tateiwa Tomb 10 in Iizuka with Bronze Mirrors. From Ōtemae Daigaku Shigaku Kenkyūjo 2010.

medium-slender type 中細形, seen most clearly in the morphology of the spear from Jar Burial 10 at Tateiwa. On the Korean peninsula this type was found at the Mahan site of P'yŏngjang-ni in Iksan, but the majority of examples, like those at Sinch'ŏn-dong in Taegu, Taho-ri in Changwŏn, and Yongjŏn-ni in Yŏngch'ŏn, have been found in the Chinhan region.

Why were Korean-type weapons in continuous use while mirrors were replaced by those made in central China? This is primarily because in this stage polities in Japan had instituted their own system to produce peninsular-style bronzes, whereas in the previous stage such production had been initiated by craftsmen who had come from southwestern Korea. This claim is well supported by the discovery of stone molds at various sites in Japan, including Suku-Okamoto in Kyushu. In short, an unprecedentedly close network had been created that involved human exchange and the sharing of information related to the technologies for producing a form of bronze weaponry that was common to both Kyushu and the Chinhan region.

Another possible explanation is that the Han commanderies may have tightly controlled the flow of their sophisticated iron-made weapons into Samhan and Wa. The Han empire must have taken measures to prevent any repetition of the considerable threat that had been posed by Wiman Chosŏn, a polity that the Han empire supported with weapons and financial resources in return for keeping the neighboring territories under control. Many iron swords have been found in tombs of the Han commanderies dating to the first century B.C., but not in those of the Wa and the Samhan.

In the Chinhan region of southeastern Korea, Chinese bronze-mirror burials continued to be accompanied in this phase by bronze daggers, spears, dagger-axes, and other types of weaponry. However, there were considerable numbers of tombs containing flat axe blades, weaponry, tools, and horse-riding equipment made of iron. Illustrative examples include Tomb 1 at Taho-ri in Ch'angwŏn, which included a single Han-style mirror, and Tomb 38 at Choyang-dong in Kyŏngju, which included four small Han-style mirrors. Also, the wood-coffin tomb at Yongjŏn-ni in Yŏngch'ŏn, which contained a broken mirror, included a bronze dagger-axe and a spear head. It also yielded large amounts of iron weaponry, flat axe blades, and tools. As will be discussed further below, this abundance of iron goods contrasts with the large quantity of Han mirrors but almost no iron artifacts found in the tombs of chiefs in Japan. In addition, at the site of Imdang-dong 林堂洞 in Kyŏngsan 慶山, the majority of wood-coffin tombs with refashioned Han mirror fragments contain iron daggers and flat axe blades instead of bronze artifacts. Although there are no complete Han mirrors in these burials, the considerable number of iron artifacts found in wood-coffin tombs is comparable to what we find in Japan. The scale of Han mirrors in burials is higher in the Kyushu region than in southern Korea, but the reverse is true for iron artifacts.

An excavation at Chŏn'gok-tong 泉谷洞 in Ulsan 蔚山 that shows evidence of an iron-ore mine in this period provides circumstantial evidence that intensive production of iron and iron goods had actively begun in the Yŏngnam region during this time. However, in Japan evidence that iron production had begun in this stage is absent. Examples of medium-thin iron dagger-axes that have not been positively confirmed in the Korean peninsula offer the possibility that there was small-scale production of iron objects in Japan as well. Finds in Kyushu of iron production tools used to process iron imported from the Korean peninsula also suggest the possibility of production, but this has not yet been verified. Discoveries of Yayoi pottery at sites in southeastern Korea, such as Nŭk-to 勒島 in Sach'ŏn 泗川

Figure 1.17 Bronze Mirrors from Ŏŭn-dong in Yŏngch'ŏn. From Kungnip Chungang Pangmulgwan 1992.

Figure 1.18 Bronze Mirrors from P'yŏngni-dong in Taegu. From Kungnip Chungang Pangmulgwan 1992.

and Chŏn'gok-tong in Ulsan, provide additional indirect evidence that polities in Japan had started to acquire information related to iron production through exchange with southeastern Korea (Takesue 2009:287–291).

Stage V—Eastern Han Mirrors (First to Second Centuries A.D.)

In the first half of this stage, roughly the first half of the first century, tombs containing mirrors of the Eastern Han period (25–220) are concentrated in the Chinhan region of southeastern Korea. Although the tombs were not excavated through proper archaeological techniques, making it difficult to draw conclusions based on their data, mirrors were recovered from tombs at Ŏŭn-dong 漁隱洞 in Yŏngch'ŏn (one serpentine dragon mirror, and two small inscribed banded-register mirrors, as well as one medium and eleven small Han imitation mirrors) (Umehara and Fujita 1925:3–29) and at P'yŏngni-dong 坪里洞 in Taegu (one serpentine dragon mirror as well as one medium and four small imitation mirrors) (Yun 1981:1–21) (Figures 1.17 and 1.18). The only mirror recovered in the course of a systematic excavation is a single serpentine dragon mirror from wood-coffin Tomb 75 at Sindae-dong 新垈洞 in Kyŏngsan (Yŏngnam Munhwajae Yŏn'guwŏn

Figure 1.19 Tomb 130 at Sara-ri in Kyŏngju with Bronze Mirrors.
From Yŏngnam Munhwajae Yŏn'guwŏn 2001.

2010). It is worth noting that the mirrors from all three of these Chinhan burials were the serpentine dragon variety. The excavation of the Ponghwang-dong 鳳凰洞 site in Kimhae also yielded one extremely rare undecorated imitation mirror from wood-coffin Tomb 3 (Tongasea Munhwajae Yŏn'guwŏn 2006) and demonstrates that bronze mirror burial in tombs had also begun in Pyŏnhan territory at this time.

After the mid-first century, only one site in the Chinhan region has yielded Han-style mirrors, that being Tomb 130 at the Sara-ri 舍羅里 site in Kyŏngju, which is an elite tomb containing large quantities of iron and lacquer artifacts and four small imitation mirrors (Yŏngnam Munhwajae Yŏn'guwŏn 2001) (Figure 1.19). During this period it was instead

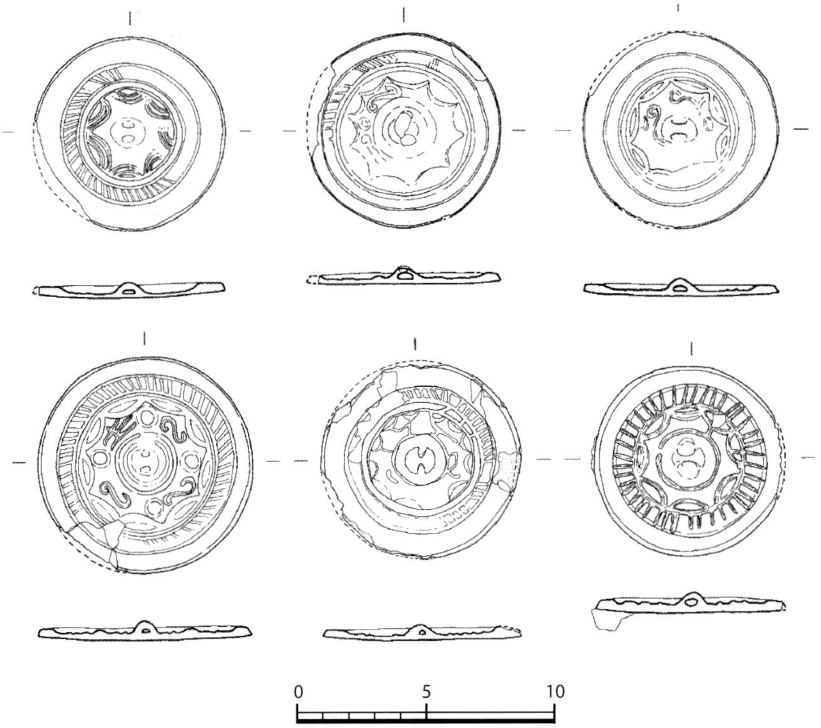

Figure 1.20 Imitative Bronze Mirrors from Tomb 162 at Yangdong-ni in Kimhae. From Im and Kwak 2000.

the Kimhae region, understood as the center of Pyŏnhan, that practiced full-scale burial of bronze mirrors in tombs. These include one TLV mirror from Tomb 19 at Naedŏng-ni 内德里; one small imitation mirror from Tomb 55 at Yangdong-ni 良洞里; and three additional small imitation mirrors from Tomb 427 at the same site. One elite wood-chamber tomb containing large numbers of iron artifacts, Tomb 162 at Yangdong-ni, dating from the latter half of Stage VI (around the mid-second century), has also yielded two small Han mirrors and eight small imitation mirrors (Im and Kwak 2000) (Figure 1.20).

As previously discussed, Han mirrors can be seen as evidence of exchange with the Han commanderies, and the pattern of distribution

Figure 1.21 Hirabaru Tomb 1 in Maebaru with Bronze Mirrors. From Yanagida Yasuo 2000.

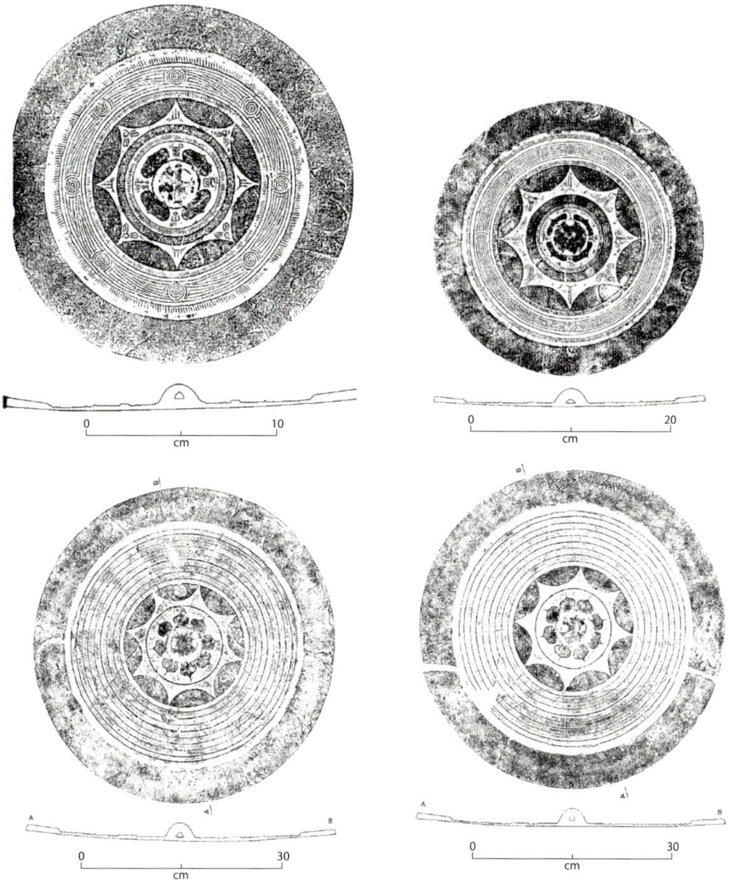

Figure 1.22 Large Imitative Bronze Mirrors from Hirabaru Tomb 1 in Maebaru. From Yanagida Yasuo 2000.

of these objects suggests that the Kŭmho River basin on the middle Naktong and the Kimhae region in the lower Naktong functioned as nodes of trade, these being understood to correspond to the sites of minor polities of Chinhan and Pyŏnhan respectively. Viewed chronologically, distributions of bronze mirrors in burials indicate that trade was first concentrated in Chinhan prior to the mid-first century A.D., after which the focus then shifted to Pyŏnhan.

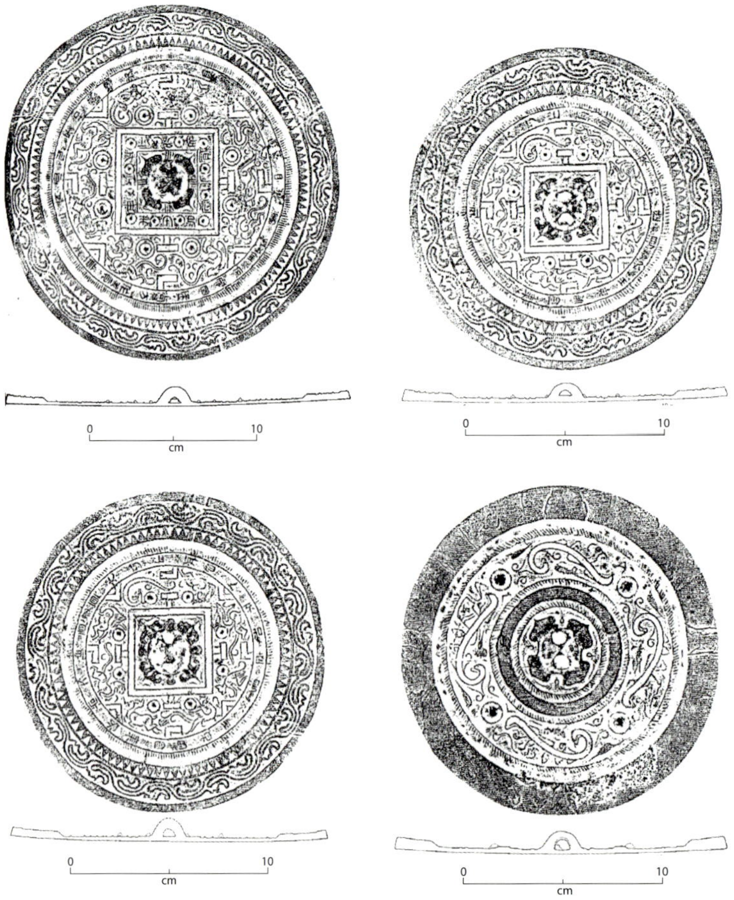

Figure 1.23 Han Mirrors from Hirabaru Tomb 1 in Maebaru.
From Yanagida Yasuo 2000.

In Japan in the first century A.D., twenty-one bronze mirror fragments, including those from eighteen checkerboard four-deity mirrors, were placed in a jar burial at the site of Ihara-Yarimizo 井原鑓溝 in Maebaru City 前原市, Fukuoka Prefecture (Nakayama 1916), while at Sakuranobaba 桜馬場 in Karatsu City, Saga Prefecture, two checkerboard mirrors were also found in a jar burial (Karatsuwan Shūhen Iseki Chōsa Iinkai 1982). At the site of Hirabaru

平原 in Maebaru City more than forty bronze mirrors, including thirty-two checkerboard four-deity mirrors and five oversized mirrors 46.5 cm in diameter with floral patterns, were discovered in a broken state in the four corners of a tomb dating to the second century. The date is disputed, however. The five oversize mirrors and one large mirror 27.1 cm in diameter are believed to be imitation mirrors produced in Japan, while the remaining thirty-four are thought to have been imported from China (Yanagida 2000:9–71) (Figures 1.21, 1.22, and 1.23).

The number and size of Central Plains–style Han mirrors found in Kyushu are overwhelmingly greater than those of the Korean peninsula, and it is argued that polities in Kyushu had a much stronger exchange capability. With regard to burial of Han mirrors in Japanese tombs, Japanese scholars emphasize mirrors as political objects invested with the authority of the Han empire, given by states of the Central Plains for the purpose of displaying long-distance exchange power (Fukunaga 2008:112–126).

Furthermore, in Japan mirrors were not simply a symbol of exchange with Chinese states—internally they came to be recognized as political prestige goods, and this concept was further developed in the subsequent Kofun period. In this context, bronze mirrors functioned as vehicles for strengthening the networks between central polities and surrounding groups and regions outside of northern Kyushu, and burials with imitation mirrors and Han mirror fragments can be explained as those with a somewhat lower status (Minami 2008:27–37). This fact contrasts with the Korean peninsula after the second century, when bronze mirrors were not important as political prestige goods.

Examples are scarce of high-status burials, like Tomb 130 at Sara-ri or Tomb 162 at Yangdong-ni in southeastern Korea, that contain bronze mirrors in addition to large quantities of flat axe blades and various iron weapons and tools. These tombs contain only four small imitation mirrors each. Furthermore, tombs believed to date to approximately the first half of the second century, such as Tomb 78 at Oksŏng-ni 玉城里 in P'ohang 浦項, contain large numbers of iron spears but no bronze mirrors whatsoever. Only Tomb 162 at Yangdong-ni in Kimhae, a wood-coffin tomb in the Pyŏnhan region dating to the mid-second century, contained two small Han mirrors along with eight imitation mirrors, in addition to forty flat axe blades and large numbers of iron spears.

Thus, in contrast with Japan, the primary grave good in elite tombs of the Chinhan and Pyŏnhan areas was not bronze mirrors but rather domestically produced iron objects, confirming that the most important components of high authority were secular considerations such as the ability to produce, control, and distribute iron. Considering the large amounts of iron procured by elites, it is likely that rather than just being able to produce iron through the specialized skills of craft workshops, they also had the ability to control the distribution of iron objects. Those who possessed the ability to control all aspects of the iron production process—from the oversight of particular groups of craftsman and the provision of raw materials to the manufacture and circulation of large amounts of iron and iron weaponry—were the paramount leaders.

In sum, in approximately the first to second century in the Chinhan and Pyŏnhan regions, the ability to administer the internal production system of iron and iron goods was the most important aspect of leadership. This contrasts with Wa, in which the most important characteristic of a leader was the ability to conduct long-distance exchange, as symbolized by Han mirrors and other Central Plains artifacts.

As noted previously, at this stage in Japan iron object prestige goods are found in considerably smaller quantities than in Chinhan and Pyŏnhan. The situation after the end of the Yayoi period in the latter half of the second century differs, as the tombs of the Kofun period contain an abundance of iron weaponry and tools. It is understood that in this period Japan could not yet conduct the level of administration and management related to the acquisition of iron material or specialized craftsman groups with a high level of skill in iron goods production. There is a possibility that iron and information related to its production were imported along with labor resources from Chinhan and Pyŏnhan in southeastern Korea.

Focusing on the temporal distribution of iron axe heads in burials, Tomb 130 at the Chinhan site of Sara-ri is chronologically earlier than Tomb 162 at the Pyŏnhan site of Yangdong-ni. This indicates that Kyŏngju became the center of iron production in Chinhan before Kimhae became the corresponding center for Pyŏnhan. Thus, assuming that iron was imported into Kyushu from the Korean peninsula, there is a strong possibility that the source of import in southeastern Korea was the Chinhan region. The Japanese-style imitation mirrors and medium-wide form of bronze dagger-axes and spears discovered in Taegu serve as additional evidence for this argument (Figure 1.24).

Since molds have not yet been discovered in the Korean peninsula, it is not certain that the production of imitation mirrors occurred in Chinhan and Pyŏnhan. However, examples similar to the medium-form imitation mirrors from Ŏŭn-dong in Yŏngch'on and P'yŏngni-dong in Taegu

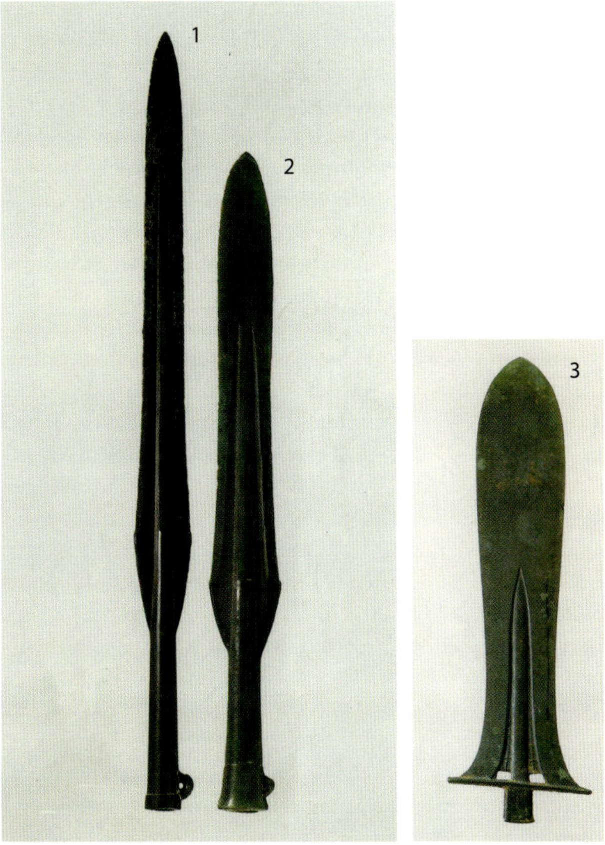

Figure 1.24 Bronze Spear Heads and Halberd from Pisan-dong in Taegu. From Kungnip Chungang Pangmulgwan 1992.

have not been found in Japan, so it is difficult to completely rule out the possibility of local production of imitation mirrors in Korea (Yi Chae-hyŏn 2003:134–136). Nevertheless, given various types of circumstantial evidence, including the fact that the vast majority of imitation mirrors have been unearthed in Kyushu, we cannot ignore the claim that a considerable number were produced in Kyushu (Tajiri 2003; Gotō 2009:307–341). If this is the case, there is a high probability that all of the imitation mirrors found in the Chinhan and Pyŏnhan regions were imported from Kyushu.

As Japanese researchers have pointed out, the production of small imitation mirrors was rather crude, and these mirrors were certainly not something that Chinhan regional craftsmen would have been unable to manufacture. Also, as stated previously, in the Chinhan and Pyŏnhan regions, the offering of Han mirrors as prestige goods in tombs was not particularly popular. In those regions such mirrors were simply gifts exchanged as symbols of goodwill, unlike the practice among the Wa, where the giving of Central Plains mirrors was vested with political meaning. This is the same case with the medium-wide and wide-form bronze spearheads excavated in Taegu, as will be discussed below.

In this stage, large numbers of medium-wide bronze swords, spearheads, and dagger-axes were produced in Japan in forms that differed from peninsular types. Therefore, the medium-wide bronze dagger-axes and spearheads discovered at Pisan-dong 飛山洞 and Manch'on-dong 晩村洞 (both in Taegu) were, based on their morphologies, most likely produced and imported from Japan (Yoshida 2003: 47–75). The bronze spearheads and dagger-axes distributed in Japan show a further development from medium-wide to wide forms, and given finds of molds for such artifacts, it is clear that these were produced in the northern Kyushu region. This development coincided with the time that the ritual of burying caches of bronze weapons in medium-wide and wide forms as religious offerings was also prevalent in Japan.

A few examples of medium-wide bronze spearheads have been found in tombs at Yangdong-ni in the Pyŏnhan region, but it was iron weaponry rather than bronze that was widely circulated in Kimhae. Bronze weapons had not only lost their practical utility in this period, but they were also not revitalized as ritual objects the same way they were in Japan, where they were ritually buried in earthen pits. As with imitation mirrors, they were probably received through exchange with Japan and did not have ideological significance.

In conclusion, in this period southeastern Korea—a short distance across the sea from Kyushu—escaped from its second-century B.C. circumstances, in which it was a peripheral area of bronze production and distribution, and become prominent as a central region for bronze and iron goods. While this was occurring, polities in Japan—with their need for a supply of strategic resources—formed close exchange relationships first with Chinhan and later with Pyŏnhan. Japanese imitation mirrors and weapon-shaped ritual goods thus appeared in the peninsula as exchange goods (Yi Hyŏn-hye 1994:35–57; Yi Chae-hyŏn 2003; Gotō 2009:335).

It is intriguing that a small imitation mirror and a wide bronze spear have been found in stone-cist Tomb 5 in Area A, and another set in Tomb 2 in Area B, at the Harō ハロウ site in Toyotama-chō 豊玉町, Tsushima City, on Tsushima Island, the midpoint of the route connecting Pyŏnhan and Wa. The fact that these two types of bronze exchange items were offered in tombs as prestige goods indirectly reflects the importance of the well-established trade network between the Wa based in Kyushu and Pyŏnhan in southeastern Korea. Although they are Wa objects produced in Kyushu, they were not buried according to Wa ritual, but instead follow the Pyŏnhan example.

Conclusions

In the first millennium B.C., multi-knobbed mirrors and Han mirrors were circulated widely in the Korean peninsula and Japan in the Old Chosŏn, Samhan, and Wa polities. Though they appeared in different times in each region, the majority of elite tombs from these polities contain bronze mirrors. Old Chosŏn can be divided into three chronological phases (early, late, and Wiman Chosŏn), and the center and level of social development changed in each stage. The center of early Old Chosŏn before the fourth century B.C. was a chiefdom polity ruled by a priestly leader who maintained loose relations with neighboring polities with which it shared a degree of cultural commonality. Initially, the center of the polity was in the Daling River basin, as suggested by the elite tomb at Shiertaiyingzi in Chaoyang, dating from roughly the eighth to seventh century B.C. The center subsequently moved to the Liao River basin, as seen in the tomb at Zhengjiawazi in Shenyang, dating to the sixth to fifth century B.C. From the time Yan advanced into the Liaoning region in the fourth century B.C., the center of later Old Chosŏn had moved to northwestern Korea. Further, elite burials with bronzes and ceramics of the type found at Zhengjiawazi began to appear in the South Ch'ungch'ŏng region of southwestern Korea, suggesting that a new minor polity connected with the earlier Old Chosŏn had settled in this region, and this is understood to be the central minor polity of early Mahan.

The existence of the central polity of later Old Chosŏn located in northwestern Korea is difficult to verify archaeologically, but it is understood to be reflected in the continuation of the tradition of multi-knobbed mirrors being the prestige goods of the highest elites and the development of Type C mirrors from Type B around the third century B.C. Then, as Old Chosŏn authority was supplanted by the state-level

Wiman Chosŏn in the early second century B.C., multi-knobbed mirrors came to be buried in the tombs of somewhat lesser elites or the leaders of peripheral groups or polities.

However, in the same period in the Mahan territory of southwestern Korea, elaborate Type C mirrors were manufactured as prestige goods and were deposited together with a variety of ceremonial bronze rattles in the tombs of religious leaders of the chiefdom-level central polity. Those individuals interred in the tombs without bronze rattles but with multi-knobbed mirrors and weaponry are understood as small-scale or lower-ranking regional leaders.

The ritual practices of Samhan leaders, involving the burial of these multi-knobbed mirrors and bronze weaponry in tombs, were also emulated in Japan beginning around the second century B.C. While bronze weaponry and tools found in burials were produced in Japan from a comparatively early stage, the Type C mirrors, the production of which required a high degree of technical skill, were most likely imported from the Mahan region. Southwestern Korea had become the earliest locus of active exchange for the Wa polities of Kyushu.

Then, in the first century B.C., as Wiman Chosŏn collapsed and the Han commanderies were established in northwestern Korea, the production and circulation of multi-knobbed mirrors ceased and Central Plains–style Han mirrors appeared. Almost none of these mirrors are found in the Mahan region, which previously had the highest concentration of multi-knobbed mirrors. Instead, a relatively larger quantity of mirrors circulated in the Chinhan region in the northern part of southeastern Korea. Also, the Kyushu region had an overwhelmingly larger number of mirrors deposited in the tombs of elites compared with southern Korea.

Based on the importation of Chinese Han mirrors and their burial in tombs, it is possible to say that there were certain distinctions among Mahan, Chinhan, Pyŏnhan, and Wa in their ability to conduct exchange with China and how they were recognized by the Han commanderies. However, it is possible that these distinctions reflect the differing lengths of time these polities had maintained the longstanding Old Chosŏn tradition of depositing multi-knobbed mirrors in tombs, which was comparatively short in the case of Wa.

Han mirrors imported from China have been unearthed in tombs dating to around the first century in large quantity in the Kyushu region, though they are also found in the Chinhan and Pyŏnhan regions. A large number of imitation mirrors were also produced and distributed in Japan, and these were imported and buried in tombs, first in the Chinhan region and somewhat later in the Pyŏnhan region. The minor Wa polities of Kyushu at that time engaged in active exchange with the Chinhan region, which had become a locus of iron and iron production from the first century B.C., to the same extent that they sought exchange with the Han commanderies and access to the advanced culture the commanderies were able to provide. At first exchange was conducted with Chinhan, but the scope of exchange later expanded to include Pyŏnhan, as evidenced by the chronological differences observed between these two regions in the deposition of Japanese imitation mirrors and ceremonial weaponry in tombs. These artifacts represent a form of trade commodity testifying to the close system of exchange that existed between the Wa and the Chinhan and Pyŏnhan polities.

References

Chang Yong-jun 張龍俊, and Hiragōri Tatsuya 平郡達哉

2009 Yujŏlbyŏngsik sŏkkŏm ŭro pon mumun t'ogi sidae maejang ŭirye ŭi kongyu 有節柄式 石劍으로 본 無文土器時代 埋葬儀禮의 共有 [The shared burial ritual of the Mumun pottery period seen through Yujŏlbyŏng-style stone daggers]. *Han'guk Kogo Hakpo* 韓國考古學報 72: 36–71.

Cho Yu-jŏn 趙由典

1984 Chŏnnam Hwasun ch'ŏngdong yumul ilkwal ch'ulto yujŏk 全南 和順 青銅遺物 一括 出土 遺蹟 [Bronze objects excavated from Hwasun in South Chŏlla Province]. In *Yun Mu-byŏng paksa hoegap kinyŏm nonch'ong* 尹武炳博士回甲紀念論叢 [Studies commemorating the sixtieth birthday of Dr. Yun Mu-byŏng], pp. 67–103. T'ongch'ŏn Munhwasa 通川文化社, Seoul.

Chŏn Yŏng-nae 全榮來

1977 *Han'guk chŏngdonggi munhwa ŭi kyebo wa p'yŏnnyŏn: tanyu kyŏng ŭi pyŏnch'ŏn ŭl chungsim ŭro* 韓國青銅器文化의 系譜와 編年: 多鈕鏡의 變遷을 中心으로 [Lineage and chronology of Korean bronze-ware culture: Focusing on the transformation of fine-line mirrors]. Chŏnbuk yujŏk chosa pogo 7 chip 全北遺蹟調査報告 7輯 [Chŏnbuk sites study report 7]. Chŏnju Sirip Pangmulgwan 全州市立博物館 [Chŏnju Municipal Museum], Chŏnju: 4–85.

Fukunaga Shin'ya 福永伸哉

2008 Seidōkyō no seijisei hōga 青銅鏡の政治性萌芽 [The germ of the political nature of bronze mirrors]. In *Girei to kenryoku* 儀礼と権力 [Ritual and power], edited by Shitara Hiromi 設楽博己, pp. 112–126. Yayoi jidai no kōkogaku 弥生時代の考古学 [Yayoi period archaeology], Vol. 7, Shitara Hiromi 設楽博己, Fujio Shin'ichirō 藤尾慎一郎, and Matsugi Takehiko 松木武彦, general editors. Dōseisha 同成社, Tokyo.

Fukuoka-ken Iizuka-shi Tateiwa Iseki Chōsa Iinkai 福岡県飯塚市立岩遺跡調査委員会 [*Ad hoc* Committee for the Investigations of the Tateiwa Site in Iizuka City, Fukuoka Prefecture]

1977 *Tateiwa iseki* 立岩遺跡 [The Tateiwa site]. Kawade Shobō Shinsha 河出書房新社, Tokyo.

Fukuoka-ken Kyōiku Iinkai 福岡県教育委員会 [Fukuoka Prefectural Municipal Board of Education]

1985 *Mikumo iseki: Minami-shōji chiku hen* 三雲遺跡: 南小路地区編 [The Mikumo site: Minami-shōji area]. Fukuoka-ken bunkazai chōsa hōkokusho 福岡県文化財調査報告書 [Report of investigations into cultural properties in the Fukuoka Prefecture] 69. Fukuoka-ken Kyōiku Iinkai 福岡県教育委員会, Fukuoka.

Fukuoka-shi Kyōiku Iinkai 福岡市教育委員会 [Fukuoka Municipal Board of Education]

1986 *Yoshitake-Takagi: Yayoi jidai maiso iseki chōsa gaiyō* 吉武高木: 弥生時代埋葬遺跡調査概要 [Yoshitake-Takaki: A preliminary report of archaeological excavations at a Yayoi period burial site]. Fukuoka-shi Kyōiku Iinkai [Fukuoka Municipal Board of Education] and Rekishi Shiryō Kan [Museum of History], Fukuoka.

Gotō Tadashi 後藤直

1996 Reigan shutsudo igata no ichi 霊巖出土鋳型の位置 [Place of a mold excavated at Yŏngam]. In *Tōhoku Ajia no Kōkogaku* 東北アジアの考古學 [The archaeology of Northeast Asia], Vol. 2, edited by Tōhoku Ajia Kōkogaku Kenkyū Kai 東北亞細亞考古學研究會, pp. 149–204. Kip'ŭn Saem 깊은샘, Seoul.

———

2009 Yayoi jidai no Wa-Kan kōshō: Wa-Sei seidōki no Kan e no ishutsu 弥生時代の倭韓交渉: 倭製青銅器の韓への移出 [Interaction between Korea and Japan during the Yayoi period: Exporting Japanese-made bronze objects to Korea]. *Kokuritsu Rekishi Minzoku Hakubutsukan kenkyū hōkoku* 国立歴史民俗博物館研究報告 [Bulletin of the National Museum of Japanese History] 151: 307–341.

Han Pyŏng-sam 韓炳三

1987 Wŏlsŏng Chuktong-ni ch'ult'o ch'ŏngdonggi ilkwal yumul 月城 竹東里出土 青銅器一括遺物 [Bronze-ware artifacts unearthed from Chuktong-ni at Wŏlsŏng]. In *Sambul Kim Wŏl-lyong kyosu chŏngnyŏn t'oeim kinyŏm nonch'ong I: Kogo p'yŏn* 三佛金元龍教授停年退任紀念論叢 1: 考古編 [Studies commemorating the retirement of Sambul Kim Wol-lyong, vol. 1: Archaeology], edited by Sambul Kim Wŏl-lyong Kyosu Chŏngnyŏn T'oeim Kinyŏm Nonch'ong Kanhaeng Wiwŏnhoe 三佛金元龍教授停年退任記念論叢刊行委員會 [Publication Committee for the Retirement Festschrift for Professor Kim Wŏl-lyong], pp. 103–120. Ilchisa 一志社, Seoul.

Han Pyŏng-sam 韓炳三 , and Yi Kŏn-mu 李健茂

1977 *Namsŏng-ni sŏkkwanmyo* 南城里石棺墓 [Stone-coffin tombs at Namsŏng-ni]. Kungnip pangmulgwan kojŏk chosa pogo che 10 ch'aek 國立博物館古蹟調查報告第10冊 [National Museum ancient remains study report 10]. Kungnip Chungang Pangmulgwan 國立中央博物館 [National Central Museum], Seoul.

Harada Dairoku 原田大六

1991 *Hirabaru Yayoi kofun: Ōhirumenomuchi no haka* 平原弥生古墳: 大日孁貴尊の墓 [The Yayoi tomb of Hirabaru: The tomb of Ōhirumenomuchi]. 2 Vols. Ashi Shobō 葦書房, Fukuoka.

Honam Munhwajae Yŏn'guwŏn 湖南文化財研究院 [Honam Institute of Cultural Properties]

2005 *Wanju Kal-tong yujŏk* 完州葛洞遺蹟 [The Kal-tong site in Wanju]. Honam Munhwajae Yŏn'guwŏn, Tamyang.

Im Hyo-t'aek 林孝澤, and Kwak Tong-ch'ŏl 郭東哲

2000 *Kimhae Yangdong-ni kobun munhwa* 金海良洞里古墳文化 [Kimhae Yangdong-ni tomb culture]. Tongŭi Taehakkyo Pangmulgwan haksul chongsŏ 7 東義大學校博物館學術叢書 7 [Tongŭi University Museum academic series 7]. Tongŭi Taehakkyo Pangmulgwan 東義大學校博物館, Pusan.

Im Pyŏng-t'ae 林炳泰

1987 Yŏngam ch'ult'o ch'ŏngdonggi yongbŏm e taehayŏ 靈巖出土 青銅器 鎔范에 대하여 [On the bronze mold excavated in Yŏngam]. In *Sambul Kim Wŏllyong kyosu chŏngnyŏn t'oe'im kinyŏm nonch'ong I: Kogohak p'yŏn* 三佛金元龍教授停年退任紀念論叢 I: 考古學編 [Studies commemorating the retirement of Sambul Kim Wollyong, vol. 1: Archaeology], edited by Sambul Kim Wŏl-lyong Kyosu Chŏngnyŏn T'oeim Kinyŏm Nonch'ong Kanhaeng Wiwŏnhoe 三佛金元龍教授停年退任記念論叢刊行委員會 [Publication Committee for the Retirement Festschrift for Professor Kim Wŏl-lyong], pp. 121–140. Ilchisa 一志社, Seoul.

Iwanaga Shōzō 岩永省三

2000 Seidō buki giki-ka no hikaku kenkyū: Kan to Wa 青銅武器儀器化の比較研究: 韓と倭 [Comparative study on the transformation process from bronze weapon to ritual paraphernalia: Cases of Korea and of Japan]. *Kogohak ŭro pon Pyŏn · Chinhan kwa Wae* 考古學으로 본 弁·辰韓과 倭 [Pyŏnhan, Chinhan, and Wa viewed through archaeology], Che-4 hoe Yŏngnam Kogo Hakhoe Kuju Kogo Hakhoe haptong kogohak taehoe 第4回 嶺南考古學會·九州考古學會 合同考古學大會 [The fourth joint archaeological conference of the Yeungnam Archaeological Society and the Kyushu Archaeological Society]: 109–127. Pusan, Korea.

Kang Kŏn-gil 池健吉

1978 Yesan Tongsŏ-ri sŏkkwanmyo ch'ŏngdong ilkwal yumul 禮山東西里石棺墓青銅一括遺物 [Bronze artifacts from stone-coffin tombs at Tongsŏ-ri in Yesan]. *Paekche Yŏn'gu* 百濟研究 9: 151–181.

Karatsuwan Shūhen Iseki Chōsa Iinkai 唐津湾周辺遺跡調査委員会 [*Ad hoc* committee for investigations into archaeological sites on the coastal areas of Karatsu Bay]

1982 *Matsurakoku* 末盧国 [Matsura polity]. Rokkō Shuppan 六興出版, Tokyo.

Kasuga-shi Na-koku no Oka Rekishi Shiryōkan 春日市奴国の丘歴史資料館 [Kasuga City Nakoku-no-Oka Historical Museum]

2000 *Na-koku ō no shutsugen to hokubu Kyūshū no kuniguni: Suku-Okamoto iseki hakken 100 shūnen kinen-ten* 奴国王の出現と北部九州のクニグニ: 須玖岡本遺跡発見100周年記念展 [The discovery of the Na-koku king and the polities of northern Kyushu: Exhibition commemorating the 100-year anniversary of the discovery of the Suku-Okamoto site]. Kasuga-shi Na-koku no Oka Rekishi Shiryōkanpō, Kasuga.

Kataoka Kōji 片岡宏二

1999 *Yayoi jidai toraijin doki to seidōki* 弥生時代渡来人と土器・青銅器 [Bronze objects, pottery, and immigrants during the Yayoi period]. Yūzankaku 雄山閣, Tokyo.

Kim Sŭng-ok 金承鈺

2007 Punmyo charyo rŭl t'onghae pon ch'ŏngdonggi sidae sahoe chojik kwa pyŏnch'ŏn 墳墓資料를 통해 본 青銅器時代 社會組織과 變遷 [Bronze Age social organization and transformation seen through tomb material]. In *Kyech'ŭng sahoe wa chibaeja ŭi ch'urhyŏn* 階層社會와 支配者의 出現 [Stratified society and the appearance of rulers], edited by Han'guk Kogo Hakhoe 韓國考古學會, pp. 61–138. Sahoe P'yŏngnon 사회평론, Seoul.

Kobayashi Seiji 小林青樹

2008a Tōhoku Ajia ni okeru dōka no kigen to nendai: Ryōsei shiki dōka no seiritsu to En-Chōsen e no eikyo 東北アジアにおける銅戈の起源と年代: 遼西式銅戈の成立と燕・朝鮮への影響 [Origin and age of bronze halberds in Northeast Asia: Beginning of the Liaoxi-style halberds and their influence on Yan and Chosŏn]. In *Higashi Ajia seidōki no keifu* 東アジア青銅器の系譜 [Genealogy of bronze in Northeast Asia], edited by Harunari Hideji 春成秀爾 and Nishimoto Toyohiro 西本豊弘 , pp. 24–38. Yūzankaku 雄山閣, Tokyo.

———

2008b Tate to ka wo mochiita girei 盾と戈をもちいた儀礼 [Rituals utilizing a shield and halberd]. In *Girei to kenryoku* 儀礼と権力 [Ritual and power], edited by Shitara Hiromi 設楽博已, pp. 32–45. Yayoi Jidai no Kōkogaku 弥生時代の考古学 [Yayoi-period archaeology] 7, Dōseisha 同成社, Tokyo.

Kungnip Chungang Pangmulgwan 國立中央博物館 [National Museum of Korea]

1992 *Han'guk ŭi Ch'ŏngdonggi munhwa* 韓國의 青銅器文化 [Bronze culture of Korea]. Pŏmusa 汎友社, Seoul.

———

2006 *Pungnyŏk ŭi munhwa yusan* 북녁의문화유산 [Cultural heritage of North Korea]. Samin 삼인, Seoul.

Kungnip Kyŏngju Pangmulgwan 國立慶州博物館 [Kyŏngju National Museum]

2003 *Kyŏngju Choyang-dong yujŏk II* 慶州 朝陽洞遺蹟 II [The Choyang-dong site in Kyŏngju, vol. 2]. Kungnip Kyŏngju Pangmulgwan haksul chosa pogo che 14 ch'aek 國立慶州博物館 學術調査報告 第13冊 [Kyŏngju National Museum academic studies report 13]. Kungnip Kyŏngju Pangmulgwan, Kyŏngju.

———

2007 *Yŏngch'ŏn Yongjŏn-ni yujŏk* 永川龍田里 遺蹟 [The Yongjŏn-ni site in Yŏngch'ŏn]. Kungnip Kyŏngju Pangmulgwan haksul chosa pogo che 19 ch'aek 國立慶州博物館 學術調査報告 第19冊 [Kyŏngju National Museum academic studies report 19]. Kungnip Kyŏngju Pangmulgwan 國立慶州博物館, Kyŏngju.

Kungnip Pangmulgwan 國立博物館 [National Museum of Korea]

1968 *Ch'ŏngdong yumul torok: 8 - 15 hu sujip* 青銅遺物圖錄: 8 · 15後 蒐集 [Selected bronze objects of the early metal period in Korea: 1945–1968]. Kungnip Pangmulgwan haksul charyojip (1) 國立博物館學術資料集 (1) [National Museum of Korea academic sourcebook, vol. 1]. Kungnip Pangmulgwan, Seoul.

Kyŏngsang-pukto Munhwajae Yŏn'guwŏn 慶尚北道文化財研究院 [North Kyŏngsang Institute of Cultural Properties]

2005 *Sŏngju Paekchŏn Yesan-ni t'oji kuhoek chŏngni saŏp chigunae munhwa yujŏk palgul chosa pogosŏ* 星州栢田禮山里 土地區劃整理事業地區内 文化遺蹟發掘調査報告書 [Report of the excavation of cultural sites in the city planning project area business district at Yesan-ni in Paekchŏn, Sŏngju]. Kyŏngsang-pukto Munhwajae Yŏn'guwŏn haksul chosa pogo che 48 ch'aek 慶尚北道文化財研究院 學術調査報告 第48冊 [North Kyŏngsang Institute of Cultural Properties academic studies report 48]. Kyŏngsang-pukto Munhwajae Yŏn'guwŏn, Kyŏngsan.

———

2008 *Kimch'ŏn-si t'enisŭ chang p'yŏnip pujinae Kimch'ŏn Mundang-dong yujŏk* 金泉市 테니스장 編入敷地内 金泉 文唐洞 遺蹟 [Site of Kimch'ŏn Mundang-dong within the Kimch'ŏn City tennis court land transfer]. Kyŏngsang-pukto Munhwajae Yŏn'guwŏn haksul chosa pogo che 91 ch'aek 慶尚北道文化財研究院 學術調査報告 第91冊 [North Kyŏngsang Cultural Properties Research Institute academic studies report 91]. Kyŏngsang-pukto Munhwajae Yŏn'guwŏn 慶尚北道文化財研究院, Kyŏngsan.

Kyōto Teikoku Daigaku Bungakubu Kōkogaku Kyōshitsu 京都帝国大学文学部考古学教室 [Kyoto Imperial University Faculty of Letters Department of Archaeology]

1930 *Chikuzen Suku shizen iseki no kenkyū* 筑前須玖史前遺跡研究 [Studies on the Suku prehistoric site in Chikuzen]. Kyōto Teikoku Daigaku Bungakubu kōkogaku kenkyū hōkoku 京都帝國大學文學部考古學研究報告 [Kyoto Imperial University literature department report on archaeological research], Vol. 11. Tōkō Shoin 刀工書院, Tokyo.

Li Dianfu 李殿福

1991 Jianping Gushanzi Liushulinzi qingtong shidai muzang 建平孤山子柳树林子青铜时代墓葬 [Bronze Age tomb at Liushulingzi in Gushanzi, Jianping]. *Liaohai Wenwu Xuekan* 辽海文物学刊: 1–6.

Mifune Haruhisa 三船温尚
2007 Ikei yumon seidōki ni okeru monyō to dōkei ittsui seihin no chūzo gijutsu 異形有文青銅器における文様と同形一対製品の鋳造技術 [Decorative pattern of variform bronze objects and casting technology of identical bronze objects in a pair]. In *Hanbando ŭi ch'ŏngdonggi chejak kisul kwa Tong Asia ŭi kogyŏng* 韓半島의 青銅器 製作技術과 東아시아의 古鏡 [Bronze production technologies of the Korean peninsula and ancient mirrors of East Asia], edited by Kungnip Kyŏngju Pangmulgwan 國立慶州博物館 and Nara Kenritsu Kashihara Kōkogaku Kenkyūjo 奈良県立橿原考古学研究所, pp. 25–58. Kungnip Kyŏngju Pangmulgwan, Kyŏngju.
Minami Kentarō 南健太郎
2008 Zen-Kan kyō no hakyō to sono kakusan keitai: Hakyō ni hodokosareru niji kakō no kento kara 前漢鏡の破鏡とその拡散形態: 破鏡に施される二次加工の検討から [Fragmentary Western Han mirrors and the nature of their distribution in Japan: Based on examination of secondary modification applied to the fragmentary bronze mirrors]. In *Ōken to buki to shinko* 王権と武器と信仰 [Kingship, weapons, and belief], edited by Sugaya Fuminori 菅谷文則, pp. 27–37. Dōseisha 同成社, Tokyo.
Miryang Taehakkyo Pangmulgwan 密陽大學校博物館 [Miryang University Museum]
2004 *Miryang Kyo-dong yujŏk* 密陽校洞遺蹟 [The Kyo-dong site in Miryang]. Miryang Taehakkyo Pangmulgwan haksul chosa pogo che 7 ch'aek 密陽大學校博物館 學術調査報告 第7冊 [Miryang University Museum academic studies report 7]. Miryang Taehakkyo Pangmulgwan 密陽大學校博物館, Miryang.
Miyazato Osamu 宮里修
2008 Tachū-saimon kyō no keishiki bunrui to hen'nen 多鈕細文鏡の型式分類と編年 [Classification and chronology of Korean fine geometric mirrors]. *Kōkogaku Zasshi* 考古学雑誌 92(1): 1–32.
———
2009 Tachū kyō no seisaku-chi 多鈕鏡の制作地 [Where were Korean geometric mirrors made?]. *Ch'ŏngdong kŏul kwa kodae sahoe palp'yo yoji* 青銅 거울과 古代社會 發表要旨 [Bronze mirrors and ancient society: Presentation summaries], 2009 nyŏn Pokch'ŏn Pangmulgwan t'ŭkpyŏljan kinyŏm haksul semina 2009年 福泉博物館 特別展記念 學術세미나 [Pokch'ŏn Museum Special Exhibition Seminar 2009]: 18–20. Pusan.
Morioka Hideto 森岡秀人
1989 Dōkyō 銅鏡 [Bronze mirrors]. *Kikan Kōkogaku* 季刊考古学 27: 47–52.

Munakata-shi Kyōiku Iinkai 宗像市教育委員會 [Munakata Municipal Board of Education]

2009 *Gaihō: Taguma-Ishihatake iseki: Fukuoka-ken Munakata-shi Taguma shozai iseki no hakkutsu chōsa gaiyō* 概報: 田熊石畑遺跡: 福岡県宗像市田熊所在遺跡の発掘調査概要 [Summary report: The Taguma-Ishihatake site: Outline on the excavation and survey of the site at Taguma in Munakata City, Fukuoka Prefecture]. Munakata-shi Bunkazai Chōsa Hōkokusho dai 61 shū 宗像市文化財調査報告書 第61集 [Munakata City cultural properties survey report, vol. 61]. Munakata-shi Kyōiku Iinkai, Munakata.

Nakayama Heijiro 中山平次郎

1916 Ōgame o hakken seru kodai iseki 1 大甕を発見せる古代遺跡 1 [Ancient sites where large jars have been discovered]. *Kōkogaku Zasshi* 考古学雑誌 11(1): 1–13.

Neimenggu Zizhiqu Wenwu Kaogu Yanjiusuo 内蒙古自治区文物考古研究所 [Inner Mongolia Autonomous Region Institute of Archaeology], and Ningchengxian Liao Zhongjing Bowuguan 宁城县辽中京博物馆 [Liao Central Capital Museum of Ningcheng]

2008 *Xiaoheishigou: Xiajiadian shangceng wenhua yizhi fajue jianbao* 小黑石沟: 夏家店上层文化遗址发掘报告 [Xiaoheishigou: Report of the excavation of the Upper Xiajiadian culture site]. Kexue Chubanshe 科学出版社, Beijing.

Oda Fujio 小田富士雄

2000 *Wajin den no kuniguni* 倭人伝の国々 [Countries in the "Account of Wa"]. Gakuseisha 学生社, Tokyo.

Ōtemae Daigaku Shigaku Kenkyūjo 大手前大学史学研究所 [Ōtemae University Historical Research Institute]

2010 *Yayoi, Kofun jidai dōkyō shutsudo jōkyō shiryōshū: Nihon kōkogaku kyōkai 2010 nendo Hyōgo taikai dai-2 bunkakai "Kofun shutsugen katei to dōkyō" shiryōshū* 弥生・古墳時代銅鏡出土状況資料集: 日本考古学協会2010年度兵庫大会第2分科会「古墳出現過程と銅鏡」資料集 [Data compendium of the archaeological contexts of the discoveries of bronze mirrors of the Yayoi and Kofun periods: Compendium from "Mirrors and the excavation of tomb mounds," Session No. 2 of the 2010 Hyōgo Assembly of the Japanese Archaeological Association]. Ōtemae Daigaku Shigaku Kenkyūjo, Nishinomiya.

Pak Sun-bal 朴淳發

2004 Yoryŏng chŏmt'odae t'ogi munhwa ŭi Hanbando chŏngch'ak kwajŏng 遼寧粘土帶土器文化의 韓半島 定着過程 [The settlement process of attached-rim pottery culture of Liaoning in the Korean peninsula]. *Kŭmgang Kogo* 錦江考古 1: 57–75.

Qiao Liang 喬梁
2004 Xinzhuangtou 30 hao mu de niandai ji qita 辛庄頭30號墓的年代及其他 [On the chronology of Tomb 30 at Xinzhuangtou]. *Huaxia Kaogu* 華夏考古, no. 2: 58–67.
Shenyang Gugong Bowuguan 沈阳故宫博物馆 [Shenyang Old Palace Museum], and Shenyangshi Wenwu Guanli Bangongshi 沈阳市文物管理办公室 [Shenyang Office of Cultural Properties Management]
1975 Shenyang Zhengjiawazi de liang zuo qingtong shidai muzang 沈阳郑家洼子的两座青铜时代墓葬 [Two Bronze Age tombs at Zhengjiawazi in Shenyang]. *Kaogu Xuebao* 考古学报, no. 1: 141–156.
Sugiyama Shigetsugu 杉山林継, and Muramatsu Yōsuke 村松洋介
2005 Tachū kyō no kansatsu to shiyō konseki ni tsuite 多鈕鏡の観察と使用痕跡について [Observation of Korean geometric mirrors and their use-wear]. *Higashi Ajia ni okeru Shin-Sekki Bunka to Nihon* 東アジアにおける新石器文化と日本 [Neolithic culture and Japan in East Asia]. Kokugakuin Daigaku 21 seiki COE Puroguramu kōkogaku chōsa kenkyū hōkoku 国学院大学21世紀 COEプログラム考古学調査研究報告 [Research reports of archaeological surveys of the twenty-first century COE program at Kokugakuin University]. Kokugakuin Daigaku 国学院大学, Tokyo: 339–381.
Suzuki Toshihiro 鈴木敏弘
2005 Yayoi bo to genshi kōeki 弥生墓と原史交易 [Yayoi-period burials and protohistoric trades]. *Kikan Kōkogaku* 季刊考古学 92: 31–34.
Tajiri Yoshinori 田尻義了
2003 Yayoi jidai kogata bōseikyō seisakuchi: Shoki kogata bōseikyō kento 弥生時代小形仿製鏡製作地: 初期小形仿製鏡検討 [Locations of the production of small Yayoi-period bronze mirrors modelled after Chinese mirrors: Examination of the early types of small Japanese mirrors modeled after Chinese mirrors]. In *Tōhoku Ajia Seidōki kara mita Kankoku Seidōki Bunka ni kansuru Kenkyū* 東北アジア青銅器文化からみた韓国青銅器文化に関する研究 [Research into the Korean bronze culture in the Northeast Asian context], special issue, *Seikyū Gakujutsu Ronshū* 青丘学術論集 22: 77–95.
Takakura Hiroaki 高倉洋彰
1972 Yayoi jidai kogata bōsei-kyō ni tsuite 弥生時代小形仿製鏡について [Small Japanese bronze mirrors modeled after Chinese mirrors during the Yayoi period]. *Kōkogaku Zasshi* 考古学雑誌 58(3): 1–30.

———

1993 Zen-Kan kyō ni arawareta ken'i no shōchōsei 前漢鏡にあらわれた権威の象徴性 [Symbol of authority as appearing in early Han Chinese mirrors in Japan]. *Kokuritsu Rekishi Minzoku Hakubutsukan Kenkyū Hōkoku* 国立歴史民俗博物館研究報告 55 [Bulletin of the National Museum of Japanese History]: 3–37.

———

1995 *Kin in kokka-gun no jidai* 金印国家群の時代 [Era of a cluster of states awarded golden seals from China]. Aoki Shoten 青木書店, Tokyo.

Takesue Jun'ichi 武末純一

2002 Yoryŏngsik tonggŏm myo wa kuk ŭi hyŏngsŏng 遼寧式銅劍墓와 國의 形成 [Liaoning dagger tombs and state formation]. *Ch'ŏnggye Sahak* 清溪史學 16/17: 27–39.

———

2009 San Kan to Wa no kōryu: Kaison no shiten kara 三韓と倭の交流: 海村の視点から [Interaction between Three Kingdoms of Korea and Japan: From the perspective of ocean villages]. *Kokuritsu Rekishi Minzoku Hakubutsukan kenkyū hōkoku* 国立歴史民俗博物館研究報告研究報告 [Bulletin of the National Museum of Japanese History] 151: 285–306.

Terasawa Kaoru 寺沢薫

2000 *Ōken tanjō* 王權誕生 [The birth of royal authority]. Kōdansha 講談社, Tokyo.

Tongasea Munhwajae Yŏn'guwŏn 東亞細亞文化財研究院 [East Asia Institute of Cultural Properties]

2006 *Kimhae Kaya ŭi sup chosŏng pujinae munhwa yujŏk palgul chosa pogosŏ* 金海 伽倻의 숲 造成敷地内 文化遺蹟發掘調査報告書 [Kimhae Kaya wooded garden construction zone cultural site excavation report]. Tongasea Munhwajae Yŏn'guwŏn palgul chosa pogosŏ che 8 chip 東亞細亞文化財研究院 發掘調査 報告書 第8輯 [Tongasea Cultural Properties Research Institute excavation report 8]. Tongasea Munhwajae Yŏn'guwŏn 東亞細亞文化財研究院, Ch'angwŏn.

Tsunematsu Mikio 常松幹雄

2006 *Saiko no ōbo: Yoshitake-Takaki iseki* 最古の王墓: 吉武高木遺跡 [Yoshitake-Takaki site: Earliest royal tomb in Japan]. Shinsensha 新泉社, Tokyo.

Umehara Sueji 梅原末治, and Fujita Ryōsaku 藤田亮策

1925 *Minami Chōsen ni okeru Kan-dai no iseki* 南朝鮮に於ける漢代の遺跡 [Han Chinese sites in the southern Korean peninsula]. Taishō jūichinendo koseki chōsa hōkoku dai 2 saku 大正十一年度古跡調査報告 第2冊. Chōsen Sōtokufu 朝鮮総督府 [Government-General of Korea], Seoul (printed in Kyoto, Japan).

Wei Haibo 魏海波

1987 Liaoning Benxi faxian qingtong duanjian mu 辽宁本溪发现青铜短剑墓 [Discovery of a bronze dagger tomb in Benxi, Liaoning]. *Kaogu* 考古, no. 2: 181–182.

Wuenyuesitu 乌恩岳斯图

2007 *Beifang caoyuan kaoguxue wenhua yanjiu: Qingtong shidai zhi zaoqi tieqi shidai* 北方草原考古学文化研究：青铜时代至早期铁器时代 [Studies of archaeological cultures of the northern plains: Bronze Age to the early Iron Age]. Kexue Chubanshe 科学出版社, Beijing: 224–251.

Yanagida Yasuo 柳田康雄

2000 Hirabaru 1-gō bo 平原1号墓 [Hirabaru no. 1 burial]. In *Hirabaru iseki* 平原遺跡 [Hirabaru site], edited by Maebaru-shi Kyōiku Iinkai 前原市教育委員會 [Maebaru Municipal Board of Education], pp. 9–71. Maebaru-shi Kyōiku Iinkai, Maebaru-shi.

Yi Chae-hyŏn 李在賢

2003 *Pyŏn·Chinhan sahoe ŭi kogohakchŏk yŏn'gu* 弁·辰韓社會의 考古學的 研究 [Archaeological investigation of Pyŏnhan and Chinhan society]. Pusan Taehakkyo Taehakwŏn paksa hakwi nonmun 釜山大學校 大學院 博士學位論文 PhD Dissertation, History Department, Pusan University, Pusan.

Yi Ch'ŏng-gyu (Lee Chungkyu) 李清圭

1997 Yŏngnam chibang ŭi ch'ŏngdonggi munhwa ŭi chŏn'gae 嶺南地方의 青銅器文化의 展開 [The spread of bronze-ware culture in the Yŏngnam region]. *Yŏngnam Kogohak* 嶺南考古學 21: 29–77.

———

2000, Kuk ŭi hyŏngsŏng kwa tanyu kyŏng pujangmyo 國의 形成과 多鈕鏡副葬墓 [State formation and fine-line mirror tombs]. *Sŏnsa wa Kodae* 先史와古代 14: 27–47.

———

2005 Ch'ŏngdonggi rŭl t'onghae pon Ko Chosŏn kwa chubyŏn sahoe 青銅器를 통해 본 古朝鮮과 周邊社會 [Old Chosŏn and peripheral society seen through bronze-ware]. In *Pukpangsa nonch'ong* 6 北方史論叢 6 [Studies on northern zone history], edited by Koguryŏ Yŏn'gu Chaedan 高句麗研究財團, pp. 7–58. Koguryŏ Yŏn'gu Chaedan 高句麗研究財團, Seoul.

———

2008 Chungguk tongbuk chiyŏk kwa Hanbando ch'ŏngdonggi munhwa yŏn'gu ŭi sŏngkwa 中國東北地域과 韓半島 青銅器文化研究의 成果 [Results of investigations into the bronze-ware culture of northeast China and the Korean peninsula]. In *Chungguk tongbuk chiyŏk kogohak yŏn'gu hyŏnhwang kwa munjejŏm* 中國東北地域 考古學 研究現況과 問題點 [Archaeology of northeast China:

The state of research and problems], edited by Tongbuga Yŏksa Chaedan [Northeast Asian History Foundation], pp. 192–262. Tongbuga Yŏksa Chaedan, Seoul.

———

2010 Tanyu kyŏng ŭi pyŏnch'ŏn kwa punp'o 多鈕鏡 型式의 變遷과 分布 [Transformation and distribution of fine-line mirror morphology]. *Han'guk Sanggosa Hakpo* 韓國上古史學報 67: 45–89.

Yi Hyŏn-hye 李賢惠

1984 *Samhan sahoe hyŏngsŏng kwajŏng yŏn'gu* 三韓社會形成過程研究 [A study of the formation processes of Samhan society]. Ilchogak 一潮閣, Seoul.

———

1994 Samhan ŭi taeoe kyoyŏk ch'egye 三韓의 對外交易體系 [The Samhan foreign exchange system]. In *Yi Ki-baek sŏnsaeng kohŭi kinyŏm Han'guk sahak nonch'ong (sang)* 李基白先生古稀紀念韓國史學論叢 (上) [Studies commemorating the seventieth birthday of Professor Yi Ki-baek, vol. 1], edited by Yi Ki-baek Sŏnsaeng Kohŭi Kinyŏm Han'guk Sahak Nonch'ong Kanhaeng Wiwŏhoe 李基白先生古稀紀念韓國史學論叢刊行委員會 [Publication Committee for the Seventieth Birthday Festschrift for Yi Ki-baek], pp. 35–57. Ilchogak 一潮閣, Seoul.

———

2003 Han'guk ch'ogi ch'ŏlgi sidae ŭi chŏngch'ich'e sujang e taehan koch'al 韓國初期鐵器時代의 政治體 首長에 對한 考察 [Analysis of the political leadership of the Korean early Iron Age]. *Yŏksa Hakpo* 歷史學報 180: 1–34.

Yi Kang-sŭng 李康承

1987 Puyŏ Kubong-ni ch'ult'o ch'ŏngdonggi ilkwal yumul 扶餘 九鳳里出土 青銅器一括遺物 [Collected bronze artifacts from Kubong-ni in Puyŏ]. In *Sambul Kim Wŏl-lyong kyosu chŏngnyŏn t'oeim kinyŏm nonch'ong I: Kogop'yŏn* 三佛金元龍教授停年退任紀念論叢 1: 考古編 [Studies commemorating the retirement of Sambul Kim Wol-lyong, vol. 1: Archaeology], edited by Sambul Kim Wŏl-lyong Kyosu Chŏngnyŏn T'oeim Kinyŏm Nonch'ong Kanhaeng Wiwŏnhoe 三佛金元龍教授停年退任記念論叢刊行委員會 [Publication Committee for the Retirement Festschrift for Professor Kim Wŏl-lyong], pp. 141–167. Ilchisa 一志社, Seoul.

———

1984 Han'gyŏng ŭl panch'urhan sehyŏng tonggŏm ŭi illye 漢鏡을 伴出한 細形銅劍의 一例 [Instances of slim bronze daggers accompanying Han mirrors]. In *Yun Mu-byŏng paksa hoegap kinyŏm nonch'ong* 尹武炳博士回甲紀念論叢 [Studies commemorating the sixtieth birthday of Dr. Yun Mu-byŏng], edited by Yun Mu-byŏng Paksa Hoegap Kinyŏm Nonch'ong Kanhaeng Wiwŏnhoe 尹武炳博士回甲記念論叢刊行委員會 [Publication Committee for the Sixtieth Birthday Festschrift for Dr. Yun Mu-byŏng], pp. 129–142. T'ongch'ŏn Munhwasa 通川文化社, Seoul.

Yi Kŏn-mu 李健茂, and Sŏ Sŏng-hun 徐聲勳

1988, *Hamp'yŏng Ch'op'o-ri yujŏk* 咸平草浦里遺蹟 [The Ch'op'o-ri site in Hamp'yŏng]. Kungnip Kwangju Pangmulgwan 國立光州博物館 [Kwangju National Museum], Kwangju.

Yi Kŏn-mu 李健茂, Yi Yŏng-hun 李榮勳, Yun Kwang-jin 尹光鎭, and Sin Tae-gon 申大坤.

1989 Ŭich'ang Taho-ri yujŏk palgul chinjŏn pogo (1) 義昌 茶戶里遺蹟 發掘進展報告 (1) [Progress report for the excavation of the Taho-ri site in Ŭich'ang, vol. 1]. *Kogohak Chi* 考古學誌 1: 1–174.

Yi Sŏng-jae 李成載

2007 Chungguk tongbuk chiyŏk chŏmt'odae t'ogi munhwa ŭi chŏn'gae kwajŏng yŏn'gu 中國東北地域 粘土帶土器文化의 展開過程 研究 [A study of the developmental processes of attached-rim pottery culture in China's northeastern regions]. Sungsil Taehakkyo sŏksa hagwi nonmun 崇實大學校碩士學位論文. Master's thesis, Department of History, Sungsil University, Seoul.

Yi Yang-su 李陽洙

2004 Tanyu semun kyŏng ŭro pon Han'guk kwa Ilbon 多鈕細文鏡으로 본 韓國과 日本 [Korea and Japan seen through fine-line mirrors]. *Yŏngnam Kogohak* 嶺南考古學 35: 37–57.

———

2006 Hanbando esŏ Han'gyŏng ŭi punbae wa yut'ong 韓半島에서 漢鏡의 分配와 流通 [Distribution and circulation of Han mirrors from Korea]. *Kogohak Chi* 考古學誌 15: 27–56.

Yi Yŏng-mun 李榮文

2002 *Han'guk chisŏngmyo sahoe yŏn'gu* 韓國 支石墓社會 研究 [Study on Korean dolmen society]. Hagyŏn Munhwasa 學研文化社, Seoul.

Yŏngnam Munhwajae Yŏn'guwŏn 嶺南文化財研究院 [Yŏngnam Institute of Cultural Properties]

2001 *Kyŏngju Sara-ri yujŏk II: Mokkwanmyo, chugŏji* 慶州舍羅里遺蹟 II: 木棺墓, 住居址 [The Sara-ri site in Kyŏngju, vol. 2: Wood-coffin tombs and dwellings]. Yŏngnam Munhwajae Yŏn'guwŏn haksul chosa pogo che 32 chip 嶺南文化財研究院 學術調査報告 第32冊 [Yŏngnam Cultural Heritage Research Institute academic studies report 32]. Yŏngnam Munhwajae Yŏn'guwŏn 嶺南文化財研究院, Taegu.

———

2010 *Kyŏngsan Sindae-ri yujŏk I* 慶山 新垈里遺蹟 I [The Sindae-ri site in Kyŏngsan, vol. 1]. Yŏngnam Munhwajae Yŏn'guwŏn haksul chosa pogo che 176 chip 嶺南文化財研究院 學術調査報告 第176冊 [Yŏngnam Cultural Heritage Research Institute academic studies report 176]. Yŏngnam Munhwajae

Yŏn'guwŏn 嶺南文化財研究院 [Yŏngnam Institute of Cultural Properties], Kyŏngbuk Ch'ilgok-kun.

Yoshida Hiroshi 吉田廣

2003 Chōsen hanto shutsudo no Wa-kei buki-gata seidōki 朝鮮半島出土の倭系武器形青銅器 [Japanese bronze weapon-shaped ritual paraphernalia excavated in the Korean peninsula]. In *Tōhoku Ajia seidōki bunka kara mita Kankoku seidōki bunka ni kansuru kenkyū* 東北アジア青銅器文化からみた韓国青銅器文化に関する研究 [Research into the Korean bronze culture in the Northeast Asian context], special issue, Seikyū Gakujutsu Ronshū 青丘学術論集 22: 47–75.

———

2008 Nihon retto ni okeru buki-gata seidōki no chūzo kaishi nendai 日本列島における武器形青銅器の鋳造開始年代 [Age of the beginning of casting bronze weapon-shaped ritual paraphernalia in Japan]. In *Higashi Ajia seidoki no keifu* 東アジア青銅器の系譜 [Genealogy of bronze in Northeast Asia], edited by Harunari Hideji 春成秀爾 and Nishimoto Toyohiro 西本豊弘, pp. 39–54. Yūzankaku 雄山閣, Tokyo.

Yun Yong-jin 尹容鎭

1980 *Kyŏngsang-pukto munhwajae chip'yo chosa pogosŏ (1)* 慶尚北道文化財地表調査報告書 (1) [Kyŏngsang-pukto Cultural Heritage index report, vol. 1]. Kyŏngbuk Taehakkyo Pangmulgwan 慶北大學校博物館, Taegu.

———

1981 Han'guk ch'ŏngdonggi munhwa yŏn'gu: Taegu P'yŏngni-dong ch'ult'o ilkwal yumul kŏmt'o 韓國青銅器文化研究: 大邱坪里洞出土一括遺物檢討 [Korean bronze culture studies: Taegu P'yŏngni-dong collected artifact examination]. *Han'guk Kogo Hakpo* 韓國考古學報 10, 11: 1–21.

Zhongguo Shehui Kexueyuan Kaogu Yanjiusuo 中国社会科学院考古研究所 [Institute of Archaeology, Chinese Academy of Social Sciences] and Neimenggu Gongzuodui 内蒙古工作队 [Inner Mongolia Work Team]

1975 Ningcheng Nanshangen yizhi fajue baogao 宁城南山根遗址发掘报告 [Report of the excavation of the Nanshangen site in Ningcheng]. *Kaogu Xuebao* 考古学报, no. 1: 117–140, 204–211.

Zhu Gui 朱贵

1960 Liaoning Chaoyang Shiertaiyingzi qingtong duanjian mu 辽宁朝阳十二台营子青铜短剑墓 [Bronze Dagger Tomb at Shiertaiyingzi in Chaoyang, Liaoning]. *Kaogu Xuebao* 考古学报, no. 1: 63–72, 130–135.

2

Interaction Between the Korean Peninsula and the Japanese Archipelago During the Yayoi Period

Iwanaga Shōzō

Abstract

In this chapter I discuss prehistoric interactions between the Yayoi (600 B.C.–200 A.D.) and Mumun periods (1500–300 B.C.) from the perspective of the Japanese archipelago. I review diachronic stages of local sociocultural evolution, and then turn to characterizing archipelago-peninsular relations in the final Jōmon (ca. seventh century B.C.) and the early Yayoi. As migrants came to western Japan from the peninsula, the Jōmon people concurrently adopted aspects of peninsular material culture. I then look at the importation and production of bronze objects and associated artifacts in terms of interactions between northern Kyushu and the southwestern part of the peninsula until the mid-second century B.C. Migration from the Korean peninsula had continued until that time, and evidence shows that bronze production subsequently began in the archipelago, including such distinctive Yayoi objects as daggers, spears, halberds, and bronze bells. I examine the development of bronze objects and social aspects of mortuary practices and how it consolidated community relations. Grave goods indicate that differences in wealth emerged from the latter Middle Yayoi and into the early part of the Late Yayoi. Iron and the influence of the Lelang commandery contributed to social changes that led to the formation of chiefdoms and the advent of a prestige system.

Yayoi Society in the Context of Social Evolution

To clarify the cultural characteristics of the interaction between the Japanese archipelago and the Korean peninsula, it is necessary to recognize which stage of social evolution the Yayoi and Mumun 無文 societies occupied in order. As the Mumun phenomena are addressed elsewhere in this volume (see the chapter by Lee), in the present study I will focus on Yayoi society.

Throughout the discussion that follows, I follow the chronological framework presented in Table 2.1. My view of calendrical dates for each stage of the Yayoi period differs somewhat from those published by the National Museum of Japanese History, and I will defend my own framework in Addendum 1 below.

The chronological stage that preceded the Yayoi period 弥生時代 was the Jōmon period 縄文時代. Some scholars argue that society in the final Jōmon phase (tenth to seventh centuries B.C.) was socially ranked, but I reject this position and suggest, in agreement with Tanaka (1999), that society in the final Jōmon phase was still at the tribal level.[1] Once methods of rice cultivation were adopted in some regions of western Japan at the end of the Jōmon period (or in the initial phase of the Yayoi period) around 600 B.C., groups were transformed into agrarian societies. From the second century A.D. (the late phase of the Late Yayoi period) the social organization became sufficiently complex and the scale of social integration became extended enough for that society to be considered as a chiefdom (Tanaka 2000).

Yayoi society developed between the sixth century B.C. and the second century A.D. From 200 B.C. (the end of the Early Yayoi period) to 100 B.C. (the middle phase of the Middle Yayoi period), there appeared in small coastal plains of northern Kyushu several locally influential communities who possessed bronze objects imported from the Korean peninsula. A few local communities produced agricultural tools in quantities far greater than they themselves needed so that they could distribute surplus tools widely in northern Kyushu. Even in this stage, specialized production and redistribution of commodities controlled by the center were not the defining aspects of the society. Consequently, I consider this stage as still representing a tribal level of development.

Settlement and mortuary remains indicate that from the early first century B.C. (the late phase of the Middle Yayoi period) to the early first century A.D. (the early phase of the Late Yayoi period), influential tribal leaders appeared in northern Kyushu in communities distributed in locations approximately twenty to thirty kilometers apart from one another. These influential tribal leaders acted as nodes of extra-local interaction and as facilitators of exchanges of prestige goods, and they were interred in rich

[1] For discussion of social evolution as used in the present study, refer to Addendum 2 at the end of this chapter.

Table 2.1
Chronological Table for Korea and Japan

Calendar Date	Korea Period	Korea Period (phase)	Korea Pottery	Japan Period	Japan Period (phase)	Japan Pottery	Japan Jar Coffin	NMJH Date
1000	MUMUN POTTERY PERIOD	INCIPIENT	Misa-ri Type	JŌMON PERIOD	LATE PHASE	Hirota Type		
10th C								
900			Karak-ni Type					
9th C								
800		EARLY				Kurokawa Type		
8th C								
700			Hŭnam-ni Type					
7th C								
600		MIDDLE	Hyuam-ni Type	YAYOI PERIOD	INCIPIENT	Yamanotera		950
6th C								
500						Yūsu Type		
5th C			Songgung-ni Type					
400					EARLY			780
4th C						Itatsuke I		
300		LATE	Susŏng-ni Type			Itatsuke II A		
3rd C						Itatsuke II B	Hakugen Type	
200			Nŭkto Type			Itatsuke II C	Kinkai Type	380
					MIDDLE	Jonokoshi Type	Jonokoshi	
2nd C						Suku I Type	Kunden Type	
100							Suku Type	
1st C	PROTO THREE KINGDOMS					Suku II Type		
B.C.							Tateiwa Type	B.C.
A.D.					LATE			A.D.
1st C								
100								
2nd C								
200					END	Shōnai Type		
3rd C								
300				KOFUN	EARLY			
4th C								
400								

Note: Chronological and pottery type boundaries are approximations.

burials with metal objects and other prestige goods. The scale of communal integration, however, does not appear to have increased significantly from the earlier period.

From the late first century A.D. (the early phase of the Late Yayoi period), the concentration and growth of the production of bronze ritual paraphernalia, the development of rituals utilizing bronze objects, and increases in the scale of social integration all took place in northern Kyushu. At the same time, as a greater number of non-local cultural elements were introduced, locally characteristic cultural traditions weakened. It also seems that the population in northern Kyushu declined. Consequently, the transition to a chiefdom society was not complete, and such a political scale was not achieved. In contrast, from the second century A.D. (the late phase of the Late Yayoi period) to the early third century A.D. (the end of the Yayoi period) social differentiation and social integration developed rapidly in such regions as the central and eastern Inland Sea, central Kinki 近畿, northern Kinki, and Hokuriku 北陸, in addition to Ōmi 近江 and Tōkai 東海. In these regions, chiefdom-level societies emerged by the early third century (the end of the Yayoi period).

Interactions with the Korean Peninsula at the Beginning of the Yayoi Period

From the Final Jōmon period (ca. seventh century B.C.) to the Initial Yayoi period (sixth and fifth centuries B.C.), a relatively small number of people skilled in the technology of wet rice cultivation migrated from the southwestern part of the Korean peninsula to northern Kyushu. The likely origins of the material culture and technological information at that time are to be found in the southern coastal regions of the Korean peninsula, especially the region of the Nam River 南江, a tributary of the Naktong River 洛東江 (Hashino 2001). Although the Liaoning-style bronze daggers 遼寧式銅劍 were present in the cultural complex of the southern coastal regions, it is likely that these daggers were local copies rather than imports.

According to Tanaka (1991, 2002), societies in western Japan during the Final Jōmon period maintained bilineal descent groups, and local Jōmon people accepted peninsular immigrants, lived with them, and, as time passed, intermarried with them. In the process, agricultural and carpentry tools, pottery, mortuary customs such as mortuary architecture, funerary offerings, and ideology, the concept of enclosing a settlement by moat, and residential structures came to be adopted and adapted from the Korean peninsula. In particular, certain types of dolmens (Hashino 2001),

Songgung-ni 松菊里 type pottery, and Liaoning-style bronze daggers were introduced at the beginning of the Yayoi period. It is important to note that the Mumun culture as a whole did not reach northern Kyushu to replace the local culture. Rather, cultural elements that were not present in the Jōmon culture were selectively and gradually introduced.

Although the number of peninsular immigrants was not negligible, neither were their numbers large. In northern Kyushu, no sites of the Initial Yayoi period exist in which all the discovered artifacts and features are of peninsular origin. Japanese artifacts of the Mumun traditions were not produced with techniques fully and precisely adopted from the peninsula. Yet, both physical and cultural impacts of the immigrants were very significant because the local population in the coastal regions of northern Kyushu was quite small. Peninsular immigrants were peacefully absorbed into the local Jomon population. Possible factors that facilitated this peaceful incorporation into local communities are: (1) a long history of interaction between the Korean peninsula and northern Kyushu such that peninsular immigrants had accumulated good knowledge of northern Kyushu and (2) local Jōmon people in northern Kyushu had great regard for wet rice cultivation that the immigrants had brought during the middle Final Jōmon phase.

Interaction with the Korean Peninsula from the Standpoint of Importation and Production of Bronze

Beginning of the Importation of Bronze and Subsequent Local Production

Beginning of the Full-Scale Importation of Bronze

While the number of people, quantities of objects, and the amount of information introduced from the Korean peninsula in the sixth and fifth centuries B.C. were relatively large, archaeological evidence for the introduction of people and cultural elements of Korean origins dated to the fourth to mid-third centuries B.C. is obscure. At the end of the third century B.C. (the end of the Early Yayoi period), a full scale introduction of bronze objects from the Korean peninsula began and continued until the late first century B.C. (late phase of the Middle Yayoi period).

Among the bronze objects imported from the Korean peninsula were bronze weapons, such as the slender-type dagger, slender-type spear, and slender-type halberd, Korean geometric mirror, and bronze bracelet. The identification of "imported" bronze objects as opposed to "locally produced" ones is based on morphologies identical or nearly identical to those

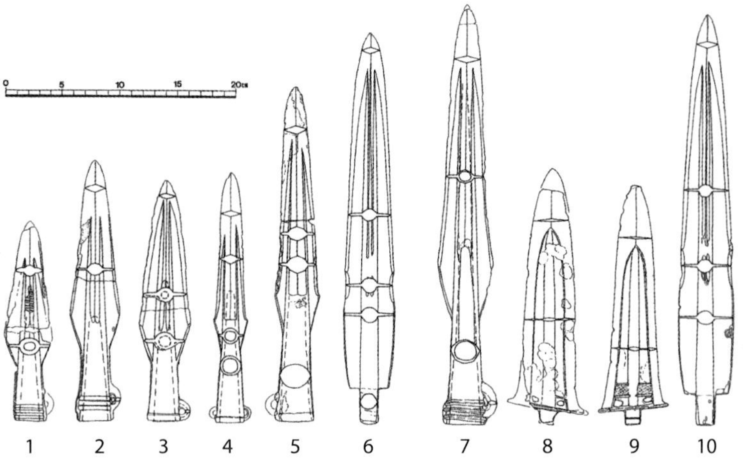

Figure 2.1 Slender-type Bronze Weapons Produced in the Korean Peninsula or the Japanese Archipelago.
1 and 2. Slender-type bronze spear with a small tab, triple-line reliefs, and short blade; 3–5. Slender-type bronze spear with a small tab, single-line relief, and short blade; 6. Relatively long, slender-type bronze dagger; 7. Slender-type bronze spear with a small tab, triple-line reliefs, and long blade; 8 and 9. Slender-type, flat and fragile bronze halberd; 10. Relatively long slender-type bronze dagger.

discovered in the Korean peninsula. It is very important to note the possibility that some types of bronze weapons were produced in the Korean peninsula and that the majority of them may have been exported to the Japanese archipelago. If such is the case, this phenomenon is a reflection of the preference and active selection of the local Yayoi people. Such bronze weapons are all early types from the end of the third century B.C. (the end of the Early Yayoi) to the second century B.C. (the early phase of the Middle Yayoi) and include (1) the slender-type bronze spear with a small tab, triple-line reliefs, and short blade; (2) the slender-type bronze spear with a small tab, single-line relief, and short blade; and (3) the relatively long, slender-type bronze dagger (1–6 in Figure 2.1).

As I will mention below, the beginning of the local production of bronze objects dates to the early- and mid-second century B.C. (the early phase of the Middle Yayoi) based on the discoveries of molds in context with pottery. Among the bronze objects that are dated to the end of the third and beginning of the second centuries B.C. (the Early/Middle Yayoi), which is earlier than the local production of bronze, three types are not found in the Korean peninsula. The three types are (1) the slender-type bronze spear with a small tab, triple-line reliefs, and long blade; (2) the slender-type, flat and fragile bronze halberd; and (3) the relatively long, slender-type bronze dagger (7–10 in Figure 2.1). Two interpretations are possible to explain these phenomena. The first is that they were produced in the Korean peninsula and exported to the Japanese archipelago, and the other is that they were all locally made in Japan. At the time of this writing we cannot conclude which interpretation is more plausible. It is in any case very important that the Yayoi people actively selected preferred forms of bronze objects after the initial adoption of those objects.

The bronze objects imported at the end of the third century and beginning of the second century B.C. (Early/Middle Yayoi) are likely to have been produced in the southwestern part of the Korean peninsula, based on the similarities of bronze goods in the two regions. On the contrary, bronze objects imported after the early and mid-second century B.C. (early phase of the Middle Yayoi) were from the southeastern part of the Korean peninsula. This change was probably the result of a shift in the locations of the bronze production in the Korean peninsula (Iwanaga 2002).

Besides bronze weapons, pottery also gives us clues to understanding the interaction with the southwestern part of the Korean peninsula at the end of the third century and beginning of the second century B.C. Korean Mumun pottery of this date has been discovered at several sites in northern Kyushu (Gotō 1979, Kataoka 1999, Hira 2001). At a few sites, a full set of functionally different forms of Mumun pottery were discovered in considerable quantities (Figure 2.2). This suggests that groups of people from the peninsula migrated to northern Kyushu, and it is possible that these groups of people brought bronze objects. This introduction took place long before the Wajil pottery appeared in the southern part of the Korean peninsula. At the same time, Yayoi pottery has also been discovered in the Korean peninsula at sites such as Nŭk-to 勒島. Interactions between the Korean peninsula and northern Kyushu were at that time direct, in both directions, and were conducted for various purposes.

At present, the discoveries of pottery originating in Japan are skewed toward the South Kyŏngsang region probably because fieldwork is itself skewed toward this region. This makes it difficult to approach the activities of the Yayoi people in the southwestern part of the Korean peninsula from the standpoint of pottery. Yet, I hypothesize that interactions with the

Figure 2.2 Mumun Pottery Vessel from the Moro-oka Site in Fukuoka. From Oda, ed. 1991.

southwestern part of the Korean peninsula were very close and frequent. Evidence for this comprises the northern Kyushu discoveries of materials characteristic of the southwestern part of the Korean peninsula, including Korean geometric-pattern mirrors, bronze cross-shaped pommels, bronze spear-shaped planes, amazonite accessories, and jade beads, as well as bronze weapons (Figure 2.3). The interactions with southwestern Korea were a continuation of interactions that took place prior to the third century B.C. (the later phase of the Early Yayoi), as evidenced by types of dolmens (Hashino 2001), Songgung-ni–type pottery, and Liaoning-style bronze daggers.

The interactions with the southwestern part of the Korean peninsula did not continue in the same scale and degree after the early and mid-second

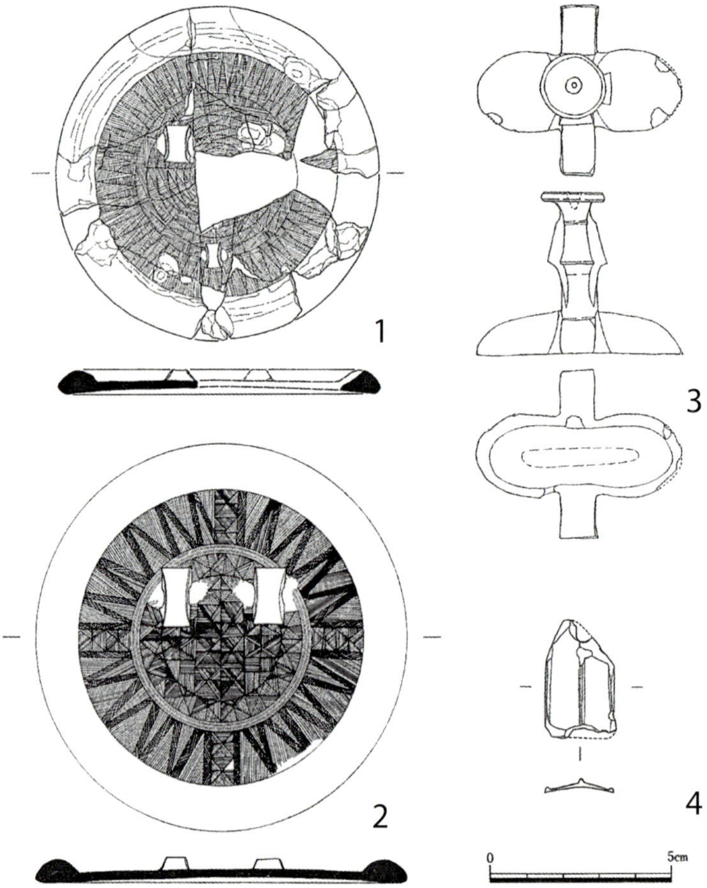

Figure 2.3 Bronze Objects Produced in Southwestern Korea, Discovered in Northwestern Kyushu.
1. Korean geometric mirror from the Masuda site, Saga Prefecture;
2. Korean geometric mirror discovered at the Honsongomori site, Saga Prefecture;
3. Cross-shaped pommel discovered at the Yoshinogari site, Saga Prefecture;
4. Spear-shaped plane discovered at the Honsongomori site.

century B.C. (the early phase of the Middle Yayoi). At sites dated to the end of the third century B.C. where considerable quantities of Mumun pottery were discovered, the quantities of Mumun pottery are significantly small. This was a result of a drastic decline in the number of immigrants from the peninsula. The production of pottery that incorporated the techniques of both Yayoi pottery and Mumun pottery began, and this would seem to be a reflection of immigrants marrying local Yayoi people and of the weakening cultural norms of the immigrants. Subsequently the production of pottery that incorporated Korean techniques ceased. While Mumun pottery was imported even after the early and mid-second century (the early phase of the Middle Yayoi), the quantities were very small in comparison to the local Yayoi pottery. In other words, this was not likely a result of immigration from the peninsula.

Unlike the case of the Initial Yayoi period, when Korean people, objects, and information all reached northern Kyushu together, immigration from Korea at the end of the third to the beginning of the second century B.C. brought only bronze objects and did not result in major cultural transformation. By the end of the third century, the Yayoi cultural system became stable, and the local Yayoi population considerably increased as a result of the adoption of wet rice agriculture. Consequently, a small number of Korean immigrants were engulfed by and assimilated into a large local Yayoi population physically and culturally.

Beginning of Bronze Production in Japan (Slender-Type Bronze Weapon)

As noted above, we do not have evidence for local bronze production in Japan at the end of the third century B.C., when, as aforementioned, some people emigrated from the peninsula to northern Kyushu. Based on discoveries of bronze molds in context with pottery, local bronze production began in the early and mid-second century B.C. (the early phase of the Middle Yayoi). In other words, the local bronze production started once immigration from the Korean peninsula declined and the immigrants became assimilated into the local Yayoi population.

The early types of Japanese bronze weapons are of the "slender type" and "medium-slender type." While the size of the former falls within the range of the Korean standard weapons, the size of the latter is larger than those of Korea. Some of the slender-type weapons made in Japan are morphologically indistinguishable from the Korean prototypes. At the same time, slender-type weapons that possessed morphological features absent in the Korean prototypes also appeared. The medium-slender type marks the origin of the uniquely Japanese types of bronze weapons, such as the medium-wide type and the wide type, and is the earliest type distinguishable from the Korean-made bronze weapons in terms of size and morphology. The

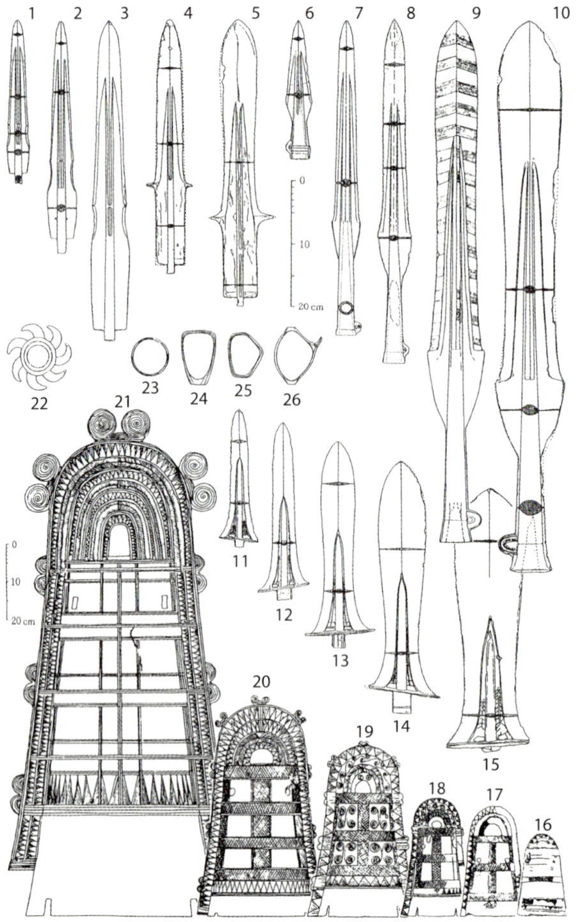

Figure 2.4 Various Bronze Objects of the Yayoi Period.
1. Slender type dagger; 2. Medium-slender type dagger (archaic style);
3. Medium-slender type dagger (new style); 4. Wide type dagger (archaic style);
5. Wide type dagger (new style); 6. Slender type spear; 7. Medium-slender type spear;
8. Medium-slender type spear (new style); 9. Medium-wide type spear;
10. Wide type spear; 11. Slender type halberd; 12. Medium-slender type (archaic style);
13. Medium-slender type halberd (new style); 14. Medium-wide type halberd;
15. Wide type halberd; 16. Type I ritual bronze bell (dōtaku);
17. Type II ritual bronze bell; 18. Type III-1 ritual bronze bell;
19. Type III-2 ritual bronze bell; 20. Type IV-2 ritual bronze bell;
21. Type IV-2 ritual bronze bell; 22. Spiral-shaped bronze object; 23-26. Bracelets.

medium-slender type bronze weapons consist of the medium-slender dagger, medium-slender spear, and medium-slender halberd (Figure 2.4). In the mid-second century B.C. (the late half of the early phase of the Middle Yayoi period), these three were present.

With the beginning of local bronze production in northern Kyushu in the early second century B.C., local craftspeople developed a uniquely Japanese style of bronze objects. In the mid-second century B.C. a consistent form of medium-slender type weapon came to be adopted. Divergence from the Korean prototype was relatively rapid in northern Kyushu. From the beginning of local bronze production, a basis existed for the production of bronze objects distinctive from those of Korea. Whether the craftspeople who produced bronze originated from the Korean peninsula or Kyushu, they were in any case kept distant from the peninsula in terms of the exchange of information and people. The appearance in northern Kyushu of types of bronze weapons or weapon-shaped ritual paraphernalia unique to the archipelago coincided with the beginning of the production of ritual bronze bells or *dōtaku* 銅鐸 in the west-central region of the archipelago, later called Kinai 畿内 (Namba 2009). In the past, the dominant hypothesis was that the production of the ritual bronze bells started at the end of the third century B.C. (Sahara 1960).

Development of Local Bronze Production and Social Change

Typological Change in Japanese Bronze Objects and Its Social Background

Once the medium-slender type appeared, bronze weapons or weapon-shaped ritual paraphernalia of the archipelago went through typological change to the medium-wide type and eventually to the wide type (Figure 2.4). Typological change is most clearly characterized by the increase in size and the loss of functionality as a weapon (i.e. the working edge became increasingly dull). Such changes rarely took place in the Korean prototypes, as is discussed below. The active selection of Korean cultural elements among the local Yayoi is apparent not only in the products themselves but also in the uses of the products. Japanese bronze weapons were not primarily deposited in graves with the dead, but were intentionally buried in caches. Japanese archaeologists suspect that this act was ritualistic in nature and that bronze weapons were thus transformed into ritual paraphernalia.

In northern Kyushu, the ritual caching of bronze objects started in the mid-second century B.C. (the late half of the early phase of the Middle

Yayoi), at the same time as the appearance of the medium-slender-type weapons. At that time, the custom of depositing bronze objects in graves with the dead was still being practiced. By the early first century B.C. (the late phase of the Middle Yayoi), however, a practice of ritual burial of bronze objects became dominant. From the early first century B.C., functional differentiation came to exist between iron weapons for deposit with the dead and medium-slender and medium-wide types of bronze spears and halberds for ritual burial. The production and use of bronze daggers were more or less discontinued in the stage of medium-slender-type weapons in northern Kyushu. In the coastal regions of the Inland Sea, however, the bronze daggers were widely adopted and developed as ritual paraphernalia.

In the early and mid-second century (the early phase of the Middle Yayoi) when bronze weapon-shaped ritual paraphernalia appeared, local communities grew in response to the population increase subsequent to the Early Yayoi period. Numerous minor "daughter" settlements split off from parental core settlements. These new minor settlements were established in reclaimed agricultural lands, and they were organized by one another (Tanaka 2000). I argue that the adoption of rituals utilizing bronze weapons was a response to the need of integrating the parental, core settlements and those newly separated from the core settlements or of organizing settlements established in newly reclaimed lands.

It is important to stress that bronze objects were not only ritually buried but also deposited with the dead in the Middle Yayoi period. In regions east of Chūgoku 中国 and Shikoku 四国, bronze objects were principally buried ritually. In northern Kyushu, two seemingly conflicting phenomena took place concurrently. That is, the appearance of influential tribal leaders with access to prestige goods of Chinese origins occurred at the same time that bronze objects began to be deposited with the dead, and an effort was expended on communal rituals utilizing bronze objects of peninsular origins.

From the late first century B.C. (the end of the Middle Yayoi) to the early first century A.D. (the beginning of the Late Yayoi period), rituals utilizing weapon-shaped bronze paraphernalia reached their peak. At that time in many regions of Japan, settlements were abandoned, and populations came to be concentrated into particular settlements (Ozawa 2000, 2002). This might be one of the outcomes of climatic cooling. As communities moved, separated from one another, or integrated together, land-based ties became stronger, and kin-based ties became weaker. Under such conditions, conflicts would have occurred among re-organized land-based communities, and the interests of land-based communities and kin-based groups that were tied weakly would have tended to clash with one another. The gradual development of social ranking also resulted in the division of groups within a given community. Therefore, it would be essential for leaders to mediate, manage, and suppress these conflicts, competitions, and contradictions. As social ranking developed, a group of a particular descent would be selected to play a role in managing society. When greater numbers of communities became integrated, the role of managing a society of a selected descent group became more diverse and complex. In order to cope with the necessity of mediating, managing, and suppressing conflicts, competitions, and contradictions, inter-regional ties among the selected descent groups of various communities would have been formed. These selected descent groups from different communities would not necessarily be tied by kinship.

Among the selected descent groups, some would have become more successful in managing society. In the process of management, these groups could have put themselves in a more advantageous position in the acquisition and maintenance of resources, not only those for survival but also those for luxury. As a result, differences in wealth emerged, which eventually turned into a tension between social positions. Those who emerged in the top strata of society were not a single chief or single family but a kin member or descent group as a whole. While selected groups including the clan head would have made efforts to accumulate their wealth and maintain their position over generations, ordinary members of the community or selected groups from other communities would have made efforts to maintain social equality.

An increase in the scale of social integration and a decrease in population weakened cultural traditions. A seeming increase in the scale of integration occurs when population increases, resulting in the branching out of "sibling" settlements. It also occurs when a society is declining and being faced with risks. I consider it important to examine a tribal confederacy from this standpoint, as well.

Under such conditions, two choices would have been possible: (1) to strengthen the cooperation and unity of a community and (2) to strengthen the authority of the selected groups in charge of social management. In the first case, bronze ritual paraphernalia would have been used to make communal rituals more highly elaborate and sophisticated and to strengthen the cooperation and unity of a community. This strategy was adopted by communities in northern Kyushu utilizing the spear-shaped and halberd-shaped bronze ritual paraphernalia and those in Chūgoku (the western end of Honshu), Shikoku, Kinki (west-central Honshu), Hokuriku (Sea of Japan coast of central Honshu), and Tōkai (Pacific coast of central Honshu) utilizing ritual bronze bells or *dōtaku*. In northern Kyushu, practices of depositing iron weapons and other items with the dead declined from the middle phase of the Late Yayoi period, and rituals utilizing weapon-shaped ritual paraphernalia flourished.

It is necessary here to clarify the role of selected groups in conducting communal rituals utilizing bronze paraphernalia. Citing Kristian Kristiansen's (1991) argument that practices of depositing metal objects with the dead in the Bronze Age were replaced by practices of ritual burial of metal objects in the Iron Age in Europe, a Japanese specialist of Yayoi-period archaeology has hypothesized that both the deposit of bronze objects with the dead and the ritual burial of bronze objects were strategies executed for the dual purpose of intentionally making bronze scarce and of displaying the prestige of the elite (Kuwabara 1995). According to him, both were merely differences in the representations of the same act of aggrandizement of the consumption of goods. This is not to say that selected groups did not play a major role in the production of bronze objects and in their utilization for communal rituals. At the same time, it is important to note that highly distinctive mounded burials with rich funerary offerings were not built when communal rituals utilizing bronze objects were practiced. Consequently, the production of bronze ritual paraphernalia and the conducting of communal rituals were not meant to accumulate the wealth of the selected groups but to promote the shared, communal benefit of all those who participated in the rituals. Such a community would probably correspond to a tribe or to a group of clans. I speculate that, in rare cases in which the interest of the selected groups and the purpose of communal rituals for the entire groups came to differ, the rise of power and authority of these selected groups was suppressed when the conducting of such communal rituals was at its peak.

On the other hand, in such regions as northern Shikoku (the southern coastal region of the Inland Sea), San'yō 山陽 (the northern coastal region of the Inland Sea), San'in 山陰 (the coastal region of western Honshu), northern Kinki, and a part of Hokuriku, communities adopted the second strategy to strengthen the authority of the selected groups in charge of social management from the late half of the Late Yayoi period. In these regions, communal rituals utilizing bronze objects, including *dōtaku*, were terminated early, and there developed highly distinctive mounded burials and mortuary rituals dedicated to those interred in the mounds. In the process, the accumulation of wealth in the hands of highly selected groups came to be justified, and we find that iron weapons were deposited with the dead in mounds. At that time, when Japanese society had not yet adopted a patrilineal descent system (Tanaka 1995), these mortuary rituals were conducted in honor of the dead chief and also unidentified ancestral spirits.

Toward the early third century A.D. (the end of the Yayoi period), communities that adopted the first strategy of conducting communal rituals for the benefit of the communities as a whole terminated those communal rituals and started building mounded burials for selected individuals, thereby conforming with communities that had adopted the second strategy. The background to this change was probably various social and political difficulties and complexities from the second to early third centuries, which necessitated increased dependency on leaders as well as interaction and cooperation with communities in other regions that had adopted the second strategy of choosing powerful leaders.

Typological Changes in Bronze Objects and Their Regional Differences

It is necessary to examine some previous interpretations proposed by Japanese bronze specialists (Kondō 1969, Okauchi 1973) that some bronze weapons in the southern part of the Korean peninsula from 100 B.C. to the late first century B.C. also went through transformation into ritual paraphernalia. Specifically, the following attributes gradually became more pronounced: decorative elements, flatness, dullness of the tip, large size unnecessary for effectiveness as a weapon, and reduced size and weakness in the joint between the blade and hilt (Figure 2.5). In many respects, transformation into ritual paraphernalia in southern Korea should be distinguished from the Japanese case. While it is true that the size of bronze weapons did increase in the southern part of the Korean peninsula, the size never exceeded that of the Japanese medium-slender-type bronze weapons, specifically 40 cm for daggers, 60 cm for spears, and 30 cm for halberds. In the case of halberds, the size in fact decreased. A more important and prominent distinction is the way in which bronze weapons were treated. In the southern part of the Korean peninsula it was the norm to deposit bronze weapons that had been morphologically transformed into "ritual paraphernalia" in graves with the dead. In the very few cases where bronze weapons were intentionally buried in the southern part of the peninsula, the weapons were of very early types, and it is unclear if they were intended for communal rituals.

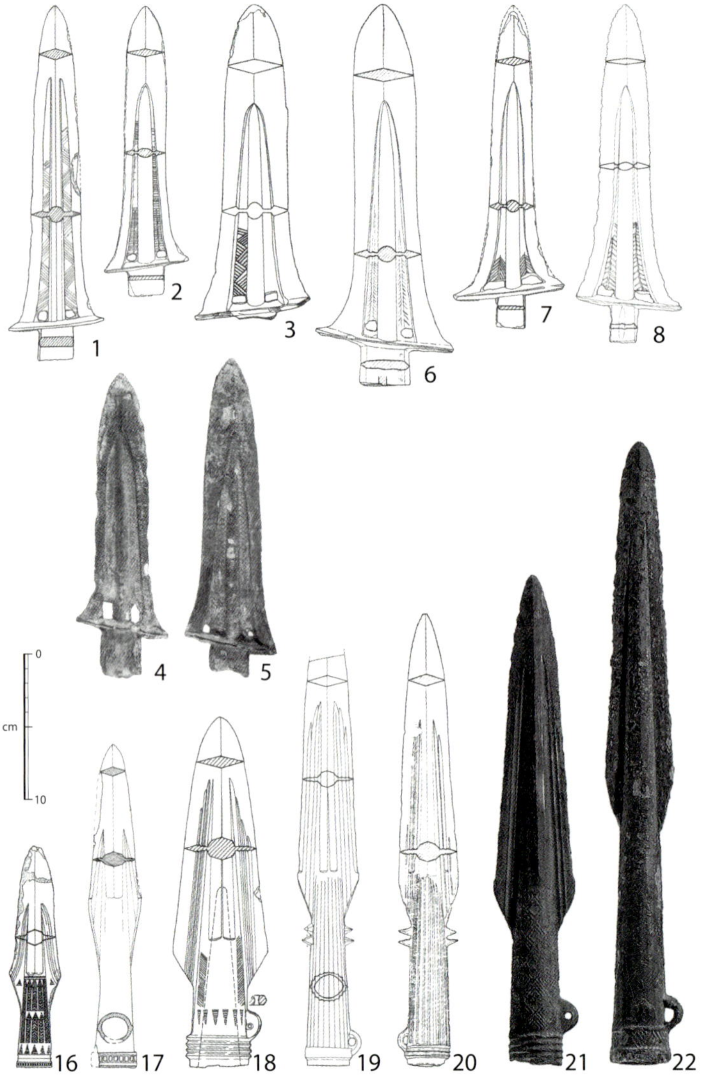

Figure 2.5 Various Types of Ritualized Bronze Weapons Excavated on the Korean Peninsula.
1–11. halberds; 12–15 daggers; 16–28. spear heads
(Nos. 24 and 26 were probably exported from the archipelago).

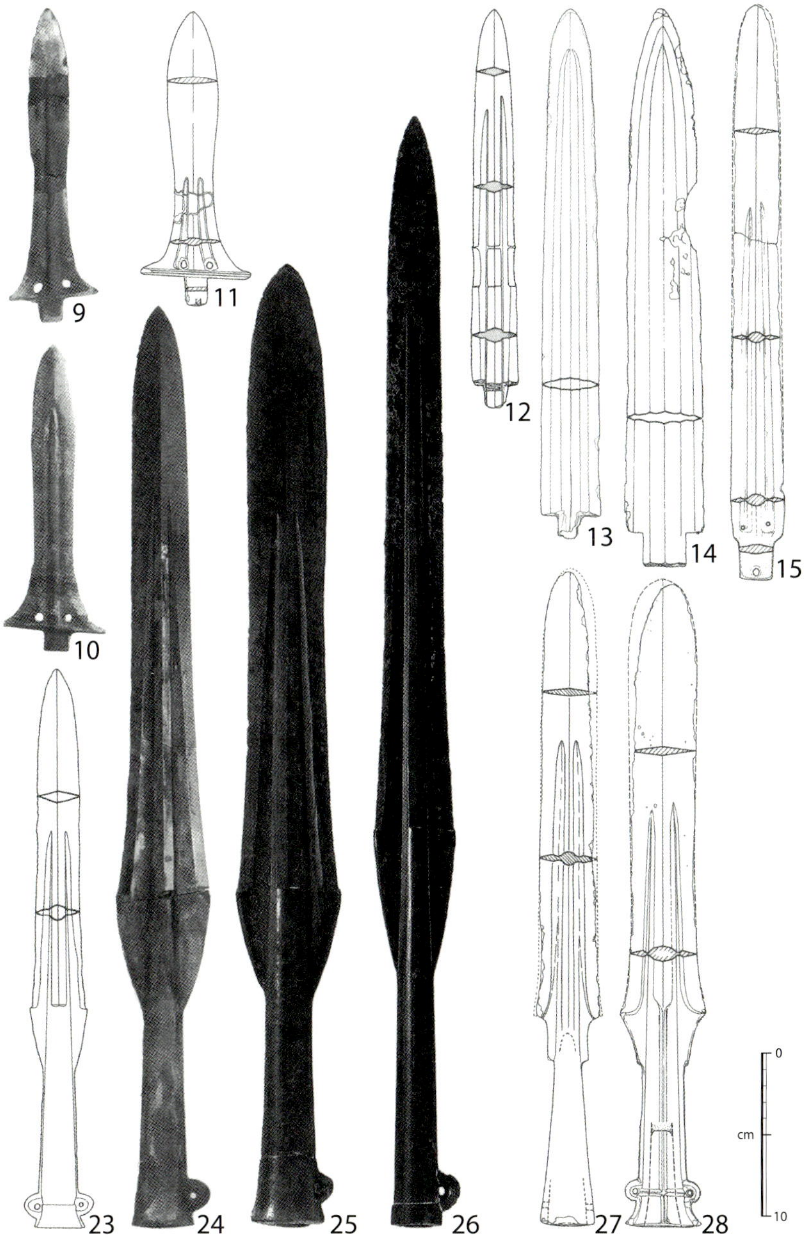
9
11
12
13
14
15
10
23
24
25
26
27
28
0
cm
10

In the southern part of the Korean peninsula, the morphological transformation of bronze weapons into ritual paraphernalia corresponded to an increase in iron weapons. This transformation was more a result of bronze being replaced by iron as the primary material for weapons. Although both southern Korea and western Japan adopted wet rice cultivation as the primary means of subsistence, it seems highly likely that bronze objects in the southern part of the Korean peninsula did not become paraphernalia for communal rituals. A possible reason for this is that the adoption of iron tools replacing stone tools was so rapid that the evolution of social organization was accelerated, and there was little time for people to develop communal rituals that would have suppressed the rise of powerful leaders and the division of social ranks. In other words, the evolution of agrarian society was very rapid, and the development of social complexity took place earlier than in Japan. In western Japan, the development of weapon-shaped bronze ritual paraphernalia corresponded to an increase in the scale of integration of communities that were tied by or shared the rituals utilizing bronze paraphernalia. Although the spatial scale of social integration expanded, the social complexity and the division of social ranks did not develop. These phenomena were in striking contrast with the southern Korean case, in which the degree of social integration increased, and the spatial scale of integrated communities did not expand. This would be one of the reasons that giant tumuli did not develop in the southern Korean peninsula where the three regional states of Paekche, Kaya, and Silla formed in competition with one another. This competition remained internally even after Silla unified the Korean peninsula.

Aspects of Korea-Japan Interactions After the Establishment of the Han Commandery of Lelang

Before the Han Emperor Wu 漢武帝 established the four commanderies in the northern part of the Korean peninsula in 108 B.C., few goods of continental origin reached southern Korea and Japan. The founding of the four commanderies in 108 B.C., or of the greater Lelang 樂浪 commandery in 75 B.C. (a restructuring and unification of the Lelang, Lintun 臨屯, and Xuantu 玄菟 commanderies), triggered a drastic increase in the introduction of Han materials to these regions. In particular, the importing of large quantities of continental products, especially bronze mirrors, started after the early first century B.C. (the late phase of the Middle Yayoi period) in northern Kyushu. It is indeed possible to consider the Han commandery of Lelang as the major partner of interaction.

Figure 2.6 Chinese Star-cloud Bronze Mirror from Tomb 1 at Taho-ri in Ch'angwŏn. From Oda, ed. 1991.

Patterns of interaction between southern Korea and western Japan changed from the end of the third century B.C. (the end of the Early Yayoi to the beginning of the Middle Yayoi) to 100 B.C., when Yayoi people of various regions of northern Kyushu maintained direct contacts with the southern part of the Korean peninsula. While the amount of Mumun pottery reaching Kyushu decreased, it was instead transported to Tsushima 対馬, Iki 壱岐, Okinoshima 沖ノ島, and other islands off the Honshu coast of the western Inland Sea. This is a reflection of the increased activities of sea-based people as middlemen in trade (Gotō 1987). All these islands form a line between the southern Korean peninsula, northern Kyushu, and the Inland Sea. Yayoi people in northern Kyushu interacted with the Lelang commandery or with the Han empire through the middlemen strategically located in the islands. In particular, considerable quantities of pottery and vessels made in imitation of Mumun pottery have recently been excavated at the Harunotsuji 原ノ辻 site on Iki island (Kataoka 2001), where Yayoi pottery made at various places in northern Kyushu has also been discovered. Furthermore, various sub-types of Suku-II 須玖 type Yayoi pottery have been excavated at the Nŭk-to 勒島 site in South Kyŏngsang Province. These sub-types retain regionally characteristic features of Tsushima of Nagasaki Prefecture and Itoshima 糸島 and Kasuya 粕屋 of Fukuoka Prefecture. This suggests that people of Tsushima and various regions of northern Kyushu visited the Nŭk-to site (Tanaka 2001). Indeed, the role of the Harunotsuji and Nŭk-to sites became considerably more important.

As a result of a relative decline of direct interaction between various places in southern Korea and northern Kyushu, concurrent types of Korean bronze objects were not imported to northern Kyushu whenever new types appeared in the areas of origin. This does not mean, however, that interaction between these two regions was discontinued. A slender-type long-blade bronze spear with a tab and some slender-type bronze halberds with a cedar-leaf pattern (*ayasugi mon* 綾杉文) in the fuller (blood groove) were probably imported from southeastern Korea. The results of lead isotope analyses of lead spears discovered at the Kuri-Ōmuta 久里大牟田 site, Karatsu 唐津 City, Saga 佐賀 Prefecture, and at the Noda 野田 site, Yame 八女 City, Fukuoka Prefecture, suggest the possibility that lead was mined in the North Kyŏngsang and Kangwŏn provinces. If this is indeed the case, these lead spears were imported in the context of interaction with southeastern Korea. In the opposite direction, from northern Kyushu to the Korean peninsula, a newer sub-type of the medium-slender-type Yayoi bronze spear was transported to southeastern Korea—they are found at the Pisan-dong 飛山洞 site in Taegu (Figure 2.5, No. 26) and at Tomb 1 at the Taho-ri 茶戸里 site in Ch'angwon 昌原 (Figure 2.5, No. 24). As for iron in the early to late first century B.C., iron daggers and iron spears increased markedly in southeastern Korea (Takaku 2000) as well as in northern Kyushu. It is possible that some iron daggers and iron spears in northern Kyushu in the first century B.C. were imported from southeastern Korea.

Recent discoveries of Western Han bronze mirrors in the southeastern part of the Korean peninsula also shed new light on our understanding about interaction between southeastern Korea and northern Kyushu (Figure 2.6). Star-cloud mirrors 星雲文鏡 (Tomb 1 at Taho-ri), illumination mirrors 日光鏡 (Chisan-dong 池山洞, Taegu; Tomb 38 at Choyang-dong

朝陽洞, Kyŏngju; Ŏŭn-dong 漁隱洞, Yŏngch'ŏn 永川), shining mirrors 昭明鏡 (Chisan-dong, Taegu; Tomb 38 at Choyang-dong, Kyŏngju), and serpentine dragon mirrors 虺龍文鏡 (Ŏŭn-dong 漁隱洞, Yŏngch'ŏn; P'yŏngni-dong 坪里洞, Taegu) were all transported to southeastern Korea and northern Kyushu. Because Western Han bronze mirrors have been discovered in larger quantities in northern Kyushu than in the Korean peninsula, Japanese archaeologists used to speculate that Yayoi people obtained Western Han mirrors directly from the Lelang commandery or from the Western Han empire. However, these recent discoveries in southeastern Korea introduce new research problems. One problem concerns whether the peoples of southeastern Korea and northern Kyushu obtained these Western Han mirrors from the Lelang commandery or the Han empire independently. Another is whether there existed a redistribution center of Western Han materials from which peoples of southeastern Korea and of northern Kyushu obtained these Western Han mirrors. These discoveries in southeastern Korea also suggest the possibility that some of the Western Han mirrors were imported from southeastern Korea to northern Kyushu.

In the first century A.D. (Late Yayoi period), large quantities of Korean slender-type bronze daggers, bronze daggers with deep fullers (blood grooves), dagger fittings, and various forms of bronze objects were imported to Tsushima (Figure 2.7). Moreover, earthenware and stoneware of the Mumun pottery tradition were imported in large quantities not only to Tsushima but also to Iki and the Itoshima plain of northern Kyushu. At the same time, Japanese medium-wide-type bronze spears, medium-wide-type bronze halberds, and wide-type bronze spears were imported to the southern part of the Korean peninsula. The Japanese medium-wide-type bronze spears have been discovered in the Kimhae 金海 area (two in Tomb 90, one in Tomb 390, and one collected on the surface at the Yangdong-ni 良洞里 site; another one from Kimhae; and yet another one said to have been discovered in Kimhae) and at the Chuch'on-myŏn 酒村面 site. medium-wide-type bronze halberds have been discovered in Taegu (one said to have been discovered at Pisan-dong; another discovered at Manch'on-dong 晩村洞). And wide-type bronze spears have been discovered in the Kimhae area (two in Tomb 200, one in Tomb 390, and one collected on the surface at the Yangdong-ni site; other ones from Myŏngbŏp-tong 明法洞 and Naedŏng-ni 内德里 Tomb 19) and at the Tongoe-dong 東外洞 site in Kosŏng 固城. During the Late Yayoi period, groups in Tsushima came to play an active role in interaction and trade between the Korean peninsula and northern Kyushu (Shimojō 1979).

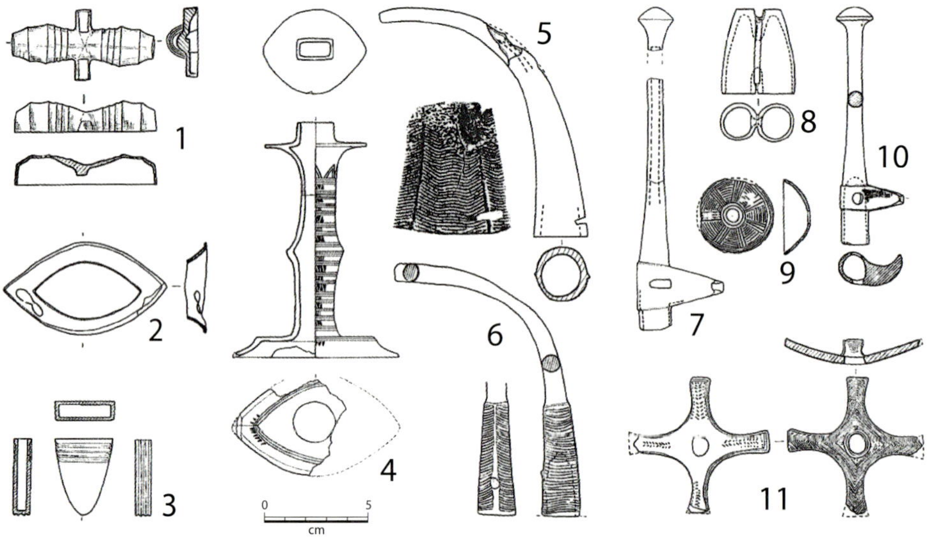

Figure 2.7 Bronze Accessories to Bronze Weapons and Other Bronze Objects Discovered in Tsushima.
1, 3, 6, 8, 9, 10 and 11. Discovered at the Tōsaki site; 2, 4, 5, and 7. Discovered at the Kisaka site.

Two phenomena are particularly noteworthy: (1) a variety of minor bronze objects that are not discovered in northern Kyushu have been excavated in Tsushima in large quantities; and (2) the Korean discoveries of Japanese medium-wide and wide-type bronze spears are concentrated in the Kimhae region and its vicinity. As aforementioned, while primary interaction with the Lelang commandery took place from ca. 100 B.C. to the late first century B.C., interaction with southeastern Korea also continued to a lesser degree at the same time. In these contexts, while groups in Tsushima were entrusted by groups of northern Kyushu to interact with Lelang and with southern Korea to obtain iron ingots, they were also engaged in localized trading with the Kimhae region. In this localized trading sphere, spears of the Japanese archipelago were exchanged north to Kimhae, and a variety of minor bronze objects were exchanged south to Tsushima. It is noteworthy that medium-wide and wide-type Japanese archipelago bronze spears were treated in Kimhae in a manner very different from that of northern Kyushu. These spears that were usually buried ritually in northern Kyushu

Figure 2.8 Wide-type Spears Deposited in a Stone Coffin at the Tōnokubi 塔ノ首 site in Tsushima. Photograph by Oda Fujio, used with permission.

were in Kimhae deposited in graves. In Tsushima, most of them were ritually buried in hoards, as in northern Kyushu. Some of them, as in the case of Kimhae, were deposited in graves as burial goods (Figure 2.8). A few of them were ritually broken prior to deposit in the graves, which was the same custom as in Kimhae. It is likely that deposit of wide-type bronze spears in graves in Tsushima was a result of a "reverse adoption" of a custom common at the mouth of the Naktong River.

Although the spatial distribution of Chinese bronze mirrors in Japan was limited to northern Kyushu in the first century A.D., quantities of bronze mirrors of continental origin declined in northern Kyushu in the second century. Instead, small quantities of bronze mirrors were transported to eastern Kyushu and the coastal regions of the Inland Sea. In the early third century (Shōnai 庄内 phase), bronze mirrors of continental origin came to be distributed in relatively small quantities from Chūgoku, Shikoku, Kinki, and Tōkai of western Honshu all the way to Kantō of eastern Honshu. From the late second to early third century A.D. (the late phase of Late Yayoi to terminal Yayoi), in addition to northern Kyushu, practices of depositing rich funerary offerings came to be adopted in northern Kinki (old provinces of Tango 丹後, Tamba 丹波, and Tajima 但馬), where the discoveries of large quantities of iron weapons and glass accessories in burial contexts have recently been reported (Figure 2.9). This practice was soon adopted in the coastal regions of the Inland Sea, such as Harima 播磨 (southwestern Kinki), Sanuki 讃岐 (northeastern Shikoku), and Awa 阿波 (eastern Shikoku), and a little later in central Kinki.

An obvious decline of Chinese bronze mirrors exported to Japan from ca. 100 (the middle phase of Late Yayoi) to the early and mid-second century (the late phase of Yayoi) was probably a result of political turmoil in mainland China and the Lelang commandery. Even in southern Korea, materials of Chinese origins declined from the early first century to the mid-second century (Takaku 2000). Quantities of funerary offerings of Chinese origins increased again in Japan from the late second to early third centuries, probably because of renewed interactions with the Gongsun 公孫 rulers of Liaodong and the Daifang 帶方 commandery founded by the Gongsun, or with the polities of Chinhan 辰韓 and Pyŏnhan 弁韓 in southern Korea. By this, I do not mean that all the iron daggers and glass objects discovered in northern Kinki came from the Gongsun. Iron weapons and glass accessories discovered in northern Kinki were probably materials of Chinese origins produced locally in southern Korea (Takaku 2000). The spatial distribution of non-local materials, such as Eastern Han bronze mirrors and iron objects, expanded eastward beyond eastern Kyushu probably because the ability of northern Kyushu polities to keep precious materials from further distribution became weak, and the political ability of other regional polities became strong. In particular, it is likely that iron weapons

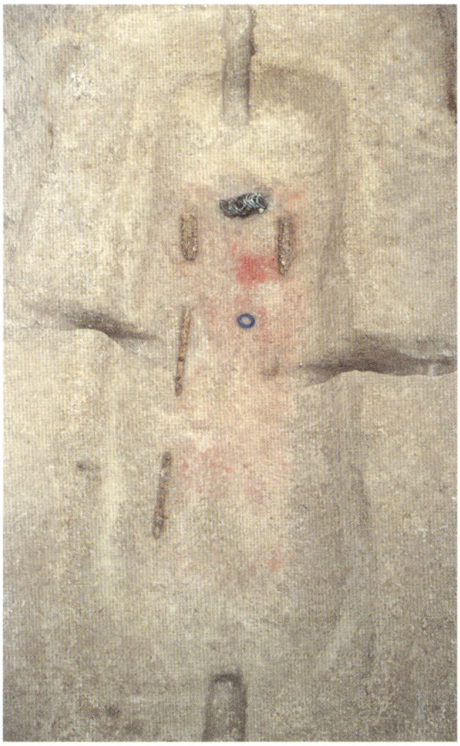

Figure 2.9 Rich Grave from the Ōburo-Minami 大風呂南 Burial Mound Group in Iwataki-chō, Kyoto. From Iwataki-chō Kyōiku Iinkai 2000. Above: view of burial pit; upper-right: glass bracelet; lower right: bronze bracelets.

and glass ornaments discovered in northern Kinki were directly imported to northern Kinki owing to the direct political relationships between polities in northern Kinki and southern Korea.

Control over Non-Local Prestige Goods and the Formation of Chiefdoms

As mentioned above, large mounded burials developed in various regions of Japan more or less simultaneously from the second to early third centuries A.D. (the late phase of the Late Yayoi to the terminal Yayoi). This phenomenon was probably related to the following: (1) a collapse of the pre-first century A.D. monopoly by the northern Kyushu polities of funerary goods of non-local or non-archipelago origin, such as bronze mirrors and projectile points, iron weapons and tools, and glass objects; (2) the adoption of the practice of depositing funerary goods in burials in regions to the east of Kyushu; and (3) an increase in the quantities of funerary goods buried with the dead in regions to the east of Kyushu. This suggests that, when the imports of materials of continental origins, such as bronze mirrors, iron weapons, and glass objects, resumed at the end of the second century, it is possible that groups and their leaders who had control over the procurement, redistribution, and trade gained and increased their own political prestige, and that they became able to levy communal labor for the building of mounded burials in return for distributing non-local goods. In this sense, the significance of and background to the appearance of mounded burials in regions to the east of Kyushu may be considered the same as the appearance of burials with very rich funerary offerings in northern Kyushu from the end of the third century B.C. to the first century A.D., and especially in the early first century B.C.

I argue that the spatial distribution of a particular type of mounded burial indicates the spatial extent of an alliance and network of local chiefs under an influential chief who controlled the procurement and redistribution of prestige goods. As in the case of northern Kyushu from the end of the third century to the late first century B.C., the import of large quantities of non-local items at the end of the second century A.D. triggered the rapid organization of various groups through the procurement, management, and redistribution of the non-local items. Furthermore, procurement routes of mostly non-local "prestige goods" shifted in the mid-first century, which necessitated the re-organization of systems that developed before ca. 100 A.D. As a result, not only intra-regional networks of chiefs in the middle and eastern Inland Sea region, central Kinki, northern Kinki, and Hokuriku, as well as Omi and Tōkai, but also an additional loose network among these aforementioned regions emerged. This loose network provided the foundation upon which Himiko 卑弥呼 was collectively selected as the leader of Yamataikoku 邪馬台国 at the end of the second century.

This network at the terminal Yayoi period was strengthened and re-organized into a unilateral alliance among chiefs with central Kinki as the center, owing to Himiko's dispatching of diplomatic missions to Wei China and a monopoly on the procurement of large quantities of prestige goods that represented a new set of values.

I want to be clear that two prestige systems existed at different times in different regions. One was in operation from the early first century B.C. in northern Kyushu and the other from the end of the second century A.D. in the eastern Inland Sea region. While I argue for the tribal nature of the Middle Yayoi society in Kyushu, even if a prestige system was in operation in Middle Yayoi in northern Kyushu (and the prestige of an influential tribal leader rose), it was quite temporary. Had prestige goods become unavailable, the whole system would have collapsed. This is the reason why influential tribal leaders in northern Kyushu declined from the middle phase of the Late Yayoi period. When the import of prestige goods resumed in the latter half of the Late Yayoi period, it was no longer tribal leaders of northern Kyushu who handled the procurement and redistribution.

Generally speaking, that the maintenance of prestige depends on the procurement of scarce items suggests that the foundation of the prestige system is weak. The system can be sustained only so long as the procurement of the non local, scarce, and exotic items is guaranteed. If the procurement of such goods becomes difficult, such that the redistribution center or trade routes have shifted, then individual political prestige declines immediately, and the whole system becomes subordinate to a new political center. This is particularly evident from the second century to the early third century when the supremacy of the northern Kinki polities (Tango, Tamba, and Tajima) weakened, and they were eclipsed first by the coastal regions of the Inland Sea (Harima, Sanuki, and Awa), and then in turn by central Kinki. In other words, the prestige goods system is heavily influenced by other historical factors, and the system no longer functions when nothing can be redistributed. Elites must inevitably seek constantly for the next prestige goods to distribute.

In this sense, I disagree with Kawano Kazutaka (1998) who considers the "saturation" of goods important in systems of prestige-good redistribution. A more serious problem is not saturation that can be controlled but the exhaustion of resources. In particular, when items for distribution are not of a chief's own production but have to be imported, the whole system becomes highly unstable. In contrast, it would be possible to establish a broad, long-distance network among local chiefs if one influential leader gained control over the procurement and distribution of prestige goods that local chiefs desired.

A broad, long-distance network formed by this process is evidenced by the distribution of keyhole tombs in the late third century A.D. As Tanaka Yoshiyuki (1995) has shown, relationships or alliances among chiefs based on the exchange of prestige goods and the return of loyalty or any contribution to the paramount chief depended on personal ties among chiefs and was not yet systematized and institutionalized in the late third century. Nor was the succession of the chiefly position stable from one generation to the next. A system had to be renewed every time a paramount chief was replaced. In the process, some of the prestige items had to be replaced, and locally produced prestige items had to be invented.

In the late fifth century, the positions of paramount chief and other local chiefs became stable, and clan groups came to be organized at central and regional nodes. Local chiefs became obliged to contribute to the central court in response to the guarantee of their positions over generations. In the sixth century, each clan group in the center was given specialized duties for the central authority, and in return each clan group was granted the right to control local people. In regions away from the center, local chiefs were incorporated into the class of provincial governors or county magistrates under centralized control, and a system was created in which the local chiefs were allowed to control and manage local groups. Gradually, a systematic and organized political system developed. This is the beginning of pre-state political formation.

Addendum 1: The Basis of Calendrical Dates for the Yayoi Period and Critique of the AMS Dating by the National Museum of Japanese History

The National Museum of Japanese History (hereafter, NMJH), utilizing the AMS (accelerator mass spectrometry) method, published the calendrical dates for the beginning of the Initial, Early, and Middle Yayoi period as 1,000 B.C., 750 B.C., and 400 B.C. Since the conventionally accepted calendrical dates for these epochs were 500–600 B.C., 350–400 B.C., and 200 B.C., respectively, the results published by NMJH were sensationally published in newspapers. I do not support their position. I first criticize their methods and then go on to clarify the basis of my views of calendrical dates.

First of all, the problem with the NMJH approach is that they utilized soot remaining on pottery surfaces as a basis for AMS dating. The soot resulted from burning woods much older than the pottery, meaning that samples that NMJH subjected to the AMS dating could well contain carbon much earlier than carbon produced at the time of pottery production.

In order to test the validity of the dates proposed by NMJH, my colleagues and I have independently conducted AMS dating of Yayoi human skeletons and deer bones (Tanaka, Mizoguchi, Iwanaga, and Higham 2004). Taking the marine reservoir effect into consideration, we have intentionally selected specimens discovered inland. I will discuss the marine reservoir effect prior to presenting the result of our dating. Water on or close to the bottom of the ocean remained stagnant for eight hundred years, during which time carbon-14 decayed, and, therefore, its content became less than that of the air above dry land. Consequently, radiocarbon dates of samples derived from marine organisms tend to be older than actual dates or dates of contemporaneous land organisms. This requires us to calibrate the radiocarbon dates utilizing carbon-13. We are aware that the carbon-13 content of the marine organisms is higher than that of organisms living outside the ocean. This allows us to calibrate the carbon-14 dates by comparing the average carbon-13 content of plants living on land with the sample value of carbon-13, which makes it possible to estimate the extent to which land organisms subsisted on marine organisms.

Tanaka, Mizoguchi, Iwanaga, and Higham (2004) have obtained the following results: seventh to fifth centuries B.C. for the Initial Yayoi period, fourth to third centuries B.C. for the beginning and early phase of the Middle Yayoi period, and second and first centuries B.C. for the late phase of the Middle Yayoi period. Since Japan is an island country, the marine reservoir effect is unavoidable, and we should expect to obtain results earlier than the reality. Even so, all of our results show dates much later than those of the National Museum. Indeed, our results correlate to the conventionally accepted dates of the Yayoi period based on chronology of pottery in association with materials of continental origin.

I would like to raise an additional point regarding the marine reservoir effect. It is likely that Yayoi people ate marine foods, and dates obtained by AMS should yield results earlier than the reality because of the marine reservoir effect. Therefore, we must calibrate the dates by taking into consideration the contribution of marine foods to the diet, measuring the $\delta 13C$ to estimate the amount of carbon derived from marine foods. It is further necessary to take into consideration that the marine reservoir effect is locally varied, and we must calibrate the date using the data of marine reservoir effect taken near northern Kyushu. When this is done, the obtained results show even later dates: the mid-third century B.C. for the end of the Early

Yayoi and first century B.C. for the late phase of the Middle Yayoi. It is the case in island countries such as Japan and New Zealand that even rain contains marine water and that plants can be affected by the marine reservoir effect. Moreover, skeletons of elderly individuals may contain carbon of old foods that were not metabolized completely. If we take these factors into consideration, the dates for the Initial and Early Yayoi periods should be even later than the NMJH results.

Since the publication of the NMJH results suggesting that the beginning of the Yayoi period was dated five hundred years earlier than originally suspected, many Japanese archaeologists published articles in support of the NMJH results. Yet, it is not simple to override the conventional view of calendrical dates of the Yayoi period because that view was also based on evidence of some degree of confidence. In order to approach calendrical dates of the Yayoi period based purely on archaeological methods, it is first essential to correlate pottery chronology between the Japanese archipelago and the Korean peninsula, between the Korean peninsula and the Liaodong peninsula (northeastern China), and between the Liaodong peninsula and the Central Plains of China. It is then necessary to depend on historically dated artifacts made in the Central Plains of China that were transported to the Korean peninsula and to the Japanese archipelago. It would be ideal if we could cross-date pottery chronologies of different regions, but this is not always possible. Generally, artifacts were transported in one direction from the Central Plains of China to the Liaodong peninsula, then to the Korean peninsula, and finally to the Japanese archipelago. Consequently, the discoveries of bronze weapons and mirrors whose dates are historically known in the Japanese contexts only indicate the *terminus ante quem*.

Despite this difficulty, calendrical dates of the late phase of the Middle Yayoi period and later can be determined based on the discoveries of Western Han, Xin, and Eastern Han bronze mirrors in the contexts of jar burials in northern Kyushu. These Chinese bronze mirrors whose dates are historically known give the oldest possible calendrical dates for each type of Yayoi pottery in association with these mirrors. If the NMJH results are correct, then we have to push back the calendrical dates of the phases prior to the early Middle Yayoi period, especially the Initial and Early periods.

Japanese archaeologists are faced with difficulties in estimating the calendrical dates for the Early Yayoi and Initial Yayoi periods. Of course, chronological correlations between Liaoning Province and the Korean peninsula are to a large extent well established, and some bronze objects produced in Liaoning reached the Japanese archipelago. A problem is that we do not know the precise date of each chronological type of Liaoning materials. To overcome this difficulty, Japanese archaeologists have traditionally taken the length of time necessary for one type of Middle Yayoi pottery to evolve to the next chronological type and applied this to the Early and Initial Yayoi case. While the length of this time is known for the Middle Yayoi pottery based on the association of chronologically different types of Chinese bronze mirrors, the length of time required for the evolution of Early and Initial Yayoi pottery is purely speculative. Therefore, calendrical dates for the Early and Initial Yayoi periods should be open to challenge.

In order to give support to the NMJH results, Japanese specialists of Chinese archaeology have started to reconsider hypothetical calendrical dates of the bronze cultures of the Liaoning region and of the Korean peninsula apart from the conventional view of calendrical dates for the Initial and Early Yayoi periods. They take advantage of a recent increase in discoveries in the western Liaoning region of Chinese bronze objects made in the Central Plains to revise the calendrical dates of the Liaoning bronze cultures. This revision will lead to another revision of the calendrical dates of bronze objects and polished stone objects, both of which were produced in the Korean peninsula and modeled after Liaoning bronze objects. Their new hypotheses on calendrical dates of Bronze Age chronologies of the Liaoning region and the Korean peninsula are very important because they attempt to give support to the NMJH dates adopting the orthodox and traditional archaeological approach. Therefore, we cannot ignore their attempt, regardless of our position concerning the NMJH dates.

Japanese specialists of Chinese archaeology in support of the NMJH dates now argue that the Initial to early Middle Yayoi period should be considered to coincide with the eighth to third centuries B.C. Their hypothesis is not valid, because their view is based on a series of speculations. Their discussion is very difficult to substantiate. If, however, we do not adopt their logic of argument, what would be an alternative argument?

First, the Type I Liaoning-style bronze dagger is dated to the ninth to sixth centuries B.C. Even if we accept the interpretation that the Type I polished stone dagger with a stepped hilt was an adaptation of the Liaoning-style bronze dagger, it is not necessary to consider the dates of the subsequent polished stone daggers with joints, those with a stepped hilt (Type II), and those without a stepped hilt contemporaneous to the Type I Liaoning-style bronze dagger. Rather, these polished stone daggers could be dated to the sixth to fourth centuries B.C. Owing to the association of these polished stone daggers with pottery, the Hyuam-ni 休岩里 and Songgung-ni types should be dated to the sixth to fourth centuries B.C. If this is indeed the case, the Japanese Yamanotera 山の寺 to Itazuke 板付 I phases (contemporary to the Hyuam-ni and Songgung-ni phases) should fall between the sixth and fourth centuries B.C.

Second, the Type V Liaoning-style bronze dagger, which morphologically seems archaic, but whose size is considerably larger than the Type I Liaoning-style bronze dagger, should be later than Type I and not contemporaneous to it. I would assume that the date of Type V would fall between the fifth and fourth centuries B.C. I disagree with some Japanese archaeologists who, by considering Type V as contemporaneous to Type I, attempt to push back the dates of polished stone daggers with no stepped hilt and stone arrowheads with a single stepped stem that are in association with Type V, thereby further attempting to push back the dates of the Hyuam-ni and Songgung-ni phases.

In the Korean peninsula, the Type II and Type III Liaoning-style bronze daggers that are morphologically close to Type 2 Liaoning bronze daggers in Liaoning Province appeared in the fifth century B.C. Owing to the association with pottery whose relative chronology is firmly established, the date of the Type V dagger (Songgung-ni sub-type) is later than the Type III dagger (Yonghŭng-ni 龍興里 sub-type). In other words, the date of the Type V bronze dagger should fall between the fifth and fourth centuries B.C. Since the slender-type bronze daggers appeared later than the Type V Liaoning-style bronze daggers, the date of the appearance of the slender-type bronze daggers should be the third century B.C., although I do not deny the possibility of their appearance in the fourth century B.C. If this is indeed the case, the date of the beginning of the Late Mumun period and the Itazuke-II phase should be later than the beginning of the third century B.C.

Bronze daggers, spears, and halberds formed a set (assemblage) in the Korean peninsula a little later than the appearance of the slender type (in the second chronological sub-type). Slender-type bronze daggers were transported to northern Kyushu at the end of the Early Yayoi period in the stage of the third chronological sub-type of the Korean peninsula. This is the stage in which bronze spears with a small tab, spears with multiple line reliefs, spears with a slightly longer blade, and halberds with decorative patterns and small fullers appeared. If the slender-type bronze daggers appeared at the beginning of the third century B.C., the end of the Early Yayoi period should be after the late third century B.C.

When I compare my archaeological view of the calendrical dates of the Initial and Early Yayoi periods with the results of AMS dating conducted on human skeletons discovered in the Yayoi context, the results of our AMS dating are far more acceptable than the NMJH result. Still, the results of our AMS dating tend to show dates fifty to two hundred years older than my archaeologically hypothetical dates of the Initial and Early Yayoi periods. This probably results from insufficient calibration of the marine reservoir effect. In any case, we should continue testing hypotheses concerning the calendrical dates of the Yayoi period, applying the AMS dating to herbivorous deer and human skeletons discovered far away from the ocean. It is also urgent to establish appropriate methods to calibrate dates taking into consideration of the local marine reservoir effect.

Addendum 2: The Classification of Chiefdom and Japanese Studies of Chiefdoms

Anthropologists of the neo-evolutionary school in the 1960s constructed a framework of cultural evolution by drawing a comparison with biological evolution and by paying attention to the following: the tendency of organisms to increase internal complexity, fissioning of particular organs to integrate and reproduce this complexity, and the process of increasing complexity by fission and integration (Service 1962). Within this framework, the chiefdom is placed as a stage prior to the state. In the chiefdom, a new organizational principle arises to exert control over conflicts of different interests. This organizational principle is a chief, perhaps with an aristocratic tier, who manages and mediates political, economic, social, and religious activities. The chiefdom, however, lacks a legal system, a bureaucracy, and a standing army to exert strong control over many communities. Economically, specialized production and redistribution of goods characterize most aspects of social activities. A chief represents the ownership of communal land and functions as a means to integrate communal production and distribution. The economic basis of chiefly power is derived from his or her role as a redistributor of commodities. While a chief receives tributes and services from people, he or she also has to distribute the accumulated wealth to people in the event of communal festivals or other communal projects in order to maintain his or her prestige as a chief.

At the same time, the chiefdom is a type of society in which clan-based ties incorporate relationships between those who rule and those who are subordinate that are represented as kin relationships or mediated by kinship ties. Kinship relationships in this sense include both blood and fictive types. Under such an arrangement, social status and rank are translated into a kinship system. Relationships between those who rule and those who are subordinate tend to appear in the context of a re-organized relationship of relatives and kin (Nakabayashi 1969).

Considerable variation exists among chiefdoms and includes the simple versus complex chiefdom dichotomy, in addition to the group-oriented chiefdom versus individualizing chiefdom. In a simple chiefdom, according to Earle's conception (1978), a conical clan is the basis of social organization and land ownership, and a chief and members of the community are tied genealogically. The rank of an individual is determined based on genealogical distance from a higher-ranking chief. While chiefly authority tends to be centralized, the authority is still weak. Lower-ranking chiefs have actual control over land. In a complex chiefdom, by contrast, economic differentiation between chief and commoners increases, and higher-ranking chiefs, rather than low-ranking chiefs, exercise the authority to control land. Political centralization takes place at a regional or supra-local level. Aristocrats at the center monopolize political power, and specialists in executive administration, military, land control, production, and other activities appear. The highest class of chiefs and the local people are no longer tied genealogically and economically. Conical clan organization does not exist for commoners. On the other hand, chiefs inter-marry within a class of chiefs, and the class maintains the structure of a conical clan. The descent system is bi-lineal rather than patrilineal.

Along with the model proposed by Service (1962), a second often-cited evolutionary model is that put forward by Morton Fried (1967). Here, I examine how Fried's notions of rank societies and stratified societies correlate to Service's notions of tribes and chiefdoms.

In rank societies, as in egalitarian societies, division of labor is based on age and sex. At the same time, a limited number of social ranks appear, and a few members of the community occupy these ranks. The occupying of a specific rank, however, does not affect the ease of access to commodities necessary for living, nor does it give special benefit or permanent prestige. In this sense, Fried's notion of rank societies may be correlated to Service's notion of a tribe.

On the other hand, Fried's notion of ranked societies includes some elements of a chiefdom, with reference to kinship. In ranked societies, kinship order is more established as an organizational principle than in egalitarian societies. Kinship relations play a major role, and ranked arrangement of kinship relations could be developed into the structure of a conical clan based on closeness to particular ancestors.

Similarly, the major principle of economic integration in ranked societies is redistribution, as in chiefdoms. Yet, high-ranking leaders are not excused from ordinary labor works, nor can they accumulate personal wealth. Directions or orders from leaders are not accompanied by any force. In this sense, leaders in ranked societies are more or less the same as tribal leaders.

Transition from an egalitarian to a ranked society is static, with economic relations unchanged. Access to commodities of daily subsistence remains equal. However, ecological demography and the appearance of redistribution are considered as factors for the appearance and maintenance of rank, and these are factors that are shared by chiefdoms. Such considerations indicate that ranked societies are basically correlated to tribes, but also characterized by some elements shared by chiefdoms.

In stratified societies, kinship systems no longer function in the management and control of social order and political integration because of the development of social stratification. Social stratification means unequal access to basic resources to sustain living. Variety exists in the degree of access toward the majority of members of a community to individuals. The stratified society would be correlated to the more evolved stage of a chiefdom, and Fried mentions that once social stratification begins, it would evolve to that stage relatively quickly. Nevertheless, because Fried's notion of ranked societies covers the range from tribes to developing chiefdoms, his notion of stratified societies should cover an extremely long span as a pre-state society; therefore I consider Fried's concept to be unrealistic.

Other scholars beside Service and Fried discuss chiefdoms, but it is beyond the scope of this section to review them all. An important point for classification of chiefdoms is whether the integrating principle of a society is based on kinship or not. This is an element that also affects the quality of political organization and how it is structured. The same idea has also been dominant in the field of ancient Japanese history. Japanese scholars consider it valid to classify chiefdoms into two large categories based on the degree of domination of kinship ties in a society (Nakabayashi 1969; Yoshida 1983). This binomial classificatory scheme is also valid for the consideration of the decline of the kin-based system of rule. Historian Yoshida Takashi adopted this framework from anthropologist Nakabayashi Nobuhiro. Following Yoshida (1983), I refer to the two categories as type A and type B.

The type A chiefdom is characterized by a social organization based on clan and lineage. In such a society, social hierarchy and position are represented by kinship organization. Social rank that is hereditary and accompanied by privilege and role is determined by proximity to the chief's lineage. Each social rank and status occupy an appropriate position within a web of kinship organization. Commoners believe that a chief can assume the role because he or she occupies a special position (Nakabayashi 1969). Type A is in ordinary terms a ramage or conical clan.

In the case of the type B chiefdom, a relationship between the ruler and the subordinated is not achieved through clan or lineage, but a mythical lineage is considered important. A chief can be a chief because he or she is a landowner or pioneer and is a conqueror. A kin relationship is of secondary importance (Nakabayashi 1969). A clan and lineage belong to the class of elite from which a chief is chosen. The relationship between a chief and commoners is not tied by a clan or lineage. This is also the case for the relationship among commoners. Yet, the whole society is made to appear to be based on kinship organization with the chief at the center.

I consider the concept of this type B chiefdom highly valid in consideration of the social change that took place in Japan from the fifth to seventh centuries A.D. The chiefdom is a more "advanced" stage of the social evolution toward a state than that of a tribe because clear and specific conflicts of interest exist and because a new form of organizational principle has developed to manage conflicts. At the same time, a chiefdom is clearly distinguished from a state because the social organization of the chiefdom is based on kinship and because class differentiation is not obvious. In this sense, the type B chiefdom may be considered as being in a stage closer to the state.

Another significant aspect of the chiefdom is the importance of ideology that supplements the instability and weakness of the social structure (Nakabayashi 1969). This aspect is relevant to a historically documented phenomenon in which Queen Himiko of the early third century A.D. served as a sacred chief protected and isolated from society by a series of taboos. In this circumstance, maintaining chiefly authority depended on an "alliance" with more powerful neighboring states. Such cases include those in which Himiko's polity depended on the authority of Wei China, and in which the five kings of Japan in the fifth century A.D. sent tributes to the Southern Dynasties of China.

Japanese archaeologists consider the concept of chiefdom important for the political and economic aspects of a society. Politically, the concept predicts the appearance of a new organizational principle to integrate conflicting positions of opposing interests. Economically, it predicts such a function as the redistribution of goods based on specialized production. The interest of Japanese archaeologists in chiefdoms is somewhat different from that of Japanese historians, who emphasize social structure based on kinship. This difference may have resulted from the fact that very few Japanese archaeologists are interested in kinship structure.

References

Earle, Timothy K.

1978 *Economic and Social Organization of a Complex Chiefdom: The Halelea District, Kaua'i, Hawaii.* Museum of Anthropology, University of Michigan, Anthropological Papers, No. 63. University of Michigan, Ann Arbor.

Fried, Morton H.

1967 *The Evolution of Political Society: An Essay in Political Economy.* Random House, New York.

Gotō Tadashi 後藤直

1979 Chōsen-kei Mumun doki 朝鮮系無文土器 [Mumun pottery originated from Korea]. In *Mikami Tsugio hakushi shōju kinen Tōyō-shi kōkogaku ronshū* 三上次男博士頌寿記念東洋史 考古学論集 [Collected theses in East Asian history and archaeology in celebration of Professor Mikami Tsugio's seventieth birthday], edited by Mikami Tsugio Hakushi Shōju Kinen Ronshū Henshū Iinkai 三上次男博士頌寿記念論集編集委員会 [Editorial Committee for the Festschrift Commemorating Professor Mikami Tsugio's Seventieth Birthday], pp. 485–529. Hōyū Shoten 朋友書店, Kyoto.

———

1987 Chōsen-kei Mumon doki sairon: Kōki Mumon doki-kei ni tsuite 朝鮮系無文土器再論: 後期無文土器系について [Further argument on Mumun pottery originated from Korea: With special reference to the later types]. In *Higashi Ajia no kōko to rekishi: Okazaki Takashi sensei taikan kinen ronshū* 東アジアの考古と歴史: 岡崎敬先生退官記念論集 [Archaeology and history of East Asia: Festschrift commemorating the retirement of Okazaki Takashi], Vol. 2, edited by Okazaki Takashi Sensei Taikan Kinen Jigyōkai Ronshū 岡崎敬先生退官記念事業会 [Committee Commemorating the Retirement of Okazaki Takashi], pp. 325–358. Dōhōsha Shuppan 同朋舎出版, Kyoto.

Hashino Shimpei 端野晋平

2001 Shisekibo no keifu to dempa yōtai 支石墓の系譜と伝播様態 [Origins and diffusion patterns of dolmens]. In *Yayoi jidai ni okeru Kyūshū Kan-hantō kōryū shi no kenkyū* 弥生時代における九州・韓半島交流史の研究 [A study on the history of interaction between the Korean peninsula and Kyushu during the Yayoi period], edited by Tanaka Yoshiyuki 田中良之, pp. 29–62. Kyūshū Daigaku Daigakuin 九州大学大学院, Fukuoka.

Hira Yoshinori 平美典

2001 Kan-hantō shutsudo Yayoi-kei doki kara mita Nikkan kōshō 韓半島出土弥生系土器から見た日韓交渉 [Interaction between Korea and Japan from the standpoint of Yayoi-type pottery excavated in the Korean peninsula]. In *Yayoi jidai ni okeru Kyūshū Kan-hantō kōryū-shi no kenkyū* 弥生時代における九州・韓半島交流史の研究 [A study on the history of interaction between the Korean peninsula and Kyushu during the Yayoi period], edited by Tanaka Yoshiyuki 田中良之, pp. 105–138. Kyūshū Daigaku Daigakuin 九州大学大学院, Fukuoka.

Iwanaga Shōzō 岩永省三

2002 Seidō buki giki-ka no kikaku kenkyū: Kan to Wa 青銅武器儀器化の比較研究: 韓と倭 [A comparative study of transformation of bronze weapons into ritural paraphernalia: Cases of Korea and Japan]. In *Kan-hantō kōkogaku ronsō* 韓半島考古学論叢 [Collected theses in the archaeology of Korean peninsula], edited by Nishitani Tadashi 西谷正, pp. 203–234. Sozusawa Shoten すずさわ書店, Tokyo.

Iwataki-chō Kyōiku Iinkai 岩滝町教育委員会 [Iwataki Township Board of Education] (editors)

2000 *Ōburo-Minami funbo-gun* 大風呂南墳墓群 [Ōburo-Minami burial mound group]. Iwataki-chō Kyōiku Iinkai, Kyoto Prefecture.

Kataoka Kōji 片岡宏二

1999 *Yayoi jidai, toraijin to doki, seidō-ki* 弥生時代・渡来人と土器・青銅器 [Immigrants, pottery, and bronze objects in the Yayoi period]. Yūzankaku 雄山閣, Tokyo.

———

2001 Kaikyō o ōrai suru hito to doki: Iki Harunotsuji iseki shutsudo no gi-Chōsen-kei Mumon doki o chūshin ni 海峡を往来する人と土器: 壱岐原ノ辻遺跡出土の擬朝鮮系無文土器を中心に [Pottery of immigrants across the straits: Korean-style Mumun pottery from the Harunotsuji site in Iki]. In *Magatama* 勾玉 [Curved jades], edited by Yamanaka Hidehiko Sensei Taishoku Kinen Ronbunshū Kankōkai 山中英彦先生退職記念論文集刊行会 [Publication Committee for Commemorative Papers on the Retirement of Yamanaka Hidehiko]. Yamanaka Hidehiko Sensei Taishoku Kinen Ronbunshū Kankōkai, Fukuoka.

Kawano Kazutaka 河野一隆

1998 Fukusō-hin seisan ryūtsū shisutemu ron 副葬品生産・流通システム論 [A hypothesis on the production and distribution system of funerary offerings]. In *Chūki kofun no tenkai to henkaku* 中期古墳の展開と変革 [Development and transformation of elite tumuli in the fifth century], edited by Maizō Bunkazai Kenkyūkai 埋蔵文化財研究会 [Japanese Association for Field Archaeologists], pp. 41–74. Maizō Bunkazai Kenkyū Shūkai 埋蔵文化財研究集会, Osaka and Fukuoka.

Kondō Takaichi 近藤喬一

1969 Chōsen, Nihon ni okeru shoki kinzokuki bunka no keifu to tenkai 朝鮮・日本における初期金属器文化の系譜と展開 [Origins and development of very early metal culture in Korea and Japan]. *Shirin* 史林 52(1): 75–115.

Kristiansen, Kristian
1991 Chiefdoms, States, and Systems of Social Evolution. In *Chiefdoms: Power, Economy, and Ideology*, edited by Timothy Earle, pp. 16–43. Cambridge University Press, Cambridge.

Kuwabara Hisao 桑原久男
1995 Yayoi jidai ni okeru seidō-ki no fukusō to mainō 弥生時代における青銅器の副葬と埋納 [Bronze objects deposited with the dead and ritually buried in the Yayoi period]. In *Nishitani Shinji sensei koki kinen ronbunshū* 西谷眞治先生古希記念論文集 [Collected theses in celebration of Professor Nishitani Shinji's seventieth birthday], edited by Nishitani Shinji Sensei no Koki o Oiwai Suru Kai 西谷眞治先生の古稀をお祝いする会 [Assembly Celebrating Nishitani Shinji's Seventieth Birthday], pp. 15–47. Benseisha 勉誠社, Tokyo.

Nakabayashi Nobuhiro 中林伸浩
1969 Tōnan Ajia shuchōsei no kōzō 東南アジア首長制の構造 [Structure of chiefdoms in Southeast Asia]. *Shisō* 思想 535: 80–107.

Namba Yōzō 難波洋三
2009 Yanagisawa iseki shutsudo no dōtaku to dōka 柳沢遺跡出土の銅鐸と銅戈 [Ritual bronze bells and bronze halberds excavated at the Yanagisawa site, Nagano Prefecture]. In *Yama o koe kawa ni sou: Shinshū Yayoi bunka no kakuritsu* 山を越え川に沿う: 信州弥生文化の確立 [Crossing mountains and going along rivers: Foundation of the Yayoi culture in the central highlands of Japan], edited by Nagano Kenritsu Rekishikan 長野県立歴史館 [Nagano Prefectural Museum of History], pp. 66–79. Nagano Kenritsu Rekishikan, Chikuma, Nagano Prefecture.

Oda Fujio 富士雄, and Han Pyŏng-sam 韓炳三
1991 *Nikkan kōshō no kōkogaku: Yayoi jidai hen* 日韓交渉の考古学: 弥生時代篇 [Archaeology of Japan-Korea Interactions: Yayoi Period]. Rokkō Shuppan 六興出版, Tokyo.

Okauchi Mitsuzane 岡内三真
1973 Chōsen shutsudo no dōka 朝鮮出土の銅戈 [Bronze halberds excavated in Korea]. *Kodai Bunka* 古代文化 25(9): 279–294.

Ozawa Yoshinori 小沢佳憲
2000 Yayoi shūraku no dōtai to kakki: Fukuoka-ken Kasuga kyūryō o kakki to shite 弥生集落の動態と画期: 福岡県春日丘陵を画期として [Temporal and spatial changes in Yayoi period settlements: With special reference to the case of the Kasuga Hill, Fukuoka Prefecture]. *Kobunka Dansō* 古文化談叢, No. 44, pp. 1–37.

———

2002 Yayoi jidai ni okeru chiiki shūdan no keisei 弥生時代における地域集団の形成 [Formation process of regional communities during the Yayoi period]. *Kyūhan* 究班 2: 135–151.

Sahara Makoto 佐原真

1960 Dōtaku no chūzō 銅鐸の鋳造 [Production of ritual bronze bells]. In *Sekai kōkogaku taikei 2: Yayoi jidai* 世界考古学大系 2: 弥生時代 [World archaeology: An outline, volume 2: Yayoi period], edited by Sugihara Sōsuke 杉原莊介, pp. 92–104. Heibonsha 平凡社, Tokyo.

Service, Elman R.

1962 *Primitive Social Organization: An Evolutionary Perspective*. Random House, New York.

Shimojō Nobuyuki 下條信行

1979 Nanboku shiyaku ko: Yayoi jidai Tsushima hakusai Chōsen-sei seidō-ki no imi 南北市糴考: 弥生時代対馬舶載朝鮮製青銅器の意味 [Consideration of active trading in all directions: Significance of Korean bronze objects transported to Tsushima Island]. *Shien* 史淵 116: 175–210.

Takaku Kenji 高久健二

2000 Rakurō gun to Ben-Shinkan no bosei 楽浪郡と弁・辰韓の墓制 [Mortuary practices in Pyŏnhan, Chinhan, and the Han commandery of Lelang]. In *Kōkogaku kara mita Ben-Shinkan to Wa* 考古学から見た弁・辰韓と倭 [Pyŏnhan, Chinhan, and Japan from the archaeological perspective], edited by Yŏngnam Kogo Hakhoe 嶺南考古學會 [Yŏngnam Archaeological Society] and Kyūshū Kōkogaku Kai 九州考古学会 [Kyushu Archaeological Society], pp. 25–57. Yŏngnam Kogo Hakhoe and Kyūshū Kōkogaku Kai, Pusan and Fukuoka.

Tanaka Yoshiyuki 田中良之

1991 Iwayuru torai setsu no sai kentō いわゆる渡来説の再検討 [Re-examination of the so-called immigration hypothesis]. In *Nihon ni okeru shoki Yayoi bunka no seiritsu* 日本における初期弥生文化の成立 [Early formation of the Yayoi culture in Japan], edited by Yokoyama Kōichi Sensei Taikan Kinen Jigyōkai 横山浩一先生退官記念事業会 [Committee Commemorating the Retirement of Yokoyama Kōichi], pp. 482–505. Bunken Shuppan 文献出版, Fukuoka.

———

1995 *Kofun jidai shinzoku kōzō no kenkyū* 古墳時代親族構造の研究 [Study of the kinship structure during the Kofun period]. Kashiwa Shobō 柏書房, Tokyo.

———

1999 Doki ga kataru Jōmon shakai 土器が語る縄文社会 [Jōmon society from the standpoint of pottery]. *Kenkyū Kiyō* 研究紀要 6: 1–22.

———
2000 Bochi kara mita shinzoku, kazoku 墓地から見た親族・家族 [Kinship structure from mortuary perspectives]. In *Kodai-shi no ronten* 古代史の論点 [Themes of debates in ancient Japanese history], Vol. 2, edited by Tsude Hiroshi 都出比呂志 and Sahara Makoto 佐原真, pp. 132–152. Shōgakukan 小学館, Tokyo.

———
2002 Yayoi jin 弥生人 [Yayoi people]. In *Kodai o kangaeru: Ine, kinzoku, senso: Yayoi* 古代を考える: 稲・金属・戦争: 弥生 [Consideration of ancient history: Rice, metal and war: Yayoi period], edited by Sahara Makoto 佐原真, pp. 47–76. Yoshikawa Kōbunkan 吉川弘文館, Tokyo.

Tanaka Yoshiyuki 田中良之, Mizoguchi Koji 溝口孝司, Iwanaga Shōzō 岩永省三, and Tom Higham
2004 Yayoi jinkotsu o mochiita AMS nendai sokutei 弥生人骨を用いた AMS 年代測定 [AMS dating on skeletons of the Yayoi period]. *Kyūshū Kōkogaku Kai, Yŏngnam Kogo Hakhoe dai-6-kai gōdō kōkogaku taikai: Nikkan kōryū no kōkogaku* 九州考古学会・嶺南考古学会第6回合同考古学大会 日・韓交流の考古学 [Archaeology of Korea-Japan interactions: The sixth joint archaeology conference of the Kyushu Archaeology Society and of Yŏngnam Archaeology Society], pp. 245–251. Yŏngnam Kogo Hakhoe 嶺南考古學會 and Kyūshū Kōkogaku Kai 九州考古学会, Pusan and Fukuoka.

Yoshida Takashi 吉田孝
1983 Ritsuryō *kokka to kodai no shakai* 律令国家と古代の社会 [The *ritsuryō* state and ancient society]. Iwanami Shoten 岩波書店, Tokyo.

3

Kaya, Silla, and Wa: Changing Relationships and Their Historical Backgrounds

Park Cheun Soo

Abstract

In this paper, I reexamine and revise our understanding of diachronic interrelations between Kaya, Silla, and Paekche in the Korean peninsula and Wa in the Japanese archipelago from the third to sixth centuries A.D. I begin by refuting the colonial historical perspective that yet persists in Japan regarding the relations between southern Korea and western Japan that are centered on the polity called Imna (J. Mimana). Historical sources indicate the existence of a strong relationship between Paekche and Wa, but archaeological evidence suggests otherwise. I hypothesize that relations between Paekche and Wa were focused on the sixth century, whereas before that time relations with the Kaya polities and Silla were more important. For example, examination of material culture in Korea and Japan indicates that the relations between the Kaya polities and Wa were important before the fifth century. Historical sources suggest that relations between Silla and Wa were hostile; however, archaeological evidence shows that the two polities had experienced periods of peace and hostility and active exchanges through the entire period, especially beginning in the early fifth century and lasting through the late sixth century. This is supported by evidence concerning certain political changes on the peninsula, including the decline of Kaya in the early fifth century, which resulted in the collapse of interregional iron trade that caused Wa to intensify its dealings with Silla.

Introduction

In the Japanese archipelago, the Kofun 古墳 period is considered an important milestone, during which society emerged from the formative

Yayoi 弥生 period and became part of the wider cultural zone of East Asia. During this period, new cultural material such as gilt-bronze ornaments, horse-riding equipment, porcelain-like earthenware, iron ingots, and iron agricultural tools were imported into the archipelago. Accompanying the introduction of these technologies into Japan were artisans who possessed advanced skills in iron production, metalwork, porcelain production, and horse bell manufacturing.

Many Japanese scholars have argued that this influx of culture from the Korean peninsula into the Japanese archipelago is related to the so-called Mimana Nihonfu 任那日本府 (K. Imna Ilbonbu) mentioned in early Japanese works such as the *Nihon shoki* 日本書記 (Chronicles of Japan, completed 720). Adherents of the Mimana hypothesis claim that Wa invaded the southern part of the Korean peninsula and governed it until the late sixth century. This hypothesis is based on entries concerning the conquest of the three peninsular kingdoms and the Mimana Nihonfu included in the "Annals of Jingu" (神功紀) chapter of the *Nihon shoki*; the record of the invasion of Wa on the King Kwanggaeto stele (Kwanggaet'o wangnŭng pi 廣開土王陵碑); and the references to the Five Wa kings 倭五王 in the "Accounts of Wa" 倭國傳 of the *Songshu* 宋書 (History of the Liu Song dynasty). This hypothesis, begun by Suga Masatomo 菅政友, Tsuda Sōkichi 津田左右吉, and Ikeuchi Hiroshi 池内宏 in the late nineteenth and early twentieth centuries, developed into a fully formulated theory in the *Mimana kōbōshi* 任那興亡史 (History of the rise and fall of Mimana) by Suematsu Yasukazu 末松保和 (Suematsu 1949). It is noteworthy that this book was published in 1949, suggesting that Japanese scholars' perspectives on the history of the ancient interchanges between the peoples of Korea and Japan remained unchanged after Japan's defeat in World War II. Supported by philological studies, the Mimana hypothesis has also remained a basic framework of interpretation in the study of ancient Korea-Japan relations in archaeological studies in Japan.

However, Korean scholars and several Japanese philologists have since come to recognize that the Mimana Nihonfu was simply an administrative office for Wa envoys, who were for a short time sent to Ara Kaya 阿羅伽倻 in Haman 咸安 in the early sixth century (Yi Yŏng-sik 2004). Despite this discovery, historical and archaeological studies on ancient Japan are still overshadowed by the Mimana hypothesis. Japanese archaeologists tend to ignore the findings of recent philological studies and maintain even today that Korean culture and artifacts were introduced to the archipelago by way of a Wa invasion of the peninsula. Although Japanese scholars may not refer to the Mimana Nihonfu as a Wa colony as before, they still use the term "advance" (*shinshutsu* 進出) in describing Wa's presence in the southern Korean peninsula during the late fourth century. They argue that through this advance, Wa established hegemony in the Japanese archipelago and founded an ancient polity there, as they were able to control various necessities such as iron as well as a system for the distribution of such goods. As the phrase "advance to Manchuria" (*Manshū shinryaku* 満洲進出) illustrates in the case of the twentieth-century Japanese invasion of Manchuria, however, an ancient "advance" to the Korean peninsula likewise implies an "invasion" (*shinryaku* 侵略). Such phrasing suggests that the views of many Japanese scholars with regard to Mimana/Imna have remained unchanged since 1945.

Furthermore, some Japanese scholars presume that the Yŏngsan River 榮山江 basin is the location of the so-called Makhan 慕韓 polity, the only reference to which occurs in the "Accounts of Wa" of the *Songshu* (97:2394–2396), and it is in this context that these scholars discuss the keyhole-shaped tombs found in that area (Kimura Makoto 2005). However, this view of Makhan is problematic in that it accepts uncritically the descriptions of Wa claims over Makhan that appear in the *Songshu* account, which is also one basis for support of the Mimana hypothesis. After claiming that the Yŏngsan River basin is part of Makhan, a region that supposedly was not subordinated to Paekche, these scholars then argue that Wa exerted influence over the southern part of the Korean peninsula, based on the concentration of keyhole-shaped tombs in the area. Further, drawing on the theory that four districts of Imna were located in the Honam region, some scholars even make the extreme argument that the keyhole-shaped tombs found in the Honam region were built during the Mimana Nihonfu period (Kobayashi Toshio 2004: 104–105).

These kinds of interpretation are rather extreme in that they do not take the following archaeological evidence into account: that the keyhole-shaped tombs suddenly appeared in the Yŏngsan River basin during the early sixth century and were constructed for only a single generation; that they did not form a cluster of tombs as they would in a political center; and that they contained prestige goods specific to Paekche royalty. Moreover, Makhan would have collapsed in the fifth century along with the Chinhan 秦韓 polity of the southeastern part of the peninsula. It is broadly accepted that Makhan and Chinhan cannot be considered to have developed as state-level polities. Therefore, the reference to Makhan in the context of Wa claims suggests clearly that such descriptions of the Korean peninsula in the "Accounts of Wa" in the *Songshu* do not reflect historical reality. In addition, a recent investigation of the Unp'yŏng-ni 雲坪里 cemetery site in Sunch'ŏn 順天 confirms that the four districts of Imna were not located in the Yŏngsan River basin, where the keyhole-shaped tombs were found, but rather in the estuary of the Sŏmjin River 蟾津江 in the territory of Tae Kaya 大伽倻. Thus, the grounds for connecting the four districts of Imna with the keyhole-shaped tombs are nonexistent.

In relation to these matters, a more fundamental problem would be whether it would have been at all possible for the Song court of China (429–479) to confer upon Wa, a remote and distant polity that did not belong to the Song feudal system, sovereign power over Silla and Kaya. It is also highly unlikely that the Song had the power to exert such rule over East Asia in the fifth century. Therefore, passages regarding the Korean peninsula in the "Accounts of Wa" in the *Songshu* may have simply recorded the political intentions of Wa leaders rather than historical facts.

By contrast, some Korean scholars claim that the keyhole-shaped tombs, which clearly evolved in the Japanese archipelago, were indigenous to the Korean peninsula. Other Korean scholars tend to avoid or deny the existence of keyhole-shaped tombs on the Korean peninsula, wary of their connection with the Mimana hypothesis. Yet since it is not possible to deny that the keyhole-shaped tombs in the Yŏngsan River basin are archaeological data related to Wa, it is necessary to address them in order to clarify the character of the Mimana Nihonfu, as this problem is unresolved in the history of Korea-Japan relations and a matter of strong interest in Japanese scholarship. I believe that the keyhole-shaped tombs indeed offer an important clue to the history of Korea-Japan relations and the nature of the Mimana Nihonfu.

Further, in discussing the transmission of culture from the Korean peninsula to the Japanese archipelago, Korean scholarship focuses only on the fact of transmission and omits any discussion of why and under what circumstances Kaya, Paekche, Silla, and even Koguryŏ transmitted, or should have transmitted, their culture to Wa. We also cannot limit our thinking on cultural and human transfer between the Korean peninsula and the Japanese archipelago to viewing it only as a unidirectional flow from the peninsula to the archipelago. The artifacts from the Japanese archipelago in the Taesŏng-dong 大成洞 cemetery in Kimhae 金海, the keyhole-shaped tombs in the Yŏngsan River basin, and the Wa-style tombs in the Kaya region show that the human and cultural flows were not unidirectional, but went both ways to some degree.

Kaya, Silla, and Wa 3

—Park Cheun Soo

Based on their philological arguments centered on records of exchange between Paekche and Wa in the late fourth century, scholars have so far understood ancient Korea-Japan relations only as those in which Kaya served as the gateway for cultural interchanges between the two parties until the late fourth century, at which point Paekche replaced Kaya. As a result, the relationship between Kaya and the Japanese archipelago has been dealt with only as a subordinate factor in the history of Paekche-Wa relations, or in the context of discussing the Mimana Nihonfu (Yŏn Min-su 2003: 29–30). Also, based on records in the *Samguk sagi* 三國史記 (History of the Three Kingdoms, completed 1146) and the *Nihon shoki*, the relationship between Silla and Wa has been understood as one of consistent hostility.

As I have discussed elsewhere, however, Kaya served as the center for interchanges between the Korean peninsula and the Japanese archipelago from the third to fifth centuries, and Paekche became the center only around the early sixth century (Pak Ch'ŏn-su 1995, 1998, 2001, 2007). Some might argue that political interchange between the peninsula and the archipelago could have occurred apart from cultural interchange. It is difficult, however, to conceive that the exchange of a necessity such as iron, prestige items such as gilt-bronze goods, and artisans who possessed the technology to manufacture such prestige items could have occurred without a parallel political interchange between the uppermost elite authorities of the polities involved. Therefore, it is necessary to revisit and revise the current views of cultural interchange that have been based solely on philology. Such a reconsideration is also supported by current archaeological data that indicate an active interchange between Silla and Wa from the early fifth to late sixth centuries, which contradict the conventional understanding that theirs was a relationship characterized by mutual hostility (Pak Ch'ŏn-su 2006, 2007, 2009a, 2010).

Therefore, working from the assumption that the current understanding of ancient Korea-Japan relations that focuses on Paekche is flawed, I will discuss the following points by focusing instead on Kaya and Silla.

During the third and fourth centuries, material culture and ideology from the Kimhae region were transmitted to the Japanese archipelago, and those from the Kinai 畿内 region of Japan were transmitted to the region associated with the Taesŏng-dong cemetery in Kimhae. Because these materials include prestige items that were exchanged between the newly emerging polities centered on Taesŏng-dong in the Kinai region, I would like to argue that the military activities of Wa that are described in the entries for the *Kyŏngja* year 庚子年 (400 A.D.) in the King Kwanggaet'o stele inscription do not represent independent expeditions, but instead relate to the Kŭmgwan Kaya 金官伽倻 polity centered on Kimhae.

I would also like to assert that, contrary to the established theoretical models, the gilt-bronze ornaments, horse gear, and iron ingots—introduced to the Japanese archipelago during the early fifth century—were produced in Silla, while the comma-shaped jadeite beads found at Silla sites were produced in the Japanese archipelago, not in the Korean peninsula. This will lead to a re-examination of the current philology-based theory regarding the Silla-Wa relationship as one of consistent hostility, and to an examination of the circumstances of their interchange. In particular, I will discuss the historical circumstances that made it necessary for Wa to seek out interchange with Silla.

Further, I will suggest that it was from Tae Kaya instead of Silla that gilt-bronze crowns, saddle frames, gold ceremonial implements, horse gear, arms, and weapon tools were introduced to Wa in the late fifth century. These archaeological data enable us to analyze the relationship between Tae Kaya and Wa—a study difficult to accomplish through written records alone. In addition, I will discuss the chronology and circumstances of Tae Kaya's growth in the context of its interchange with the Japanese archipelago.

I hypothesize that intensive interchange between Paekche and the Japanese archipelago occurred only in the early sixth century, a time when Paekche artifacts were abundantly introduced to the Japanese archipelago and the keyhole-shaped tombs were constructed in the Yŏngsan River basin. Further, Wa-style tombs, whose occupants were brought in by Tae Kaya at this time, were placed in the region of Taesa 帶沙, Kimun 己汶, and the four districts of Imna—a zone contested between Paekche and Tae Kaya. This placement suggests they were facing off against those buried in the keyhole-shaped tombs of the Yŏngsan River basin, who were placed there by Paekche. I will therefore examine the circumstances of their appearance with a focus on their arrangement on the southern coastal region.

I also note that the number of Silla artifacts imported to the Japanese archipelago in the sixth century, including those excavated from the Fujinoki 藤ノ木 tomb in Nara, far exceeded the number of Paekche artifacts known to have been imported to Japan. I will examine the circumstances in which the interchange between Silla and Wa resumed at the same time as artifacts from the Northern Qi 北齊 court of China (550–577) were introduced to the Japanese archipelago.

Moreover, this study also notes that during the early fifth century, a time in which the construction of oversized keyhole-shaped tombs shifted from the Nara basin to southern Osaka, Silla artifacts were imported to southern Osaka while artifacts from the Japanese archipelago were introduced to the Silla region. In particular, I will explore the circumstances of the Yamato state's emergence in the context of its interchange with Silla by illustrating that the gilt-bronze horse gear excavated from the Maruyama Tomb 丸山古墳 (the *baichō* 陪冢, or attendant tomb, of the royal Konda Gobyōyama Tomb 誉田御廟山古墳) in Osaka is a product of Silla, and that the gold helmet and armor excavated from the Daisen Tomb 大仙古墳 (traditionally the tomb of Emperor Nintoku 仁徳天皇), also in Osaka, were made by Silla artisans.

Interchange Between Kaya and Wa During the Third and Fourth Centuries

The northern-style bronze cauldron excavated from Tomb 235 as well as the Chinese bronze cauldron and the Japanese wide-blade bronze spearhead excavated from Tomb 322 at Yangdong-ni 良洞里 in Kimhae suggests that trade in that part of East Asia was centered on the Kuya 狗耶 polity located in that region. This hypothesis is supported by the "Accounts of Han" in the *Sanguozhi* 三國志 (Chronicles of the Three Kingdoms), which state: "Their country produces iron, and the Han, Ye, and Wa all come to trade for it. In their various markets they use iron to purchase goods, the same as coins are used in China. They also provide iron to the two commanderies [Lelang 樂浪郡 and Daifang 帶方郡]" (*Sanguozhi* 30:853). Another passage in the same source indicates that the Kuya polity was a junction on a route from the Daifang commandery through the southwestern coast to Wa: "To reach Wa from the [Daifang] commandery, one must first travel by sea along the coast past the Han polities, southward then eastward, reaching the Kuya Han polity on the coast to the north, a distance of over seven thousand *li*, upon which one first crosses the sea, reaching the Tsushima polity at a distance of over a thousand *li*." Further, the earliest record from the Japanese archipelago that mentions the Korean peninsula appears in the *Nihon shoki* (Sujin 65/7; 1:253–254), in which an account dated to the sixty-fifth year of the reign of Sujin 崇神 refers to an envoy from the polity of Imna (Mimana).

According to the burial items excavated from the Taesŏng-dong cemetery, built beside the Ponghwang earthen fortification 鳳凰土城, which served as a new center for the Kimhae region, artifacts from the Japanese archipelago replaced Chinese mirrors and northern-style bronze cauldrons during the fourth century. The collapse of the Lelang and Daifang commanderies in the

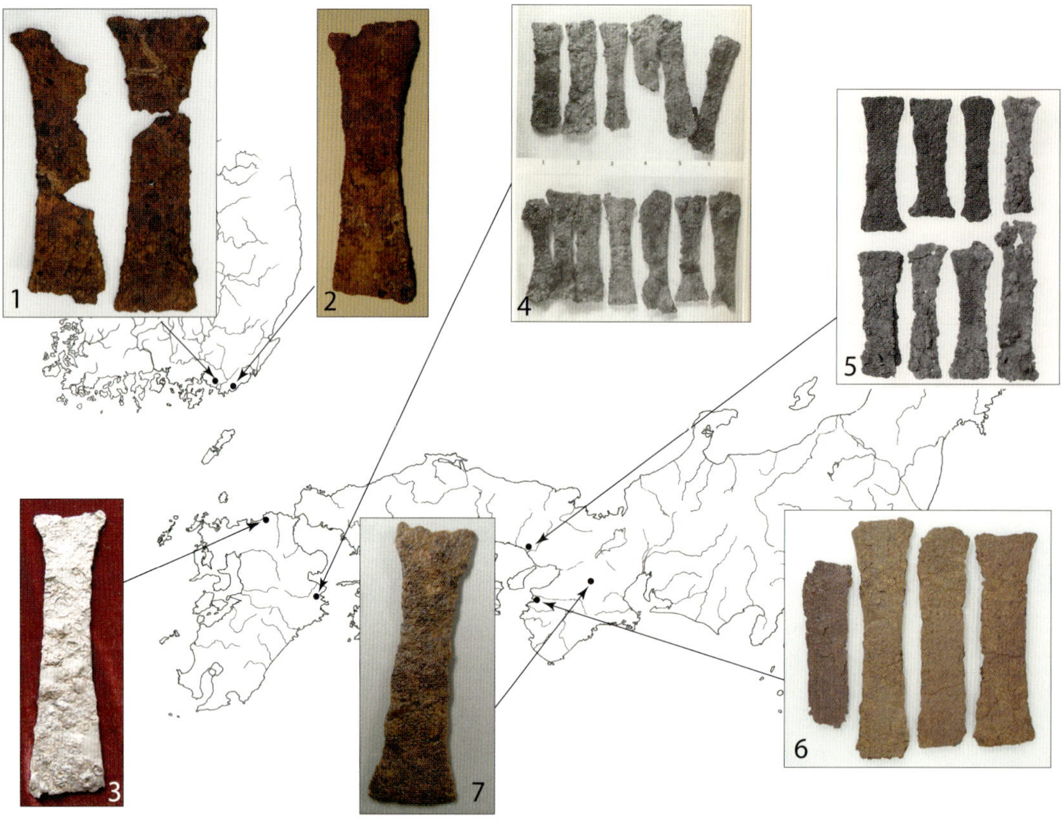

Figure 3.1 Iron Ingots Recovered from the Japanese Archipelago During the Late Fourth Century (Products of Kŭmgwan Kaya).
1. Tomb 2 at Taesŏng-dong in Kimhae; 2. Tomb 54 at Pokch'ŏn-dong in Pusan;
3. The Waribatake 割畑 tomb in Fukuoka; 4. The Shimoyama 下山 tomb in Ōita;
5. The Gyōja-zuka Tomb in Hyōgo; 6. The Maruyama Tomb in Wakayama;
7. Minamiyama Tomb 4 in Nara.

early fourth century appears to have precipitated a transition in Kaya's trading partner, making the Japanese archipelago its new focus of trade.

In addition, concerning goods from the archipelago, shields with bronze spiral-shaped ornaments and stone tools from the Kinai area replaced the Kyushu-produced mirrors and wide bronze spearheads excavated from the Yangdong-ni cemetery. Along with cylindrical bronze implements, iron ingots excavated from the Okinoshima 沖ノ島 site in Fukuoka 福岡, the Gyōja-zuka Tomb 行者塚 in Hyōgo 兵庫 Prefecture, the Yawata-Ōtsuka Tomb 八幡大塚 in Kyoto, and the Maruyama 丸山 Tomb in Wakayama 和歌山 Prefecture are thought to have been produced in the Kimhae region based on their shape: both ends are straight and both sides symmetrical without irregularities (Figure 3.1).

Artifacts from Kŭmgwan Kaya in the late fourth-century Japanese archipelago and those from Kinai in the elite Taesŏng-dong cemetery in the Kimhae region suggest a close interchange between Kŭmgwan Kaya and Wa at the time. This shows that northern Kyushu was the center of long-distance interchange in the archipelago during the period in which the Kuya polity was active in Kimhae. Northern Kyushu had in fact served as the point of entry to the archipelago since prehistoric times, but this center began shifting to the Kinai region during the Kŭmgwan Kaya period.

In particular, cylindrical bronze implements, thought to have been utilized by the uppermost elites in the northern Nara region to symbolize their alliances with newly emergent neighboring powers, appear to have been given, along with iron, by the central authorities of Kŭmgwan Kaya, who were the builders of the tombs at Taesŏng-dong. At the same time, stone ornaments and shields decorated with bronze spiral ornaments seem to have been specifically produced and given in turn by the power holders in northern Nara to the group in Kimhae that had built the Taesŏng-dong cemetery (Kawamura Yoshimitsu 1995). Such exchanges appear to have had a more symbolic than economic meaning as a means of confirming an alliance. Armor and iron spears with attached cylindrical bronze implements made in Kŭmgwan Kaya and shields with bronze spiral ornaments and quivers containing stone arrowheads produced in the archipelago represented the status of, and alliance between, the leaders of Kŭmgwan Kaya and Wa. They were gifts presented to each other to commemorate their solidarity (Suzuki Yasutami 1995).

At this time, Kŭmgwan Kaya was facing an external threat from Koguryŏ and Silla, while it was competing with Ara Kaya, a coalition of powers around the Nam River 南江 basin, the Naktong River basin, and the southern coast. The above-described archaeological data from the Kimhae and Kinai regions are noteworthy in relation to the account in the Kwanggaet'o stele inscription, which states that Wa, after invading the Silla capital (新羅城), had retreated to Imna Kara 任那加羅, believed to be in the Kimhae region, after its defeat by Koguryŏ in 400 A.D.

Together with the account in the stele inscription stating that Wa retreated to Imna Kara, the artifacts that were produced in Kŭmgwan Kaya and excavated in the archipelago and the artifacts originating from the Kinai region excavated from the Taesŏng-dong cemetery argue strongly against the theory that Wa had independently dispatched a military expedition to the peninsula at this time. Instead, this military expedition appears to be primarily related to Imna Kara—that is, Kŭmgwan Kaya. Also, had Wa launched an independent military expedition, its forces should have retreated to Yŏngil Bay 迎日灣 or Ulsan Bay 蔚山灣 near Kyŏngju 慶州, where its ships should have been at anchor. That the Wa retreated instead to the region around the former Kimhae Bay suggests that the expedition was perhaps a joint operation conducted with Kŭmgwan Kaya.

Some scholars argue that the Wa mentioned on the Kwanggaet'o stele was not the Kinai group, but rather a group from the southern Korean peninsula or a group from another region in the archipelago. However, it is clear from artifacts excavated from both the Okinoshima site in Fukuoka and the Taesŏng-dong cemetery that the group in question was the Saki 佐紀 polity of northern Nara, who were the group centered on the kingly authority of Wa. We may surmise that the Saki group, the newly emergent power of northern Nara, tried to gain hegemony in the center of the Kinai region by allying itself with Kŭmgwan Kaya, through which it could acquire prestige goods and necessities such as iron from Kŭmgwan Kaya in exchange for military support.

The motivations behind the Wa mobilization in 400 A.D. may have been complex, but the most direct cause appears to have been Kŭmgwan Kaya's forceful response to Silla's accelerating threat to the Kimhae region, especially its growing influence over the elites of Pokch'ŏn-dong 福泉洞 in the Tongnae 東萊 region, which lay within Kŭmgwan Kaya's influence network from the late fourth century.

Interchange Between Silla and Wa During the First Half of the Fifth Century

From the fifth century, iron ingots imported to the Japanese archipelago differed greatly in morphology and size from those previously imported from Kŭmgwan Kaya. Iron ingots excavated from Tomb 6 at Ōyamato 大和 in Nara have been considered products of Kŭmgwan Kaya, as they were similar to those excavated from Tombs 21 and 22 at Pokch'ŏn-dong. However, iron ingots excavated from the latter tombs are different from those excavated

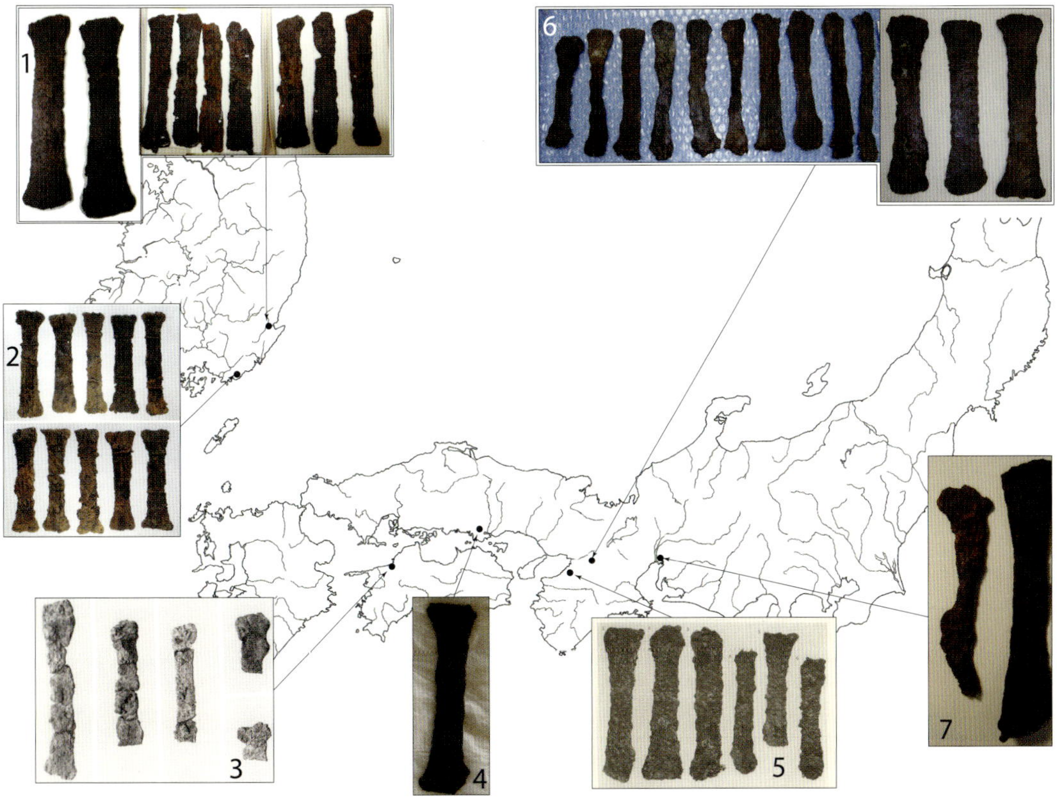

Figure 3.2 Iron Ingots Recovered from the Japanese Archipelago During the Early Fifth Century (Products of Silla).
1. The southern mound of the Great Tomb at Hwangnam in Kyŏngju; 2. Tomb 21 at Pokch'ŏn-dong in Pusan; 3. The Shussaku 出作 site in Ehime; 4. The Kuboki-Yakushi site in Okayama; 5. The Nonaka tomb in Osaka; 6. Tomb 6 at Ōyamato in Nara; 7. The Iseyama Chūgakkō site in Aichi.

from Tomb 54, which have straight ends and symmetrical sides, suggesting that they were produced in Kŭmgwan Kaya. Rather, with their arc-shaped 40-cm-long ends and asymmetrical sides, ingots from Tombs 21 and 22 appear to be products of Silla similar to iron ingots excavated from Tomb 6 at Wŏlsŏng-no 月城路 in Kyŏngju, Tombs G5 and G6 at Imdang-dong 林堂

洞 in Kyŏngsan 慶山, and the southern mound at the Great Tomb at Hwangnam 皇南大塚 in Kyŏngju. Therefore, we may conclude that most of the large iron ingots excavated from Tomb 6 at Ōyamato were imported from Silla.

According to a study based on chemical tests of the iron ingots excavated from the Pokch'ŏn-dong cemetery, the ingots excavated from Tomb 39 contained a high quantity of copper, like the iron ingots from the Ch'angnyŏng 昌寧 area and Tomb 6 at Ōyamato (Murakami Einosuke 1993). In light of this finding, we can surmise that all these ingots were made from iron ore produced in the same region, namely, Silla. In particular, the small iron ingots from Tomb 6 at Ōyamato were likely supplied from Silla, as they are exactly the same in form and dimension as those produced in the Kyŏngju area: they all have arc-shaped ends and asymmetrical sides with exaggerated indentations. In addition, despite an earlier theory that assumed mid- to small-size iron ingots excavated from the Kuboki-Yakushi 窪木薬師 site in Okayama Prefecture, the Nonaka 野中 tomb in Osaka, Tomb 4 at Minamiyama 南山 in Nara, and the Iseyama Chūgakkō 伊勢山中学校 site in Aichi 愛知 Prefecture were products of the Kaya region, it is more likely that they were imported from Silla, as they are all similar in form and dimension to iron ingots excavated from the Kyŏngju area sites. Moreover, iron ingots recovered from the Pusan area were supplied from Silla during the early fifth century (Figure 3.2).

Iron ingots used to manufacture the tremendous amount of iron armor and weapons that suddenly appeared in the middle period of ancient burial mounds have so far been generally attributed to Kaya, but they were in fact products of Silla, a polity that has thus far been understood to have maintained a constantly hostile relationship with the archipelago. At the time of their production, gold handicrafts also appeared in the archipelago, instead of the greenstone items used earlier for magical purposes. Most scholars have so far considered these gold handicrafts to be products of Paekche or Kaya due to their bias concerning the nature of the relationship between Silla and Wa. This view, however, ignores the fact that the most gold handicrafts were produced in Silla during this period. Based on the items excavated from the Pokch'ŏn-dong cemetery in Pusan, it has been clarified that gold handicrafts excavated from the Japanese archipelago were in fact products of Silla, instead of Kaya as previously thought (Takada Kanta 2003; Pak Ch'ŏn-su 2006).

Gold handicrafts of this period that clearly indicate Silla origin are the gold crown ornaments, neck ornaments, dangling ear ornaments, hair ornaments, and finger rings excavated from Tomb 126 at Niizawa Senzuka 新沢

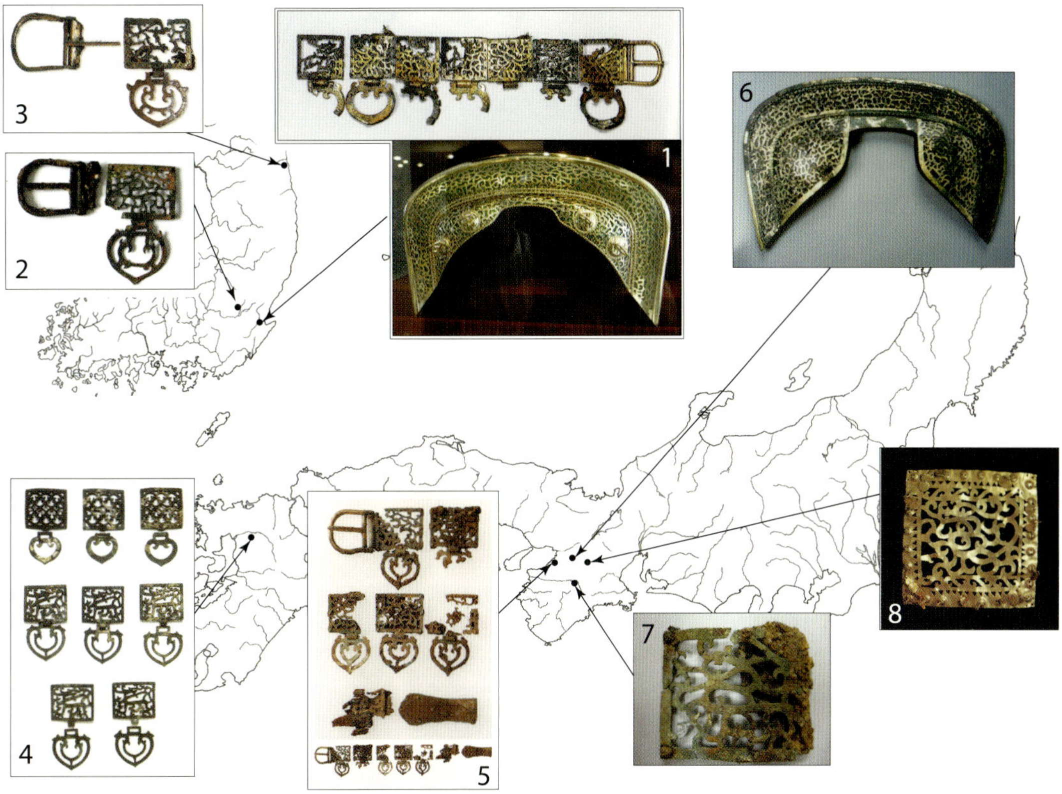

Figure 3.3 Gold Handicrafts of the Early Fifth Century Recovered from the Japanese Archipelago.
1. The southern mound of the Great Tomb at Hwangnam in Kyŏngju; 2. Tomb 7 at Imdang-dong in Kyŏngsan; 3. Tomb A-1 at Chodang-dong in Kangnung; 4. The Tsukino-oka tomb in Fukuoka; 5. The Shichikan tomb in Osaka; 6. The Maruyama Tomb in Osaka; 7. The Nekozuka tomb in Nara; 8. The Niizawa Senzuka 126 tomb in Nara.

千塚 in Nara. It is also clear that the glass vessels recovered along with these ornaments were imported by way of Silla. The same is true of gilt-bronze saddle frames, neck armor, and visored helmets excavated from the Gojō-Nekozuka 五條猫塚 tomb in Nara; gilt-bronze saddle frames, neck armor, quivers, saddles, and visored helmets excavated from the Tsukinooka 月の岡

tomb in Fukuoka; gilt-bronze dragon-pattern saddle frames in the Shichikan 七観 tomb in Osaka; and gilt-bronze horse gear in Tomb 1 at Shingai 新開 in Shiga 滋賀 Prefecture (Figure 3.3).

In particular, a glass cup was discovered together with gold armor in the front quarter of the Daisen Tomb in Osaka (traditionally, the tomb of Nintoku), which is associated with a royal tomb. As glass cups were buried in general in royal tombs in Silla, and as it was found in Tomb 126 at Niizawa Senzuka along with gold handicrafts from Silla, it appears to have been imported from Silla. Accordingly, considering that a headdress characteristic of Silla was attached to the helmet and armor with gold ornaments excavated from the Daisen Tomb, and that they were accompanied by a glass cup imported via Silla, it is highly likely that they were made by Silla artisans.

Early in the fifth century, the techniques of riveting and iron casing were introduced in the manufacture of armor in the Japanese archipelago. The riveting technology is considered as a breakthrough technological development in the manufacture of armor in the Japanese archipelago, and this has come to be understood as an introduction from the southern part of the Korean peninsula, particularly the Kaya region. The morphology of rivets and the riveting technique seen in iron saddle frames are the same for both regions, as is the iron casing technique used for the saddle frames, suggesting that these techniques had been brought in by immigrants, though the genealogy is not clear (Tsukamoto Toshio 1993). It is noteworthy, however, that these riveting and iron casing techniques were both evident in horse gear produced in Silla, such as that recovered from the Kurazuka 鞍塚 tomb in Osaka, Tomb 1 at Shingai in Shiga, and the Nakahachiman 中八幡 tomb in Gifu 岐阜 Prefecture as well as from Coffins 3 and 4 in Tomb 109 at Hwangnam-dong 皇南洞 in Kyŏngju and Tomb Na-39 at Sinhŭng-ni 新興里 in Sangju 尚州. I therefore surmise that these two breakthrough developments in the production of armor in the archipelago were in fact introduced from Silla along with the technique for producing gilt-bronze armor (Pak Ch'ŏn-su 2009a).

Moreover, it is noteworthy that immigrants from Silla were in the Japanese archipelago during this period, examples being those interred in the Gojō-Nekozuka tomb in Nara, which, although small in size, contained Silla-style gilt-bronze artifacts and forging implements; in the Miyayama 宮山 tomb in Hyōgo 兵庫 Prefecture, the main burial pit of which was lined with stones in the style found in the Naktong River estuary and that contained gold artifacts and iron items made in Silla; and in Tomb 126 at the

Niizawa Senzuka in Nara. These discoveries suggest that there were active interchanges between Silla and Wa during this period.

Also worth our attention are the numerous curved jadeite beads, made in the Japanese archipelago and found in Silla. Curved jadeite beads began to be imported to Silla in the late fourth century, as shown in Tomb Ka-13 at Wŏlsŏng-no in Kyŏngju and Tomb G6 at Imdang-dong in Kyŏngsan. After that, large numbers of curved jadeite beads were buried in tombs throughout Silla. For example, large numbers of high-quality curved jadeite beads crafted in the Japanese archipelago were found attached to the gold crowns discovered in tombs associated with royal burials like the northern mound of the Great Tomb at Hwangnam (seventy-seven pieces), Ch'ŏnmach'ong 天馬塚 (fifty-eight pieces), Kŭmgwanch'ong 金冠塚 (fifty-eight pieces), and Sŏbongch'ong 瑞鳳塚 (forty-one pieces). Curved jadeite beads crafted in the Japanese archipelago were also found as hanging ornaments in the gold saddle frames and neck ornaments discovered in the northern and southern mounds of the Great Tomb at Hwangnam, Ch'ŏnmach'ong, Kŭmgwanch'ong, and Kŭmnyŏngch'ong 金鈴塚. In addition, hundreds of curved jadeite beads were excavated from chiefly tombs in the Silla region distributed around royal tombs in Kyŏngju, including Tomb 55 at Talsŏ 達西 in Taegu 大邱, Tomb 7 at Kyo-dong 校洞 in Ch'angnyŏng, Tomb 1 at Pokch'ŏn-dong in Pusan, and the Husband-and-Wife Tomb 夫婦塚 in Yangsan 梁山.

The color and shape of the comma-shaped jadeite beads produced in the Japanese archipelago changed between the end of the early phase and the early middle phase of the Yayoi period (ca. 400–100 B.C.). The curved jadeite beads of the earlier period have a translucent and lucid green hue and vary greatly in size and shape. They also have perforations on one side or both sides made by stone implements. From the middle period they were crafted from opaque, white jadeites that were neither translucent nor green in hue, and their form and size ceased to vary significantly. They were also perforated on one side by iron implements with a sharp tip (Ōga Katsuhiko 2005). Interestingly, the same change can be observed in the peninsula, particularly in the Silla region. The northern mound of the Great Tomb at Hwangnam yielded gold crowns with highly translucent jadeites, but the crowns recovered from later tombs like Kŭmgwanch'ong and Sŏbongch'ong contained jadeites with relatively low translucence. The gold crowns from Ch'onmach'ong, the tomb latest in date, used primarily white jadeites with very low translucence.

Ch'oe Ŭnju as well as Saotome Masahiro and Hayakawa Yasuhiro has analyzed the curved jadeite beads using X-ray florescence in order to understand them through scientific methods. Ch'oe Ŭnju analyzed the curved jadeite beads collected by Kim Yang-sŏn at Soongsil University and discovered that microelements such as strontium and zirconium, commonly detected in curved jadeite beads from the Japanese archipelago, were not detected in them (Ch'oe Ŭn-ju 1986). In light of this finding, Ch'oe argued that the curved jadeite beads recovered from Silla tombs were products of the Korean peninsula. In contrast, Saotome Masahiro and Hayakawa Yasuhiro analyzed the curved jadeite beads excavated from the Husband-and-Wife Tomb in Yangsan, a chiefly tomb in the Silla region in the custody of the Tokyo National Museum, and detected strontium and zirconium in them (Saotome Masahiro and Hayakawa Yasuhiro 1997). More recently, Warashina Tetsuo analyzed the curved jadeite beads recovered from the cemetery in the vicinity of King Mich'u's tomb 味鄒王陵 in Kyŏngju and the Imdang-dong cemetery in Kyŏngsan and determined that they were crafted in Itoigawa 糸魚川 in Niigata 新潟 Prefecture (Warashina Tetsuo 2008).

Despite the above-mentioned example that seems to suggest that some curved jadeite beads were made in the Korean peninsula, I would argue that these beads were made in the Japanese archipelago for the following reasons: no known production centers have ever been confirmed in the peninsula; they appeared in the Japanese archipelago several hundred years before they did in the Korean peninsula; and it was confirmed through scientific analysis that the curved jadeite beads recovered from Silla tombs such as the cemetery near King Mich'u's Tomb in Kyŏngju and the Husband-and-Wife Tomb in Yangsan were made in Itoigawa.

We can surmise that the interchange between Silla and Wa was the result of their converging mutual interests. Although Wa had an absolute need for a new trade partner in order to secure iron and prestige items like Silla gold metalwork after the weakening of Kŭmgwan Kaya, Silla also needed to control peninsular trade with Wa and mend their previously antagonistic relationship.

Silla was geographically closest to Wa and could provide it with the gold metalwork and iron goods that it greatly needed. The archaeological indicator for Silla is the large amount of gold metalwork and iron goods excavated from the southern mound of the Great Tomb at Hwangnam in Kyŏngju, built in the mid-fifth century. The admiration of Wa for Silla's gold metalwork is obvious in an entry in the annals of Emperor Chuai 仲哀天皇 in the *Nihon shoki*, in which Silla is called "the country of dazzling gold and silver" (眼炎之金銀彩色多在其國) (Chuai 8/9; 1:326–327).

Some argue that the dragon-pattern *pique-a-jour* gilt-bronze saddle frames excavated from the early fifth-century Maruyama Tomb, which is an attendant tomb of the Konda Gobyōyama Tomb in Osaka (traditionally, the tomb of Emperor Ōjin 應神天皇), were not manufactured in Silla (Isahaya Naoto 2012). However, their structure, the dragon-pattern *pique-a-jour*, and the accompanying horse gear all suggest that they were most likely imported from Silla. This theory is also supported by the fact that horse gear, gilt-bronze ornaments, iron ingots, iron agricultural and machine tools, and craftsmen came from Silla during this period. When we consider the genealogy of artifacts introduced to the Japanese archipelago, we have to take other imported artifacts during the same period into account. The same is true of gilt-bronze hanging pendants and bridle cheek plates excavated from the Ōtani 大谷 tomb in Wakayama Prefecture and gilt-bronze saddle accessories excavated from the Fujinoki tomb in Nara.

In my opinion, the following strongly suggests an amicable interchange between the royal powers of Silla and Wa: the inclusion of the dragon-pattern *pique-a-jour* gilt-bronze saddle frames in the early fifth-century Maruyama Tomb, which is an attendant tomb of the Konda Gobyōyama Tomb in Osaka, and the likelihood that the curved jadeite beads attached to the gold crowns and gold saddle frames discovered in tombs associated with royal tombs such as the northern mound of the Great Tomb at Hwangnam, Kŭmgwanch'ong, and Ch'ŏnmach'ong were made at Itoigawa in Niigata. This interpretation is also supported by the fact that the Silla-produced gilt-bronze saddle frames and the archipelago-produced curved jadeite beads were both ornamental prestige goods that had symbolic political significance for the relationship between the royal power and provinces. In particular, the introduction of Silla-produced weapons and tools, such as iron spearheads, helmets, armor, and bow-cases, to the Japanese archipelago as well as the manufacturing of helmets and armor with gold ornaments in the archipelago by Silla artisans using the technique of riveting, speaks to the nature of the interchange between the two. It would be difficult to imagine polities with a hostile relationship sharing prestige items like arms and armor. In particular, the helmets and armor with gold ornaments excavated from the square portion of the royal Daisen Tomb support this theory (Figure 3.4).

The *Samguk sagi* contains numerous accounts of hostile engagements between Silla and Wa, but the account (Silsŏng 1/3; 27) describing the dispatch to Wa of Misahun 未斯欣 in the first year of the reign of King Silsŏng 實聖王 (402) and the records in the *Nihon shoki* (Ōjin 31/8; 1:377; Nintoku 11/10; 1:394–395) of Silla craftsmen dispatched to Wa in the thirty-first year of Emperor Ōjin (420) and in the eleventh year of Emperor Nintoku

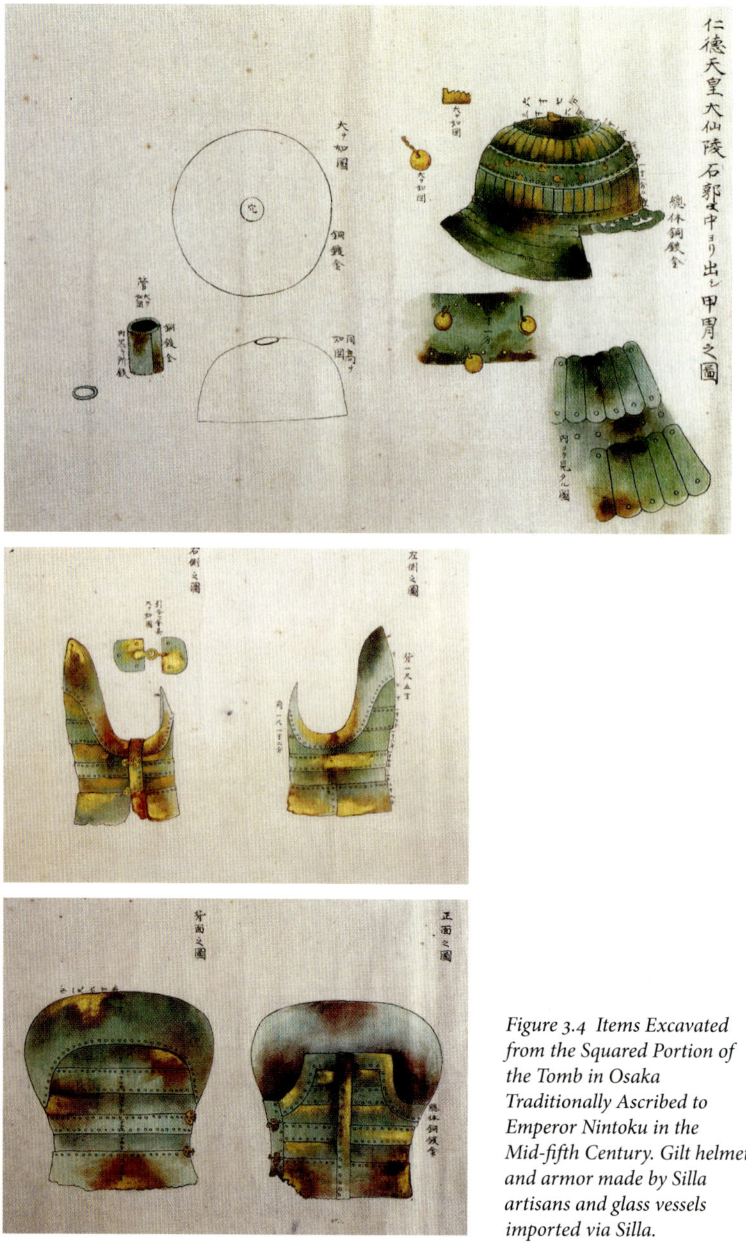

Figure 3.4 Items Excavated from the Squared Portion of the Tomb in Osaka Traditionally Ascribed to Emperor Nintoku in the Mid-fifth Century. Gilt helmet and armor made by Silla artisans and glass vessels imported via Silla.

(443) all suggest a dynamic political interaction between Silla and Wa. The *Nihon shoki* entries for the reign of Emperor Ingyō 允恭 contain only the accounts of Wa interchanges with Silla, and none with Paekche or Kaya. The accounts of Wa's dispatch of an envoy to Silla, the dispatch of Silla doctors in the third year of Emperor Ingyō to Wa (Ingyō 3/1; 1:436–437), and the records of Silla's messengers of condolence dispatched in the forty-second year of Emperor Ingyō (Ingyō 42/1; 1:448–449) all suggest a friendly relationship between Silla and Wa during that period.

We can surmise that Silla's active diplomatic relations with Wa had to do with its need to check the pressures not only from Paekche and Kaya, but also Koguryŏ. It is possible that in order to free itself from the pressure exerted by Koguryŏ, Silla adopted the strategy of playing one enemy against another—checking Koguryŏ, its former ally, by way of Wa, its former enemy. It appears that the withdrawal of the Koguryŏ troops that had been pressuring Silla in the mid-fifth century was related to the sudden estrangement of Silla and Wa. This can be interpreted as reflecting that Silla no longer needed its alliance with Wa after securing the territory east of the Naktong River and along the coast of the East Sea, as well as acquiring freedom from Koguryŏ's pressure.

Although scholars have considered only internal factors in understanding Silla's advance toward the territory east of the Naktong River and subsequent developments, I suggest that Silla's accumulation of wealth through trading iron and gold metalwork with Wa and securing the safety of the home front also played an important role.

Interchanges Between Tae Kaya and Wa During the Late Fifth Century

In the mid-fifth century, Tae Kaya, based in Koryŏng 高靈, grew into a large polity, controlling a broad area including the Hwang River 黄江 basin, the middle and upper reaches of the Nam River, the Sŏmjin River basin, the southern coast of the peninsula, and the upper reaches of the Kŭm River 錦江.

Gold hanging pendants, saddle frames with gilt-bronze ornaments, and crowns crafted in Tae Kaya during this period appear throughout the Japanese archipelago (Figure 3.5). Also, horse bits combining F-shaped gilt-bronze cheek plates and necktie-shaped pendants, manufactured in Tae Kaya and replacing horse gear imported from Silla during the early fifth century, have been recovered in all regions of the archipelago, suggesting

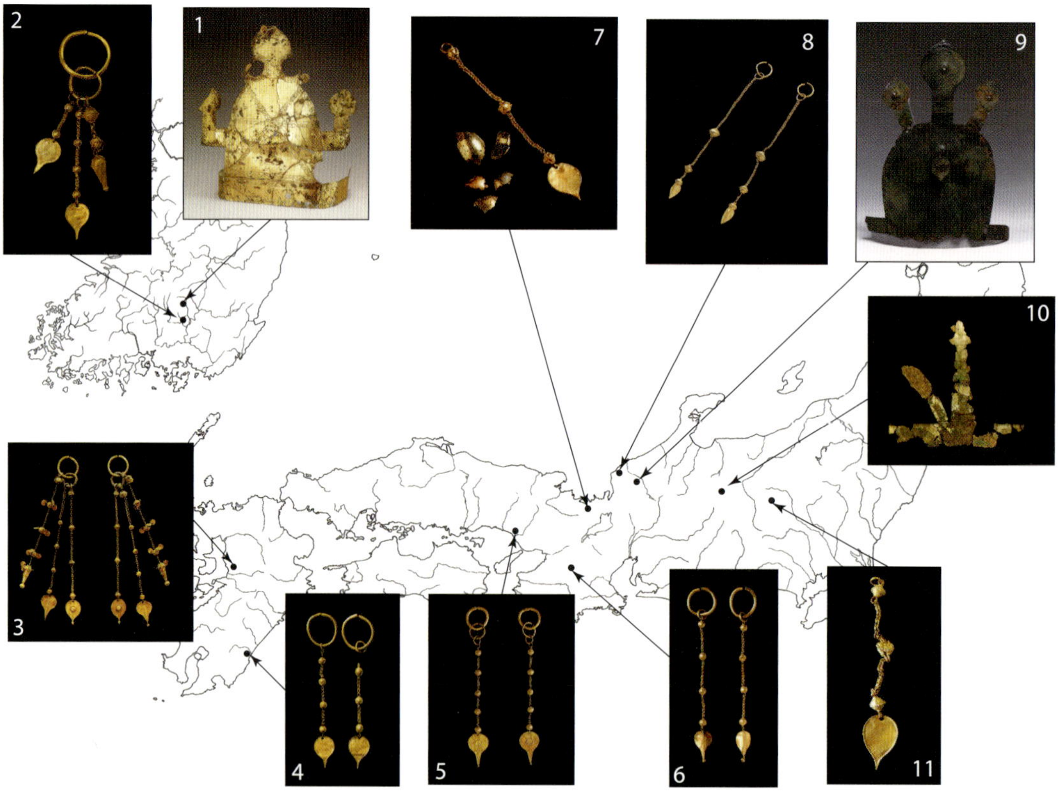

Figure 3.5 Ornaments from the Japanese Archipelago of the Late Fifth Century (Products of Tae Kaya).
1. Tomb 32 at Chisan-dong in Koryŏng; 2. Tomb 28 at Okchŏn in Hapch'ŏn;
3. The Eta-Funayama tomb in Kumamoto; 4. The Shimokitakata 下北方 *No. 5 underground-tunnel tomb in Miyazaki;*
5. The Kansuzuka カンス塚 *tomb in Hyogo; 6. Tomb 109 at Niizawa Senzuka in Nara;*
7. Tomb 1 at Mukaiyama 向山 *in Fukui; 8. Tomb 7 at Tenjinyama* 天神山 *in Fukui;*
9. The Nihonmatsuyama 二本松山 *tomb in Fukui; 10. The Sakuragaoka* 櫻ヶ丘 *tomb in Nagano;*
11. The Kenzaki-Nagatoro-Nishi 剣崎長瀞西 *site in Gunma.*

that this was the primary type of horse gear used during this period. Further, horse remains excavated from various sites in Japan appear to represent horses imported from Tae Kaya, as they were found along with Tae Kaya–produced horse gear. Examples include Pit SC16 at Yamasaki-Uehara 山崎上原 and Pit SK02 at Shimauchi 島内, in Miyazaki 宮崎 Prefecture; Pit

SK105 at Ōsato-nishioki 大里西沖 in Mie 三重 Prefecture; and Pit 64 by Tomb SM03 at the Miyagaito 宮垣外 site and Tomb 12 at Araibara 新井原, in Nagano 長野 Prefecture.

At the same time, the following artifacts that were produced in the Japanese archipelago were newly imported to the inland area of Tae Kaya territory: helmets and armor excavated from Tomb 32 and Tomb 1 at Chisan-dong 池山洞 in Koryŏng, Tomb 28 at Okchŏn 玉田 in Hapch'ŏn 陝川, and the Sangbaeng-ni 上柏里 cemetery in Hamyang 咸陽; noctilucent ladles produced at Amami-Ōshima 奄美大島 from Tomb 44; mirrors from Tomb 45; and small jars with a wide mouth and perforations from Tombs 1 to 5 at Chisan-dong.

In the past, the development of Tae Kaya was considered to be closely linked to the decline of the southern Kaya polities of Kŭmgwan Kaya and Ara Kaya as a result of Koguryŏ's southward campaign. When the two southern polities declined, Tae Kaya expanded by intensifying iron production in the Yaro 冶爐 region in Hapch'ŏn, an area connected to the Koryŏng region through the Allim Stream 安林川. However, I think it unlikely that the rapid rise of Tae Kaya as well as the introduction of a substantial number of Tae Kaya–produced artifacts into the Japanese archipelago during the late fifth century was possible only through its cultivation of iron production in the Yaro region, which enabled its domination over the Sŏmjin River route and the occupation of Taesa-jin 帶沙津 in Hadong 河東. Regarding this issue, it is important to examine why Paekche so persistently invaded the four districts of Imna as well as Taesa and Kimun (Chŏn Yŏng-nae 1985).

Some Japanese scholars still argue that the four districts of Imna were located near the Yŏngsan River basin, where keyhole-shaped tombs were discovered. For example, Tanaka Toshiyaki places Tari 哆唎 in Kwangju 光州 and Yŏngam 靈巖, east of the Yŏngsan River; Sata 娑陀 in Hamp'yŏng 咸平 and Mujang 茂長; and Moru 牟婁 in Yŏnggwang 靈光 and Muan 務安 west of the Yŏngsan River (Tanaka Toshiaki 2008). This, however, is a flawed argument, reflecting neither the circumstances of the time nor the archaeological data. First of all, it conflates Imna with Kaya, assuming that both names describe the same political and cultural area. Although the Yŏngsan River basin has been considered a single jar-burial cultural area, mortuary practices of certain areas of the basin, including Naju 羅州, Kwangju, and Haenam 海南, where large mounded tombs have been discovered, were clearly different from those of other areas, making it unreasonable to group this area together under the single name "Imna." It is even less likely that areas north of the Noryŏng Mountains 蘆嶺山脈 would have fallen within Imna territory. Therefore, in order to identify the location of names related to historical events, it is necessary to review archaeological data.

Regarding the four districts of Imna as well as Kimun and Taesa, I surmise that they were located on the border between Paekche and Tae Kaya, as they were areas of contention between those two polities. Accordingly, it is unreasonable to place the four districts of Imna in the Yŏngsan River basin. Historical records state that Paekche began attacking the four districts of Imna in 512 and advanced to Kimun and Taesa in 513, so we can assume that the two regions were near each other. Therefore, the locations of Kimun and the four districts of Imna should be determined based on the location of Taesa, which scholarship has almost universally interpreted as contemporary Hadong. Moreover, we may hypothesize, based on records of Paekche's attacks on the Tae Kaya localities of Kimun and Taesa, that the four districts of Imna were likewise territories of Tae Kaya, even though surviving historical records do not explicitly make an association between the four districts and Tae Kaya. This also agrees with the recent hypothesis that relates Tari and Kimun of the four districts of Imna to the Tari 達已 and the upper and lower Kimul 奇物 mentioned in relation to the twelve songs of Urŭk 于勒 (Kim T'ae-sik 2002: 262–263).[1]

Moreover, the recent discovery of the Andong 雁洞 tomb in Kohŭng 高興, built during Paekche's Hansŏng period (漢城時代, trad. 18 B.C–475 A.D.) and containing Paekche prestige items, confirms Paekche's influence on the Kohŭng region during the Hansŏng period. This discovery clearly suggests that the four districts of Imna, which had not belonged to Paekche territory until then, were located east of the Kohŭng peninsula. Accordingly, we can place Paekche's southeastern border in the early sixth century at Yŏsu 麗水, where the Korak 鼓樂山城 and Ch'ŏksan 尺山山城 fortresses were built; Sunch'ŏn 順天, where the Kŏmdan fortress 劍丹山城 was built; and Kwangyang 光陽, where the Maro fortress 馬老山城 was built, rather than at the Noryŏng Mountains. It is also clear that we can place the four districts of Imna as well as Kimun and Taesa in Yŏsu, Sunch'ŏn, and Kwangyang on the border between Paekche and Tae Kaya.

[1] Editor's Note: This refers to the twelve songs said to have been composed by the Kaya musician Urŭk in the mid-sixth century. For a list and descriptions of the songs, refer to *Samguk sagi* 32:317 (Music, Kayagŭm).

Considering the mortuary practices and pottery recently excavated from the Unp'yŏng-ni cemetery in Sunch'ŏn and the Hŭngnyŏng-ni 興龍里 cemetery in Hadong, Tae Kaya appears to have first advanced to the upper reaches of the Nam River and then southward to the Namwŏn 南原 basin and Kurye 求禮. It then eventually took control of the Yŏsu, Sunch'ŏn, and Kwangyang regions, supposedly the four districts of Imna, by securing Hadong, the port in the estuary of the Sŏmjin River. As Tae Kaya could not secure the safety of its sea routes only by acquiring Hadong, it should have occupied the Yŏsu region, a place of strategic military importance located in the middle of the southern coast, and a long protruding peninsula (Pak Ch'ŏn-su 2007).

Inferior gold metalwork produced by Tae Kaya suddenly appeared in the Japanese archipelago in the late fifth century, replacing both the artifacts produced by Kŭmgwan Kaya imported until the fourth century, as well as the Silla-produced gold metalwork imported until the early fifth century. This change may have been due to the advance of Tae Kaya. By gaining control of the sea route, Tae Kaya was able to exercise considerable influence over the traffic between Paekche and Wa as well as that between Wa and China. These circumstances may have led Wa to import gold metalwork from Tae Kaya instead of Silla.

During this period prestige items manufactured by Tae Kaya, such as gilt-bronze ornaments, horse gear, and iron arms and armor, were buried in the tombs of newly emerging chiefs all over the archipelago, including the Sakitama-Inariyama 埼玉稲荷山 tomb in Sakitama 埼玉 Prefecture in the Kantō region, the Ōtani tomb in Wakayama Prefecture in the Kinki 近畿 region, and the Eta-Funayama 江田船山 tomb in Kumamoto 熊本 Prefecture in the western region. The presence of such burial goods appears to be closely related to the political shift in the late fifth-century Japanese archipelago (Tsude Hiroshi 1988; Pak Ch'ŏn-su 1995). Powerful clans that had depended on Silla until then must have declined, and new clans in alliance with Tae Kaya must have begun to emerge as power holders.

Regarding the alliance between Tae Kaya and powerful clans in the archipelago, it is worth noting an account recorded in the *Nihon shoki* for the eighth year of the reign of Emperor Yūryaku 雄略天皇 (464), which states that a king of Imna sent three men to attack Koguryŏ (Yūryaku 8/2; 1:476–479). Given the political situation at the time, it seems likely that the king of Imna mentioned in this record was a king of Tae Kaya. Further, because Koguryŏ was the target of the attack, this should not have been an independent military expedition by Wa, but must instead have been related to Tae Kaya, as Wa's previous military expedition in 400 had been related to Kŭmgwan Kaya. Another relevant record in the *Nihon shoki* is that for the third year of the reign of Emperor Kenzō 顯宗天皇 (487), which records that Ki no Oiwa no Sukune 紀生磐宿禰 (K. Ki Saengban Sungni), who was stationed in Imna, attacked Paekche in alliance with Koguryŏ, taking advantage of a plan crafted by a man from Imna (Kenzō 3/4; 1:524–527). Since the surname of this person is Ki 紀, and he is mentioned in connection with Imna (that is, Tae Kaya), he could have been someone dispatched from Wa to attack Paekche. In particular, there appears to have been a special relationship between the Ki 紀 family and Tae Kaya, as Tae Kaya–produced artifacts, including gilt-bronze horse gear and iron horse armor, were buried in the Ōtani tomb in Wakayama, the Ki family's stronghold. It is interesting that the same kind of transverse beam structure found in the Tomb of the Heavenly Kings and Earthly Spirits (*Ch'ŏnwangjisin ch'ong* 天王地神塚) of Koguryŏ is also seen in the corridor-style horizontal burial chambers in the Iwase-Senzuka 岩橋千塚 cemetery in Wakayama. It is also possible that the structure of Stone Chamber B of Tomb 1 at Songhak-tong 松鶴洞 in Kosŏng 固城 originated from this region.

Given the above evidence, we can surmise that in order to counter the military advances of Koguryŏ and Silla, Tae Kaya formed an alliance with Wa elites as well as with powerful clans in various regions in the archipelago in exchange for the goods it produced.

Philological and archaeological scholarship attempting to establish the time of development of the Tae Kaya polity have in the past relied solely on the record of the dispatch of a mission to the Southern Qi court in 479 included in the *Nan Qishu* 南齊書 (History of the Southern Qi), which suggests a date in the late fifth century. However, archaeological data suggest a time in the mid-fifth century, when Tae Kaya products began to appear on the upper reaches of the Nam River and when artifacts produced by Tae Kaya began to appear in the Japanese archipelago at the same time as goods from the archipelago began to appear in the Tae Kaya region. During this time, Silla, then in an antagonistic relationship with Tae Kaya, dominated the Naktong River estuary. The competing polity of So Kaya had its own forces arrayed in the Sach'ŏn 泗川 and Kosŏng Bays. Therefore, Tae Kaya needed to secure the Sŏmjin River route in order to trade with the archipelago. Tae Kaya cultural material appearing in the archipelago in the mid-fifth century also indicates that it controlled the Sŏmjin River basin in the eastern part of the Honam region.

The Eta-Funayama tomb in Kumamoto and the Sakitama-Inariyama tomb in Sakitama, in which Tae Kaya artifacts were buried in large quantities, are known for large swords and iron daggers with inlaid inscriptions. It has been vaguely assumed that the artisans of the inlay technique must have come from Paekche or China. Regarding this, it is noteworthy that the large dragon-pattern sword with a ringed pommel in the possession of the Tokyo National Museum, considered a product of Tae Kaya based on the dragon pattern, also has inlaid inscriptions. The inscriptional style and the inlay technique are quite similar to those of inscribed iron daggers excavated from the Sakitama-Inariyama tomb. Similarly, the inscribed ring-handled large sword excavated from Tomb 11 at Kyo-dong in Ch'angnyŏng from the same period has the same hanging arc pattern 綾森文 found in horse gear from Tae Kaya inscribed on its side (Tōno Haruyuki 1992). Like the large dragon-and-phoenix sword with a round handle excavated from the neighboring Tomb 10 at Kyo-dong, this may also have been a product of Tae Kaya (Figure 3.6).

Therefore, given that the inscriptional style seen in the inlaid inscription on the iron dagger recovered from the Sakitama-Inariyama tomb is similar to that of the large sword with a round handle in the Tokyo National Museum, and since other large swords with inlaid inscriptions were manufactured in Tae Kaya, we can hypothesize that they were manufactured in the Japanese archipelago by artisans from Tae Kaya (Pak Ch'ŏn-su 2009b). We can also infer from these objects that Tae Kaya had developed a relative proficiency in the use of writing in Chinese and that artisans from Tae Kaya must have participated in producing large inscribed swords in the Japanese archipelago during the late fifth century.

In the same period, Wa elites distributed large swords with inscriptions produced by Tae Kaya artisans as prestige items among powerful clans in various regions. The system of distributing large ornamental swords as prestige items in the Japanese archipelago is similar to the sword system of Tae Kaya, which used large ornamental swords like the gilt-bronze–decorated dragon-and-phoenix–patterned large ring-handled swords and the silver-decorated large swords with a pentagon handle as prestige items to control its territory. Unlike the system of crown distribution in Silla and Paekche, the system in Tae Kaya and Wa during this period was based on ornamental large swords.

The gold and gilt-bronze ornaments and horse gear, among the material culture that Tae Kaya transmitted to the Japanese archipelago during the late fifth century, indicate the qualitative difference between the competitive power of Tae Kaya and Kŭmgwan Kaya, as these items were far superior in quality to the iron artifacts transmitted from Kŭmgwan Kaya to Japan in the

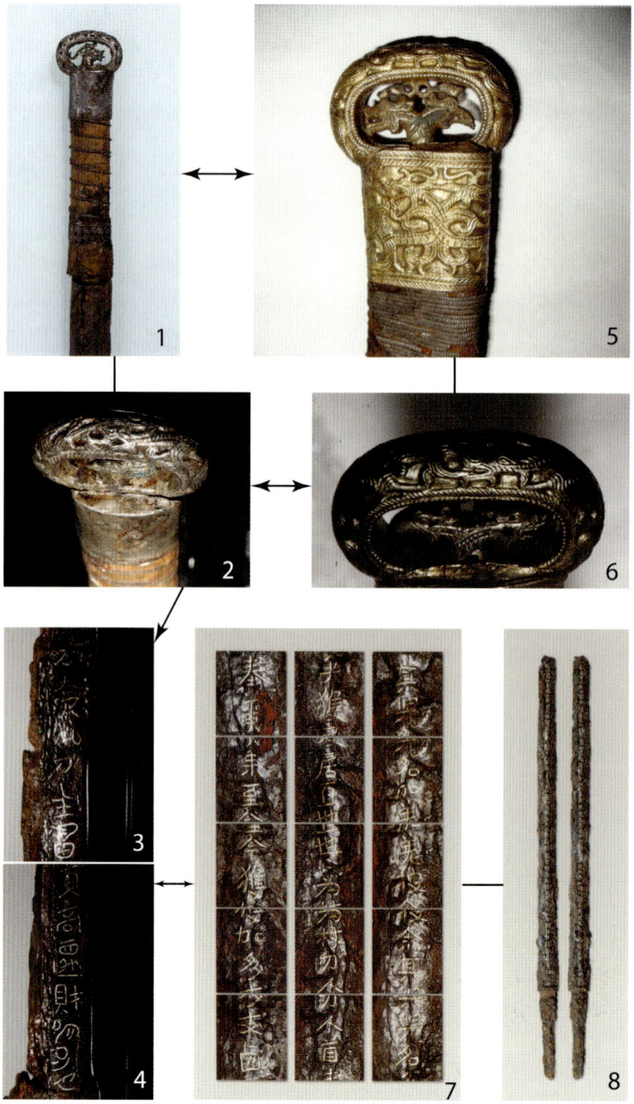

Figure 3.6 Genealogy of Large Swords with Inlaid Inscriptions of the Late Fifth Century from the Japanese Archipelago. 1–4. Articles excavated in the Kaya region; 5–6. Tomb M4 at Okchŏn in Hapch'ŏn; 7–8. Inariyama tomb in Saitama.

fourth century. Also, Tae Kaya contributed to the societies of the Japanese archipelago by sending horses and the techniques to raise them and by fully developing the use of writing, essential to improving its political system.

By the early sixth century, Paekche had occupied the four districts of Imna and Taesa-jin, and as a result Tae Kaya lost its control of the sea route along the southern coast as well as its trade ports. Along with this occupation, Paekche-produced cultural artifacts far superior to those produced in Tae Kaya entered the Japanese archipelago, and trade between Tae Kaya and the archipelago dwindled, reflecting Tae Kaya's decline.

Interchange Between Tae Kaya and Wa During the Sixth Century

In the early sixth century, when Paekche made a significant foray into the Yŏngsan River basin and the Kaya region, the import of material culture from the Kaya region into the Japanese archipelago rapidly decreased, while imports from Paekche briskly increased. Paekche material culture flowed into the Japanese archipelago in the early sixth century in accordance with Wa's need to import culture associated with Buddhism and Confucianism, advanced forms of religion essential to the improvement of its political system. Wa did not have to depend on Kaya as much as before, because it had begun to produce iron in the archipelago and no longer needed to import iron ingots from Kaya.

At this time, keyhole-shaped tombs began to appear in the Yŏngsan River basin in Honam. Scholars have two contrasting theories regarding the occupants of these keyhole-shaped tombs. Some argue that they were Wa leaders, while others argue that they were indigenous leaders. However, they could not have been indigenous leaders for the following reasons. First, they appeared abruptly and are unrelated to the nearby tombs of indigenous leaders, especially those in the Pannam 潘南 cemetery in Naju and the Pongdŏng-ni 鳳德里 cemetery in Koch'ang 高敞, the largest settlement centers of the time in the Honam region. Second, these tombs were built during only a single generation. Third, the styles of the mound, the ritual use of *haniwa*, the structure of the stone chambers, and the burial goods are all characteristic of Wa.

Given the following facts, we can surmise that those interred in the keyhole-shaped tombs in the Yŏngsan River basin were Paekche officials with a Wa lineage, dispatched from the Paekche court to this region in order to check the power of the indigenous clans, develop diplomatic relations with the Japanese archipelago, and subjugate Tae Kaya. First, the construction of these tombs was limited to the late Ungjin 熊津 period (475–538) of

Paekche. Second, their locations were intentionally spatially scattered. Third, an ornamental wood coffin, gilt-bronze crown, and horse gear—all products of Paekche—were buried in the Sindŏk 新德 tomb in Hamp'yŏng, and Chinese ceramics of a type known to have been imported to Paekche were buried in the Yongdu-ri 龍頭里 tomb in Haenam (Pak Ch'ŏn-su 2002).

Paekche is likely to have dispatched Wa people to the Yŏngsan River basin since its government, temporarily in disarray after the fall of Hansŏng in 475, did not have the capacity to rule the southern region on its own after moving its capital from Hansŏng to Ungjin. It certainly did not have sufficient military power to wage war against both Koguryŏ and Tae Kaya. Arms and armor buried in Wa-style tombs, including the keyhole-shaped tombs, indicate that those interred there played a military role.

During this period, tombs with stone-lined chambers as the main burial pit, such as northern Kyushu-style tombs, appeared in the Kaya region, including Tomb 1 at Kyŏngsan-ni 景山里 and Tomb 1 at Ungong-ni 雲谷里 in Ŭiryŏng 宜寧; Tomb 1 at Songhak-tong in Kosŏng; the Sŏnjin-ni 船津里 tomb in Sach'ŏn; and the Changmok 長木 tomb in Kŏje 巨濟. Those interred in these Wa-style tombs cannot be indigenous leaders, as they all appeared abruptly without any relation to indigenous leadership lineages in the surrounding areas, as in the case of the occupants of the keyhole-shaped tombs in the Yŏngsan River region, the stone-lined chamber B of Tomb 1 at Songhak-tong being an exception. In addition, the fact that they were built for only a single generation, along with the structure of the stone chambers, the ritual use of *haniwa*, and the types of burial goods, shows that these tombs could not have been those of the indigenous leaders. Those interred in these Wa-style tombs in the Kaya region appear to have been elites from the Chikugogawa 筑後川 and Hikawa 氷川 regions, where the Tae Kaya–produced goods were buried and similar-style tombs were concentrated. Also, judging from the region in which these tombs were constructed and the style of the burial goods they contained, especially prestige items produced in Tae Kaya, those interred in the Wa-style tombs in the Kaya region must have been Wa individuals with a connection to Tae Kaya.

From the abundance of battle gear included as burial goods, it appears likely that those interred in these Wa-style tombs in the Kaya territories were Wa individuals transplanted by Tae Kaya and So Kaya to check the diplomatic and military activities of Paekche, the Japanese archipelago, and Silla. They would in particular have served to check the actions in support of Paekche of those buried in the keyhole-shaped tombs on the Yŏngsan River, who had been settled in that region by Paekche for a similar purpose.

The keyhole-shaped tombs on the Yŏngsan River and the Wa-style tombs in the Kaya region are dispersed and arranged with the regions of Kimun, Taesa, and the four districts of Imna in the middle. This arrangement, along with the facts that the period of their construction was limited to the early sixth century and that each tomb contained prestige items from either Paekche or Tae Kaya, suggests that Wa people from northern Kyushu were employed by both Paekche and Tae Kaya to serve as troops in the struggles of those polities to control the regions of Kimun, Taesa, and the four districts of Imna (Map 3.1).

It appears that Paekche and Tae Kaya employed powerful clans from northern Kyushu not only because of their geographical locations, but also because the leaders of these polities wanted to use the networks they each had built in the late fifth century between the East Sea and the Inland Sea coast. The royal authorities of Paekche and Tae Kaya chose powerful clans from northern Kyushu instead of those from Kinai, because those three polities had convergent goals.

After the Rebellion of Iwai in 527, mentioned in the *Nihon shoki* in the account for that year in the reign of Emperor Keitai 継体 (527) (Keitai 21/8; 2:36–37), most Paekche officials with a Wa lineage had been replaced by members of powerful clans from the Kinai region. The Wa people from northern Kyushu appear to have been active participants in the military and diplomatic spheres of both Paekche and Tae Kaya and to have functioned as agents supplying prestige goods from Paekche and Tae Kaya to their own groups and to the entire Japanese archipelago. I propose that these circumstances are consistent with the hitherto unexplained sudden rise of the Kyushu powers during the late fifth and early sixth centuries, symbolized in their construction of tombs decorated with wall murals.

In other words, the respective alliances between Paekche royalty and Wa and between Tae Kaya elites and Wa were possible only because they served Paekche's and Tae Kaya's goal of expanding their influence within the Korean peninsula and the Japanese archipelago, as well as the northern Kyushu clans' goal of strengthening their influence within the archipelago. The war between Wa elites and the powerful clans of the northern Kyushu region, symbolized by the Rebellion of Iwai in 527, has so far been understood only in the context of the alliance of the northern Kyushu clans with Silla. However, this war must have been possible because the clans in this area were at the height of their power thanks to their diplomatic efforts and the ensuing growth of their influence to a level that could threaten Wa elites.

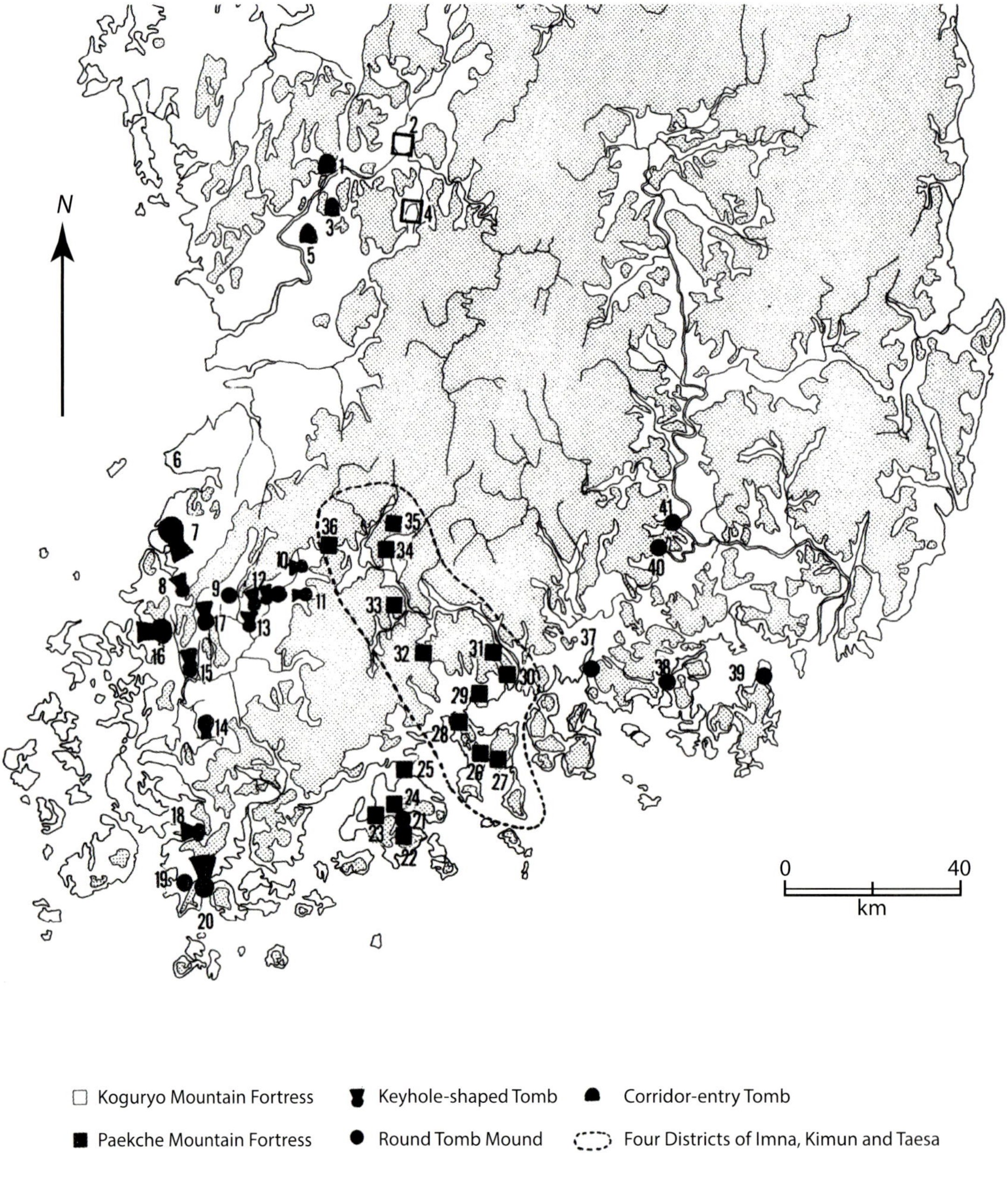
N
0
40
km
Koguryo Mountain Fortress
Keyhole-shaped Tomb
Corridor-entry Tomb
Paekche Mountain Fortress
Round Tomb Mound
Four Districts of Imna, Kimun and Taesa

The construction of keyhole-shaped tombs in the Yŏngsan River basin and the Wa-style tombs in the Kaya region ceased along with Paekche's direct rule of this area after Paekche's move of its capital to Sabi in 538, the completion of its expedition to Tae Kaya in the early sixth century, and the decline of the Kyushu clans after the Iwai Rebellion.

Interchange Between Silla and Wa During the Late Sixth Century

The following archaeological evidence suggests that there was an active interchange between Silla and Wa during the early sixth century. First, the Fujinoki tomb in Nara, the Watanuki-Kan'non'yama 綿貫観音山 tomb in Gunma 群馬 Prefecture, and the Shōgunyama 将軍山 tomb in Sakitama, in which many Silla-produced prestige items including horse gear and bronze bowls were buried, were the burial sites of Wa chiefs. Second, Silla-produced horse gear was consecrated at the state ritual site of Okinoshima in Fukuoka on the sea route between the peninsula and the archipelago.

Debate continues concerning the place of origin of the horse-riding equipment, especially the saddle, discovered in the Fujinoki tomb. Arguments have been made for its manufacture in China based on the inlaid patterns, in Silla based on the style of horse equipment, in Paekche based on manufacturing technique, and more recently and strongly, the Japanese archipelago. However, saddles excavated from the Fujinoki tomb were most likely made in Silla, judging from their structural characteristics and from other horse gear excavated with them (Kamiya Masahiro 2002; Chiga

Map 3.1 Wa-style Tombs and Related Sites in the Southern Korean Peninsula During the Early Sixth Century. 1. Horizontal-entry tomb at Tanji-ri in Kongju; 2. Namsan'gol mountain fortress in Ch'ŏngwon; 3. Horizontal-entry tomb at Anyŏng-ni in Kongju; 4. Wŏlp'yŏng-dong mountain fortress in Taejŏn; 5. Horizontal-entry tomb at Nŭngsan-ni in Puyŏ; 6. Chungmak-tong ritual site in Puan; 7. Ch'iram-ni tomb in Koch'ang; 8. Wŏlgye tomb in Yŏnggwang; 9. Yŏngch'ŏn-ni tomb in Changsŏng; 10. Kosŏng-ni tomb in Tamyang; 11. Sŏngwŏl-li tomb in Tamyang; 12. Tombs 1 and 2 at Wŏlgye-dong and the Ssangam-dong tomb in Kwangju; 13. Myŏnghwa-dong tomb in Kwangju; 14. Chara-bong tomb in Yŏngam; 15. P'yosan tomb in Hamp'yŏng; 16. Changgo-san tomb in Hamp'yŏng; 17. Sindŏk tomb in Hamp'yŏng; 18. Yongdu-ri tomb in Haenam; 19. Chosan tomb in Haenam; 20. Changgo-san tomb in Haenam; 21. Andong tomb in Kohŭng; 22. Paekch'i fortress in Kohŭng; 23. Handong-ni mountain fortress in Kohŭng; 24. Tokch'i fortress in Kohŭng; 25. Namyang-ni mountain fortress in Kohŭng; 26. Korak mountain fortress in Yŏsu; 27. Ch'ŏksan fortress in Yŏsu; 28. Kŏmdan mountain fortress in Sunch'ŏn; 29. Maro mountain fortress in Kwangyang; 30. Pongam mountain fortress in Kwangyang; 31. Puram mountain fortress in Kwangyang; 32. Sŏngam mountain fortress in Sunch'ŏn; 33. Pongsŏng mountain fortress in Kurye; 34. Hammi mountain fortress in Kurye; 35. Ch'ŏngmun-ni mountain fortress in Namwŏn; 36. Horŏmŏni mountain fortress in Sunch'ang; 37. Sŏnjin-ni tombs in Sach'ŏn; 38. Tomb 1 at Songhak-tong in Kosŏng; 39. The Changmok tomb in Kŏje; 40. Tomb 1 at Ungong-ni in Ŭiryŏng; 41. Tomb 1 at Kyŏngsan-ni in Ŭiryŏng.

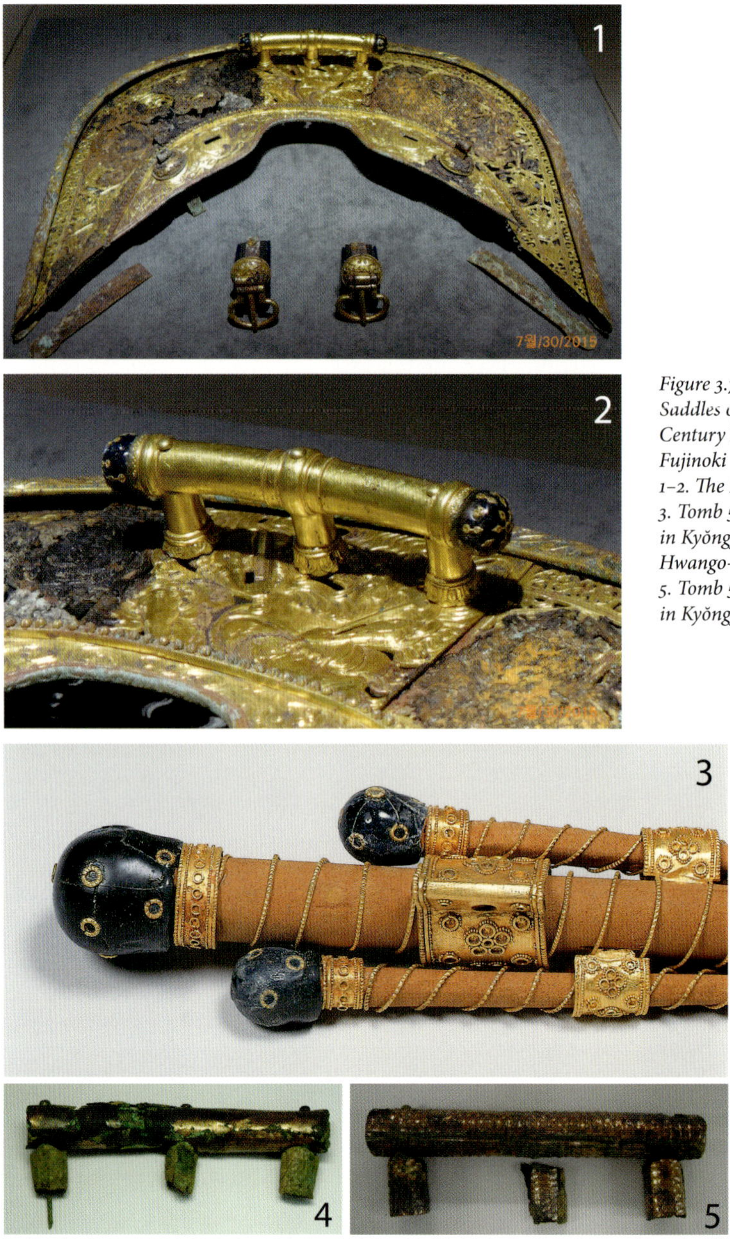

Figure 3.7 Silla-made Saddles of the Late Sixth Century Excavated from the Fujinoki Tomb in Nara. 1–2. The Fujinoki tomb; 3. Tomb 52 at Hwango-dong in Kyŏngju; 4. Tomb 37 at Hwango-dong in Kyŏngju; 5. Tomb 5A at Imdang-dong in Kyŏngju.

Hisashi 2003) (Figure 3.7). Moreover, Yi Hyŏn-jŏng discovered that saddles with a three-footed handle, similar to those excavated from the Fujinoki tomb, were concentrated in tombs in late fifth-century Silla territory, including the northern mound of the Great Tomb of Hwangnam; Tomb 37 at Hwango-dong in Kyŏngju; Tomb 5A at Imdang-dong in Kyŏngsan; and Tomb 38 at Sŏngsan-dong in Sŏngju. She argues that this distribution suggests that the three-footed handle was one of the characteristics of Silla-produced saddles (Yi Hyŏn-jŏng 2007). I interpret this finding as meaning it is highly likely that the saddles excavated from the Fujinoki tomb were products of Silla, as they are structurally similar to those found in the Silla tombs just mentioned. As this horse gear is a prestige item, it could not have been introduced to the archipelago without an interchange between the elites of Silla and Wa.

After the late sixth century, curved jadeite beads were not buried in tombs, but enshrined in ornamented Buddhist reliquaries or used as goods buried during the ground-breaking ceremony for monasteries. They were found at the wooden pagoda site and at the western main hall at the Hwangnyong Monastery 皇龍寺 and at the brick pagoda at the Punhwang Monastery 芬皇寺. Curved jadeite beads were no longer produced or used in the Korean peninsula after they had been enshrined as *sari* relics in the Sŏkka Pagoda 釋迦塔 in Pulguk Monastery 佛國寺 in the eighth century. This coincides with the period in which the use of curved jadeite stopped in the Japanese archipelago, which indicates that the supply from Wa ceased during this period. The Silla-produced bronze bowl and saddle frame excavated from Tomb 2 at Ōza-nishi 大座西 at Oki 隱岐 Island in Shimane 島根 Prefecture indicate an active use of the sea route connecting Yŏngil Bay through Ullŭng 鬱陵 Island to Oki and eventually to the mainland.

The account of the twenty-first year of the reign of Emperor Kinmei 欽明 (560) in the *Nihon shoki* records that Silla and Wa first engaged in diplomatic relations immediately after the collapse of Kaya (Kinmei 21/6; 2:118–119). We can understand this to indicate that Silla dispatched a mission to Wa at that time as a political gesture related to the impending collapse of Tae Kaya in 562. At a time when Silla had already brought the southern part of Kaya into its domain and was forging plans to incorporate the northern regions as well, Silla would have needed to sever the military alliance between Paekche and Wa.

In 555 Paekche sent its final mission to Wa headed by Prince Hye 惠 after having previously dominated interchange with the archipelago. There

Figure 3.8 Chinese Ceramics of the Late Sixth Century Excavated from the Sōroku Tomb in Nagasaki, with Related Data.
1, 2, and 4. Sōroku tomb; 3. Anapchi in Kyŏngju;
5. Sŏk-tong cemetery 石洞古墳群 *in Chinhae* 鎮海.

followed a twenty-year period during which no exchanges between the two polities took place. From this it can be surmised that Silla proposed to the Wa court that it replace Paekche as the supplier of cultural products to the archipelago (Kim Ŭn-suk 1994). During this period, when the Southern Courts of China collapsed and the political and cultural center shifted to northern China, the relationship between Paekche and China became distant, and Silla built strong ties with the Northern Courts after occupying the lower reaches of the Han River. This was also followed by Wa's import of advanced culture from Silla instead of Paekche (Kim Hyŏn-gu 1985).

In relation to this change, it is noteworthy that a white-glazed bowl with green color featuring circle reliefs, was excavated from the Sōroku 双六 tomb at Iki 壱岐 in Nagasaki 長崎 Prefecture. This bowl has a form similar to that of a bowl excavated in Northern Qi, and a similar article was excavated from Anapchi Pond 雁鴨池 in Kyŏngju. Excavation of pottery vessels in the style of late Silla and of Silla-produced horse gear from the Sōroku tomb at Iki along with the bowl indicates that it must have been introduced to the archipelago via Silla (Yuba Tadanori 2006: 90) (Figure 3.8). Moreover, the bronze water bottle excavated from the Watanuki-Kan'non'yama tomb in Gunma is similar to an artifact excavated from the tomb of Shedi Huiluo 厍狄迴洛 in Northern Qi. Scholars think that the water bottle must have made its way to the archipelago either directly from China or via Paekche, as it was excavated together with the same kind of mirror as that excavated from the tomb of Paekche's King Muryŏng 武寧王 (r. 501–523). However, given the historical circumstances of this period as well as the facts that no other Chinese goods were recovered from this tomb and that the water bottle was accompanied by Silla-produced horse gear, it would be more reasonable to conclude that the bottle had not come directly from China, but via Silla.

As Silla occupied the lower reaches of the Han River from the 550s, it would have secured an advantageous position in its interchanges with China. Silla's occupation of the eastern part of the southern coast that had previously been held by Kaya made it difficult for Paekche and Wa to trade with each other. In other words, this change in geopolitics forced Wa to import elements of advanced culture from China through Silla instead of Paekche.

Political Change in the Japanese Archipelago Seen Through the Ancient Interchange Between Korea and Japan

The very-large-scale keyhole-shaped tombs in the Japanese archipelago first appeared in the southeastern part of the Nara basin in the mid-third century, moved to the northern region of Nara, and then moved again to the southern Osaka region during the late fourth to early fifth centuries. There are two theories about the shift in location of this type of tomb from northern Nara to southern Osaka: one explains it as the removal of the site of burial to a new location and the other as the removal of the center of political power.

According to a recent study, the Gosashi 五社神 tomb (length 276 m), which had been thought to be a royal tomb and among the earliest tombs in the Saki 佐紀 cemetery, was in fact one of the latest in that cemetery (Shiraishi Taichirō 2008: 452). Therefore, we have to revise the previous theory that royal power had already shifted to the south of Osaka at the time of the Tsudō-Shiroyama 津堂城山 tomb (length 208 m) in the late fourth century. We should instead presume that the stronghold of Wa power was located in the northern Nara basin during the late fourth century.

The locus of Wa power shifted three times during the fourth to sixth centuries. It was first transferred during the period in which the placement of very-large-scale keyhole-shaped tombs (those thought to be royal burials), shifted from the southeastern to the northern part of the Nara basin in the early fourth century. The next transfer of royal power occurred in the early fifth century, the period in which tomb-building shifted from the Nara basin to the Osaka plain. The third transfer occurred in the early sixth century, the period in which tomb-building moved from the southern to the northern part of the Osaka plain. This continuation and interruption of elite power in the Japanese archipelago, manifested in the shifting of the building of very-large-scale keyhole-shaped tombs, was closely related to changing circumstances in the southern Korean peninsula. In particular, the establishment of the Kawachi 河内 dynasty and that of the Keitai dynasty were related to interchanges with the royal powers in Silla and Paekche, indicating the important role played by external factors.

First, let us take a look at circumstances influencing the shifting of tomb-building from the southeastern Nara basin to the Saki cemetery in the northern Nara basin in the context of the political situation in the Korean peninsula. The Makimuku 纏向 site, representing a large-scale settlement associated with the Ōyamato 大和 and Yanagimoto 柳本 cemeteries, rapidly declined during the period in which the very-large-scale keyhole-shaped tombs were built at the Saki cemetery. Therefore, I argue that powerful elites in the southeastern Nara basin moved not just the location of their graveyards but also their entire locus of power to the north.

It is noteworthy that the Lelang and Daifang commanderies collapsed under Koguryŏ's attack in 313. These events resulted in the obstruction of the route by which the power holders in the southeastern Nara basin imported Chinese artifacts, including prestige items like bronze mirrors featuring rims in triangular cross-section and divine animal motifs (三角緣神獸鏡). Accordingly, their ability to command royal power in the Japanese archipelago declined, since this had been largely based on their ability to display their access to Chinese authority as embodied in such Chinese prestige items as these mirrors. During this period, iron ingots, iron helmets and armor, and cylindrical bronze implements like those buried in the Taesŏng-dong cemetery were exported to the Japanese archipelago and buried in the tombs of powerful leaders there. The appearance of Kinai-produced prestige items in the Taesŏng-dong cemetery in Kimhae at this time cannot be a coincidence. It was probably related to the activities of the newly emerging power holders based in the northern Kinai basin. This newly emerging group must have acquired hegemony within the central group in Kinai by bringing cylindrical bronze implements and iron items from Kŭmgwan Kaya, replacing the Chinese prestige items previously imported by way of its military alliance with Kŭmgwan Kaya.

Therefore, from the Kŭmgwan Kaya–produced iron artifacts introduced to the Japanese archipelago in the late fourth century and the bronze spiral ornaments and jadeite ornaments excavated from the Taesŏng-dong cemetery in Kimhae, we can surmise that Kŭmgwan Kaya had maintained exchanges with the Saki 佐紀 group, which commanded power in the Kinai region during this period. It appears that the Saki group distributed prestige items such as bronze spiral ornaments and jadeite ornaments in exchange for the bronze mirrors with divine animal motifs (Tanaka Shinsaku 2009). The Saki group likely obtained power by introducing iron goods and prestige items from Kŭmgwan Kaya, replacing the southeastern Nara basin group that declined when its interchange with China was hindered after Koguryŏ destroyed Lelang and Daifang in 313. In light of the philological data that describe Wa's retreat to Imna Kara, along with archaeological data like the Kŭmgwan Kaya–produced artifacts in the Japanese archipelago and the Kinai-produced artifacts in the Taesŏng-dong cemetery, I surmise that it was the Saki group that waged war against Koguryŏ in 400.

It is noteworthy that Silla-produced horse gear, iron ingots, and iron helmets suddenly appear in the Kurazuka 鞍塚 tomb and the Shukinzuka 珠金塚 tomb next to the Nakatsuyama 仲津山 tomb (traditionally the tomb of Nakatsu-hime 仲津媛; length 286 m) in the Furuichi 古市 cemetery, built in the late fourth to early fifth centuries. Similar items also appear abruptly in the Shichikan 七観 tomb, which is an attendant tomb of the

Figure 3.9 Mozu Tumulus Group in Osaka.
Photograph courtesy of Sakai-shi Kyōiku Iinkai 堺市教育委員會 (Sakai Municipal Board of Education).

Kami-ishizu-Misanzai 上石津ミサンザイ tomb (traditionally the tomb of Emperor Richū 履中天皇, length 365 m) in the Mozu 百舌鳥 cemetery. Scholars have considered the horse gear recovered from both tombs to be products of Kŭmgwan Kaya, based on their similarity to the horse gear excavated from the Pokch'ŏn-dong cemetery in Pusan. But, judging from the similarity in form, they are clearly products of Silla dating to the period when the horse gear from the outer coffins 3 and 4 of Tomb 109 at Hwangnam-dong in Kyŏngju was produced (Pak Ch'ŏn-su 2009a). Moreover, curved jadeite beads of the same high quality as those excavated from Tomb G6 at Imdang-dong in Kyŏngsan and Tomb Ka-13 at Wŏlsŏng-no in Kyŏngju also appeared suddenly during the same period.

In short, horse gear from Silla was introduced to southern Osaka and curved jadeite beads from the Japanese archipelago were introduced to Silla before the early fifth century. As curved jadeite beads were mainly buried in tombs in the southern Osaka region, such as the Koganezuka 黃金塚 tomb and the Shukinzuka tomb, the curved jadeite beads recovered in Silla are likely to have been imported from the southern Osaka group.

Accordingly, we can surmise that the newly emerging southern Osaka authority had already begun exchanges with Silla during the time when Kŭmgwan Kaya was engaged in interchange with the Saki group, which obtained power in the northern Nara basin. In other words, during the time when very-large-scale keyhole-shaped tomb construction shifted from northern Nara to southern Osaka, and especially when the Konda Gobyōyama Tomb (traditional tomb of Ōjin) and Daisen Tomb (traditional tomb of Nintoku) were built, Wa elites changed their trading partner from Kŭmgwan Kaya to Silla. As the two powerful groups in the late fourth century, one located in northern Nara and the other in southern Osaka, interchanged with Kŭmgwan Kaya and Silla, respectively, their rise and fall were closely influenced by the rise and fall of their partners.

As a result of the southward advance of Koguryŏ in 400, the Saki group of northern Nara, in alliance with Kŭmgwan Kaya, declined, while the emerging southern Osaka group obtained royal power.

Accordingly, I argue that the shift in the location of very-large-scale keyhole-shaped tombs from northern Nara to southern Osaka is not a simple removal of a burial ground, but instead a dynastic shift. Moreover, the prosperity of the Kawachi dynasty that constructed the very-large-scale keyhole-shaped tombs was possible because of the introduction of basic necessities such as iron, of prestige items such as gold goods, and of artisans skilled in advanced technologies (Figure 3.9). We can also surmise that Silla had engaged in interchange with Wa, in which it exported iron to Wa, a result of which was a military alliance through which Silla could counter the pressures exerted upon it by Koguryŏ and thereby maintain its own security. It is against this background that Silla was able to advance towards the area east of the Naktong River and the eastern coast of the peninsula, which previously had been held by Koguryŏ.

However, in the late fifth century, artifacts produced by Tae Kaya found in Japan replaced those produced by Silla. It appears that Tae Kaya, because of its iron production, influenced not only traffic between Paekche and Wa but also traffic between Wa and China during this period by securing control of the sea routes along the southern coast, along with developing the Sŏmjin River route. Accordingly, Tae Kaya, although located inland, secured competitive superiority over Silla and Paekche by trading with Wa. This also reflects that Silla no longer needed Wa after securing the region east of the Naktong River and the eastern coast, freeing itself from Koguryŏ's pressure.

Tae Kaya, previously understood as a minor inland polity, emerged in the late fifth century through sea trade, exporting iron, gold, and gilt-bronze items produced inland to the entire Japanese archipelago. The independent dispatch of an envoy by Tae Kaya to Southern Qi in China in 479 supports this theory of its activities through sea routes along the southern coast.

Material culture of this period produced by Tae Kaya include gold and gilt-bronze ornaments, gilt-bronze horse gear, horses, and horse-breeding methods. In addition, Tae Kaya appears to have contributed to the societies of the Japanese archipelago by introducing the use of writing. Tae Kaya–produced culture and artifacts in the Japanese archipelago demonstrate the power of Tae Kaya in the regional context, one that may have equaled that of Silla and Paekche in the late fifth century.

The agent of interchange with Wa elites in the Korean peninsula shifted during the early sixth century, a period when the Imashirozuka 今城塚 tomb in Osaka, considered to be the tomb of Emperor Keitai, was constructed following the migration of Wa elites from south to north.

Around the early sixth century, the source for the artifacts exported to the Japanese archipelago changed from Tae Kaya to Paekche, and at the same time, Japanese artifacts, previously imported to the Kaya region, were found concentrated in the Yŏngsan River basin under Paekche's control. Paekche-produced artifacts in the Eta-Funayama tomb in Kumamoto, as well as the umbrella-pine (*kōyamaki* 高野槇) from the Japanese archipelago used as coffin material in the tomb of King Muryŏng, symbolize that Paekche took the initiative in the interchange with the Japanese archipelago, surpassing Kaya, which previously had dominated trade with Wa since the late fourth century.

The relationship between King Muryŏng and Emperor Keitai is also confirmed through the mirror with human figures recovered from the Suda-Hachiman Shrine 隅田八幡神社 in Wakayama. The inscription on this mirror names both Muryŏng and Keitai (as Sama 斯麻 and Futo 孚弟, respectively), and gives the year of its manufacture as 503, the year after King Muryŏng's coronation according to philological studies, before Keitai's enthronement. This date is confirmed by the mirror's form as well (Kurumazaki Masahiko 1993).

In relation to this, it is also very noteworthy that beginning in the early sixth century Paekche-produced artifacts and Paekche-style pillar-wall building sites came to be concentrated in the Wakasa 若狭 Bay region and on the shores of Lake Biwa 琵琶湖, areas associated with Keitai facing the East Sea. Such sites include the Jūzen'nomori 十善の森 tomb in Fukui Prefecture and the Kamo-Inariyama 鴨稲荷山 tomb in Shiga. It appears that the Kyushu authority, which had formed a large network around the area near the East Sea and the Inland Sea, played the role of mediator between Paekche royalty and the Keitai dynasty with regard to Keitai's enthronement. This is supported by the fact that the main form of burial for powerful leaders in the Hokuriku 北陸 region is the Kyushu-style stone chamber, an example being the Jūzen'nomori tomb in Fukui, a tomb related to Keitai.

By excluding the Kaya polities, which had traditionally held a close relationship with the Kawachi authority, in favor of accessing advanced goods through engagement with Paekche, the Keitai authorities appear to have attempted to differentiate themselves from the Kawachi in order to secure an advantage in Kinai. Accordingly, we can surmise that such interchange with the peninsular polities played an important role in the shifts of power within the Kinai central polity. It is also worth noting that there was probably a mutual connection between the political changes in Wa during the shift of power from Yūryaku to Keitai, and the political changes in Paekche during the shift of power from Tongsŏng 東城王 (r. 479–501) to Muryŏng.

Conclusion

Based solely on the written sources, the relationship between the peninsula and the archipelago after the late fourth century has been understood in terms of Paekche's continuing initiation of an interchange with Wa, with Kaya depending on this relationship and Silla having a consistently antagonistic relationship with Wa. However, archaeological evidence reveals that Kŭmgwan Kaya–produced artifacts were introduced into the Japanese archipelago while many prestige items produced in the archipelago were included as burial goods in the Taesŏng-dong cemetery, a cemetery for the elite tombs of Kŭmgwan Kaya. Such exchanges occurred even during the late fourth century, a time in which there was a record of interchanges between Paekche and Wa and during which the seven-branched sword of the Isonokami Shrine 石上神宮 in Tenri 天理 was introduced to the archipelago. Likewise, even during the late fifth century, artifacts from Tae Kaya were introduced to the Japanese archipelago and vice versa, suggesting that the center for interchange between the peninsula and the archipelago was Tae Kaya during this period, as it had been Kŭmgwan Kaya during the late fourth century.

3 Kaya, Silla, and Wa —Park Cheun Soo

Although there had been continuous political interchange between Paekche and Wa from the late fourth century, considering the peninsula-produced artifacts in the Japanese archipelago and the archipelago-produced artifacts in the Korean peninsula, the major player in the interchange between peninsula and archipelago was clearly Kaya before the fifth century, the time when the keyhole-shaped tombs appeared in the Yŏngsan River basin and Paekche-produced artifacts were imported into the archipelago.

Moreover, although the relationship between Silla and Wa has been traditionally understood, based solely on philological data, to be one of hostility, we see quite a different picture when we examine the archaeological data. Not only did the interchange between the two polities last through the Three Kingdoms period, but Silla moreover emerged as the center of this interchange during the early fifth and late sixth centuries. This suggests the limitations of the traditional study of Korea-Japan relations, which has been based solely on philological data.

The exclusion of Kaya from the ancient history of Korea-Japan interchanges, the focus on the relationship between Paekche and Wa, and the view that the relationship between Silla and Wa was one of consistent hostility can all be explained in the context of international relations in the eighth century. It is relevant that Paekche historical material was utilized in the compilation of the *Nihon shoki*. Migrants from Paekche, who were hostile to Silla and considered Kaya a subordinate polity, participated in its compilation. Now we can determine that the relationship between Silla and Wa was not consistently hostile, but varied over time, ranging from peace to war.

Korea-Japan relations during the Three Kingdoms period were not always constant, but very complicated and dynamic depending on the political situation of both regions.

I expect that in the future Korea-Japan relations during the Three Kingdoms period will be illuminated by combining rich archaeological data from both countries with philological data, rather than depending solely on the latter.

Powerful clans, including the uppermost elites of the Japanese archipelago, had to rely on the southern Korean peninsula for iron, the most important material necessity, until the fifth century. They also had to import cultural goods, including prestige items from the Korean peninsula, in order to maintain their authority. Paekche, Silla, and Kaya also needed to form diplomatic and military alliances with Wa in order to defeat each other. It is difficult to deny that Wa was in a relatively advantageous position in

Korea-Japan relations, because the Korean peninsula was divided into four competing polities. We should remember, however, that Wa was a polity that had to depend on the Korean peninsula for certain necessities. In particular, the collapse of interregional iron trade networks during the early fifth century due to the decline of Kŭmgwan Kaya made it inevitable that Wa would approach Silla. Likewise, we can surmise that a similar situation was created in the late sixth century as a result of Silla's advance to the Han River basin and to the southern peninsular coast after the collapse of Kaya.

The fact that the ancient relationship between the archipelago and the peninsula has always been portrayed as one of invasion, confrontation, domination, and subjugation can be understood as the result of looking at the relationship between Silla and Wa as one of antagonism. This approach needs to be thoroughly revised.

Also, although dynastic change in the Japanese archipelago has been understood mainly in the context of internal factors or through a vague East Asian context, I have tried to discuss external factors in this study, especially since the emergence and flourishing of the Kawachi dynasty was related to its interchange with Silla and the emergence of the Keitai dynasty to its interchange with Paekche.

3 Kaya, Silla, and Wa
—Park Cheun Soo

References

Chiga Hisashi 千賀久

2003 Nihon shutsudo "Shiragikei" basōgu no keifu 日本出土『新羅系』馬装具の系譜 [The genealogy of "Silla-lineage" horse trappings excavated in Japan]. In *Higashi Ajia to Nihon no kōkogaku 3: Kōryū to kōeki* 東アジアと日本の考古学 3: 交流と交易 [Archaeology of East Asia and Japan, vol. 3: Exchange and trade], edited by Gotō Tadashi 後藤直 and Mogi Masahiro 茂木雅博, pp. 101–127. Dōseisha 同成社, Tokyo.

Ch'oe Ŭn-ju 崔恩珠

1986 Han'guk kogok ŭi yŏn'gu 韓國 曲玉의 硏究 [Study of Korea's curved jades]. *Sungsil Sahak* 崇實史學 4: 1–150.

Chŏn Yŏng-nae 全榮來

1985 Paekche nambang kyŏngyŏk ŭi pyŏnch'ŏn 百濟南方境域의 變遷 [Vicissitudes of the southern border of Paekche]. In *Ch'ŏn Kwan-u Sŏnsaeng hwannyŏk kinyŏm Han'guk sahak nonch'ong* 千寬宇先生還曆記念韓國史學論叢 [Ch'on Kwan-u's sixtieth birthday commemoration issue of the Korean Historical Studies Collection of Treatises], edited by Ch'ŏn Kwan-u Sŏnsaeng Hwannyŏk Kinyŏm Han'guk Sahak Nonch'ong Kanhaeng Wiwŏnhoe 千寬宇先生還曆紀念韓國史學論叢刊行委員會, pp. 135–162. Chŏngŭm Munhwasa 정음문화사, Seoul.

Isahaya Naoto 諫早直人

2012 *Tōhoku Ajia ni okeru kiba bunka no kōkogakuteki kenkyū* 東北アジアにおける騎馬文化の考古学的研究 [An archaeological study of horse-riding culture in Northeast Asia], Yūzankaku 雄山閣, Tokyo.

Kamiya Masahiro 神谷正弘

2002 Fujinoki kufun shutsudo kondō sōan ni tsuite 藤ノ木古墳出土金銅装鞍について [On the gilt-bronze decorated saddle excavated from the Fujinoki tomb]. *Kōkogaku Jānaru* 考古学ジャーナル 482: 17–20.

Kawamura Yoshimitsu 河村好光

1995 Umi o watatte kita zoku-gata hekigyoku seihin 海をわたってきた鏃形碧玉製品 [Arrowhead-shaped jadeite ornaments from across the sea]. In *Tembō kōkogaku: Kōkogaku Kenkyūkai 40-shūnen kinen ronshū* 展望考古学: 考古学研究会40周年記念論集 [Collection of papers commemorating the fortieth anniversary of the Archaeological Society of Japan], edited by Kōkogaku Kenkyūkai 考古学研究会 [Archaeological Society of Japan], pp. 117–124. Kōkogaku Kenkyūkai, Okayama.

Kim Hyŏn-gu 金鉉球

1985 *Yamato seiken no taigai kankei kenkyū* 大和政権の対外関係研究 [A study of interregional relations of the Yamato court]. Yoshikawa Kōbunkan 吉川弘文館, Tokyo.

Kim T'ae-sik 김태식
2002 *Miwan ŭi munmyŏng ch'ilbaengnyŏn Kayasa* 미완의 문명 7백년 가야사 [The incomplete history of seven hundred years of Kaya]. 3 vols. Purun Yŏksa 푸른역사, Seoul.
Kim Ŭn-suk 金恩淑
1994 6-segi huban Silla-wa Wae-guk ŭi kukkyo sŏngnip kwajŏng 6世紀 後半 新羅와 倭國의 國交成立過程 [The process of establishing the diplomatic relationship between Silla and Wa in the late sixth century]. In *Silla ŭi taeoe kwan'gyesa yŏn'gu* 新羅의對外關係史硏究 [Studies of the history of Silla's interregional relations], edited by Silla Munhwajae Haksul Palp'yohoe 新羅文化祭學術發表會, pp. 179–223. Silla Munhwa Sŏnyanghoe 新羅文化宣揚會, Kyŏngju.
Kimura Makoto 木村誠
2005 Chōsen Sangoku to Wa 朝鮮三国と倭 [The Three Kingdoms of Korea and Wa]. In *Kodai o kangaeru: Nihon to Chōsen* 考える: 日本と朝鮮 [Considering the ancient past: Japan and Korea], edited by Takeda Yukio 武田幸男, pp. 90–91. Yoshikawa Kōbunkan 吉川弘文館, Tokyo.
Kobayashi Toshio 小林敏男
2004 Nihon kodai kokka keisei katei: 5-6 seiki o chūshin ni 日本古代国家形成過程: 五' 六世紀を中心に [The state formation processes of ancient Japan: Focused on the fifth and sixth centuries]. In *Shinbojiomu Wajin no kuni kara Nihon e: Higashi Ajia kara miru Nihon kodai kokka no kigen* シンポジウム倭人のクニから日本へ: 東アジアからみる日本古代国家の起源 [Symposium: From the country of the Wa people to Japan: The origins of the ancient Japanese state in East Asia], edited by Suzuki Yasutami 鈴木靖民 and Ueda Masaaki 上田正昭, pp. 88–105. Gakuseisha 学生社, Tokyo.
Kurumazaki Masahiko 車崎正彦
1993 Wa kyō no sakusha 倭鏡の作者 [The makers of Wa mirrors]. In Tokushū: Kagami no kataru kodai-shi 特集: 鏡の語る古代史 [Mirrors speak of ancient history], special issue, *Kikan Kōkogaku* 季刊考古學 43: 68–72.
Murakami Einosuke 村上英之介
1993 Kankoku Fukusendō kofun tettei no biryō seibun bunseki to jakkan no kōsatsu 韓国福泉洞古墳鉄鋌の微量成分分析と若干の考察 [Trace component analysis of iron ingots from the Pokch'ŏn-dong cemetery in Korea and some considerations]. In *Kodaigaku hyōron* 古代学評論 [Review of the study of ancient times], Vol. 3, edited by Kodai o Kangaeru Kai 古代を考える会, pp. 131–138. Kodai o Kangaeru Kai, Osaka.
Ōga Katsuhiko 大賀克彦
2005 Inadō kofun-gun no tama-rui ni tsuite: Kofun jidai chūki kōhan ni okeru tama no densei 稲童古墳群の玉類について: 古墳時代中期後半における玉の伝世

[On the jade from the Inadō cemetery: Inheritance of the jade of the latter half of the middle Kofun period]. In *Inadō kofun-gun: Fukuoka-ken Yukuhashi-shi Inadō shozai no Inadō kofun-gun chōsa hōkoku* 稲童古墳群: 福岡県行橋市稲童所在の稲童古墳群調査報告 [The Inadō cemetery: Report of investigations of the Inadō cemetery at Inadō in Yukuhashi City, Fukuoka Prefecture], edited by Yukuhashi-shi Kyōiku Iinkai 行橋市教育委員会, pp. 286–297. Yukuhashi-shi Kyōiku Iinkai, Yukuhashi.

Pak Ch'ŏn-su (Pak Cheun Soo) 朴天秀

1995 Torai-kei bumbutsu kara mita Kaya to Wa ni okeru seijiteki hendō 渡来系文物からみた伽耶と倭における政治的変動 [Political change in Kaya and Wa seen through imported goods]. In *Machikaneyama ronsō Shigaku hen* 待兼山論叢 史学篇 [Memoirs of the faculty of arts at Osaka University history section] 29, pp. 53–84. Ōsaka Daigaku Bungakubu 大阪大学文学部, Osaka.

———

1998 Kōkogaku kara mita kodai no Kan-Ni kōshō 考古学から見た古代の韓·日交渉 [Ancient Korea-Japan exchanges seen through archaeology]. *Seikyū Gakujutsu Ronshū* 青丘学術論集 12: 77–122.

———

2001 Sankoku-Kofun jidai ni okeru Kan-Nichi kōshō 三国·古墳時代における韓·日交渉 [Korea-Japan exchanges during the Three Kingdoms and Kofun periods]. In *Torai bunka no nami: 5–6 seki no Kii no kuni o saguru* 渡来文化の波: 5–6世紀の紀伊国を探る [Waves of culture from abroad: Exploring the Kii polity of the fifth and sixth centuries], edited by Wakayama Shiritsu Hakubutsukan 和歌山市立博物館, pp. 69–90. Wakayama Shiritsu Hakubutsukan, Wakayama.

———

2002 Eisan-kō ryūiki ni okeru zempō-kōen-fun no hisōsha no shutsuji to sono seikaku 栄山江流域における前方後円墳の被葬者の出自とその性格 [The origin and nature of those buried in the keyhole tombs in the Yŏngsan River basin]. *Kōkogaku Kenkyū* 考古学研究 49(2): 42–59.

———

2006 3–6 segi Hanbando wa Ilbon yŏlto ŭi kyosŏp 3–6世紀 韓半島와 日本列島의 交涉 [Interchange between the Korean peninsula and the Japanese archipelago between the third and sixth centuries]. *Han'guk Kogo Hakpo* 韓国考古學報 61: 4–41.

———

2007 *Saero ssŭnŭn kodae Han-Il kyosŏpsa* 새로 쓰는 고대 한일교섭사 [History of ancient Korea-Japan exchange written anew]. Sahoe P'yŏngnon 사회평론, Seoul.

———

2009a Kogohak ŭl t'onghae pon Silla wa Wae 考古學을 통해 본 新羅와 倭 [Silla and Wa viewed through archaeology]. *Hosŏ Kogohak* 湖西考古學 21: 164–197.

———

2009b *Ilbon yŏlto sok ŭi Tae Kaya munhwa* 日本列島 속의 大加耶文化 [Culture of Tae Kaya in the Japanese archipelago]. Kyŏngbuk Taehakkyo 慶北大學校 [Kyungpook National University], Taegu, Koryŏng-gun.

———

2010 *Kaya t'ogi* 加耶土器 [Kaya Pottery]. Chininjin 진인진, Seoul.

Saotome Masahiro 早乙女雅博, and Hayakawa Yasuhiro 早川康弘

1997 Nikkan kōgyoku-sei magatama no shizen kagakuteki bunseki 日本硬玉製勾玉の自然科学的分析 [Natural scientific analysis of Japanese magatama made of jadeite]. *Chōsen Gakuhō* 朝鮮学報162: 21–42.

Shiraishi Taichirō 白石太一郎

2008 Wa koku ōbo zōeichi idō no imi surumono 倭国王墓造営地移動の意味するもの [The meaning of the shift in location of Wa royal tombs]. In *Kinki chihō ni okeru ōgata kofun-gun no kisoteki kenkyū* 近畿地方における大型古墳群の基礎的研究 [Fundamental studies of the large-scale cemeteries in the Kinki region], edited by Shiraishi Taichirō, pp. 451–457. Nara Daigaku Bungakubu 奈良大学文学部, Nara.

Suematsu Yasukazu 末松保和

1949 *Mimana kōbōshi* 任那興亡史 [History of the rise and fall of Mimana]. Ōyashima Shuppan 大八洲出版, Tokyo.

Suzuki Yasutami 鈴木靖民

1995 Kaya no tetsu to Wa-ōken ni tsuite rekishi-teki paasupekutiibu 伽耶の鉄と倭王権について歴史的パースペクテイーヴ [Historical perspective of Kaya iron and the Wa central authority]. In *Nihon kodai kokka no tenkai* (Jō) 日本古代国家の展開 (上) [Development of the ancient state in Japan, vol. 1], edited by Kadowaki Teiji 門脇貞二, pp. 23–47. Shibunkaku 思文閣, Tokyo.

Takada Kanta 高田貫太

2003 5.6 seki Naktong-gang ŭi tong chiyŏk kwa Ilbon yŏlto ŭi kyosŏp e kwanhan yech'al 5.6世紀 洛東江以東地域과 日本列島의 交渉에 관한 豫察 [A study of the interchange between the area east of the Naktong River and the Japanese archipelago during the fifth and sixth centuries]. *Han'guk Kogo Hakpo* 韓國考古學報 50: 97–120.

Tanaka Shinsaku 田中晋作

2009 *Tsutsugata-dōki to seiken kōtai* 筒形銅器と政権交替 [Tube-shaped bronze objects and replacement of the central polity]. Gakuseisha 学生社, Tokyo.

Tanaka Toshiaki 田中俊明

2008 5–6 segi Namhaean chiyŏk ŭi Kaya, Paekche, Wa 5–6世紀南海岸地域의 加耶.百濟.倭 [Kaya, Paekche, and Wa on the southern coast during the fifth and sixth centuries]. In *Chŏnnam tongbu chiyŏk ŭi Kaya munhwa* 전남동부지역의 가야문화 [The culture of Kaya in the eastern part of South Chŏlla Province], edited by Sanggosa Hakhoe 上古史學會, pp. 56–88. Sanggosa Hakhoe, Sunch'ŏn.

Tōno Haruyuki 東野治之

1992 Meibun no kaidoku 銘文の解読 [Reading inscriptions]. In *Shūri hōkoku: Yūmei kantō tachi* 修理報告: 有銘環頭大刀 [Report of repairing artifacts: Inscribed swords with ring pommels], edited by Tōkyō Kokuritsu Hakubutsukan 東京国立博物館 [Tokyo National Museum], pp. 22–26. Tōkyō Kokuritsu Hakubutsukan, Tokyo.

Tsude Hiroshi 都出比呂志

1988 Kofun jidai shuchō keifu no danzoku to danzetsu 古墳時代首長系譜の断続と断絶 [Continuation and interruption in the genealogy of chiefs in the Kofun period]. In *Machikaneyama ronsō Shigaku hen* 待兼山論叢 史学篇 [Memoirs of the faculty of arts at Osaka University history section] 22, pp. 1–16. Ōsaka Daigaku Bungakubu 大阪大学文学部, [Osaka University Faculty of Letters], Osaka.

Tsukamoto Toshio 塚本敏夫

1993 Bagu (Kinki): Shoki bagu kara mita toraikei kōjin no dōkō to 5-seiki no tekki seisan taisei 馬具(近畿): 初期馬具から見た渡来系工人の動向と 5世紀の鉄器生産体制 [Horse gear (Kinki): Trends of emigrant craftsmen and the fifth-century iron production system viewed through early horse gear]. In *Kofun jidai ni okeru Chōsenkei bumbutsu no dempa*, 古墳時代における朝鮮系文物の伝播 [The spread of Korean-style artifacts in the Kofun period], Dai 34-kai maizō bunkazai kenkyū shūkai 第34埋蔵文化財研究集会 [Proceedings of the thirty-fourth Buried Cultural Properties research meeting], pp. 171–185. Maizō Bunkazai Kenkyūkai 埋蔵文化財研究会 [Japanese Association for Field Archaeologists], Nara.

Warashina Tetsuo 藁科哲男

2008 Hanbando ongnyu ŭi ihwahakchŏk punsŏk kwa yut'ong 韓半島 玉類의 理化學的 分析과 流通 [Physical and chemical analysis of jades in the Korean peninsula and their circulation]. In *Hosŏ chiyŏk ŭmnak sahoe ŭi pyŏnch'ŏn* 湖西地域 邑落社會의 變遷 [Vicissitudes of the village societies in the Hosŏ region], edited by Hosŏ Kogo Hakhoe 湖西考古學會 [Hosŏ Archaeological Society], pp. 65–75. Hosŏ Kogo Hakhoe, Ch'ŏngju.

Yi Hyŏn-jŏng 李炫娅

2007 Silla kobun ch'ult'o an'gyo sonjabi siron 신라고분 출토 안교손잡이 시론 [An essay on saddlebow handles excavated from Silla tombs]. *Yŏngnam Kogohak* 嶺南考古學 41: 5–43.

Yi Yŏng-sik 이영식

2004 Kaya wa Wae, kŭrigo "Imna Ilbonbu" 가야와 왜, 그리고 '임나일본부' [Kaya, Wa, and the "Mimana Nihonfu"]. In *Kaya, itch'yŏjin irŭm, pinnanŭn yusan* 가야 잊혀진 이름 빛나는 유산 [Kaya, forgotten name and splendid legacy], edited by Kayasa Chŏngch'aek Yŏn'gu Wiwŏnhoe 가야사정책연구위원회 [Kaya History Policy Research Committee], pp. 111–129. Hyean 혜안, Seoul.

Yŏn Min-su 延敏洙

2003 *Kodae Han-Il kyoryusa* 古代韓日交流史 [History of ancient Korea-Japan relations]. Hyean 혜안, Seoul.

Yuba Noritomo 弓場紀知

2006 Iki Sōroku Kofun shutsudo no hakuyū ryokusai enmon wan: Sono nendai to Chūgoku tōshi shijō no ichidzuke 壱岐双六古墳出土の白釉緑彩円文碗: その年代と中国陶瓷史上の位置づけ [A white-glazed bowl with green color featuring circle reliefs excavated from the Sōroku tomb in Iki: Its date and its place in the history of Chinese ceramics]. In *Sōroku kofun* 双六古墳 [The Sōroku tomb], edited by Iki-shi Kyōiku Iinkai 壱岐市教育委員会 [Iki Municipal Board of Education], pp. 82–92. Iki-shi Kyōiku Iinkai, Iki.

4

Interactions Between Paekche and Wa in the Third to Sixth Centuries A.D. Based on Patterns of Trade and Exchange

Woo Jae-Pyoung

Abstract

This chapter presents an investigation of the nature of historical interactions between Paekche 百濟 and Wa 倭 (Japan) based on the patterns of trade and exchange between the two polities in the third to sixth centuries A.D. The main axis of trade between the peninsula and the archipelago in the third to fourth centuries A.D. ran through the Kŭmgwan Kaya polity on the estuary of the Naktong River. Around the second half of the fifth century A.D. this trade system expanded to include direct trade contacts between Paekche and Wa. Archaeological evidence for interactions between Paekche and Wa around the fifth to sixth centuries A.D. has been found at peninsular sites such as the Chungmak-tong ritual site in Puan and the Wa-style keyhole-shaped tombs in southwestern Korea. Evidence on the archipelago includes Paekche-style wood-burning stove-type furnaces as well as Paekche-type corridor-style horizontal burial chamber tombs, both of which spread during the sixth century from the central region of Wa. I suggest that Paekche introduced Wa-style keyhole-shaped tombs in the southwestern regions for provincial heads as a sign of its peer polity amity with Wa. This suggests a new strategy adopted by Wa that prioritized relations with Paekche, and it is likely that a strategic alliance between Paekche and Wa in the fifth and sixth centuries was deemed necessary to overcome the instability on the Korean peninsula caused by Koguryŏ's attacks against Kaya and Paekche.

Introduction

The Asuka and Nara periods in Japan (seventh and eighth centuries A.D.) include the so-called *ritsuryō* 律令 period, in which the state was governed through a law-based political system known as "ritsuryō-sei." One of the main contributing factors to this political development ushering in the *ritsuryō* period was Japan's exchange with ancient states of the Korean peninsula. The adoption of new knowledge and elements of advanced culture through exchanges with peninsular polities served as a catalyst for Japan's transformation into law-based polities. The flourishing of Asuka culture in Japan beginning in the early seventh century was in part a result of the introduction of the advanced material culture from Paekche. Ironically, though, the demise of Paekche occurred soon thereafter, as it succumbed to the attacks of the Tang-Silla military alliance in the second half of the seventh century.

The goal of this study is to cast light on the nature of the interaction between Paekche and Wa in the period leading up to the historical drama of the seventh century that is highlighted by Paekche's defeat and Japan's dramatic growth. The interaction between Paekche and Wa presupposes the existence of political and economic exchanges between the two states. Therefore, I focus on the questions of long-distance maritime trade between the archipelago and the peninsula and mutual adoption of burial practices, as well as the introduction of Paekche-style cooking and heating systems by Wa in order to gain a more fine-grained sense of the nature of the exchanges that occurred during this period between the two regions.

The importing of iron from Korea, which was an essential commodity in Wa's economy, played a key role in the process of state formation on the Japanese archipelago. It appears that this economic structure, which depended on imported metals from Korea, lasted until around the fifth century. Based on the records of the "Account of Han" 韓傳 in the *Sanguozhi* 三國志 (Chronicles of the Three Kingdoms) (30:849–853) and archaeological analysis of metal materials, it is likely that the main regions that exported iron to Japan during this period were those of Pyŏnhan 弁韓 and Chinhan 辰韓 located in the southeastern part of the peninsula (Tsude 1989:48–52).

The existing trade system between Wa and Kŭmgwan Kaya 金官加耶 in the estuary of the Naktong River 洛東江, on the other hand, was dealt a serious blow as a result of Koguryŏ's attacks beginning around 400 against the Kaya region in the southeastern part of the peninsula. Signs of the long-distance trade that existed between Paekche and Wa beginning in the latter half of the fifth century have been discovered at sites associated with ancestral rituals on the western coastal region of Paekche, an area that served as the sea route between the two polities. It appears that the influence of

Paekche-type cooking and heating systems as well as of mortuary practices quickly spread in Wa after the second half of the fifth century. This kind of archaeological data allows us to take a closer look at the nature of bilateral exchanges between the peninsula and the archipelago and strongly suggests the existence of a close interaction between the two involved polities as a precondition for political and economic cooperation.

The analyses of archaeological data presented in this paper are based on the assumption that Japan and Korea were connected by a sea route in the fifth century, which made possible communication between the two. This study also relies on the analysis of the following four phenomena of the fifth and sixth centuries, a time when the exchange between the two polities appears to have sharply increased.

First, some of the remains discovered at archaeological sites along the sea routes in Paekche's western coastal region, dating from the fifth to the sixth centuries, suggest that Wa-style ancestral rituals were performed there. Second, at approximately the same time, Wa-style keyhole-shaped tombs were adopted for the burial of regional chiefs in certain parts of the southwestern regions of Paekche. Third, also during this period, Paekche-style mortuary architecture characterized by horizontal-entry-style stone chambers was adopted in Wa, first in the central region and then spreading to the other parts of the archipelago. And lastly, along with the spread of horizontal-entry-style stone-chamber tombs, other elements of Paekche culture such as wood-burning stove-type cooking and heating systems were also introduced in Wa. In my conclusion, I attempt to draw a comprehensive portrayal of the historical interaction between Paekche and Wa in the fifth and sixth centuries based on the issues emerging from the discussion of the above four phenomena.

Maritime Trade Routes Between Paekche and Japan: Changes Between the Third to Fourth Centuries and the Fifth to Sixth Centuries

Maritime Trade Routes Developed in the Third to Fourth Centuries Between the Korean Peninsula and the Japanese Archipelago Centered on Kŭmgwan Kaya

The Taesŏng-dong 大成洞 cemetery site in Kimhae 金海, located in the estuary of the Naktong River, served as the burial site of the ruling class of Kŭmgwan Kaya from the third to fifth centuries. The excavation of these ancient tombs revealed evidence corroborating the description in historical records of Kŭmgwan Kaya as an ancient state, the thriving economy of which was based on iron production and exports. Another reason this site has received much attention from the international community is the discovery of prestige goods related to the central Kinai 畿内 region of Japan, including pinwheel-shaped bronze ornaments, arrow quivers (Figure 4.1), spindle-whorl–shaped stone implements, arrowhead-shaped stone implements, and other artifact types (Kyŏngsŏng Taehakkyo Pangmulgwan 2000).

Meanwhile, the excavation of the Yangdong-ni 良洞里 cemetery site in Kimhae has yielded important clues about the nature of trade relations between the Korean peninsula and the Japanese archipelago in the preceding period of the first to the second centuries, prior to the formation of Kŭmgwan Kaya. Artifacts such as large bronze spearheads, slender bronze daggers, and imitative bronze mirrors were found in this burial area, with tombs presumed to belong to members of the Pyŏnhan ruling class (Tongŭi Taehakkyo Pangmulgwan 2000). These artifacts are likely to have been imported from northern Kyushu or, at least, to be related to that region given that similar items are found primarily in northern Kyushu. The archaeological finds from the Yangdong-ni site, therefore, suggest that the exchange between the Korean peninsula and the Japanese archipelago during the first and second centuries took place primarily between Pyŏnhan in the southeastern part of the peninsula and northern Kyushu.

The excavation of artifacts related to Wa from the Yangdong-ni and Taesŏng-dong cemetery sites in Kimhae strongly suggests shifts in the patterns of exchange over time between the Kaya region and the Japanese archipelago. Thus, in the case of southeastern Korea, occupied by Pyŏnhan during the first and second centuries, artifacts have been discovered that appear to have been imported through exchanges with northern Kyushu. Meanwhile, archaeological sites associated with Kŭmgwan Kaya dating from the third to the fifth centuries, such as Taesŏng-dong, contain artifacts from Japan, in this case originating from the central Kinai region of Japan, mainly Nara and Osaka. This suggests that the polity of the southeastern part of the Korean peninsula, as it evolved both politically and economically from Pyŏnhan into what later became Kŭmgwan Kaya, further expanded its trade relations with central powers in Wa during the period in question.

It appears that in the third to fifth centuries changes were introduced in existing trade relations with Korea by political forces in the northern Kyushu region. The discovery of a significant number of artifacts from Japan's central region in Kŭmgwan Kaya following the formation of central

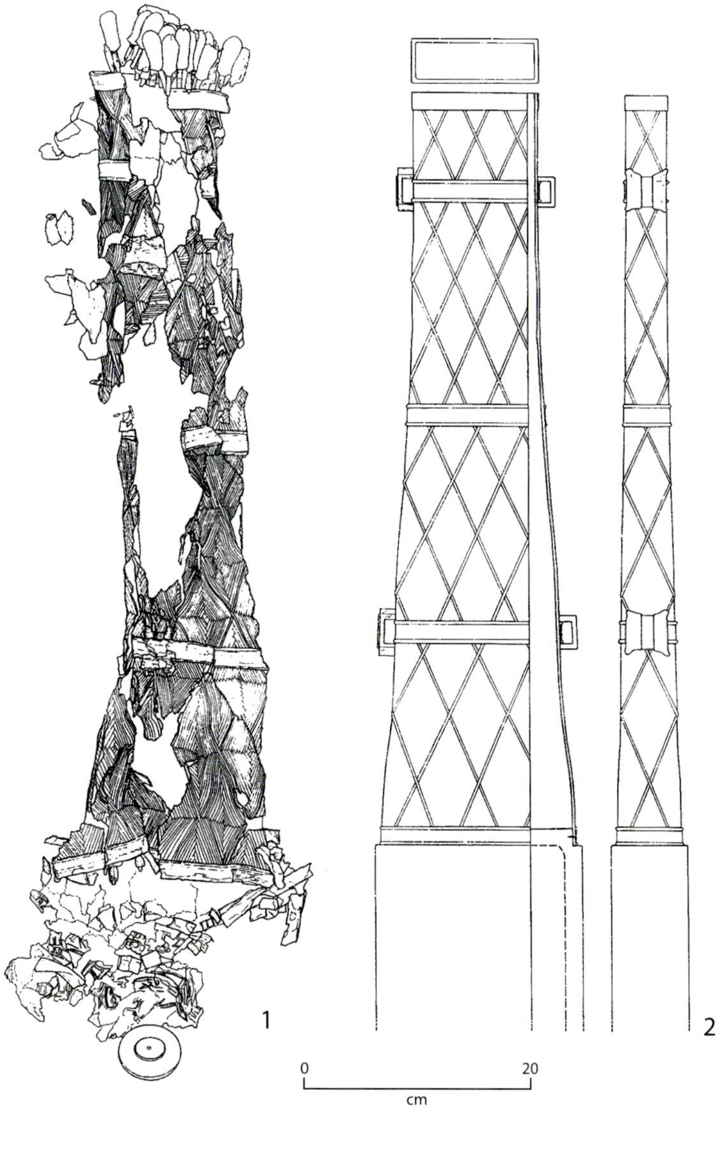

Figure 4.1 Quiver Excavated from the Yukinoyama Tumulus in Shiga Prefecture.
After Sugii 1996.
1. Side view of quiver; 2. Restoration.

power in Kinai suggests that Japan became more deeply involved in trade with Kŭmgwan Kaya, both directly and indirectly. This important change seems, in turn, related to the rise of the Yamato regime sometime in the latter half of the third century, symbolized by the emergence of keyhole-shaped tombs. Hence, around the mid-third century and thereafter, the main agent of trade and exchange with Kŭmgwan Kaya appears to have become the central ruling power in a Japan that was undergoing political transformations toward the early state (Tsude 2005:95–105).

Among the tombs of the Taesŏng-dong cemetery site in Kimhae, most artifacts of Japanese provenance are concentrated in wood-frame tombs (*mokkwak myo* 木槨墓) dating from the early fourth century to the early fifth century. This suggests that the maritime trade route connecting the Japanese archipelago with the Korean peninsula during that period went through Kŭmgwan Kaya. Therefore, it can be assumed that trade between Paekche and Wa in this period was mostly indirect via Kŭmgwan Kaya. However, this trade route connecting the archipelago with the peninsula seems to have rapidly changed following the decline of Kŭmgwan Kaya as a result of attacks by Koguryŏ. Thus, in the second half of the fifth century and thereafter, the trade system between Korea and Japan, which had previously been centered on trade relations between Kŭmgwan Kaya and Wa, underwent important changes and focused primarily on direct trade contacts with Paekche.

Maritime Trade Routes During the Fifth and Sixth Centuries: New Ties Between Paekche and Japan and the Resulting Changes in Trade and Exchange Patterns

Archaeological evidence found in the Paekche region suggestive of close, friendly ties between Paekche and Wa in the fifth and sixth centuries comes from the Chungmak-tong 竹幕洞 ritual site in Puan 扶安 on the west coast, as well as from thirteen keyhole-shaped tombs found in southwestern Korea (Map 4.1).

The excavation of the Chungmak-tong ritual site, situated atop a cliff on the western coast of Korea, has received a great deal of attention, largely owing to the discovery of important evidence pointing to maritime trade relations between Paekche and Japan in the fifth and sixth centuries. Alongside artifacts originating from Kaya and from the Southern Dynasties of China dating to the fifth and sixth centuries, a series of stone implements imitative of those widely used in ancestor-worship rituals in Wa were discovered (Kungnip Chŏnju Pangmulgwan 1994).

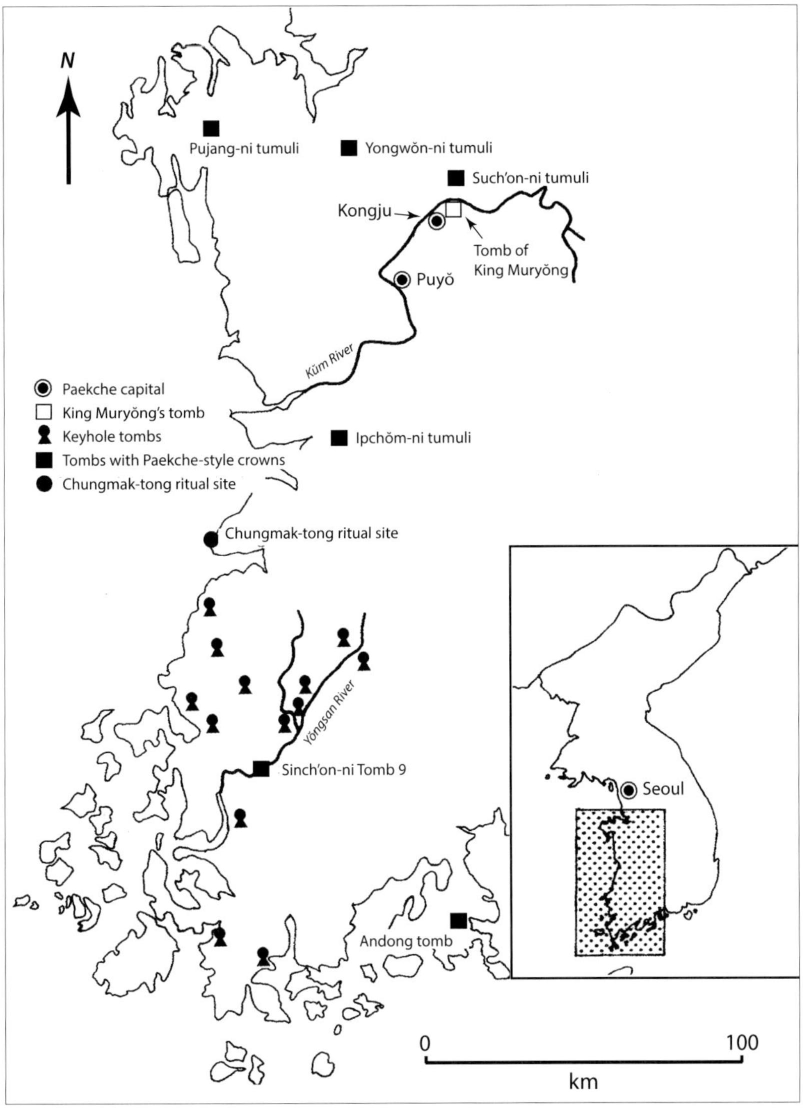

Map 4.1 Locations of Tombs Yielding Crowns, the Chungmak-tong Site, and Keyhole-shaped Tombs in the Paekche Region in the Fifth to Sixth Centuries. Data from Chŏnnam Taehakkyo Pangmulgwan 2000 and Wŏn'gwang Taehakkyo Mahan Paekche Munhwa Yŏn'guso 2000.

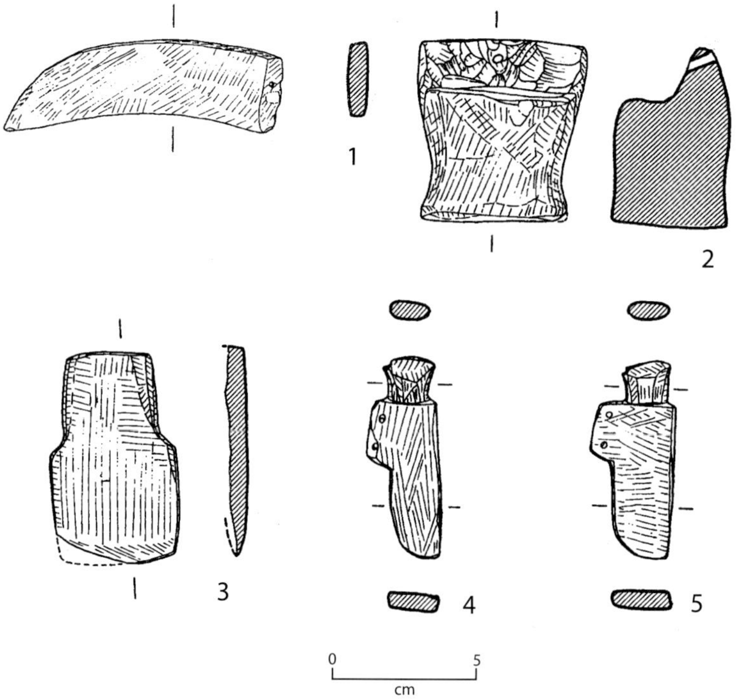

Figure 4.2 Wa-style Stone Implements Excavated from the Chungmak-tong Ritual Site. After Kungnip Chŏnju Pangmulgwan 1994.

The discovery of these imitative Japanese-type stone implements (Figure 4.2) at the Chungmak-tong site suggests the existence of maritime trade between Paekche and Japan at that time. More specifically, I suggest that extra-local merchant ships with Wa individuals on board would pass through this area, and Wa seafarers would participate in local ancestor worship at the site. Furthermore, the Chungmak-tong site is located in the area through which all ships of Japanese provenance bound for Paekche's capital (Seoul, Kongju, and later Puyŏ) had to pass. With this in mind, the main purpose of these ancestral rituals held at that site was presumably to pray for the safe passage of Wa vessels to their destination. While the use of imitative stone implements in ancestral rituals in Japan's coastal regions, and especially in Okinoshima 沖ノ島, is quite well known, in the case of Korea these were found for the first time at the Chungmak-tong site.

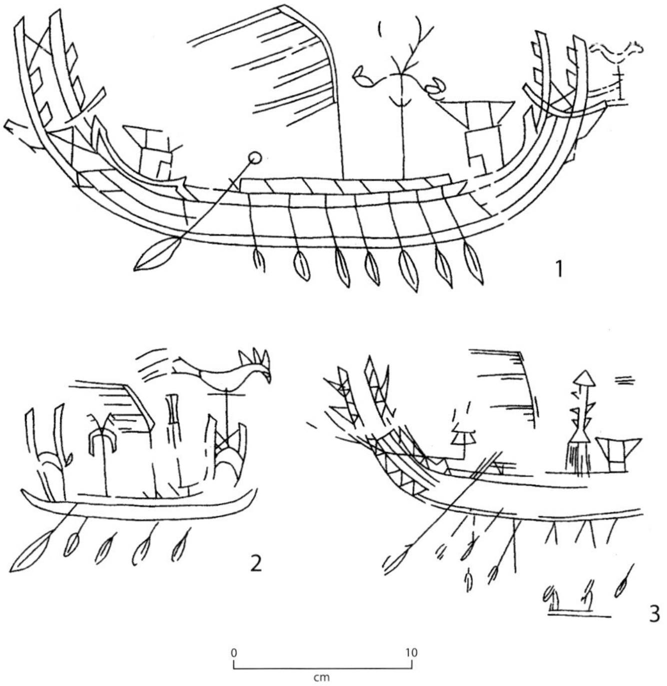

Figure 4.3 Boat-shaped Figures Incised on Haniwa *from the Higashi-tonozuka Tumulus in Tenri. After Tenri-shi Kyōiku Iinkai 2000.*

If the assumption expressed above is correct, Wa travelers going from the Kinai region to the Paekche capital must have had to take one of three routes in order to be able to participate in ancestor rites at the Chungmak-tong site.

The first is a direct sea route between central Wa and central Paekche. One should bear in mind that shipbuilding and navigation between the two polities at the time were probably based on the use of man-powered rowboats rather than wind-driven sailboats (Wu Chae-byŏng 2002:178–189; Figure 4.3). For instance, ancient ships restored on the basis of boat-shaped earthenware vessels recovered from Tomb 2 at the Nagahara-Takamawari 長原高廻り site in Osaka, which were used between Korea and Japan in an experimental archaeology sailing project, provide a clue as to Wa shipbuilding and navigation practices at the time. As a result of this evidence, we know that long-distance sea travel between Korea and Japan was

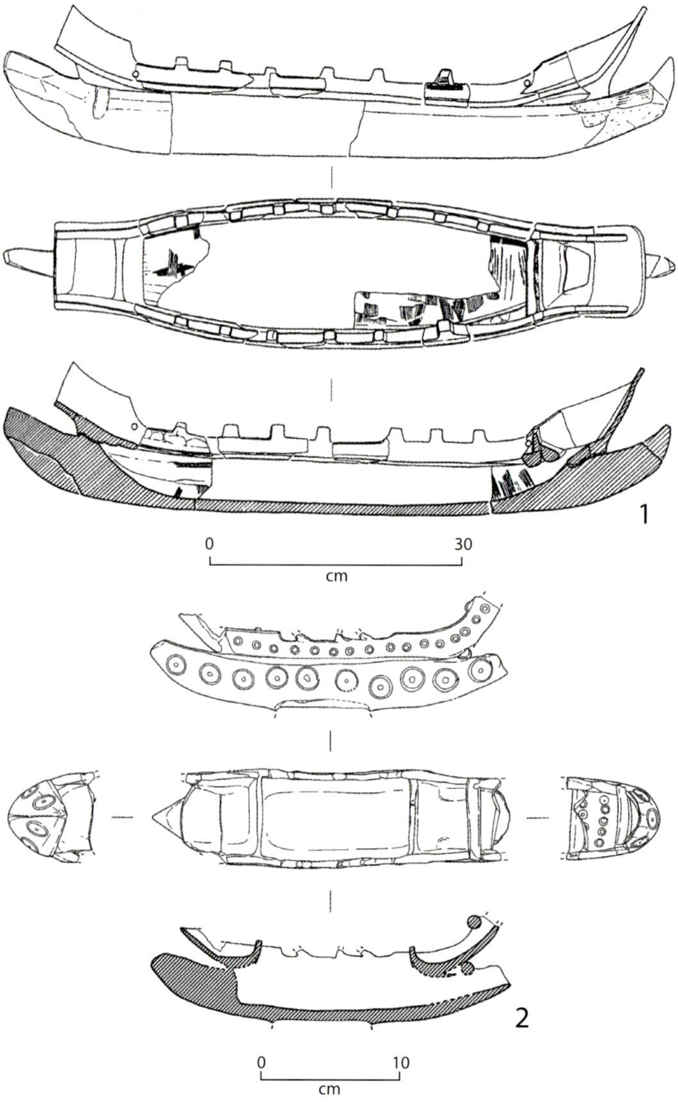

Figure 4.4 Boat-shaped Clay Figures Excavated in Japan and Korea.
1. From the Nigore tumulus in Kyoto (after Okita 1988);
2. From shaft feature no. 12 at the P'yŏngch'on-ni site in Talsŏng (after Kyŏngsang-pukto Munhwajae Yŏn'guwŏn 2010).

possible also on the type of ships that did not have sails, but were powered by oarsmen (Ōsaka shi Kyōiku Iinkai 1989:9–24).

Furthermore, examples excavated from the remains of the Kyūhōji 久宝寺 site in Osaka are quite well known, although the actual material used for this type of boat was wood (Takahashi 1989:26–27). The appearance of this type of boat can be found in images painted on cylindrical earthenware vessels (*haniwa* 埴輪) discovered from the ancient tombs at the Higashi-tonozuka 東殿塚 tomb in Tenri 天理 (Figure 4.3, no. 2).

On the other hand, examples of this type of boat-shaped earthenware vessel (Figure 4.4, no. 1) from the Japanese archipelago, mainly in the central regions of Wa, are relatively well known. However, the same kind of objects have been recently discovered at the P'yŏngch'on-ni 坪村里 site in Talsŏng 達成, located on the bank of the Naktong River in southeastern Korea (Kyŏngsang-pukto Munhwajae Yŏn'guwŏn 2010:247–257). Given that similar boat-shaped earthenware vessels have been discovered both in Korea and Japan dating to the fifth and sixth centuries, we can hypothesize that shipbuilding and navigation in various ancient states on the Korean peninsula and in Wa were at the time at a comparable level.

Given the similarities in shipbuilding and navigation between Paekche, Kaya, and Wa, the Wa ships departing from northern Kyushu and going through Iki 壱岐, Tsushima 対馬, Okinoshima, and other islands would have first cast their anchors in the ports of the Kŭmgwan Kaya region. Here, after possibly making a rest stop, getting the necessary supplies, and engaging in some trade, Wa ships would have continued their journey to the Paekche region. After passing through the main ports along the southern and western coast of the Korean peninsula on their way to the final destination in Paekche's central region, these boats would have made a stop in the ports near the Chungmak-tong site. It is likely that the crews of ships traveling to Seoul, Kongju, or Puyŏ—the three capitals of Paekche at various times—would have disembarked from their ships as they passed the Chungmak-tong site. The sea route leading to Paekche's central regions would have been considered to be a treacherous one for ships, so the crews would have participated in ancestral rites at the Chungmak-tong site to pray for safety during the remainder of their journey (Figure 4.5, no. 1).

The second route that might have been used by Wa sailors would take them to a port in the Kŭmgwan Kaya region near the estuary of the Naktong River. It is possible that at this point they would change from their own boats into Kaya or Paekche vessels to complete the remaining stretch to the final destination in central Paekche. Under this scenario, the Wa

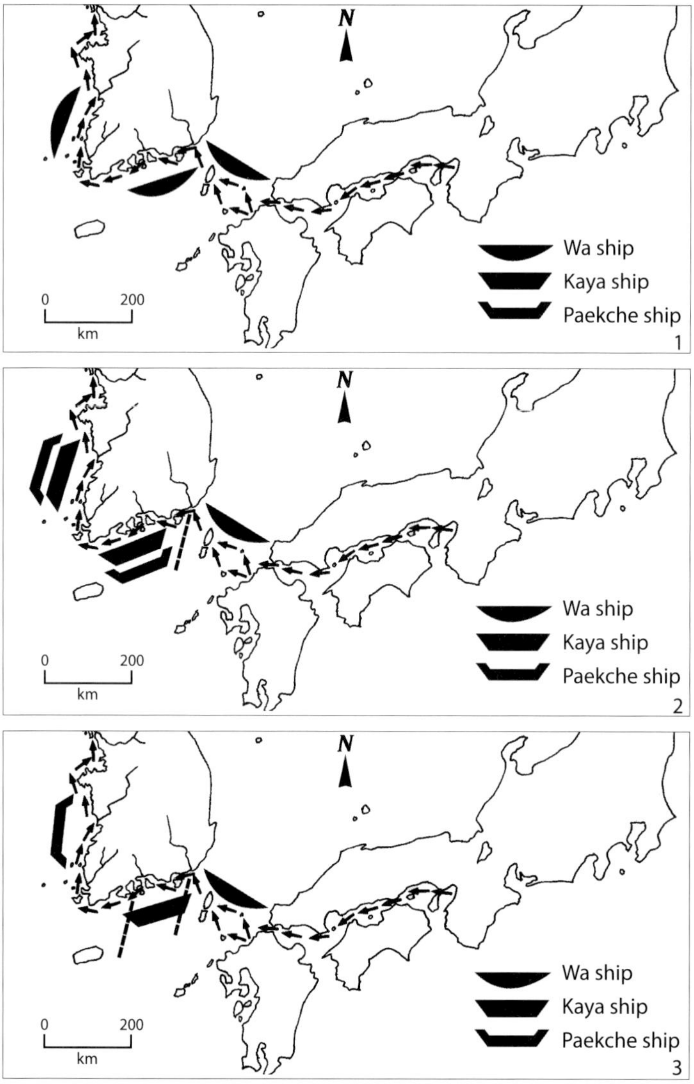

Figure 4.5 Three Methods of Sea Travel from Wa to Paekche in the Fifth and Sixth Centuries.
1. Direct travel by Wa; 2. Transfer to Kaya or Paekche ships at Kimhae; 3. Multiple transfer via Wa, Kaya, and Paekche ships.

travelers would have participated in rituals at the Chungmak-tong site as the passengers of a Kaya or Paekche ship when their boat would make a stop at a port near this site (Figure 4.5, no. 2).

The third possible route would have the Wa reaching the Kŭmgwan Kaya region on their own ships and, once there, changing into Kaya boats, loading also the goods they brought with them for trading. The Kaya ship would then take the Wa passengers and their goods to the border between Kaya and Paekche, where the latter would again change to a Paekche ship with all their goods. The Paekche ship boarded with Wa passengers, now on its way to central Paekche, would cast anchor near the Chungmak-tong ritual site to participate in the ritual to pray for safe seafaring (Figure 4.5, no. 3).

Each of these three hypothetical scenarios is equally plausible as an itinerary used by ancient Japanese to travel to central Paekche. Yet, given that seafarers of these regions traveled at that time mainly on rowboats rather than sailboats, they probably needed to make frequent stops so that the oarsmen could recover from the exertion. Traveling along the southern and western seaboards would have made this possible. Nevertheless, navigating through the waters of the southern and western coasts of the Korean peninsula along their jagged coastlines crowded with obstacles, all the way to the final destination in Paekche, must not have been easy for Wa ships. Therefore, the most likely scenario was for the Wa to depart aboard their own ships, then board a Kaya ship once they reached the Kaya region, and finally a Paekche ship once in the Paekche-controlled territory (Wu 2009:216). It should be noted, however, that archaeological evidence for such scenarios has not yet been discovered.

Rituals are thought to have been held at the Chungmak-tong site starting in the mid-fourth century and continuing until the early seventh century. However, stone ritual items discovered at the site are quite similar to those used in Japan during the middle to late Kofun period. This fact, along with the estimated period during which large-scale jars were used inside burial mounds in the Paekche region, allows us to narrow the time frame for activity at Chungmak-tong to a period from the late fifth century to the early sixth century (Kungnip Chŏnju Pangmulgwan 1994:239–263).

As a result of the archaeological finds from the Chungmak-tong ritual site described above, it appears that the peer polity strategy of Wa toward the Korean peninsula changed around the fifth and sixth centuries. In other words, the existing trade system the Wa had maintained with the Korean peninsula, which was once centered primarily on Kŭmgwan Kaya, changed

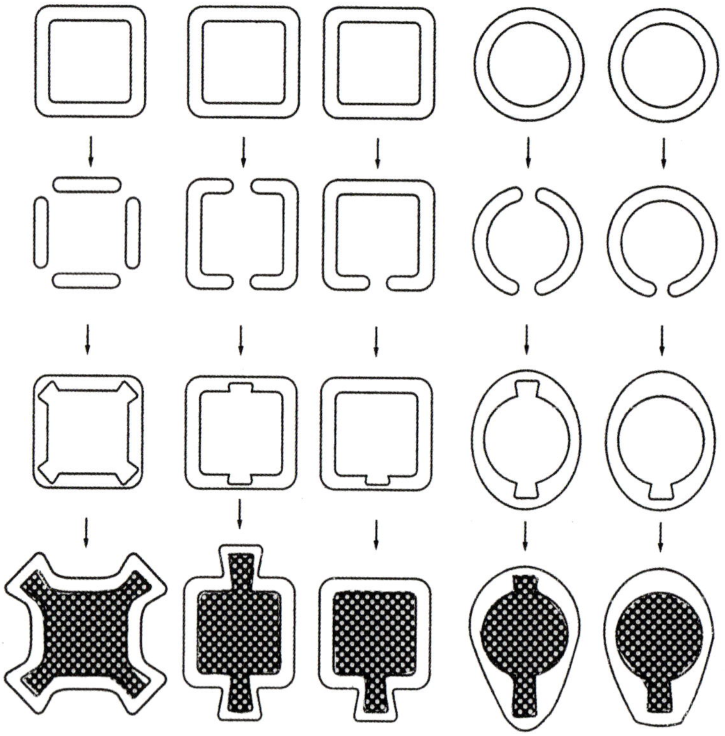

Figure 4.6 Changes in Tomb Shape During the Yayoi Period. After Tsude 1998.

into a new system that privileged trade relations with Paekche. Also, the hypothesis that Wa traders may have attended seafaring rituals at the Chungmak-tong site alongside Paekche sailors suggests that the two polities had by then developed close ties.

The political situation on the Korean peninsula in the early fifth century probably also compelled the Wa to engage in amicable relations with Paekche. Kaya sustained a major attack from Koguryŏ around this time, and the fortunes of Kŭmgwan, the leading Kaya polity, rapidly ebbed. Paekche's close relationship with the Southern Dynasties of China is likely to have been another factor pushing the Wa ruling group to seek closer ties with the peninsular kingdom.

For its part, Paekche was forced to move its capital to Kongju when its early capital in Seoul was overrun and occupied by Koguryŏ in the latter part of the fifth century. Thus, the evidence that Wa sailors participated in Wa-style ancestral rites at the Chungmak-tong site during the fifth and sixth centuries suggests that Paekche probably sought closer relations with neighboring Wa to ward off the threat from Koguryŏ.

Keyhole-Shaped Tombs in the Paekche Region

Wa-Style Keyhole-Shaped Tombs Found in Paekche Territory

The Japanese-style keyhole-shaped tombs found in the southwestern region of the Korean peninsula, particularly in the basin of the Yŏngsan River 榮山江, also constitute important archaeological evidence suggesting that Paekche and Wa forged close ties with each other toward the fifth and sixth centuries.

The keyhole-shaped tomb is a burial form that looks like a round mound attached to a square mound in a layout resembling a keyhole. Based on typological studies carried out in Japan, this is the style of tomb that was standardized across the Japanese archipelago after the second half of the third century and was prevalent from the fourth to sixth centuries during the Kofun period (Figure 4.6). It appears that these keyhole-shaped tombs developed from round-shaped tombs of the Yayoi 弥生 period (Figure 4.7). Although there have been efforts to find the origins of keyhole-shaped tombs in continental China and on the Korean peninsula, these studies have not produced any conclusive evidence. Yet, the emergence of keyhole-shaped tombs in the Japanese archipelago testifies to at least some influence from the continent. In light of the most recent archaeological discoveries, we now have a theoretical model proposing that keyhole-shaped tombs were standardized and became the prevalent mortuary type for the upper ruling class in Wa (Tsude 1998:40–60).

To date, thirteen burial mounds in the shape of a keyhole have been discovered through archaeological surveys in the southwestern region of Paekche (Chŏnnam Taehakkyo Pangmulgwan 2000; Wŏn'gwang Taehakkyo Mahan Paekche Munhwa Yŏn'guso 2000). These tombs were presumed to have been constructed over a period between the late fifth century and the early sixth century, but actually were mostly erected in the early sixth century. In other words, these burials roughly date to the time of the reign of Paekche's King Muryŏng 武寧王 (r. 501–523).

Figure 4.7 Hierarchical Divisions in the Form of Tombs During the Kofun Period. After Tsude 1998.

There is no evidence that the keyhole-shaped tombs found in the southwestern part of the Korean peninsula emerged through an endogenous process of stylistic and architectural transformation. Given the fact that these keyhole-shaped tombs were highly popular in Japan from the late third century to the sixth century, it would be reasonable to suppose that similar tombs found in the southwestern part of the Korean peninsula began to appear under influence from Wa. Archaeologists from both Korea and Japan are mostly in agreement with each other in thinking that the keyhole-shaped tombs constructed in the southwestern part of the Korean peninsula in the early sixth century were mortuary structures created under extra-local influence.

However, scholarly opinions are divided as to how Japanese mortuary architecture came to have an influence in the southwestern part of the Korean peninsula. In order to explain this, one must first establish whether the southwestern part of the Korean peninsula was under Paekche's control in the early sixth century. And if this region was indeed under Paekche's control during the time of King Muryŏng, the next important question to consider is how it was governed. Concretely, the question would concern whether this region was governed by Paekche indirectly through local clan chiefs appointed by the center or was instead ruled directly through officials dispatched by the Paekche court.

Of the many theories that have been proposed concerning the emergence of keyhole-shaped tombs on the Korean peninsula during the early sixth century, the four most noteworthy are the following.

According to the first model, the region of what is currently South Chŏlla Province was not yet under the complete rule of Paekche between the second half of the fifth century and the first half of the sixth century. Instead, control rested in the hands of local political powers who maintained active exchanges with various regions of the Japanese archipelago, but primarily with northern Kyushu. Thus, based on gilt-bronze ornaments found among the mortuary goods of keyhole-shaped tombs of the South Chŏlla region as well as other evidence, keyhole-shaped tombs in this area are believed to be a result of independent activities of powerful regional clans buried in these places, although relations with Paekche admittedly existed even during this period (Habuta 2000:19–21).

In the second model, since tombs in the Yŏngsan River basin used burial architecture not seen in the central region of Paekche and yielded prestige goods such as gilt-bronze crowns, thus probably belonging to the heads of independent polities, it is difficult to conceive of this region as Paekche territory. Scholars adhering to this theory think that this area was controlled until the mid-sixth century by an indigenous group of Mahan lineage who formed a polity independent from Paekche in the Yŏngsan River valley (Im 2002:25).

The third model suggests that the keyhole-shaped tombs in the Yŏngsan River basin belonged to Wa individuals who were dispatched by Paekche as a temporary measure to govern the area since it lacked the capability to rule over the southwestern part of the Korean peninsula directly following the move of the Paekche capital to Kongju in 475 (Pak Ch'ŏn-su 2002:42–59).

The fourth model suggests that the keyhole-shaped tombs in the Yŏngsan River basin were a result of the migration during the fifth century of various groups from regions of northern Kyushu into this area. Individuals from these groups were responsible for the construction of these tombs in concert with local forces (Azuma 2002:166–167).

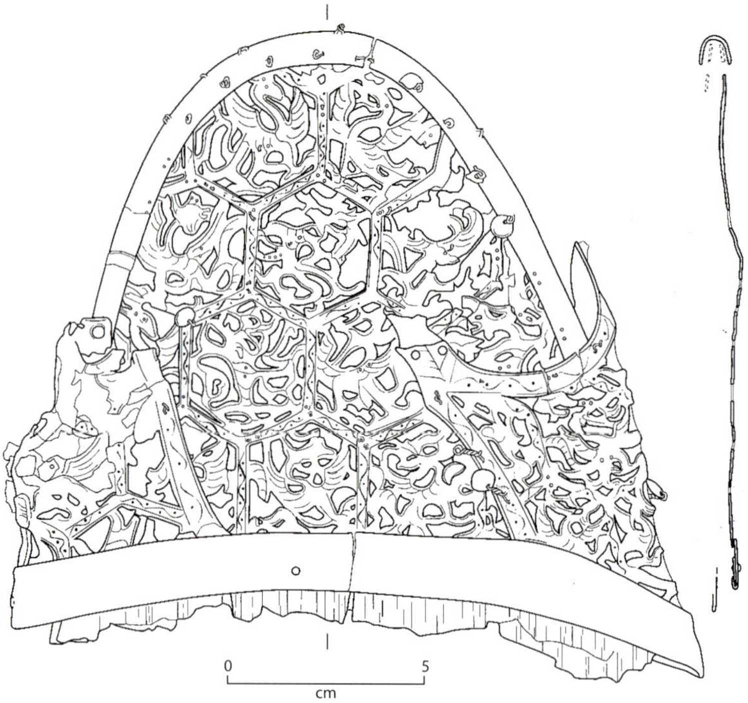

Figure 4.8 Gilt-bronze Cap from Tomb 5-1 at Pujang-ni in Sŏsan. After Ch'ungch'ŏng-namdo Yŏksa Munhwa Yŏn'guwŏn 2008.

Of these four models, the second theory proposing that the Yŏngsan River valley was not a Paekche domain at that time, based on the idea that the existence of keyhole-shaped tombs containing gilt-bronze crowns suggests that it was an independent polity, has become increasingly difficult to maintain in light of recent archaeological discoveries of gilt-bronze crowns and caps (Figure 4.8) in various parts of the southwestern region of Korea. Such artifacts are similar to those found within the Paekche territorial heartland (Yi Han-sang 2009:134–166; Yi Hun 2010:157–187).

A gilt-bronze crown closely resembling examples found in central Paekche was also discovered in the late fifth-century Andong tomb 雁洞古墳 located in Kohŭng 高興, at the southernmost tip of the southwestern part of the Korean peninsula. Accordingly, most scholars now propose that these gilt-bronze crowns were bestowed upon local chieftains by the Paekche court (Yi Hun 2006:1–21; Yi Han-sang 2006:45–53; Yi Nam-sŏk 2008:453–468).

Therefore, based on the discovery and distribution of gilt-bronze crowns (Map 4.1), it is hard to maintain the second model's hypothesis that local powers of Mahan lineage centered in the Yŏngsan River basin were politically independent from Paekche before the middle of the sixth century. Neither have any traces of fifth- and sixth-century Wa settlements related to keyhole-shaped tombs in the Yŏngsan River basin been found. Thus, the fourth model is also difficult to corroborate on the basis of existing archaeological evidence. On the other hand, a number of important status goods (Kungnip Kwangju Pangmulgwan 2008:6) made of gold, glass, jade, and other materials discovered in Wa-style keyhole-shaped tombs in the southwestern region of Paekche bear a resemblance to objects recovered from the tomb of King Muryŏng (Kungnip Kongju Pangmulgwan 2007:104–158).

Based on the evidence presented above, it is quite clear that the southwestern part of the Korean peninsula was controlled to some degree by Paekche in the early sixth century, around the time of King Muryŏng. Uncertainty remains, however, as to how exactly this territory was governed: whether it was administered by local clan chiefs appointed by the Paekche ruler or through officials dispatched from the Paekche court. Archaeological research, meanwhile, has suggested that there were periodic changes in the methods through which the Paekche court conferred local official titles on regional leaders. Archaeological data indicate that in the late sixth century, the central government of Paekche implemented a system in which clan chiefs would be given crown-frill ornaments made of silver as a symbol of their status as local officials. Therefore, the Paekche method of controlling its newly annexed territories by awarding status symbols changed over the centuries, from bestowing gilt-bronze crowns and caps to silver crown and cap ornaments. More recently, some historians have suggested that the earlier period in which the Paekche court bestowed gilt-bronze crowns and caps on local chiefs was a period of indirect rule, whereas the later period, during which gilt-bronze crowns and caps were replaced with silver crown and cap ornaments, corresponds to a period of direct rule (Kang 2005:243–250; Yi Nam-sŏk 2008:463–472).

The archaeological finds of gilt-bronze crowns, caps, and frill ornaments support the idea that the southwestern part of the Korean peninsula was under some degree of Paekche control already toward the late fifth and early sixth centuries.

4 Interactions Between Paekche and Wa—Woo Jae-Pyoung

The Emergence of Wa-Style Keyhole-Shaped Tombs in Southwestern Korea

Having now established the hypothesis that the southwestern part of the Korean peninsula was under Paekche's rule from the late fifth until the early sixth century, we can turn to the historical background related to the emergence of Wa-style keyhole-shaped tombs in this region. Let us begin by examining the plausibility of the argument that these keyhole-shaped tombs were those of Wa individuals. According to this view, the Wa who migrated from the archipelago and settled in groups in the Yŏngsan River valley (Azuma 2002:166–167) would have relied on coercion or military force to erect keyhole-shaped tombs. The same might have been true of Wa individuals hired by Paekche to rule on its behalf over the outlying territory (Pak Ch'ŏn-su 2001:28–29).

I propose that, based on written records, those interred in the keyhole-shaped tombs found on the Korean peninsula included individuals of extra-local origin who were recognized at the time as Paekche officials of Wa descent. Thus, the Wa settlers who were appointed by Paekche as local chiefs are likely to have had their tombs built in the locations to which they had been sent by the central government. However, there are two chronological issues related to identifying all keyhole-shaped tombs found in the southwestern part of the peninsula with Paekche officials of Wa descent.

First, the majority of keyhole-shaped tombs discovered in Korea appear to have been constructed in the early sixth century during the reign of King Muryŏng. But according to the *Nihon shoki* 日本書紀 (Chronicles of Japan), Paekche officials of Wa origin mainly appear in Paekche only starting in the middle of the sixth century.

Second, if we assume that all keyhole-shaped tombs found in the southwestern region of the Korean peninsula belonged to Paekche officials of Wa origin, it is necessary first to bear in mind that no record of this exists in the *Nihon shoki*. Further, if these individuals had died in Paekche and keyhole-shaped tombs were constructed for their interment, we should expect to find keyhole-shaped tombs in Paekche that reflect various periods of construction. However, as noted above, the majority of keyhole-shaped tombs in Korea seem to have been constructed around the same time in the early sixth century during the reign of King Muryŏng. Thus, if we subscribe to the view that those interred in the tombs are Wa individuals appointed by the Paekche government to official positions, then we should account for this temporal discrepancy. In light of this evidence, however, it is rather difficult to maintain this position.

4 Interactions Between Paekche and Wa—Woo Jae-Pyoung

In my discussion of keyhole-shaped tombs on the peninsula, I have pointed out that they all appear to have been built around the same time in the early sixth century. We also need to mention the following two important changes related to tomb construction, which occurred at roughly the same time in the early sixth century, both in central Paekche and in its outlying regions.

First, Paekche royal tombs in this period, such as that of King Muryŏng, adopted the architectural style of brick-chamber tombs utilized by the Chinese Southern Dynasties. Besides the tomb of King Muryŏng, the only other brick-chamber tomb of this continental style discovered in the Paekche region is Tomb 6 at the Songsan-ni 宋山里 site in Kongju. In the early sixth century Paekche abruptly adopted the brick-chamber style of tomb from the Southern Dynasties in place of the traditional horizontal-entry-style stone-chamber tomb. The inscribed funerary tablet recovered from the tomb of King Muryŏng shows clearly that this brick-chamber tomb did not belong to a Chinese individual, but was erected for Paekche's King Muryŏng, who received the title of "Grand General" (*da jiangjun* 大將軍) from the Southern Dynasties.

In the late fifth century, Paekche removed its capital from Seoul to Kongju as a result of Koguryŏ attacks. King Muryŏng was faced with managing a state still in crisis in the years following the removal of the capital (Best 2006:102–148). To understand why a Chinese Southern Dynasties–style brick-chamber tomb was suddenly chosen for King Muryŏng, we first need to look at the historical context of this time period. Paekche appears to have adopted a new political strategy that prioritized close, amicable relations with the Southern Dynasties in order to ward off an imminent state crisis. That King Muryŏng received the title of "Grand General" from the Southern Dynasties courts attests to the success of this strategy.

In my opinion, the choice of such a style of tomb for the king's personal interment was also a conscious decision made in the context of this same strategy to strengthen ties with powerful continental neighbors. Funerals of royal family members or of the nobility functioned as an important channel of information exchange between the ancient states in those times. Therefore, the fact that the deceased Paekche king had been interred in a Southern Dynasties–style brick-chamber tomb would have been quickly transmitted to Koguryŏ and other kingdoms in the region by way of the official envoys who attended the funeral. This, in turn, must have sent a message to its neighbors that Paekche had forged a political alliance with the Chinese courts. Thus, the adoption of a Chinese-style tomb for the royal burial can be viewed as a political strategy designed to keep Koguryŏ's ambitions in check through a visible display of a newly formed intimate relationship between Paekche and the Chinese courts. This new diplomacy emphasizing funerary display seems to have been a successful strategy that temporarily helped to ensure the security of Paekche and to restore stability in the kingdom during the reign of King Muryŏng and the subsequent reign of King Sŏng 聖王 (r. 523–554).

On the other hand, the fact that the Southern Dynasties would permit Paekche, among the various peninsular states, to build this style of elite tomb may reflect a new Chinese strategy that prioritized relations with Paekche. At the time, Paekche played a key geographical and strategic role in connecting the Southern Dynasties with Kaya, Wa, and other polities both on the Korean peninsula and on the Japanese archipelago through maritime trade routes. This function seems to have served as a compelling motivation for the Chinese courts to engage in closer relations with this peninsular state.

Second, the construction of keyhole-shaped tombs in southwestern Korea for burial of local clan chiefs also began around the time of the construction of the Southern Dynasties–style brick-chamber tomb for King Muryŏng in the early sixth century. The southwestern part of the Korean peninsula, located along the main trade route between central Paekche and the Japanese archipelago, where Japanese-style keyhole-shaped tombs have been discovered, appears to have been a region directly involved in trade with coastal Japan. In other words, the southwestern area of Korea played a role similar to that played by northern Kyushu as a gateway for trade for the Japanese archipelago.

Considering the concurrent timing of the two events, I hypothesize that the adoption of Wa-style keyhole-shaped tombs was related to the adoption of a Southern Dynasties–style brick-chamber tomb for the Paekche king's burial. In other words, we can regard these two changes in tomb construction as strategic moves that were closely associated with the political situation in Paekche at the time. It appears that the adoption of foreign styles in funerary architecture at this time was a means to publicize these newly formed alliances. It is noteworthy that both types of burial architecture adopted from China and Japan were intended for the uppermost elites in their polities of origin (Figure 4.7), which clearly points to the underlying political motivations of the Paekche court with regard to borrowing these particular styles. I believe that the construction of keyhole-shaped tombs, as well as the adoption of brick-chamber tombs, was part of a political strategy employed by the Paekche government as a deterrent against new military threats from Koguryŏ (Figure 4.9) (Wu 2004:73–78).

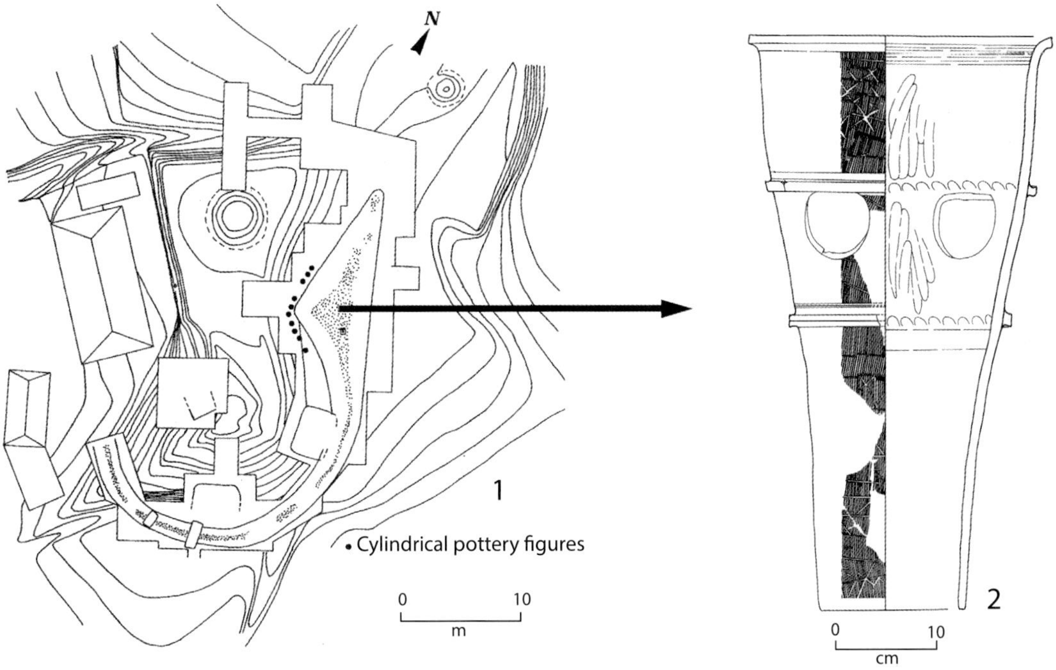

*Figure 4.9 Wa-style Keyhole-shaped Tomb in Paekche's Southwestern Region.
After Kungnip Kwangju Pangmulgwan 1996.
1. Myŏnghwa-dong tomb in Kwangju;
2. Cylindrical pottery from the Myŏnghwa-dong tomb.*

As to why Japanese-style keyhole-shaped tombs were constructed in Paekche's southern borderland province while the Paekche court itself adopted the new burial architecture from the Southern Dynasties, the answer lies in the hierarchical structure of Paekche society. It is likely that the social position of a deceased person determined the choice of a tomb, even the choice between two tomb styles of foreign origin. It appears that hierarchy according to social rank was quite pronounced in Paekche at the time of the adoption of foreign funerary practices, as regional chiefs were forbidden from interment in Southern Dynasties–style tombs, apparently reserved exclusively for royal burials. Thus, perhaps Wa-style keyhole-shaped tombs were regarded as being on a lower level of formality and therefore not appropriate for use by the uppermost elite. With this in mind, it stands to reason that the choice of a particular tomb style during this period was contingent on the place of the deceased individual within the social hierarchy (Figure 4.7).

On the other hand, Tomb 9 at Sinch'on-ni 新村里 in Naju 羅州 (Kungnip Munhwajae Yŏn'guso 2001), assumed to be that of a high-ranking local chief, did not adopt the keyhole mortuary architecture. Instead, it was built in a classical square-mound style native to Paekche. The keyhole-shaped tombs, on the other hand, found in the southwestern section of Paekche, such as Tomb 1 at Wŏlgye-dong 月桂洞 in Kwangju 光州 (Im 1994) and the tomb at Myŏnghwa-dong 明花洞 also in Kwangju (Kungnip Kwangju Pangmulgwan 1996; Figure 4.9), appear to have belonged to local chiefs of relatively lower status. Thus, even in the southwestern region, Wa-style keyhole-shaped tombs were not adopted uniformly—the choice of a particular architectural style depended on the social standing of the deceased.

The ethnic identity of the owners of these Wa-style keyhole-shaped tombs in the southwestern part of the peninsula, meanwhile, remains an unresolved issue as their tombs left no inscribed epitaphs of the sort found in King Muryŏng's tomb. It is unlikely that they were all built to inter Wa officials appointed by Paekche. If all such tombs in the southwest interred Wa individuals, they would have shown uniformity in their architectural style, as many of the Wa remained in Korea as long-term settlers. However, keyhole-shaped tombs appear only briefly during the time of King Muryŏng in the early sixth century and gradually disappear thereafter. I propose that those interred in most of the keyhole-shaped tombs in southwestern Korea were in fact not Wa at all, but local clan chiefs of areas directly involved in trade between Paekche and Wa.

With this in mind, it is difficult to see keyhole-shaped tombs as evidence of the Paekche government sending Wa individuals to govern in the southwest. For instance, findings from Tomb 9 at Sinch'on-ni, thought to be that of a top-ranking local chief of the southwestern province of Paekche at this time, show neither traces of a hostile relationship between the locals and the Wa, nor the existence of any governance mechanism involving Wa. On the contrary, the keyhole-shaped tombs appear to have been constructed for some of the local chiefs as symbols of amity with Wa. Tomb 9 at Sinch'on-ni, although a representative tomb of the Yŏngsan River basin in an overall square shape, has *haniwa*-like cylindrical pottery figures on the top of the mound on its four corners (Figure 4.10). Thus, although the tomb did not adopt the type of mound used in keyhole-shaped tombs, it adopted some

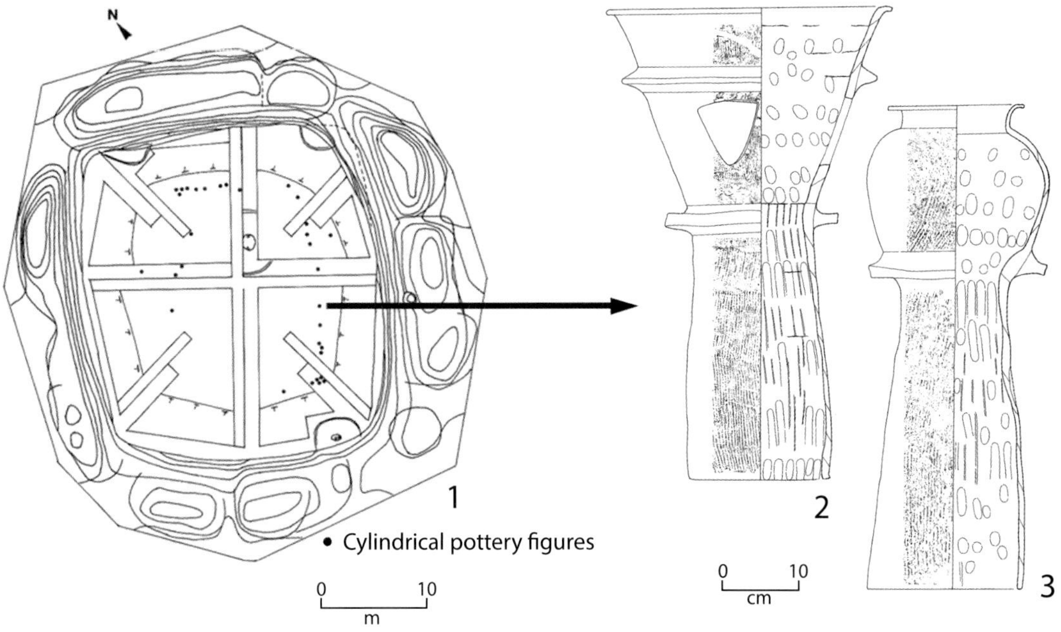

Figure 4.10 Cylindrical Pottery from the Top of Tomb 9 at Sinch'on-ni in Naju. After Kungnip Munhwajae Yŏn'guwŏn 2001.
1. Layout of Tomb 9 at Sinch'on-ni; 2–3. Cylindrical pottery from Tomb 9.

elements associated with such tombs (Teramura 2003:98–108; Figure 4.11). Such detail would be inexplicable if the occupant of Tomb 9 at Sinch'on-ni was an individual who had a hostile relationship with the Wa or was involved in any other kinds of contentious relationship with them. If anything, the occupant of Tomb 9 was an individual who was close enough to the Wa to integrate Wa-style ornamentation into his or her tomb.

Toward the late sixth century, when political stability was restored in Paekche following another change of the capital, this time from Kongju to Puyŏ, the construction of brick-chamber tombs in its central region and keyhole-shaped tombs in the southwestern borderland disappeared. In other words, after the diplomacy of close, amicable relations with China and Japan had achieved positive results and restored political stability, the use of extra-local-style mortuary types began to decline.

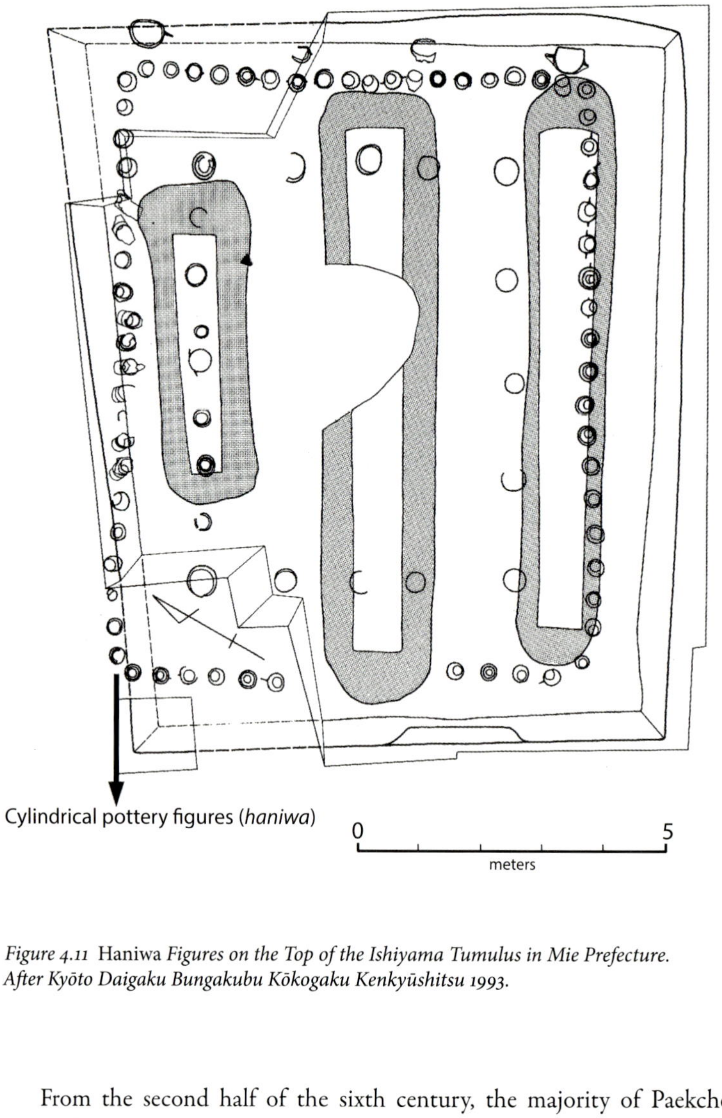

Figure 4.11 Haniwa *Figures on the Top of the Ishiyama Tumulus in Mie Prefecture. After Kyōto Daigaku Bungakubu Kōkogaku Kenkyūshitsu 1993.*

From the second half of the sixth century, the majority of Paekche tombs for members of the royal family and high-ranking nobility were of a new style that combined a horizontal-entry-style stone-chamber tomb with a round tomb mound and a square-shaped mound. In particular, after the transfer of the capital from Kongju to Puyŏ, Sabi-style (泗沘型), horizontal-entry-style stone chamber tombs began to spread from the Paekche center into the outlying regions. Tomb 2 at Sindŏk 新德 in Hamp'yŏng 咸平, which was constructed close to a keyhole-shaped tomb built in the early part of the sixth century, is an example of a Sabi-style 泗沘型 horizontal-entry stone-chamber tomb, attesting to changes that had occurred in burial styles in Paekche (Kim Nak-chung 2009:268–272). Hence, the use of non-local burial styles in Paekche was a rather short-lived phenomenon.

The position I have just presented does not contradict the views of numerous scholars, both in Korea and Japan, regarding the background of keyhole-shaped tomb discoveries on the Korean peninsula. However, the current debate on keyhole-shaped tombs found in the southwestern region of Korea and the historical background of their emergence continues among scholars with a hope that future archaeological discoveries will yield further strong evidence that will allow them to reshape the contours of the ongoing discussion.

The Spread of Paekche-Style Tombs and Cooking and Heating Systems in Wa in the Fifth and Sixth Centuries

The Adoption of Horizontal-Entry-Style Stone-Chamber Tombs from Paekche by Central Wa in the Early Sixth Century

During the fourth to fifth centuries, the prevailing type of burial structure used for powerful elites in the Kinai region, the political center of Japan, was a traditional vertical-pit-style tomb similar to the vertical-pit-style stone-chamber tomb. Starting in the early sixth century, however, a sudden change occurred in the architectural style of tombs used for the burial of members of the ruling class based in the Kinai region, as Wa adopted horizontal-entry-style stone-chamber tombs from Paekche. In the vertical-pit-style stone-chamber tomb, the deceased is placed in a narrow stone coffin, around which the outer coffin is tightly sealed with a stone slab on top, whereas the horizontal-entry-style stone-chamber tomb has a wide entrance on the side of the chamber and a plan that allowed for an easy passage into and out of the tomb. Therefore, the horizontal-entry-style stone-chamber tomb allows the interment of additional individuals into the same tomb chamber even after the burial of its primary occupant (Figure 4.12). This type of horizontal-entry-style stone-chamber tomb originated in Han China and became popular in Koguryŏ and the former Lelang region in the northern part of the Korean peninsula, as well as in Paekche in the southwest (Ichinose 2005:83).

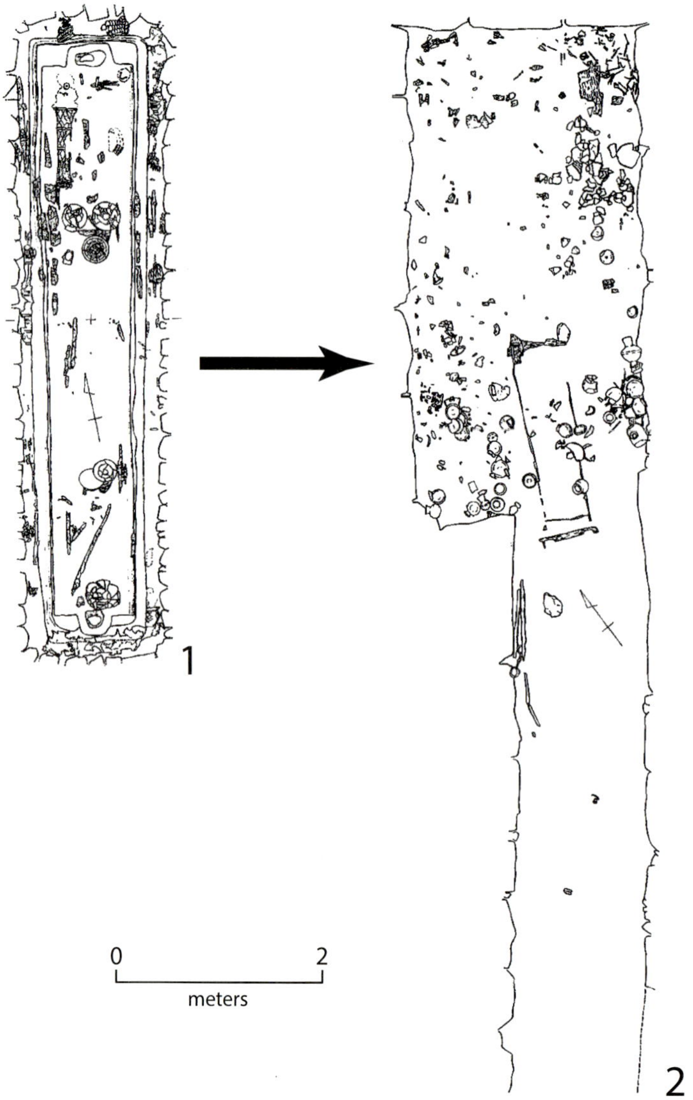

Figure 4.12 Development from Pit-style Stone Cist Tombs to Horizontal-entry-style Stone-chamber Tombs in Japan.
1. Yukinoyama tumulus in Shiga Prefecture (after Yukinoyama Kofun Hakkutsu Chōsadan 1996);
2. Inouchi Inarizuka tomb in Kyoto (after Ōsaka Daigaku Inarizuka Kofun Hakkutsu Chōsadan 2005).

The first appearance of horizontal-entry-style stone-chamber tombs in the Japanese archipelago dates back to the late fourth century. In the early sixth century, Paekche-style tombs of this type were newly reintroduced to the Kinai region and then spread from there to all other regions of the archipelago. Contemporary examples of horizontal-entry-style stone-chamber tombs from northern Kyushu dating back to the late fourth century include the Rōji 老司 and the Sukisaki 鋤崎 tombs. There are currently two opinions regarding the origin of these tomb types on the Japanese archipelago. According to one theory, this was a result of Paekche's influence on the archipelago at the time (Yanagisawa 1989:132–134), while the other view is that the Wa adopted the idea of a horizontal-entry-style stone-chamber tomb from the Korean peninsula and combined it with the traditional vertical-pit-style stone-chamber tomb common in northern Kyushu during that period (Shiraishi 2007:8–10).

Nevertheless, horizontal-entry-style stone-chamber tombs that appeared toward the end of the fifth century in the Kinai region in Osaka and Nara assumed a completely different style from those that had been built in the late fourth century. Representative of this period is the Takaidayama 高井田山 tomb in Osaka, which contained Paekche-style bronze pans used for ironing. This new type of horizontal-entry-style stone-chamber tomb, which was strongly influenced by Paekche-style tombs after the move of the capital to Kongju, became the primary type of tomb used for the burial of upper elites in the Kinai region toward the end of the sixth century. Over time, this tomb type adopted from Paekche was gradually enlarged and changed into what later became known as the Kinai-style horizontal-entry-style stone-chamber tomb (Ichinose 2005:62–76).

Examples of tombs belonging to clan chiefs built in the style of Paekche horizontal-entry-style stone-chamber tombs in the early sixth century include the Inouchi Inarizuka 井ノ内稲荷塚 tomb in the Kyoto area and the Shōfukuji 勝福寺 tomb in Hyōgo Prefecture, both of which are located in the Kinai region. Some regard this revolution in burial style that introduced horizontal-entry-style stone-chamber tombs from Paekche around the early sixth century as related to major political shifts inside Wa administrative structures that led to the birth of the Keitai 継体 regime (Fukunaga 2005:217–218; Fukunaga 2007:430–433).

After their adoption in the Kinai region as mortuary features for powerful clan chiefs, Paekche-style horizontal-entry-style stone-chamber tombs spread to surrounding regions as well. Paekche-style mortuary features were apparently not only used in burials of the highest level of elite in the Wa central region, but were also adopted in cemeteries for lower-level members of society in the same region, indicating their further widespread adoption on the archipelago (Morioka 1989:209–219).

The fact that Paekche-style horizontal-entry-style stone-chamber tombs were built not only for clan chiefs of the Kinai region, but also adopted in burials of power holders in the peripheral regions and used in non-elite cemeteries as well constitutes important archaeological evidence suggesting the strengthening of relations between Paekche and Wa in the sixth century. This means, in other words, that the new Wa central authority, emerging from the re-organization of power relations within Japan's political leadership in the early sixth century, embraced the burial architecture of Paekche as part of a new pro-Paekche political strategy. Funerals of high-ranking Wa officials in Paekche-style tombs would have been an effective means of demonstrating both internally and externally the formation of a new close relationship between the two polities. Wa's central power could thus provide a broad-reaching visual demonstration of this new alliance by way of the delegations, both domestic and foreign, that were sent to attend these high-profile funerals. In other words, through these funerary forms the Wa central authorities could demonstrate their close relations with the advanced Paekche polity, and this would also have had the effect of internally stabilizing their own power base. On the diplomatic side as well, Wa would have been able to announce the adoption of a Paekche-oriented policy.

The formation of close relations between Paekche and Wa is further illustrated by an analysis of foreign-made artifacts recovered from the early sixth-century tomb of Paekche's King Muryŏng. Although most foreign goods buried in King Muryŏng's tomb were imports from the Southern Dynasties (Kwŏn O-yŏng 2005:195–197), the material used for the wooden coffin came from high-quality Japanese umbrella pine (*Sciadopitys verticillata*) imported from Wa (Pak Wŏn-gyu et al. 2002:113–131). In addition, the bronze mirrors discovered in this tomb appear to be related to similar mirrors found in Japan, providing further archaeological evidence of the close relationship between King Muryŏng and the ruler of Wa (Fukunaga 2007:430–433).

Thus, Paekche could demonstrate its new close alliance with the Southern Dynasties through the adoption of brick-chamber tomb architecture and the inclusion of the highest-quality goods, such as Chinese celadon, in its burial of King Muryŏng. The use of expensive Japanese pine wood for the king's coffin, on the other hand, would have been a visible testament to Paekche's new alliance with Wa. Thus, the adoption of Wa-style keyhole-shaped tombs in some regions of Paekche and the use of Japanese wood for

King Muryŏng's coffin strongly suggest that along with its adoption of a Southern Dynasties–oriented diplomatic policy in the early sixth century, Paekche had also begun to pursue a pro-Wa peer polity strategy.

The political destabilization of the Korean peninsula after the Koguryŏ attacks in the late fifth century forced the removal of Paekche's capital to Kongju would have been perceived as a security threat to Wa as well. In such a situation, Paekche would naturally have sought ways to strengthen its close relationship with Wa. From the Wa perspective, closer ties with Paekche would have provided a means to counter the growing military threat from Koguryŏ that could have jeopardized the trade and exchanges with the Korean peninsula that brought advanced culture and technology to the archipelago. It was clearly a common interest in security that brought Paekche and Wa closer to each other toward the early sixth century. The mutual adoption of funerary customs in this period should, therefore, be understood as a visible symbol of a new political configuration in the region.

Wa Adoption of Paekche-Style Cooking and Heating Systems in the Fifth and Sixth Centuries

In the fifth to sixth centuries, major changes took place in the cooking and heating systems used in Wa dwellings. The core change had to do with a transition from a simple fire hearth to a wood-burning stove-type furnace that was then prevalent in the Korean peninsula. The wood-burning stove of this period was a type of furnace made of clay or mixed clay and stone, with furnaces and smoke ducts placed inside the dwelling. The smoke ducts used in this type of furnace were exposed above the floor and ran along the walls, and in this respect they were distinct from the peninsular *ondol* system, in which stone smoke ducts ran under the floor. Since starting a fire in wood-burning stoves would also heat the clay furnaces and smoke ducts, this type of heating had a higher thermal efficiency than the simple fire furnace previously used in Wa (Figure 4.13).

On the other hand, examples of what are thought to be peninsula-style *ondol* heating systems are known from the Anō 穴太 site in Shiga 滋賀, dating to the latter half of the sixth century (Hanada 2002:212–216). However, this type of *ondol* heating that would heat the floors inside a dwelling did not spread in the archipelago as widely as did the wood-burning stove. In any event, given the climate of the archipelago, the wood-burning stove-type system seems to have been more suitable for the heating of houses there.

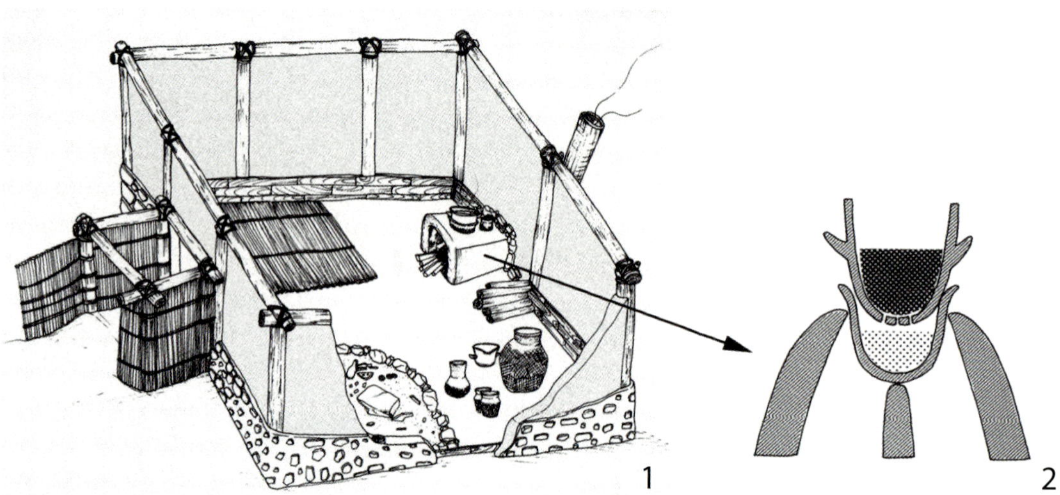

Figure 4.13 Wood-burning Stove-type Cooking and Heating Systems as Used in a Dwelling.
1. Restoration of stove-type cooking system in a dwelling (after Kim Sang-suk 2005);
2. Restoration of use of the system with a jar and steamer (after Wu Chae-byŏng 2006).

Peninsula-style wood-burning stoves first appeared in the archipelago sometime during the late third century in the northern Kyushu region. The Nishijin-machi 西新町 site in Fukuoka, a coastal settlement not far from the eastern coast of the Korean peninsula, is a representative settlement site in which several foundations of peninsula-style wood-burning stoves dating from the latter half of the third century have been excavated. The archaeological finds from this site include, in addition to peninsula-style wood-burning stoves, large quantities of earthenware items of peninsular origin. The excavated pottery ranged from Kaya-style ceramics from the southeastern region of the peninsula to large steamers and other pottery used for cooking from southwestern Korea.

Furthermore, the discovery of large, flat iron axes at the Nishijin-machi site, apparently imported from Kaya, has led some scholars to suggest that the site may have functioned as a long-distance trade port in antiquity, used by various political groups who were involved in the trade of iron from the Kaya region and who traveled back and forth between the peninsula and the archipelago (Takesue 2000:100–104).

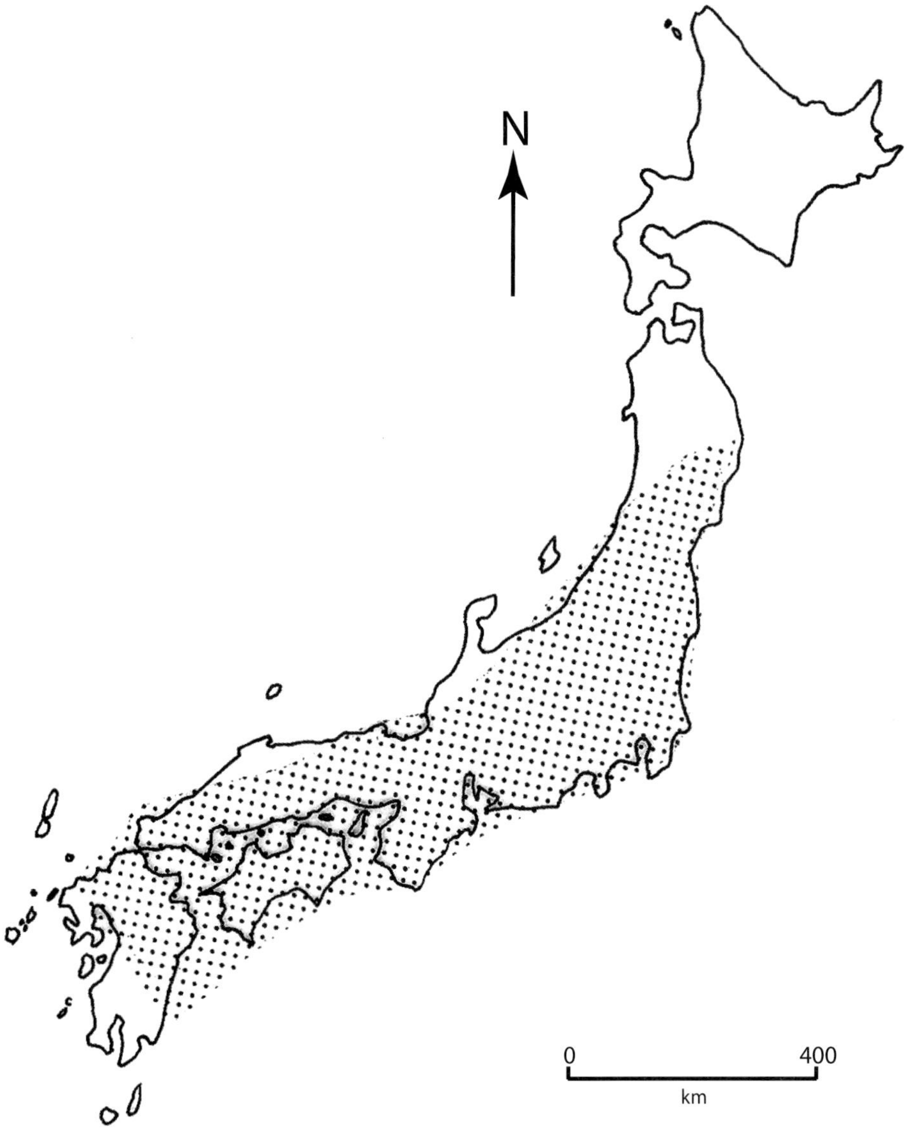

Map 4.2 Distribution of Wood-burning Stove-type Cooking and Heating Systems in the Japanese Archipelago in the Sixth Century. After Sugii 1999.

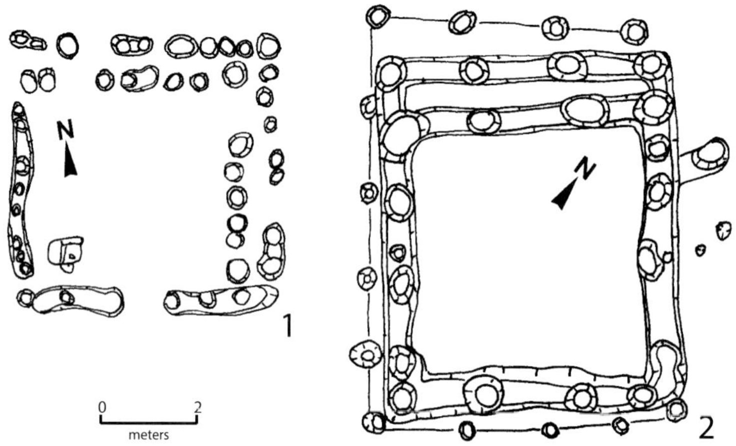

Figure 4.14 Comparison of Large-walled Dwelling Structures in the Central Regions of Paekche and in the Kinki Region of Japan.
1. Feature S-4 at Kunsa-ri in Puyŏ (after Ch'ungnam Taehakkyo Paekche Yŏn'guso 2003);
2. Feature SB-4 at the Anō site in Shiga Prefecture (after Hanada 2002).

However, late third-century peninsula-style heating and cooking systems, which used wood-burning stoves, steamers, and jars (Figure 4.13, no. 2), discovered at the Nishijin-machi site on the coastal region of northern Kyushu, do not appear to have continued to spread to other parts of the archipelago. The widespread diffusion of the peninsula-style heating and cooking systems had to wait, in fact, until the fifth and sixth centuries. In other words, their widespread diffusion coincided with the adoption and spread of Paekche-style horizontal-entry-style stone-chamber tombs across the archipelago.

Peninsula-style cooking and heating systems did not become widespread in Japan during the third and fourth centuries—the period of strong influence of Kŭmgwan Kaya on the archipelago. However, in the fifth and sixth centuries, when Paekche-style funerary architecture appeared in the archipelago, reflecting a new influence of Paekche culture, peninsula-style cooking and heating systems also began to spread widely. The analysis of the construction materials used for peninsula-style wood-burning stoves dating from the fifth and sixth centuries, as well as their flat-surfaced design and the types of steamers discovered along with them (Wu 2006:62–69),

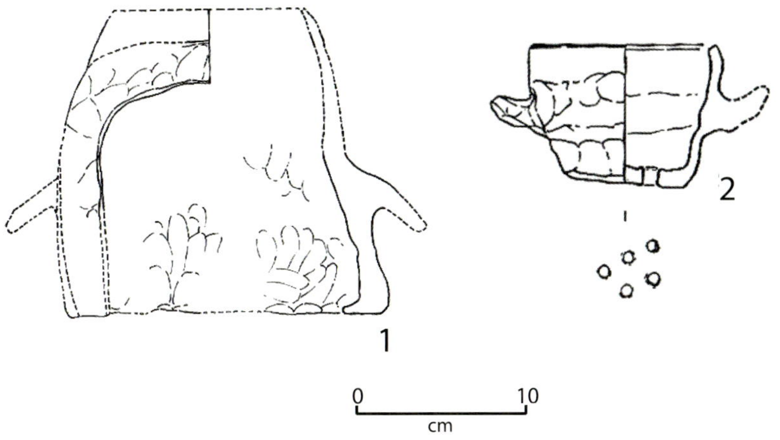

Figure 4.15 Clay Stove and Steamer from Tomb No. WA20 at the Ichisuka Cemetery in Osaka. After Ōsaka-fu Kyōiku Iinkai. 1. Clay stove; 2. Clay steamer.

suggests a strong Paekche influence on the process of their diffusion, with many of the furnaces assuming a style specifically associated with Paekche.

Although the exact timing of the adoption of the Paekche-style heating and cooking system in the Japanese archipelago varies depending on the region, its widespread diffusion can be said to have started around the fifth century. Once into the sixth century, Paekche-style heating and cooking systems appear to have been present, in the case of the Kyushu region, as far as the Kumamoto 熊本 Plain (Sugii 2001:91–94). In the southern part of the Tōhoku region, they had almost completely replaced the earlier native hearth (Kikuchi 1999:218–220; Map 4.2).

Sites featuring a type of large-walled house that was apparently introduced to the archipelago by peninsular emigres settled in the Kinai region show similarity to large-walled house sites excavated in Paekche territory (Hanada 2002:253–257; Figure 4.14). Further, wood-burning stoves and steamers modeled on Paekche styles have been discovered in cemeteries with tombs that adopted the horizontal-entry mortuary style from Paekche (Figure 4.15). Considering these facts, it appears that the new settlers from the peninsula played a key role in the process of diffusion of these cooking and heating systems throughout Japan in the fifth and sixth centuries.

The fact that the Paekche-style heating and cooking system was imported into Japan during the fifth and sixth centuries is certainly another piece of archaeological evidence attesting to the close ties between the two polities. The spread of the Paekche-style heating and cooking systems was not merely a result of the superior thermal efficiency of this system or of the large influx of settlers of Paekche origin. It probably also served the desire of the Wa leadership to showcase, both domestically and interregionally, the close relationship between Wa and Paekche. Hence, the broad diffusion of the Paekche-style heating and cooking system in the Japanese archipelago during the fifth and sixth centuries, along with the closely related adoption of horizontal-entry-style tombs in the sixth century, may be seen to reflect a Paekche-oriented political strategy by its ruling regime.

Conclusions

As I have argued in this article, analyses of mortuary culture and heating and food preparation systems provide traces of an active exchange between Paekche and Wa during the fifth and sixth centuries. This, in turn, suggests that close ties were formed between the two polities during this period. The evidence of this active exchange can be found in the diplomatic strategies adopted by the two polities in prioritizing relations with one another.

Starting in the fifth century, Paekche was subjected to continuous attacks by Koguryŏ. Koguryŏ's attacks against Kaya polities in the early fifth century, followed by attacks on Paekche in the late fifth century that forced the Paekche government to move its capital from Seoul to Kongju, were the primary factor contributing to instability on the Korean peninsula during this period. This military threat affected not only Paekche but also the whole economic structure of trade and exchange between the Japanese archipelago and the Korean peninsula. This structure provided Wa with access to essential raw materials such as iron and non-local products from a more technologically advanced culture. Therefore, Wa's adoption of Paekche-type tombs and heating and cooking systems can be interpreted as archaeological evidence for a close strategic relationship between the two polities.

Archaeological discoveries from the Yangdong-ni and Taesŏng-dong cemetery sites in Kimhae suggest that up until the fourth century, the southeastern part of the Korean peninsula was the Japanese archipelago's principal gateway for accessing iron products and other technologies. Subsequently, in the fifth century, as once-thriving Kŭmgwan Kaya fell to the forces of Koguryŏ and the established long-distance trade system between the archipelago and peninsula began to crumble, Wa set out to develop new trade relations with Paekche as its principal partner. This is clear if we look at the traces of Wa-style ritual in the southwestern region of Paekche from the Chungmak-tong site as well as the selection by elites of Wa-style keyhole-shaped tombs in the same region, both of which appeared in the late fifth and early sixth centuries.

Toward the late fifth century, Wa traders traveling to Paekche left Wa-style stone artifacts and other traces of their participation in rituals at the Chungmak-tong ritual site, located along their sea route in the western coastal waters of the peninsula. The Chungmak-tong site is located at an important transit route to the Paekche capital for Wa ships. The results of the excavations at this site suggest that toward the fifth to sixth centuries, ships piloted by Wa individuals on their way to the Paekche capital made stops at Chungmak-tong. The archaeological finds from this site also suggest that Wa people attended rituals there to ensure their safe journey.

The Wa-style stone artifacts and large jars found at the Chungmak-tong ritual site lead us to conclude that rituals were performed there over a period spanning the late fifth to the early sixth centuries. I have emphasized in my discussion of the Chungmak-tong site the fact that Wa participation in these rituals was contemporary to, and in fact related to, the construction of Wa-style keyhole-shaped tombs for some of the local chieftains of Paekche's southwestern borderland region.

Concerning the historical background to the appearance of Wa-style keyhole-shaped burial mounds in the Korean peninsula, I have drawn attention to the following three points. First, the majority of keyhole burial mounds found in the southwestern part of the Korean peninsula were constructed during the reign of King Muryŏng in the earlier part of the sixth century. Second, archaeological discoveries related to the forms and distribution of Paekche gilt-bronze crowns and headpieces indicate that the southwestern part of the Korean peninsula had already been brought under Paekche's control by the first half of the sixth century. And third, two brick-chamber tombs in the style of the Southern Dynasties were constructed in Paekche during the early sixth century—one for King Muryŏng and another for a ruling-class member of royal rank.

These three special features appear to be closely related to the construction of no more than one or two Wa-style keyhole-shaped tombs in each of various locations in Paekche's southwestern regions during the early sixth century. Meanwhile, the short-lived adoption of Wa-style burial structures in the early sixth century for some of the local chieftains in Paekche's southwestern regions seems to be closely related to a similarly short-lived adoption of Southern Dynasties–style brick-chamber tombs for royal burials. If we connect these two inferences, it seems logical that there must have been some compelling reason behind the simultaneous adoption by the Paekche court of two different types of non-local mortuary architecture.

Toward the late fifth century, after the relocation of its capital, Paekche was compelled to cement ties with the Southern Dynasties as well as with Wa as a way of keeping Koguryŏ's ambitions in check through the help of its allies. Paekche's adoption of the Southern Dynasties– and Wa-style mortuary forms in its capital and in its southwestern regions respectively appears to have been part of a larger effort. Funerals of the Paekche king and local clan chiefs were high-profile events attended by envoys from neighboring polities and thus served as strategic vehicles for the sharing of information and news beyond the borders of the kingdom. The Southern Dynasties–style brick-chamber tomb built to house the remains of King Muryŏng and the Wa-style keyhole-shaped burial mounds for deceased local clan chiefs therefore functioned as visible signs of Paekche's new strategic ties with the Chinese states and Wa.

On the other hand, Paekche-style horizontal-entry-style stone-chamber tombs appeared in central Wa in the early sixth century and then spread to other parts of the polity. As was the case with Paekche's adoption of Wa burial architecture, the Wa political leadership may have used horizontal-entry-style tombs as visible symbols of their strengthened ties with Paekche. Hence, the securing of a stable route of import for advanced cultural goods from Paekche would have been an important issue for the Wa central authorities at a time when they faced the growing military threat from Koguryŏ. The adoption of Paekche-style tombs also served internal purposes, as it also helped strengthen the government's political base at home.

Meanwhile, along with horizontal-entry-style stone-chamber tombs, the Paekche-style heating and cooking systems, including Paekche wood-burning stoves and steamers, were also imported by Wa in the fifth century. By the sixth century, the Paekche-style heating and cooking systems had spread all the way to the Kumamoto Plain in Kyushu and appeared in almost every dwelling in the southern part of Tōhoku. The widespread diffusion of the Paekche-style heating and cooking system appears to have been facilitated by the influx of settlers of Paekche origin. The superior thermal efficiency of this system compared to simple furnaces previously used in Japan must also have been a contributing factor. However, in addition to its practical aspect, we should not overlook the political dimension of this change, as the diffusion of the Paekche heating and cooking systems proceeded against the background of strengthened relations between Paekche and Wa. In any event, the widespread adoption of the Paekche-style heating and cooking systems and mortuary architecture constitutes an important piece of archaeological evidence attesting to the close relationship between the two polities.

Based on the archaeological evidence I have presented, it appears that political, economic, and military necessities compelled Paekche and Wa to form closer ties with each other from the fifth century. Toward the early sixth century, these ties appear to have further strengthened. Around this period, Paekche not only was actively seeking closer relations with the Southern Dynasties, but was also looking to form a closer political alliance with Wa in an effort to keep Koguryŏ in check.

In the fifth century Koguryŏ launched attacks into the Kaya region, from which the Wa had imported advanced goods such as iron, and late in the century it also destroyed Paekche's capital in Seoul. It was thus in Wa's interest to strengthen its ties with Paekche as a way to counter Koguryŏ's military strength, which had become a threat to the security of the southern part of the peninsula and extending even to the archipelago. Securing stable access to advanced cultural goods must also have been a factor that pushed Japan to seek Paekche's support. There is no evidence suggesting the existence of asymmetrical political relations between Paekche and Wa such as those that existed between the Southern Dynasties and Paekche. Nevertheless, they appear to have maintained close interactions with each other at a political, economic, and military level.

I view the close relationship that existed between Paekche and Wa as corresponding to the concept of peer polity interaction (Renfrew and Cherry 1986). Of course, if one places emphasis only on the broad dissemination in Wa of Paekche-style mortuary forms and heating and cooking systems, it may be difficult to view the interactions between the two polities as based on equality. However, when simultaneously considering the adoption of Wa-style mortuary systems by some elites in Paekche's southwestern regions, it becomes reasonable to view the character of relations between the two polities as peer polity interaction.

This study has described the interchanges between Paekche and Wa during the fifth and sixth centuries as peer polity interaction. However, due to a paucity of data, I am presently unable to explore specific details of the political, economic, and military support that they may have received from each other to counter the instability created by Koguryŏ's military aggressions. I hope to pursue the investigation of this topic further as relevant new archaeological data become available.

References

Azuma Ushio 東潮

2002 Wa to Eisan-kō ryūiki 倭と榮山江流域 [Wa and the Yŏngsan River basin]. In *Zempō-kōen-fun to kodai Nitchō kankei* 前方後円墳と古代日朝関係 [Keyhole-shaped tombs and ancient Japan-Korea relations], edited by Chōsen Gakkai 朝鮮学会 [Society for Korean Studies], pp. 127–172. Dōseisha 同成社, Tokyo.

Best, Jonathan W.

2006 *A History of the Early Korean Kingdom of Paekche*. Harvard University Asia Center, Cambridge (Massachusetts) and London.

Chŏnnam Taehakkyo Pangmulgwan 전남대학교박물관 [Chŏnnam University Museum]

2000 *Chŏnnam chiyŏk kobun ch'ŭngnyang pogosŏ* 전남지역 고분 측량보고서 [Survey report of mounded burials in the Chŏnnam region]. Chŏnnam Taehakkyo Pangmulgwan, Kwangju.

Ch'ungnam Taehakkyo Paekche Yŏn'guso 충남대학교 백제연구소 [Chungnam National University Paekche Research Institute]

2003 *Sabi t'osŏng* 사비都城 [The Sabi capital]. Ch'ungnam Taehakkyo Paekche Yŏn'guso, Taejŏn.

Ch'ungch'ŏng-namdo Yŏksa Munhwa Yŏn'guwŏn 충청남도 역사문화연구원 [Chungnam Institute of History and Culture]

2008 *Sŏsan Pujang-ni yujŏk* 서산 부장리유적 [The Pujang-ni site in Sŏsan]. Ch'ungch'ŏng-namdo Yŏksa Munhwa Yŏn'guwŏn, Kongju.

Fukunaga Shin'ya 福永伸哉

2005 Kofun no hyōka 古墳の評価 [Evaluation of the Inouchi-Inarizuka tumulus]. In *Inouchi-Inarizuka kofun no kenkyū* 井ノ内稲荷塚古墳の研究 [Studies of the Inouchi-Inarizuka tumulus], edited by Ōsaka Daigaku Inarizuka Kofun Hakkutsu Chōsadan 大阪大学稲荷塚古墳発掘調査団 [Osaka University Team for Archaeological Investigations of the Inarizuka Tumulus], pp. 217–218. Ōsaka Daigaku Inarizuka Kofun Hakkutsu Chōsadan, Osaka.

———

2007 Keitai ōken to Kan-hantō no zempō-kōen-fun 継体王権と韓半島の前方後円墳. In *Shōfukuji kofun no kenkyū* 勝福寺古墳の研究 [Studies of the Shōfukuji tumulus], edited by Ōsaka Daigaku Bungaku Kenkyūka Kōkogaku Kenkyūshitsu 大阪大学文学研究科考古学研究室 [Osaka University Faculty of Letters Department of Archaeology], pp. 425–434. Ōsaka Daigaku Bungaku Kenkyūka Kōkogaku Kenkyūshitsu, Toyonaka.

Habuta Yoshiyuki 土生田純之

2000 Han-Il chŏnbang huwŏn pun ŭi pigyo kŏmt'o 韓・日 前方後圓墳의 比較檢討 [Comparative analysis of keyhole-shaped tombs in Korea and Japan]. In *Han'guk ŭi chŏnbang huwŏn pun* 韓國의 前方後圓墳 [Korea's keyhole-shaped tombs], edited by Ch'ungnam Taehakkyo Paekche Yŏn'guso 충남대학교 백제연구소 [Chungnam National University Paekche Research Institute], Paengma Haksul Ch'ongsŏ 백마학술총서 [Paengma Academic Collection series], Vol. 11, pp. 19–21. Ch'ungnam Taehakkyo Ch'ulp'anbu 충남대학교 출판부, Taejŏn.

Hanada Katsuhiro 花田勝広

2002 *Kodai no tetsu seisan to toraijin* 古代の鉄生産と渡来人 [Ancient iron production and migrants]. Yūzankaku 雄山閣, Tokyo.

Ichinose Kazuo 一瀬和夫

2005 *Daiōbo to zenpō kōenfun* 大王墓と前方後円墳 [Large royal burials and keyhole-shaped tombs]. Yoshikawa Kōbunkan 吉川弘文館, Tokyo.

Im Yŏng-jin 임영진

1994 Kwangu Wŏlgye-dong changgo pun 2 ki 광주 월계동 長鼓墳2基. [Two tombs at Changgo in Wŏlgye-dong, Kwangju]. *Han'guk Kogo Hakpo* 한국고고학보 31: 237–264.

———

2002 Kankoku no fun-shū doki. 韓國の墳周土器 [Pottery from tomb peripheries in Korea]. In *Higashi Asia to Nihon no kōkogaku 2* 東アジアと日本の考古学 2 [Archaeology of East Asia and Japan, volume 2]. Edited by Gotō Tadashi 後藤直 and Mogi Masahiro 茂木雅博, pp. 3–26. Dōseisha 同成社, Tokyo.

Kang Chong-wŏn 강종원

2005 Han-sŏng malgi chibang chibae wa Such'on-ni Paekche kobun'gun 漢城말기 지방지배와 수촌리 백제고분군 [Regional control in the late Han-sŏng period and the Such'on-ni mounded burials of Paekche]. *Ch'ungch'ŏnghak kwa Ch'ungch'ŏng Munhwa* 충청학과 충청문화 4(1): 235–251.

Kikuchi Yoshiro 菊地芳朗

1999 Tōhoku chihō ni okeru kofun jidai chū-kōki no torai-kei bunka 東北地方における古墳時代中–後期の渡来系文化 [Imported culture of the middle and late Kofun period in the Tōhoku region]. In *Torai bunka no juyō to tenkai* 渡来文化の受容と展開 [Reception and development of imported culture], edited by Dai-46 Kai Maizō Bunkazai Kenkyū Shūkai Jikkō Iinkai 第46回埋蔵文化財研究集会実行委員会 [Executive Committee for the Forty-Sixth Assembly for Buried Cultural Properties], pp. 217–231. Maizō Bunkazai Kenkyū Kai 埋蔵文化財研究会 [Japanese Association for Field Archaeologists], Nara.

Kim Nak-chung 김낙중

2009 *Yŏngsan-gang yuyŏk kobun yŏn'gu* 영산강유역 고분 연구 [Research on the mounded burials of the Yŏngsan River basin]. Hagyŏn Munhwasa 학연문화사, Seoul.

Kim Sang-suk 김상숙

2005 Han'guk kodae kudŭl sisŏl e taehayŏ 한국 고대 구들시설에 대하여 [On the ancient Korean floor heating features]. Haksa hagwi nonmun 학사학위 논문 [Unpublished undergraduate graduation thesis], 충남대학교 [Chungnam National University], Taejŏn.

Kungnip Chŏnju Pangmulgwan 국립전주박물관 [Chŏnju National Museum]

1994 *Puan Chungmak-tong chesa yujŏk* 부안 죽막동 제사유적 [The Chungmak-tong ritual site in Puan]. Kungnip Chŏnju Pangmulgwan 국립전주박물관, Chŏnju.

Kungnip Kongju Pangmulgwan 국립공주박물관 [Kongju National Museum]

2007 *Muryŏngwang nŭng: Ch'ult'o yumul punsŏk pogosŏ 3* 무녕왕릉: 출토유물 분석보고서 3 [Report on the analysis of artifacts excavated from the tomb of King Muryŏng, volume 3]. Kungnip Kongju Pangmulgwan 국립공주박물관, Kongju.

Kungnip Kwangju Pangmulgwan 국립광주박물관 [Kwangju National Museum]

1996 *Kwangju Myŏnghwa-dong kobun* 광주 명화동고분 [The Myŏnghwa-dong mounded burial]. Kungnip Kwangju Pangmulgwan 국립광주박물관, Kwangju.

———

2008 Haenam Yongdu-ri kobun palgul chosa: Chido wiwŏnhoe ŭi charyo 해남 용두리고분 발굴조사: 지도위원회의 자료 [Unpublished advisory committee briefs of the excavations of the Yongdu-ri mounded burials, Haenam]. Kungnip Kwangju Pangmulgwan 국립광주박물관, Kwangju.

Kungnip Munhwajae Yŏn'guso 국립문화재연구소 [National Research Institute for Cultural Heritage]

2001 *Naju Sinch'on-ni 9-ho pun* 나주 신촌리9호분 [Tomb 9 at Sinch'on-ni, Naju]. Kungnip Munhwajae Yŏn'guso, Taejŏn.

Kwŏn O-yŏng 권오영

2005 *Kodae Tong Asia munmyŏng kyoryusa ŭi pit: Muryŏngwang nŭng* 고대 동아시아 문명교류사의 빛: 무령왕릉 [The tomb of King Muryŏng: Illuminating the history of exchange among civilizations in East Asia]. Tolbegae 돌베개, P'aju.

Kyŏngsang-pukto Munhwajae Yŏn'guwŏn 경상북도 문화재연구원 [North Kyŏngsang Institute of Cultural Properties]

2010 *Talsŏng P'yŏngch'on-ni Yehyŏn-ni yujŏk* 달성 평촌리·예현리유적 [The P'yŏngch'on-ni and Yehyŏn-ni sites at Talsŏng]. Kyŏngsang-pukto Munhwajae Yŏn'guwŏn, Yŏngch'ŏn.

Kyŏngsŏng Taehakkyo Pangmulgwan 경성대학교박물관 [Kyŏngsŏng University Museum]

2000 *Kimhae Taesŏng-dong kobun'gun 1* 김해 대성동고분군 1 [The Taesŏng-dong cemetery in Kimhae, volume 1]. Kyŏngsŏng Taehakkyo Pangmulgwan, Pusan.

Kyōto Daigaku Bungakubu Kōkogaku Kenkyūshitsu 京都大学文学部考古学研究室 [Kyoto University Faculty of Letters Department of Archaeology]

1993 *Shikinzan kofun to Ishiyama kofun* 紫金山古墳と石山古墳 [The Shikinzan and Ishiyama tumuli]. Kyōto Daigaku Bungakubu Hakubutsukan 京都大学文学部博物館, Kyoto.

Morioka Hideto 森岡秀人

1989 Gunshūfun no keisei 群集墳の形成 [Formation of clustered tombs]. In *Kodai o kangaeru: Kofun* 古代を考える: 古墳 [Considering the ancient past: Tombs], edited by Shiraishi Taichirō 白石太一郎, pp. 207–245. Yoshikawa Kōbunkan 吉川弘文館, Tokyo.

Okita Masaaki 置田雅昭

1988 Fune gata haniwa 船形埴輪 [Boat-shaped *haniwa*]. In *Nigore kofun* ニゴレ古墳 [The Nigore tumulus], edited by Tenri Daigaku Hakubutsukangaku Kenkyūshitsu 天理大学博物館学研究室 [Tenri University Museology Laboratory], pp. 97–105. Yasaka Chō Kyōiku Iinkai 弥栄町教育委員会 [Yasaka Board of Education], Kyoto Prefecture.

Ōsaka Daigaku Inarizuka Kofun Hakkutsu Chōsadan 大阪大学稲荷塚古墳発掘調査団 [Osaka University Team for Archaeological Investigations of the Inarizuka Tumulus]

2005 *Inouchi-Inarizuka kofun no kenkyū* 井ノ内稲荷塚古墳の研究 [Studies of the Inouchi-Inarizuka tumulus]. Ōsaka Daigaku Inarizuka Kofun Hakkutsu Chōsadan, Osaka.

Ōsaka-fu Kyōiku Iinkai 大阪府教育委員会 [Osaka Prefectural Board of Education]

1992 *Ichisuka kofun gun shiryō mokuroku 1* 一須賀古墳群資料目録 1 [Catalogue of tomb data from the Ichisuka cemetery, volume 1]. Ōsaka-fu Kyōiku Iinkai, Osaka.

Ōsaka-shi Kyōiku Iinkai 大阪市教育委員会 [Osaka Municipal Board of Education]

1989 *Yomigaeru kodai sen to 5-seiki no Ōsaka* よみがえる古代船と5世紀の大阪 [Reconstructed ancient boats and fifth-century Osaka]. Ōsaka-shi Kyōiku Iinkai, Osaka.

Pak Ch'ŏn-su (Park Cheun Soo) 朴天秀

2001 Eisan-kō ryūiki no kofun 榮山江流域の古墳 [Tombs of the Yŏngsan River basin]. In *Higashi Asia to Nihon no kōkogaku 1* 東アジアと日本の考古学 1 [Archaeology of East Asia and Japan, volume 1]. Edited by Gotō Tadashi 後藤直 and Mogi Masahiro 茂木雅博, pp. 3–31. Dōseisha 同成社, Tokyo.

———

2002 Eisan-kō ryūiki ni okeru zempō-kōen-fun no hisōsha no shutsuji to sono seikaku 榮山江流域における前方後円墳の被葬者の出自とその性格 [The origin and nature of those buried in the keyhole tombs in the Yŏngsan River basin]. *Kōkogaku Kenkyū* 考古学研究 49(2): 42–59.

Pak Wŏn-gyu 박원규, Pak Sang-jin 박상진, and Kang Ae-gyŏng 강애경

2002 Muryŏngwang nŭng ch'ult'o kwanmok punsŏk ŭl t'onghan kodae Han-Il kwan'gye 무녕왕릉 출토 棺木 분석을 통한 고대 韓日關係 [Ancient Korea-Japan relations through the analysis of wood from the coffin of the tomb of King Muryŏng]. *Paekche munhwa rŭl t'onghae pon kodae Tong Asia segye* 백제문화를 통해 본 고대 東아시아世界 [The world of East Asia as seen through Paekche culture], pp. 113–131. Kongju Taehakkyo Paekche Munhwa Yŏn'guso 공주대학교 백제문화연구소 [Kongju University Paekche Research Institute], Kongju.

Renfrew, Colin and John F. Cherry (editors)

1986 *Peer Polity Interaction and Socio-Political Change*. Cambridge University Press, Cambridge.

Shiraishi Taichirō 白石太一郎

2007 Yokoanashiki sekishitsu tanjō 横穴式石室誕生 [The birth of corridor-style horizontal burial chamber tombs]. In *Yokoanashiki sekishitsu tanjō: Yominokuni no seiritsu* 横穴式石室誕生: 黄泉国の成立 [The birth of corridor-style horizontal burial chamber tombs: The establishment of Yominokuni], edited by Ōsaka Furitsu Chikatsu Asuka Hakubutsukan 大阪府立近つ飛鳥博物館 [Osaka Prefectural Asuka Museum], pp. 8–15. Ōsaka Furitsu Chikatsu Asuka Hakubutsukan, Kanan, Osaka.

Sugii Takeshi 杉井健

1996 Yugi no kōzō to sono seiritsu no haikei 靫の構造とその成立背景 [Structure of Kofun period quivers and the historical background to their appearance]. In *Yukinoyama kofun no kenkyū: Kōsatsu hen* 雪野山古墳の研究: 考察篇 [Studies of the Yukinoyama tumulus: Analysis volume], edited by Yukinoyama Kofun Hakkutsu Chōsadan 雪野山古墳発掘調査団 [Team for Archaeological Investigations of the Yukinoyama Tumulus], pp. 107–144. Yukinoyama Kofun Hakkutsu Chōsadan 雪野山古墳発掘調査団, Yōkaichi.

———

1999 Suihan yōshiki kara mita tōzai Nihon no chiiki sei 炊飯様式からみた東西日本の地域性 [Regionality of eastern and western Japan from the perspective of cooking styles]. In *Nihonjin no kigen to chiikisei* 日本人の起源と地域性 [Origins and regionality of the Japanese people], edited by Sahara Makoto 佐原真 and Tanaka Migaku 田中琢, pp. 103–124. Kodaishi no ronten 古代史の論点 [Issues in ancient history], Vol. 6, Kanaseki Hiroshi 金関恕, Sahara Makoto, Tanaka Migaku, and Tsude Hiroshi 都出比呂志, general editors. Shōgakukan 小学館, Tokyo.

———

2001 Chōsen hantō-kei torai bunka no dōkō to kofun no hikaku kenkyū shiron 朝鮮半島系渡来文化の動向と古墳の比較研究試論 [Trial comparative study of tombs and trends in culture imported from the Korean peninsula]. *Kōkogaku Kenkyū* 考古学研究 47(4): 90–104.

Takahashi Takumi 高橋工

1989 Kodai no fune 古代の船 [Ancient boats]. In *Yomigaeru kodai sen to 5-seiki no Ōsaka* よみがえる古代船と5世紀の大阪 [Reconstructed ancient boats and fifth-century Osaka], edited by Ōsaka-shi Kyoiku Iinkai 大阪市教育委員会 [Osaka Municipal Board of Education], pp. 26–31. Ōsaka-shi Kyoiku Iinkai, Osaka.

Takesue Jun'ichi 武末純一

2000 Hokubu Kyūshū no Kudara-kei doki: 4-5-seiki o chūshin ni 北部九州の百済系土器: 4–5世紀を中心に [Paekche-type pottery in northern Kyushu: with a focus on the fourth to fifth centuries]. In *Fukuoka Daigaku sōgō kenkyūjo hō: Sōgō Kagaku hen dai-3 gō* 福岡大学総合研究所報: 総合科学編 第3号 [Fukuoka University comprehensive research report: Comprehensive science volume no. 3], edited by Fukuoka Daigaku Sōgō Kenkyūjo 福岡大学総合研究所 [Fukuoka University Comprehensive Research Institute], pp. 99–114. Fukuoka Daigaku Sōgō Kenkyūjo, Fukuoka.

Tenri-shi Kyōiku Iinkai 天理市教育委員会 [Tenri City Board of Education]

2000 *Nishitonozuka kofun, Higashitonozuka kofun* 西殿塚古墳・東殿塚古墳 [The Nishitonozuka and Higashitonozuka tombs]. Tenri-shi Kyōiku Iinkai, Tenri.

Teramura Hiroshi 寺村裕史

2003 Hōkei haniwa retsu to jikeiretsu hensen to kakki 方形埴輪列の時系列変遷と画期 [Temporal change and epoch in a practice of standing *haniwa* cylinders in line forming a square], *Kōkogaku Kenkyū* 考古学研究 50(1): 98–110.

Tongŭi Taehakkyo Pangmulgwan 동의대학교박물관 [Tongŭi University Museum]

2000 *Kimhae Yangdong-ni kobun munhwa* 김해 양동리 고분문화 [Tomb culture at Yangdong-ni in Kimhae]. Tongŭi Taehakkyo Pangmulgwan, Pusan.

Tsude Hiroshi 都出比呂志

1989 *Kofun jidai no ō to minshū* 古墳時代の王と民衆 [The king and people of the Kofun period]. Kodai-shi fukugen 6 古代史復元 6 [Recovering ancient history, volume 6], Tanaka Migaku 田中琢 and Sahara Makoto 佐原真, general editors. Kodansha 講談社, Tokyo.

———

1998 *Kodai kokka no taidō* 古代国家の胎動 [Beginnings of the ancient state]. Nihon Hōsō Shuppan Kyōkai 日本放送出版協会, Tokyo.

———

2005 *Zempō-kōen-fun to shakai* 前方後円墳と社会 [Keyhole-shaped tombs and society]. Hanawa Shobō 塙書房, Tokyo.

Wŏn'gwang Taehakkyo Mahan Paekche Munhwa Yŏn'guso [Wonkwang University Mahan Paekche Research Institute]

2000 *Koch'ang ŭi pun'gu myo* 고창의 분구묘 [Mounded burials of Koch'ang]. Wŏn'gwang Taehakkyo Mahan Paekche Munhwa Yŏn'guso, Iksan.

Wu Chae-byŏng (Woo Jae Pyoung) 우재병

2002 4-5 segi Wae esŏ Kaya Paekche ro ŭi kyoyŏk rut'ŭ wa kodae hangno 4–5세기 왜에서 가야 · 백제로의 교역루트와 고대항로 [Ancient seaways and exchange routes from Wa to Kaya and Paekche]. *Hosŏ Kogohak* 湖西考古學 67: 165–199.

———

2004 Yŏngsan-gang yuyŏk chŏnbang huwŏn pun ŭi ch'urhyŏn kwa kŭ paegyŏng 榮山江流域 前方後圓墳의 출현과 그 배경 [The emergence of keyhole-shaped tombs in the Yŏngsan River basin and its background]. *Hosŏ Kogohak* 湖西考古學 10: 63–82.

———

2006 5–6-segi Paekche chugŏ nanbang myoje munhwa ŭi Wae-guk chŏnp'a wa paegyŏng 5–6세기 백제 주거·난방·묘제문화의 왜국 전파와 그 배경 [The advance to Wa of Paekche's dwelling, heating, and burial culture in the fifth to sixth centuries]. *Han'guksa Hakpo* 한국사학보 23: 59–93.

———

2009 5–6-segi Paekche Kaya Wae sai ŭi kwangyŏk kyoyŏk ch'egye chaep'yŏn kwa kŭ paegyŏng 5–6세기 백제·가야·왜사이의 廣域交易體系 再編과 그 배경 [Reorganization of broad trade systems among Paekche, Kaya, and Wa in the fifth to sixth centuries]. *Sŏnsa wa Kodae* 선사와 고대 31: 197–226.

Yanagisawa Kazuo 柳澤一男

1989 Kofun no henshitsu 古墳の変質 [Changes in ancient tombs]. In *Kodai o kangaeru: Kofun* 古代を考える: 古墳 [Considering the ancient past: Tombs], edited by Shiraishi Taichirō 白石太一郎, pp. 107–141. Yoshikawa Kōbunkan 吉川弘文館, Tokyo.

Yi Han-sang 이한상

2006 Silla wa Paekche kwanmo ŭi pigyo 신라와 백제 冠帽의 비교 [Comparing Silla and Paekche crowns]. *Ch'ungch'ŏnghak kwa Ch'ungch'ŏng Munhwa* 충청학과 충청문화 5(2): 45–68.

———

2009 *Changsin'gu sayŏ ch'eje ro pon Paekche ŭi chibang chibae* 裝身具 賜與체제로 본 백제의 지방지배 [Paekche control of regions as seen through its system of ornament bequeathment]. Sŏgyŏng Munhwasa 서경문화사, Seoul.

Yi Hun 이훈
2006 Kongju Such'on-ni Paekche kŭmdong kwan ŭi kogohakchŏk sŏngkyŏk 공주 수촌리 백제 금동관의 고고학적 성격 [The archaeological character of the gilt-bronze crown of Paekche from Such'on-ni, Kongju]. *Ch'ungch'ŏnghak kwa Ch'ungch'ŏng Munhwa* 충청학과 충청문화 5(2): 3–32.

———

2010 Kŭmdong kwan ŭl t'onghae pon 4–5-segi Paekche ŭi chibang t'ongch'i 金銅冠을 통해 본 4–5세기 백제의 지방통치. Paksa hagwi nonmun 박사학위논문 [Unpublished Ph.D. dissertation], Kongju Taehakkyo Taehagwŏn 공주대학교 대학원 [Graduate School, Kongju University], Kongju.

Yi Nam-sŏk 이남석
2008 Paekche kwanmo kwansik kwa chibang t'ongch'i ch'eje 백제 冠帽·冠飾과 지방통치체제 [Paekche's official crowns and local governance system]. *Han'guksa Hakpo* 한국사학보 33: 443–478.

Yukinoyama Kofun Hakkutsu Chōsadan 雪野山古墳発掘調査団 [Team for Archaeological Investigations of the Yukinoyama Tumulus]
1996 *Yukinoyama kofun no kenkyū* 雪野山古墳の研究 [Studies of the Yukinoyama tumulus]. Yukinoyama Kofun Hakkutsu Chōsadan, Yōkaichi.

5

Ancient Kibi, Western Japan, and the Korean Peninsula

Kameda Shūichi

Abstract

This chapter attempts to reconstruct interactions between the Korean peninsula and the western Japanese archipelago between the fifth and seventh centuries A.D., drawing upon a variety of available sources. I focus on the Kibi region of western Japan because a dominant polity, somewhat independent of the central polity, existed in Kibi. Within Kibi, evidence for interaction with the Korean peninsula becomes clear from the early fifth century in southern Bitchū, southern Bizen, and southeastern Bizen. In the southern Bitchū area in particular, giant keyhole tumuli as large as the imperial mausolea in the Kinai central polity appeared in the early to mid-fifth century. The power symbolized by the size of the keyhole tumuli may to some extent be owed to this area's interactions with the Korean peninsula. Although the Kibi polity fell under the control of the Kinai central polity in the late fifth century, new immigrants from the peninsula were sent to Kibi by the central polity in the mid-sixth century, when the central polity established the royal estate. Owing to immigrants' introduction of new technology, iron production began in Kibi and subsequently developed.

Introduction

The Japanese archipelago spans an area of approximately two thousand kilometers from the northern tip of Hokkaido to the southernmost part of Kyushu, a distance equivalent to that between Beijing and Hong Kong, and between New York and Miami, Florida (Map 5.1). The islands of the archipelago are narrowly distributed in the northeast–southwest direction. Generally speaking, the Japanese archipelago is divided into western

5 Ancient Kibi, Western Japan, and the Korean Peninsula—Kameda Shūichi

Map 5.1 East Asia with Location of Kibi in Japan.
Map by Mark E. Byington after author's original.

and eastern halves. This chapter covers western Japan, while the chapter by Habuta in this volume covers eastern Japan.

By "western Japan" archaeologists and ancient historians tend to mean regions to the west of the Kinki 近畿 district (inclusive of Kinki) where Kyoto and Osaka are located. In western Japan are northern Kyushu (Tsukushi 筑紫) and San'in 山陰 (the Sea of Japan coastal region of western Honshu) where interactions with the Korean peninsula were more direct than Kibi 吉備, the focus of this chapter, and central Kinki, a region that later came to be called Kinai 畿内 and where the central polity and government were located throughout the Kofun period. This chapter focuses on the Kibi region because evidence for interactions with the Korean peninsula as well as with the central polity in Kinai is very clear.

Kibi (present Okayama 岡山 Prefecture) is a region situated on the northern coast of the Inland Sea in western Japan. The regional polity of Kibi is often discussed as a local power in ancient Japanese history and archaeology, along with Tsukushi (northern Kyushu), Izumo 出雲 (Sea of Japan coast of western Honshu), Owari 尾張 (Pacific coast of central Japan), and Kenu 毛野 (north of Tokyo). The regional polity of Kibi is distinguished not only because of the presence of two exceptionally large keyhole tumuli of more than 300 m in length, comparable to the imperial mausoleum in Yamato, but also due to many other regional characteristics, such as high agricultural output owing to fertile plains, iron production, transportation by the Inland Sea, and salt production owing to a dry climate. Among these characteristics, the focus of this chapter is transportation to and from the Korean peninsula and resultant immigration from the peninsula.

In order to approach aspects of interaction between Kibi and the Korean peninsula, I will examine data from the fifth to seventh centuries A.D., a period for which we have very good archaeological evidence for interaction with Korea (Kameda 1997a). Although Kibi was historically divided into four provinces, Bitchū 備中, Bizen 備前, Mimasaka 美作, and Bingo 備後 (Map 5.2), I will focus on southern Kibi—the old provinces of Bitchū and Bizen—because southern Bitchū and southern Bizen compose the core area of Kibi. Southern Bitchū may be related to the Shimotsumichi 下道 family of the later historic period, and southern Bizen is related to the Kamitsumichi 上道 family of the later historic period. There is good archaeological evidence for Korean interaction in these areas. I will first examine archaeological evidence, then historic sources, and, finally, I will integrate interpretations of archaeological and historical evidence.

In this chapter, I use the term "immigrants" (*toraijin* 渡来人) to refer to people from the Korean peninsula who came to and settled in Japan as well as peninsular people who visited Japan on business and later returned to their home. I am aware of the importance of this difference, but it is not always simple to distinguish archaeologically between foreigners who settled in Japan and those who only visited. I have discussed this issue at length elsewhere in Japanese (Kameda 1993, 2003).

My analyses have led me to the following conclusions. I suspect that immigrants from the southeastern part of the Korean peninsula settled in the southern Bitchū area in the early fifth century, based on a marked increase in the quantities of archaeological data of Korean origins. It seems

Map 5.2 Kibi Region in Western Japan, showing Bingo, Bitchū, Bizen, and Mimasaka.

that these immigrants were involved in iron tool production and transportation by sea under the supervision of the secondary-level chiefs who were under the control of the highest-ranking chiefs interred in keyhole tumuli of more than 300 m in length. Local polities in Kibi remained weak from the late fifth century to the early sixth century, probably due to the failed Kibi rebellion against Emperor Yūryaku 雄略 in 463. When two *miyake* or royal estates were established by the central authority of Yamato in 555 and 556, new Korean immigrants were dispatched by the central authority to these royal estates. Iron smelting in southern Bitchū commenced on the basis of new technologies and information the inhabitants brought from the Korean peninsula.

Archaeologists surmise that immigrants from the southeastern part of the Korean peninsula settled in the southern Bizen area somewhat later than in Bitchū from the early fifth to early sixth centuries in the vicinity of the Ryōgūzan 両宮山 keyhole tumulus of more than 200 m in length. This interpretation is based on the discoveries of large quantities of archaeological data of Korean origins. In the Oku 邑久 area in southeastern Bizen, some archaeological data of Korean origin are dated to the late fifth century. Historic sources suggest that the Kibi no Ama no Atai 吉備海部直 family resided in the Oku area and were in charge of diplomatic negotiations with polities in the Korean peninsula from the late fifth to the end of the sixth centuries. After the establishment of the royal estates in 555 and 556, it is probable that this family was involved in the management of *sue*-stoneware production and salt production.

In sum, in ancient Kibi two polities existed in the fifth century in southern Bitchū and southern Bizen, and both interacted with polities in the Korean peninsula. Although their power was comparable to that of the central polity of Yamato, in the late fifth century the two polities in Kibi were suppressed by the central polity. An exception to the decline in power in Kibi in the late fifth century was a local polity in the Oku area of southeastern Bitchū. It maintained its relatively autonomous position owing to information and maritime technology introduced from the Korean peninsula. The Oku polity or the Kibi no Ama no Atai family interacted not only with the dominant polities of Kibi but also with the central polity of Yamato. This suggests that three different areas in Kibi were relatively autonomous and interacted with polities of the Korean peninsula and the central polity of Yamato independently. Below, I will present archaeological and historical data to support the claims presented above.

Kibi and the Korean Peninsula as Evidenced by Archaeological Data

The Relationship Between Bitchū and the Korean Peninsula

Material culture of Korean origins in southern Bitchū is commonly excavated in the vicinity of two exceptional keyhole tumuli: Zōzan 造山 (No. 22 in Figure 5.1; Figure 5.2; Nishikawa 1986a) and Sakuzan 作山 (No.

5 Ancient Kibi, Western Japan, and the Korean Peninsula—Kameda Shūichi

Figure 5.1 Sites in the Bitchū Region Where Korean Artifacts and Features Have Been Discovered.

35 in Figure 5.1; Kuzuhara 1986; Kameda 2004a).[1] The former, at 360 m in length, is the fourth largest tumulus in Japan, and it was built at the beginning of the fifth century A.D., or Phase 5 to 6 of the Kofun period.[2] The

[1] Editor's Note: Although the Sino-Japanese characters differ, the tumuli here called Zōzan and Sakuzan are both pronounced *tsukuriyama*, literally meaning man-made mound. Zōzan and Sakuzan are different pronunciations of the respective site names. The translator uses these pronunciations throughout this chapter to avoid confusion.

[2] These phases are based on Kondo (1991). Editor's Note: Kameda mentions these phases because Japanese archaeologists consider relative chronology more

Figure 5.2 Aerial Photograph of the Tsukuriyama (Zōzan) Tumulus and the Sakakiyama Tumulus.
Photograph courtesy of the Okayama Municipal Board of Education.

reliable. While the great majority of Japanese archaeologists agree on the relative date of Zōzan (Phase 5 to 6), many archaeologists debate the calendrical dates of individual tumuli.

Figure 5.3 Horse-shaped Buckles Discovered at the Sakakiyama Tumulus. Upper left 10.4 cm. Reproduced with permission of the Imperial Household Agency, National Government of Japan.

latter is 286 m in length and the ninth largest tumulus in Japan, and it was built after Zōzan and is dated to the early fifth century (Phase 6). These two are indeed comparable to the imperial mausolea in Kinai (Kameda 2008).

Material culture of Korean origins deposited with the dead in tumuli in the vicinity of Zōzan include: (1) horse-shaped belt hooks (Figure 5.3) and stoneware of Kaya origin discovered at the Sakakiyama 榊山 tumulus (No. 23 in Figure 5.1; Wada 1919; Shimazaki 1982; Fukuo 2006); and (2) *haji*-earthenware jars modeled after Korean stoneware, the earliest type of *sue* stoneware made in Kibi, and the earliest type of *sue*-stoneware pedestalled bowl modeled after *haji* earthenware discovered at Tumulus No. 37 of the Hōren 法蓮 tumulus group (No. 21 in Figure 5.1; Sōja-shi Kyōiku Iinkai 1985). The Sakakiyama tumulus is a circular mound 35 m in diameter built in the early fifth century (Phases 5 to 6). The Hōren tumulus group consists of some forty small circular and square tumuli, and No. 37 is dated to the early fifth century. Approximately five kilometers north-northwest of Zōzan in the Zuian 随庵 tumulus (No. 15 in Figure 5.1; Kamaki et al. 1965), a full set of imported ironsmith tools were deposited, and the deceased was placed in a wooden coffin with iron clamps. The burial, dated to the early fifth century (Phase 6), is a scallop-shaped mound with small projections and is 40 m in length. The full set of imported ironsmith tools represents an extremely rare find from the early fifth century, and the use of iron clamps was likewise highly unusual at that time (Kameda 2004b).

Evidence for Korean interaction was also discovered at settlement sites and production sites. At the Kuboki-Yakushi 窪木薬師 site (No. 20 in Figure 5.1), approximately two kilometers northeast of Zōzan, pit dwelling No. 13 (early fifth century) adopted a very early example of an earthen stove, and in the dwelling were the earliest type of *sue* stoneware, earthenware made using a Korean technique, iron arrowheads, iron ingots, iron slag, and whetstones (Okayama-ken Kyōiku Iinkai 1993b). The iron arrowheads are very similar to those discovered in Tombs 21 and 22 of the Pokch'ŏn-dong 福泉洞 site in the Kaya region (Pusan Taehakkyo Pangmulgwan 1990). Although iron production at the Kuboki-Yakushi site continued until the early seventh century, it seems likely that people who had emigrated from Kaya originally settled at this site, started an ironsmith workshop, and produced iron tools.

Another settlement site with good evidence for Korean immigration is the Takatsuka 高塚 site (No. 14 in Figure 5.1), located 1.7 km east of the Kuboki-Yakushi site. Some 100 pit dwellings dated from the early fifth to late sixth centuries were excavated. Approximately 50 pit dwellings were dated to the fifth century, 25 of which had earthen stoves, and of those 25, a total of 16 pit dwellings yielded ceramics made with Korean techniques. Among the 25 pit dwellings with earthen stoves, the earliest ones were dated to the early fifth century. Together with the early fifth-century dwellings with earthen stoves at the Kuboki-Yakushi site, they are the earliest-dated examples of earthen stoves in Kibi. A lid of the earliest type of *sue* stoneware discovered in dwelling No. 147 is morphologically very similar to the one discovered in the Hōren No. 37 tumulus. Moreover, slag from iron production was discovered in five of the fifth-century dwellings. I would speculate that some of the craftsmen who worked in iron production at the Kuboki-Yakushi site may have lived at the Takatsuka settlement.

The sites mentioned above are all located within a five-km radius from Zōzan, and I argue that these sites formed an inter-related system at that time. The regional paramount chief buried in the Zōzan keyhole tumulus occupied the highest rank. Second-ranking chiefs were probably those buried in the Sakakiyama circular tumulus and Zuian tumulus. The Sakakiyama chief probably had opportunities to visit the Korean peninsula, and the Zuian chief was in any case in a position to obtain the most advanced ironsmith tools. Under these second-ranking chiefs, Korean immigrants worked as iron specialists at the Kuboki-Yakushi settlement, resided at the Takatsuka settlement, and were buried in the Hōren tumulus group.

A similar system may be hypothesized for the area surrounding the Sakuzan keyhole tumulus. Approximately four kilometers to the north of the Sakuzan is the Okugatani 奥ケ谷 kiln site (No. 41 in Figure 5.1), where the earliest type of *sue* stoneware of the Kaya tradition was locally fired in the early fifth century (Okayama-ken Kyōiku Iinkai 1997). Earthenware cooking jars with brush-marks fired at this kiln were characterized by features similar to those at the Suemura-Obadera 陶邑大庭寺 kiln in Osaka, where the production of *sue* stoneware was introduced from the Korean peninsula for the first time in Japan (Ōsaka-fu Kyōiku Iinkai 1995). Still, I would argue for the possibility that pottery craftsmen at the Okugatani kiln came from Kaya independently of those who resided at Suemura.

Approximately four kilometers to the south of the Sakuzan is the Sugō Shōgakkō Urayama 菅生小学校裏山 (a hill behind the Sugō Elementary School) site (No. 30 in Figure 5.1), where a wide variety of pottery in the Korean tradition has been excavated (Okayama-ken Kyōiku Iinkai 1993a; Nakano 1993). Although archaeologists have not discovered identifiable pier features, they do suspect that the site was a port because of its location on the shore of the Achi 阿智 inlet. The pottery recovered from this site includes both stoneware and earthenware, made with techniques characteristic of Kaya, Silla, Paekche, and the Chŏlla 全羅 region, as well as the earliest type of locally made *sue* stoneware, all dated to the early fifth century. In sum, the Bitchū region in the early fifth century maintained close relationships with the Korean peninsula, including the incorporation of immigrants.

Sixth-century evidence for Korean interaction in Bitchū is scarce, especially in the neighborhood of Zōzan and Sakuzan. Yet, it is possible to speculate that immigrants came from the Korean peninsula and were involved in the production of iron and iron tools. Among the scarce evidence, the discovery of an iron tri-pronged hoe discovered in a pit dwelling of the early to late sixth century at the Kuboki 窪木 site (No. 18 in Figure 5.1) is important (Okayama-ken Kyōiku Iinkai 2008). This site is located approximately 500 m northwest of the Kuboki-Yakushi site. The three-pronged iron hoe is a Korean artifact and is extremely unusual in Japan. Besides the Kuboki example, only five have been discovered in Japan in fourth- and fifth-century contexts. In a ditch 800 m northeast of this pit dwelling, earthenware made with Korean techniques was discovered in association with iron slag and mid-sixth-century *sue* stoneware (Okayama-ken Kyōiku Iinkai 1998). Approximately 1.2 km west of the Kuboki site is the Fukui-Ōtsuka 福井大塚 No. 12 Tumulus, where a late sixth-century *sue* stoneware pan with grooved handle was discovered (Takahashi 1994). The grooved handle reflects a Korean tradition, and this type of pan is unusual in the sixth-century context. In the vicinity of the tumulus is a place named Kanakuro-ike 金黒池 (Black Iron Pond), which suggests that the place was related to iron production.

Seventh-century evidence for Korean interaction in Bitchū is still extremely scarce, but roof tiles give clues to our understanding about such interaction (Minato and Kameda 2006). The earliest roof tiles not only in Bitchū but also in Kibi as a whole were discovered at the Kamo-Mandokoro 加茂政所 site (No. 11 in Figure 5.1; Okayama-ken Kyōiku Iinkai 1999). The roof tiles are dated to the early seventh century and are of the Okuyama-Kume-dera 奥山久米寺 type. This type is in the Paekche tradition and of the "Kinai mainstream"[3] type adopted by Buddhist temples erected by the Soga 蘇我 family in Asuka, then the capital of Japan. It is likely that a small Buddhist hall-like structure was erected at the site, but the details are unclear. The roof tiles were fired at the Suenooku 末ノ奥 kiln (No. 28 in Figure 5.1), approximately 4.2 km southwest of the site (Hinoura 2003). A terminal ridge-end tile with lotus-pattern design fired at this kiln is known to have been transported all the way to Yamato, 190 km to the east (Iuchi 1992).

The earliest Buddhist temple in Kibi (and in Bitchū) is the Hadawara 秦原 Temple site (No. 43 in Figure 5.1) in Hadawara Ward, Shimotsumichi 下道 County (Kuzuhara 1987). It was erected in the second quarter of the seventh century. The name Hada, or Hata 秦, suggests a connection with the Hata family in Yamashiro 山背 Province (southern Kyoto Prefecture). Indeed, the roof tiles used at the Hadawara Temple were very similar to the round eaves tiles with simple-petal lotus-flower pattern excavated at the Kōryū Temple 広隆寺 (Ishida 1936), southern Kyoto Prefecture, erected

[3] Editor's Note: The author refers to the types of roof tiles adopted by major Buddhist temples erected by the Soga family and the Imperial Court in Kinai, such as the Asuka-dera type, Okuyama-Kume-dera type, Yamada-dera type, Kawara-dera type, as the Kinai-mainstream type. By contrast, the author refers to the kinds of roof tiles adopted by local Korean immigrants and minor regional chiefs independently from the central government as the "non-mainstream" type (Kameda 1994).

by the Hata family. The Hata family was one of several immigrant families who were very influential in the central government.

In the mid-seventh century, the Kayadera 栢寺 temple site (No. 19 in Figure 5.1) was erected in the Hattori 服部 Ward, Kaya 賀夜 County (Okayama-ken Kyōiku Iinkai 1979). It is considered to be the family temple of the Kaya 賀夜 family. The type of round eaves tiles with simple-petal lotus-flower pattern adopted at the time of the initial construction is not of Japanese Kinai origin, but is possibly of Korean origin. Another line of evidence suggesting that the Kayadera temple had a close relationship with the Korean peninsula is that the molds for the Kayadera round eaves tiles were used for the production of roof tiles in the establishment of another Buddhist temple possibly erected by a Paekche priest in Bingo (Okamoto 1992). This temple is now known as the Bingo Teramachi 寺町 temple site (Hiroshima-ken Kusadosengen-chō Iseki Hakkutsu Chōsa Kenkyūjo 1980–1982) and is considered to be the site of Mitani-dera 三谷寺. The Mitani-dera is recorded in the *Nihon ryōiki* 日本霊異記 (Part 1, Section 7, p. 90)[4] as having been built by the Paekche priest Gusai (K. Hongje 弘濟), who went to Bingo along with an ancestor of Lord Tairyō 大領 of Mitani 三谿 County, and who fought at the battle of the Paekch'on River 白村江 in 663.

In the late seventh century, the Hibata 日畑 temple (No. 6 in Figure 5.1) was erected in Ekiya 駅家 Ward, Tsu'u 都宇 County (Kurashiki-shi Kyōiku Iinkai 2005). The type of round eaves tiles with simple-petal lotus-flower pattern adopted at the time of the initial construction of the temple bears an impression of cloth on the back of the eaves section. The production technique that left a cloth impression on the back of the eaves part of a roof tile was not adopted in Kinai at that time. This type of roof tile has been discovered at the Kyejok mountain fortress 鷄足山城 on the border of Paekche and Silla (Sim and Kong 1994; Ch'ungnam Taehakkyo Paekche Yŏn'guso 2005) and at other sites in the Korean peninsula. I speculate that the technique was introduced to Bitchū without the involvement of the Kinai central government (Kameda 1996; 2006).

[4] The *Nihon ryōiki* [Miraculous Stories from Japan], compiled in 822, is the earliest-dated collection of Buddhist episodes.

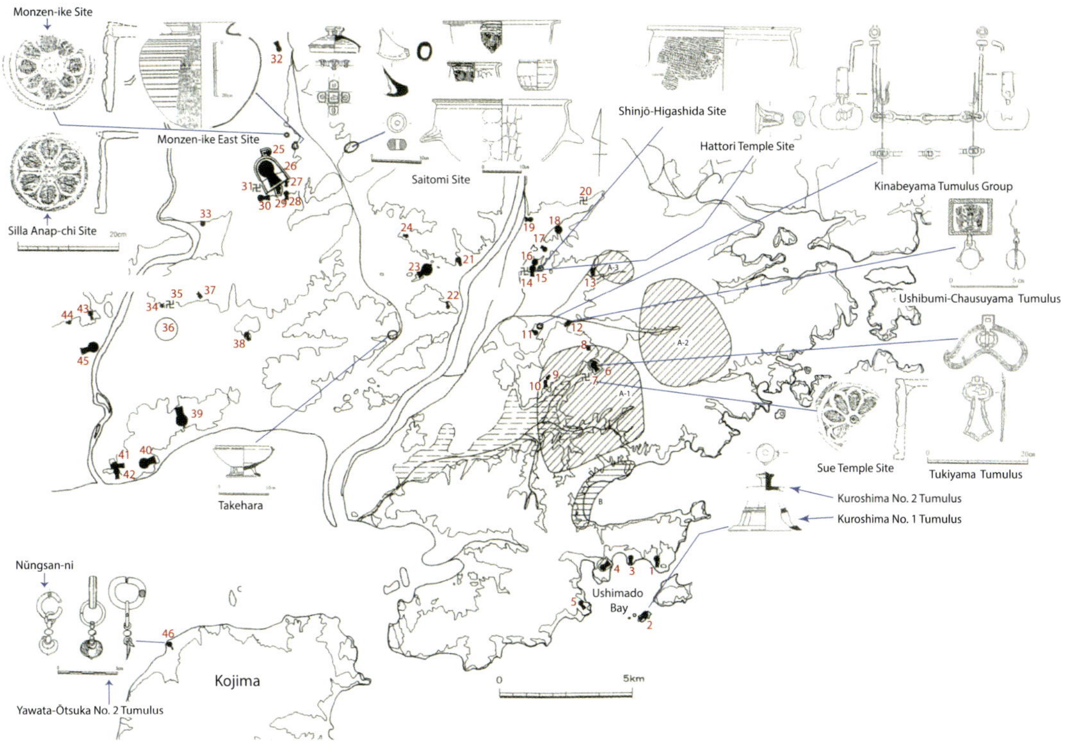

Figure 5.4 Sites in the Bizen Region Where Korean Artifacts and Features Have Been Discovered.

The Relationship Between Bizen and the Korean Peninsula

Cases of the Oku Area in Bizen

The Oku area that occupies the southeastern corner of Kibi is culturally distinct from the "core area" of Kibi, as defined at the beginning of this chapter, and I consider it necessary to discuss this region separately (Figure 5.4). While keyhole tumuli of more than 200 m in length are located in the core areas of Bitchū and Bizen, there are no keyhole tumuli of more than 100 m in Oku. Even when the construction of keyhole tumuli declined in the late fifth and early sixth centuries in the core areas, probably because of pressure exerted by the Yamato authority, the construction of keyhole tumuli of 60 to 90 m continued throughout the fifth and sixth centuries in Oku. Although our hypothetical reconstruction of the history of Oku is not conclusive because archaeological excavations in Oku are not carried out as often as in the core areas of Bitchū and Bizen, it appears that iron and iron tool production did not take place in Oku. On the contrary, *sue* stoneware was produced in Oku, and salt was produced on the coast of the same region, which is not the case in the core areas of Kibi. Based on historical sources, we speculate that the local chief of Oku was involved in transportation by the Inland Sea. Given the coastal location of Oku, we would argue for the possibility that the local chief of Oku directly interacted not only with Yamato but also with the Korean peninsula. Here, I introduce some archaeological evidence for such interaction.

First, some earthenware made with Korean techniques has been discovered in this area. A pan with a handle, presumably dated to the fourth century, was collected at the Shinjō-Higashida 新庄東田 site in Bizen City (near Nos. 15 and 16 in Figure 5.4; Hirai 1987). Approximately 600 m to the west of this site, the grooved handle of either a steamer or pan was excavated at the Maruyama 丸山 site, which occupies the lower stratum of the Hattori 服部 temple site (No. 14 in Figure 5.4) in Osafune 長船, Setouchi 瀬戸内 City (Osafune-chō Kyōiku Iinkai 1997). The handle is considered to have been made at the beginning of the fifth century.

Second, fragments of Korean stoneware have been excavated in the Kuroshima 黒島 No. 1 and No. 2 Tumuli (No. 2 in Figure 5.4; Ito and Shimazaki 1984; Kameda 1997b, 1997c). This type of Korean stoneware is common on the eastern bank region of the Naktong 洛東 River, encompassing the Kaya and Silla regions. We speculate that the excavated Korean stoneware was made in the early fifth century. The Kuroshima No. 1 Tumulus is a keyhole tumulus of 81 m in length, while the Kuroshima No. 2 Tumulus is a circular tumulus of approximately 11 m in diameter, located to the northeast of the No. 1 Tumulus.

Regarding metal objects of Korean origins, a cast iron axe has been discovered in the Hanaena はなえな tumulus in Oku, Setouchi City (Nishikawa 1975). The precise context of the discovery is unclear, but we suspect that it was made around the fifth century because similar examples in Kibi are mostly dated around the fifth century. Such discoveries are very few in Kibi. Representative examples are from the Kanakurayama 金蔵山 tumulus in Okayama City (No. 39 in Figure 5.4; Nishitani and Kamaki 1959) and Tonoyama 殿山 No. 8 Tumulus, Sōja 総社 City (No. 32 in Figure 5.1; Okayama-ken Kyōiku Iinkai 1982).

A few horse trappings discovered in this area are possibly imported from the Korean peninsula rather than locally made. Such examples include a gilt-bronze bit with an f-shaped cheek plate and decorative pendants for a horse harness (*gyōyō* 杏葉) discovered in the late fifth-century Tsukiyama 築山 tumulus (No. 6 in Figure 5.4) and an iron bit with ovoid cheek plate discovered in the Kinabeyama 木鍋山 tumulus group (Emi 1998; Kameda 1998a). Iron bits similar to the latter have been discovered in Tomb Ka-A of the Pan'gyeje 磻溪堤 site in Hapch'ŏn 陜川 (Kungnip Chinju Pangmulgwan 1987).

A highly unusual belt fitting with a zoomorphic relief has been discovered in the Ushibumi-Chausuyama 牛文茶臼山 tumulus in Osafune, Setouchi City (No. 12 in Figure 5.4; Nishikawa 1986b; Kameda 1998b, 2001). Based on the typology of other artifacts discovered in association with this belt fitting, archaeologists consider it to date to the end of the fifth century. The tumulus is scallop-shaped and 48 m long. In Japan, there are only two other known discoveries of belt fittings with zoomorphic relief. They are at the Yoroizuka 鎧塚 No. 2 Tumulus in northern Shinano (Suzaka-shi Kyōiku Iinkai 2000) and Jūzen'nomori 十善の森 tumulus in Fukui Prefecture (Saitō 1970). In the Korean peninsula, similar belt fittings with zoomorphic reliefs have been excavated in Tombs 2 and 5 of the Songsan-ni 宋山里 cemetery, located in the Paekche capital of Ungjin 熊津 (present-day Kongju 公主) (Nomori and Kanda 1935). The Korean examples are all dated to the end of the fifth century. The Ushibumi-Chausuyama chief probably obtained the belt fitting in the context of relationship with Paekche or Kaya in the late fifth century.

In the mid-seventh century, Silla-style round eaves tiles were adopted at the Sue 須恵 temple site in Osafune, Setouchi City (No. 7 in Figure 5.4, historically, Sue Ward of Oku County; Kameda 1998c, 2001). This style of round eaves tile is characterized by a groove between the central portion and its surrounding petal reliefs. This feature is present in round eaves tiles of the pre-unification Silla period (prior to 668) and is very scarce in Japan. It was not adopted at major Buddhist temples in Kinai, where the central government was located, and archaeologists do not know of a possible route of importing that style of eaves tile. Either they were brought directly from the Korean peninsula to Kibi, or through polities peripheral to Kinai. In any case, they are an example of a non-mainstream type of roof tile.

Figure 5.5 Paekche-style Gold Earrings
Excavated in the Yawata-Ōtsuka No. 2 Tumulus. 5.4 cm in length.
Property of the Agency for Cultural Affairs.
Photograph courtesy of the Okayama Prefectural Museum.

Interaction Between the Core Bizen Area and the Korean Peninsula

There is relatively strong evidence for interaction with Korea in the vicinity of the Ryōgūzan tumulus (No. 26 in Figure 5.4; Akaiwa-shi Kyōiku Iinkai 2005). It is a giant keyhole tumulus of 206 m in length, enclosed by inner and outer moats, and is dated to the mid-fifth century (Phase 7 of the Kofun period). While we do not have secure evidence for iron tool manufacture in the mid-fifth century in the neighborhood of this large keyhole tumulus, it is safe to speculate that people who interacted with the Korean peninsula resided in this area and worked using Korean techniques. Archaeologists made relevant discoveries at the Monzen'ike-Tōhō 門前池東方 and Saitomi 斎富 sites. The former is located approximately 1.6 km to the northeast, and the latter approximately 3 km to the southeast of the Ryōgūzan keyhole tumulus. The following artifacts and features were excavated at the Monzen'ike-Tōhō site: early fifth-century Korean stoneware; iron slag in a late sixth-century pit dwelling with *ondol* features (Korean floor-heating system); and (beyond the scope of this study) first-century A.D. tall cup-shaped pottery of Lelang 樂浪 style (Noritake et al. 1994).

At the Saitomi 斎富 site, a lid of a stoneware pedestalled bowl in the tradition of the region along the eastern bank of the Naktong River was discovered in association with gilt-bronze iron-core crupper joints in a late fifth-century pit dwelling. Archaeologists speculate that horse trappings may have been repaired in this particular residence. Other artifacts of Korean origin discovered at this site include large quantities of iron slag in a ditch dated to the end of the fifth or beginning of the sixth century; horn-shaped *sue* stoneware and earthenware made with Korean techniques in a pit dwelling of the early sixth century; and an abacus-bead-shaped spindle-whorl found in occupation debris.

A round eaves tile of the Silla style was discovered at the Monzen'ike 門前池 site, approximately 1.5 km north-northeast of the Ryōgūzan tumulus (Okayama-ken Kyōiku Iinkai 1975). Archaeologists consider the roof tile to be dated to be the mid-seventh century. A distinguishing feature of this round eaves tile is the concave center of the central portion. No similar round eaves tiles have been discovered in Japan, but similar examples have been excavated at the Anapchi Pond 雁鴨池 site in Kyŏngju 慶州 (Kungnip Kyŏngju Pangmulgwan 2000). I consider the Monzen'ike round eaves tile to be in the Silla tradition.

Although somewhat peripheral to the core Bizen area, Paekche-style gold earrings were excavated in the Yawata-Ōtsuka 八幡大塚 No. 2 Tumulus in Kojima 児島 (No. 46 in Figure 5.4; Figure 5.5; Kamaki and Kameda 1986; Yi 2001). The tumulus is circular, 35 m in diameter, and is dated to the end of the sixth or beginning of the seventh century. Kojima was at that time an island, and the tumulus was situated on its northern coast, facing the Bizen coast of the Inland Sea. Kojima happens to be the site of the Kojima Miyake 児島屯倉, one of the royal estates established and maintained by the central government. Because of the geographical proximity, we may speculate that the Yawata-Ōtsuka chief obtained the earrings from the royal estate or the central government.

Interactions Between Kibi and the Korean Peninsula as Evidenced by Historical Sources

Archaeologists must be cautious about applying descriptions of written sources to the interpretations of archaeological data. It is still important to note that for Kibi in comparison to other regions we have relatively many descriptions of interactions with the Korean peninsula (Table 5.1).

Table 5.1
List of Articles in Japanese Historic Sources Mentioning Interaction Between Kibi and the Korean Peninsula

Year/ Month	Individuals and Activities	Source
463/8	Kibi-no-Shimotumichi-no-Omi Sakitsuya 吉備下道臣前津屋 was executed for his alleged attempt to rebel against Yūryaku.	*NS*
463/	Kibi-no-Kamitsumichi-no-Omi Tasa 吉備上道臣田狭 (also, Mimana-no-Kuni-no-Mikotomochi Tasa-no-Omi 任那国司田狭臣) and his son Otokimi 弟君 revolted against Yūryaku in Imna. Yūryaku ordered Kibi-no-Ama-no-Atai Akao 吉備海部直赤尾 and Otokimi to visit Paekche, but they did not join the rebellion. Instead, the two brought back Tanasue-no-Tehito 手末才伎 from Paekche.	*NS*
464/2	Kibi-no-Omi Onashi 吉備臣小梨 was advised by the King of Imna 任那 to assist Silla in fighting against Koguryŏ.	*NS*
465/3	Kibi-no-Kamitsumichi no Uneme-no-Ōshiama 吉備上道采女大海 married Ki-no-oyumi no Sukune 紀小弓宿禰, who was a general in the military expedition to Silla.	*NS*
465/5	According to the narrative on the birth of Kibi-no-Kamitsumichi no Kashimada-no-Murano Yakehitora 吉備上道蚊嶋田邑家人部, upon the death of Ki-no-oyumi no Sukune, Uneme-no-Ōshiama returned to Kibi.	*NS*
530/9	Kenu no Omi 毛野臣, who was stationed in Imna 任那, killed Kibi-no-Karako-natari 吉備韓子那多利 and Shihuri 斯布利.	*NS*
541/4	Mimana-no Yamato-no Mikotomochi Kibi-no-Omi 任那日本府吉備臣 (Otokimi 弟君) visited Paekche with Kanki 旱岐 of Imna.	*NS*
544/3	Kibi-no-Omi 吉備臣 (Otokimi 弟君) disagreed with King Sŏngmyŏng 聖明 of Paekche on plan to revive Imna.	*NS*
544 /11	King Sŏngmyŏng 聖明 of Paekche begged King Kinmei to send Kibi-no-Omi back to Japan.	*NS*
555/7	Soga-no-Ō'omi Iname-no-Sukune 蘇我大臣稲目宿禰 dispatched Hozumi no Iwayumi-no-Omi 穂積磐弓臣 to Kibi, and established the Royal Estate of Shirai 白猪 in five counties of Kibi.	*NS*
556/7	King Kinmei dispatched Soga-no-Ō'omi Iname-no-Sukune 蘇我大臣稲目宿禰 to Kojima 児島 County, Bizen 備前 Province, established a royal estate [miyake] at Kojima, and appointed Kazuragi-no-Yamada-no-Atai Mitsuko 葛城山田直瑞子 as magistrate (田令 tatsukai) of the Kojima Royal Estate.	*NS*
569 /1	Itsu (Tangjin in Chinese) 胆津, a nephew of Ō Jinni (Wang Chin-i in Korean) 王辰爾, inspected the family registers of peasants residing in the Shirai 白猪 Royal Estate.	*NS*

569/4	Itsu 胆津 was praised for the inspection of the family registers of the Shirai 白猪 Royal Estate, was granted the name Shirai no Fuhito 白猪史, and appointed as magistrate [tatsukai] of the royal estate.	*NS*
573/5	Kibi-no-Ama-no-Atai Naniwa 吉備海部直難波 was appointed as an ambassador who would accompany Koguryŏ diplomatic envoys returning to Koguryŏ.	*NS*
573/7	Ambassador Naniwa threw the two Koguryŏ diplomatic envoys into the sea, and returned to Japan.	*NS*
573/8	Ambassador Naniwa filed a false report of the mission.	*NS*
574/7	Naniwa's report was found out to be false, and he was punished.	*NS*
574/10	Soga no Umako 蘇我馬子 increased the productivity of the Shiari 白猪 Royal Estate and granted the Royal Estate to Itsu 胆津.	*NS*
583/7	Kibi-no-Ama-no-Atai Hashima 吉備海部直羽島 visited Paekche in an attempt to bring back Nichira 日羅 (?–583), who was a Japanese bureaucrat serving Paekche.	*NS*
583/10	King of Paekche refused Hashima's request, and Nichira was asked to stay in Paekche.	*NS*
583/	Hashima spoke in the Han 韓 language to convince the Paekche government, and successfully brought back Nichira to Japan. Representatives of the Japanese government acknowledged Nichira's services at the Kojima no Miyake 児島屯倉.	*NS*
661/	According to the narratives of the Nima 二万 ward, Shimotsumichi 下道 County, 20,000 soldiers were recruited to assist the Paekche troops.	*BKF*
Late 7th c.	Paekche Buddhist priest Gusai 弘濟 (Hongje in Korean) was thrown into the Inland Sea near the Hone 骨 Island, Bizen 備前 Province. Gusai was saved by a turtle, and arrived on the coast of Bitchū 備中 Province.	*NR*
Late 7th c.	Paekche Buddhist priest Gusai 弘濟 (Hongje in Korean) was attacked by a pirate and thrown into the Inland Sea near the Hone 骨 Island, Bizen 備前 Province. He was saved by a turtle and arrived at the coast of Bingo 備後 Province.	*KM*
759/9	Several provincial governments on the northern coast of the Inland Sea were ordered to build 161 ships to send troops to Silla.	*SN*
779/7	Shimotsumichi-no-Ason Nagahito 下道朝臣長人, Ambassador to Silla, returned to Japan, accompanying Japanese diplomatic officers sent to Tang China.	*SN*

All months are of the lunar calendar.

Source Abbreviations
NS = *Nihon shoki* 日本書紀 (Chronicles of Japan)
BKF = *Bitchū no kuni fudoki* 備中国風土記 (History of Bitchū)
NR = *Nihon ryōiki* 日本霊異記 (Miraculous Stories from Japan)
KM = *Konjaku monogatari* 今昔物語 (Tales of Times Now Past)
SN = *Shoku Nihongi* 続日本紀 (Later Chronicle of Japan)

5 Ancient Kibi, Western Japan, and the Korean Peninsula—Kameda Shūichi

Here I list a few descriptions from historical sources relevant to Kibi. The *Nihon shoki* or Chronicle of Japan records that in the eighth month of 463 (seventh year of the reign of Emperor Yūryaku), Kibi no Shimotsumichi no Sakitsuya 吉備下道前津屋 was executed because he attempted to rebel against Emperor Yūryaku (Yūryaku 7/8; 1:472–475). The *Nihon shoki* also records that in the same year, Kibi no Kamitsumichi no Omi Tasa 吉備上道臣田狭 was appointed as provincial governor of Imna 任那 (J. Mimana) on the southern tip of the Korean peninsula, led a rebellion in Imna, and failed (Yūryaku 7/8; 1:474–477). At that time, Kibi no Ama no Atai Akao 吉備海部直赤尾 accompanied Tasa's son Otokimi 弟君 but did not join the rebellion. When he returned to Kibi, he brought back some technicians from Paekche. From the late fifth century to the end of the sixth century, local lords of Kibi frequently visited the Korean peninsula. In a few cases, local women from the peninsula bore the children of local lords of Kibi. These include Kibi no Karako Natari 吉備韓子那多利 and Shifuri 斯布利 (Karako meaning a Korean son), who were, according to the *Nihon shoki*, killed by a lord of Kenu 毛野 stationed in Imna. These records indicate that local lords of Kibi maintained very close relationships with local people in Korea, including marital relationships.

As these lists above show, historical sources frequently mention activities of the Kamitsumichi 上道 family and the Kibi no Ama no Atai 吉備海部直 family. The head of the former was a powerful local lord in Kibi who controlled the core area of Bizen, and the Ryōgūzan tumulus would be the burial of one of the members of this family. As the name Ama 海部 (sea specialist) suggests, the Kibi no Ama no Atai family was involved in works related to the sea. It is generally thought that the family was based in the Oku area (Kondō 1956; Yoshida 1984). Although members of the Shimotsumichi 下道 family were dominant local lords in Bitchū, the family's interactions with the Korean peninsula were not recorded.

These are examples of direct relationships between Kibi and the southern part of the Korean peninsula. Historical sources also record that Korean immigrants and their descendants were dispatched to Kibi by the central government of Japan. After the 463 rebellion, the central government of Yamato established *miyake*, or royal estates, in 555 and 556 in Kibi (Kanō 2005). They were the Shirai no Miyake 白猪屯倉 and the Kojima no Miyake 児島屯倉, respectively. They were meant to achieve more direct and better control over the Kibi province. The establishment of these two *miyake* was actually done by Soga no Iname 蘇我稲目, who was the paramount aristocrat in the central government in the sixth century. It is noteworthy that the head of the Shirai no Miyake dispatched from the central government was Itsu 胆津, who was a nephew of Korean immigrant Wang Chin-i 王辰爾. Upon the appointment, Itsu was granted the title and name Shirai no Fuhiko Itsu 白猪史胆津 by the central government in 569 (the thirtieth year of the reign of Emperor Kinmei 欽明).

Besides Itsu, the central government dispatched descendants of several Korean immigrants to Kibi, and they subsequently settled there. According to *Bitchū no kuni taizei fu shibō nin chō* 備中国大税負死亡人帳 (Notes on deceased taxpayers in the province of Bitchū), written in 739, their surnames were Hata 秦 for Bizen and Kawachi no Aya 西漢人, Yamato no Aya 東漢人, and Oshinumi 忍海 for Bitchū (*Bitchū no kuni*, 316–319). Thus, historical sources give us insight, suggesting that not only did Korean immigrants arrive in Kibi directly from their homeland, but that they also were dispatched by the central government of Japan. The latter interaction may be considered as an indirect, "secondary migration."

Interaction Between Kibi and the Korean Peninsula as Evidenced by Archaeological Data and Historical Sources

Iron and Iron Tool Production and Korean Immigrants in Southern Bitchū

My discussion above frequently touches on the archaeological evidence of iron. I have also published an article elsewhere on this issue (Kameda 2000a). Here, I intend to discuss the production of iron and iron tools and the role Korean immigrants played in southern Bitchū from both archaeological and historical perspectives. In particular, I would like to point out the possibility that Korean immigrants dispatched by the central government of Japan (Yamato) were involved in the production of iron and iron tools in southern Kibi and that the two *miyake* established in Kibi had some impact on that production.

Iron tool production in Kibi started in the Yayoi period and became large-scale in the early fifth century. The center of iron tool production in the fifth century was, I suspect, the Kuboki-Yakushi site, where evidence for interaction with Kaya was discovered. The regional paramount chief buried in Zōzan was likely involved in the plan to expand iron tool production, and with the intention of the paramount chief, Korean immigrants from the lower tributary area of the Naktong River probably participated in the management of the Kuboki-Yakushi iron workshop. The production of iron tools at this site declined in the late fifth century and expanded again in the second quarter of the sixth century. These phenomena correspond very well to descriptions in historical sources indicating that production decreased after the failure of Kibi no Shimotsumichi no Sakitsuya's rebellion in 463, that the production gradually recovered once the Yamato authority gave the workshop some support prior to the establishment of the Shirai no Miyake, and that full-scale production was revitalized when the Yamato authority established the *miyake* in 555. The establishment of the Shirai no Miyake very likely had some impact on the iron and iron tool production in Kibi (Kameda 2000b).

In the late sixth century, shortly after the establishment of the Shirai no Miyake, iron smelting and iron tool production started at the Sembiki-Kanakurodani 千引カナクロ谷 site (No. 16 in Figure 5.1; Sōja-shi Kyōiku Iinkai 1999), which is at present the earliest-dated iron smelting site in Japan. In my opinion, the establishment of the *miyake* triggered the introduction of new iron smelting technology and iron tool production to Kibi, thereby increasing the output of iron and iron tools from Kibi, which were then transported to Yamato in large quantities.

The Sembiki-Kanakurodani site is a part of the Okusaka 奥坂 site cluster, which includes six iron smelting sites in the neighborhood of the Sembiki-Kanakurodani site. Altogether, archaeologists have excavated twenty iron smelting furnaces and twenty-four charcoal production kilns in the site cluster, dating from the late sixth century to the early eighth century. Indeed, the cluster as a whole is a representative site of iron smelting in Kibi.

The area where the Okusaka site cluster is located was in the eighth century a part of the Aso 阿蘇 ward in Kaya 賀夜 County. The aforementioned *Bitchū no kuni taizei fu shibō nin chō* (Notes on deceased taxpayers in the province of Bitchū) lists deceased taxpayers who resided in the Aso ward. The document was written in 739, when the iron smelting sites in Okusaka were nearing the end of their operation. In the document, we find such foreign names as Kawachi no Ayahito-be Maro 西漢人部麻呂 residing in the Sōbu 宗部 village, Fuhitobe no Achimasa 史戸阿遅麻佐 residing in the Iwahara 磐原 village, and Kawachi no Ayahito-be Kotonashime 西漢人部事无売 (*Bitchū no kuni*, 316–319). Long before the archaeological excavations of the Sembiki-Kanakurodani site, historian Naoki Kōjirō 直木孝次郎 (1983) argued that these foreign immigrants were involved in iron production.

The document also lists the name of Yamato no Aya no Torate 東漢人部刀良手 who resided in the Ōi 大井 ward, Kaya County, the eastern neighbor of the Aso ward. Coincidentally, an excavation at the Nara Imperial Palace yielded a wooden tablet with an inscription reading "ten [iron] hoes from Ōi" (大井鍬十口). It is likely that the Ōi mentioned in this wooden tablet inscription is the Ōi ward in Kaya County, Bitchū. All the evidence suggests that iron was smelted in this area and that new technology was adopted from Korea. Tools such as hoes were manufactured, and the iron tools were transported to the Nara capital. Regarding the village of Sōbu 宗部, historian Yoshida Akira 吉田晶 (1990:103) points out that the name was a contraction of Soga-be 宗我部. If this is indeed the case, this area is somewhat related to the Shirai and Kojima no Miyake, both of which were established by Soga no Iname.

The *Bitchū no kuni taizei fu shibō nin chō* also mentions the placename Miyake 三宅 in the Niwase 庭瀬 ward, Kaya County, which also suggests that those related to the *miyake* were located in the Miyake village. The document also lists Oshinumi no Ayabe no Mamaro 忍海漢部真麻呂 who resided in the Miyake village. Oshinumi no Ayabe no Mamaro may have been a descendant of an immigrant who originally settled in the Katsuragi 葛城 region of Yamato Province. We know from historical records that Emperor Yūryaku weakened the power of the Katsuragi family in the late fifth century and that the Soga family took over the rights and interests of the Katsuragi family (Katō 1983). We may therefore speculate that the ancestor of Oshinumi no Ayabe no Mamaro was forced to move to Kibi when Soga no Iname established the two miyake in Kibi in 555 and 556.

Furthermore, historian Seki Akira 関晃 (1966) argues that the Oshinumi be 忍海部 originally participated in the production of weapons and armor based on a description in the *Hizen no kuni fudoki* 肥前国風土記 (History of Hizen Province) stating that Oshinumi no Ayahito 忍海漢人, who resided in Ayabe 漢部 Ward in Mine 三根 County, fabricated weapons (*Hizen no kuni fudoki*, 49). Although Miyake Village is 6.5 km away from the Kuboki-Yakushi site, which belonged to the Hattori 服部 ward, different from the Niwase ward, I would venture to point out the possibility that Oshinumi no Ayabe was involved in the production of iron arrowheads, knives, and swords in the sixth century at the Kuboki-Yakushi site.

In the late sixth century, soon after production at the Kuboki-Yakushi site was revitalized, the Kōmorizuka こうもり塚 keyhole tumulus (No. 25 in Figure 5.1) was constructed, which was the largest keyhole tumulus in western Japan in the sixth century outside of Kinai. It is 100 m long and contains a corridor-style horizontal burial chamber of 19.4 m in length, which was the fourth largest in Japan. Among the rich funerary offerings, iron slag was also deposited in the burial chamber (Kuzuhara et al. 1986). The discovery of iron slag suggests the possibilities that the paramount regional chief at that time, who was buried in the Kōmorizuka tumulus, may have

Figure 5.6 Tumuli Located in the Ushimado Bay Area.
Photograph courtesy of the Seto Municipal Board of Education, Okayama Prefecture.

administered the production of iron and iron tools and that he may have been involved in the production at the Kuboki-Yakushi sites and other sites under the control of the Shirai no Miyake.

The Kibi no Ama no Atai Clan in the Oku Area of Bizen and Interactions with the Korean Peninsula

Archaeologists and historians generally suspect that the Kibi no Ama no Atai family resided in the Oku area, especially in an area called Ushimado 牛窓 (Figure 5.6), based on spatial and temporal distribution of tumuli in the area and the association of its coastal location with the name

Ama (sea specialist). Descriptions in the *Nihon shoki* suggest that members of the Kibi no Ama no Atai family acted as guides to the Korean peninsula for the Yamato authority (Table 5.1) and were *de facto* diplomats.

As mentioned previously, the *Nihon shoki* records that when Kibi no Ama no Atai Akao and Otokimi (the son of Kibi no Kamitsumichi no Omi Tasa) were dispatched to fight against Silla in 463 (seventh year of Emperor Yūryaku's reign), Kibi no Ama no Atai Akao brought back some technical specialists from Paekche. In addition, the *Nihon shoki* records other visits to the Korean peninsula by members of the Kibi no Ama no Atai family. In 573 (second year of Emperor Bidatsu's 敏達 reign), Kibi no Ama no Atai Naniwa 吉備海部直難波 was ordered to accompany the Koguryŏ diplomats on their homeward return (Bidatsu 2/5; 2:135–137). Instead, Naniwa threw the Koguryŏ diplomats overboard into the sea from a ship, and for this he was punished by the Yamato authority. In 583 (the twelfth year of Emperor Bidatsu's reign), Kibi no Ama no Atai Hashima 吉備海部直羽島 negotiated with the king of Paekche and successfully brought back a Paekche man, Illa 日羅, to Japan (Bidatsu 12/7; 2:142–143). The Yamato authority was very pleased with this success, and recognized his service at the Kojima no Miyake. It is possible to speculate that Akao, Naniwa, and Hashima were buried in keyhole tumuli in the Ushimado area.[5] Since archaeological excavations rarely take place in the Oku area (Ushimado area), it is at present difficult to verify the activities of the Kibi no Ama no Atai family archaeologically.

Still, it is safe to assume that members of the Kibi no Ama no Atai family were deeply involved in transportation by sea, including transportation to the Korean peninsula. Because Hashima was competent in the Paekche language, he must have been very active in diplomatic relationships between Japan and states in the Korean peninsula. It is also apparent that members of the family were associated with the core of the Yamato authority. Under the directives of the Yamato authority, members of the family often took ships to the Korean peninsula and must have had numerous opportunities to acquire current information, culture, materials and technologies of the Korean peninsula, which they probably brought back to their home, Oku, though we do not know how much time they spent in the Korean peninsula.

[5] While the precise calendrical date of the construction of the Futatsukayama tumulus, the latest keyhole tumulus at Ushimado, is unclear, scholars strongly suspect that it was built toward the end of the late sixth century. If Hashima was indeed buried in Ushimado, he would be the one who was buried in the Futatsukayama tumulus.

I would argue that the artifacts of Korean origin discussed previously in connection with Oku were brought to that area through the interactions of the Kibi no Ama no Atai family with individuals of the Korean peninsula. In particular, we may understand the discovery of the highly unusual belt fitting with a zoomorphic relief deposited in the Ushibumi-Chausuyama tumulus at the end of the fifth century in this context. If the horse trappings discovered in the Tsukiyama tumulus and in the Kinabeyama tumulus group were indeed produced in Korea, their presence in these burials should be results of direct interaction with the Korean peninsula in the late fifth century. Coincidentally, it was in the late fifth century, in 463, that Kibi no Ama no Atai Akao visited the Korean peninsula and brought back Paekche technicians.

Conclusion

The influence and strength of the Kibi polity reached its peak at the beginning of the fifth century when the exceptionally large Zōzan keyhole tumulus, which was comparable in size to imperial mausolea, was built. This was followed by the construction of the Sakuzan and Ryōgūzan tumuli of more than 200 m in length, which were comparable to imperial mausolea and tumuli in which the paramount lords in Kinai were buried. There must have been several factors that allowed the paramount chiefs of Kibi to build such giant keyhole tumuli, and one of the most likely was their interaction with the Korean peninsula when the political situation there was in turmoil from the end of the fourth to the early fifth century. The paramount chiefs of Kibi, while maintaining ties with the Yamato authority, independently interacted with the Korean peninsula and brought back immigrants from the lower tributary region of the Naktong River, together with their technologies and information.

The construction of major keyhole tumuli halted for some one hundred years in Kibi until the late sixth century, when the Kōmorizuka was built. This gap in the mid-fifth century was probably a reflection of the rebellion attempt by Kibi no Shimotsumichi no Sakitsuya against Emperor Yūryaku in 463, as recorded in the *Nihon shoki* (Yūryaku 7/8; 1:472–475). As regional polities of Kibi weakened after the rebellion attempt, the Yamato authority gained stronger control over Kibi and established the Shirai no Miyake and Kojima no Miyake in 555 and 556. After the establishment of the two *miyake*, polities in Kibi became more closely associated with the Yamato authority not only politically but also economically. The production of iron and iron tools, salt, and *sue* stoneware in Kibi was beneficial to the Yamato authority, and the Kibi region benefitted from the recognition of these services. Indeed, it seems that Kibi was incorporated into a regional system under the Yamato authority in the late fifth century. I would speculate that not only Korean immigrants who had previously arrived in Kibi but also those who were newly dispatched by the Yamato authority contributed to the further growth of the production of iron and iron tools as well as *sue* stoneware. Even after the Yamato authority achieved stronger control over Kibi in the sixth century, the construction of Kōmorizuka, the largest keyhole tumulus in western Japan outside Kinai, would indicate that polities in Kibi maintained a considerable degree of their own power.

Along with the core areas of Kibi, the Oku polity in southeastern Bizen also played a role in interactions with the Korean peninsula. We presume that the Kibi no Ama no Atai family led the Oku polity, and the family not only maintained ties with central polities of Kibi but also associated with the Yamato authority. A group of keyhole tumuli at Ushimado are considered to be the graves of the successive heads of the family. This tumulus group is very unusual in the Kofun period because the construction of keyhole tumuli continued without any hiatus from the fourth to the end of the sixth centuries, as follows: Ushimado-Tenjinyama 牛窓天神山 (85 m) in the late fourth century (Kameda 1997d); Kuroshima 黒島 No. 1 (81 m) in the early fifth century; Kabuyama 鹿歩山 (84 m) in the late fifth century (Kameda 1997e); Hakayama 波歌山 (60 m) at the end of the fifth to the beginning of the sixth century (Kameda 1997f); and finally Futatsukayama 二塚山 (55 m) in the late sixth century (Kameda 1997g). Although the tumulus group is not exceptionally large-scale for western Japan, it is the third largest in Kibi. It is highly noteworthy that from the late fifth to early sixth centuries, when "chiefly" burial mounds could not be distinguished in the core areas of Kibi, the construction of keyhole tumuli of 84 m and 60 m continuously took place at Ushimado. This indicates that the Oku polity was somewhat independent from the dominant polities in the core areas of Kibi and associated with the Yamato authority in its own way. The strength of the Oku polity was made possible by its involvement in sea transportation, not only to regions neighboring the Inland Sea, but also to Kyushu and the Korean peninsula.

In the seventh century, Buddhist temples that had become a cultural symbol of the strength of the Yamato authority were introduced into all the polities in Kibi. Yet, the earliest-dated full-scale Buddhist temple in Bitchū and in the whole of Kibi, the Hadawara temple site, adopted roof tiles of the "non-mainstream Korean type" related to the immigrant Hata family. Similarly, cloth impressions on the back of round eaves tiles at the Hibata temple site of Bitchū indicate the application of manufacturing techniques that were absent in Kinai and its surroundings. These observations make it difficult to interpret these Buddhist temples as fully under the control of the Kinai polity. It is also important to note that the molds for eaves tiles of the Kayadera temple site of Bitchū were used for a Buddhist temple said to have been erected by a Paekche priest, as described in the *Nihon ryōiki*. This also suggests that this temple in Kibi had ties to Paekche. Furthermore, round eaves tiles with compound-petal lotus-flower patterns that were prevalent in Bitchū from the late seventh to the early eighth century were an example of the non-mainstream Korean type that the Korean immigrants settled in Kinai were involved in creating. This type is highly distinctive from eaves tiles of the Kawaradera type (one of the mainstream types) adopted in the peripheral areas in Kibi. Bizen shows yet another case of adopting roof tiles independently from Kinai. Around the mid-seventh century, the roof tiles introduced to Bizen were of the old Silla type, which was different from those of Kinai and of Bitchū. This type of roof tile was absent in other regions and unique. These observations suggest that, while polities in Kibi had come to be pressured by the central authority of Kinai, they were not under its full control. These polities interacted somewhat independently with Korean immigrants settled in Kinai, and the pattern of interaction was very complex.

Finally in the early to mid-eighth century, polities in Kibi adopted eaves tiles of the Nara Imperial Palace. Along with the local establishment of county offices and provincial headquarters by the Yamato authority from the end of the seventh to early eighth century, the *ritsuryō* 律令 legal and political system was gradually adopted all over Japan. In this context, polities in Kibi were fully incorporated into the political and legal system of the Yamato authority.

It is my position that polities in Kibi fell nominally under the control of the Yamato authority in the early eighth century. To this end, societies in Kibi went through several stages, including the "rebellion" against Emperor Yūryaku in the late fifth century and the local establishment of *miyake* by the Yamato authority in the middle of the sixth century during the reign of Emperor Kinmei. I think I have successfully reconstructed this process of social change in Kibi based on several lines of evidence, including material culture of Korean origin, written sources, and immigration from Korea.

References

Akaiwa-shi Kyōiku Iinkai 赤磐市教育委員会 [Akaiwa Municipal Board of Education]

2005 *Ryōgūzan kofun* 両宮山古墳 [The Ryōgūzan tumulus]. Akaiwa-shi Bunkazai chōsa hōkoku 赤磐市文化財調査報告 [Report of investigations into the cultural heritage of Akaiwa city] No. 1. Akaiwa-shi Kyōiku Iinkai, Akaiwa.

Ch'ungnam Taehakkyo Paekche Yŏn'guso 忠南大學校百濟研究所 [Chungnam National University Paekche Research Institute]

2005 *Taejŏn Kyejok-sansŏng* 大田鷄足山城 [Kyejok mountain fortress in Taejŏn]. Ch'ungnam Taehakkyo Paekche Yŏn'guso haksul yŏn'gu ch'ongsŏ 忠南大學校百濟研究所學術研究叢書 [Chungnam National University Paekche Research Institute Academic Research Collection] No. 13. Ch'ungnam Taehakkyo Paekche Yŏn'guso, Taejŏn.

Emi Masami 江見正己

1998 Kinabeyama iseki 木鍋山遺跡 [The Kinabeyama site]. In *Osafune-chō shi: Shiryō hen (jō)* 長船町史: 史料編(上) [History of Osafune town: Historic sources, volume 1], edited by Osafune-chō Shi Hensan Iinkai 長船町史編纂委員会 [Osafune Town History Compilation Committee], pp. 229–236. Osafune-chō 長船町 [Osafune Township], Osafune.

Fukuo Masahiko 福尾正彦

2006 Kunai-chō shoryō-bu hokan no uma-gata taikō ni tsuite: Shutsudo chi no sai-kentō 宮内庁書陵部保管の馬形帯鉤について: 出土地等の再検討 [Horse-shaped buckles in the possession of the Division of Mausoleums and Documents, Agency for the Imperial Household]. In *Higashi Ajia chiiki ni okeru seidōki bunka no inyū to hen'yō oyobi ryūtsū ni kansuru takakuteki hikaku kenkyū* 東アジア地域における青銅器文化の移入と変容および流通に関する多角的比較研究 [Multi-faceted comparative studies on the introduction, evolution, and exchange of the bronze culture in East Asia], edited by Fujio Shin'ichirō 藤尾慎一郎, pp. 121–133. Kokuritsu Rekishi Minzoku Hakubutsukan 国立歴史民俗博物館 [National Museum of Japanese History], Sakura.

Hinoura Hiroyuki 日野浦弘幸

2003 Sueno'oku kama-ato 末ノ奥窯跡 [Sueno'oku kiln site]. In *Yamate son shi: Shiryō hen* 山手村史: 資料編 [History of the Yamate village: Historical data], edited by Yamate-son Shi Kankō Iinkai 山手村史刊行委員会 [Publication Committee for the History of Yamate Village], pp. 120–124. Yamate-son 山手村 [Yamate Village Government], Yamate.

Hirai Noriko 平井典子

1987 Bizen-shi Shinjō Nishi Hatakeda iseki, Shinjō Higashida iseki saishū no shiryō 備前市新庄西畑田遺跡・新庄東田遺跡採集の資料 [Artifacts collected at the

Shinjō Nishi Hatakeda and Shinjō Higashida sites, Bizen city]. *Kodai Kibi* 古代吉備 9: 71–86.

Hiroshima-ken Kusadosengen-chō Iseki Hakkutsu Chōsa Kenkyūjo 広島県草戸千軒町遺跡調査研究所 [Hiroshima Prefectural Institute for the Kusadosengen-chō Site Excavations]

1980–1982 *Bingo Teramachi haiji: Suitei Mitani-dera hakkutsu chōsa gaihō: Dai 1-ji kara dai 3-ji* 備後寺町廃寺: 推定三谷寺発掘調査概報: 第1次〜第3次 [Preliminary report of archaeological excavations at the Teramachi Buddhist temple site, possibly the historically known Mitani-dera (seasons 1 to 3)]. Hiroshima-ken Kusadosengen-chō Iseki Hakkutsu Chōsa Kenkyūjo, Hiroshima.

Ishida Mosaku 石田茂作

1936 *Asuka jidai ji'in shi no kenkyū* 飛鳥時代寺院址の研究 [Study on Buddhist temples built during the Asuka period]. Shōtoku Taishi Hōsan Kai 聖徳太子奉賛會 [Society Dedicated to the reverence of Prince Shōtoku], Nara.

Itō Akira 伊藤晃, and Shimazaki Azuma 島崎東

1984 Chūgoku chihō: Okayama-ken 中国地方: 岡山県 [Okayama Prefecture, Chūgoku district]. In *Nihon tōji no genryū* 日本陶磁の源流 [Origins of Japanese ceramics and porcelains], edited by Ōtani Joshi Daigaku Shiryōkan 大谷女子大学資料館 [Ōtani Women's University Museum], pp. 149–167. Kashiwa Shobō 柏書房, Tokyo.

Iuchi Kiyoshi 井内潔

1992 Yagawara enkakuchi seisan no ichi-sokumen 屋瓦遠隔地生産の一側面 [An aspect of local roof-tile production far away from the center]. *Kodai Bunka* 古代文化 44(1): 48–51.

Kamaki Yoshimasa 鎌木義昌, and Kameda Shūichi 亀田修一

1986 Yawata-Ōtsuka 2-gō fun 八幡大塚2号墳 [Yawata-Ōtsuka No. 2 tumulus]. In *Okayama-ken shi* 岡山県史 [History of Okayama Prefecture], Vol. 18 (Archaeology), edited by Okayama-ken Shi Hensan Iinkai 岡山県史編纂委員会 [Okayama Prefecture History Compilation Committee], pp. 271–273. Okayama-ken 岡山県 [Okayama Prefectural Government], Okayama.

Kamaki Yoshimasa 鎌木義昌, Makabe Tadahiko 間壁忠彦, and Makabe Yoshiko 間壁葭子

1965 *Zuian kofun* 随庵古墳 [Zuian tumulus]. Sōja-shi Kyōiku Iinkai 総社市教育委員会 [Sōja Municipal Board of Education], Okayama Prefecture.

Kameda Shūichi 亀田修一

1993 Kōkogaku kara mita toraijin 考古学から見た渡来人 [Immigrants as evidenced by archaeology]. *Kobunka Dansō* 古文化談叢 30(2): 747–778.

———

1994 Kawara kara mita Kinai to Chōsen hantō 瓦から見た畿内と朝鮮半島 [Kinai and the Korean peninsula from the standpoint of roof tiles]. In *Yamato ōken to kōryū no shosō* ヤマト王権と交流の諸相 [Various aspects of interaction and the Yamato kingship], Kodai ōken to kōryū 古代王権と交流 [Interaction and ancient kingship] Vol. 5, edited by Araki Toshio 荒木敏夫, pp. 173–205. Meicho Shuppan 名著出版, Tokyo.

———

1996 Kan hantō nambu chiiki no gatō rimen nunome nokimaru-gawara 韓半島南部地域の瓦当裏面布目軒丸瓦 [Round eaves tiles with cloth impressions on the back, discovered in the southern Korean peninsula]. In *Sŏgo Yun Yong-jin Kyosu chŏngnyŏn t'oeim kinyŏm nonch'ong* 碩晤尹容鎭教授停年退任紀念論叢 [Collected papers in celebration of Professor Yun Yong-jin's retirement], edited by Sŏgo Yun Yong-jin Kyosu Chŏngnyŏn T'oeim Kinyŏm Nonch'ong Kanhaeng Wiwŏnhoe 碩晤尹容鎭教授停年退任紀念論叢刊行委員會 [Publication Committee for the Collected Papers in Celebration of Professor Yun Yong-jin's Retirement], pp. 641–661. Sŏgo Yun Yong-jin Kyosu Chŏngnyŏn T'oeim Kinyŏm Nonch'ong Kanhaeng Wiwŏnhoe, Taegu.

———

1997a Kōkogaku kara mita Kibi no toraijin 考古学から見た吉備の渡来人 [Immigrants in ancient Kibi from an archaeological standpoint]. In *Chōsen shakai no shiteki tenkai to Higashi Ajia* 朝鮮社会の史的展開と東アジア [Social evolution in the Korean peninsula in the East Asian context], edited by Takeda Yukio 武田幸男, pp. 131–178. Yamakawa Shuppansha 山川出版社, Tokyo.

———

1997b Kuroshima 1-gō fun 黒島1号墳 [Kuroshima No. 1 tumulus]. In *Ushimado-chō shi: Shiryō hen 2* 牛窓町史: 資料編 2 [History of Ushimado town: Historical data, volume 2], edited by Ushimado-chō Shi Hensan Iinkai 牛窓町史編纂委員会 [Ushimado Town History Compilation Committee], pp. 138–148. Ushimado-chō 牛窓町 [Ushimado Township Government], Ushimado.

———

1997c Kuroshima 2-gō fun 黒島2号墳 [Kuroshima No. 2 tumulus]. In *Ushimado-chō shi: Shiryō hen 2* 牛窓町史: 資料編 2 [History of Ushimado town: Historical data, volume 2], edited by Ushimado-chō Shi Hensan Iinkai 牛窓町史編纂委員会 [Ushimado Town History Compilation Committee], pp. 149–150. Ushimado-chō 牛窓町 [Ushimado Township Government], Ushimado.

———

1997d Ushimado Tenjinyama kofun 牛窓天神山古墳 [Ushimado Tenjinyama tumulus]. In *Ushimado-chō shi: Shiryō hen 2* 牛窓町史: 資料編 2 [History of Ushimado town: Historical data, volume 2], edited by Ushimado-chō Shi Hensan Iinkai 牛窓町史編纂委員会 [Ushimado Town History Compilation Committee], pp. 132–137. Ushimado-chō 牛窓町 [Ushimado Township Government], Ushimado.

———

1997e Kabuyama kofun 鹿歩山古墳 [Kabuyama tumulus]. In *Ushimado-chō shi: Shiryō hen 2* 牛窓町史: 資料編 2 [History of Ushimado town: Historical data, volume 2], edited by Ushimado-chō Shi Hensan Iinkai 牛窓町史編纂委員会 [Ushimado Town History Compilation Committee], pp. 150–156. Ushimado-chō 牛窓町 [Ushimado Township Government], Ushimado.

———

1997f Hakayama kofun 波歌山古墳 [Hakayama tumulus]. In *Ushimado-chō shi: Shiryō hen 2* 牛窓町史: 資料編 2 [History of Ushimado town: Historical data, volume 2], edited by Ushimado-chō Shi Hensan Iinkai 牛窓町史編纂委員会 [Ushimado Town History Compilation Committee], pp. 157–173. Ushimado-chō 牛窓町 [Ushimado Township Government], Ushimado.

———

1997g Futatsukayama kofun 二塚山古墳 [Futatsukayama tumulus]. In *Ushimado-chō shi: Shiryō hen 2* 牛窓町史: 資料編 2 [History of Ushimado town: Historical data, volume 2], edited by Ushimado-chō Shi Hensan Iinkai 牛窓町史編纂委員会 [Ushimado Town History Compilation Committee], pp. 174–184. Ushimado-chō 牛窓町 [Ushimado Township Government], Ushimado.

———

1998a Tsukiyama kofun 築山古墳 [Tsukiyama tumulus]. In *Osafune-chō shi: Shiryō hen (jō)* 長船町史: 史料編 (上) [History of Osafune town: Historical data, volume 1], edited by Osafune-chō Shi Hensan Iinkai 長船町史編纂委員会 [Osafune Town History Compilation Committee], pp. 65–77. Osafune-chō 長船町 [Osafune Township Government], Osafune.

———

1998b Ushibumi Chausuyama kofun 牛文茶臼山古墳 [Ushibumi Chausuyama tumulus]. In *Osafune-chō shi: Shiryō hen (jō)* 長船町史: 史料編 (上) [History of Osafune town: Historical data, volume 1], edited by Osafune-chō Shi Hensan Iinkai 長船町史編纂委員会 [Osafune Town History Compilation Committee], pp. 78–88. Osafune-chō 長船町 [Osafune Township Government], Osafune.

———
1998c Sue Hai-ji 須恵廃寺 [Sue Buddhist temple site]. In *Osafune-chō shi: Shiryō hen (jō)* 長船町史：史料編（上）[History of Osafune town: Historical data, volume 1], edited by Osafune-chō Shi Hensan Iinkai 長船町史編纂委員会 [Osafune Town History Compilation Committee], pp. 282–303. Osafune-chō 長船町 [Osafune Township Government], Osafune.

———
2000a Tetsu to toraijin: Kofun jidai no Kibi o taishō toshite 鉄と渡来人：古墳時代の吉備を対象として [Immigrants and iron: With special reference to Kofun-period Kibi]. In *Fukuoka Daigaku Sōgō Kenkyūjo hō* 福岡大学総合研究所報 240 [Bulletin of the central research institute, Fukuoka University: Humanities and social sciences, no. 240], edited by Fukuoka Daigaku Sōgō Kenkyūjo 福岡大学総合研究所 [Fukuoka University Central Research Institute], pp. 165–184. Fukuoka Daigaku Sōgō Kenkyūjo, Fukuoka.

———
2000b Kodai Kibi no tetsu to tekki seisan 古代吉備の鉄と鉄器生産 [Iron and iron tool production in ancient Kibi]. In *Osafune-chō shi: Tōken hen, tsūshi* 長船町史：刀剣編，通史 [History of Osafune town: Volume on iron swords; history], edited by Osafune-chō Shi Hensan Iinkai 長船町史編纂委員会 [Osafune Town History Compilation Committee], pp. 43–129. Osafune-chō 長船町 [Osafune Township Government], Osafune.

———
2001 Chōsen hantō tono kōryū 朝鮮半島との交流 [Interaction with the Korean peninsula]. In *Osafune-chō shi: Tsūshi hen* 長船町史：通史編 [History of Osafune town: Cultural history], edited by Osafune-chō Shi Hensan Iinkai 長船町史編纂委員会 [Osafune Town History Compilation Committee], pp. 170–178. Osafune-chō 長船町 [Osafune Township Government], Osafune.

———
2003 Toraijin no kōkogaku 渡来人の考古学 [The archaeology of immigrants]. *Nanakuma Shigaku* 七隈史学 4: 1–14.

———
2004a 5-seiki no Kibi to Chōsen hantō: Zōzan kofun, Sakuzan kofun no shūhen o chūshin ni 5 世紀の吉備と朝鮮半島：造山古墳・作山古墳の周辺を中心に [Kibi and the Korean peninsula in the fifth century: With particular reference to the vicinities of the Zōzan and Sakuzan tumuli]. *Kibi Chihō Bunka Kenkyū* 吉備地方文化研究 14: 1–19.

———
2004b Nihon no shoki no kugi, kasugai ga katarumono 日本の初期の釘・鎹が語るもの [Hypotheses based on iron nails and clamps of early Japan]. In *Bunka*

no tayōsei to hikaku kōkogaku: Kōkogaku Kenkyū Kai 50-shūnen kinen ronbunshū 文化の多様性と比較考古学: 考古学研究会50周年記念論文集 [Cultural diversity and comparative archaeologies: Collected papers in celebration of the 50th anniversary of the Society for Archaeological Studies], edited by Kōkogaku Kenkyū Kai 考古学研究会 [Society for Archaeological Studies], pp. 29–38. Kōkogaku Kenkyū Kai, Okayama.

———

2006 *Nikkan kodai kawara no kenkyū* 日韓古代瓦の研究 [A study of ancient roof tiles of Korea and Japan]. Yoshikawa Kōbunkan 吉川弘文館, Tokyo.

———

2008 Kibi to Yamato 吉備と大和 [Kibi and Yamato]. In *Kofun jidai no jitsuzō* 古墳時代の実像 [Realistic image of the Kofun period], edited by Habuta Yoshiyuki 土生田純之, pp. 19–71. Yoshikawa Kōbunkan 吉川弘文館, Tokyo.

Kanō Hisashi 狩野久

2005 Hakui Miyake to Soga-shi 白猪屯倉と蘇我氏 [Hakui Miyake and Soga families]. In *Kodai o kangaeru: Kibi* 古代を考える: 吉備 [Consideration of ancient history: Kibi], edited by Kadowaki Teiji 門脇禎二, Kanō Hisashi, and Kuzuhara Katsuhito 葛原克人, pp. 185–207. Yoshikawa Kōbunkan 吉川弘文館, Tokyo.

Katō Kenkichi 加藤謙吉

1983 *Soga-shi to Yamato ōken* 蘇我氏と大和王権 [The Yamato kingship and the Soga family]. Yoshikawa Kōbunkan 吉川弘文館, Tokyo.

Kinojō Gakujutsu Chōsa Iinkai 鬼ノ城学術調査委員会 [Committee for Scholarly Investigations into the Kinojō Site]

1980 *Kinojō* 鬼ノ城 [The Ki fortress]. Kinojō Gakujutsu Chōsa Iinkai, Sōja City, Okayama Prefecture.

Kondō Yoshirō 近藤義郎

1956 Ushimado wan o meguru kofun to kofun-gun 牛窓湾をめぐる古墳と古墳群 [Tumuli and tumulus groups in the Ushimado bay area]. *Watakushitachi no Kōkogaku* 私たちの考古学 3(2): 2–10.

——— (editor)

1991 *Zempō-koenfun shūsei: Chūgoku, Shikoku hen* 前方後円墳集成: 中国・四国編 [Compendium of keyhole tumuli: Chūgoku and Shikoku districts]. Yamakawa Shuppan 山川出版社, Tokyo.

Kungnip Chinju Pangmulgwan 國立晋州博物館 [Chinju National Museum]

1987 *Hapch'ŏn Pan'gyeje kobun'gun: Hapch'ŏn taem sumol yejŏng chigu palgul chosa pogo 1* 陜川磻溪堤古墳群: 陜川댐水没豫定地域発掘調査報告 1 [The Pan'gyeje cemetery in Hapch'ŏn: Excavation reports in the locality in the Hapch'ŏn dam floodway, volume 1]. Kungnip Chinju Pangmulgwan, Chinju.

Kungnip Kyŏngju Pangmulgwan 國立慶州博物館 [Kyŏngju National Museum]
2000 *Silla wa chŏn: Arŭmdaun Silla wa kŭ ch'ŏnnyŏn sumgyŏl* 新羅瓦塼: 아름다운 신라와 그천년 숨결 [An exhibition of Silla roof tiles: The beauty of Silla and the breath of a millennium]. Kungnip Kyŏngju Pangmulgwan, Kyŏngju.

Kurashiki-shi Kyōiku Iinkai 倉敷市教育委員会 [Kurashiki Municipal Board of Education]
2005 *Hibata hai-ji hakkutsu chōsa hōkoku-sho* 日畑廃寺発掘調査報告書 [Report of archaeological excavations at the Hibata Buddhist temple site]. Kurashiki-shi maizō bunkazai hakkutsu chōsa hōkoku 倉敷市埋蔵文化財発掘調査報告 [Report of archaeological investigations in Kurashiki city] No. 11. Kurashiki-shi Kyōiku Iinkai, Kurashiki.

Kuzuhara Katsuhito 葛原克人
1986 Sakuzan kofun 作山古墳 [Sakuzan tumulus]. In *Okayama-ken shi* 岡山県史 [History of Okayama Prefecture], Vol. 18 (Archaeology), edited by Okayama-ken Shi Hensan Iinkai 岡山県史編纂委員会 [Okayama Prefecture History Compilation Committee], pp. 348. Okayama-ken 岡山県 [Okayama Prefectural Government], Okayama.

———
1987 Hatabara hai-ji 秦原廃寺 [Hatabara Buddhist temple site]. In *Sōja-shi shi: Kōko shiryo hen* 総社市史: 考古資料編 [History of Sōja City: Archaeology], edited by Sōja-shi Shi Hensan Iinkai 総社市史編纂委員会 [Sōja City History Compilation Committee], pp. 336–348. Sōja-shi 総社市 [Sōja Municipal Government], Sōja.

Kuzuhara Katsuhito 葛原克人, Kondō Yoshirō 近藤義郎, and Kamaki Yoshimasa 鎌木義昌
1986 Kōmorizuka kofun こうもり塚古墳 [Kōmorizuka tumulus]. In *Okayama-ken shi* 岡山県史 [History of Okayama Prefecture], Vol. 18 (Archaeology), edited by Okayama-ken Shi Hensan Iinkai 岡山県史編纂委員会 [Okayama Prefecture History Compilation Committee], pp. 372–375. Okayama-ken 岡山県 [Okayama Prefectural Government], Okayama.

Minato Tetsuo 湊哲夫, and Kameda Shūichi 亀田修一
2006 *Kibi no kodai jiin* 吉備の古代寺院 [Ancient Buddhist temples of Kibi]. Kibito Shuppan 吉備人出版, Okayama.

Nakano Masami 中野雅美
1993 Sugō Shogakkō Urayama iseki shutsudo no shoki sueki 菅生小学校裏山遺跡出土の初期須恵器 [The earliest type of *sue* stoneware discovered at the Sugō Shōgakkō Urayama site]. In *Kanshiki-kei doki kenkyū* 韓式系土器研究 [Studies of pottery of Korean origins], Vol. 4, edited by Kanshiki-kei Doki Kenkyū Kai 韓式系土器研究会 [Society for Study of Pottery of Korean Origins], pp. 107–119. Kanshiki-kei Doki Kenkyū Kai, Osaka.

Naoki Kōjirō 直木孝次郎

1983 Kibi no toraijin to gōzoku 吉備の渡来人と豪族 [Immigrants and influential local chiefs in Kibi]. In *Okayama no rekishi to bunka* 岡山の歴史と文化 [Culture and history of Okayama], edited by Fujii Shun Sensei Kiju Kinen Kai 藤井駿先生喜寿記念会 [Society for the Celebration of Professor Fujii Shun's Seventy-seventh Birthday], pp. 73–91. Fukutake Shoten 福武書店, Tokyo.

Nishikawa Hiroshi 西川宏

1975 *Kibi no kuni* 吉備の国 [The old province of Kibi]. Gakuseisha 学生社, Tokyo.

———

1986a Zōzan kofun 造山古墳 [The Zōzan tumulus]. In *Okayama-ken shi* 岡山県史 [History of Okayama Prefecture], Vol. 18 (Archaeology), edited by Okayama-ken Shi Hensan Iinkai 岡山県史編纂委員会 [Okayama Prefecture History Compilation Committee], pp. 342–343. Okayama-ken 岡山県 [Okayama Prefectural Government], Okayama.

———

1986b Ushibumi Chausuyama kofun 牛文茶臼山古墳 [The Ushibumi Chausuyama tumulus]. In *Okayama-ken shi* 岡山県史 [History of Okayama Prefecture], Vol. 18 (Archaeology), edited by Okayama-ken Shi Hensan Iinkai 岡山県史編纂委員会 [Okayama Prefecture History Compilation Committee], pp. 211–212. Okayama-ken 岡山県 [Okayama Prefectural Government], Okayama.

Nishitani Shinji 西谷真治, and Kamaki Yoshimasa 鎌木義昌

1959 *Kanakurayama kofun* 金蔵山古墳 [The Kanakurayama tumulus]. Kurashiki Kōkokan 倉敷考古館 [Kurashiki Museum of Archaeology], Kurashiki City.

Nomori Ken 野守健, and Kanda Sōzō 神田惣蔵

1935 *Chūsei-nandō Kōshū Sōsan-ri kofun chōsa hōkoku* 忠清南道公州宋山里古墳調査報告 [Report of the excavation of the Songsan-ni mounded burial in Kongju, South Chungch'ŏng]. Shōwa 2-nendo koseki chōsa hōkoku 2 昭和2年度古蹟調査報告 2 [Report of investigations of ancient sites for the second year of Shōwa, volume 2]. Chōsen Sōtokufu 朝鮮總督府 [Government-General of Korea], Keijō (Seoul).

Noritake Tadanao 則武忠直, Oka Hideaki 岡秀昭, and Shiomi Masayasu 塩見真康

1994 Okayama-ken Sanyō-chō Monzen'ike Tōhō iseki no Chōsen hantō-kei shiryō 岡山県山陽町門前池東方遺跡の朝鮮半島系資料 [Archaeological materials of Korean origins discovered at the Monzen'ike Tōhō site, Sanyō town, Okayama Prefecture]. *Kobunka Dansō* 古文化談叢 32: 47–52.

Okamoto Hirohisa 岡本寛久

1992 "Mizukiri kawara" no kigen to dempa no igi 「水切り瓦」の起源と伝播の意義 [Significance of the origins and diffusion of the rounded eaves tiles with "pointed bottoms"]. In *Kibi no kōkogaku-teki kenkyū* 吉備の考古学的研究

[Archaeological studies of Kibi], edited by Kondō Yoshirō 近藤義郎, pp. 349–384. San'yō Shimbunsha 山陽新聞社, Okayama.

Okayama-ken Kyōiku Iinkai 岡山県教育委員会 [Okayama Prefectural Board of Education]
1975 *Monzen'ike iseki* 門前池遺跡 [The Monzen'ike site]. Okayama-ken maizō bunkazai hakkutsu chōsa hōkoku 岡山県埋蔵文化財発掘調査報告 [Report of archaeological excavations in Okayama Prefecture] No. 9. Okayama-ken Kyōiku Iinkai, Okayama.

———
1979 *Kayadera hai-ji kinkyu hakkutsu chōsa hōkokuksho* 栢寺廃寺緊急発掘調査報告書 [Report of emergency salvage excavations at the Kayadera Buddhist temple site]. Okayama-ken maizō bunkazai hakkutsu chōsa hōkoku 岡山県埋蔵文化財発掘調査報告 [Report of archaeological excavations in Okayama Prefecture] No. 34. Okayama-ken Kyōiku Iinkai, Okayama.

———
1982 *Tonoyama iseki, Tonoyama kofun-gun* 殿山遺跡・殿山古墳群 [Tonoyama site and Tonoyama tumulus group]. Okayama-ken maizō bunkazai hakkutsu chōsa hōkoku 岡山県埋蔵文化財発掘調査報告 [Report of archaeological excavations in Okayama Prefecture] No. 47. Okayama-ken Kyōiku Iinkai, Okayama.

———
1993a *San'yō jidōsha dō kensetsu nitomonau hakkutsu chōsa* 5 山陽自動車道建設に伴う発掘調査 5 [Archaeological excavations conducted prior to the construction of the San'yō expressway, volume 5]. Okayama-ken maizō bunkazai hakkutsu chōsa hōkoku 岡山県埋蔵文化財発掘調査報告 [Report of archaeological excavations in Okayama Prefecture] No. 81. Okayama-ken Kyōiku Iinkai, Okayama.

———
1993b *Kuboki-Yakushi iseki* 窪木薬師遺跡 [The Kuboki-Yakushi site]. Okayama-ken maizō bunkazai hakkutsu chōsa hōkoku 岡山県埋蔵文化財発掘調査報告 [Report of archaeological excavations in Okayama Prefecture] No. 86. Okayama-ken Kyōiku Iinkai, Okayama.

———
1996 *Saitomi iseki* 斎富遺跡 [The Saitomi site]. Okayama-ken maizō bunkazai hakkutsu chōsa hōkoku 岡山県埋蔵文化財発掘調査報告 [Report of archaeological excavations in Okayama Prefecture] No. 105. Okayama-ken Kyōiku Iinkai, Okayama.

———
1997 *Yabuta kofun-gun, Kanakuro Ike Higashi iseki, Okugatani kama-ato, Nakayama iseki, Nakayama kofun-gun, Nishiyama iseki, Nishiyama kofun-gun, Hattori iseki, Kita-Mizote iseki, Kuboki iseki, Tanakamatsu-Tanaka iseki* 藪田古墳群・金

黒池東遺跡・奥ヶ谷窯跡・中山遺跡・中山古墳群・西山遺跡・西山古墳群・服部遺跡・北溝手遺跡・窪木遺跡・高松田中遺跡 [The Yabuta tumulus group, Kanakuro Ike Higashi site, Okugatani kiln site, Nakayama site, Nakayama tumulus group, Nishiyama site, Nishiyama tumulus group, Hattori site, Kita-Mizote site, Kuboki site, and Tanakamatsu-Tanaka site]. Okayama-ken maizō bunkazai hakkutsu chōsa hōkoku 岡山県埋蔵文化財発掘調査報告 [Report of archaeological excavations in Okayama Prefecture] No. 121. Okayama-ken Kyōiku Iinkai, Okayama.

———

1998 *Kuboki iseki 2* 窪木遺跡 2 [The Kuboki site, volume 2]. Okayama-ken maizō bunkazai hakkutsu chōsa hōkoku 岡山県埋蔵文化財発掘調査報告 [Report of archaeological excavations in Okayama Prefecture] No. 124. Okayama-ken Kyōiku Iinkai, Okayama.

———

1999 *Kamo-Mandokoro iseki* 加茂政所遺跡 [The Kamo-Mandokoro site]. Okayama-ken maizō bunkazai hakkutsu chōsa hōkoku 岡山県埋蔵文化財発掘調査報告 [Report of archaeological excavations in Okayama Prefecture] No. 138. Okayama-ken Kyōiku Iinkai, Okayama.

———

2000 *Takatsuka iseki, Mitsute iseki 2* 高塚遺跡・三手遺跡 2 [The Takatsuka site and Mitsute site, volume 2]. Okayama-ken maizō bunkazai hakkutsu chōsa hōkoku 岡山県埋蔵文化財発掘調査報告 [Report of archaeological excavations in Okayama Prefecture] No. 150. Okayama-ken Kyōiku Iinkai, Okayama.

———

2008 *Minami Mizote iseki, Kuboki iseki* 南溝手遺跡・窪木遺跡 [The Minami-Mizote site and Kuboki site]. Okayama-ken maizō bunkazai hakkutsu chōsa hōkoku 岡山県埋蔵文化財発掘調査報告 [Report of archaeological excavations in Okayama Prefecture] No. 214. Okayama-ken Kyōiku Iinkai, Okayama.

Osafune-chō Kyōiku Iinkai 長船町教育委員会 [Osafune Township Board of Education]
1997 *Hattori hai-ji* 服部廃寺 [The Hattori Buddhist temple site]. Osafune-chō maizō bunkazai hakutsu chōsa hōkoku 長船町埋蔵文化財発掘調査報告 [Report of archaeological excavations in Osafune town] No. 2. Osafune-chō Kyōiku Iinkai, Osafune.

Ōsaka-fu Kyōiku Iinkai 大阪府教育委員会 [Osaka Prefectural Board of Education]
1995 *Suemura-Obadera iseki 4* 陶邑・大庭寺遺跡 4 [The Suemura-Obadera site, volume 4]. Ōsaka-fu maizō bunkazai kyokai chōsa hōkoku-sho 大阪府埋蔵文化財協会調査報告書 [Report of archaeological investigations conducted by the Osaka Prefectural Association for Archaeological Heritage Management] No. 90. Ōsaka-fu Kyōiku Iinkai, Osaka.

Pusan Taehakkyo Pangmulgwan 釜山大学校博物館 [Pusan National University Museum]
1990 *Tongnae Pokch'ŏn-dong kobun'gun 2* 東來福泉洞古墳群 2 [The Pokch'ŏn-dong mounded burials in Tongnae, volume 2]. Pusan Taehakkyo Pangmulgwan yujŏk chosa pogo 14 釜山大学校博物館遺蹟調査報告14 [Pusan National University Museum site excavation report 14]. Pusan Taehakkyo Pangmulgwan, Pusan.

Saitō Masaru 斎藤優
1970 *Wakasa Kaminaka machi no kofun* 若狭上中町の古墳 [Tumuli in Kaminaka town, old province of Wakasa]. Kaminaka-chō Kyōiku Iinkai 上中町教育委員会 [Kaminaka Township Board of Education], Kaminaka.

Seki Akira 関晃
1966 *Kika-jin* 帰化人 [Immigrants]. Shibundō 至文堂, Tokyo.

Shimazaki Azuma 島崎東
1982 Bitchū Sakakiyama kofun saishū no ibutsu ni tsuite 備中榊山古墳採集の遺物について [Artifacts collected at the Sakakiyama tumulus in Bitchū]. *Okayama-ken Shi Kenkyū* 岡山県史研究 3: 96–104.

Sim Chŏng-bo 沈正輔, and Kong Sŏk-ku 孔錫龜
1994 *Kyejok-sansŏng sŏmunji chosa kaebo* 鶏足山城西門址調査概報 [Summary report on the excavations of the west gate site of Kyejok mountain fortress]. Taejŏn Sanŏp Taehakkyo Hyangt'o Munhwa Yŏn'guso 大田産業大学校郷土文化研究所 [Taejŏn Industrial University Local Culture Research Center]. Taejŏn Sanŏp Taehakkyo Hyangt'o Munhwa Yŏn'guso, Taejŏn.

Sōja-shi Kyōiku Iinkai 総社市教育委員会 [Sōja Municipal Board of Education]
1985 *Hōren kofun-gun* 法蓮古墳群 [Hōren tumulus group]. Sōja-shi maizō bunkazai hakkutsu chōsa hōkoku 総社市埋蔵文化財発掘調査報告 [Report of archaeological excavations in Sōja City] No. 2. Sōja-shi Kyōiku Iinkai, Sōja.

———
1999 *Okusaka iseki-gun* 奥坂遺跡群 [Okusaka site cluster]. Sōja-shi maizō bunkazai hakkutsu chōsa hōkoku 総社市埋蔵文化財発掘調査報告 [Report of archaeological excavations in Sōja City] No. 15. Sōja-shi Kyōiku Iinkai, Sōja.

Suzaka-shi Kyōiku Iinkai 須坂市教育委員会 [Suzaka Municipal Board of Education]
2000 *Nagano-ken shiseki Hacchō Yoroizuka* 長野県史跡 八丁鎧塚 [Hacchō Yoroizuka tumulus, nationally designated historic site, Nagano Prefecture]. Suzaka-shi Kyōiku Iinkai, Suzaka.

Takahashi Shin'ichi 高橋進一
1994 Fukui Shinden chiku hojō seibi jigyō ni tomonau hakkutsu chōsa 福井新田地区ほ場整備事業に伴う発掘調査 [Archaeological excavations at Shinden locality in Fukui, conducted prior to the re-organization of rice paddies]. *Sōja-shi maizō bunkazai chōsa nempō* 総社市埋蔵文化財調査年報 [Annual report of archaeological investigations in Sōja City] 4: 28–29.

5 Ancient Kibi, Western Japan, and the Korean Peninsula—Kameda Shūichi

Wada Senkichi 和田千吉

1919 Bitchū no kuni Tsukubo gun Shinjō-shita kofun 備中国都窪郡新庄下古墳 [Shinjō-shita tumulus in Tsukubo County, old province of Bitchū]. *Kōkogaku Zasshi* 考古学雑誌 9(11): 33–45.

Yi Han-sang 李漢祥

2001 Ilbon ch'ult'o Paekche isik ŭi yŏndae 일본 출토 백제이식의 연대 [Approximate dates of Paekche-made earrings discovered in Japan]. *Kodae Yŏngu* 古代研究 8: 63–78.

Yoshida Akira 吉田晶

1984 Kodai Oku chiiki ni kansuru ichi kosatsu 古代邑久地域史に関する一考察 [Thoughts on the Oku area of ancient Japan]. *Okayama-ken Shi Kenkyū* 岡山県史研究 7: 1–25.

———

1990 Kibi no *Be* min 吉備の部民 [Be people in ancient Kibi]. In *Okayama-ken shi* 岡山県史 3 [History of Okayama Prefecture, volume 3] (Ancient period, part 2), edited by Okayama-ken Shi Hensan Iinkai 岡山県史編纂委員会 [Okayama Prefecture History Compilation Committee], pp. 97–120. Okayama-ken 岡山県 [Okayama Prefectural Government], Okayama.

6

Archaeological Investigations at the Ōmuro Cairn Cluster in the Central Highlands of Japan: With Reference to Korean Immigrants in the Fifth and Sixth Centuries A.D.

Sasaki Ken'ichi

Abstract

This chapter reports on the major results of archaeological investigations conducted at the Ōmuro cairn and earthen mound group in Nagano City, in the northern central highlands of Japan. The site is a cemetery consisting of more than five hundred mounded tombs and dates to the middle fifth to seventh centuries A.D. The site is very unusual because of the presence of numerous cairns, about thirty of which have "vaulted" burial chambers, which are very rare in Kofun-period Japan. Some of the fieldwork yielded clues to understanding the interaction between the Korean peninsula and the central highlands of Japan. It is likely that equestrian specialists invited from the Korean peninsula were buried in some of the mounds at Ōmuro. The name "Ōmuro" appears in a tenth-century historic source in a list of national pastures for raising horses under the central government, and it seems that horse breeding had already started at Ōmuro in the middle fifth century. Since the way in which horses were treated at Ōmuro differs from other regions of Japan, the author proposes the possibility that local elites in Nagano invited equestrian specialists from the Korean peninsula independently from the central polity in the fifth century.

Introduction

This chapter reports the major results of archaeological investigations at the Ōmuro 大室 cairn and earthen mound group and discusses their

6 Archaeological Investigations at the Ōmuro Cairn Cluster—Sasaki Ken'ichi

Map 6.1 Location of Ōmuro.

Figure 6.1 Vaulted Burial Chamber. Photograph by author.

significance in the broader context of Japanese history, with special reference to issues related to Korea-Japan interaction. Staff of the Archaeology Program, Faculty of Arts and Letters, Meiji University conducted the archaeological investigations between 1984 and 1996 (Ōtsuka et al. 1993; Ōtsuka and Kobayashi 2006; Kobayashi et al. 2008; Sasaki et al. 2015). The site is located in Nagano City in the central highlands of Japan (Map 6.1), where the Winter Olympic Games were held in 1998, and dates from the middle fifth to the end of the seventh century or perhaps to the beginning of the eighth century. In Japanese archaeology, these dates correspond to the middle and late Kofun period and the historic Asuka period.

This site has attracted scholarly attention for a long time for several reasons. First, this group of burial mounds includes numerous cairns, which is very unusual among burial mounds of the Kofun period but is not particularly unusual in the Korean peninsula. Many of the cairns were accompanied by "vaulted" burial chambers, characterized by two or three pairs of stone slabs leaning against each other, thereby forming the roof of a burial chamber (Figure 6.1). In Japan, some fifty or so vaulted chambers are known archaeologically, some thirty of which exist in the Ōmuro cairn and earthen mound group. Since similar burial chambers are known in the

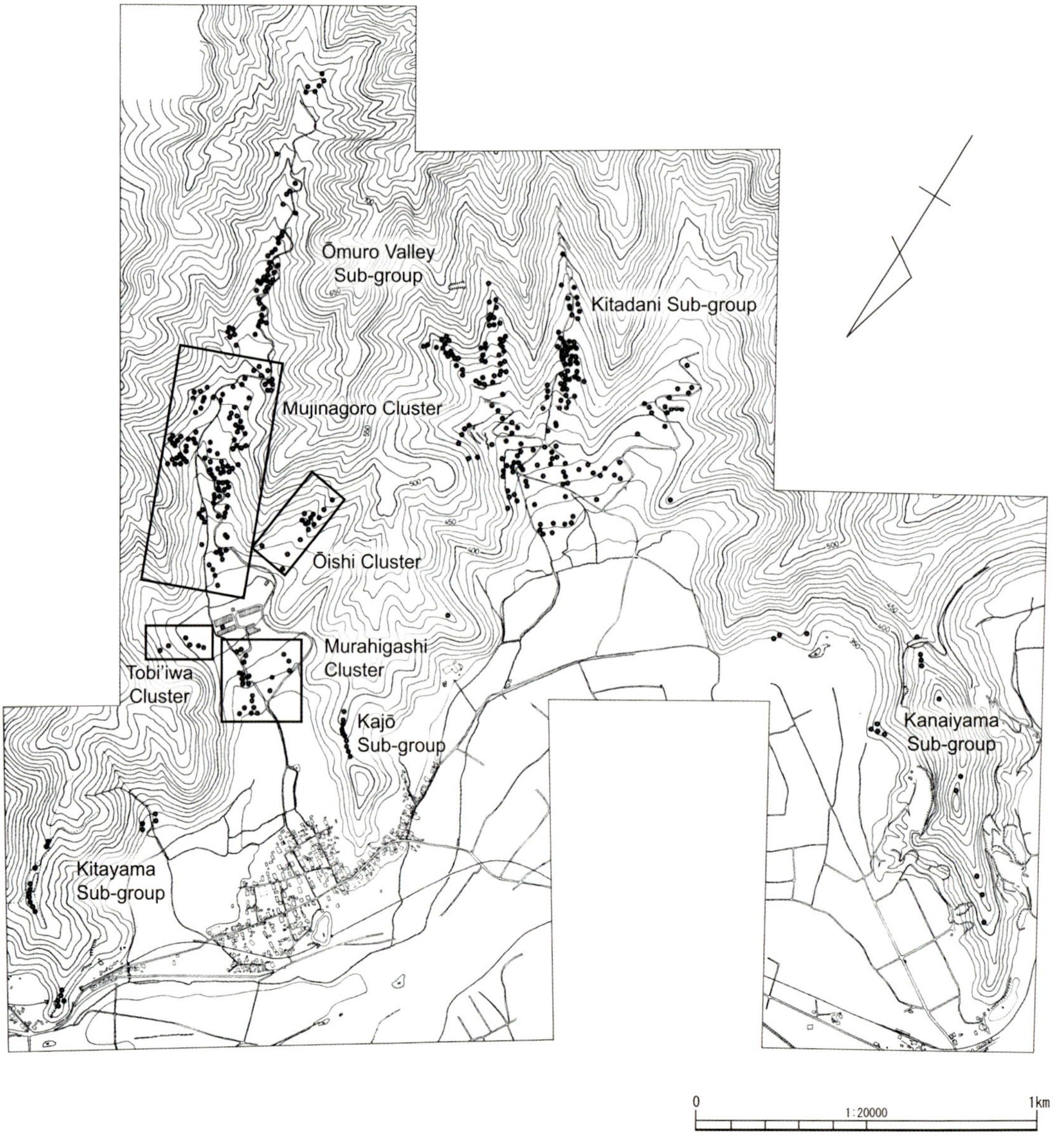

Map 6.2 Spatial Divisions Within the Ōmuro Cairn and Earthen Mound Group.

Korean peninsula, some Japanese archaeologists have previously speculated that the vaulted burial chambers were burials of immigrants from the Korean peninsula (e.g. Nishiyama 2014).

Secondly, the place name Ōmuro is mentioned in the early tenth-century document, *Engishiki* 延喜式 (Codes compiled in the Engi era [901-923]), as one of the official pastures where horses were raised and produced for the central government. Horses were not native to Japan, but were introduced from the Korean peninsula. Because raising and breeding horses required specialized skills and knowledge, equestrian specialists had to be invited from the Korean peninsula. Together with the possibility of Korean immigrants being buried in the Ōmuro cairn and earthen mound group, some Japanese archaeologists have speculated that a practice of raising horses started in the Ōmuro region much earlier than the ninth century (e.g. Ōtsuka 1969).

The results of Meiji University's long-term excavations have clarified temporal change in the construction pattern of cairns and earthen mounds in the Ōmuro Valley sub-group of this mound group. The results also provided invaluable data that give us insight into Korea-Japan interactions from the fifth to seventh centuries.

Overview of the Site and Issues Related to Burial Chambers

The Ōmuro cairn and earthen mound group consists of some 500 burial mounds in an area of 2.5 square kilometers. It is the largest in scale of all mound groups in this region. The mound group is situated on the western slope of the hills that mark the eastern side of the Nagano Basin, and on the eastern bank of the Chikuma 千曲 River that flows into the Sea of Japan (East Sea). The mound group is spatially divided into five sub-groups (Map 6.2), namely (from the north) Kitayama 北山 (21 mounds), Ōmuro Valley, Kajō 霞城 (13 mounds), Kitadani 北谷 (179 tombs, most of which are cairns, 6 of which are accompanied by vaulted burial chambers), and Kanaiyama 金井山 (17 mounds). Among these, the largest is the Ōmuro Valley sub-group, where 241 burial mounds are distributed. The Ōmuro Valley sub-group is further spatially divided into clusters, distributed from west to east, or from the lower to the higher altitude: Murahigashi 村東, Tobi'iwa 鳶岩, Ōishi 大石, and Mujinagōro ムジナゴーロ.

Although such spatial units as "sub-groups" and "clusters" are today based purely on spatial distributions of mounds, these divisions must have had some meaning during the Kofun period. For example, although *haniwa* 埴輪 ceramic cylinders were used only in the fifth century in the Ōmuro

Valley sub-group, the practice of standing *haniwa* ceramic cylinders on the tops of mounds continued into the sixth century in the Kitadani sub-group. These spatially distinctive sub-groups are tied together by the common existence of very unusual cairn and vaulted burial chambers.

Although a cluster is also a matter of spatial division, we speculate that this division had some meaning when the Ōmuro Valley functioned as a cemetery from the middle fifth to seventh centuries. The formation of both the Ōishi and Mujinagōro clusters started with the construction of a cairn with a vaulted burial chamber. The construction of cairns continued until the early sixth century in both of the clusters, as well as in the Murahigashi cluster where fifth-century cairns have been destroyed, but a very early sixth-century cairn with a vaulted burial chamber was excavated (Kazama 2011). In the middle sixth century, corridor-style horizontal burial chambers were introduced to these three clusters. In other words, temporal change in construction patterns seems both independent and parallel from cluster to cluster. This independence might indicate, for example, a difference in the lineages of people who were buried in each cluster.

In the Ōmuro mound group as a whole, some one hundred burials are cairns constructed purely with locally available rocks. Around three hundred mounds are constructed with internal stone structures, and the spaces enclosed by the internal stone structures are filled with earth. Some Japanese archaeologists even consider the latter type as cairns in order to distinguish them from ordinary earthen burial mounds constructed principally with earth. In this paper, we maintain a strict definition of the cairn as a burial constructed purely with rocks (Kobayashi Saburō 2006), as is true of cairns in other regions of the world.

The Ōmuro mound group appeared in the middle fifth century, when the construction of cairns started there. Prior to this, relatively large keyhole tombs of 68 to 99 m in length were built in the Nagano Basin in successive generations beginning in the late third century. Each keyhole tomb occupied the top of a ridge extending into the Nagano Basin. A Japanese archaeologist hypothesized that a system of circular succession was then practiced in the Nagano Basin—that is, local elites from different lineages took turns occupying the highest-ranking position in the Nagano Basin (Iwasaki 1964). This old hypothesis has been widely accepted. In the middle fifth century, however, the construction of large keyhole tombs stopped. Around the same time, the formation of the Ōmuro mound group started. We do not know whether these two phenomena were aspects of the same social process, but they do not seem to be entirely coincidental.

6 Archaeological Investigations at the Ōmuro Cairn Cluster—Sasaki Ken'ichi

The construction of mounds in the Ōmuro mound group continued until the seventh century, and additional interments in previously constructed burial chambers took place until the end of the seventh century or perhaps the early eighth century, when the Nara capital or Heijō Kyō 平城京 was already active. Cairns with vaulted burial chambers were constructed until the beginning of the sixth century. In the second quarter of the sixth century or a little later, corridor-style horizontal burial chambers were introduced to the Nagano Basin, and most of the mounds in the Ōmuro mound group constructed after that date featured this type of burial chamber.

Before discussing the major results of the work at the Ōmuro mound group, we consider it necessary to discuss issues related to "vaulted" burial chambers (Figure 6.1). This type of burial facility is extremely unusual in Japan; it is found only in the Ōmuro mound group and in Yamanashi 山梨 Prefecture, a southeastern neighbor of Shinano 信濃 (Kobayashi Hideo 1978; Iijima 2003a, 2003b). Japanese archaeologists were aware of this very rare type of burial chamber both in the Nagano Basin (Morimoto 1926) and in the Korean peninsula (Saitō 1944) as early as the 1930s, when Japan occupied the Korean peninsula. Because this type of burial chamber is very rare in Japan, and because similar types of burial chamber have been discovered in the southern part of the Korean peninsula, some Japanese archaeologists have argued for their origin in Paekche (e.g. Saitō 1944; Nishiyama 1996, 2000). One example of such a burial in a Korean context is that at Simok-tong 柿木洞 in Kongju 公州. All the stone slabs that constitute parts of the burial chamber are well carved, which suggests that this burial chamber is dated to the seventh century. For this reason, Japanese archaeologists used to believe that vaulted burial chambers in the Nagano Basin should be dated to the seventh century or later.

As archaeological excavations in the Ōmuro mound group progressed in the 1980s, however, Ōtsuka and Kobayashi (2006) found that some of the vaulted chambers were constructed in the third quarter of the fifth century or possibly earlier. This date is much earlier than Japanese archaeologists used to believe, and much earlier than the known Korean counterparts. Japanese archaeologists who maintain the Korean origin of vaulted burial chambers in the Nagano Basin suspect that there must be much earlier Korean examples of vaulted chambers waiting to be discovered (e.g. Kirihara 1989). In any case, the appearance of vaulted burial chambers in the Nagano Basin was sudden and without any precedent. At the same time, it is important to note that uniquely Japanese *haniwa* ceramic cylinders stood on the surface of cairns with vaulted burial chambers. It is not, therefore, simple to consider vaulted burial chambers as evidence for Korean immigrants in the Nagano Basin.

Another important aspect of vaulted chambers is that a body was placed in the chamber from the side rather than from the top, as in a pit-style burial chamber. In the Early and Middle Kofun periods (middle third to fifth centuries A.D.), the pit-style burial chamber was the dominant form of interment. In this burial style, a large pit was dug at the top of the burial mound, in which the burial chamber was constructed. Then the body was placed in the chamber by lowering it from the top. In the case of a vaulted burial chamber, by contrast, the body was carried into the chamber from the side, although the chamber itself was installed in the mound from the top. It was the practice to carry the body horizontally into corridor-style, horizontal burial chambers. This practice came to be widely adopted in the sixth century or the Late Kofun period. The idea of the corridor-style, horizontal burial chamber was adopted from the Korean peninsula. The case of the Nagano Basin is the earliest example in Japan of the practice of carrying a body horizontally to a burial chamber with the exception of Kyushu, where corridor-style, horizontal burial chambers were introduced from the Korean peninsula in the early fifth century.

In the middle sixth century, corridor-style burial chambers were introduced to the Nagano Basin. Generally speaking, corridor-style burial chambers evolved from those constructed with numerous small rocks to those constructed with fewer, very large rocks as technology progressed to bridge larger rocks over the top of two side walls. A corridor-style burial chamber usually consists of a main burial chamber where one or more coffins were placed, and a corridor leading to the main burial chamber. In corridor-style burial chambers of a very early type, the widths of the main burial chamber and the corridor are the same. In the second stage of evolution, the main burial chamber became wider than the corridor (Ozaki 1966).

History of Archaeological Investigations

Because the Ōmuro mound group has attracted scholarly attention for a long time, there was already a very long history of investigations before Meiji University launched a long-term archaeological project in 1984. In the late 1920s, a local learned society surveyed the Ōmuro mound group. Then, in an archaeological project whose results formed the foundation for investigations that have continued up to the present, a local schoolteacher, Kuribayashi Kidō 栗林紀道, identified and numbered some five hundred mounds as part of a comprehensive survey conducted in the late

1940s. The results of this work were published in 1952, and, although additional burial mounds were discovered and some mounds identified by Kuri-bayashi were later revealed not to be burial mounds, we still use the identification numbers he designated.

In 1951, Gotō Shuichi 後藤守一, Professor of Archaeology at Meiji University, conducted excavations and surveys of the Ōmuro mound group. Ōtsuka (1969) participated in this project as a young graduate student and published the major results of the investigations after Gotō's death. The Meiji University team excavated Tomb No. 107 in the Ōmuro Valley sub-group and No. 358 in the Kitadani sub-group. Besides these two burials, the team mapped the mounds and burial chambers of fifteen mounds in the Ōmuro Valley, Kitadani, and Kanaiyama sub-groups. This was the first problem-oriented, systematic archaeological project conducted in the Ōmuro mound group.

In 1969, a part of the Kitadani sub-group was excavated prior to the construction of the Nagano Prefectural Center for Agriculture (Kamimura 1970). These excavations resulted in the discovery of corridor-style burial chambers of a rather unusual type. Ordinarily, the side walls of corridor-style burial chambers are constructed by piling up flat stones. However, the morphology of this unusual type of corridor-style burial chambers is characterized by "standing" side walls—that is, flat stones constituting the side walls are placed upright. This type is rather rare in Japan and may be traced to an origin in the Korean peninsula. I will discuss this in some detail in relation to Tomb No. 187 of the Mujinagōro cluster.

From 1970 to 1972, in 1978, and again in 1980, Nagano City and the Komazama University cooperatively conducted very comprehensive surveys of the entire Ōmuro mound group (Kurata 1981). They identified a total of 454 mounds: 21 in the Kitayama sub-group, including one keyhole tomb probably dating to the early fifth century, 13 in the Kajō sub-group, 17 in the Kanaiyama sub-group, 179 in the Kitadani sub-group, and 224 in the Ōmuro Valley sub-group. Cairns constituted considerable portions of the Kitadani and Ōmuro Valley sub-groups. The results of their comprehensive survey confirmed the validity of the results of the surveys personally conducted by Kuribayashi in the late 1940s.

In 1984, the staff of the Archaeology Program at Meiji University launched a long-term archaeological investigation in the Ōmuro Valley sub-group under the direction of Ōtsuka Hatsushige, now Professor Emeritus of Meiji University. Ōtsuka chose the Ōmuro Valley sub-group because its cairns and earthen mounds are situated in close proximity, and by excavating both he expected to explore their temporal and perhaps their cultural relationships (Ōtsuka et al. 1993). The project lasted until 1996, and the major results of this series of excavations and mappings are reported in this chapter.

The results of this work contributed to our understanding about previously unknown aspects of Kofun culture. Owing to these results, the Ōmuro Valley sub-group was designated as a Historic Site by the national government, and will be protected against any future destruction. In 1989 and 1990, six mounds in the Murahigashi cluster of the Ōmuro Valley sub-group were fully excavated prior to the construction of an expressway (Ōtsuka et al. 1991). Since the Meiji team mapped one of the six mounds and surveyed their vicinity in 1984, this team was put in charge of the excavations. Among the six mounds, the burial chamber and mound of Tomb No. 23 were completely dismantled and re-built at a different location. Since 1997, the Nagano City government has been conducting excavations of the Murahigashi cluster in order to turn the site into a park (Shimizu et al. 2007; Shimizu and Iijima 2008; Kazama 2013, 2014, 2016).

Major Results of Archaeological Investigations by Meiji University: Murahigashi Cluster

Staff of the Archaeology Program at Meiji University conducted surveys, mapping, and excavations in the Murahigashi, Ōishi, and Mujinagōro clusters of the Ōmuro Valley sub-group. As aforementioned, the spatial differentiations into clusters must have had some meaning in the Kofun period, and therefore the results of archaeological investigations in each cluster are presented separately. In each section, the results of excavations are given in the chronological order in which the mounds were constructed. The mounds are grouped into two chronological categories: fifth century to the beginning of the sixth century, when cairns were primarily built, and the middle sixth century and later, when earthen mounds with corridor-style burial chambers were primarily built. These two categories are tentatively referred to as "the age of cairns" and "the age of corridor-style burial chambers" (Sasaki et al. 2015).

Fifth Century to the Beginning of the Sixth Century: Age of Cairns

The Murahigashi cluster occupies the lowest part and the western end of the Ōmuro Valley sub-group. As in the cases of the Ōishi and Mujinagōro clusters, the formation of the Murahigashi cluster probably started with a cairn with a vaulted burial chamber, though fifth-century cairns have been

Figure 6.2 Discovery of a Vaulted Burial Chamber of Tomb No. 241. Photograph courtesy of the Nagano Municipal Board of Education.

destroyed. The Meiji University team discovered only fragments of fifth-century *haniwa* ceramic cylinders in the vicinity of Tomb No. 241 during excavations and surveys in 1984, but none of them were *in situ* (Ōtsuka et al. 1993). During an excavation of cairn Tomb No. 241 in 2009, staff of the Nagano Municipal Board of Education discovered a vaulted burial chamber dated to the beginning of the sixth century A.D. (Figure 6.2) (Kazama 2011). This vaulted burial chamber is the latest example so far excavated in the Ōmuro Valley sub-group.

The excavation also resulted in discoveries of horse trappings and iron arrowheads. This is highly noteworthy in that one of the iron arrowheads is a type characteristic of those discovered in large keyhole tombs. Despite the small size of this cairn, its occupant might have been an elite of very high rank. I will raise this important issue in the conclusion of this chapter.

Middle Sixth Century to Seventh Century:
Age of Corridor-Style Horizontal Burial Chambers

In this cluster, the Meiji University team mapped Tombs Nos. 23, 26, 239, 240, 243, and 244 in the summer of 1984 and excavated Tombs Nos. 244 and 248 from October 27 to November 8, 1984. In the process, the team discovered two previously unknown mounds, namely Tombs A and B. Furthermore, the team participated in rescue excavations of Tombs 21, 22, 23, 24, 25, and 二 (*ni*) in 1989 and 1990. Among these, Tomb No. 22 was revealed not to be a tomb (Ōtsuka et al. 1993). All of these tombs were destroyed during the construction of the expressway, with the exception of Tomb No. 23, which was dismantled, moved, and rebuilt near Tomb No. 244. In this section, I report the results of archaeological investigations at Tombs 23, 26, 239, 240, 243, 244, and 248. I incorporate the results of the rescue excavations at Tomb 23 and of excavations by the Nagano Municipal Board of Education at Tombs 26, 239, 240, 243, and 244 from 1998 to 2004 (Shimizu et al. 2007; Shimizu and Iijima 2008; Kazama 2013, 2014, 2016) as necessary.

Tomb No. 239 is a circular mound of approximately 12 m in diameter (Figure 6.3). It is accompanied by a corridor-style horizontal burial chamber (Figures 6.4 and 6.5). The burial chamber is structurally divided into the main burial chamber of 4.3 m in length and 1.15 m in width with a corridor 2.57 m in length leading to the main burial chamber. Because the widths of the main burial chamber and of the corridor are more or less the same, and because the chamber is constructed with small rocks, the burial chamber is considered as an early type. Among the burial mounds in the Murahigashi cluster, this is the earliest type. Based on this observation, this mound

Figure 6.3 Tomb No. 239. Photograph by author.

may have been constructed in the middle sixth century. The mound is constructed primarily of earth.

Tomb No. 240 is also a circular mound of 7.5 by 9.0 m (Figure 6.6). The mound was originally 10 m in diameter, but the front portion, where the entrance to a corridor-style horizontal burial chamber opens, has been destroyed. It is accompanied by a corridor-style burial chamber, but the corridor leading to the main burial chamber was destroyed. The main burial chamber is 4.1 m in length, 1.8 m in width at the back wall, and 2.2 m in maximum width (Figures 6.7 and 6.8). The burial chamber is characterized by a plan in which the central part is wider than the two ends, which was common in the seventh century. The back wall of this chamber is

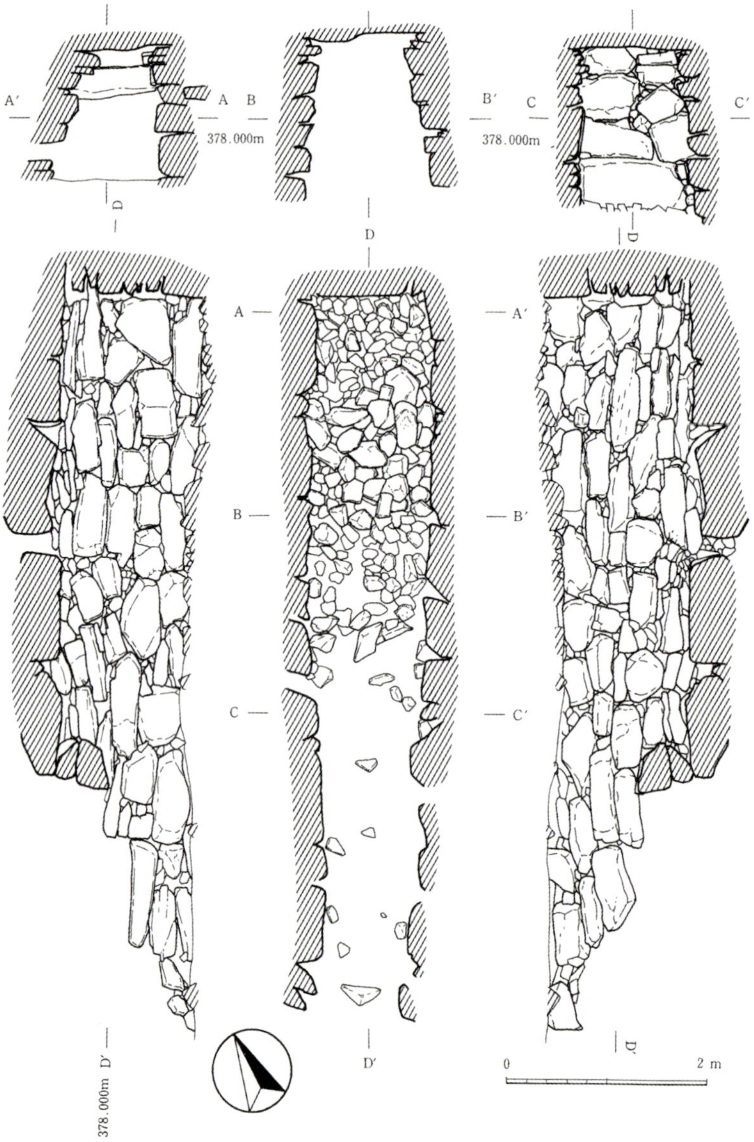

Figure 6.4 Corridor-style Burial Chamber of Tomb No. 239. From Ōtsuka et al. 1993, Fig. 79.

Figure 6.5 View of the Exit and Corridor from the Main Burial Chamber of Tomb No. 239. Photograph by author.

Figure 6.6 Tomb No. 240. Photograph by author.

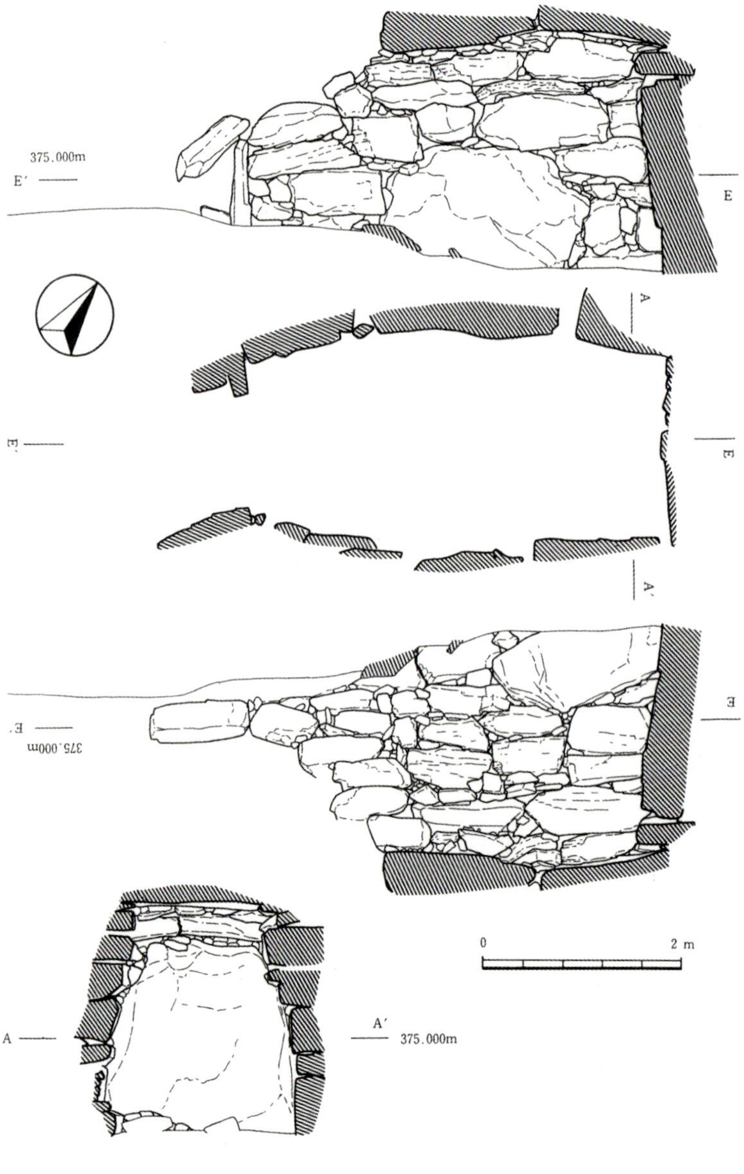

Figure 6.7 Corridor-style Burial Chamber of Tomb No. 240.
From Ōtsuka et al. 1993, Fig. 82.

Figure 6.8 Back Wall of the Burial Chamber of Tomb No. 240. Photograph by author.

Figure 6.9 Tomb No. 243. Photograph by author.

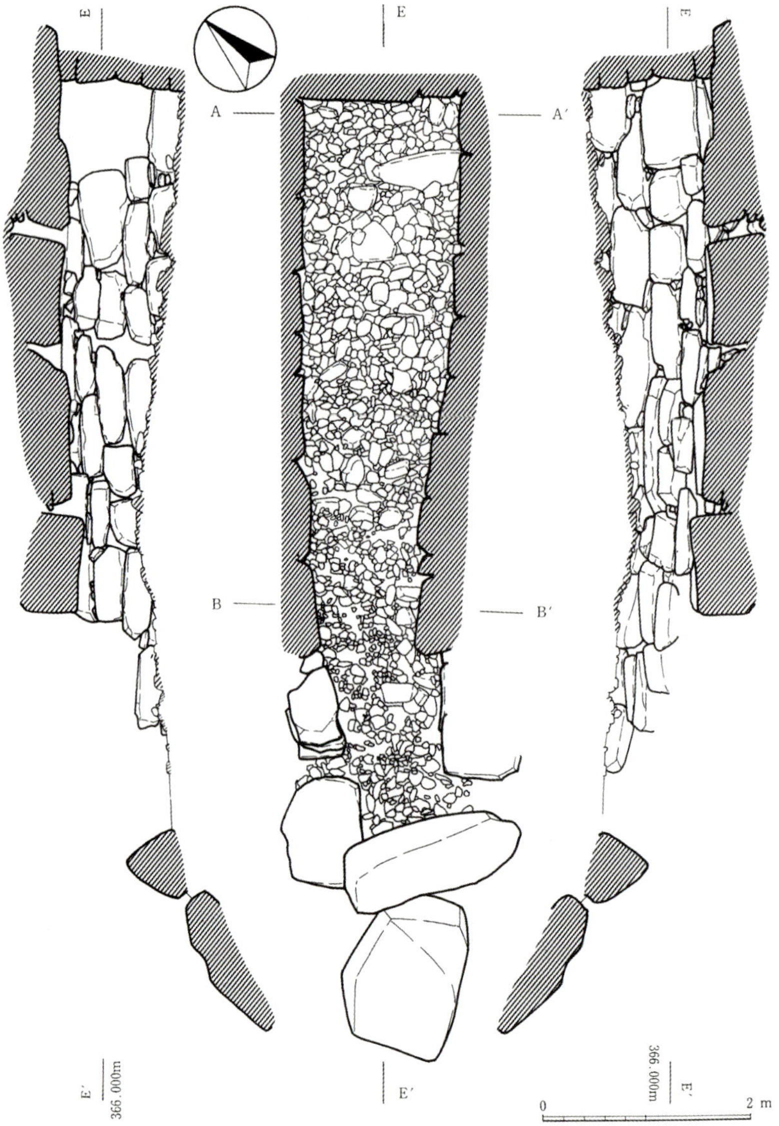

*Figure 6.10 Corridor-style Burial Chamber of Tomb No. 243.
From Ōtsuka et al. 1993, Fig. 86.*

Figure 6.11 Tomb No. 244. Photograph by author.

constructed primarily with a single flat rock, which also suggests that the chamber is of a later type. Based on these observations, this mound may be dated to the seventh century. The mound is constructed primarily of earth.

Tomb No. 243 is also a circular mound of 9.5 by 9.0 m (Figure 6.9). Almost half of the mound was destroyed to the extent that the exterior of a side wall of a corridor-style burial chamber, which is usually completely covered by the mound, is exposed. The corridor-style burial chamber is 7.6 m in length. The main burial chamber is 5.0 m in length, 1.5 m in width at the back wall, and 1.4 m in width at the center of the main chamber (Figure 6.10). A part of the corridor leading to the main burial chamber was destroyed, and we do not know the length of the corridor. The width of the corridor is more or less the same as the main burial chamber. The burial chamber is constructed with relatively small stones. This mound may be dated to the middle to late sixth century.

Tomb No. 244 is the largest and tallest circular mound in the Ōmuro Valley sub-group. It is 18.1 m by 15.2 m because it is situated on a slope, and the remaining height is 8.5 m (Figure 6.11). Its corridor-style burial chamber

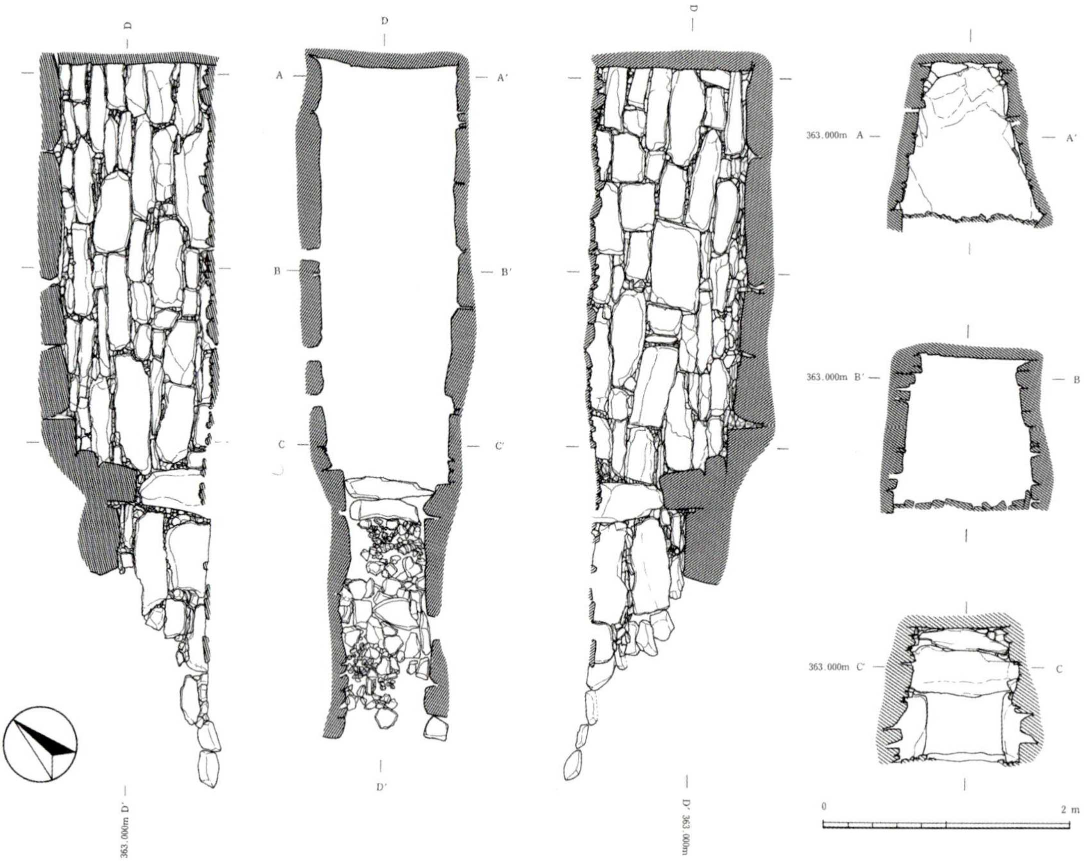

Figure 6.12 Corridor-style Burial Chamber of Tomb No. 244.
From Ōtsuka et al. 1993, Figs. 91 and 92.

is also of the largest scale (Figures 6.12 and 6.13). The total length is 11.7 m. The main burial chamber is 6.5 m in length, 2.2 m in width at the back wall, 2.3 m in the center, and 1.9 m at the entrance, and 2.5 m in the internal height. A corridor leading to this main burial chamber is 4.25 m in length, 1.5 m in width at the entrance to the main burial chamber and 1.3 m at the entrance to the corridor, and 1.5 m in internal height. Since the back wall of the burial chamber is constructed with a single giant slab, I estimate that the mound

Figure 6.13 View of the Exit and Corridor from the Main Burial Chamber of Tomb No. 244. Photograph by author.

*Figure 6.14 Moat Enclosing the Mound of Tomb No. 244.
Photograph by author.*

was built toward the end of the sixth century or perhaps the beginning of the seventh century.[1] The mound is characterized by a very steep slope, and the surface is covered with flat stones. The mound gives an impression considerably distinct from that given by ordinary circular mounds of the Kofun period. This mound is distinguished from others of the Ōmuro Valley subgroup by the moat enclosing the mound (Figure 6.14). Because of the large scale of the mound and burial chamber, I would consider this as the burial of a chief of the highest rank, although it is not keyhole-shaped. I will come back to this issue in the conclusion of this chapter.

Tomb No. 23 is a roughly circular mound of 17.85 by 13.23 m, accompanied by a corridor-style burial chamber (Figures 6.15, 6.16, and 6.17). The burial chamber is 7.15 m long. The main burial chamber is 4.05 m long, 1.40 m in width at the back wall, 1.65 m at its maximum width, 1.30 m in width at the entrance, and 2.4 m in internal height. A corridor leading to the main

[1] While a report of this excavation (Ōtsuka et al. 1993) does not mention the date of this tomb, Ōtsuka (2000) mentions that it was built in the late sixth century.

Figure 6.15 Tomb No. 23.
Photograph by Mihoko Sudō.

burial chamber is 3.10 m in length, 1.15 m in width at the entrance to the main burial chamber, 0.95 m in width at the entrance, and 1.40 m in internal height. The entrance to the main burial chamber was demarcated by the construction of a gate. The back wall was constructed with a single large slab. These observations suggest that this burial chamber was of a later type.

Since this tomb was fully excavated, we have gained considerable understanding about the internal structure of the burial mound. First, the burial chamber was constructed and then was covered by rocks. In this stage, this mound was in reality a cairn. This "cairn" portion may be referred to as a "primary" mound. Then, this cairn was enclosed by an inner stone wall and outer stone wall. Finally, spaces enclosed by these internal stone structures were filled with earth. This earthen mound may be referred to as a "secondary" mound.

During the excavation, the following artifacts were discovered: one glass bead, twenty-seven iron arrowheads, and some *haji* earthenware in the main burial chamber; *haji* earthenware and *sue* stoneware in the corridor to the main burial chamber; and *haji* earthenware and *sue* stoneware

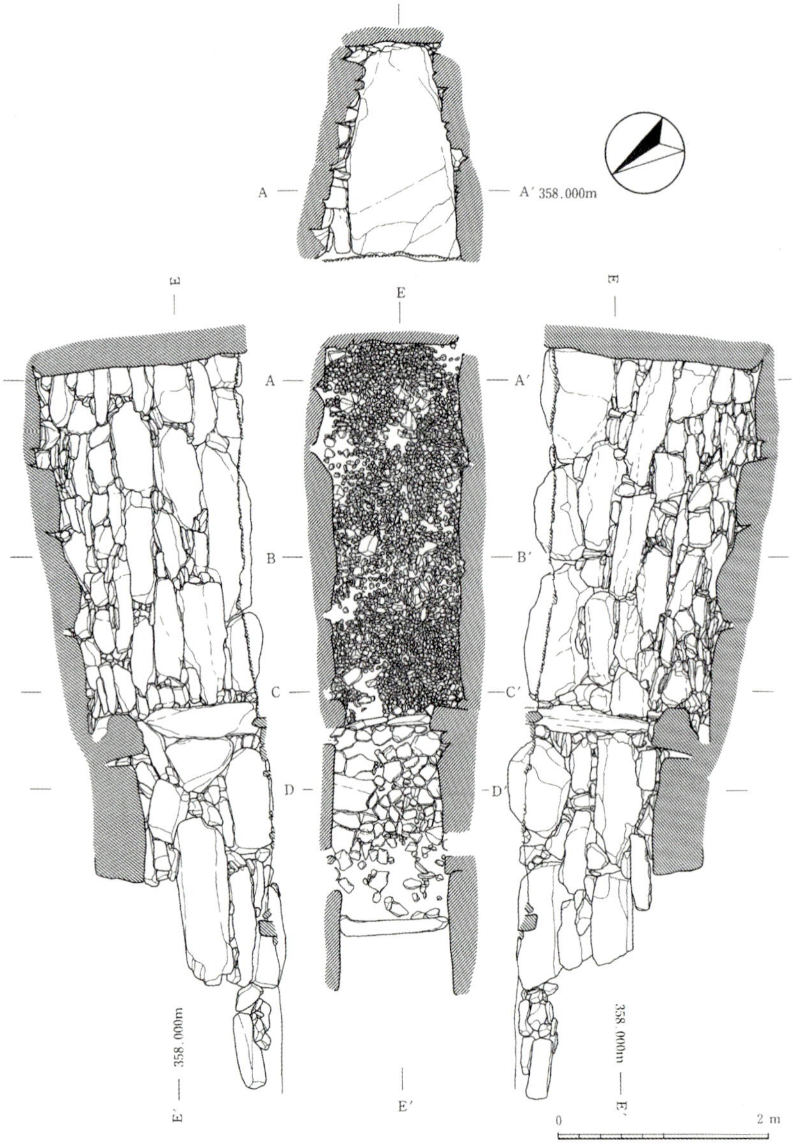

*Figure 6.16 Corridor-style Burial Chamber of Tomb No. 23.
From Ōtsuka et al. 1993, Fig. 16.*

*Figure 6.17 Back Wall of the Burial Chamber of Tomb No. 23.
Photograph by Mihoko Sudō.*

in the earth constituting the mound. Most of the *haji* earthenware are pedestalled bowls, presumably for ritual. The arrowheads are of types typical of the early seventh century. Therefore, this tomb may be dated to the early seventh century, which does not contradict the characteristics of the burial chamber. Some of the *sue* stoneware is of a type dated to the early eighth

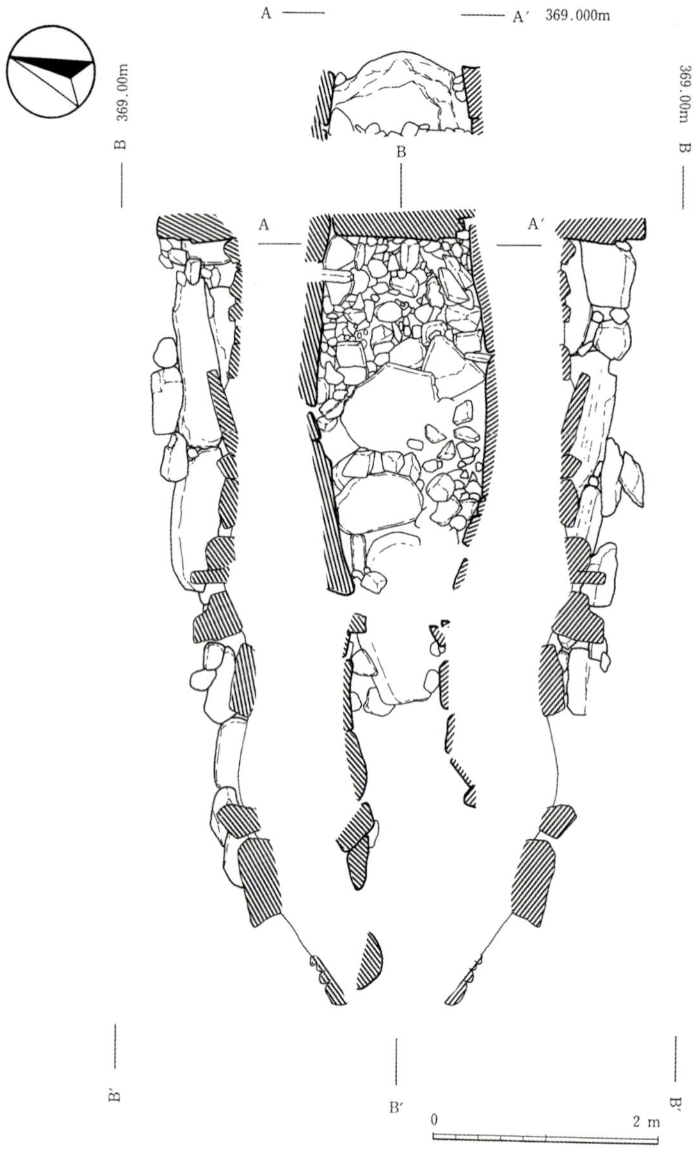

Figure 6.18 Corridor-style Burial Chamber of Tomb No. 26. From Ōtsuka et al. 1993, Fig. 71.

century. Pottery of later date probably resulted from an additional interment that took place after the initial construction of this tomb. It is noteworthy that *haji*-earthenware pedestalled bowls are of a type common in the early and middle sixth century. The excavators interpret the pedestalled bowls as of an earlier type that were mixed with the earth constituting the mound (Ōtsuka et al. 1993:51–52). I propose an alternative interpretation and suggest that those who built this mound intentionally produced pedestalled bowls of an archaic style for ritual purposes.[2] This was probably the case for Tomb No. 186 in the Mujinagōro cluster.

Tomb No. 26 is a circular mound of 18 m in diameter, accompanied by a corridor-style burial chamber of 5 m in length. The top portion of the mound was destroyed to the extent that the top of the burial chamber is exposed. In fact, the top portion of the burial chamber was removed, and the original height remains unknown. The chamber consists of the main burial chamber and the corridor leading to it. The plan of the main burial chamber is characterized by two sides expanding like an arc. The length of the main burial chamber is 3.4 m. Its width is 1.3 m at the back wall, 1.5 m at the center, and 0.6 m at the entrance. The corridor is 1.6 m in length and 0.8 m in width (Figure 6.18). Because the morphology of the main burial chamber with a wider central portion is characteristic of the seventh century, it is likely that this tomb was constructed in the seventh century.

Major Results of Archaeological Investigations by Meiji University: Ōishi Cluster

There are only nine tombs in this cluster, which is spatially distant from the Murahigashi and Mujinagōro clusters, and Ōtsuka and Kobayashi (2006) speculated that this cluster is distinctive in other respects. If this is indeed the case, they might be able to approach, for example, differences in lineage groups within the Ōmuro Valley sub-group. The second reason they chose this cluster for the early phase of long-term investigations was that cairns with vaulted burial chambers and ordinary mounds with corridor-style burial

[2] Japanese archaeologists traditionally speculated that pottery of an earlier type was used for ritual purposes. This speculation turned out to be valid during excavations of the Kuroimine site, Gunma Prefecture. The site is called the "Pompeii of Japan" because the site was instantly buried and packed with volcanic ash resulting from an eruption of Mount Haruna in the early sixth century. In one of the pit dwellings, archaeologists excavated a household shrine. Before this shrine, pottery of a type earlier than household pottery was offered.

Figure 6.19 Vaulted Burial Chamber of Tomb No. 225.
Photograph by Kenri Satō.

chambers coexisted side by side. By excavating all of them, they hoped to gain important information about possible relationships between the two very different kinds of mortuary practices. They also hoped that the results of excavations in this small cluster would help them plan long-term excavations of the Mujinagōro cluster, where scores of cairns and earthen mounds exist (Ōtsuka and Kobayashi 2006).

Fifth Century to the Beginning of the Sixth Century: Age of Cairns

The tomb construction in the Ōishi cluster started with Tomb No. 225, a cairn, in the middle fifth century (Figures 6.19 and 6.20). Since the earliest dated tomb in the Mujinagōro cluster of the Ōmuro Valley sub-group is also a cairn dated to the middle fifth century, it is likely that the construction of the Ōmuro mound group started with cairns in the middle fifth century. A single-adult-size vaulted burial chamber is installed in the cairn. Archaeological excavations yielded the discoveries of iron arrowheads, iron sickles, *haji*-earthenware vessels, and *haniwa* ceramic cylinders.

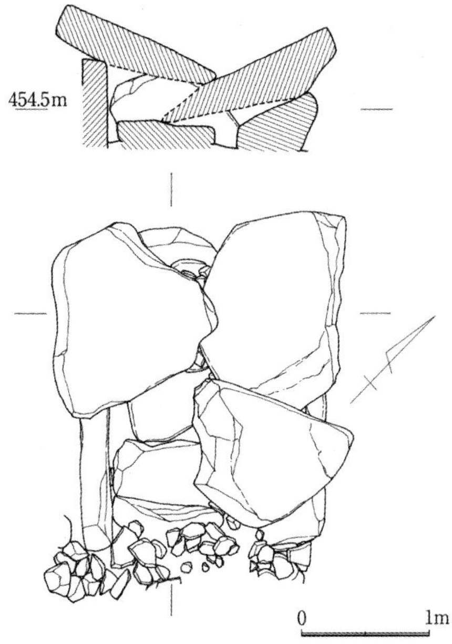

Figure 6.20 Vaulted Burial Chamber of Tomb No. 225. From Ōtsuka and Kobayashi 2006, Fig. 61.

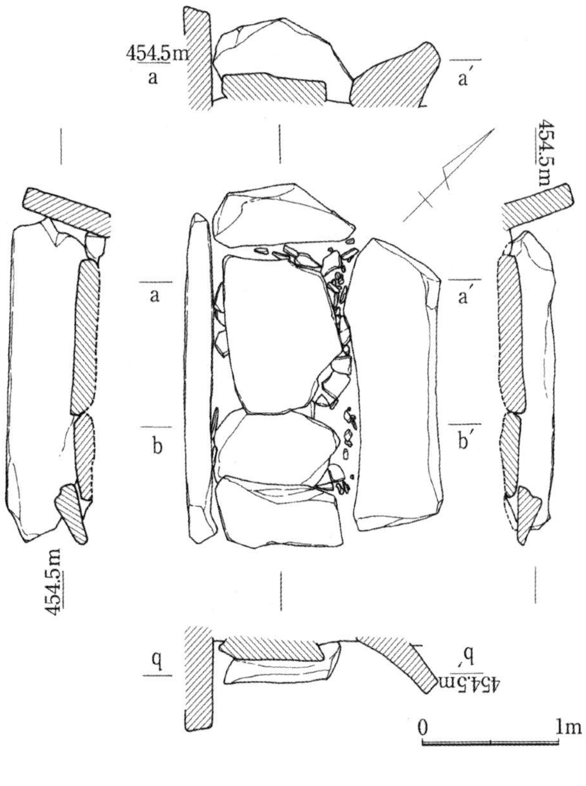

The second-earliest tomb in this cluster is Tomb No. 221 (Figures 6.21 and 6.22), which is also a cairn. Its date would be toward the end of the fifth or perhaps the beginning of the sixth century. The burial structure is the same type as that of Tomb No. 225. An iron sword, iron knives, iron arrowheads, *haji*-earthenware vessels, *haniwa* ceramic cylinders, and various types of beads have been excavated.

Figure 6.21 Vaulted Burial Chamber of Tomb No. 221. Photograph by author.

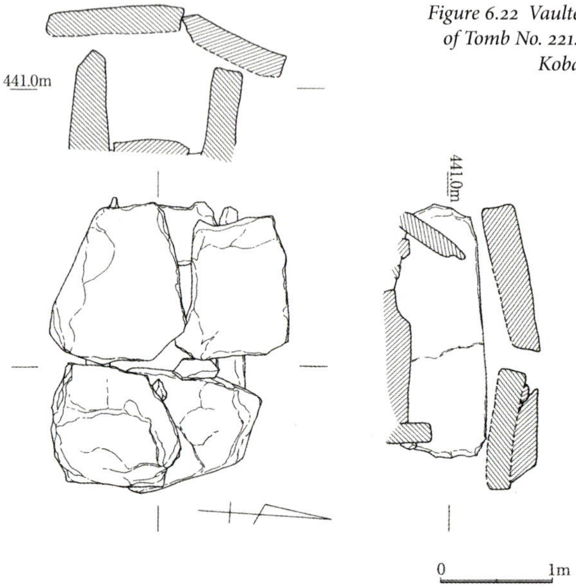

Figure 6.22 Vaulted Burial Chamber of Tomb No. 221. From Ōtsuka and Kobayashi 2006, Fig. 15.

Figure 6.23 Corridor-style Burial Chamber of Tomb No. 227. Photograph by Kenri Satō.

Prior to the middle fifth century, Feature No. 226 was formed. It is a concentration of cobbles. *Haji*-earthenware vessels from earlier than the middle fifth century were discovered in the concentration. Our excavation has revealed no evidence of burials, and we interpret this concentration as a result of ritual activity. Tombs 225 and 221 and Feature No. 226 are all located on the same ridge, close to one another.

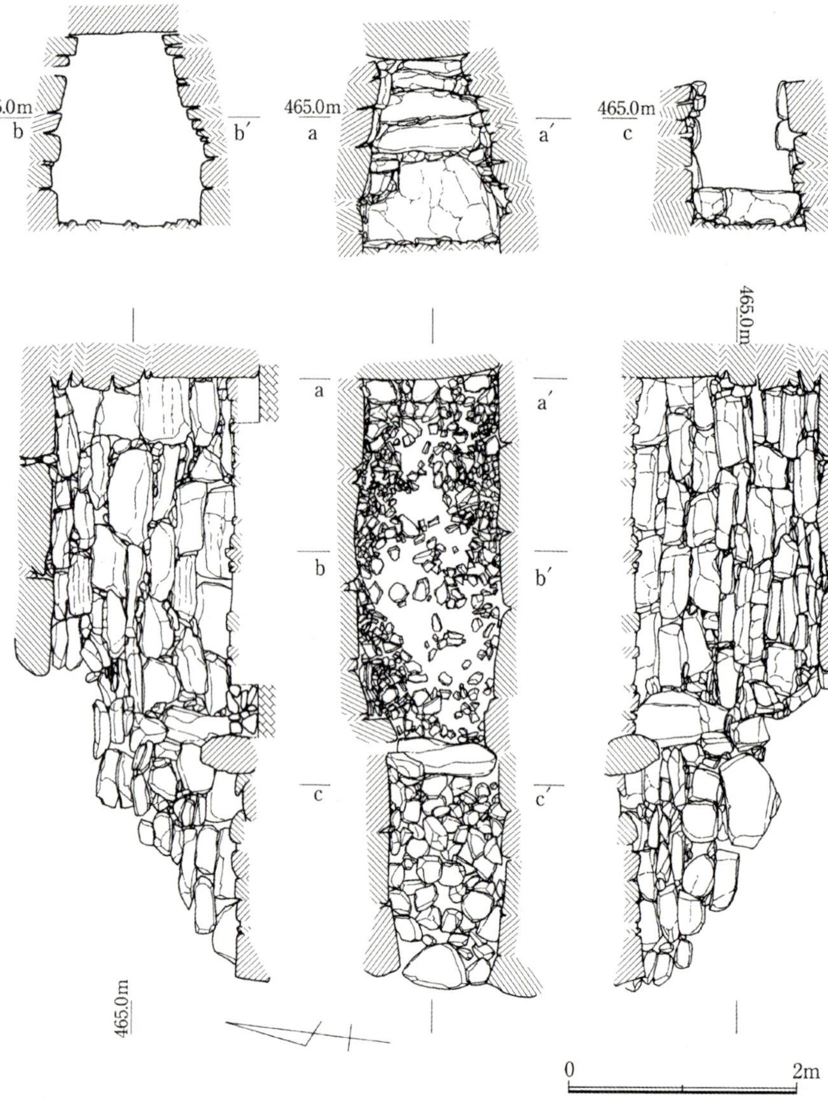

Figure 6.24 Corridor-style Burial Chamber of Tomb No. 227.
From Ōtsuka and Kobayashi 2006, Fig. 76.

Figure 6.25 Corridor-style Burial Chamber of Tomb No. 222. Photograph by author.

Middle Sixth Century to Seventh Century: Age of Corridor-Style Horizontal Burial Chambers

No mound construction took place in the early half of the sixth century in this cluster. In this time period, corridor-style burial chambers were introduced to the Ōmuro mound group. Indeed, several corridor-style burial chambers were adopted in other sub-groups in the early sixth century. The question of why the tomb construction was temporarily halted in the Ōishi cluster remains to be discussed.

In the late sixth century, tomb construction in the Ōishi cluster resumed with the appearances of Tomb No. 227 (Figures 6.23 and 6.24) and Tomb No. 222 (Figures 6.25 and 6.26). Both are basically earthen mounds, with corridor-style burial chambers in the center of the mounds. All the burial chambers in the Ōishi cluster face southwest. It is probable that two mounds of this type were constructed as a pair in this cluster. Strictly speaking, the mound construction technique is characterized by the adoption of stone walls encircling a corridor-style burial chamber, and earth is packed between the stone walls.

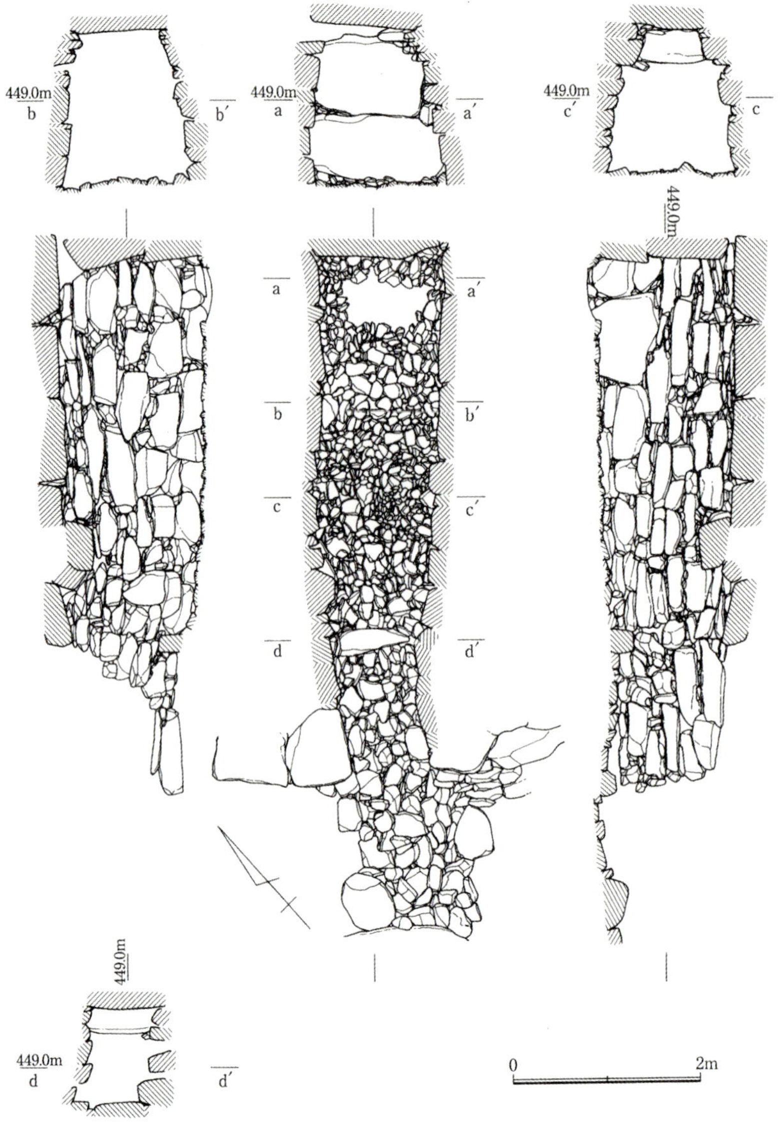

Figure 6.26 Corridor-style Burial Chamber of Tomb No. 222.
From Ōtsuka and Kobayashi 2006, Fig. 25.

Figure 6.27 Corridor-style Burial Chamber of Tomb No. 220. Photograph by Kenri Satō.

Tomb No. 227 is located on the same ridge as the two cairns, which might suggest an earlier date for this tomb than for Tomb No. 222 located on the bottom of the valley. However, typological analysis of corridor-style burial chambers and artifacts discovered in these tombs does not give particularly strong support for an earlier date of Tomb No. 227. Tomb 227

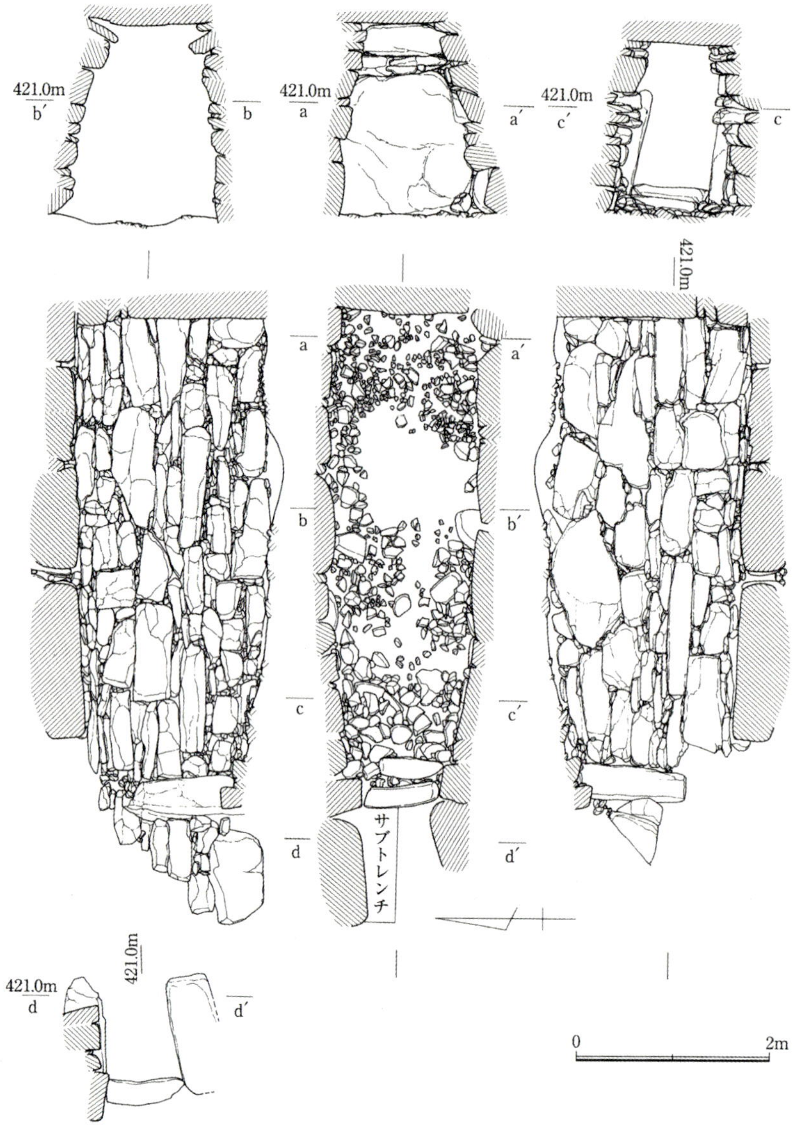

Figure 6.28 Corridor-style Burial Chamber of Tomb No. 220.
From Ōtsuka and Kobayashi 2006, Fig. 8.

Figure 6.29 Corridor-style Burial Chamber of Tomb No. 224. Photograph by author.

yielded iron knives, iron arrowheads, earrings, *haji*-earthenware vessels, and *sue*-stoneware vessels. The iron arrowheads were moved from their original place in the burial chamber, which suggests that an additional interment took place after the late sixth century.

In Tomb 222, iron arrowheads, iron nails, whetstones, *haji*-earthenware vessels, and *sue*-stoneware vessels were discovered. Some of the artifacts are of the early seventh century, which clearly indicates that an additional interment took place at that time.

In the early seventh century, Tomb No. 220 (Figures 6.27 and 6.28) and Tomb No. 224 (Figures 6.29 and 6.30) were constructed. Both of them are characterized by the same mound construction technique as Tombs No. 227 and No. 222 and by the adoption of corridor-style burial chambers. Excavations of Tomb No. 220 yielded the discoveries of an iron long sword, iron knives, iron arrowheads, horse trappings, *haji*-earthenware vessels, and *sue*-stoneware vessels. In Tomb No. 224, a wealth of artifacts have been discovered, including a sword hilt, a sword sheath, iron knives, iron arrowheads, fragments of horse trappings, earrings, whetstones, *haji*-earthenware

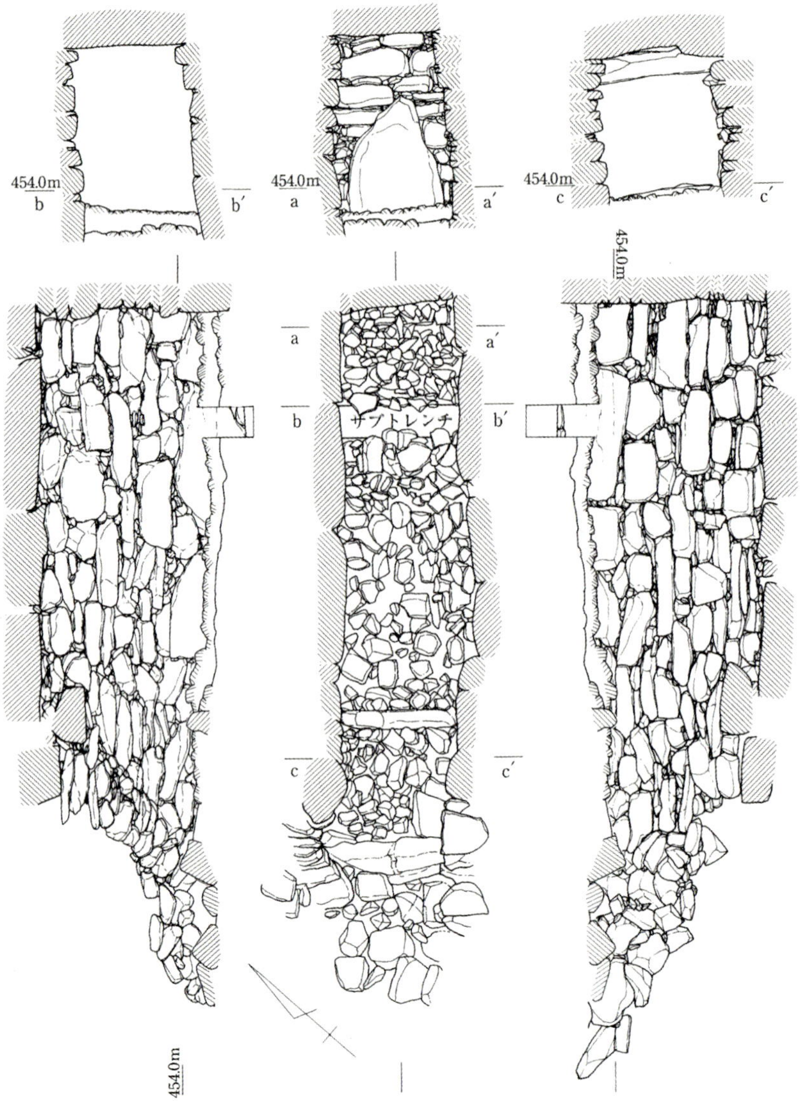

Figure 6.30 Corridor-style Burial Chamber of Tomb No. 224.
From Ōtsuka and Kobayashi 2006, Fig. 45.

Figure 6.31 Corridor-style Burial Chamber of Tomb No. 223. Photograph by author.

vessels, *sue*-stoneware vessels, and various types of beads. Since at least two bodies were buried in the chamber, additional interments must have taken place, but over a relatively short period of time. This is based on the observation that all of the funerary offerings date to the seventh century.

The construction of these two tombs was followed by that of Tomb No. 223 (Figures 6.31 and 6.32) and Tomb No. 230 (Figures 6.33 and 6.34) in the late seventh century. We know that Tomb No. 223 predates Tomb No. 230 because the size of the corridor-style burial chamber is smaller in Tomb No. 230. Although corridor-style burial chambers were first adopted in the early sixth century for the purpose of multiple interments, over time they decreased in size, eventually accommodating only a single interment. Indeed, the length of the chamber of No. 230 is only 2.21 m. In Tomb No. 223, gilt-bronze fittings, a pedestalled metal vessel, a sword sheath, *haji*-earthenware vessels, and *sue*-stoneware vessels were discovered. Among these artifacts, the gilt-bronze fittings are rather unusual. The funerary offerings for Tomb No. 230 are few, but the possibility exists that at least two bodies were interred in the small burial chamber. In any case, Tomb

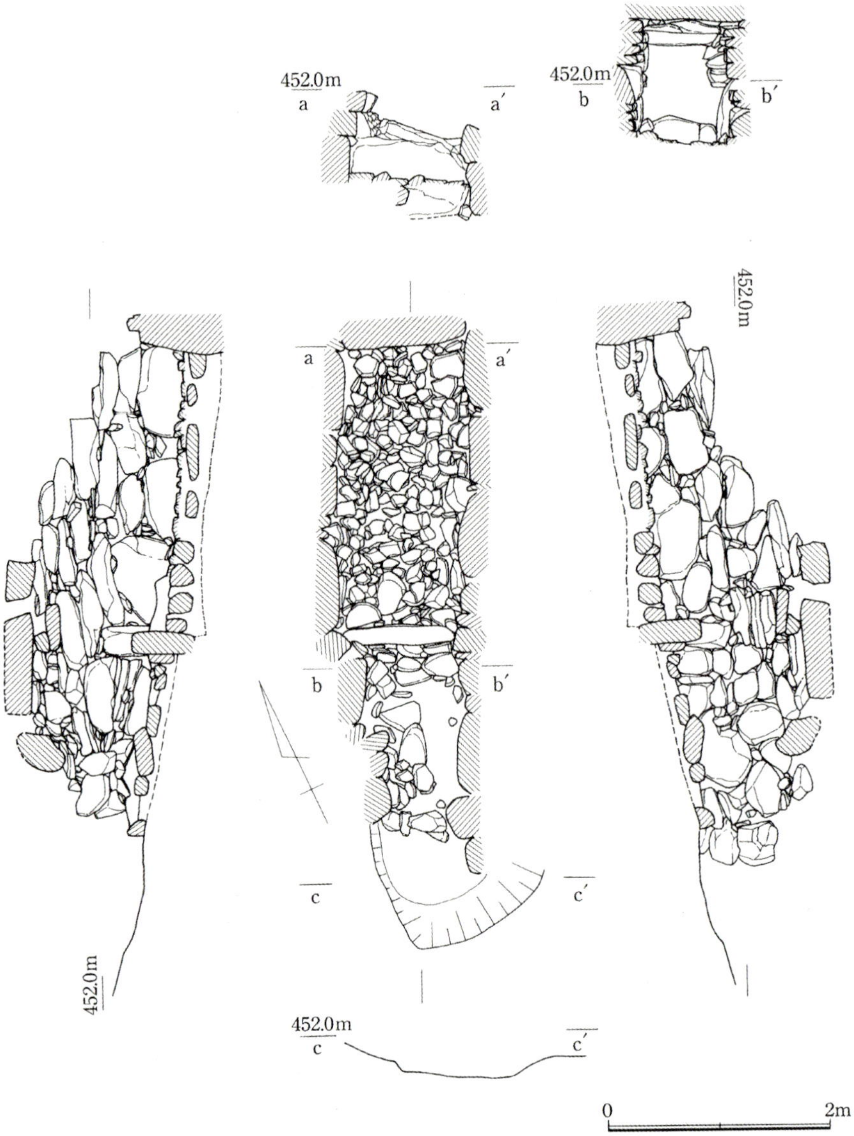

Figure 6.32 Corridor-style Burial Chamber of Tomb No. 223.
From Ōtsuka and Kobayashi 2006, Fig. 36.

Figure 6.33 Corridor-style Burial Chamber of Tomb No. 230. From Ōtsuka and Kobayashi 2006, Pl. 29.

No. 230 marks the end of interment not only in the Ōishi cluster but also in the Ōmuro mound group as a whole.

In conclusion, the results of investigations of the Ōishi cluster are significant in many respects. First, our investigations have revealed that cairns with cists are the earliest in the Ōmuro mound group. They were followed by the adoption of the corridor-style burial chamber. As in the cases of other regions of Japan, the corridor-style burial chambers at Ōmuro were created for the purpose of making multiple interments. We now know that the interments ended at Ōmuro around the end of the seventh century or the beginning of the eighth century.

Major Results of Archaeological Investigations by Meiji University: Mujinagōro Cluster

Fifth Century to the Beginning of the Sixth Century: Age of Cairns

The formation of the Mujinagōro cluster, like that of the Ōishi cluster, started in the middle fifth century with the construction of a cairn with a

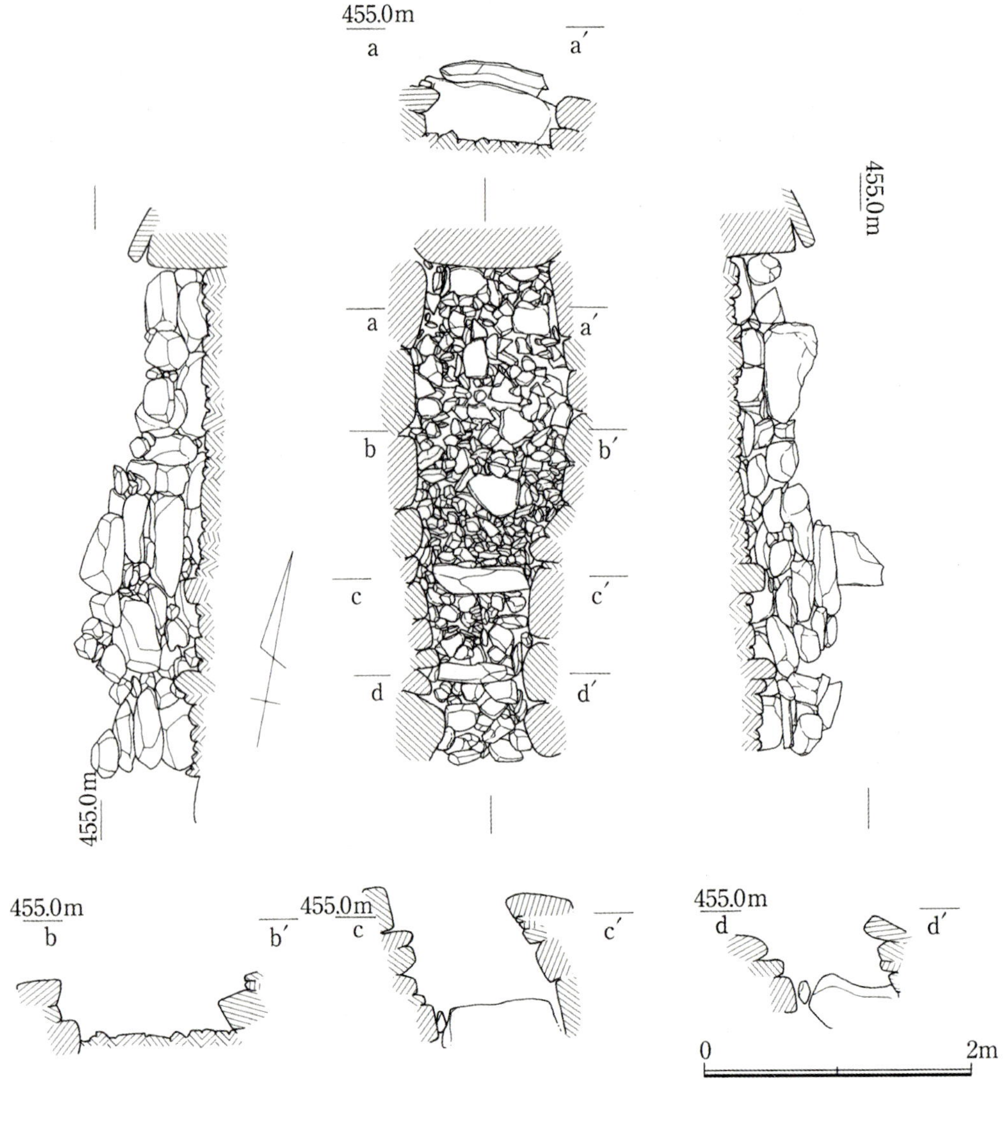

Figure 6.34 Corridor-style Burial Chamber of Tomb No. 230.
From Ōtsuka and Kobayashi 2006, Fig. 85.

Figure 6.35 Vaulted Burial Chamber of Tomb No. 156. Photograph by author.

vaulted burial chamber. Because there are numerous tombs in the cluster, and because they are well preserved, a variety of types of mounded tomb, including cairns, are represented (Sasaki et al. 2015).

Tomb No. 156 is a cairn of 8 m in diameter, with a vaulted stone burial chamber (Figures 6.35 and 6.36). It may be dated to the early or middle fifth century, A.D. It is the earliest dated tomb so far investigated in the Ōmuro Valley sub-group, based on the fact that no *sue* stoneware was discovered. The construction of this tomb may well predate the introduction of *sue* stoneware in the middle fifth century. The vaulted burial chamber is 1.8 m in internal length, 0.8 m in internal width, and 0.85 m in internal height from the floor to the top. The height of the side wall is 0.45 m, and the height of the front wall only 0.2 m. No artifacts have been excavated from inside the burial chamber. Excavations of trenches placed in the mound yielded some *haji*-earthenware pots.

The next-earliest tombs are Tomb No. 165 and Tomb No. 168, both of which are dated to the third quarter of the fifth century. Tomb No. 165 is a roughly circular cairn of 9.5 m north-south by 10.5 m east-west. It

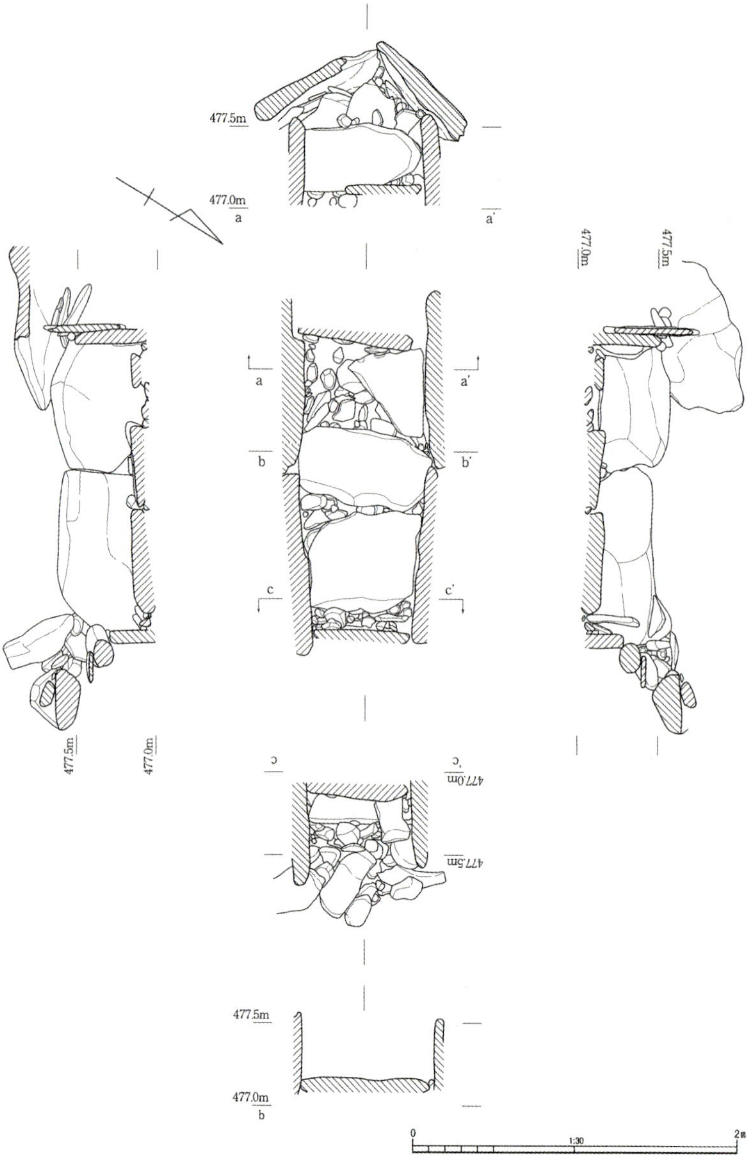

*Figure 6.36 Vaulted Burial Chamber of Tomb No. 156.
From Sasaki et al. 2015, Fig. 42.*

Figure 6.37 Vaulted Burial Chamber No. 1 of Tomb No. 165. Photograph by the Archaeology Program, Meiji University.

is accompanied by two vaulted burial chambers. Although the stone slabs that would have constituted the top of the burial chambers are gone, the morphology of the back walls with pointed tops clearly indicates that the burial chambers were vaulted. Burial chamber No. 1 (Figures 6.37 and 6.38) is situated 44 degrees eastward from due north. In other words, the axes of the two chambers almost form a right angle. The secondary chamber is 1.8 m in internal length, 0.68 m in internal width, and 0.75 m in height from the floor to the top. The height of a side wall is 0.40 m and of the front wall is 0.2 m. No artifacts have been excavated in this burial chamber. Chamber No. 2 (Figures 6.39 and 6.40) is situated at the center of the mound and 29 degrees westward from due north. It is 1.5 to 1.85 m in internal length and 0.6 m in internal width. The height of the side wall is 0.5 m. Probably because of looting, the stone stabs for the floor are gone. No artifacts have been excavated. Because no skeletons have been excavated, it is impossible to determine a relationship between the two individuals buried in the primary and secondary burial chambers.

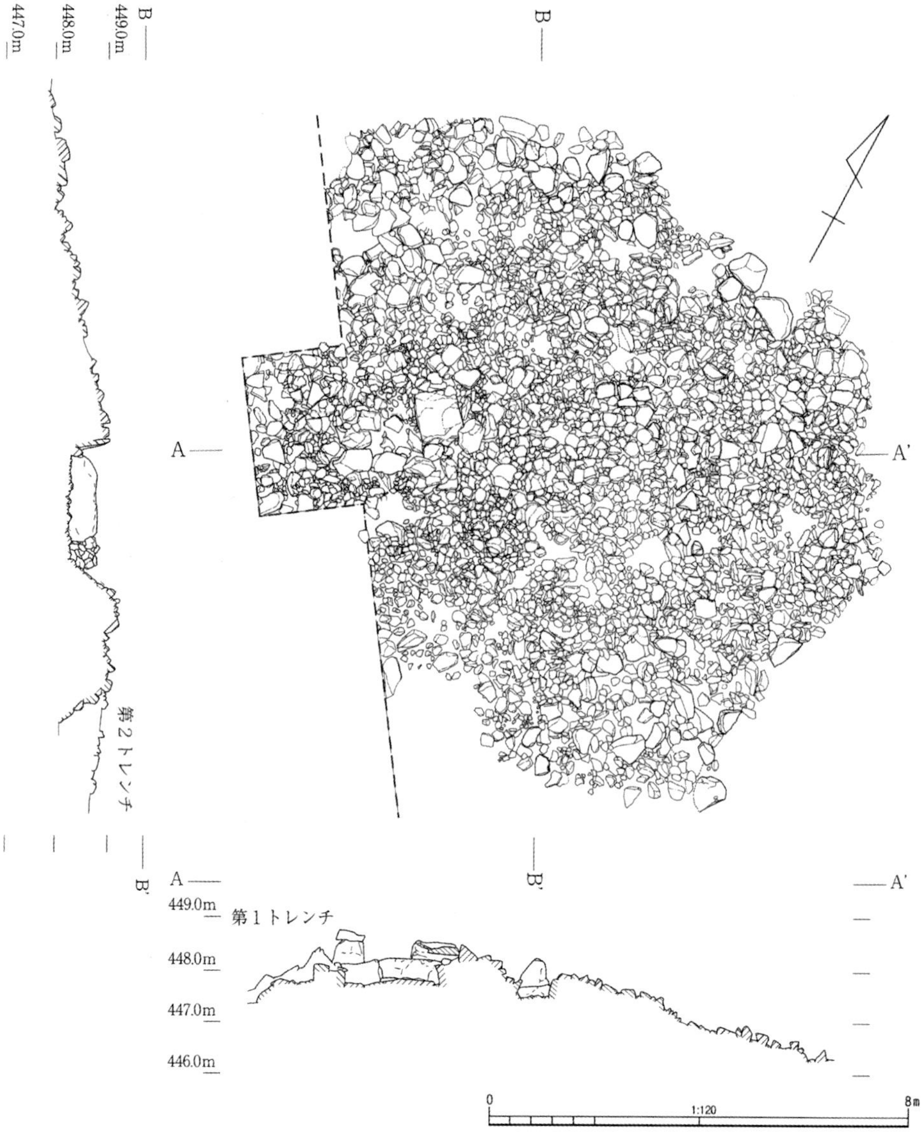

Figure 6.38 Vaulted Burial Chamber No. 1 of Tomb No. 165. From Sasaki et al. 2015, Fig. 44.

Figure 6.39 Vaulted Burial Chamber No. 2 of Tomb No. 165. Photograph by Kenri Satō.

Tomb No. 168 is also a roughly circular cairn (Kobayashi et al. 2008). Since it is situated on a slope of eight degrees in gradient, the lower foot of this mound (northwestern corner) is at 470.0 m in altitude, and the higher foot of this mound (southeastern corner) is at 472.0 m in altitude. Owing to this location, diameter varies from one direction to another.

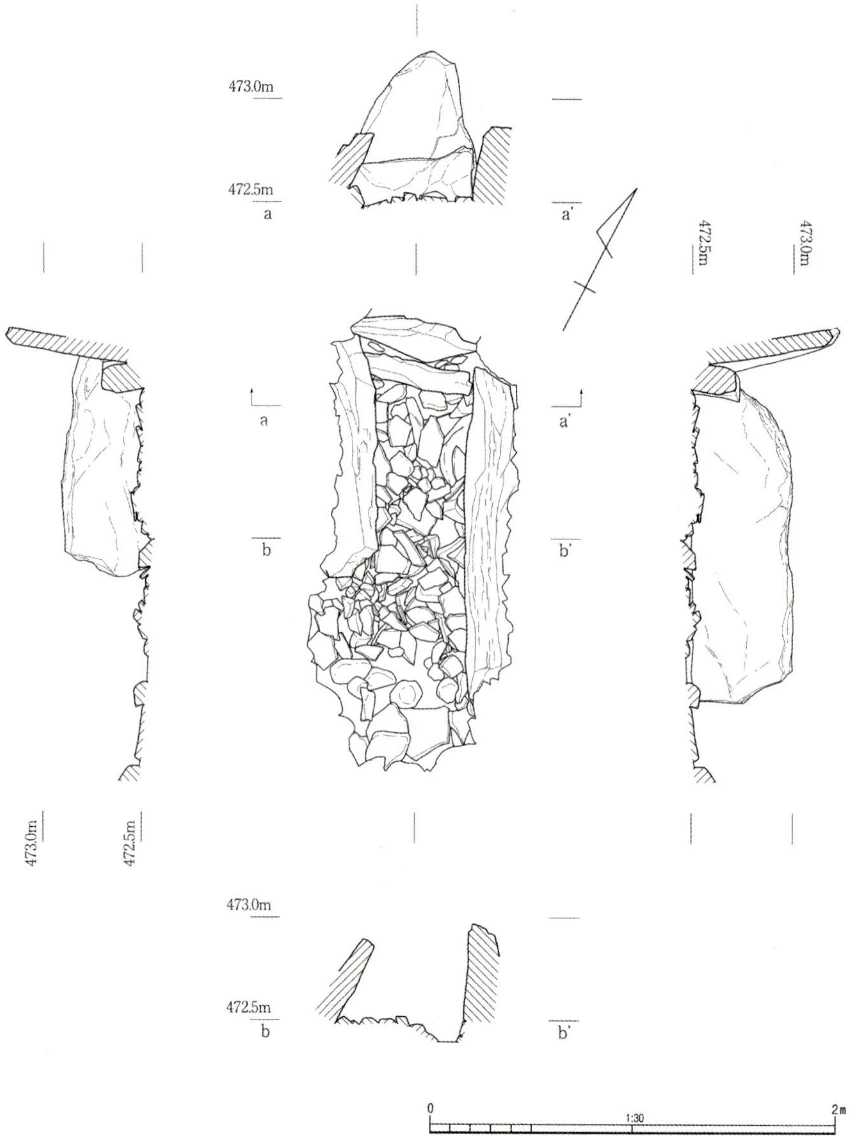

Figure 6.40 Vaulted Burial Chamber No. 2 of Tomb No. 165.
From Sasaki et al. 2015, Fig. 46.

Figure 6.41 Vaulted Burial Chamber of Tomb No. 168. Photograph by the Archaeology Program, Meiji University.

Its diameter is as follows: along the east-west axis 11.2–12.4 m; along the north-south axis 12.2–13.0 m or 14.5–15.0 m, including a line of stones in the upper slope; along the axis of the burial chamber 13.3–14.4 m; and in the direction perpendicular to the axis of the burial chamber 12.1 m or 12.9 m, including the line of stones in the upper slope. The height of the cairn is more than 0.96 m from the upper slope and 2.96 m from the lower slope.

The burial chamber of Tomb No. 168 is constructed with a combination of stone slabs (Figures 6.41 and 6.42). It is situated 56 degrees east of due north, and it opens to the southwest. The direction of the axis is parallel to a contour line. In other words, the selection of this axis direction was a result of this tomb's having been situated on a slope. The length of the coffin is 1.82 m, and the width is 0.83 m (southwestern end) and 0.86 m (northeastern end). Its height including the top is 0.92 to 1.06 m. The height of the northwestern side wall is 0.6 m, and that of the southeastern side wall is 0.75 m. The height of the southwestern end wall is 0.38 m, and

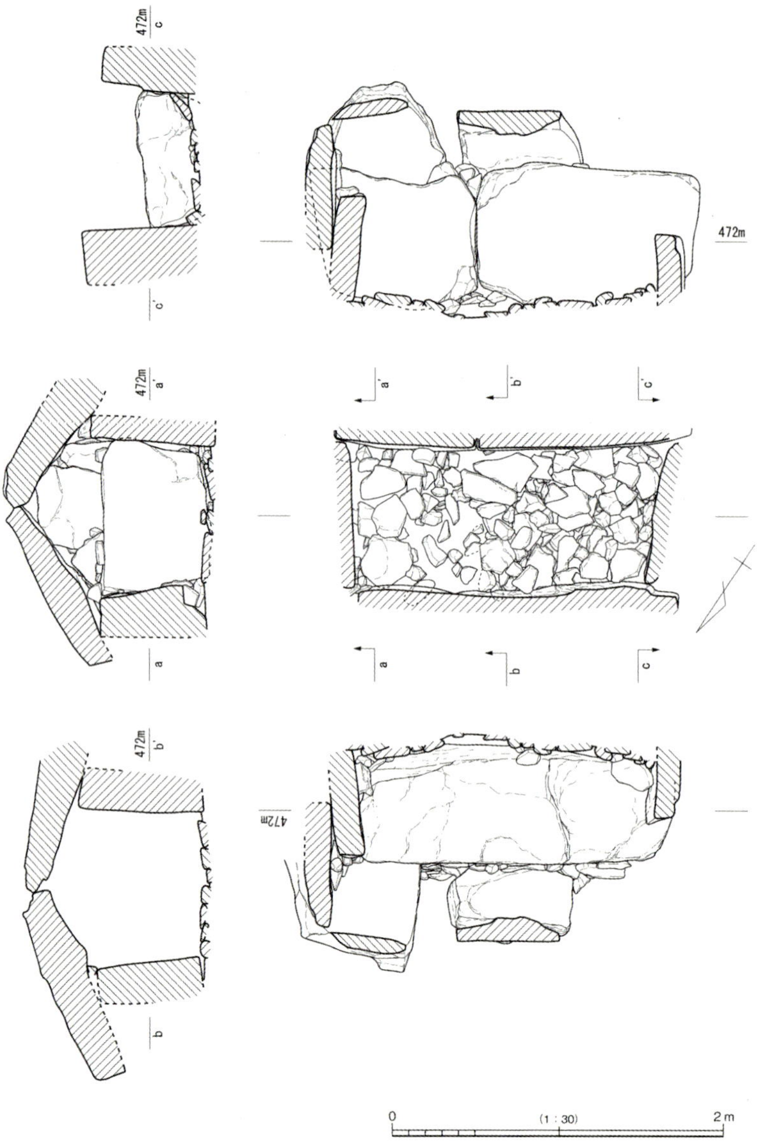

Figure 6.42 Vaulted Burial Chamber of Tomb No. 168.
From Kobayashi et al. 2008.

Figure 6.43 Horse-shaped Ceramic Model Discovered at Tomb No. 168. Photograph courtesy of the Nagano Municipal Board of Education.

Figure 6.44 Tomb No. 155, Cairn. Photograph by Kenri Satō.

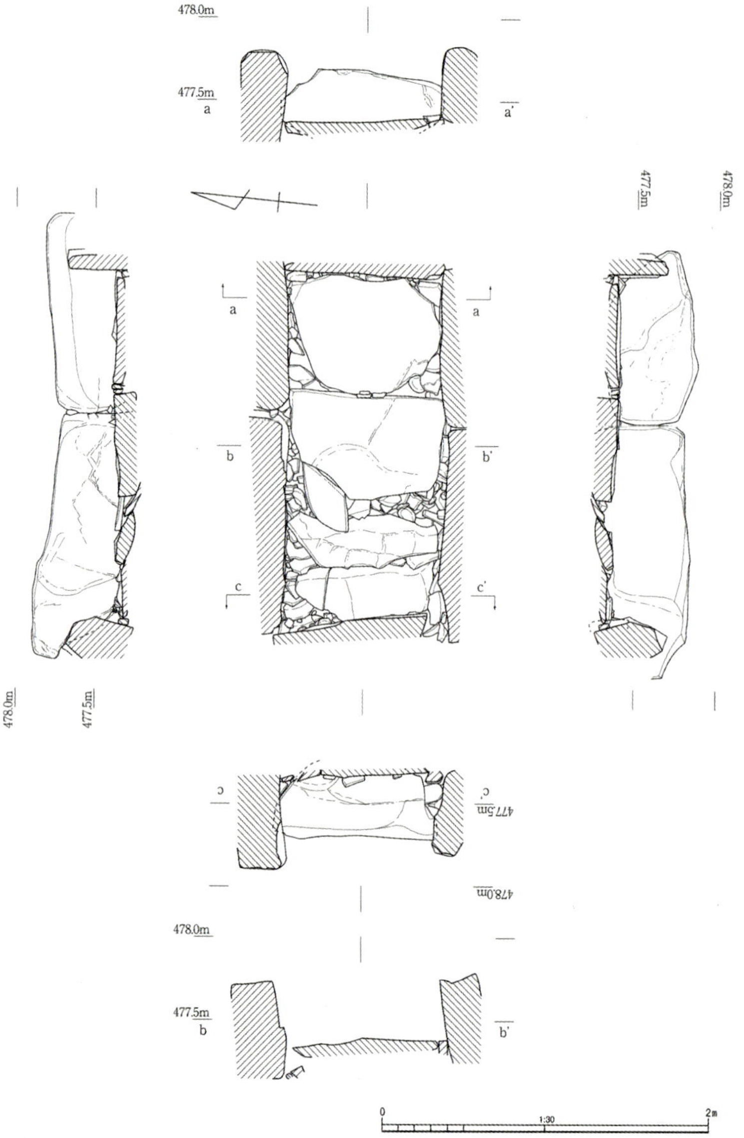

Figure 6.45 Vaulted Burial Chamber of Tomb No. 155. From Sasaki et al. 2015, Fig. 35.

that of the northeastern end wall is 0.58 m. A few small slabs were placed on the top of the wall at the northeastern end to fill a gap between the top and the end wall. The low southwestern end wall and an opening between the top and the southwestern end wall indicate that the southwestern end functioned as the "entrance" or the "front" of this coffin. The small size of this coffin might suggest the possibility of a delayed interment. A few iron daggers and a knife were discovered in the coffin. It is likely that more objects were deposited with the dead.

Once the construction of the mound and the coffin was completed, considerable numbers of *haji*-earthenware vessels, *sue*-stoneware vessels, and *haniwa* ceramic cylinders were placed on and at the foot of the mound. None of the ceramic artifacts were buried in the course of the mound construction. Among those ceramic artifacts, the most notable is a horse-shaped ceramic figurine (Figure 6.43) discovered at the southern foot of the mound. It is possible that the horse-shaped figurine was intentionally broken, because some body parts were missing. Presumably, this figurine was used at a mortuary ritual. It also suggests that whoever was buried in Tomb No. 168 was an equestrian, and that a pasture at Ōmuro might have been utilized as early as the fifth century.

At the same time, it is important to note that ordinary Japanese *haniwa* ceramic cylinders were placed on and at the foot of the mound. It is not a simple matter to consider this cairn as a burial of an immigrant from the Korean peninsula.

Tomb No. 155 is a roughly circular cairn, 9.2 by 10.4 m in diameter (Figure 6.44), with a presumably vaulted stone burial chamber (Figure 6.45), though the top of the burial chamber was lost. The foot of the cairn was not clearly demarcated, but it seems that rocks somewhat larger than the other rocks of the cairn were used for the foot. Excavations of the cairn itself resulted in the discoveries of fragments of *haniwa* ceramic cylinders, large jars of *sue* stoneware, and *haji*-earthenware pots.

The burial chamber of Tomb No. 155 is oriented toward 86 degrees eastward from due north. It is approximately 2.12 m in length and 1.00 m in width. The height of the side wall is approximately 0.45 m, and that of the end wall is 0.35 m. Based on the discovery of slabs that were presumably used for the top of this burial chamber, and of a slab presumably used as the back wall, we suspect that this burial chamber was vaulted. Two fragments of an iron dagger and thirteen iron arrowheads were discovered in the burial chamber. It is noteworthy that the iron arrowheads were discovered beneath the floor of the burial chamber. We may speculate that the arrowheads were

Figure 6.46 Cist Grave of Tomb No. 185.
Photograph by the Archaeology Program, Meiji University.

placed there as a result of ritualistic activity in the course of construction of this cairn. Based on the typology of pottery and iron arrowheads, we estimate the date of this tomb to be the third or fourth quarter of the fifth century.

Tomb No. 185 is a cairn of approximately 8 m in diameter, with a cist grave (Figures 6.46 and 6.47). The cist grave is badly disturbed; only a floor and one side wall remain. Based on this fragmentary information, we estimate that the cist grave was 2.2 m in length and 0.5 m in width. Since the cist grave was constructed on a slope, cobbles were accumulated to level the

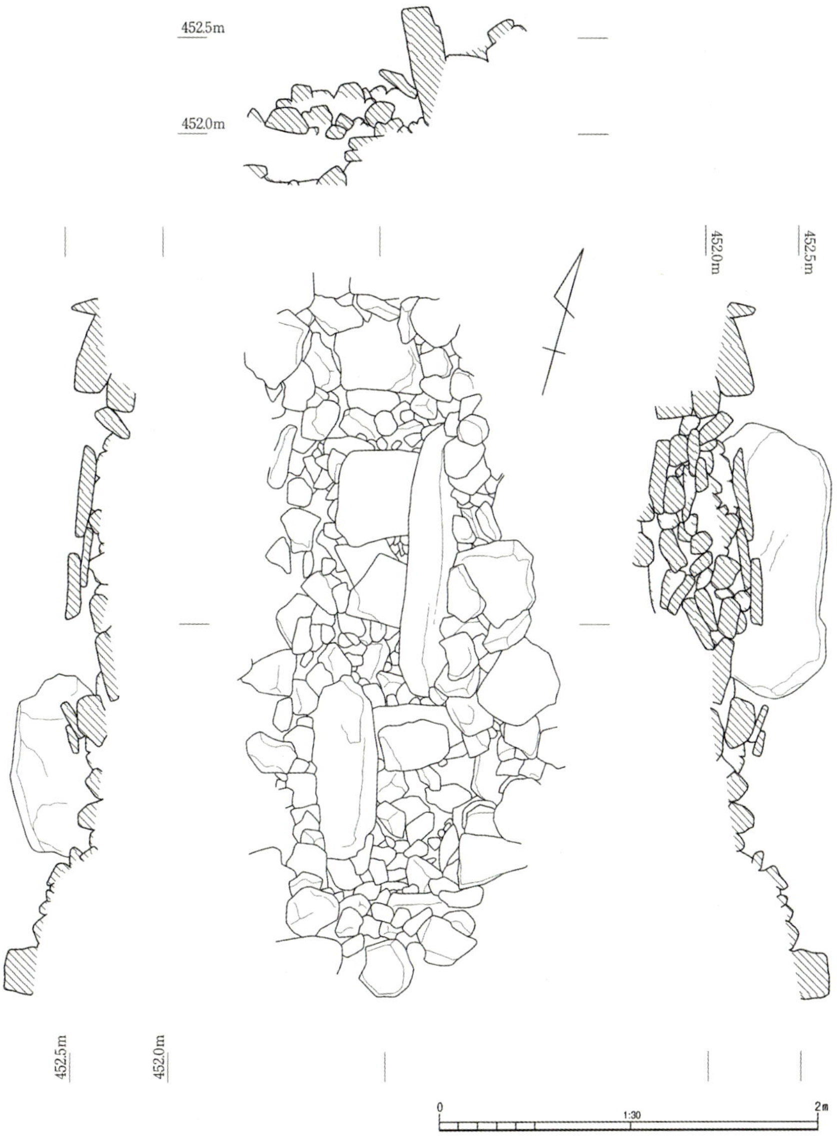

Figure 6.47 Cist Grave of Tomb No. 185.
From Sasaki et al. 2015, Fig. 52.

Figure 6.48 Cist Grave of Tomb No. 189.
Photograph by the Archaeology Program, Meiji University.

bottom, and then flat slabs were put in place. On top of the flat slabs, six or seven flat stones of 35 to 40 cm were placed as the floor of the grave. Outside of the side wall were cobbles packed to reinforce the side wall.

We excavated only *haji* earthenware from this burial. One finely polished bowl was discovered beneath the floor. Several jars were discovered at the foot of this cairn, as if to enclose it. Since these jars had bottoms with holes intentionally drilled, and since one of them had a hole intentionally drilled in its belly, the jars did not function as storage jars but rather as *haniwa* cylinders that marked the foot of a mound. Based on pottery typology, this cairn may be dated to the late fifth century.

Tomb No. 189 is also a cairn of some 10 m in diameter, with a cist grave (Figures 6.48 and 6.49). The cairn is constructed with large stones of 70 cm in the lower portion and stones of 30 cm in the higher part, where the cist grave is situated at the center. The cist grave is 1.6 to 1.9 m in internal length, and 0.5 to 0.6 m in internal width. The height of

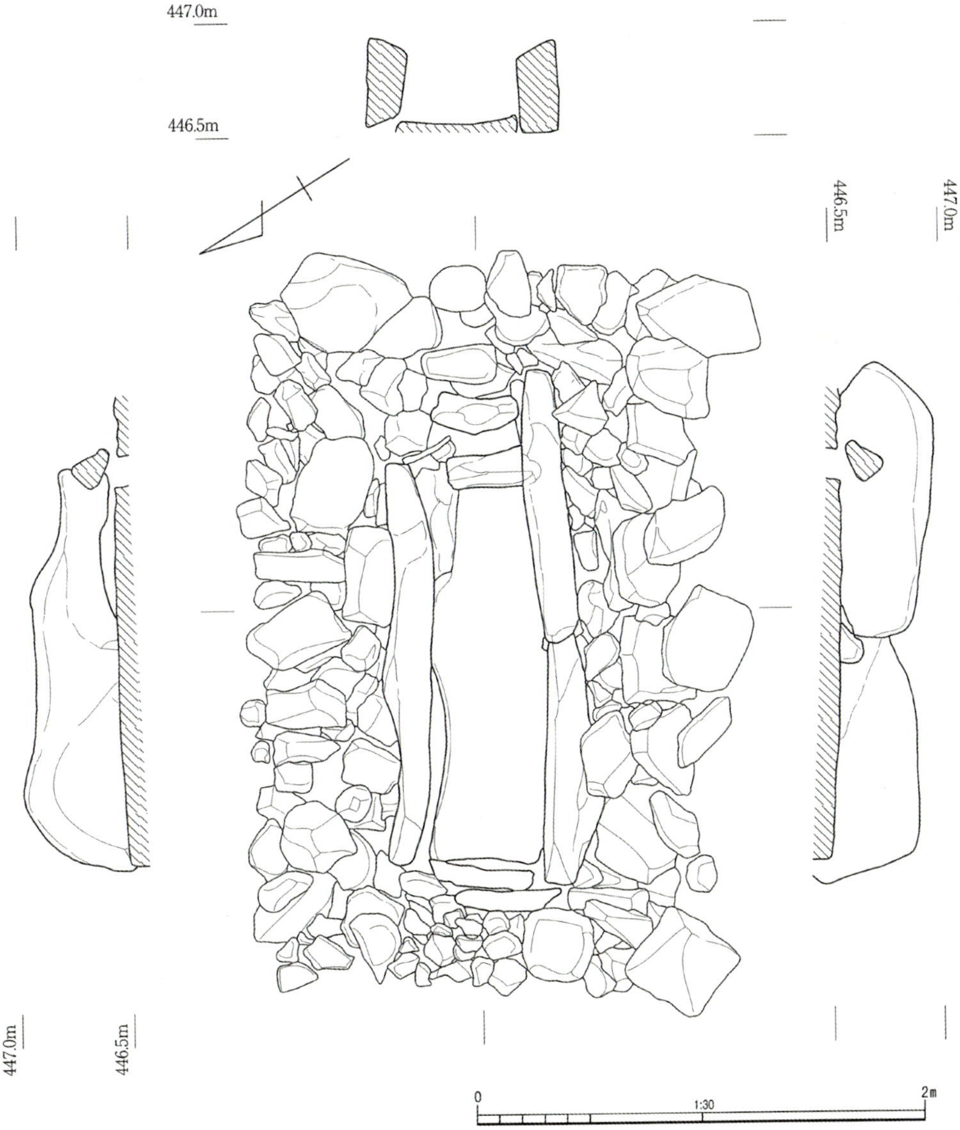

Figure 6.49 Cist Grave of Tomb No. 189.
From Sasaki et al. 2015, Fig. 75.

Figure 6.50 Vaulted Burial Chamber of Tomb No. 196.
Photograph by the Archaeology Program, Meiji University.

the side wall is 0.3 m. No artifacts have been excavated in the cist grave, probably because the grave itself was exposed long before our excavation. A variety of pottery has been discovered in the mound. The *haji* earthenware discovered here includes jars with a stepped rim, jars with holes drilled through the base, and pedestalled bowls. A *sue*-stoneware pedestalled bowl has also been discovered. Based on the pottery typology, this tomb may be dated to the late fifth century.

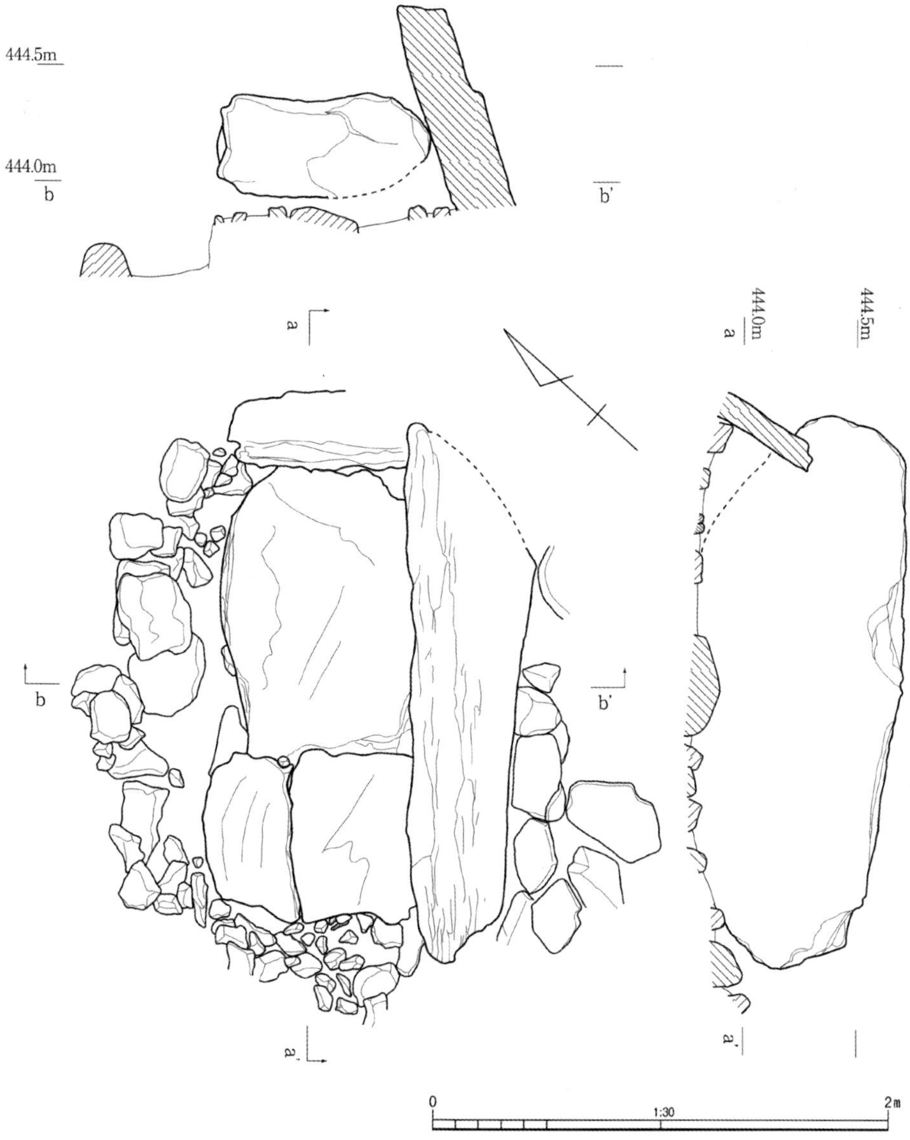

Figure 6.51 Vaulted Burial Chamber of Tomb No. 196. From Sasaki et al. 2015, Fig. 89.

*Figure 6.52 Fragments of Iron Cuirass Discovered at Tomb No. 196.
Photograph courtesy of the Archaeology Program, Meiji University.*

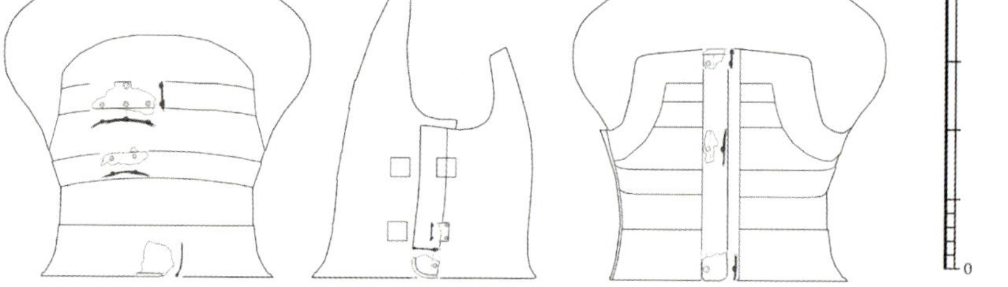

*Figure 6.53 Reconstruction of Iron Cuirass at Tomb No. 196.
From Uchiyama 2015, Fig. 1.*

Figure 6.54 Bronze Mirror Discovered at Tomb No. 196. Photograph courtesy of the Archaeology Program, Meiji University.

Tomb No. 196 is a cairn of 19 m in diameter, with the central part of 10 m in diameter constructed solely with rocks, and the outer part with a mixture of rocks and earth. This cairn had a large, presumably vaulted stone burial chamber, but it has been very badly looted and destroyed; the north side wall was removed, and slabs constituting the top and the slab of the west end wall have fallen into the burial chamber (Figures 6.50 and 6.51). Based on this fragmentary information, we estimate that the chamber was 2.3 m in length and 1.1 m in width, which is considerably larger than ordinary vaulted stone burial chambers at Ōmuro.

A variety of artifacts have been excavated in the burial chamber and looter's pit. The artifacts include fragments of a riveted iron cuirass (Figures

Figure 6.55 Chamber A of Tomb No. 195.
Photograph by the Archaeology Program, Meiji University.

6.52 and 6.53), fragments of iron horse trappings such as bits and the joint of a leather harness, fragments of a Japanese bronze mirror (Figure 6.54), iron arrowheads, iron knives, glass beads, comma-shaped glass beads, cylindrical jades, whetstone, and iron daggers. The excavation of a trench placed to the south of the chamber resulted in the discovery of *haji*-earthenware pots and pedestalled bowls, a *sue*-stoneware wine server, and fragments of iron horse trappings. Additional examples of *haji* earthenware and *sue* stoneware were discovered on the surface of this cairn. Based on the typology of the *sue* stoneware, this tomb is dated to the fourth quarter (toward the end) of the fifth century.

Tomb No. 196 is significant for several reasons. First, iron armor was the symbol of authority in the fifth century, and is usually associated with giant keyhole-shaped mounded tombs or the small satellite mounded tombs that accompany them. It is rather unusual to find iron armor in such a small cairn unassociated with a giant keyhole-shaped tomb. Second, the discovery of a small bronze mirror is also unusual in the old province of Shinano because so far fewer than fifteen discoveries of bronze mirrors of this type have been reported in Shinano. Third, the discovery of horse trappings of a very early type is also important because, along with the use of iron armor, horse trappings and the practice of horse riding would become symbols of authority in the sixth century. In fact, Shinano is the region where the second-largest quantities of horse trappings have been discovered in the Kofun-period context, after the old provinces of Chikuzen 筑前 and Chikugo 筑後 (Fukuoka Prefecture). Still, the discovery of a very early type is rather unusual. Based on these observations, I would like to argue that Tomb No. 196 was an elite burial despite its very small size and its circular (as opposed to keyhole-shaped) form. I will come back to this issue in the conclusion.

Middle Sixth Century to Seventh Century:
Age of Corridor-Style Horizontal Burial Chambers

Tomb No. 195 is situated northwest of Tomb No. 187 and west of Tomb No. 189. It is a cairn of roughly 12 m in diameter, but it was impossible to identify the foot of the cairn. This cairn is very unusual because it features two burial chambers, 3 m apart from each other, and because both of the burial chambers are of a pit style, the dominant form of burial chambers in the Early and Middle Kofun period. The smaller chamber A is situated somewhat in the western half of the mound and oriented 40 degrees westward from due north (Figures 6.55 and 6.56). Its internal dimension is 1.94 m in length and 0.9 m in width. While the side walls were constructed by piling up slabs, standing slabs were used for the end walls. Nine iron arrowheads, one iron knife, and one iron sword have been discovered in chamber A. The larger chamber B is situated somewhat in the northern half of the mound and oriented parallel to chamber A (Figures 6.57 and 6.58). It is 3.4 m in length and 1.2 m in width. All of the four walls were constructed by piling up slabs, most of which have been lost. The artifacts discovered in

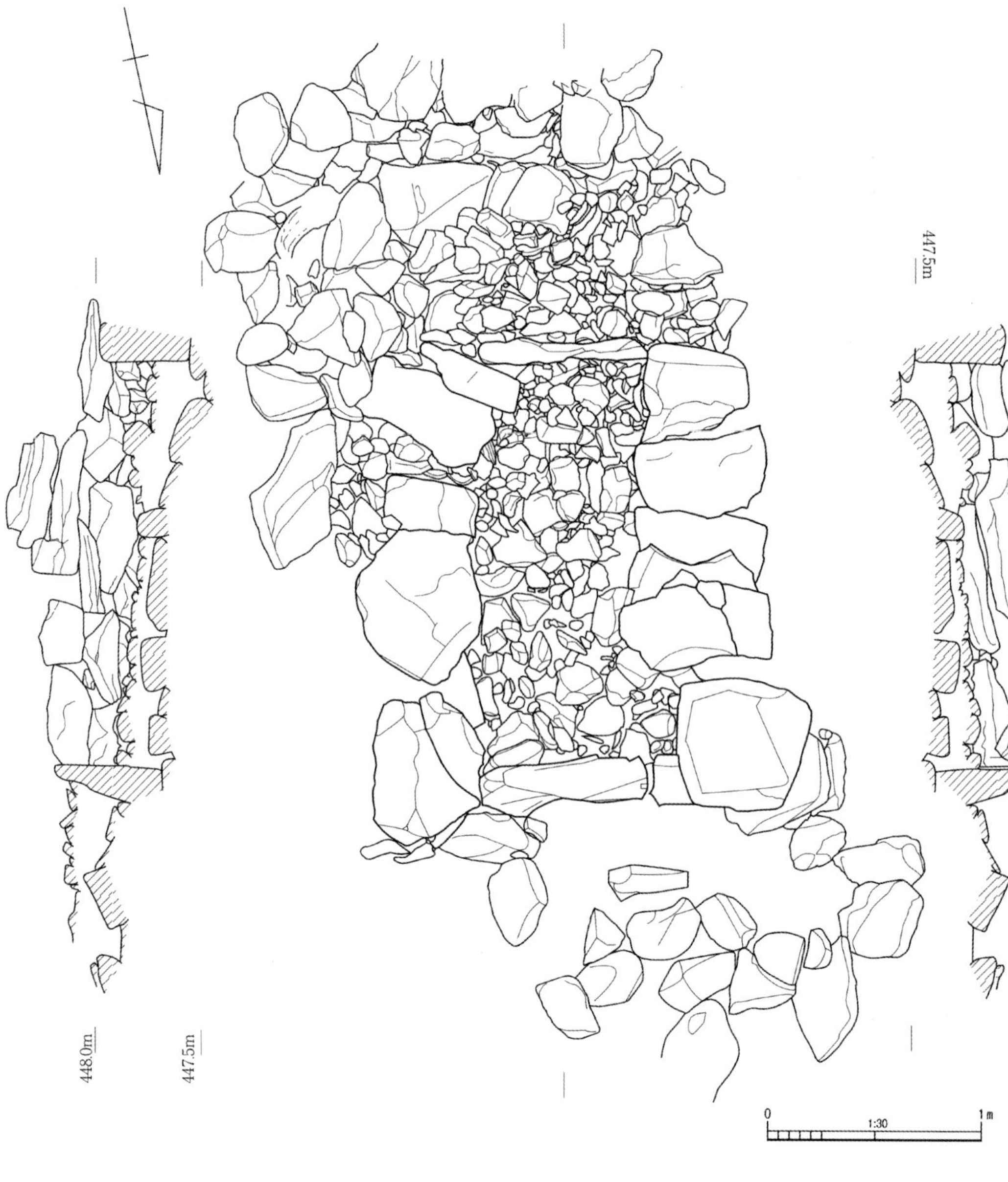

Figure 6.56 Chamber A of Tomb No. 195.
From Sasaki et al. 2015, Fig. 82.

Figure 6.57 Chamber B of Tomb No. 195.
Photograph by the Archaeology Program, Meiji University.

chamber B included four iron arrowheads, two knives, three strap-distributors used as part of horse trappings, and a bronze bell. Excavations of the cairn itself yielded the discovery of *haji*-earthenware pedestalled bowls in pieces as well as fragments of large jars of *sue* stoneware, pedestalled bowls, and wine pitchers. All of these artifacts tend to suggest a date of the middle sixth century, although a few of them are of an earlier date. Since a portion of this mound was destroyed in the process of the construction of Tomb No. 187, dated to the late sixth century, Tomb No. 195 is considered to have

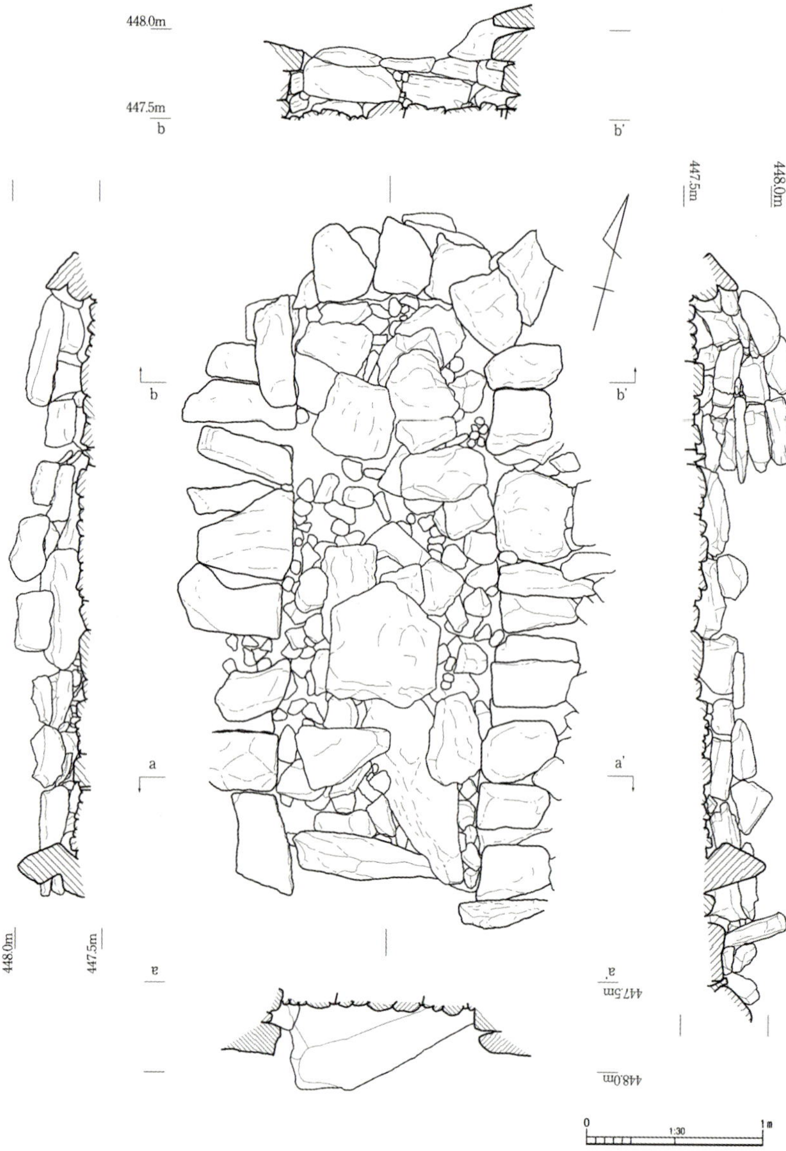

Figure 6.58 Chamber B of Tomb No. 195.
From Sasaki et al. 2015, Fig. 83.

Figure 6.59 Corridor-style Horizontal Burial Chamber of Tomb No. 187. Photograph by the Archaeology Program, Meiji University.

been constructed in the second quarter of the sixth century. Some artifacts, such as horse trappings, that are of much later date, toward the end of the sixth century or early seventh century, are probably a result of additional interment, although this does not commonly occur.

Tomb No. 187 is a circular cairn 12.4 m in diameter and 1.5 m in remaining height. At the center of the mound was a corridor-style horizontal burial chamber of 5.04 m in length and 0.98 m in width (Figures 6.59 and 6.60). The morphology of this corridor-style burial chamber is very unusual because it is characterized by six pairs of "standing" side walls. Ordinarily, the side walls of corridor-style burial chambers are constructed by piling up flat stones. In fact, the corridor leading to the main burial chamber of Tomb No. 187 was constructed by this method. At Ōmuro, the corridor-style burial chambers of Tomb No. 190 in the Mujinagōro cluster, Tombs No. 362, 429, and 436 in the Kitadani sub-group (Kamimura 1970), and Tomb D in the Murahigashi cluster (unexcavated) are examples of the type

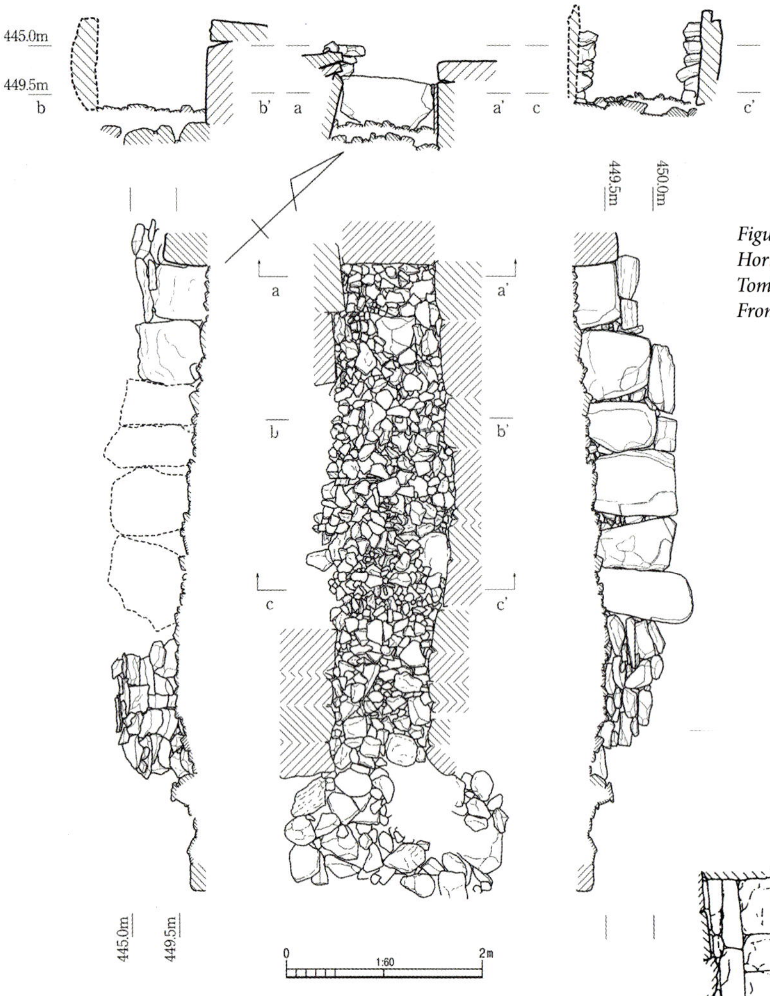

Figure 6.60 Corridor-style Horizontal Burial Chamber of Tomb No. 187. From Sasaki et al. 2015, Fig. 69.

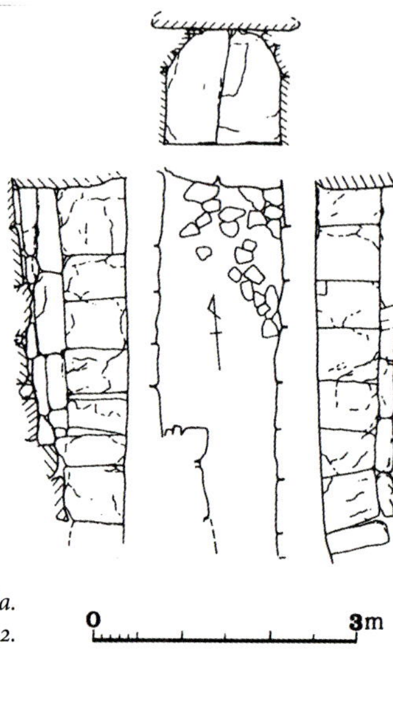

Figure 6.61 Tomb 1 at Kundun in North Chŏlla. From Ch'oe et al. 1992.

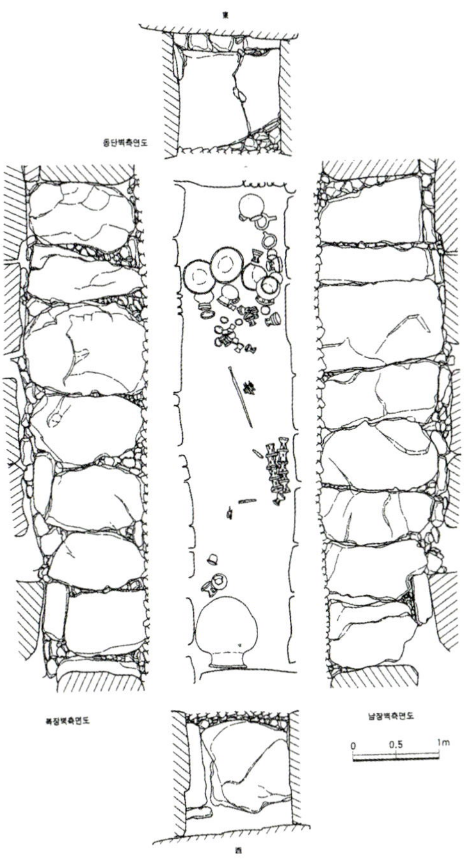

Figure 6.62 Yangmok Tomb in Ch'ilgok, Near Taegu. From Yi and Pak 1997.

Figure 6.63 Corridor-style Horizontal Burial Chamber of Tomb No. 197. Photograph by the Archaeology Program, Meiji University.

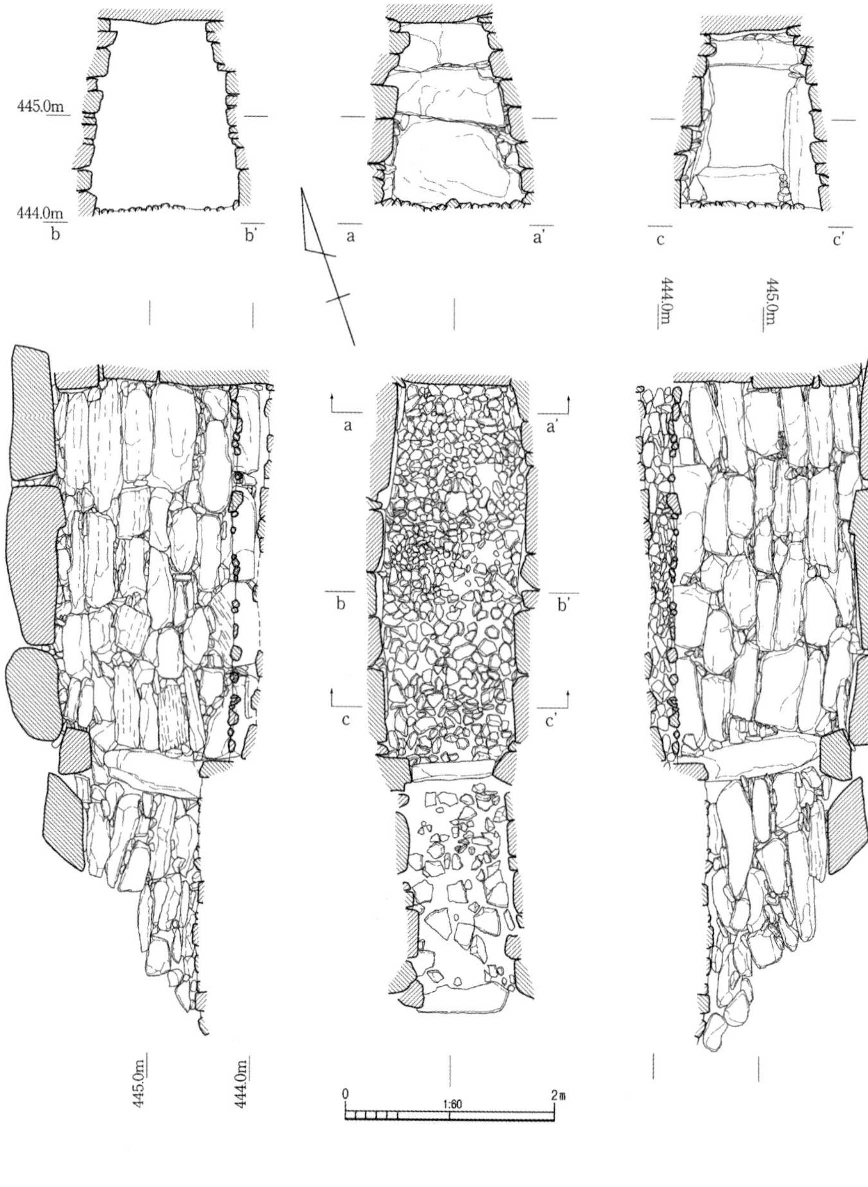

Figure 6.64 Corridor-style Horizontal Burial Chamber of Tomb No. 197. From Sasaki et al. 2015, Fig. 96.

Figure 6.65 Tomb No. 186.
Photograph by the Archaeology Program, Meiji University.

Figure 6.66 Inside the Corridor-style Burial Chamber of Tomb No. 186.
Photograph by the Archaeology Program, Meiji University.

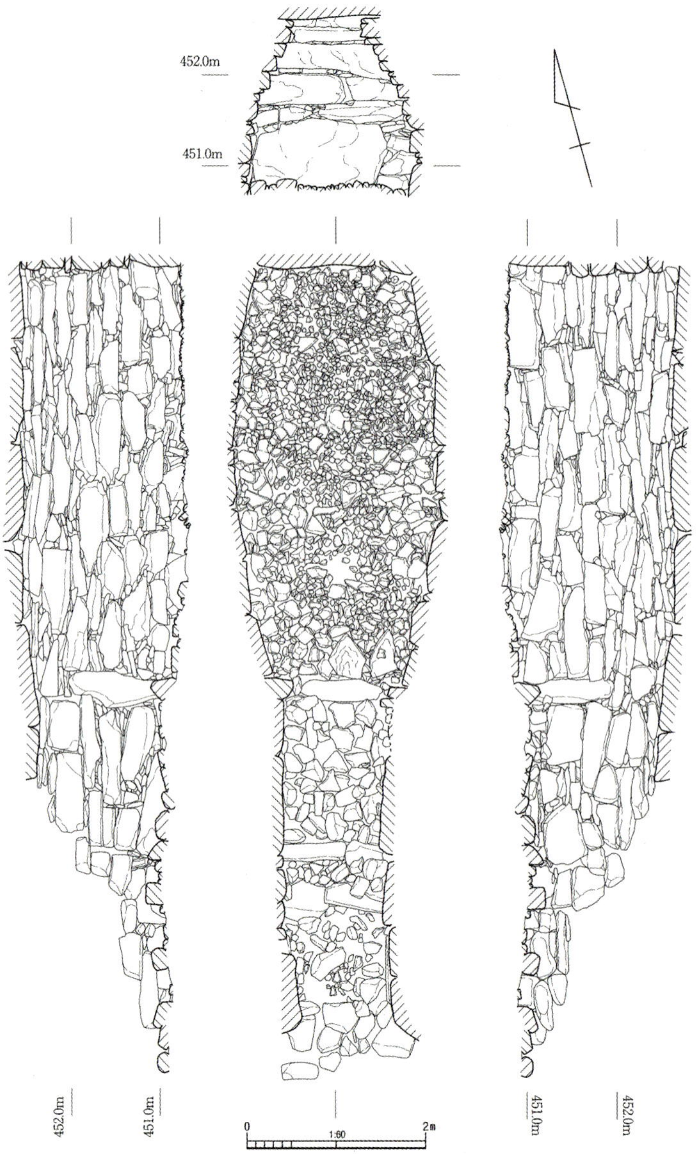

Figure 6.67 Corridor-style Burial Chamber of Tomb No. 186. From Sasaki et al. 2015, Fig. 56.

Figure 6.68 Parts of Iron Cuirass Discovered at Tomb No. 186. Photograph courtesy of the Archaeology Program, Meiji University.

that characterizes No. 187. In Japan, there are very few examples of this type, a few in the Iida 飯田 Basin in southwestern Nagano and a few in Kyushu. Kusumoto (1996) and Habuta (1997, 2000) find similar examples in the Korean peninsula, such as Tomb 1 at Kundun 軍屯 in North Chŏlla (Figure 6.61) and the Yangmok 若木 tomb in Ch'ilgok 漆谷, near Taegu (Figure 6.62). Both of these tombs have a pit-style burial chamber, but they are characterized by side walls made of standing slabs. In the Iida Basin, archaeologists found horses buried in pits at the foot of mounded tombs. Although evidence is still weak, the possibility that these tombs represent an adaptation of a Korean method of constructing burial chambers cannot be denied.

Numerous artifacts have been discovered in the main burial chamber. Five iron swords were placed along the back wall and along the side walls near the back wall, as if to surround the head of the deceased. One of the iron swords was accompanied by a sword guard. In the center of the burial chamber were an iron horse bit, iron knives, and silver earrings. Nineteen iron arrowheads were discovered on the floor of the corridor leading to the main burial chamber. Typologically, the horse bit may date to the middle to late sixth century and the iron arrowheads to the late sixth century. The date of Tomb No. 187 may be estimated to date from the third to the fourth quarter of the sixth century, and it is thought to be the latest cairn in the Ōmuro Valley sub-group. We may surmise that a practice of constructing cairns continued until the third or fourth quarter of the sixth century even after corridor-style burial chambers were introduced to the Nagano Basin in the middle sixth century.

Tomb No. 197 is a roughly circular mound of 18.5 by 15 m, the morphology being a result of its placement on a slope. The height of the mound is 1.2 m at the higher point and 33.5 m at the foot. A corridor-style horizontal burial chamber housed in this mound is oriented 46 degrees eastward from due north. The chamber was 6.5 m in length, including the corridor leading to the main burial chamber (Figures 6.63 and 6.64). The main burial chamber was 3.5 m in length, 1.7 m in height, and 1.3 m in width. Although the tomb had been looted, an iron knife, iron arrowheads, and an earring were discovered in the main burial chamber, and *sue*-stoneware vessels were discovered in the corridor. Some *haji*-earthenware vessels and *sue*-stoneware vessels were discovered in pieces in the mound. The typologies of the artifacts suggest that the tomb dates to the end of the sixth century.

Tomb No. 186 is also a small circular mound of 12.5 by 13.5 m (Figure 6.65). A corridor-style horizontal burial chamber was housed in this mound. The chamber is 8.4 m in total length, and the main burial chamber is 4.6 m in length, 1.8 m in height, 1.8 m in width at the back wall, and 2.2 m in maximum width (Figures 6.66 and 6.67). The floor plan of the main burial chamber is not rectangular, but the left and right walls form a convex arc. The corridor leading to the main burial chamber is 1.6 m in width and 1.4 m in height. The burial chamber is oriented fourteen degrees westward from due north, and the entrance opens to the south. On the eastern

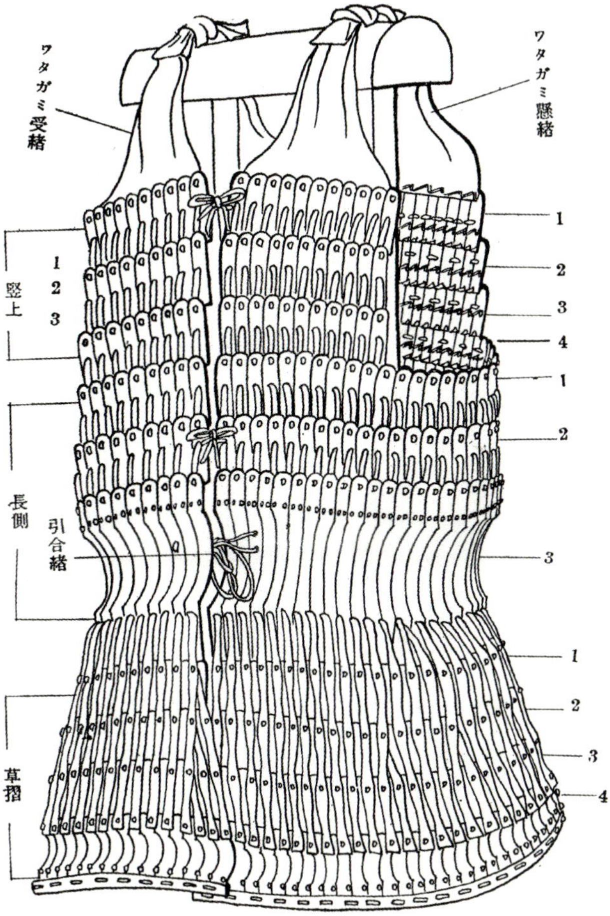

Figure 6.69 Reconstruction of an Iron Cuirass of the Same Type. From Suenaga 1934, Fig. 8.

Figure 6.70 Pedestalled Jar Discovered at Tomb No. 244. Photograph courtesy of the Archaeology Program, Meiji University.

Figure 6.71 Corridor-style Burial Chamber of Tomb No. 190. Photograph by the Archaeology Program, Meiji University.

side of the entrance were large jars of *sue* stoneware in pieces but *in situ*, as well as a concentration of *haji*-earthenware pots and pedestalled bowls. On the western side of the entrance were the remains of a horse. Since the head of the horse was discovered without any other body parts, the head might have been ritually severed and placed near the entrance of the burial chamber. The presence of a horse that might have been ritually sacrificed also suggests the possibility that an equestrian specialist was buried in this tomb. The pottery typology suggests a date toward the end of the sixth century for this tomb.

Excavations of the burial chamber yielded an iron cuirass, two gilt-bronze earrings, large quantities of beads, two iron arrowheads, seven fragments of iron swords, and human bones. The iron cuirass is a type composed of numerous small iron scale-like pieces that were tied by leather threads, which gave the wearer considerable flexibility (Figures 6.68 and 6.69). This type appeared in the late fifth century and is considered as an adaptation to horse riding. The arrowheads are of a type typical of the fourth quarter of the sixth century, which gives support for the date of this tomb based on the typology of pottery discovered outside the entrance to the burial chamber. In addition, large quantities of *haji*-earthenware pedestalled bowls were discovered in the corridor and entrance to the burial chamber, which were also presumably used for rituals. It is very interesting to note that these pedestalled bowls are morphologically of a type older than the late sixth century. It might be the case that older-style pottery was specially used for ritual purposes, as in the case of Tomb No. 23 in the Murahigashi cluster. The discovery of the iron cuirass is also significant because iron armor had been a symbol of authority since the fifth century. Despite the small size of the mound and its circular form, this tomb might well be an elite burial, as is the case with Tomb 196. This interpretation gains support from the discovery of pedestalled jars of the same type as one discovered in Tomb No. 244 (Figure 6.70), the largest of the Ōmuro mound group.

Tomb No. 190, like Tomb 187, is characterized by a corridor-style burial chamber with side walls made of standing slabs (Figures 6.71 and 6.72). It is a circular, primarily earthen mound of approximately 10 m in diameter, although a part of the mound was destroyed during the construction of a road, and the foot of the mound was not confirmed. The burial chamber is 4.6 m in length. The main burial chamber is 2.6 m in length and 1.45 m in maximum width. The side walls are concave in plan, like those of Tomb No. 186. The corridor leading to the main burial chamber is 2.0 m in length, 0.87 m in width, and 0.8 m in height. Since all the pottery discovered is in small fragments, it is very difficult to determine the date of this tomb based on pottery typology. Because a corridor-style burial chamber with side walls curving outward became common in the seventh century, I would suggest that this tomb was built in the seventh century. Since Tomb No. 186 with side walls of standing slabs, similar to Tomb No. 190, is dated to the end of the sixth century, I tend to assume that the construction of this tomb took place in the very early seventh century.

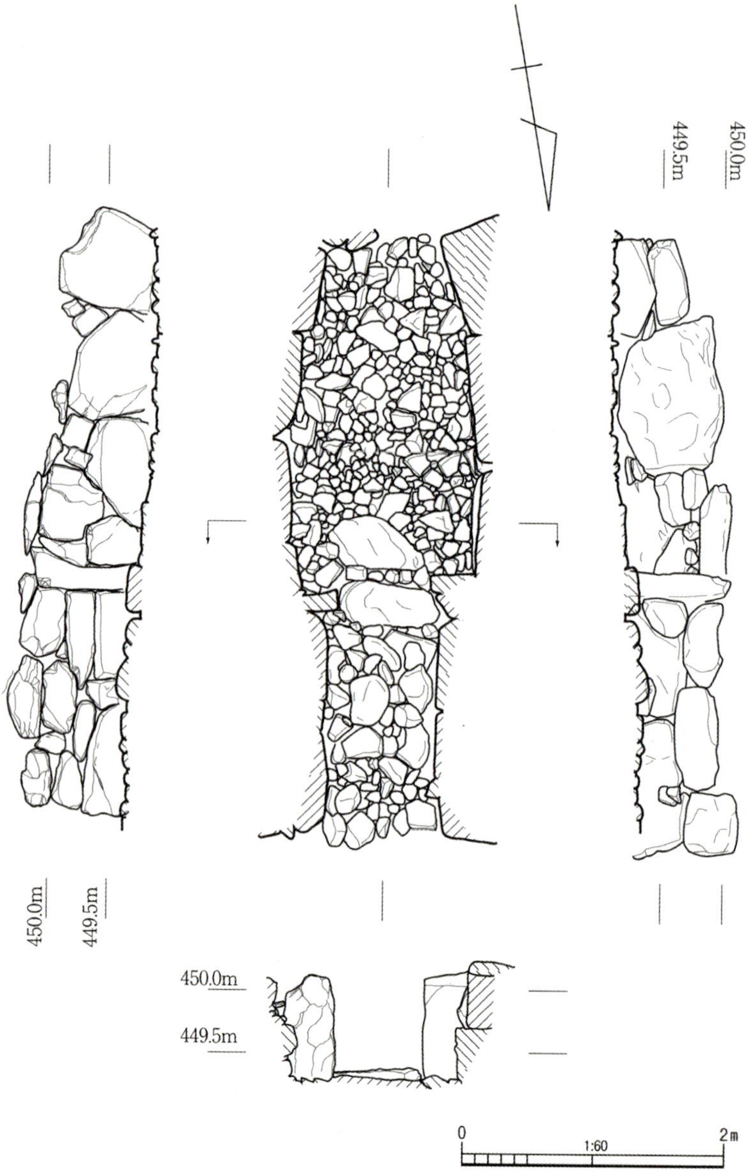

Figure 6.72 Corridor-style Burial Chamber of Tomb No. 190. From Sasaki et al. 2015, Fig. 79.

Figure 6.73 Corridor-style Burial Chamber of Tomb No. 198. Photograph by the Archaeology Program, Meiji University.

Tomb No. 198 is a roughly circular cairn of 10 by 8.5 m and is approximately 2 m in height. This cairn houses a corridor-style burial chamber of 4.4 m in length (Figures 6.73 and 6.74). The main burial chamber is 2.7 m in length, 1.1 m in maximum width, and 1.7 m in height. The side walls of the main burial chamber are concave in plan. The length of the corridor leading to the main burial chamber is 1.7 m.

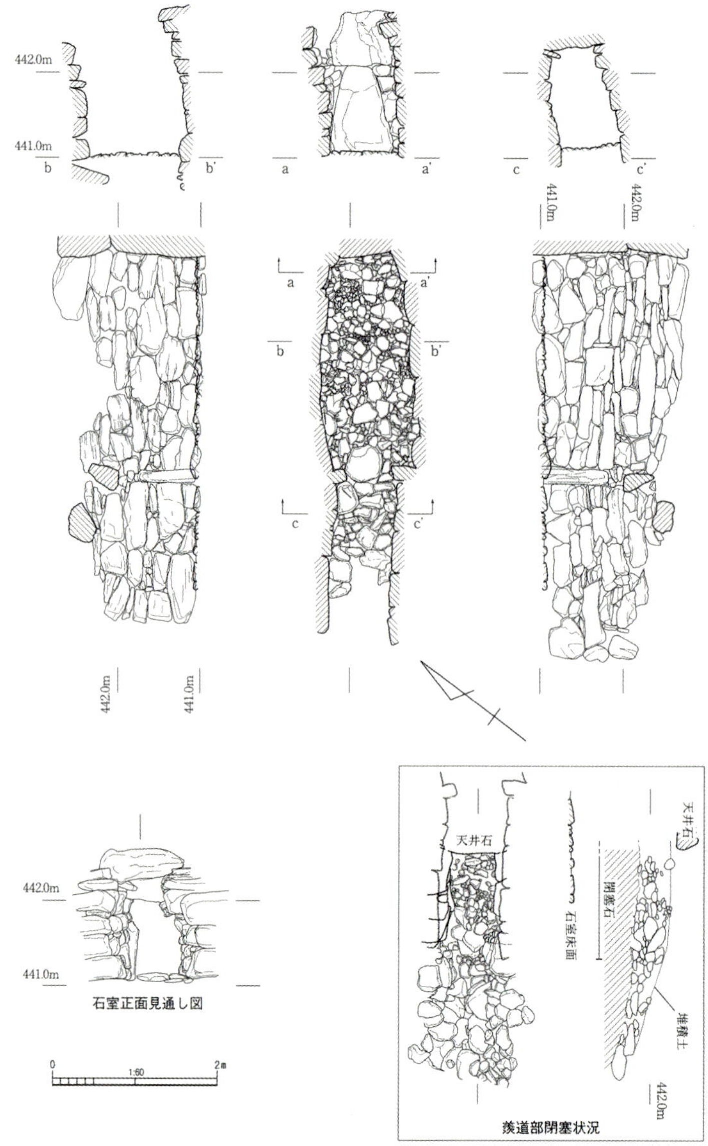

Figure 6.74 Corridor-style Burial Chamber of Tomb No. 198. From Sasaki et al. 2015, Fig. 101.

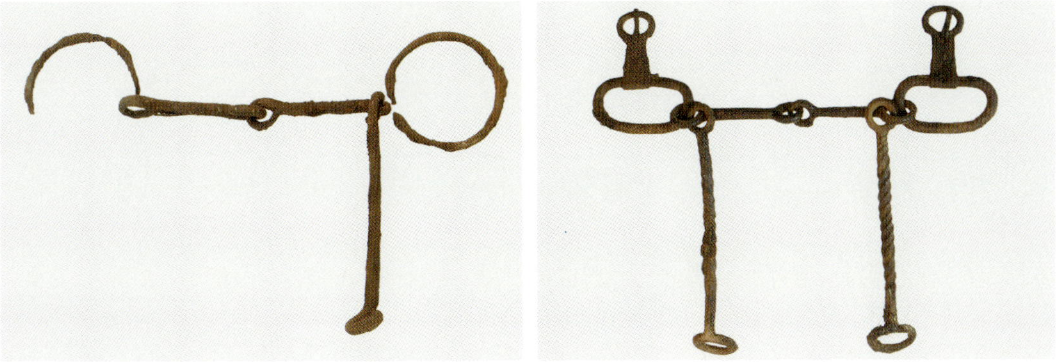

Figure 6.75 Horse Bit Discovered in the Burial Chamber of Tomb No. 198. From Sasaki et al. 2015, Fig. 104.

Figure 6.76 Corridor-style Burial Chamber of Tomb No. 200. Photograph by Masanori Kawano.

Slabs that presumably covered the burial chamber have been lost except for one. Yet, the burial chamber was not looted at all, probably because earth of more than 1 m in thickness covered the floor of the chamber. Thirty-three iron arrowheads were placed on the floor along the right side wall. A silver horse bit (Figure 6.75) was placed inside the gate of the main burial chamber. Other discoveries include iron knives and ornaments for

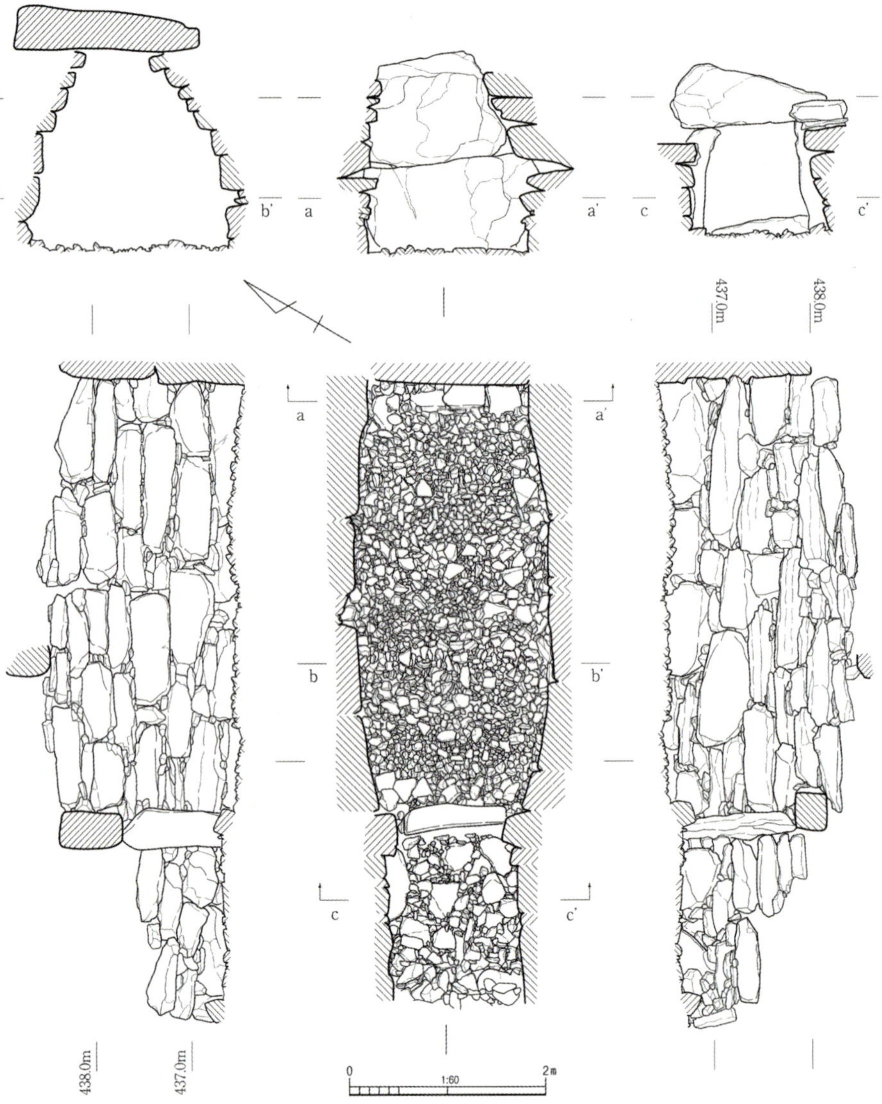

Figure 6.77 Corridor-style Burial Chamber of Tomb No. 200. From Sasaki et al. 2015, Fig. 8.

Figure 6.78 Corridor-style Burial Chamber of Tomb No. 201. Photograph by the Archaeology Program, Meiji University.

bows. Pottery was not placed in the main burial chamber but in the corridor leading to it, near the entrance to the corridor. The pottery assemblage consists of both *haji* earthenware and *sue* stoneware. The typology of the *sue*-stoneware vessels suggests that the date of this tomb should be the middle to late seventh century. The horse bit and iron arrowheads are types very common in the middle to late seventh century.

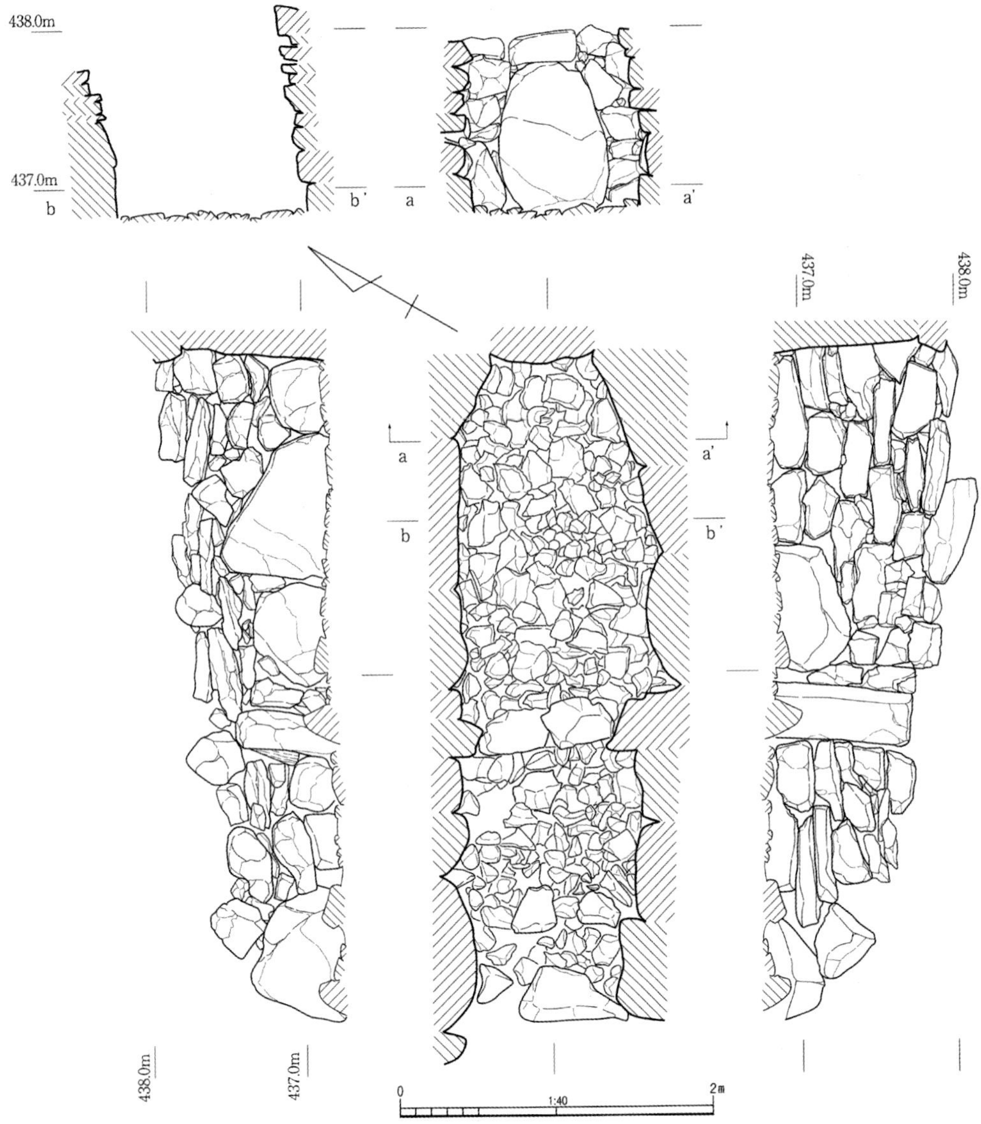

Figure 6.79 Corridor-style Burial Chamber of Tomb No. 201. From Sasaki et al. 2015, Fig. 24.

Tomb No. 200 is a small circular mound of 10.4 by 11.8 m in diameter, constructed with earth and rocks. The height of the mound is 2.4 m on the upper slope and 3.2 m on the lower slope. This mound housed a corridor-style burial chamber of 4.3 m in length (Figures 6.76 and 6.77). The main burial chamber was 2.7 m in length, 1.3 m in maximum width, and 1.7 m in height. The floor plan of the main burial chamber is not rectangular, but the left and right walls form a convex arc. The corridor was 1.6 m in length and 0.9 m in width. Excavations in the main burial chamber resulted in the discovery of a bronze bracelet, an iron end-fitting of a sheath, three earrings, nine comma-shaped beads, one cylindrical bead, five spherical beads, and sherds of *sue* stoneware and *haji* earthenware. The typology of pottery discovered at the entrance to the burial chamber suggests that this burial mound was built at the end of the sixth or beginning of the seventh century. It is likely that pottery was "offered" in the process of mound construction, probably as part of a ritual. Based on the relative dates of the artifacts in the main burial chamber, no additional interments took place once the body was buried at the completion of the mound. After the mound was completed, however, pottery was offered again in the early seventh century, probably as a ritual conducted in memory of the dead.

Tomb No. 201 is a very small, circular mound of 8.0 by 9.6 m, constructed with earth and rocks. The top of the mound has been lost, and we do not know its height. This mound houses a corridor-style horizontal burial chamber that is oriented 104 degrees westward from due north. The main burial chamber is 2.3 m in length, 1.2 m in maximum width, 0.6 m in width at the back wall, and 0.8 m in width at the gate to the main burial chamber (Figures 6.78 and 6.79). One of the side walls is concave while the other is straight at the base.

Excavations in the main burial chamber resulted in the discovery of an iron sword, twenty-eight iron arrowheads of at least three distinctive types, and four iron knives. Several *haji*-earthenware bowls and various *sue*-stoneware vessels were discovered just outside the entrance of the corridor leading to the main burial chamber. The pottery assemblage represents three different chronological phases in the seventh century. This suggests the possibility that interment took place three times, or that rituals took place sometime after one interment, because the burial chamber is very small. Another interesting aspect of the pottery assemblage is that pottery fired apparently at different kilns in the Nagano Basin was offered. This suggests to me that people from different places in the Nagano Basin participated in mortuary rituals at this tomb.

Conclusion: Significance of the Ōmuro Investigations

The results of our long-term archaeological excavations at the Ōmuro Valley sub-group of the Ōmuro cairn and earthen mound group are significant in many ways. First, the Ōmuro Valley sub-group is spatially divided into clusters, such as Murahigashi, Ōishi, and Mujinagōro. While this may simply be a matter of spatial division, it may have some historical significance because the formation of all the clusters started with a cairn with vaulted burial chambers. In all the clusters the construction of cairns with vaulted chambers ended by the beginning of the sixth century. Also, in all the clusters corridor-style horizontal burial chambers were introduced in the middle to late sixth century. In this section, I discuss the significance for the period before and leading up to the beginning of the sixth century (age of cairns) and the period since the middle sixth century (age of the corridor-style burial chamber). I will also touch on issues related to Korean immigrants.

Fifth Century to the Beginning of the Sixth Century: Age of Cairns

The formation of the Ōmuro cairn and earthen mound group started in the middle fifth century in the Nagano Basin in northern Shinano at a time when the construction of keyhole-shaped mounded tombs was in a decline. In the Nara Basin, where the central polity of the Kofun period was located, large groups of small burial mounds appeared. These are considered a precursor of "clustered tombs" or *gunshū fun* 群集墳, consisting of a large number of small circular and square mounded tombs, typical of the sixth and seventh centuries. The appearance of clustered tombs is interpreted as a reflection of the central polity attempting to gain more direct control over people by granting rights to construct mounded tombs (Nishijima 1961) and of more local people rising to the class of low-ranking elite who could build their own mounded tombs (Kondō 1952). The appearance represented an important epoch in the history of the Kofun period, and Wada (1992) even considers this phenomenon as marking the beginning of the Late Kofun period.

Debating whether the middle fifth century or the beginning of the sixth century marks the beginning of the Late Kofun period is beyond the scope of this chapter. Still, it is important to note that the Ōmuro cairn and earthen mound group is one of the rather unusual large-scale mound groups that appeared in the middle fifth century. Japanese archaeologists who contributed to the study of tomb clusters that appeared in the fifth century and lasted until the sixth or seventh centuries, such as Terasawa (1982), Wada (1992), and Kyōjima (1997), consider the appearance of clustered tombs as a reflection of the central polity attempting to incorporate immigrants from the Korean peninsula into the social system in the fifth century.

In the context of the regional history of the Nagano Basin, it is noteworthy that once the Ōmuro mound group appeared, keyhole-shaped mounded tombs were no longer constructed in the Nagano Basin. In order to explain why the construction of keyhole-shaped mounded tombs declined in the Nagano Basin in the middle fifth century, a hypothesis has been proposed suggesting that the seat of the highest-ranking elite moved from the Nagano Basin to the Iida Basin in southwestern Shinano, where the construction of keyhole-shaped mounded tombs started in the fifth century (e.g. Nishiyama 2003). This hypothesis is backed by the observation that one characteristic technique of *haniwa* production diffused from the Nagano Basin to the Iida Basin in the middle fifth century (Tanaka 2013).

In this chapter, I propose the alternative hypothesis that higher-ranking elites remained in the Nagano Basin even after the construction of keyhole-shaped mounded tombs declined and that the elite class emerged newly and independently in the Iida Basin. I argue that locally high-ranking elites who would have been buried in keyhole-shaped mounded tombs in the fourth century were in fact buried in some of the small circular cairns in the Ōmuro mound group. Tomb No. 196, where an iron cuirass, bronze mirror, and horse trappings were deposited with the dead, may well be considered an elite burial. The special status of the individual buried in Tomb No. 196 may be inferred from the larger size of the vaulted burial chamber as well as the lavish burial goods. If Tomb No. 196 was indeed an elite burial, as I suspect, it would suggest that less significance was attached to keyhole-shaped mounded tombs in this region in the late fifth century and that social ranking was represented differently here than it was in the central polity.

Moreover, less significance attached to keyhole-shaped mounded tombs indicates that local elites in the late fifth century did not observe a practice of differentiating the form and size of burial mounds as an indicator of an elite social hierarchy. This would further lead us to the interpretation that local elites were relatively autonomous. I will come back to this issue of autonomy below.

The Issue of Korean Immigrants

Archaeological excavations at Tombs No. 168 and No. 186 have resulted in the discoveries of a horse-shaped figurine and a horse skeleton, respectively. These constitute strong evidence that equestrian specialists themselves, or those who were closely related to them, such as their managers, were buried in the Ōmuro mound group. Horses were not native to Japan. Horses had to be imported, and more importantly, equestrian specialists had to be invited from the Korean peninsula. The introduction of horses to Japan was undoubtedly initiated by the central polity of Yamato toward the end of the fourth century. Indeed, evidence for early introduction of horses along with Korean ceramics has recently been excavated in Shijōnawate 四条畷 City, northern Osaka Prefecture, within the region under the direct control of the central polity (Iwase et al. 2009). At the same time, I suspect that it was difficult for the highest-ranking chief in the central polity to produce large numbers of horses at once on his or her own and that he or she had to depend on local elites, such as those in the Nagano Basin, for raising and reproducing horses.

I suggest that the local elites in the Nagano Basin invited equestrian specialists from the Korean peninsula independently from the central polity because horses were treated very differently in the Nagano Basin than they were in Shijōnawate City. At sites in Shijōnawate City, the entire bodies of horses were buried in pits at the foot of circular mounded tombs. This is also the case in the Iida Basin (Shibuya 2012). By contrast, at Tomb 186, dated to the end of the sixth century, the head of a horse was presumably cut off ritually and placed on the slope of the mound. In the case of Tomb 168, a horse-shaped figurine was offered, together with other ceramics, at the foot or on the slope of the mound. I suspect that a group of equestrian specialists different from those who were settled in the present Shijōnawate region were invited to the Nagano Basin. My hypothesis must be tested, for example, by the DNA examination of horses discovered in the Nagano Basin and in Shijōnawate City.

Furthermore, I suggest the possibility that the equestrian specialists in the Nagano Basin came to Nagano directly from the Korean peninsula, without traveling through the Osaka-Nara region. My hypothesis is based on: (1) the aforementioned difference in the treatment of horses in the Nagano Basin and in the Shijōnawate region; (2) the Chikuma River, which flows through the Nagano Basin and eventually flows into the Sea of Japan (East Sea in Korean), facilitating transportation between the Sea of Japan coast and the Nagano Basin; and (3) my suspicion that local polities in Kyushu in the Early Kofun period were so autonomous that they could interact with polities in the southern part of the Korean peninsula independently from the central polity. My suspicion is based on the late third-century Furu-type 布留 pottery originally invented in Yamato, discovered in southeastern Korea, and made in northern Kyushu, which indicates to

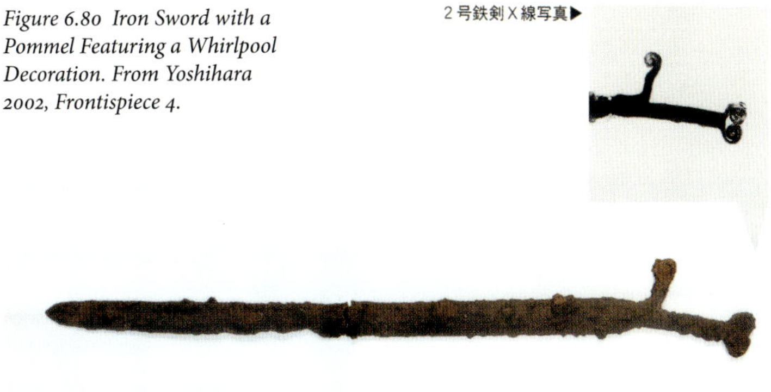

Figure 6.80 Iron Sword with a Pommel Featuring a Whirlpool Decoration. From Yoshihara 2002, Frontispiece 4.

me that the central polity of Yamato did not fully monopolize diplomatic rights (Sasaki 2010). Even in the fifth century, this was probably the case in the Nagano Basin.

Local elites in the Nagano Basin in the fifth century could invite Korean specialists of horse production without major difficulty because Korean people had visited and stayed in the Nagano Basin since the first or second century A.D. For example, an iron sword with whirlpool-pattern decorations (Figure 6.80) was discovered at the site of the first- to second-century Nezuka 根塚 burial mound in the northeastern Nagano Basin (Yoshihara 2002), and is very likely to have been brought from southern Korea. There are no other discoveries of this type of iron sword in Japan, but several iron swords of this type have been discovered at the Yangdong-ni 良洞里 cemetery site in Kimhae 金海 (Tongŭi Taehakkyo Pangmulgwan 2000). Habuta (2006: 181; 2012: 7–8; this volume) argues that this sword was transported directly from the southern Korean peninsula without going through, for example, northern Kyushu or the Nara Basin. I entirely agree with Habuta because local polities in the Sea of Japan coastal regions of western Japan, such as San'in 山陰 and Tango 丹後, independently interacted with polities in southern Korea during the Late Yayoi period (first to middle third centuries A.D.).

Another piece of evidence for interaction between polities in the Nagano Basin and those in the southern Korean peninsula before the fifth century is a horse-shaped bronze buckle (Figure 6.81) discovered at the Asakawabata 浅川端 site in the central Nagano Basin (Shimizu and Kazama 2005). It is basically the same type as one discovered at the Ch'ŏngdang-dong 清堂洞 site, in particular Tomb No. 5, in Ch'ŏnan 天安 City, and is

Figure 6.81 Horse-shaped Bronze Buckle Discovered at the Asakawabata Site. From Shimizu and Kazama 2005, Frontispiece.

also likely to have been brought from the Korean peninsula. The buckle is dated to the third century A.D. based on typological analysis (Kazama 2006). As in the case of the Nezuka iron sword, I argue for the possibility that these materials were directly brought to the Nagano Basin without going through the intermediation of the central polity of Yamato. The basis of my argument is the same as that for the travel route of equestrian specialists settled in the Nagano Basin.

It is highly likely that the local elites in the Nagano Basin welcomed immigrants from the Korean peninsula beginning in the second century. Because of this longstanding practice, it was easy for them to invite equestrian specialists from the Korean peninsula in the fifth century. By this time, local elites were also familiar with Korean-style mortuary facilities, including the cairn burial. The cairn appeared in the Nagano Basin without any precursor, and its origin should be traced to outside regions, such as the Korean peninsula. I speculate that cairns in the Ōmuro mound group were constructed in the fifth century under the direction or advice of second- or third-generation descendants of Korean immigrants.

My hypothesis explains why cairns were constructed in the third century or earlier in the Korean peninsula and in the Nagano Basin in the fifth century. My hypothesis can also explain why Japanese *haniwa* ceramic cylinders were placed on the surface of cairns and Japanese *sue* stoneware was offered to cairns in the Ōmuro mound group. When the central polity began allowing low-ranking elites, who could not have built their own burials in the fourth century, to build their own burial mounds in the middle fifth century, they built burial mounds of their own taste and style. This shift in the policy of the central polity is reflected in the appearance of clustered mounded tombs in the middle fifth century. At the same time, by the fifth century, second- or third-generation descendants of Korean immigrants were well adapted to Japanese customs, and when they started building cairns, they also decorated cairns with Japanese *haniwa* ceramic cylinders.

Middle Sixth Century to Seventh Century:
Age of Corridor-Style Horizontal Burial Chambers

A hiatus exists between the end of the practice of construction of cairns at the beginning of the sixth century and the introduction of corridor-style horizontal burial chambers to Ōmuro in the middle sixth century. This hiatus in the construction of burial mounds exists in other regions of Japan, such as the Kantō 関東 region of eastern Japan and Kibi 吉備 of western Japan. We do not have any idea why this would be so. It might be a result of political turmoil following the death of the powerful Emperor Keitai 継体 in 527 or 531. In any case, the introduction of corridor-style burial chambers indicates an increase in the influence of the central polity upon local regions, including the Nagano Basin. The introduction was made to almost all regions of mainland Japan, Shikoku, and Kyushu, with only a very few exceptions, such as southern Hitachi 常陸 (50 miles northeast of Tokyo).

It is likely that Tomb No. 186 was built under this influence of the central polity of Yamato. The buried person was high-ranking or maybe even the highest-ranking elite in the Nagano Basin. Although the tomb is small, a set of cuirass armor was deposited with the dead. Moreover, the corridor-style burial chamber is comparable in size to those of the second highest-ranking burials in the central polity, such as the Kaihōzuka 海北塚 tomb in northern Osaka Prefecture, in which a sarcophagus, a decorated sword, and three full sets of horse trappings were discovered (Umehara 1937). While the size of the main burial chamber of Tomb No. 186 is 4.6 m in length, 2.2 m in maximum width, and 1.8 m in height, the size of the main burial chamber of the Kaihōzuka tomb is 4.6 m in length, 2.5 m in width, and 3.3

m in height. In addition, the tomb's occupant was probably involved in raising and breeding horses, as in the case of Tomb No. 168, because the head of a horse was ritually offered. This strongly suggests that elite lineages continued in the Nagano Basin throughout the sixth century, though keyhole-shaped mounded tombs were no longer built in the Nagano Basin.

Besides a difference in size, differences in the structure and style of corridor-style burial chambers are apparent in the Mujinagōro cluster. For example, the burial chambers of Tombs No. 187 and No. 190 in the Mujinagōro cluster and Tombs No. 362, 429, and 436 in the Kitadani sub-group (Kamimura 1970) are characterized by side walls standing upright, rather than side walls constructed by piling up rocks. A similar phenomenon is observed in the Iida Basin, where keyhole-shaped mounded tombs with variously structured corridor-style burial chambers coexisted in the sixth century. Shiraishi (1983) has argued that the differences in structure among corridor-style burial chambers indicated individual elites interacting with competing higher-ranking elites within the central polity. While this hypothesis is convincing in the case of the Iida Basin, where these keyhole-shaped mounded tombs are spatially set apart from one another, this hypothesis cannot explain the Ōmuro case, where corridor-style burial chambers of different structure are situated side by side. In traditional Japan, members of the same clan tended to be buried in a single cemetery. The Ōmuro case might be a reflection of a difference in kinship, such as closeness to or distance from a Korean ancestor. Tombs No. 187, No. 190, No. 362, No. 429, and No. 436 may be the burials of clan members who had close Korean relatives.

In conclusion, the results of long-term archaeological investigations into the Ōmuro cairn and earthen mound group are invaluable for understanding Kofun-period history as a whole. The investigations have revealed previously unknown aspects of mortuary practices in peripheral regions of Japan, far away from the central polity, as well as temporal changes in these practices. The results suggest that local elites in the Nagano Basin, especially in the fifth century, were relatively autonomous and independent from the central polity. It might also be the case that the central polity did not fully monopolize the diplomatic relationship with the Korean peninsula. These contributions are important because research into the Kofun period tends to be skewed toward understanding the central polity.

References

Ch'oe Wan-kyu 崔完奎, Kim Chong-mun 金鍾文, and Yi Sin-hyo 李信孝 (editors)

1992 *Okku Changsang-ni Paekche kobun'gun palgul chosa pogosŏ* 沃溝將相里百濟古墳群 發掘調査報告書 [Report of the excavation of a Paekche cemetery at Changsang-ni in Okku]. Wŏn'gwang Taehakkyo Pangmulgwan 圓光大學校博物館 [Wonkwang University Museum], Iksan.

Habuta Yoshiyuki 土生田純之

1997 Shinano ni okeru yokoanashiki sekishitsu no juyō 信濃における横穴式石室の受容 [Adoption of corridor-style burial chambers in Shinano]. *Shinano* 信濃 49(4–5): 294–308.

———

2000 Tsumi'ishizuka kofun to gasshōgata sekishitsu no sai-kentō: Ōmuro Kofun-gun o chūshin toshite 積石塚古墳と合掌形石室の再検討: 大室古墳群を中心として [Re-examination of cairns and vaulted stone burial chambers: With focus on the Ōmuro Tomb Group]. *Fukuoka Daigaku Sōgō Kenkyūjo Hō* 福岡大学総合研究所報, no. 240 (Sōgō Kagaku Hen, no. 3): 131–154.

———

2006 Nihon shutsudo no uma-gata taikō no shiteki igi 日本出土の馬形帯鉤の史的意義 [Historical significance of horse-shaped buckles discovered in Japan]. In *Higashi Ajia chiiki ni okeru seidōki bunka no inyū to hen'yō oyobi ryūtsū ni kansuru takakuteki hikaku kenkyū* 東アジア地域における青銅器文化の移入と変容および流通に関する多角的比較研究 [Multi-faceted comparative studies on the introduction, evolution, and exchange of the bronze culture in East Asia], edited by Fujio Shin'ichirō 藤尾慎一郎, pp. 179–200. Kokuritsu Rekishi Minzoku Hakubutsukan 国立歴史民俗博物館 [National Museum of Japanese History], Sakura.

———

2012 Tōgoku ni okeru toraijin no isō to Tako-gun ken-gun 東国における渡来人の位相と多胡郡建郡 [Aspects of immigrants in eastern Japan and the establishment of Tako County]. In *Tako-hi ga kataru kodai Nippon to toraijin* 多胡碑が語る古代日本と渡来人 [Immigrants and ancient Japan from the perspectives of the Tako stele], edited by Habuta Yoshiyuki 土生田純之, and Takasaki-shi 高崎市 [Takahashi Municipal Government], pp. 1–47. Yoshikawa Kōbunkan 吉川弘文館, Tokyo.

Iijima Tetsunari 飯島哲也

2003a Shinano ni okeru tsumi'ishi funkyū no kofun: Iwayuru tsumi'ishizu Kofun no funkyū kōzō bunrei 科野における石積み墳丘の古墳: いわゆる積石塚古墳の墳丘構造分類 [Cairns in Shinano: Their classifications based on structures]. In *Kansai Daigaku Kōkogaku Kenkyūshitsu Kaisetsu 50-shūnen*

Kinen Kōkogaku Ronsō 関西大学考古学研究室開設五拾周年記念考古学論叢 [Collected theses in archaeology in celebration of the fiftieth anniversary of the Archaeology program at Kansai University], Vol. 1, pp. 449–476. Kansai Daigaku Kōkogaku Kenkyūshitsu 関西大学考古学研究室 [Archaeology Program, Kansai University], Osaka.

———

2003b Gasshō-gata tenjō no maisō shisetsu ni tsuite 合掌形天井の埋葬施設について [Burial chambers with "vaulted" top]. *Teikyō Daigaku Yamanashi Bunkazai Kenkyūjo Kenkyū Hōkoku* 帝京大学山梨文化財研究所研究報告 [Bulletin of the Teikyō University Institute for Research into Cultural Properties at Yamanashi], no. 11: 131–148.

Iwasaki Takuya 岩崎卓也

1964 Nagano Ken ni okeru kofun no chi'iki-teki ha'aku 長野県における古墳の地域的把握 [Regional approach to the Kofun period mounded tombs in Nagano Prefecture]. In *Nihon rekishi ronkyū: Kōkogaku minzokugaku hen* 日本歴史論究: 考古学・民俗学編 [Discussion on Japanese history: Archaeology and folklore section], edited by Tokyo Kyōiku Daigaku Shōshi Kai 東京教育大学昭史会 [Society for History at Tokyo University of Education], pp. 67–83. Bungadō Ginkō Kenkyūsha 文雅堂銀行研究社, Tokyo.

Iwase Tōru 岩瀬透, Fujita Michiko 藤田道子, Miyazaki Taiji 宮崎泰史, and Fujinaga Masa'aki 藤永正明 (editors)

2009 *Shitomiya-Kita iseki 1* 蔀屋北遺跡 1 [Shitomiya-Kita site, volume 1]. Ōsaka-fu Kyōiku Iinkai 大阪府教育委員会 [Osaka Prefectural Board of Education], Osaka.

Kamimura Tōru 神村透 (editor)

1970 *Ōmuro kofun-gun Kitadani shigun kinkyū hakkutsu chōsa hōkoku sho* 大室古墳群北谷支群緊急発掘調査報告書 [Report of rescue excavations at the Kitadani sub-group of the Ōmuro mound group]. Nagano-ken 長野県 [Nagano Prefecture] and Ōmuro Kofun-gun Chōsakai 大室古墳群調査会 [*Ad hoc* committee for excavations of the Ōmuro mound group], Nagano.

Kazama Eiichi 風間栄一

2006 Uma-gata taikō no bunrui to keiretsu ha'aku: Nihon shutsudo no uma-gata taikō o megutte 馬形帯鉤の分類と系列把握: 日本出土の馬形帯鉤をめぐって [Classification and chronology of horse-shaped buckles: With focus on those discovered in Japan]. In *Higashi Ajia chiiki ni okeru seidōki bunka no inyū to hen'yō oyobi ryūtsū ni kansuru takakuteki hikaku kenkyū* 東アジア地域における青銅器文化の移入と変容および流通に関する多角的比較研究 [Multi-faceted comparative studies on the introduction, evolution, and exchange of the bronze culture in East Asia], edited by Fujio Shin'ichirō 藤尾慎一郎, pp. 145–178. Kokuritsu Rekishi Minzoku Hakubutsukan 国立歴史民俗博物館 [National Museum of Japanese History], Sakura.

———

2011 Shiseki Ōmuro kofun-gun no hakkutsu chōsa to seibi katsuyō 史跡大室古墳群の発掘調査と整備活用 [Archaeological excavations at the Ōmuro mound group and utilizing the site for the present society]. *Gekkan Bunkazai* 月刊文化財, no. 572: 27–31.

———(editor)

2013 *Shiseki Ōmuro kofun-gun (2): Entoransu Zōn Ōmuro 238, 239, 240 gōfun no hakkutsu chōsa* 史跡 大室古墳群(2): エントランスゾーン 大室238号墳・239号墳・240号墳の発掘調査 [Ōmuro mound group historic site (2): Archaeological excavations of Ōmuro Tomb Nos. 238, 239, and 240 in the entrance zone]. Nagano-shi Kyōiku Iinkai 長野市教育委員会 [Nagano Municipal Board of Education], Nagano.

———(editor)

2014 *Shiseki Ōmuro kofun-gun (3): Entoransu Zōn Ōmuro 31, 32, 33 gōfun no hakkutsu chōsa* 史跡 大室古墳群(3): エントランスゾーン 大室31号墳・32号墳・33号墳の発掘調査 [Ōmuro mound group historic site (3): Archaeological excavations of Ōmuro Tomb Nos. 31, 32, and 33 in the entrance zone]. Nagano-shi Kyōiku Iinkai 長野市教育委員会 [Nagano Municipal Board of Education], Nagano.

———(editor)

2016 *Shiseki Ōmuro kofun-gun (4): Entoransu Zōn Ōmuro 26, 27, 242 gōfun no hakkutsu chōsa* 史跡 大室古墳群(4): エントランスゾーン 大室26号墳・27号墳・242号墳の発掘調査 [Ōmuro mound group historic site (4): Archaeological excavations of Ōmuro Tomb Nos. 26, 27, and 242 in the entrance zone]. Nagano-shi Kyōiku Iinkai 長野市教育委員会 [Nagano Municipal Board of Education], Nagano.

Kirihara Ken 桐原健

1989 *Tsumi'ishi-zuka to toraijin* 積石塚と渡来人 [Immigrants and cairns]. Tōkyō Daigaku Shuppankai 東京大学出版会 [University of Tokyo Press], Tokyo.

Kobayashi Hideo 小林秀夫

1978 Gasshō-gata sekishitsu no sho-mondai 合掌形石室の諸問題 [Various issues of "vaulted" burial chambers]. In *Chūbu kōchi no kōkogaku* 中部高地の考古学 [Archaeology of the central highlands of Japan], edited by Nagano-ken Kōkogaku Kai 長野県考古学会 [Society for Archaeology in Nagano Prefecture], pp. 212–230. Nagano-ken Kōkogaku Kai, Nagano.

Kobayashi Saburō 小林三郎

2006 Ōmuro kofun-gun Ōmuro-dani shigun Ōishi tan'i shigun no chōsa seika to kadai 大室古墳群・大室谷支群・大石単位支群の調査成果と課題 [Results of archaeological investigations at the Ōishi cluster, Ōmuro Valley sub-group, Ōmuro mound group and their issues]. In *Shinano Ōmuro tsumi'ishizuka kofun-gun no kenkyū 2: Ōmuro shigun, Ōishi tan'i shigun no chōsa* 信濃大室積石塚古墳群の研究 2: 大室谷支群・大石単位支群の調査 [Study of Ōmuro cairn and earthen mound group in the old province of Shinanao, vol. 2: Investigations in the Ōmuro and Ōishi sub-groups], edited by Ōtsuka Hatsushige 大塚初重 and Kobayashi Saburō, pp. 160–169. Meiji Daigaku Jinbun Kagaku Kenkyūjo 明治大学人文科学研究所 [Meiji University Institute of Humanities] and Tōkyōdō Shuppan 東京堂出版, Tokyo.

Kobayashi Saburō 小林三郎, Ōtsuka Hatsushige 大塚初重, Ishikawa Hideshi 石川日出志, Sasaki Ken'ichi 佐々木憲一, and Kusano Jumpei 草野潤平 (editors)

2008 *Shinano Ōmuro tsumi'ishizuka kofun-gun no kenkyū 3: Ōmuro shigun, Mujinagōro tan'i shigun dai-168 gōfun no chōsa* 信濃大室積石塚古墳群の研究 3: 大室谷支群・ムジナゴーロ単位支群第168号墳の調査 [Study of the Ōmuro cairn and earthen mound group in the old province of Shinanao, vol. 3: Investigations at Tomb 168, Ōmuro and Mujinagōro sub-groups]. Meiji Daigaku Bungakubu Kōkogaku Kenkyūshitsu 明治大学文学部考古学研究室 [Archaeology Program, Faculty of Arts and Letters, Meiji University] and Rokuichi Shobō 六一書房, Tokyo.

Kondō Yoshirō 近藤義郎

1952 Mondai no shozai 問題の所在 [Problem orientation]. In *Sarayama kofun-gun no kenkyū* 佐良山古墳群の研究 [Study on the Sarayama mound group], edited by Kondō Yoshirō, pp. 41–53. Tsuyama-shi Kyōiku Iinkai 津山市教育委員会 [Tsuyama Municipal Board of Education], Okayama Prefecture.

Kurata Yoshirō 倉田芳郎 (editor)

1981 *Nagano Ōmuro kofun-gun: Bumpu chōsa hōkoku sho* 長野・大室古墳群: 分布調査報告書 [Ōmuro mound group in Nagano: A report of survey]. Komazawa Daigaku Kōkogaku Kenkyūshitsu 駒澤大学考古学研究室 [Archaeology Program, Komazawa University], Tokyo.

Kuribayashi Kidō 栗林紀道

1952 *Ōmuro kofun-gun ryakuzu: Dai-shi kai kiso chōsa* 大室古墳群畧図: 第四回基礎調査 [Map of the Ōmuro mound group: Fourth basic survey]. Private publication.

Kusumoto Tesuo 楠本哲夫

1996 Shinano Ina-dani Zakōji chiku no 3 sekishitsu 信濃伊那谷座光寺地区の3石室 [Three corridor-style burial chambers in the Zakōji area in the Ina basin, old province of Shinano]. *Kenkyū Kiyō* 研究紀要 [Research Bulletin] 3: 13–32. Yura-Yamato Kobunka Kenkyūkai 由良大和古文化研究会 [Yura Society for the Studies of Ancient Cultures of Yamato], Nara.

Kyōjima Satoru 京嶋覚

1997 Shoki gunshūfun no keisei katei 初期群集墳の形成過程 [Formation processes of mound clusters in fifth-century Japan]. In *Ritsumeikan Daigaku Kōkogaku Ronshū 1* 立命館大学考古学論集 1 [Collection of papers on archaeology, Ritsumeikan University, volume 1], pp. 213–226. Ritsumeikan Daigaku Bungakubu Kōkogaku Kenkyūshitsu 立命館大学文学部考古学研究室 [Archaeology Program, Faculty of Letters, Ritsumeikan University], Kyoto.

Morimoto Rokuji 森本六爾

1926 *Kingaisan kofun no kenkyū* 金鎧山古墳の研究 [A study on the Kingaisan mounded tomb, Nagano]. Yūzankaku 雄山閣, Tokyo.

Nishijima Sadao 西嶋定生

1961 Kofun to Yamato seiken 古墳と大和王権 [Mounded tombs and the Yamato central polity]. *Okayama Shigaku* 岡山史学, no. 10: 154–207.

Nishiyama Katsumi 西山克己

1996 Shinano no tsumi'ishizuka kofun to gasshōgata sekishitsu 信濃の積石塚古墳と合掌形石室 [Cairns and vaulted burial chambers in Shinano]. In *Nagano-ken no kōkogaku* 長野県の考古学 [Archaeology in Nagano Prefecture], Vol. 1, edited by Nagano-ken Maizō Bunkazai Sentaa 長野県埋蔵文化財センター [Nagano Prefectural Center for Archaeological Operations], pp. 181–221. Nagano-ken Maizō Bunkazai Sentaa, Nagano.

———

2000 Shinano no tsumi'ishizuka kofun to gasshōgata sekishitsu 科野の積石塚古墳と合掌形石室 [Cairns and vaulted burial chambers in Shinano]. In *Ōtsuka Hatsushige Sensei shōju kinen kōkogaku ronshū* 大塚初重先生頌寿記念考古学論集 [Collected theses in archaeology in celebration of Professor Ōtsuka Hatsushige's seventieth birthday], edited by Shōju Kinenkai 頌寿記念会, pp. 160–196. Tōkyōdō Shuppan 東京堂出版, Tokyo.

———

2003 Shinano no Kofun jidai chūki to sono mae, sono ato: Shinrai bunka juyō no nisō kita-minami シナノの古墳時代中期とその前・その後: 新来文化受容の二相北南 [Fifth century Shinano and its before and after: Two aspects of the adoption of foreign cultures in the southern and northern parts of Shinano]. In *Teikyō Daigaku Yamanashi Bunkazai Kenkyūjo Kenkyū Hōkoku* 帝京大学山梨文化財研究所研究報告 [Bulletin of the Teikyō University Institute for Research into Cultural Properties at Yamanashi], no. 11: 111–130.

———

2014 *Shinano ni okeru Kofun jidai shakai no hatten kara Ritsuryō ki heno tenbō* シナノにおける古墳時代社会の発展から律令期への展望 [Development of Kofun-period society toward the *Ritsuryō* era in Shinano]. Yūzankaku 雄山閣, Tokyo.

Ōtsuka Hatsushige 大塚初重

1969 Nagano-ken Ōmuro kofun gun 長野県大室古墳群 [Ōmuro mound group in Nagano Prefecture], *Kōkogaku Shūkan* 考古学集刊 4(3): 73–105.

———

2000 Tsumi'ishizuka kofun to gasshōgata sekishitsu 積石塚古墳と合掌形石室 [Cairns and vaulted burial chambers]. In *Nagano-shi shi 2: Rekishi hen genshi, kodai, chūsei* 長野市誌 2: 歴史編 原始・古代・中世 [Nagano City Gazetteer, vol. 2: Protohistory, ancient and medieval history], edited by Nagano-shi Shi Hensan Iinkai 長野市誌編纂委員会 [Nagano Gazetteer Editorial Committee], pp. 213–231. Nagano-shi 長野市 [Nagano Municipal Government], Nagano.

Ōtsuka Hatsushige 大塚初重, and Kobayashi Saburō 小林三郎 (editors)

2006 *Shinano Ōmuro tsumi'ishizuka kofun-gun no kenkyū 2: Ōmuro shigun, Ōishi tan'i shigun no chōsa* 信濃大室積石塚古墳群の研究 2: 大室谷支群・大石単位支群の調査 [Study of Ōmuro cairn and earthen mound group in the old province of Shinanao, vol. 2: Investigations in the Ōmuro and Ōishi sub-groups]. Meiji Daigaku Jinbun Kagaku Kenkyūjo 明治大学人文科学研究所 [Meiji University Institute of Humanities] and Tōkyōdō Shuppan 東京堂出版, Tokyo.

Ōtsuka Hatsushige 大塚初重, Kobayashi Saburō 小林三郎, and Hirata Sadafumi 平田禎文 (editors)

1991 *Jōshin'etsu jidōsha-dō maizō bunkazai hakkutsu chōsa hōkoku sho 3: Nagano shinai, sono 1; Ōmuro kofun gun* 上信越自動車道埋蔵文化財発掘調査報告書3: 長野市内 その1: 大室古墳群 [Report of archaeological excavations prior to the construction of the Jōshin'etsu expressway, no. 3: Nagano City: Ōmuro mound group]. Nihon Dōro Kōdan Nagoya Kensetsu Kyoto 日本道路公団名古屋建設局 [Nagoya Construction Branch, Japan Expressway Construction Public Corporation], Nagano-ken Kyōiku Iinkai 長野県教育委員会 [Nagano Prefectural Board of Education], and Nagano-ken Maizō Bunkazai Sentaa 長野県埋蔵文化財センター [Nagano Prefectural Center for Archaeological Operations], Nagano.

Ōtsuka Hatsushige 大塚初重, Kobayashi Saburō 小林三郎, and Ishikawa Hideshi 石川日出志 (editors)

1993 *Shinano Ōmuro tsumi'ishizuka kofun-gun no kenkyū 1: Ōmuro shigun, Murahigashi tan'i shigun no chōsa* 信濃大室積石塚古墳群の研究 1: 大室谷支群・村東単位支群の調査 [Study of the Ōmuro cairn and earthen mound group in the old province of Shinanao, vol. 1: Investigations in the Ōmuro and Murahigashi sub-groups]. Meiji Daigaku Jinbun Kagaku Kenkyūjo 明治大学人文科学研究所 [Meiji University Institute of Humanities] and Tōkyōdō Shuppan 東京堂出版, Tokyo.

Ozaki Kisao 尾崎喜佐雄

1966 *Yokoana-shiki kofun no kenkyū* 横穴式古墳の研究 [A study of the corridor-style burial chambers]. Yoshikawa Kōbunkan 吉川弘文館, Tokyo.

Saitō Tadashi 斎藤忠

1944 Yane-gata tenjō o yūsuru sekishitsu-fun ni tsuite 屋根型天井を有する石室墳に就いて [Burial chambers with vaulted top]. *Kōkogaku Zasshi* 考古学雑誌 35, no. 3: 129–136.

Sasaki Ken'ichi 佐々木憲一

2010 Kofun shutsugen zengo ni okeru Kinai-gata kame-gata doki no seiho kakusan ni kansuru kenkyū 古墳出現前後における畿内型甕形土器の西方拡散に関する研究 [Distribution of the Kinai-type cooking ware in third-century western Japan: Approach to early state formation]. *Meiji Daigaku Jinbun Kagaku Kenkyūjo Kiyō* 明治大学人文科学研究所紀要 [Bulletin of the Meiji University Institute of Humanities] 66: 251–312.

Sasaki Ken'ichi 佐々木憲一, Kawano Masanori 河野正訓, Takahashi Tōru 高橋透, and Arai Satoru 新井悟 (editors)

2015 *Shinano Ōmuro tsumi'ishizuka kofun-gun no kenkyū 4: Ōmuro shigun, Mujinagōro tan'i shigun no chōsa* 信濃大室積石塚古墳群の研究 4: 大室谷支群・ムジナゴーロ単位支群の調査 [Study of the Ōmuro cairn and earthen mound group in the old province of Shinanao, vol. 4: Investigations into the Ōmuro and Mujinagōro sub-groups]. Meiji Daigaku Bungakubu Kōkogaku Kenkyūshitsu 明治大学文学部考古学研究室 [Archaeology Program, Faculty of Arts and Letters, Meiji University] and Rokuichi Shobō 六一書房, Tokyo.

Shibuya Emiko 澁谷恵美子

2012 *Iida kofun-gun* 飯田古墳群 [Iida mound group]. Nagano-ken Iida-shi Kyōiku Iinkai 長野県飯田市教育委員会 [Iida Municipal Board of Education], Nagano Prefecture.

Shimizu Ryūta 清水竜太, and Kazama Eiichi 風間栄一

2005 Nagano-shi Asakawabata iseki shutsudo no uma-gata taikō 長野市浅川端遺跡出土の馬形帯鉤 [Horse-shaped buckle discovered at the Asakawabata site, Nagano City]. *Kōkogaku Zasshi* 考古学雑誌 89, no. 2: 76–87.

Shimizu Ryūta 清水竜太, Tokinobu Takeshi 時信武史, and Iijima Tetsunari 飯島哲也

2007 *Kuni shiseki Ōmuro kofun-gun: Entoransu Zōn B-D ku ikō hen* 国史跡大室古墳群: エントランスゾーンB〜D区遺構編 [Ōmuro mound group, a nationally designated historic site: Archaeological features of the Localities B through D in the Entrance Zone]. Nagano-shi Kyōiku Iinkai 長野市教育委員会 [Nagano Municipal Board of Education], Nagano.

Shimizu Ryūta 清水竜太, and Iijima Tetsunari 飯島哲也

2008 *Kuni shiseki Ōmuro kofun-gun: Entoransu Zōn A, E ku ikō hen* 国史跡大室古墳群: エントランスゾーンA·E区遺構編 [Ōmuro mound group, a nationally designated historic site: Archaeological features of the Localities A and E in the Entrance Zone]. Nagano-shi Kyōiku Iinkai 長野市教育委員会 [Nagano Municipal Board of Education], Nagano.

Shiraishi Taichirō 白石太一郎

1983 [2006] Ina-dani no yokoanashiki sekishitsu 伊那谷の横穴式石室 [Corridor-style burial chambers in the Ina basin]. *Shinano* 信濃 49, no. 7 (Pt. 1), and no. 8 (Pt. 2). Reprinted in *Shinano no Ōbo no kōkogaku* シナノの王墓の考古学 [Archaeology of royal tombs in Shinano], edited by Kawasaki Tamotsu, pp. 159–194. Yūzankaku 雄山閣, Tokyo.

Suenaga Masao 末永雅雄

1934 *Nihon jōdai no katchū* 日本上代の甲冑 [Armor in ancient Japan]. Oka Shoin 岡書院, Tokyo.

Tanaka Yutaka 田中裕

2013 Ina-dani no haniwa to sono keifu 伊那谷の埴輪とその系譜 [Origins of *haniwa* ceramic objects in the Ina valley]. In *Iida kofun-gun: Ronkō hen* 飯田古墳群: 論考編 [Iida mound group: Discussion], pp. 45–79. Nagano-ken Iida-shi Kyōiku Iinkai 長野県飯田市教育委員会 [Iida Municipal Board of Education], Nagano Prefecture.

Terasawa Tomoko 寺澤知子

1982 Shoki gunshūfun no ichi yōsō 初期群集墳の一様相 [An aspect of clustered mounds in the fifth century]. In *Kōkogaku to kodai shi* 考古学と古代史 [Archaeology and ancient history], edited by Mori Kōichi 森浩一. Dōshisha Daigaku Kōkogaku Shiriizu 同志社大学考古学シリーズ [Dōshisha University Series in Archaeology], Volume 1, pp. 255–264. Dōshisha Daigaku Kōkogaku Shiriizu, Tokyo.

Tongŭi Taehakkyo Pangmulgwan 東義大学校博物館 [Tongŭi University Museum]

2000 *Kimhae Yangdong-ni kobun munhwa* 金海良洞里古墳文化 [Mounded tomb culture of the Yangdong-ni site in Kimhae]. Tongŭi University Museum haksul ch'ongsŏ 東義大学校博物館學術叢書 [Tongŭi University Museum Academic Series], No. 7. Tongŭi Taehakkyo Pangmulgwan, Pusan.

Uchiyama Toshiyuki 内山敏行

2015 Ōmuro 196-gō fun no byōdome tankō 大室196号墳の鋲留短甲 [Riveted iron cuirass discovered at Tomb No. 196 of Ōmuro]. In *Shinano Ōmuro tsumi'ishizuka kofun-gun no kenkyū 4: Ōmuro shigun, Mujinagōro tan'i shigun no chōsa* 信濃大室積石塚古墳群の研究4: 大室谷支群·ムジナゴーロ単位支群の調査 [Study of Ōmuro cairn and earthen mound group in the old province of

Shinanao, vol. 4: Investigations into the Ōmuro and Mujinagōro sub-groups], edited by Sasaki Ken'ichi 佐々木憲一, Kawano Masanori 河野正訓, Takahashi Tōru 高橋透, and Arai Satoru 新井悟, pp. 141–146. Meiji Daigaku Bungakubu Kōkogaku Kenkyūshitsu 明治大学文学部考古学研究室 [Archaeology Program, Faculty of Arts and Letters, Meiji University] and Rokuichi Shobō 六一書房, Tokyo.

Umehara Sueji 梅原末治

1937 Settsu Fukui no Kaihōzuka kofun 摂津福井の海北塚古墳 [Kaihōzuka mounded tomb at Fukui, old province of Settsu]. *Nihon Ko-Bunka Kenkyūjo Hōkoku* 日本古文化研究所報告 [Bulletin of the Institute for Ancient Japanese Culture] 4: 56–67.

Wada Seigo 和田晴吾

1992 Gunshūfun to shūmatsuki kofun 群集墳と終末期古墳 [Clustered mounds and seventh-century mounded tombs]. In *Shinban kodai no Nihon* 新版古代の日本 [Ancient Japan: A new edition], Vol. 5, edited by Yamanaka Ichiō 山中一郎 and Kanō Hisashi 狩野久, pp. 325–350. Kadokawa Shoten 角川書店, Tokyo.

Yi Paek-kyu 李白圭, and Pak Ch'ŏn-su 朴天秀 (editors)

1997 *Kyŏng-Pu kosok ch'ŏldo Taegu-Kyŏngbuk kwŏn yujŏk palgul yebi chosa pogosŏ* 京釜高速鐵道大邱·慶北圈遺蹟發掘豫備調查報告書 [Report on preparatory survey for the excavation of sites in the region of the high-speed rail in Taegu and North Kyŏngsang]. Kyŏngbuk Taehakkyo Pangmulgwan 慶北大學校博物館 [Kyungpook University Museum], Taegu.

Yoshihara Yoshi'ichi 吉原佳市

2002 *Nezuka iseki* 根塚遺跡 [Nezuka site]. Kijimadaira-mura Kyōiku Iinkai 木島平村教育委員会 [Kijimadaira Village Board of Education], Nagano Prefecture.

7

Japan-Korea Interaction Viewed from Eastern Japan During the Kofun Period

Habuta Yoshiyuki

Abstract

The Kofun period of Japan represents a transition from the stage of regional differentiation and autonomy to the stage of a unified state under the ritsuryō *code. The Kofun period may be divided into the three phases of Early (middle third to late fourth centuries A.D.), Middle (end of the fourth to late fifth centuries), and Late (end of the fifth to the beginning of the seventh centuries). There was during this time significant temporal change in the relationships between the "center" and local regions. This chapter approaches the processes behind these changes, drawing upon archaeological evidence of eastern Japan. I focus on the end of the Yayoi period (early third century), the latter half of the Middle Kofun period (late fifth century), and the latter half of the Late Kofun period (late sixth to the beginning of the seventh centuries). These are the time periods when considerable quantities of material culture of Korean peninsular origin were introduced to Japan. These time periods also marked episodes in state formation. Here I employ an inductive approach that characterizes the tradition of Japanese archaeology, avoiding the deductive approach. I pay particular attention to what archaeological data can tell us and lead us to understand.*

Introduction

In this chapter, I discuss the material culture of Korean origin and Korean immigrants in eastern Japan during the Kofun period (middle third to the beginning of the seventh centuries). I focus on the following three time periods when material culture of Korean origin was particularly conspicuous: (1) the transition from the Yayoi to Kofun periods (early to middle third century); (2) the late fifth century; and (3) from the end of the sixth to the beginning of the seventh centuries. In the third century, local polities in eastern Japan independently maintained their own trade routes with the Korean peninsula, and the power of the Yamato central authority to control local polities was absent. In the late fifth century, large numbers of Korean immigrants settled in various areas of eastern Japan, their primary activity being horse raising. Immigration to these areas from the Korean peninsula occurred during roughly the same time period and was facilitated by the policy of the central Yamato authority. These disparate locales were not necessarily closely interrelated with one another, and the social status that the immigrants held differed from place to place. The difference was due to the fact that the Yamato authority as the central polity lacked the power to interfere with the social structure of each local polity.

For the time from the end of the sixth to the beginning of the seventh century, I focus on the case of western Gunma 群馬 Prefecture (western Kamitsuke 上毛) where large quantities of Korean material culture from this period are discovered. I argue that these Korean materials were distributed by the Yamato authority, and it is likely that the highest-ranking chief in Kamitsuke redistributed the Korean materials to local elites. From the late sixth century on, the control of the Yamato authority was very well asserted in numerous local areas, which was a solid step toward the formation of a unified state.

Background

Before presenting the archaeological evidence for interactions between the Korean peninsula and eastern Japan in detail, I consider it necessary to explain some background to the Kofun-period archaeology that Japanese archaeologists practice. These practices involve (1) a deductive approach, (2) information derived from mortuary data and its significance, and (3) issues of "center" and periphery in the process of state formation. Eastern Japan is considered as a periphery during the Kofun period.

First of all, I approach the subject title above by faithfully adopting the definition of archaeology proposed by Professor Hamada Kōsaku (1922:11): "Archaeology is a discipline by which one studies and investigates the past by interpreting material remains." Hamada was an archaeologist who is considered to be the founding father of Japanese archaeology as an empirical and scientific discipline. He founded the first independent department of archaeology in Japan, at Kyoto Imperial University, and published the above-mentioned statement in his introductory textbook of archaeology. After Hamada studied in Europe for three years, from 1913 to 1916, during which time he learned directly from W. M. Flinders Petrie at University College in London, he laid out the foundation for study of modern Japanese archaeology. Even now, Japanese archaeologists share Hamada's definition of archaeology, and consider it essential to observe, grasp, analyze, and interpret material remains. Owing to this practice, Japanese archaeologists have produced important scholarly works.

Because they adhere to this attitude even now, however, the contributions of archaeologists are undervalued; critics claim that studies of Japanese archaeology remain in the stage of observation and grasp of material remains and do not achieve the level of analysis and discussion of history. It is undeniable that the Japanese practice of developing theories in the process of examining individual factual cases is difficult for scholars who have conducted research under a cultural system in which scholars discuss theories as a starting point. Such a cultural system is very different from that of Japan. Still, I emphasize that Hamada defined archaeology clearly as a discipline of pursuing the past in reference to material remains. By pursuing the human past, Hamada meant to reconstruct the reality of human culture and society in the past as a whole, thereby gaining insight into understanding our future. The place of archaeology within the broader academic world was the same as the place of history from Hamada's perspective. This is the starting point of this chapter. While this study deals with the interaction between Korea and Japan, I focus my discussion on material culture of Korean origin. I am aware of the need to pay attention to interaction in both directions, but material culture of Japanese origin discovered in the Korean peninsula will have to be discussed in a future study.

Second, the discussion in this chapter focuses primarily on material of Korean origin that has been excavated from tumuli. This should not be interpreted to suggest that items of Korean origin were only deposited with the dead. Archaeologists tend to depend on mortuary data because the archaeological contexts of such data are usually secure and because archaeological data in general are simply skewed toward burials. In addition, the differential treatment of the dead is correlated with their social ranking as well as with their differences in social status.

While tumuli functioned primarily as graves in the Kofun period, they were also monuments with political and social significance. As symbols of ancestor worship, their social significance is apparent. Large keyhole

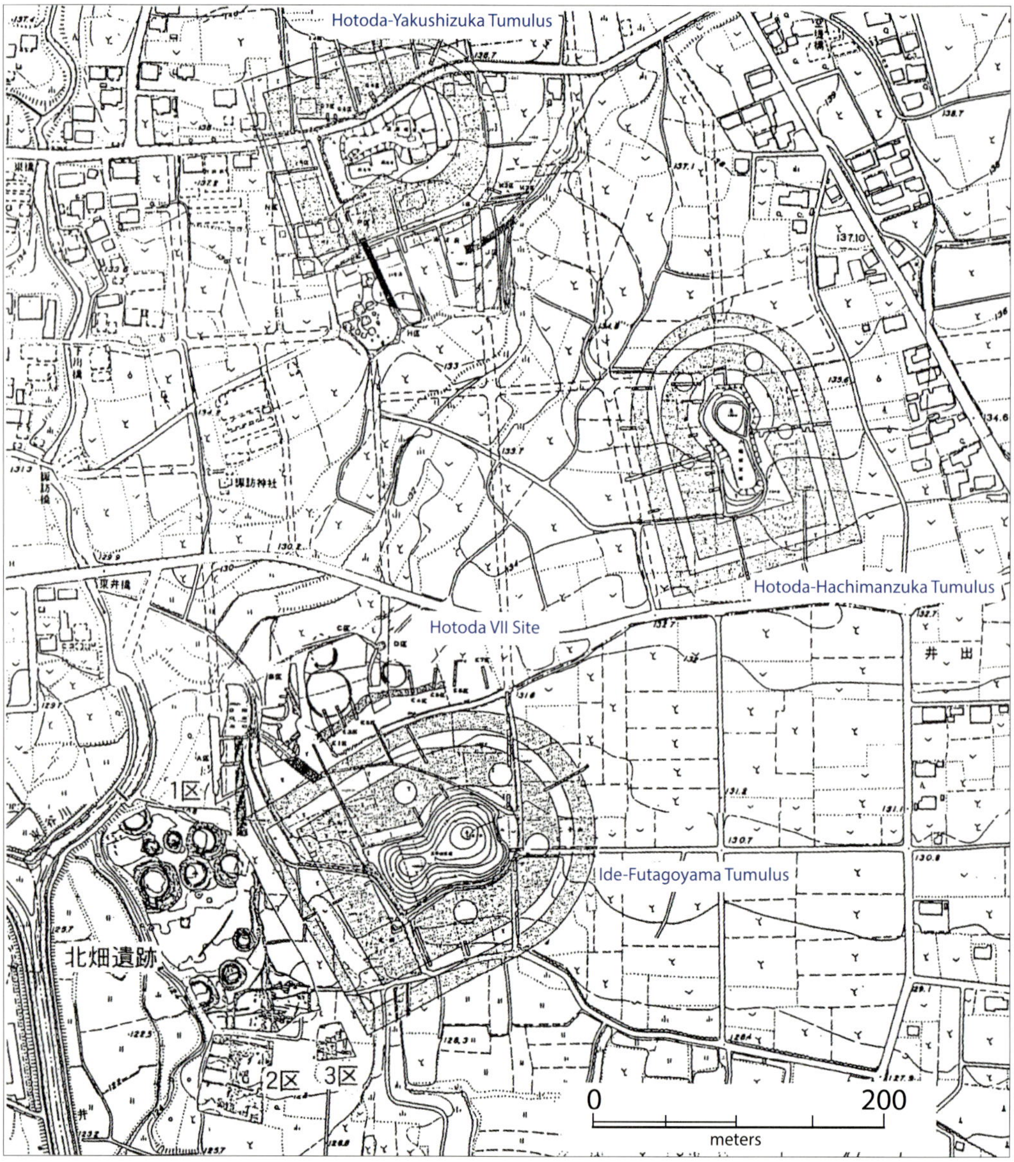

Figure 7.1 Small Circular Tumuli in the Vicinity of the Ide-Futagoyama Keyhole Tumulus. From Shimizu and Otsuka 2003.

tumuli remained to be revered in later times as symbols of the unity of a family and clan, through which the deceased ancestor maintained his or her "social life." Here, I present the example of the Hotoda 保渡田 tumulus group in Takasaki 高崎 City, Gunma Prefecture, some 64 km northwest of Tokyo (Figure 7.1). The group principally consists of three large keyhole tumuli of 90 to 105 m, namely Ide-Futagoyama 井出二子山, built in the third quarter of the fifth century, Hotoda-Hachimanzuka 保渡田八幡塚, built in the fourth quarter of the fifth century, and Hotoda-Yakushizuka 保渡田薬師塚, built in the first quarter of the sixth century. These three mounds were constructed in close proximity, only 100 m apart, with their main axes parallel or perpendicular to one another. Moreover, both Ide-Futagoyama and Hotoda-Hachimanzuka were characterized by the presence of four circular "islands" in the moats enclosing the keyhole tumulus. Since this feature of four "islands" in a moat enclosing a mounded tomb is present only in these two tumuli, the sharing of such an unusual plan suggests to Japanese archaeologists that the two were built by local chiefs belonging to a single lineage. Furthermore, because the three tumuli are all characterized by dug-out stone coffins of the same type, Japanese archaeologists believe that a local chief buried in the Hotoda-Yakushizuka tumulus was also from the same lineage as the other two, although the moat of Hotoda-Yakushizuka remains unexcavated.

Ide-Futagoyama is distinguished from the other two mounds. In its close vicinity, thirteen small circular tumuli were built by the late sixth century (Shimizu and Ōtsuka 2003), nearly 100 years after its original construction. Hotoda-Hachimanzuka and Hotoda-Yakushizuka are not accompanied by small circular tumuli in their vicinities, although the other two keyhole tumuli are characterized by approximately the same mound size and the same quantity and quality of grave goods. For those buried in the thirteen small circular tumuli and their relatives, it meant a great deal to build their graves in close vicinity to the founding ancestor of their lineage, who developed the land. We see similar phenomena at *kofun* in Nagano 長野 Prefecture and Yamagata 山形 Prefecture. Such phenomena clearly indicate that tumuli were more than graves and had social significance in the Kofun period.

Third and finally, it is also necessary to defend my decision to use the concept of the "center" in relation to the notion of a tumulus as a political monument. The "center" during the Kofun period was always located in present-day Nara, Osaka, and southern Kyoto prefectures, a region that

Figure 7.2 Urama-Chausuyama Keyhole Tumulus in Okayama. The tumulus (shown in black) was built as half of the Hashihaka tumulus (shown in red) according to the same construction plan. After Hōjō 1986.

came to be referred to as "Kinai" 畿内 in historic times.[1] In the Early and Middle Kofun period, however, the Kinai polity was not in control or command of all the local regions and areas. Rather, it acted as a representative of all the local polities. Nevertheless, I use the term "center" for the following reasons.

Keyhole tumuli were the most representative of all the burial mounds during the Kofun period, and their morphology changed over time. The largest keyhole tumulus in each chronological phase of the Kofun period is located in Kinai. More importantly, one-half-, one-third-, or one-sixth-scale versions of the largest keyhole tumulus are distributed in various regions of Japan (Wada 1981; Hōjō 1986; Figure 7.2). Whenever a giant keyhole tumulus of a slightly evolved morphology appeared in Kinai, its smaller-scale copies were built in several local regions.

In addition to the "standard keyhole plan," prestige goods were also distributed by the central polity in Kinai. Such prestige goods include Chinese bronze mirrors and jade bracelets, as well as *haniwa* ceramic cylinders and figurines that stood on the mound surface. Chinese bronze mirrors were imported by the central polity, and jade bracelets were made in Kinai. In the case of Wei-dynasty Chinese bronze mirrors with triangular cross-section rims, Kobayashi Yukio (1960, 2006) demonstrated that the highest-ranking chief of the central polity in Kinai distributed extra mirrors cast from the same mold to local elites in many different areas of Japan as a symbol of alliance. Ceramics were locally made with the techniques that craftsmen learned in Kinai. These prestige goods were necessary for local chiefs to distinguish themselves from ordinary people, and local chiefs apparently had to depend on the central polity in Kinai for their procurement. This was the major reason why the central polity in Kinai could maintain itself as the "center." It is also important to note that the political relationship between the "center" and periphery was symbolized by mortuary practices.

[1] The geographical concept or definition of "Kinai" probably did not exist in the Kofun period. However, spatial distribution of exceptionally large keyhole tumuli and extremely rich burial goods correlate with a region that would be called "Kinai" in the eighth century. For this reason, I use the term "Kinai" throughout this chapter to denote a geographical region.

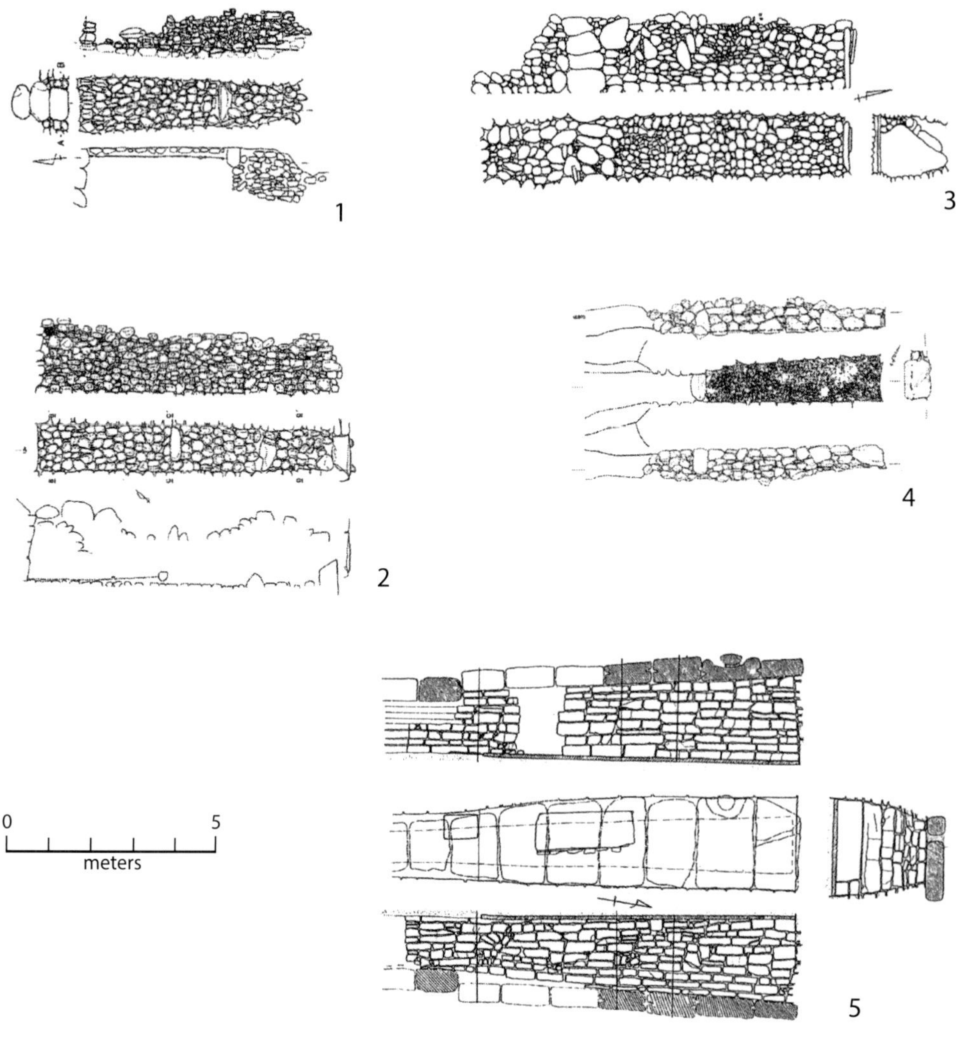

Figure 7.3 Corridor-style Horizontal Burial Chambers in the Sixth Century.
1. Kamiechi No. 1; 2. Uehara No. 1; 3. Hisano No. 4; 4. Shimoyako No. 7;
5. Kinreizuka in the Bōsō peninsula. While 1 through 4 are all circular tumuli located in Kanagawa Prefecture, a western neighbor of Tokyo, and are typical of this area, Kinreizuka was the keyhole tumulus of a very high-ranking chief; the morphology of the Kinreizuka burial chamber was a result of the availability of rocks.

Japan-Korea Interaction Viewed from Eastern Japan—Habuta Yoshiyuki 7

Methodological Frameworks for Archaeological Reconstruction of Prehistoric Interactions

It is necessary to explain methodological frameworks for the interpretation of regional interactions. For the purpose of this chapter, I classify them into three categories.

First, I approach the matter from the perspective of the transportation of materials and objects. In other words, interpretation starts with the recognition of non-local materials and objects. If we can discover the evidence for bilateral transportation from origin to destination and vice versa, an interpretation of mere coincidence would be very unlikely. The larger the quantities of non-local artifacts, the greater the validity of an interpretation becomes. We can draw different interpretations according to, for example, artifacts representing daily utensils or ritual paraphernalia. Archaeologists must be cautious because in some cases, objects and materials were transported indirectly by the hands of several agencies. It is also necessary to make distinctions among objects transported from a certain place of origin, those locally made with the production technique accurately adopted from the place of origin, and those locally imitated without mastering the original technique. Such distinctions require extremely careful observation of artifacts. Scientific techniques such as sourcing raw clay for pottery give support for archaeological observations.

The second category is to approach interaction from the perspective of archaeological features of a non-local nature. Archaeological features are not transportable; thus it is unlikely that "middle men" would have transported a feature from the origin to a destination. Such a feature would be good evidence for foreign people settled in a different region or local people having traveled to a foreign region and mastered foreign customs of building, for example, residences and graves. This approach leads us to a more robust interpretation of interaction. At the same time, it is often difficult to determine whether a feature is of a foreign origin because such a feature may be locally adapted.

One example is the case of corridor-style horizontal burial chambers in Late Kofun–period Japan (Figure 7.3). In the western Bōsō 房総 peninsula, very narrow corridor-style horizontal burial chambers were adopted as the tombs of local chiefs. This is in marked contrast with other regions, where very narrow corridor-style horizontal burial chambers are usually found in the tombs of low-ranking elites. Usually, wide and large corridor-style horizontal burial chambers would have been appropriate for high-ranking elite tombs. Such an adaptation in the Bōsō peninsula was necessary because high-quality rock hard enough to allow bridging both sides of a wide burial chamber was unavailable in the Bōsō region. Consequently, local chiefs in the Bōsō region built narrow but unusually long burial chambers to increase the floor area. This case indicates that when people immigrated to a new region and built their residences in new locations, it was sometimes necessary to modify the structures to adapt to the local environment. There are other factors that influence the structure and appearance of architectural features, and a comparison of such architectural features demands caution.

The third category is to approach the problem of interaction from the standpoint of ideology based on analyses of evidence of rituals. A reconstruction of rituals in an effort to determine human cognition is not impossible when archaeologists have very good data in secure archaeological contexts and adopt appropriate steps of interpretation and logic. It is possible to argue for close interactions between two regions if unprecedented rituals suddenly come to be adopted in one region and are subsequently continued in the other region. In the case of adopting burial chambers of extra-local tradition, highly capable craftsmen might be able to construct a burial chamber of foreign style with the appropriate construction methods and techniques, based on precise information about the burial chambers of the extra-local region.[2] In this sense, an approach from the standpoint of human cognition as evidenced by rituals is useful for the interpretation of regional interaction because it would be difficult to imitate rituals of foreign origin. In order to imitate rituals, participants must master not only the physical movements but also the thoughts and ideas that lay behind these movements in their place of origin. If we find the same rituals practiced in different regions, we might suspect that a movement of people took place between these regions. With these three frameworks in mind, I proceed to analyze Kofun-period material culture thought to be of Korean origin.

Approach to Material Culture of Korean Origins in Eastern Japan

It is well accepted that cultures of the Yayoi and Kofun periods constantly received cultural and technological stimuli and influence from the Korean peninsula. Furthermore, numerous Japanese archaeologists maintain a strong preconception that the Korean material influence was first

[2] Of course, a burial chamber built in a foreign region may undergo morphological transformations that distinguish it from those of the place of origin. In any case, we must carefully observe the style and structure as well as evidence for construction methods and techniques.

received in northern Kyushu, then transmitted to Kinai, and finally diffused to other regions of Japan (e.g. Kirihara 2001; Nishitani 2001; Ōtsuka 2001). Based on the geographical proximity of northern Kyushu to the Korean peninsula and the discoveries of large quantities of material of Korean origin in northern Kyushu, I agree with these views in that the main route of importing Korean material culture ran through northern Kyushu. At the same time, I am against the position of those scholars who deny the possibility of other routes of importing Korean material culture. I emphasize that, even in medieval Japan (fourteenth to sixteenth centuries A.D.) when Japan was already in the stage of a mature state,[3] we know from written sources that locally influential lords independently maintained active trade relationships with foreign countries. This is particularly the case with Tsushima Island, where local lords were loyal to and subjected to both Japan and Korea at the same time (Murai 1993). These examples strongly suggest the unlikelihood of adopting modern national boundaries and trade relations under the centralized control of early Japan.[4]

Keeping in mind the possibility of various routes for the importing of Korean material culture, I will review a few chronologically representative examples of Korean material culture discovered in eastern Japan. These include an iron sword and bronze belt hook dating to the end of the Yayoi period (early third century) in the central highlands of Japan; cairns that appeared in the late fifth century in various regions of eastern Japan (present-day Aichi 愛知, Shizuoka 静岡, Nagano, Yamanashi 山梨, and Gunma prefectures); and artifacts of Silla origin in the late sixth to the beginning of the seventh centuries in present-day Gunma Prefecture. These illustrate a temporal change in patterns of Japanese interaction with Korea.

Historically, eastern Japan is defined as the regions to the east of the three ancient barrier stations (the *sankan* 三関, or three checkpoint gates). The three are Fuwa 不破 in present-day Gifu Prefecture, Arachi 愛発 in present-day Fukui Prefecture, and Suzuka 鈴鹿 in present-day Mie

[3] Other archaeologists and historians have various ideas about when Japan reached the stage of a mature state, but it is beyond the scope of this paper to review this important debate. All scholars agree that by the seventh century A.D. a mature state had formed in Japan.

[4] I am aware that fortresses were built in Tsushima, which is clearly a reflection of a Japanese consciousness of the boundary with Korea. Such forts were built in Japan only when the central government was strong and when tension with neighboring polities was high. Indeed, these historical phenomena were very limited.

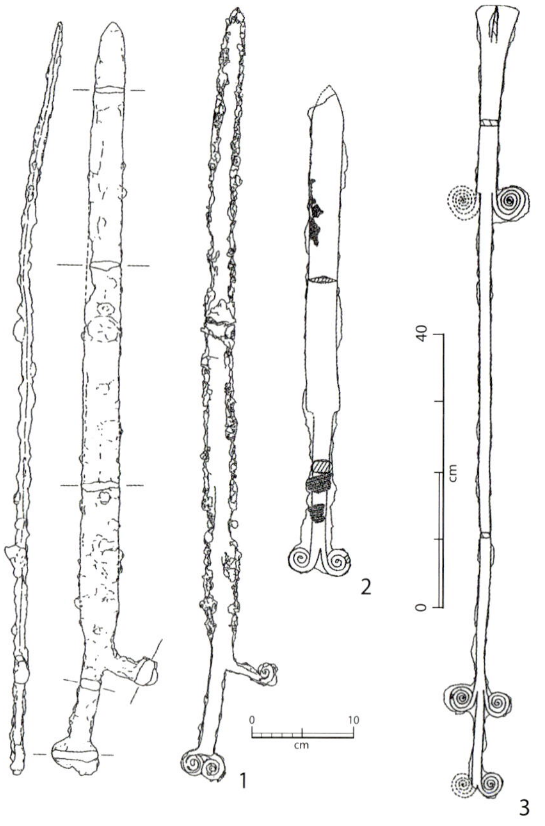

Figure 7.4 Iron Swords and Objects with Whirlpool-pattern Decorations.
1. Iron sword discovered at the Nezuka site, northern Shinano (Yoshihara 2002);
2. Iron sword discovered at Tomb 212 at Yangdong-ni, Kimhae (Tongŭi Taehakkyo Pangmulgwan 2000);
3. Iron object discovered at Tomb 212 at Yangdong-ni, Kimhae (Tongŭi Taehakkyo Pangmulgwan 2000).

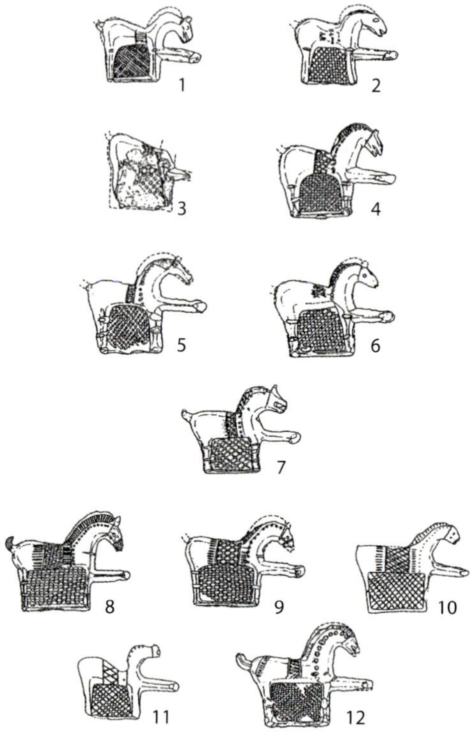

Figure 7.5 Horse-shaped Bronze Belt Buckles. From Kazama 2006. 1–6, 8, 9, and 12. From the Ch'ŏngdang-dong site in Ch'ŏnan; 7. From the Asakawabata site in northern Shinano; 10 and 11. From the Sŏngdong-ni site in Sangju.

Prefecture. Eastern Japan was a world very different from western Japan, where several regions were under the direct control of the central authority in Kinai. Although the spatial extent of eastern Japan varied slightly over time, in this chapter I adopt the definition described above.

Material Culture of Korean Origin at the End of the Yayoi Period in the Central Highlands of Japan

While calendrical dates for the Yayoi period are being hotly debated (Imamura et al. 2003; see Iwanaga, this volume), I consider the date of the Late Yayoi period as first to early third century A.D. and the beginning of the Kofun period as the middle to late third century A.D. In this section, I examine an iron sword with whirlpool-pattern decoration discovered at the Nezuka 根塚 site, Kijimadaira 木島平 Village (Figure 7.4), and a horse-shaped bronze belt hook discovered at the Asakawabata 浅川端 site, Nagano City (Figure 7.5), both in northern Nagano Prefecture (see Map 7.1 for locations).

The iron sword in question is the only one of its kind ever discovered in Japan. It is 74 cm long, with whirlpool-pattern decorations attached to the end of the hilt and at the sword-guard. It was one of two iron swords discovered in Zone B of the Nezuka site and was apparently buried intentionally with pottery dated to the early to middle third century A.D. (late Hakoshimizu 箱清水 type). Although the character of the archaeological feature of this discovery is not clear, archaeologists speculate that it was a burial. The site itself is situated on a very low elevation of 7 to 10 m above the present level of the surrounding rice paddies, and archaeological features ranging from the Jōmon to medieval periods have been discovered there (Yoshihara 2002).

Although this sword is extremely unusual in Japan, whirlpool patterns were commonly adopted in the southeastern part of the Korean peninsula during the proto-Three Kingdoms to the Three Kingdoms period, especially in the Kimhae and Ulsan regions. In particular, excavations of the Yangdong-ni 良洞里 cemetery site (Tongŭi Taehakkyo Pangmulgwan 2000) yielded several iron swords with whirlpool-pattern decorations.

Besides the Nezuka sword, another line of evidence that gives strong support for close interaction with the Kimhae region is the discovery of a Yayoi pottery sherd with the inscribed Chinese character *da* 大. It is a sherd of Hakoshimizu-type pottery discovered in Zone I of the Nezuka site. After pottery was fired, a sharp, spatula-like object was used first to engrave the character 入, and then a stroke of 一 was added from right to left. The stroke

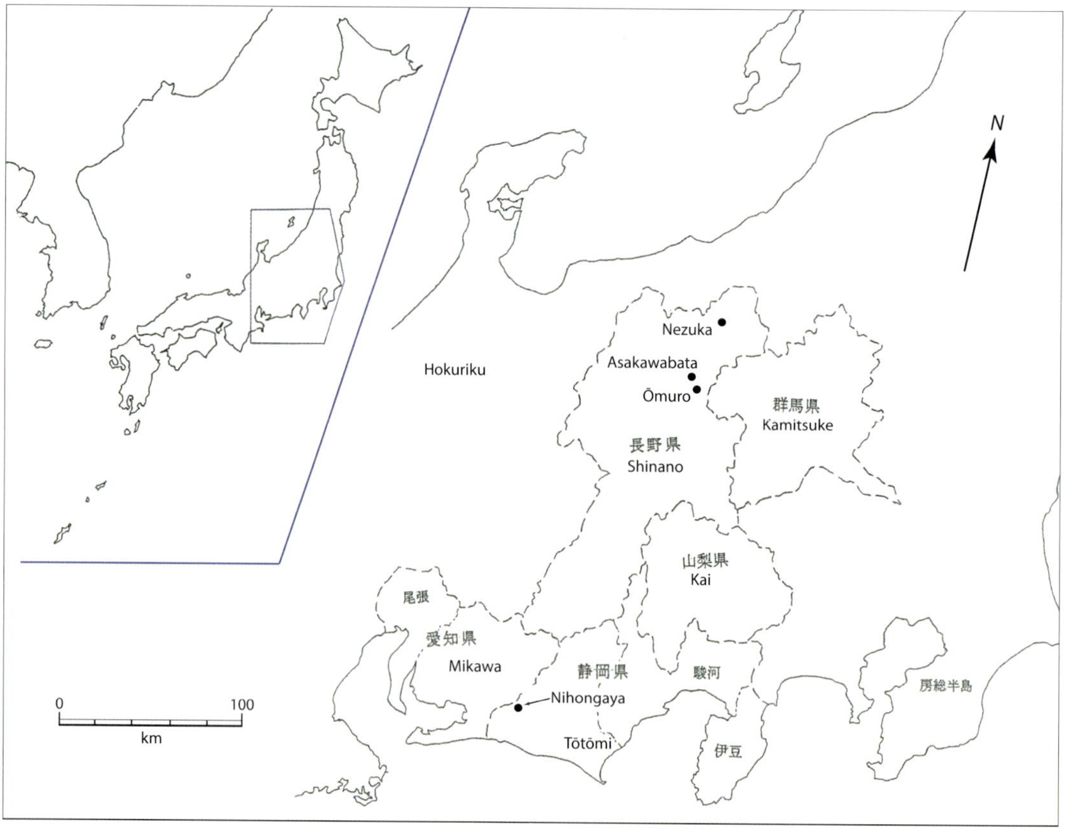

Map 7.1 Regions and Sites Mentioned in This Chapter.

order is the reverse of the usual. It is important to note that this stroke order was adapted to inscriptions on sixth-century pottery in the Korean peninsula (Hirakawa 2002). Moreover, at the Taho-ri 茶户里 site in Ch'angwŏn 昌原, the western neighbor of Kimhae, a brush dating to the late first century B.C. was discovered (Yi et al. 2008), suggesting that a writing system had reached the southern tip of the Korean peninsula by that time. Therefore, it is likely that the engraving of 大 on the Nezuka sherd was a result of interaction with the southern part of the Korean peninsula.

Another line of evidence suggestive of interaction with the Korean peninsula is a horse-shaped bronze belt buckle discovered at the Asakawabata site. Although the belt buckle was discovered in occupational debris (Shimizu and Kazama 2005), it was probably made in the third century, owing to chronological frameworks presented by Taketani (1997) and Kim (2000) and to careful and detailed typological analyses by Kazama (2006). Belt buckles discovered in the Korean peninsula went through three phases of change, and the earliest type is represented by one discovered at the Ŏŭn-dong 漁隱洞 site in Yŏngch'ŏn 永川 (Phase 1). In the second phase, belt buckles became prevalent in the southern Korean peninsula in places such as Kyŏngju and Kimhae. Then the spatial distribution extended to the west-central regions such as Kyŏnggi 京畿 Province. The Asakawabata example shares "representations of a tail, mouth, and ears" with one discovered in Tomb 5 at the Ch'ŏngdang-dong 清堂洞 site in Ch'ŏnan 天安 (Kazama 2006:153). Several other similar examples have been discovered at this site, and they are characterized by "a mane depicted in lines, a series of dots from the neck to body, and a diagonal lattice pattern on the back and saddle flap" (Kazama 2006:146). Therefore, Kamaza concludes that the Asakawabata belt buckle is contemporaneous to the examples from the Ch'ŏngdang-dong site in Ch'ŏnan and dated to the third century A.D. While the Asakawabata belt buckle may be traced back to the west-central regions of the Korean peninsula, a possibility exists that the belt buckle was brought to Japan via the Kimhae region.

I argue that these artifacts of Korean origin were imported without the intermediation of polities in Kinai but rather directly to the Hokuriku 北陸 region (Sea of Japan coast of central Japan). Archaeological evidence that would give support to my hypothesis is the spatial distribution of a particular type of bronze bracelet and iron sword in Nagano Prefecture. Bronze bracelets comprise 40 percent of the metal artifacts dated to the Late Yayoi period in Nagano Prefecture (Nozawa 2002). The type of bronze bracelet in question is distributed only in eastern Japan and is ring- or spiral-shaped and characterized by an oval cross-section. Similar bracelets have been discovered at the P'yŏngni-dong 平里洞 site in Taegu, Korea. In Nagano, these bracelets are primarily discovered in burial contexts, as in the Korean case. The spatial distributions of the bronze bracelets and iron swords overlap in Nagano, where the largest quantities of iron objects have been discovered in eastern Japan. Therefore, I consider it likely that polities in the central highlands of Japan had control over the distribution of iron in eastern Japan, which was imported via the Sea of Japan (East Sea).

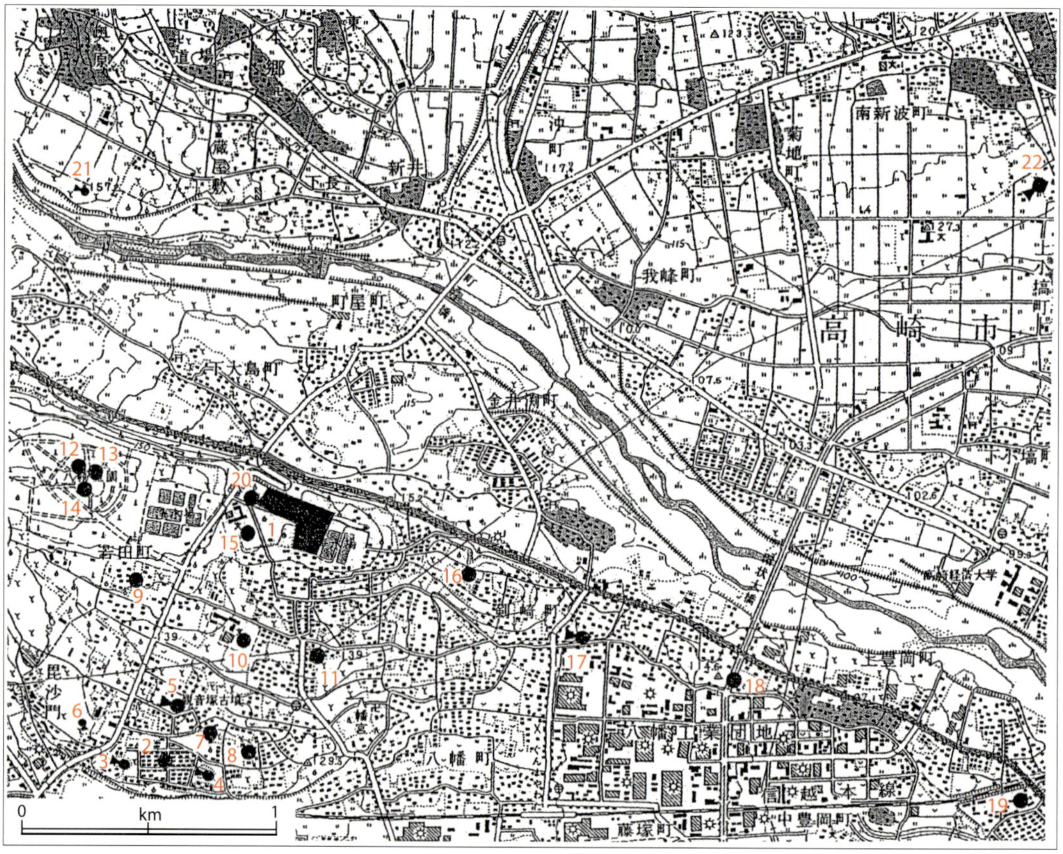

Figure 7.6 Vicinity of the Kenzaki-Nagatoro-Nishi Site. From Habuta 2003.
1. Kenzaki-Nagatoro-Nishi; 2. Hiratsuka keyhole tumulus; 3. Yawata-Kan'nonzuka.

At present, archaeologists do not have solid archaeological evidence for polities in the Hokuriku region directly trading with the Korean peninsula. The records for Emperor Kinmei 欽明 in the *Nihon shoki* 日本書紀 (Chronicles of Japan) (Kinmei 31/4–5; 2:128–129) state that a local chief in Hokuriku misrepresented himself as the ruler of Japan to Koguryŏ people who had been adrift at sea and had reached land at Hokuriku in 570 A.D. By the late sixth century, the central polity of Kinai gained unparalleled power over local polities in Japan (Naoki 1958).[5] Yet, the central government of Kinai could not hide the reality of a local polity autonomously interacting with foreign regions. This leads me to suspect that direct interaction between the Korean peninsula and the Hokuriku region took place in the Late Yayoi period and that material culture of Korean origin reached the central highlands of Japan via Hokuriku.

Late Fifth-Century Evidence for Immigrants from Korea in Eastern Japan

In the late fifth century, a highly distinctive burial custom of constructing cairns started in many different regions of eastern Japan, such as eastern Mikawa 三河 (present Aichi), western Tōtōmi 遠江 (Shizuoka), northern Shinano 信濃 (Nagano), Kai 甲斐 (Yamanashi), and western Kamitsuke (Gunma) (Map 7.1). These regions did not share cultural traits nor form a political unity. I discuss possible reasons why cairns appeared in these regions, with special reference to western Kamitsuke, where I have conducted fieldwork. I argue that patterns of interaction with the Korean peninsula and ways in which local Japanese people interacted with Korean immigrants differed from one region to another. In other words, because these local regions remained relatively autonomous in the fifth century, each region on its own initiative interacted with people of the Korean peninsula.

In western Kamitsuke, at the Kenzaki-Nagatoro-Nishi 剣崎長瀞西 cemetery site, we have discovered good evidence for immigrants from the Korean peninsula (Kuroda 2002; Habuta 2003). The site is located in the present Takasaki City, western Kamitsuke region (present-day Gunma Prefecture). The site is situated on a hill extending east–west, and is spatially divided into two clusters of archaeological features bisected in the center by a north–south hollow. The western half is Zone I, and the eastern half is Zone II. Archaeological features range from pit dwellings of the Late Yayoi period to seventh-century tumuli, and I focus on the late fifth-century features (Figures 7.6 and 7.7).

[5] In the late fifth century, locally influential lords were incorporated into the rudimentary system of the central government, called the *hito* system. Under this system, locally influential lords paid visits to the center for greetings. In the middle sixth century, the central government for the first time appointed provincial governors in all the regions of western Japan and part of eastern Japan. However, these provincial governors were all selected from locally influential lords and were not dispatched from the central government.

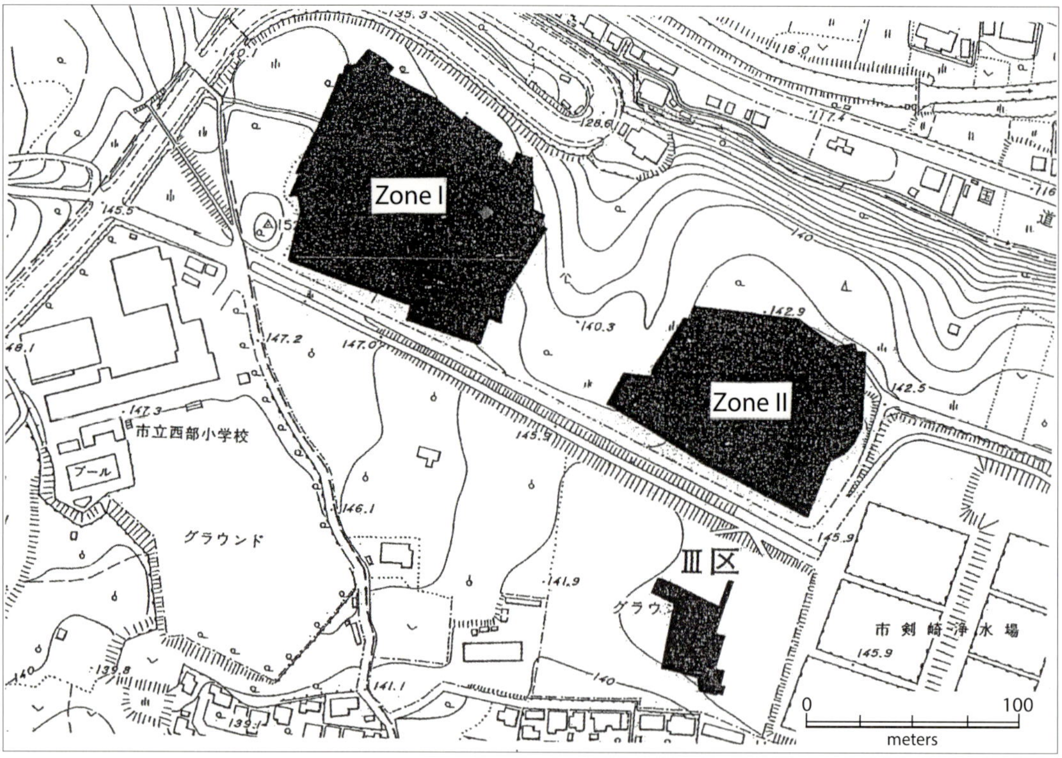

Figure 7.7 The Kenzaki-Nagatoro-Nishi Site.
From Habuta 2003.

In the late fifth century, while the western half (Zone I) was designated as a cemetery, the eastern half (Zone II) was a residential compound. Among the thirty-one late fifth-century pit dwellings excavated, twenty-six were accompanied by earthen stoves. Since earthen stoves became prevalent in the late sixth century in eastern Japan, the exceptionally early date of the earthen stoves at this site suggests that Korean immigrants resided there.

The eastern half of the cemetery consists of square mounds, some of which are cairns, and circular mounds (Figure 7.8, Table 7.1). Sixteen of the mounds were excavated, two of which turned out to date to the late sixth or seventh century (Nos. 8 and 19). Cairns are entirely constructed with

Table 7.1
List of Tomb Mounds at the Kenzaki-Nagatoro-Nishi Site

No.	Mound form	Size (m)	Artifacts	Other features
1	Circular	22	*haniwa* ceramic objects	terrace in the middle of the slope; enclosed by a moat of 2 m in width
2	Circular	10	*haniwa* ceramic objects, earthenware bowl	
3	Circular	17	*haniwa* ceramic objects	terrace in the middle of the slope; enclosed by a moat of 2 m in width
4	Circular	16	*haniwa* ceramic objects	terrace in the middle of the slope
5	Square	6.6x5.7	iron sword	pit-style burial chamber (2.5 by 0.5 m)
6	Circular	10	*haniwa* ceramic objects, earthenware bowl	pit-style burial chamber (1.8 by 0.4 m)
7	Circular	10	*haniwa* ceramic objects	
9	Square	10x9		terrace in the middle of the slope?
10	Square	9x8.2	gold earring, Korean-type pottery	
11	Cairn	2.6x2.3		pit-style burial chamber (1.1 by 0.4 m)
14	Cairn	2.9x2.3		pit-style burial chamber (0.9 by 0.4 m)
15	Cairn	1.6x1.1		pit-style burial chamber (0.9? by 0.3 m)
16	Cairn	2.2?x0.9		pit-style burial chamber (0.9? by 0.3 m)
18	Circular	14	*haniwa* ceramic objects	enclosed by a moat
20	Circular	14	*haniwa* ceramic objects	enclosed by a moat
100	Cairn	4.2x3.7	*haniwa* ceramic objects, earthenware bowl	pit-style burial chamber (1.5? by 0.4 m)

All figures are approximate.
Sixth-century tombs, such as No. 8 and No. 19, are omitted.
No. 12 is a pit-style burial chamber only and not accompanied by a mound.
No. 13 is a pit where a horse was buried.

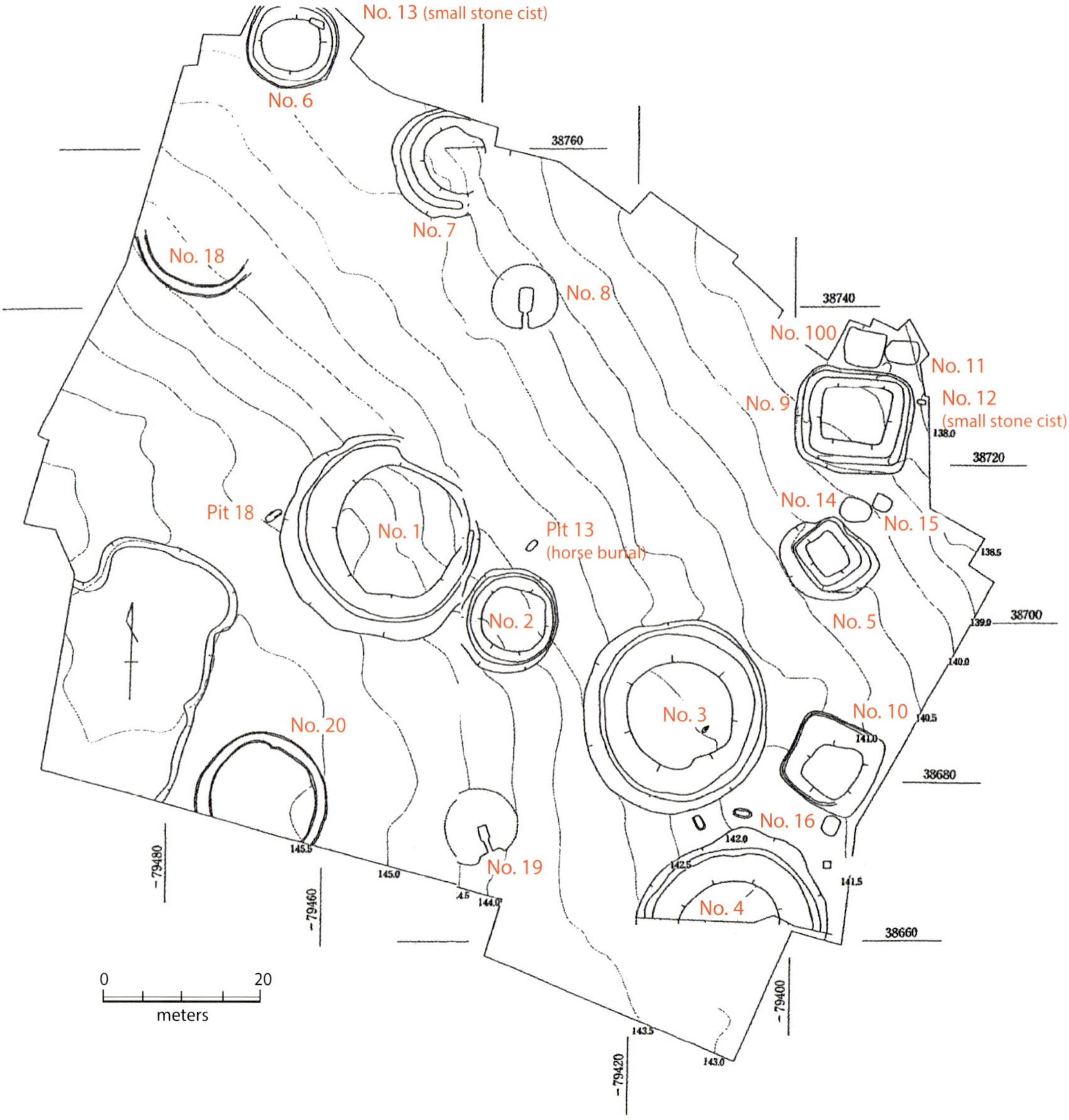

Figure 7.8 Spatial Distribution of Burial Mounds in Zone I of the Kenzaki-Nagatoro-Nishi Site. From Habuta 2003.

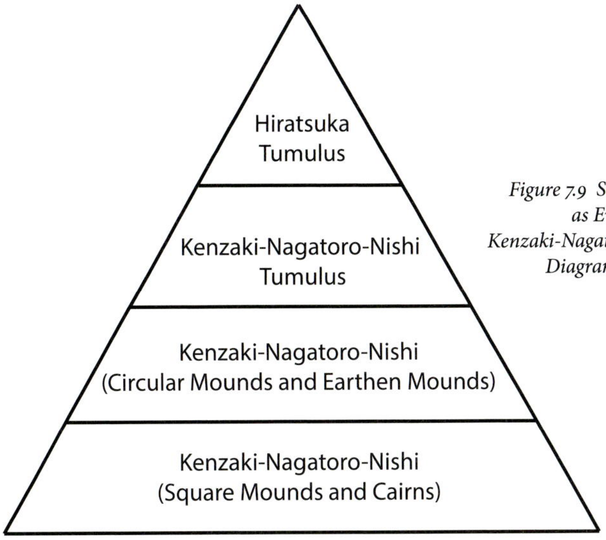

Figure 7.9 Social Hierarchy as Evidenced by the Kenzaki-Nagatoro-Nishi Area. Diagram by the author.

cobbles, and the square tombs are "cairns" placed on the top of the earthen foundations. Archaeologists consider them to be the burials of immigrants from the peninsula, while the circular mounds are the burials of local indigenous people. Square mounds are distinguished from the ordinary circular mounds in many respects. The square mounds are in general smaller than the circular mounds. Ceramics made with Korean techniques and gold earrings were discovered only in square tombs, and the square mounds lack the traditional Japanese *haniwa* ceramic objects. Moreover, the discovery of a horse with horse trappings made in the Naktong 洛東 River region, sacrificed and buried in a pit in the middle of the cemetery, also suggests the presence of Korean immigrants at this site because the custom of horse riding was introduced from the Korean peninsula in the fifth century. It is also likely that the Korean immigrants' primary activity was to raise and breed horses.[6]

At the same time, the construction technique for both the circular and square mounds is the same. An earthen foundation was carved out from the

[6] While the largest number of Kofun-period horse trappings have been discovered in Nagano Prefecture, the second largest number have been discovered in Gunma Prefecture. At the Shiroi sites in Gunma Prefecture, archaeologists discovered a horse pasture with numerous hoofprints of horses.

Figure 7.10 Aerial Photograph of Zone I of the Kenzaki-Nagatoro-Nishi Site. Photograph courtesy of the Takasaki-shi Kyōiku Iinkai 高崎市教育委員会 *(Takasaki Municipal Board of Education).*

Figure 7.11 Gold Earring Discovered in Tomb No. 10 of the Kenzaki-Nagatoro-Nishi Site. Photograph courtesy of the Takasaki-shi Kyōiku Iinkai 高崎市教育委員会 *(Takasaki Municipal Board of Education).*

ground. A smaller mound was placed on the earthen foundation, thereby leaving the space of a terrace. A small pit-style burial chamber was constructed in the smaller mound on the foundation. The smaller-scale mounds lack a terrace. In the case of the well-preserved Mound No. 6, the mound top was paved with cobbles, and a small pit-style burial chamber was placed at the center. The surface of the mound was covered with cobbles. Even the circular, earthen mounds have an appearance similar to that of cairns.

Analyses of the Kenzaki-Nagatoro-Nishi cemetery indicate some degree of social differentiation among people in western Kamitsuke in the late fifth century (Figure 7.9). The paramount chief of this region was buried in the Hiratsuka tumulus, a keyhole tomb of 105 m in length, located 1.5 km to the southwest of the Kenzaki-Nagatoro-Nishi cemetery site. It was built in the late fifth century and has a dug-out stone coffin that is a symbol of alliance among high-ranking elites in western Kamitsuke at that time. *Haniwa* ceramic cylinders discovered at the Hiratsuka tumulus are contemporaneous with those discovered in the Kenzaki-Nagatoro-Nishi cemetery. A local chief who probably held power over both the local Japanese people and Korean immigrants is buried in the Kenzaki-Nagatoro-Nishi tumulus, situated at the highest point of the cemetery, in its southwestern part. It has a circular mound of 36 m in diameter with a projection. An excavation of the tumulus yielded rich burial goods, including a bronze mirror, iron cuirass, iron spear, and talc models of various objects. The local chief buried in the Kenzaki-Nagatoro-Nishi tumulus is presumed to be an "intermediate class" elite.

Under the Kenzaki-Nagatoro-Nishi chief, it seems that those buried in the circular mounds occupied a slightly higher social status than those buried in the square mounds at the Kenzaki-Nagatoro-Nishi tumulus group. Not only are the circular mounds larger, but the square mounds are clustered in a smaller area. The sacrificial horse pit that is a representation of Korean custom is situated by a circular mound, rather than a square mound. These suggest that the Korean immigrants occupied a slightly lower social status than local Japanese people, and perhaps that the immigrants were not allowed to build circular mounds. The gold earring deposited in a square mound, which otherwise would have been an elite status symbol (Takada 1998), probably indicates the Korean identity of the individual buried in the mound (Figures 7.10 and 7.11).

Yet, the social differentiation between those buried in the circular mounds and those in the square mounds is not marked. The structure of the mounds is basically the same for both. Both groups lived in pit

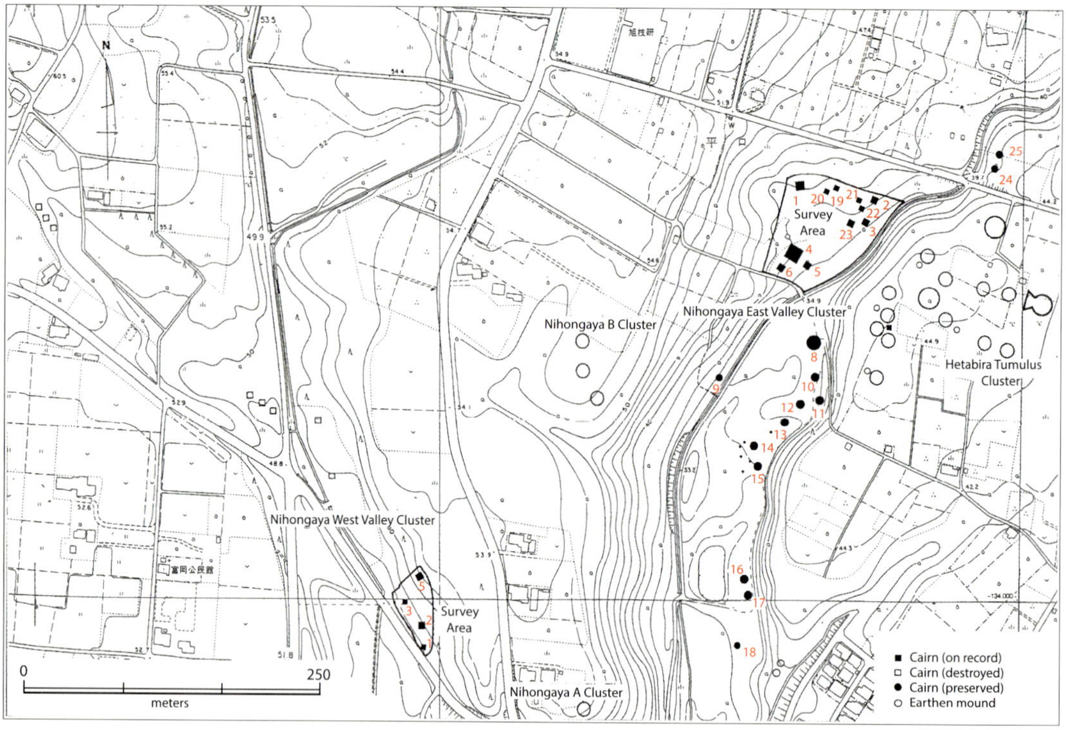

Figure 7.12 Nihongaya and Hetabira Tumulus Groups. Cairns (filled in black) located on the bottom of a valley constitute the Nihongaya tumulus group, and earthen mounds (filled in white) located in the upland region constitute the Hetabira tumulus group. From Kuno et al. 2000.

dwellings with earthen stoves (Zone II). Because the social differentiation was not marked, both groups came to adopt circular mounds by the end of the sixth century. Although archaeologists have not discovered mounds dated to the early sixth century in the Kenzaki-Nagatoro-Nishi area, all the mounds built after the end of the sixth century are circular and constructed of earth. The social status of the descendants of Korean immigrants rose, or perhaps they were assimilated into the local Japanese population. I will return to this point at the end of this chapter.

Figure 7.13 Nihongaya Tumulus Group. Photograph by author.

The context of the construction of cairns in the late fifth century in western Tōtōmi is similar to that of Kamitsuke, as evidenced by the Nihongaya 二本ケ谷 tumulus group (Figures 7.12 and 7.13; Kuno, Suzuki et al. 2000). In northern Shinano, however, the context is considerably different from that of western Kamitsuke and western Tōtōmi. Apparently, there was no strong authority in this region to determine the size and form of burial mounds according to social status in the late fifth and sixth centuries. At the Ōmuro 大室 cemetery, Nagano City (northern Shinano), more than 550 burial mounds were constructed, the majority of which are cairns. The construction of cairns started in the third quarter of the fifth century, and the construction of earthen mounds started in the middle sixth century (Figures 7.14, 7.15, and 7.16; Otsuka et al. 1993; Otsuka and Kobayashi 2006; Kobayashi Saburō et al. 2008; Sasaki et al. 2015; Sasaki, this volume). All of them are circular mounds, and it is impossible to distinguish the tombs of immigrants from those of local people. There are no burials of prominent chiefs after the early fifth century in this area, which suggests that there was no authority to control newly arrived Korean immigrants as well as local people.

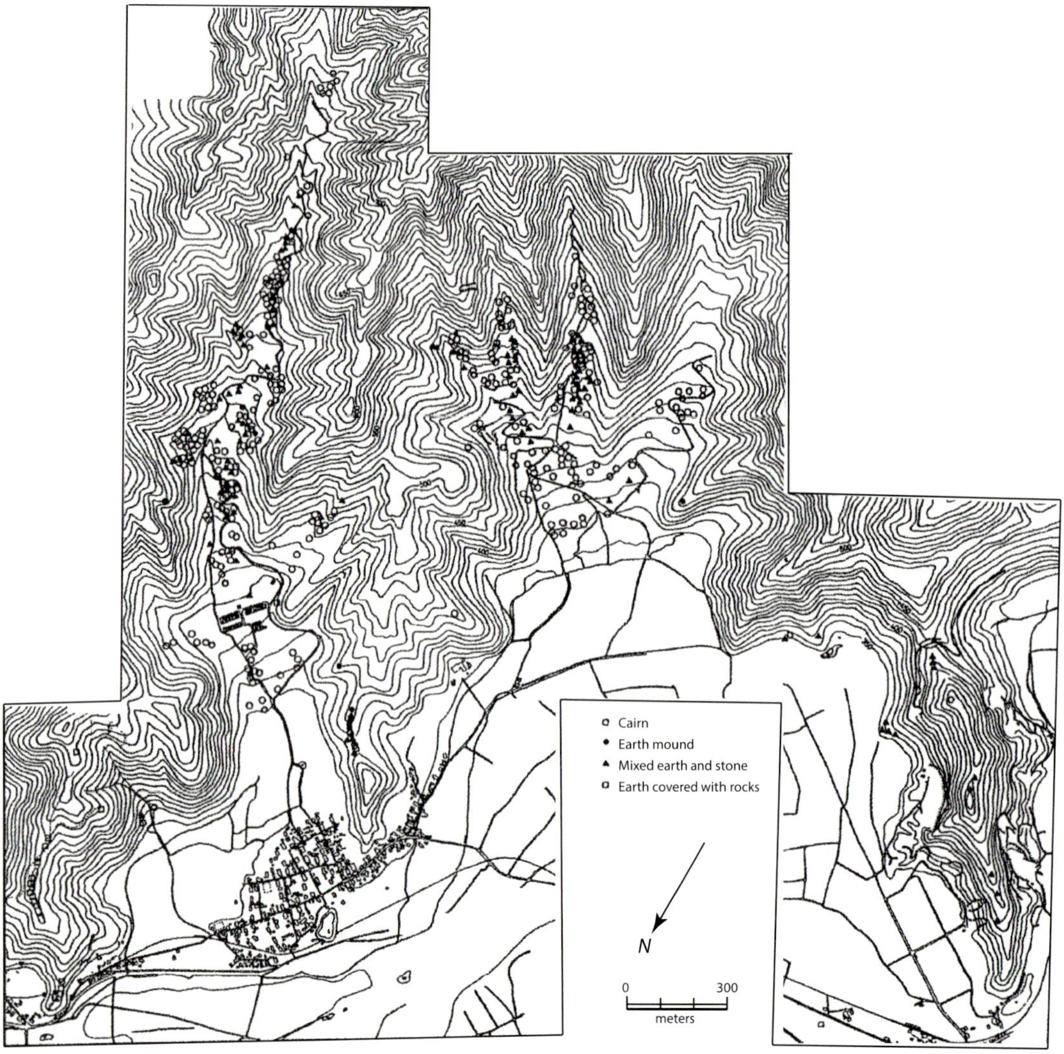

Figure 7.14 Ōmuro Tumulus Group. White circles: cairns; black dots: earthen mounds; black triangles: mounds constructed with cobbles and earth; white squares: earthen mounds with surface covered with cobbles. After Kurata 1981.

Figure 7.15 Ōmuro Tumulus Group. Photograph by author.

Yet another case of incorporating Korean immigrants into local Japanese populations is evidenced in the Ina 伊那 basin in southern Shinano. In this region, the custom of sacrificing horses was introduced in the middle fifth century (Shibuya 2007), which is exceptionally early for eastern Japan. Because the custom of horse sacrifice is an ideological matter and cannot easily be imitated (the third methodological framework discussed above), it is undoubtedly the case that people moved there from the Korean peninsula in the middle fifth century and later. Furthermore, residences with earthen stoves and *sue* stoneware appeared in the middle fifth century, which is also extremely early for eastern Japan. These phenomena give support for my suspicion regarding the presence of Korean immigrants from the middle fifth century.

Recently, three very small cairns have been discovered at the Kitakata Nishinohara site, Iida City. The three are less than 2 m square and 25 to 35 cm in height, and the burial chambers were constructed underground. Typological analysis of the iron knives and arrowheads recovered from the cairns suggests that the three were constructed in the late fifth century

Figure 7.16 Ōmuro Tumulus Group. Photograph by author.

(Shibuya and Furukawa 2017). As in the case of the Kenzaki-Nagatoro-Nishi site in Gunma Prefecture, the cairns might be evidence for Korean immigrants in this region.

The construction of several keyhole tumuli of 50 to 90 m started suddenly in the middle fifth century (Yamashita 2003). The reasons for the unprecedented construction of keyhole tumuli in the middle fifth century would be that the Yamato authority considered the Iida 飯田 basin strategically important for breeding horses and that the basin was chosen to be part of a route to eastern Japan from Yamato. In the sixth century, when dense clusters of small circular mounds appeared in many regions of Japan, the construction of such clustered mounds did not take place in this region. While the local social organization did not develop to be complex and ranked, the Yamato authority raised the social status of local chiefs. Therefore, a system of social ranking reflected by differences in mortuary practices did not fully function in the Ina society during the Kofun period. Because of the lack of such a system, neither local Japanese people nor Korean immigrants built conspicuous tombs at that time.

Material Culture of Korean Origin in Western Kamitsuke in the Late Kofun Period

After the early sixth century, material culture originating from a few specific locations in Korea came to be widely distributed in eastern Japan. This is probably a reflection of the Yamato authority gaining monopoly power over diplomatic and economic relationships with the Korean peninsula, although local polities in Japan still maintained some right to interact with polities in the peninsula independently from the Yamato authority. In this section, I examine the phenomenon of the centralized distribution of the Korean materials with reference to western Kamitsuke (Map 7.2).

In western Kamitsuke, material culture of Korean origin is excavated in tumuli of the late sixth and beginning of the seventh centuries. These tumuli were the burials of local chiefs or those very close to them (Habuta 2009). Archaeologists have not discovered such materials in the burials of Korean immigrants or ordinary local Japanese people. Among the materials of Korean origin, I pay particular attention to those produced in Silla.[7] Relevant materials have been excavated at the Watanuki-Kan'non'yama 綿貫観音山 keyhole tomb of the late sixth century (97.5 m; a in Map 7.2), the Yawata-Kan'nonzuka 八幡観音塚 keyhole tomb of the beginning of the seventh century (97 m; b in Map 7.2; Figures 7.17, 7.18, 7.19), the Koizumi-Ōtsukagoshi 小泉大塚越 No. 3 keyhole tomb of the late sixth century (55 m; c in Map 7.2), the Koizumi-Nagatsuka 小泉長塚 No. 1 mound of the late sixth century (mound form and size unknown; c in Map 7.2), the Kinkanzuka 金冠塚 keyhole tomb of the late sixth century (37 m; d in Map 7.2), and the Ishihara-Inariyama 石原稲荷山 circular tumulus of the end of the sixth century (30 m in diameter; e in Map 7.2). Individual artifacts are listed in Table 7.2. All of the tumuli of the late sixth century contained corridor-style horizontal burial chambers constructed with hornblende andesite, which symbolized an alliance of local chiefs in western Kamitsuke. I suspect that local chiefs did not obtain the Silla materials independently from one another.

[7] Thus far Japanese archaeologists have paid great attention to material culture of Paekche origin and little to that of Silla origin because it is historically known that Japan maintained friendly diplomatic relationships with Paekche and hostile relationships with Silla. Recently, however, Takada Kanta (2004, 2006) has called for greater attention to the material culture of Silla origin discovered in Japan. I support his position.

Table 7.2
Artifacts of Korean Origins from Tombs in Western Kamitsuke

Tomb	Mound form	Mound size	Date	Artifacts of Korean origins (Silla, Paekche)
Watanuki-Kan'non'yama	Keyhole-shaped	97.5 m	late sixth century	sword with egg-shaped gilt-bronze pommel, sword with club-shaped openwork pommel, sword with silver dragon design, iron knife with silver fitting, iron cuirass and armor with fittings, bit with gilt-bronze cheek plates, saddle, gilt-bronze heart-shaped decorative pendant (*gyōyō*) for horse, bronze ring with bells, gilt-bronze petal-shaped decorative pendant for horse, bronze water pitcher, gilt-bronze semi-spherical objects, gilt-bronze belt with bells, bronze mirror with beast pattern (cast from an identical mold with one discovered at King Muryŏng)
Yawata-Kan'nonzuka	Keyhole-shaped	97 m	beginning of seventh century	sword with silver-covered hilt, sword with cockscomb-shaped pommel, silver fitting with arabesque pattern of a sheath, iron knife with silver fitting, silver nock for a bow, gilt-bronze openwork pendant (*gyōyō*) for horse, harness fittings with gilt-bronze bells, gilt-bronze heart-shaped openwork decorative pendants for horse, gilt-bronze flower-shaped decorative pendant for horse, bronze bowl with a lid, lozenge silver object, iron cuirass and armor
Koizumi-Ōtsukagoshi No. 3	Keyhole-shaped	55 m	late sixth century	gilt-bronze crown, sword with ring pommel, bronze bell (part of horse trapping)
Koizumi-Nagatsuka No. 1	Unknown		late sixth century	gilt-bronze crown, sword with ring pommel
Kinkanzuka	Keyhole-shaped	37 m	late sixth century	gilt-bronze crown, gilt-bronze belt, iron helmet, iron cuirass
Ishihara-Inariyama	Circular	30 m	end of sixth century	bronze bowl, gilt-bronze flower-shaped decorative pendant (*gyōyō*) for horse

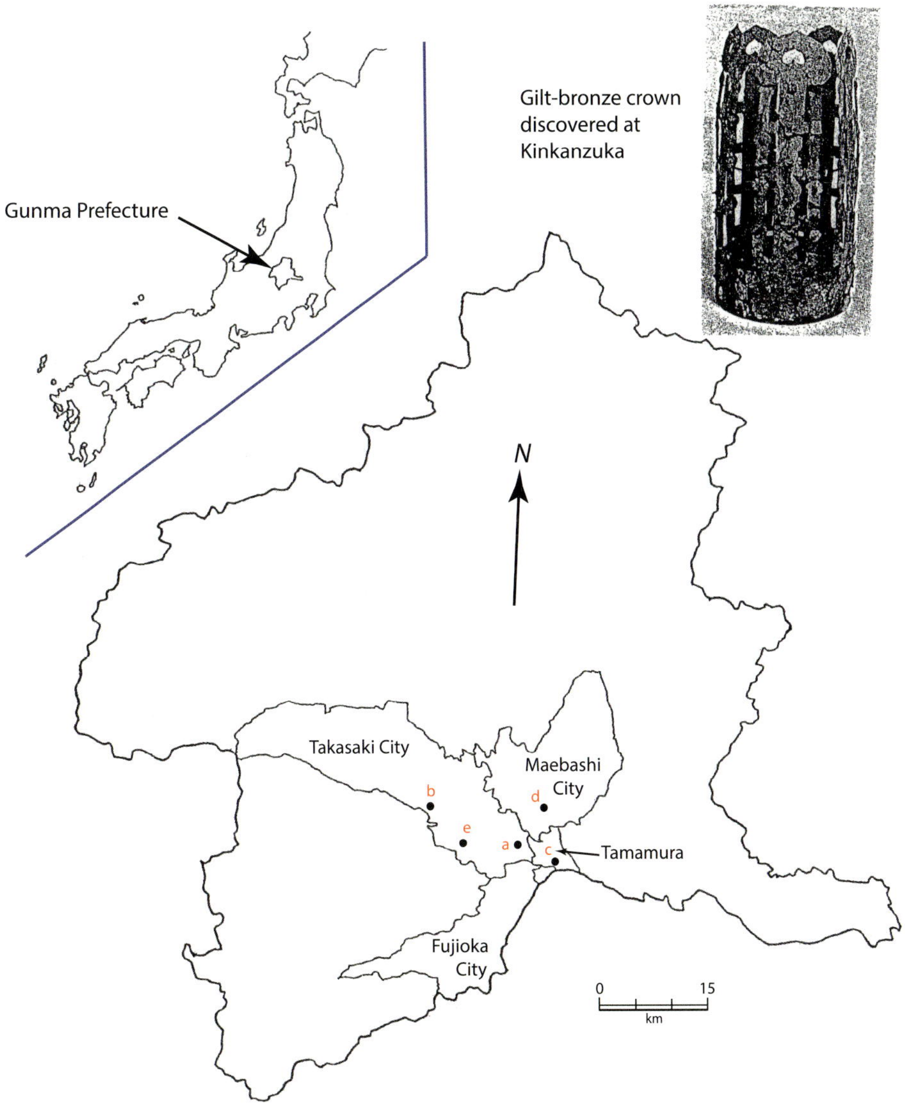

Map 7.2 Sites in Western Kamitsuke (Gunma Prefecture) Mentioned in This Chapter.
a. Watanuki-Kan'non'yama; b. Kenzaki-Nagatoro-Nishi and Yawata-Kan'nonzuka;
c. Koizumi-Ōtsukagoshi No. 3 and Koizumi-Nagatsuka No. 1;
d. Kinkanzuka; e. Ishihara-Inariyama.

Figure 7.17 Aerial Photograph of Yawata-Kan'nonzuka.
Photograph courtesy of the Takasaki-shi Kyōiku Iinkai 高崎市教育委員会 *(Takasaki Municipal Board of Education).*

Descriptions in the *Nihon shoki* give some insight into the distribution of the Silla materials in the late sixth century.[8] Since the late sixth century, Silla began to donate "tax in kind from Silla" (*Shiragi no chō* 新羅の調) to Japan. This was Silla's "tribute" (*kōnōhin* 貢納品) to Japan in exchange for Japan's renouncement of war against Silla. Of course, the term "tribute" indicates the Japanese perspective, whereas from Silla's perspective Silla would have "bestowed" these materials upon Japan. Silla also donated "tax in kind from Imna" 任那 (J. Mimana) to Japan to compensate for Japan's loss of rights and interests in Kaya, after Silla defeated Tae Kaya in 562. Again, this represents the Japanese perspective, and Silla had its own rationale for giving out "tax in kind from Imna." In any case, large quantities of Silla materials were imported to Japan or the Yamato authority.

[8] Examples being records dating to the following reign years: Kinmei 21/9 (560); 22 (561); 23/7 (562); Bidatsu 3/11 (574); 4/6 (575); 8/10 (579); 9/6 (580); and 11/10 (582).

Figure 7.18 Horse Bit and Cheek Plate Discovered at Yawata-Kan'nonzuka. Photograph courtesy of the Takasaki-shi Kyōiku Iinkai 高崎市教育委員会 *(Takasaki Municipal Board of Education).*

Figure 7.19 Pendant Ornaments Belonging to Horse-trappings Discovered at Yawata-Kan'nonzuka. Photograph courtesy of the Takasaki-shi Kyōiku Iinkai 高崎市教育委員会 *(Takasaki Municipal Board of Education).*

The Yamato authority distributed these Silla materials to local chiefs. Among these chiefs, the Yamato authority considered local chiefs in western Kamitsuke to be strategically important because of their military strength. Therefore, the authority had to pacify them, and in order to take advantage of their military strength, it had to give precious imported prestige goods to them. It is also likely that the local chiefs in western Kamitsuke in turn gave out these prestige goods to low-ranking elites. To be specific, higher-ranking chiefs who were buried in such large keyhole tumuli as Watanuki-Kan'non'yama and Yawata-Kan'nonzuka re-distributed the prestige goods to second- or third-ranking elites who were buried in Koizumi-Ōtsukagoshi No. 3 keyhole tumuli, Koizumi-Nagatsuka No. 1 mound, Kinkanzuka keyhole tumulus, and the Ishihara-Inariyama circular tumulus.

Korean Immigrants in Sixth- and Seventh-Century Kamitsuke

The aforementioned descendants of Korean immigrants who were buried in the Kenzaki-Nagatoro-Nishi cemetery occupied a slightly higher social status than did their antecedents of the late fifth century, and they were not buried in cairns but in earthen mounds. At the same time, some descendants of Korean immigrants continued to occupy a low social status. In the early sixth century, they moved farther north of the Kenzaki-Nagatoro-Nishi cemetery to the present Shibukawa City of Gunma Prefecture and continued their involvement in raising and breeding horses. This is evidenced by a large number of cairns in the vicinity of Shibukawa City, such as the Arise 有瀬 tumulus, the Ikuma 伊熊 tumulus, and the Karasawa 空沢 tumulus group, dated to the early to late sixth century. All the cairns are circular tumuli.

In the seventh century, cairns appeared farther north of Shibusawa City, the northern tip of Gunma Prefecture, in a very mountainous area. The Kawahakeikusabara 川額軍原 tumulus group consists of thirteen small, square cairns of 2 to 7 m per side. Cairns continued to be built in later phases of the Kofun period farther north in mountainous areas. This suggests that descendants of Korean immigrants whose social status remained low were compelled to remain in charge of raising and breeding horses and developing mountainous land. In the seventh century, their vocation in horse raising was more pronounced than their Korean ancestors' contributions.[9]

[9] From the Late Kofun period to the period of the *ritsuryō* state of the eighth century, those involved in raising and breeding horses belonged to an organization called the *Umakai be* 馬飼部 (*umakai* meaning raising horses, *be* meaning

Conclusion: Three Patterns of Importing Korean Materials to Japan

I have analyzed three different phases of importing and adopting material culture of Korean origin into eastern Japan from the end of the Yayoi to the Late Kofun period. These phases more or less correspond to stages of the formation and development of the "central" authority in Japan. First, at the end of the Yayoi period, a local area such as the central highlands of Japan that did not maintain the center of direct interaction with foreign polities was able to import materials via the neighboring Hokuriku region on the coast of the Sea of Japan (East Sea), without going through the western part of Japan that would grow to be the center. Naturally, other local areas must have maintained their own independent routes of interacting with the Korean peninsula. At that time, there was no central authority that would control or limit non-local interaction.

In the late fifth century in various regions of eastern Japan, cairns and pit dwellings with earthen stoves appeared contemporaneously. These are obviously related to Korean immigrants settled in these regions. It is important to note that there were no precursors to these phenomena in these regions. This leads me to suspect that these were not mere coincidence, but were the outcome of several interrelated factors. A clue to understanding these phenomena is the overlapping spatial distribution of horse trappings in these regions in the late fifth century (Momosaki 1993). The late fifth century corresponds to the reign of the Emperor Yūryaku 雄略, during which the Yamato authority gained enough power to assert control over numerous local regions. The Yamato authority at that time also made efforts to introduce and adopt several new "revolutionary" technologies in Japan. One such revolutionary technology was raising horses, and another example was firing *sue* stoneware, introduced at the beginning of the fifth century. It is likely that the Yamato authority in cooperation with several local chiefs transferred Korean specialists of horse raising in their areas and started raising horses. As I have shown in this chapter, however, the ways in which Korean immigrants were incorporated into local populations were distinctive from one region to another. This indicates that the Yamato authority at that time did not have enough power to influence the internal social structure of these areas.

From the late sixth to the beginning of the seventh century, the Yamato authority distributed prestige goods imported from the Korean

specialists). Most of them were immigrants, but they were more or less looked down upon as outcasts.

peninsula to regional chiefs in western Kamitsuke. By this time, a system was operational so that the Yamato authority almost monopolized the acquisition of prestige goods of extra-local origins and redistributed them to local chiefs. At the same time, those who obtained the prestige goods from the Yamato authority maintained the right further to redistribute the prestige goods to lower-tier elites. This indicates that the Yamato authority seemingly gained control over most regions of Japan, but local control by the Yamato authority was indirect and was dependent upon the control of regionally influential chiefs.

In the late seventh century the Yamato authority gained direct control over most of the local regions of Japan when the *ritsuryō* 律令 codified government system was established. Even after the seventh century, however, whenever the power of the central government became weak, it became impossible for the central government to restrict foreign interaction initiated by local chiefs. The Yamato authority could not pay attention to foreign interactions of very small scale initiated by local chiefs, either. Because a political system armed with a well-defined territorial boundary and centralized authority is a rare phenomenon in human history, we scholars must be conscientious about avoiding assumptions based on the influence of the present-day political systems when making our interpretations.

References

Habuta Yoshiyuki 土生田純之

2009 Kofun jidai kōki ni okeru Sei-mō no torai-kei bunbutsu 古墳時代後期における西毛の渡来系文物 [Sixth-century material culture of Korean origins discovered in western Kamitsuke]. In *Samguk sidae ch'ŏngdong yumul naptong wiwŏnso rŭl iyong han sanji ch'ujong yŏn'gu* 삼국시대 청동유물 납동위원소를 이용한 산지추정 연구 [Research on estimating the source of pseudo elements of copper lead used in bronze artifacts of the Three Kingdoms period], edited by Han'guk Kungnip Chungang Pangmulgwan 韓國國立中央博物館 [National Museum of Korea], pp. 24–43. Han'guk Kungnip Chungang Pangmulgwan, Seoul.

——— (editor)

2003 *Kenzaki-Nagatoro-Nishi 5*, 27, 35-gō fun 剣崎長瀞西5, 27, 35号墳 [Tombs 5, 27, and 25 at Kenzaki-Nagatoro-Nishi]. Senshū Daigaku Bungaku-bu Kōkogaku Kenkyūshitsu 専修大学文学部考古学研究室 [Archaeology Laboratory, Faculty of Letters, Senshū University], Tokyo.

Hamada Kōsaku 濱田耕作

1922 *Tsūron kōkogaku* 通論考古学 [Introduction to archaeology]. Daishokaku 大鐙閣, Tokyo.

Hirakawa Minami 平川南

2002 Nezuka iseki shutsudo kokusho doki 根塚遺跡出土刻書土器 [Pottery with an engraved character discovered at the Nezuka site]. In *Nezuka iseki* 根塚遺跡 [The Nezuka site], edited by Yoshihara Yoshi'ichi 吉原佳市, pp. 49–50. Kijimadaira-mura Kyōiku Iinkai 木島平村教育委員会 [Kijimadaira Village Board of Education], Nagano Prefecture.

Hōjō Yoshitaka 北條芳隆

1986 Funkyū ni hyōji sareta zenpōkōenfun no teishiki to sono hyōka: Seiritsu tōsho no Kinai to Kibi no taihi kara 墳丘に表示された前方後円墳の定式とその評価: 成立当初の畿内と吉備の対比から [The standard of keyhole tumuli as seen from the mound morphology and its evaluation: Comparison of the cases in Kinai and Kibi at the beginning of the Kofun period]. *Kōkogaku Kenkyū* 考古学研究 32(4): 42–66.

Imamura Mineo 今村峯雄, Fujio Shin'ichirō 藤尾慎一郎, et al.

2003 *Tanso-14 nendai sokutei to kōkogaku* 炭素14年代測定と考古学 [Radiocarbon dating and archaeology]. Kokuritsu Rekishi Minzoku Hakubutsukan 国立歴史民俗博物館 [National Museum of Japanese History], Sakura.

Kazama Eiichi 風間栄一

2006 Uma-gata taikō no bunrui to keiretsu ha'aku: Nihon shutsudo no uma-gata taikō o megutte 馬形帯鉤の分類と系列把握: 日本出土の馬形帯鉤をめぐって

[Classification and chronology of horse-shaped buckles: With focus on those discovered in Japan]. In *Higashi Ajia chiiki ni okeru seidōki bunka no inyū to hen'yō oyobi ryūtsū ni kansuru takakuteki hikaku kenkyū* 東アジア地域における青銅器文化の移入と変容および流通に関する多角的比較研究 [Multi-faceted comparative studies on the introduction, evolution, and exchange of the bronze culture in East Asia], edited by Fujio Shin'ichirō 藤尾慎一郎, pp. 145–178. Kokuritsu Rekishi Minzoku Hakubutsukan 国立歴史民俗博物館 [National Museum of Japanese History], Sakura.

Kim Ku-gun 金邱軍

2000 Hohyŏng taegu ŭi hyŏngsik pullyu wa p'yŏnnyŏn 虎形帶鉤의 形式分類와 編年 [Morphological classification and chronology of tiger-shaped belt buckles]. In *Kyŏngbuk Taehakkyo Kogo Illyu Hakgwa 20 chunyŏn kinyŏm nonch'ong* 慶北大學校考古人類學科20周年記念論叢 [Collected essays in honor of the 20th anniversary of the Department of Archaeology and Anthropology, Kyŏngbuk National University], edited by Kyŏngbuk Taehakkyo Inmundae Kogo Illyu Hakkwa 慶北大學校人文大學考古人類學科 [Department of Archaeology and Anthropology, Faculty of Humanities, Kyŏngbuk National University], pp. 163–220. Kyŏngbuk Taehakkyo Inmundae Kogo Illyu Hakkwa, Taegu.

Kirihara Ken 桐原健

2001 Kodai Shinano to toraijin 古代信濃と渡来人 [Immigrants and ancient Shinano]. In *Nezuka iseki to Kaya* 根塚遺跡と加耶 [Nezuka site and Kaya], edited by Nezuka Iseki Hakkutsu Chōsadan 根塚遺跡発掘調査団 [Nezuka Site Excavation Team], pp. 41–48. Kijimadaira-mura Kyōiku Iinkai 木島平村教育委員会 [Kijimadaira Village Board of Education], Nagano Prefecture.

Kobayashi Saburō 小林三郎, Ōtsuka Hatsushige 大塚初重, Ishikawa Hideshi 石川日出志, Sasaki Ken'ichi 佐々木憲一, and Kusano Jumpei 草野潤平

2008 *Shinano Ōmuro tsumi'ishizuka kofun-gun no kenkyū* 信濃大室積石塚古墳群の研究 [Study of the Ōmuro cairn group in Shinano], Vol. 3. Meiji Daigaku Bungaku-bu Kōkogaku Kenkyūshitsu 明治大学文学部考古学研究室 [Archaeology Program at the Meiji University] and Rokuichi Shobō 六一書房, Tokyo.

Kobayashi Yukio 小林行雄

1960 *Kofun jidai no kenkyū* 古墳時代の研究 [A study of the Kofun period]. Aoki Shoten 青木書店, Tokyo.

———

2006 "Treatise on duplicate mirrors," translated by Walter Edwards. In *Capital and Countryside in Japan, 300–1180: Japanese Historians Interpreted in English*, edited by Joan R. Piggott, pp. 54–76. Cornell East Asia Series, Ithaca.

Kuno Masahiro 久野正博, Sano Seiko 佐野聖子, and Suzuki Kyōtarō 鈴木京太郎
2000 *Uchino kofun-gun* 内野古墳群 [The Uchino cemetery]. Hamakita-shi Kyōiku Iinkai 浜北市教育委員会 [Hamakita Municipal Board of Education], Shizuoka Prefecture.
Kurata Yoshirō 倉田芳郎 (editor)
1981 *Nagano Ōmuro kofun-gun: Bumpu chōsa hōkoku sho* 長野大室古墳群: 分布調査報告書 [Report of surface survey at the Ōmuro cairn group, Nagano City]. Komazawa Daigaku Kōkogaku Kenkyūshitsu, Tokyo.
Kuroda Akira 黒田晃 (editor)
2002 *Kenzaki-Nagatoro-Nishi iseki* 剣崎長瀞西遺跡 [The Kenzaki-Nagatoro-Nishi site], Vol. 1. Takasaki-shi Kyōiku Iinkai 高崎市教育委員会 [Takasaki Municipal Board of Education], Gunma Prefecture.
Momosaki Yūsuke 桃崎祐輔
1993 Kofun ni tomonau gyūba kugi no kentō: Nihon rettō, Chōsen hantō, Chūgoku tōhoku chihō no jirei o hikaku shite 古墳に伴う牛馬供犠の検討: 日本列島・朝鮮半島・中国東北地方の事例を比較して [Examination of rituals utilizing cows and horses at mounded tombs: Comparison of cases from the Japanese archipelago, Korean peninsula, and northeastern China]. *Kobunka Dansō* 古文化談叢 31: 1–141.
Murai Shōsuke 村井章介
1993 *Chūsei Wajin-den* 中世倭人伝 [Medieval history of Japanese people]. Iwanami Shoten 岩波書店, Tokyo.
Naoki Kōjirō 直木孝次郎
1958 *Nihon kodai kokka no kōzō* 日本古代国家の構造 [The Structure of the ancient Japanese state]. Aoki Shoten 青木書店, Tokyo.
Nishitani Tadashi 西谷正
2001 Kaya to Wa 加耶と倭 [Kaya and Wa]. In *Nezuka iseki to Kaya* 根塚遺跡と加耶 [Nezuka site and Kaya], edited by Nezuka Iseki Hakkutsu Chōsadan 根塚遺跡発掘調査団 [Nezuka Site Excavation Team], pp. 49–57. Kijimadaira-mura Kyōiku Iinkai 木島平村教育委員会 [Kijimadaira Village Board of Education], Nagano Prefecture.
Nozawa Seiichi 野澤誠一
2002 Dō-kushiro, tekken kara mita higashi Nihon no Yayoi shakai 銅釧・鉄剣からみた東日本の弥生社会 [Yayoi society in eastern Japan from the standpoint of bronze bracelets and iron swords]. *Nagano Kenritsu Rekishikan Kenkyū Kiyō* 長野県立歴史館研究紀要 8: 2–20.
Ōtsuka Hatsushige 大塚初重
2001 Kōkogaku jō kara mita tōgoku to toraikei minzoku 考古学上から見た東国と渡来系民族 [Eastern Japan and immigrants from an archaeological

standpoint]. In *Nezuka iseki to Kaya* 根塚遺跡と加耶 [Nezuka site and Kaya], edited by Nezuka Iseki Hakkutsu Chōsadan 根塚遺跡発掘調査団 [Nezuka Site Excavation Team], pp. 59–68. Kijimadaira-mura Kyōiku Iinkai 木島平村教育委員会 [Kijimadaira Village Board of Education], Nagano Prefecture.

Ōtsuka Hatsushige 大塚初重, Kobayashi Saburō 小林三郎, and Ishikawa Hideshi 石川日出志

1993 *Shinano Ōmuro tsumi'ishizuka kofun-gun no kenkyū* 信濃大室積石塚古墳群の研究 [Study of the Ōmuro cairn group in Shinano], Vol. 1. Tokyo-dō 東京堂 and Meiji Daigaku Jinbun Kagaku Kenkyūjo 明治大学人文科学研究所 [Meiji University Institute of Humanities], Tokyo.

Ōtsuka Hatsushige 大塚初重, and Kobayashi Saburō 小林三郎

2006 *Shinano Ōmuro tsumi'ishizuka kofun-gun no kenkyū* 信濃大室積石塚古墳群の研究 [Study of the Ōmuro cairn group in Shinano], Vol. 2. Tokyo-dō 東京堂 and Meiji Daigaku Jinbun Kagaku Kenkyūjo 明治大学人文科学研究所 [Meiji University Institute of Humanities], Tokyo.

Sasaki Ken'ichi 佐々木憲一, Kawano Masanori 河野正訓, Takahashi Tōru 高橋透, and Arai Satoru 新井悟 (editors)

2015 *Shinano Ōmuro tsumi'ishizuka kofun-gun no kenkyū 4: Mujinagōro tan'i shigun no chōsa* 信濃大室積石塚古墳群の研究 4: 大室谷支群・ムジナゴーロ単位支群の調査 [Study of the Ōmuro cairn and earthen mound group in the old province of Shinanao, vol. 4: Investigations into the Ōmuro and Mujinagōro sub-groups]. Meiji Daigaku Bungakubu Kōkogaku Kenkyūshitsu 明治大学文学部考古学研究室 [Archaeology Program, Faculty of Arts and Letters, Meiji University] and Rokuichi Shobō 六一書房, Tokyo.

Shibuya Emiko 渋谷恵美子 (editor)

2007 *Iida ni okeru kofun no shutsugen to tenkai* 飯田における古墳の出現と展開 [The appearance and evolution of tumuli in the Iida basin]. Iida-shi Kyōiku Iinkai 飯田市教育委員会 [Iida Municipal Board of Education], Nagano Prefecture.

Shibuya Emiko 澁谷恵美子, and Furukawa Yutaka 古川豊

2017 *Kitakata Nishinohara iseki* 北方西の原遺跡 [Kitakata Nishinohara site]. Iida-shi Kyōiku Iinkai 飯田市教育委員会 [Iida Municipal Board of Education], Nagano Prefecture.

Shimizu Ryūta 清水竜太, and Kazama Eiichi 風間栄一

2005 Nagano-shi Asakawabata iseki no uma-gata taikō 長野市浅川端遺跡の馬形帯鉤 [A horse-shaped buckle discovered at the Asakawabata site]. *Kōkogaku Zasshi* 考古学雑誌 89(2): 76–87.

Shimizu Yutaka 清水豊, and Ōtsuka Emiko 大塚恵美子

2003 *Ide-Kitabatake iseki* 井出北畑遺跡 [The Ide-Kitabatake site]. Gunma-ken Gunma-machi Kyōiku Iinkai 群馬県群馬町教育委員会 [Gunma Township Board of Education], Gunma Prefecture.

Takada Kanta 高田貫太

1998 Suishoku-tsuki mimikazari o meguru chiikikan kōshō 垂飾付耳飾をめぐる地域間交渉 [Regional interaction as seen from earrings with accessories]. *Kobunka Dansō* 古文化談叢 41: 55–75.

———

2004 5, 6 seiki Nihon retto to Rakutō-kō itō chiiki no chiikikan kōshō 5, 6世紀日本列島と洛東江以東地域の地域間交渉 [Interaction between the Japanese archipelago and regions to the east of Naktong River in the Korean peninsula in the fifth and sixth centuries]. In *Bunka no tayōsei to hikaku kōkogaku: Kōkogaku Kenkyū Kai 50-shūnen kinen ronbunshū* 考古学研究会50周年記念論文集: 文化の多様性と比較考古学 [Cultural diversity and comparative archaeologies: A collection of theses in celebration of the 50th anniversary of the Society for Archaeological Studies], edited by Kōkogaku Kenkyū Kai 考古学研究会 [Society for Archaeological Studies], pp. 29–48. Kōkogaku Kenkyū Kai, Okayama.

———

2006 5, 6 seiki no Ni-tchō kōshō to chiiki shakai 5, 6世紀の日朝交渉と地域社会 [Korea-Japan interactions and local societies in the fifth and sixth centuries]. *Kōkogaku Kenkyū* 考古学研究 53(2): 24–39.

Taketani Toshio 竹谷俊夫

1997 Chōsen hantō shutsudo no seidō-sei uma-gata taikō ni tsuite: Tenri Sankōkan zōhin no shiryō shōkai o kanete 朝鮮半島出土の青銅製馬形帯鉤について: 天理参考館蔵品の資料紹介をかねて [Bronze horse-shaped buckles discovered in the Korean peninsula: Introducing collections of the Tenri Sankōkan Museum]. In *Katada Tadashi sensei koki kinen ronbunshū* 堅田直先生古希記念論文集 [Collected theses in celebration of Professor Katada Tadashi's seventieth birthday], edited by Katada Tadashi Sensei Koki Kinen Ronbunshū Kankōkai 堅田直先生古希記念論文集刊行会 [Publication Committee for the Collected Theses in Celebration of Professor Katada Tadashi's Seventieth Birthday], pp. 893–911. Shin'yōsha 真陽社, Kyoto.

Tongŭi Taehakkyo Pangmulgwan 東義大学校博物館 [Tongŭi University Museum]

2000 *Kimhae Yangdong-ni kobun munhwa* 金海良洞里古墳文化 [Mounded tomb culture of the Yangdong-ni site in Kimhae]. Tongŭi University Museum haksul ch'ongsŏ 東義大学校博物館學術叢書 [Tongŭi University Museum Academic Series], No. 7. Tongŭi Taehakkyo Pangmulgwan, Pusan.

Wada Seigo 和田晴吾
1981 Mukō-shi Itsukahara kofun no sokuryō chōsa yori 向日市五塚原古墳の測量調査より [Mapping the Itsukahara mound tomb in Mukō City, Kyoto Prefecture]. In *Ōryō no hikaku kenkyū* 王陵の比較研究 [Comparative studies of imperial mausolea], edited by Onoyama Setsu 小野山節, pp. 49–63. Kyōto Daigaku Bungakubu Kōkogaku Kenkyūshitsu 京都大学文学部考古学研究室 [Department of Archaeology, Kyoto University], Kyoto.

Yamashita Seiichi 山下誠一
2003 Iida bonchi ni okeru Kofun jidai zen, chūki shūraku no dōkō: Hakkutsu chōsa sareta tateana jūkyo-shi o moto ni shite 飯田盆地における古墳時代前·中期集落の動向: 発掘調査された竪穴住居址を基にして [Settlements in the early and middle Kofun period in the Iida basin: Based on archaeologically excavated pit dwellings]. *Iida-shi Bijutsu Hakubutsukan Kenkyū Kiyō* 飯田市美術博物館研究紀要 13: 125–142.

Yi Kŏn-mu 이건무, Song Ŭi-jŏng 송의정, Yun T'ae-yong 윤태용, An Kyŏng-suk 안경숙, and Pak Chin-il 박진일
2008 *Kaltaebat sok ŭi nara, Taho-ri: Kŭ palgul kwa kirok* 갈대밭 속의 나라, 茶戸里: 그발굴과 기록 [A country in a field of reeds, Taho-ri: The excavation and its records]. Kungnip Chungang Pangmulgwan t'ŭkpyŏljŏn 국립중앙박물관특별전 [National Museum of Korea special exhibition catalogue]. Kungnip Chungang Pangmulgwan 국립중앙박물관 [National Museum of Korea], Seoul.

Yoshihara Yoshi'ichi 吉原佳市
2002 *Nezuka iseki* 根塚遺跡 [The Nezuka site]. Kijimadaira-mura Kyōiku Iinkai 木島平村教育委員会 [Kijimadaira Village Board of Education], Nagano Prefecture.

CONTRIBUTORS

MARTIN T. BALE is a professor of archaeology at Yeungnam University in Kyŏngsan, Korea. He is engaged in research on prehistoric Northeast Asia. In particular, Bale is interested in social change and identity as they are manifested through households, settlements, and mortuary features. He has published articles on specialized craft production, surplus grain, storage, agricultural origins, agricultural intensification, and other topics. Bale was a researcher and then a postdoctoral fellow at Harvard University 2009–2012, a postdoctoral associate at Yale University 2012–2013, and an adjunct professor at a number of national universities in Korea 2013–2015. Bale received an M.A. from the University of British Columbia and a PhD from the University of Toronto in Canada.

MARK E. BYINGTON is an Associate in Research at the Department of Anthropology at Harvard University and the President and co-founder of the Cambridge Institute for the Study of Korea. He previously served as the founding director of the Early Korea Project at the Korea Institute, Harvard University. His research has focused on the archaeology, early history, and prehistory of the Korean peninsula and northeastern China. He has researched and written on state formation processes associated with the Puyŏ and Koguryŏ polities of northeastern China and Korea, and has served as editor for the *Early Korea* series and the Early Korea Project Occasional Series. He received his M.A. (1996) and PhD (2003) from Harvard University.

HABUTA YOSHIYUKI is a professor of history (archaeology) at Senshū University in Tokyo, Japan. His research originally encompassed the origins of mortuary architecture and mounded tombs of the Kofun period in addition to concepts of the afterlife based on material cultural evidence. More recently, Habuta has written on society, political organization, and Japanese-Korean relations in the Kofun period. He was formerly an assistant curator in the Division of Documents and Mausoleums at the National Agency for the Imperial Household. Habuta received his M.A. and D.Lit degrees in History from Kansai University in Osaka, Japan.

IWANAGA SHŌZŌ is a professor and the assistant director of the Kyushu University Museum in Fukuoka, Japan. His research interests range widely from archaeological survey to early metallurgy and tools in Japan, the development of Yayoi chiefly culture, the development of mortuary culture, Yayoi culture in an East Asian context, the complex social structure of elite authority in eighth-century Japan, and theoretical models of the origin and growth of complex societies, as well as other subjects. Iwanaga was formerly an associate curator at the Nara National Research Institute for Cultural Properties. He received an M.A. in archaeology from Kyushu University in Fukuoka, Japan.

KAMEDA SHŪICHI is a professor of anthropology and archaeology at the Okayama University of Science in Okayama, Japan. His research has focused on his interest in Yayoi and Kofun pottery. More recently, Kameda's research has moved toward ceramic roof tiles of ancient Korea and Japan, which was the subject of his doctoral dissertation and of a comprehensive publication. He has also expanded the scope of his research to include the Kofun period, and has written broadly on various aspects of the archaeology of the Kofun and early historic periods, including Korea-Japan interactions in the Kibi region of Japan. He received his M.A. and D.Lit. from Kyushu University in Fukuoka, Japan.

LEE CHUNGKYU is a professor of archaeology at Yeungnam University in Kyŏngsan, Korea. He engages with the material culture of early bronze metallurgy in his research on the Bronze Age of the Korean peninsula and northeastern China. A recent theme of Lee's research has been identity and ethnic formation in Northeast Asia. He is also an expert on the archaeology of prehistory and early history of Cheju Island, Korea. Lee has served as the head of the Department of Cultural Anthropology at Yeungnam University and as head of the Yŏngnam Archaeological Society, the Society for Korean Bronze Culture, and the Korean Archaeological Society. Lee's B.A., M.A. and PhD are from Seoul National University in Korea.

PARK CHEUN SOO is a professor of archaeology at Kyungpook National University in Taegu, Korea. His research covers Kaya history, the history of the Yŏngsan River valley, ancient relations between the Korean peninsula and the Japanese archipelago, ancient glass in Korean and Japanese mortuary contexts, and the Silk Road. Park strives to present an unbiased view of the ancient Korea-Japanese world through the analysis of material culture, and he has consistently found evidence to demonstrate that the modern boundaries of nation states had no bearing on early historic cultural changes in the region. He received his B.A. and M.A. from Kyungpook National University in Korea and his PhD from Osaka University in Japan.

SASAKI KEN'ICHI is a professor of archaeology at Meiji University in Tokyo, Japan. His research has addressed such issues as houses and settlement patterns in pre- and protohistoric Japan, mounded burial culture in Kantō, Hitachi, and other regions of eastern Japan, political organization in Kofun Japan, the history of archaeology in the USA, archaeological education, and the evolution of elite symbolism in mortuary and religious contexts. He was a visiting scholar at the Reischauer Institute of Japanese Studies at Harvard University 2009—2010. Sasaki received a B.A. from the University of Michigan, studied at Osaka University in Osaka, Japan, in the process of dissertation research, and received a PhD from Harvard University in Cambridge, Massachusetts.

WOO JAE-PYOUNG is a professor of archaeology at Chungnam National University in Taejŏn, Korea. Woo's research lies at the intersection of early historic polities in the Korean peninsula and the Japanese archipelago. Woo has addressed issues such as the spread of the technological and cultural systems of burials, food preparation, and heating, as well as the trade and exchange routes between the two regions. He has served as the head of the Department of Archaeology at Chungnam National University and as the director of the Paekche Research Institute of Chungnam National University. He received his B.A. and M.A. from Korea University in Korea and his PhD from Osaka University in Japan.

INDEX